C

IN A NUTSHELL

Second Edition

Peter Prinz and Tony Crawford

US

Beijing · Boston · Farnham · Sebastopol · Tokyo

C in a Nutshell, Second Edition

by Peter Prinz and Tony Crawford

Copyright © 2016 Peter Prinz and Tony Crawford. All rights reserved.

Printed in the United States of America.

Published by O'Reilly Media, Inc., 1005 Gravenstein Highway North, Sebastopol, CA 95472.

O'Reilly books may be purchased for educational, business, or sales promotional use. Online editions are also available for most titles (*http://safaribooksonline.com*). For more information, contact our corporate/institutional sales department: 800-998-9938 or *corporate@oreilly.com*.

Editors: Rachel Roumeliotis and Katie Schooling	**Indexer:** Angela Howard
Production Editor: Kristen Brown	**Interior Designer:** David Futato
Copyeditor: Gillian McGarvey	**Cover Designer:** Karen Montgomery
Proofreader: Jasmine Kwityn	**Illustrator:** Rebecca Demarest

December 2005: First Edition
December 2015: Second Edition

Revision History for the Second Edition

2015-12-07: First Release
2015-02-19: Second Release

See *http://oreilly.com/catalog/errata.csp?isbn=9781491904756* for release details.

978-1-491-90475-6

[LSI]

Table of Contents

Part I.   Language

Part II.   Standard Library

Part III.   Basic Tools

Preface

This book is a complete reference to the C programming language and the C runtime library. As an "In a Nutshell" book, its purpose is to serve as a convenient, reliable companion for C programmers in their day-to-day work. It describes all the elements of the language and illustrates their use with numerous examples.

The present description of the C language is based on the 2011 international C standard, ISO/IEC 9899:2011, widely known as C11. This standard supersedes the C99 standard, ISO/IEC 9899:1999, and its Technical Corrigenda, TC1 of 2001, TC2 of 2004, and TC3 of 2007. The first international C standard, ISO/IEC 9899:1990, was published in 1990 and supplemented in 1995 by Normative Addendum 1 (ISO/IEC 9899/AMD1:1995). The 1990 ISO/IEC standard corresponds to the ANSI standard X3.159, which was ratified in late 1989 and is commonly called ANSI C or C89.

The new features of the 2011 C standard are not yet fully supported by all compilers and standard library implementations. In this book, we have therefore labeled 2011 features—such as multithreading, type-generic macros, and new standard library functions—with the abbreviation C11. Extensions that were introduced by the C99 standard are labeled with the abbreviation C99.

This book is not an introduction to programming in C. Although it covers the fundamentals of the language, it is not organized or written as a tutorial. If you are new to C, we assume that you have read at least one of the many introductory books, or that you are familiar with a related language, such as Java or C++.

How This Book Is Organized

This book is divided into three parts. The first part describes the C language in the strict sense of the term; the second part describes the standard library; and the third part describes the process of compiling and testing programs with the popular tools in the GNU software collection.

Part I

Part I, which deals with the C language, includes Chapters 1 through 15. After Chapter 1, which describes the general concepts and elements of the language, each chapter is devoted to a specific topic, such as types, statements, or pointers. Although the topics are ordered so that the fundamental concepts for each new topic have been presented in an earlier chapter—types, for example, are described before expressions and operators, which come before statements, and so on—you may sometimes need to follow references to later chapters to fill in related details. For example, some discussion of pointers and arrays is necessary in Chapter 5 (which covers expressions and operators), even though pointers and arrays are not described in full detail until Chapters 8 and 9.

Chapter 1, "Language Basics"
Describes the characteristics of the language and how C programs are structured and compiled. This chapter introduces basic concepts such as the translation unit, character sets, and identifiers.

Chapter 2, "Types"
Provides an overview of types in C and describes the basic types, the type void, and enumerated types.

Chapter 3, "Literals"
Describes numeric constants, character constants, and string literals, including escape sequences.

Chapter 4, "Type Conversions"
Describes implicit and explicit type conversions, including integer promotion and the usual arithmetic conversions.

Chapter 5, "Expressions and Operators"
Describes the evaluation of expressions, all the operators, and their compatible operands.

Chapter 6, "Statements"
Describes C statements such as blocks, loops, and jumps.

Chapter 7, "Functions"
Describes function definitions and function calls, including recursive and inline functions.

Chapter 8, "Arrays"
Describes fixed-length and variable-length arrays, including strings, array initialization, and multidimensional arrays.

Chapter 9, "Pointers"
Describes the definition and use of pointers to objects and functions.

Chapter 10, "Structures, Unions, and Bit-Fields"
Describes the organization of data in these user-defined derived types.

Chapter 11, "Declarations"
Describes the general syntax of a declaration, identifier linkage, and the storage duration of objects.

Chapter 12, "Dynamic Memory Management"
Describes the standard library's dynamic memory management functions, illustrating their use in a sample implementation of a generalized binary tree.

Chapter 13, "Input and Output"
Describes the C concept of input and output, with an overview of the use of the standard I/O library.

Chapter 14, "Multithreading"
Describes the use of the C11 multithreading features, including atomic operations, communication between threads, and thread-specific storage.

Chapter 15, "Preprocessing Directives"
Describes the definition and use of macros, conditional compiling, and all the other preprocessor directives and operators.

Part II

Part II, consisting of Chapters 16, 17, and 18, is devoted to the C standard library. It provides an overview of standard headers and also contains a detailed function reference.

Chapter 16, "The Standard Headers"
Describes contents of the headers and their use. The headers contain all of the standard library's macros and type definitions.

Chapter 17, "Functions at a Glance"
Provides an overview of the standard library functions, organized by areas of application (e.g., mathematical functions, date and time functions, etc.).

Chapter 18, "Standard Library Functions"
Describes each standard library function in detail, in alphabetical order, and contains examples to illustrate the use of each function.

Part III

The third part of this book, which includes Chapters 19 through 20, provides the necessary knowledge of the C programmer's basic tools: the compiler, the *make* utility, and the debugger. The tools described here are those in the GNU software collection. Finally, the use of these tools in an integrated development environment (IDE) for C is described using the Eclipse IDE as an example.

Chapter 19, "Compiling with GCC"
Describes the principal capabilities that the widely used compiler offers for C programmers.

Chapter 20, "Using make to Build C Programs"
> Describes how to use the *make* program to automate the compiling process for large programs.

Chapter 21, "Debugging C Programs with GDB"
> Describes how to run a program under the control of the GNU debugger and how to analyze programs' runtime behavior to find logical errors.

Chapter 22, "Using an IDE with C"
> Describes the use of an integrated development environment (IDE) for unified, convienient access to all the tools for developing C programs.

Further Reading

In addition to works mentioned at appropriate points in the text, there are a number of resources for readers who want more technical detail than even this book can provide. The international working group on C standardization has an official home page at *http://www.open-std.org/jtc1/sc22/wg14*, with links to the latest version of the C standard and current projects of the working group.

For readers who are interested in not only the *what* and *how* of C, but also the *why*, the WG14 site also offers links to some of its drafts and rationales. These documents describe some of the motivations and constraints involved in the standardization process. Furthermore, for those who may wonder how C "got to be that way" in the first place, the originator of C, the late Dennis Ritchie, wrote an article titled "The Development of the C Language" (*https://www.bell-labs.com/usr/dmr/www/ chist.html*). This and other historical documents are still available on his Bell Labs website, *https://www.bell-labs.com/usr/dmr/www/index.html*.

Readers who want details on floating-point math beyond the scope of C may wish to start with David Goldberg's thorough introduction, "What Every Computer Scientist Should Know About Floating-Point Arithmetic," currently available online at *http://docs.sun.com/source/806-3568/ncg_goldberg.html*.

Conventions Used in This Book

The following typographical conventions are used in this book:

Italic
> Highlights new terms; indicates filenames, file extensions, URLs, directories, and Unix utilities.

`Constant width`
> Indicates all elements of C source code: keywords, operators, variables, functions, macros, types, parameters, and literals. Also used for console commands and options, and the output from such commands.

Constant width bold
> Highlights the function or statement under discussion in code examples. In compiler, *make*, and debugger sessions, this font indicates command input to be typed literally by the user.

Constant width italic
> Indicates parameters in function prototypes, or placeholders to be replaced with your own values.

Plain text
> Indicates keys such as Return, Tab, and Ctrl.

 This element signifies a tip or suggestion.

 This element signifies a general note.

 This element indicates a warning or caution.

Using Code Examples

Supplemental material (code examples, exercises, etc.) is available for download at *https://github.com/oreillymedia/c-in-a-nutshell-2E*.

This book is here to help you get your job done. In general, if example code is offered with this book, you may use it in your programs and documentation. You do not need to contact us for permission unless you're reproducing a significant portion of the code. For example, writing a program that uses several chunks of code from this book does not require permission. Selling or distributing a CD-ROM of examples from O'Reilly books does require permission. Answering a question by citing this book and quoting example code does not require permission. Incorporating a significant amount of example code from this book into your product's documentation does require permission.

We appreciate, but do not require, attribution. An attribution usually includes the title, author, publisher, and ISBN. For example: "*C in a Nutshell*, 2nd Edition by

Peter Prinz and Tony Crawford (O'Reilly). Copyright 2016 Peter Prinz, Tony Crawford, 978-1-491-90475-6."

If you feel your use of code examples falls outside fair use or the permission given above, feel free to contact us at *permissions@oreilly.com*.

Safari® Books Online

 *Safari Books Online* is an on-demand digital library that delivers expert content in both book and video form from the world's leading authors in technology and business.

Technology professionals, software developers, web designers, and business and creative professionals use Safari Books Online as their primary resource for research, problem solving, learning, and certification training.

Safari Books Online offers a range of plans and pricing for enterprise, government, education, and individuals.

Members have access to thousands of books, training videos, and prepublication manuscripts in one fully searchable database from publishers like O'Reilly Media, Prentice Hall Professional, Addison-Wesley Professional, Microsoft Press, Sams, Que, Peachpit Press, Focal Press, Cisco Press, John Wiley & Sons, Syngress, Morgan Kaufmann, IBM Redbooks, Packt, Adobe Press, FT Press, Apress, Manning, New Riders, McGraw-Hill, Jones & Bartlett, Course Technology, and hundreds more. For more information about Safari Books Online, please visit us online.

How to Contact Us

Please address comments and questions concerning this book to the publisher:

O'Reilly Media, Inc.
1005 Gravenstein Highway North
Sebastopol, CA 95472
800-998-9938 (in the United States or Canada)
707-829-0515 (international or local)
707-829-0104 (fax)

We have a web page for this book, where we list errata, examples, and any additional information. You can access this page at *http://bit.ly/C_Nutshell_2e*.

To comment or ask technical questions about this book, send email to *bookquestions@oreilly.com*.

For more information about our books, courses, conferences, and news, see our website at *http://www.oreilly.com*.

Find us on Facebook: *http://facebook.com/oreilly*

Follow us on Twitter: *http://twitter.com/oreillymedia*

Watch us on YouTube: *http://www.youtube.com/oreillymedia*

Acknowledgments

Both of us want to thank everyone at O'Reilly for their fantastic work on our book, and especially our editors, Rachel Roumeliotis and Katie Schooling, for all their guidance along the way. We also thank our technical reviewers, Matt Crawford, David Kitabjian, Chris LaPre, John C. Craig, and Loïc Pefferkorn, for their valuable criticism of our manuscript, and we're grateful to our production editor, Kristen Brown, and our copyeditor, Gillian McGarvey, for all their attention to making our book look good and bringing our style up to date. Finally, thanks to Jonathan Gennick for setting the whole project in motion all those years ago.

Peter

I would like to thank Tony, first of all, for the excellent collaboration. My heartfelt thanks also go to all my friends for the understanding they showed again and again when I had so little time for them. Last but not least, I dedicate this book to my daughters, Vivian and Jeanette—both of them now PhDs in computer science—who strengthened my ambition to carry out this book project.

Tony

I thank Peter for letting me take all the space I could fill in this project.

Language

Language Basics

This chapter describes the basic characteristics and elements of the C programming language.

Characteristics of C

C is a general-purpose, procedural programming language. Dennis Ritchie first devised C in the 1970s at AT&T Bell Laboratories in Murray Hill, New Jersey, for the purpose of implementing the Unix operating system and utilities with the greatest possible degree of independence from specific hardware platforms. The key characteristics of the C language are the qualities that made it suitable for that purpose:

- Source code portability
- The ability to operate "close to the machine"
- Efficiency

As a result, the developers of Unix were able to write most of the operating system in C, leaving only a minimum of system-specific hardware manipulation to be coded in assembler.

C's ancestors are the typeless programming languages BCPL (the Basic Combined Programming Language), developed by Martin Richards; and B, a descendant of BCPL, developed by Ken Thompson. A new feature of C was its variety of data types: characters, numeric types, arrays, structures, and so on. Brian Kernighan and Dennis Ritchie published an official description of the C programming language in 1978. As the first de facto standard, their description is commonly referred to simply as *K&R*.[1] C owes its high degree of portability to a compact core language that contains few hardware-dependent elements. For example, the C language proper has no file access or dynamic memory management statements. In fact, there aren't even any statements for console input and output. Instead, the extensive C standard library provides the functions for all of these purposes.

This language design makes the C compiler relatively compact and easy to port to new systems. Furthermore, once the compiler is running on a new system, you can compile most of the functions in the standard library with no further modification, because they are in turn written in portable C. As a result, C compilers are available for practically every computer system.

Because C was expressly designed for system programming, it is hardly surprising that one of its major uses today is in programming embedded systems. At the same time, however, many developers use C as a portable, structured high-level language to write programs such as powerful word processor, database, and graphics applications.

The Structure of C Programs

The procedural building blocks of a C program are *functions*, which can invoke one another. Every function in a well-designed program serves a specific purpose. The functions contain *statements* for the program to execute sequentially, and statements can also be grouped to form *block statements*, or *blocks*. As the programmer, you can use the ready-made functions in the standard library, or write your own when no standard function fulfills your intended purpose. In addition to the C standard library, there are many specialized libraries available, such as libraries of graphics functions. However, by using such nonstandard libraries, you limit the portability of your program to those systems to which the libraries themselves have been ported.

Every C program must define at least one function of its own, with the special name main(), which is the first function invoked when the program starts. The main() function is the program's top level of control, and can call other functions as subroutines.

Example 1-1 shows the structure of a simple, complete C program. We will discuss the details of declarations, function calls, output streams, and more elsewhere in this book. For now, we are simply concerned with the general structure of the C source code. The program in Example 1-1 defines two functions, main() and circularArea(). The main() function calls circularArea() to obtain the area of a circle with a given radius, and then calls the standard library function printf() to output the results in formatted strings on the console.

---

1 The second edition, revised to reflect the first ANSI C standard, is available as *The C Programming Language*, 2nd ed., by Brian W. Kernighan and Dennis M. Ritchie (Englewood Cliffs, NJ: Prentice Hall, 1988).

Example 1-1. A simple C program

```
// circle.c: Calculate and print the areas of circles

#include <stdio.h>                  // Preprocessor directive

double circularArea( double r );  // Function declaration (prototype form)

int main()                        // Definition of main() begins
{
  double radius = 1.0, area = 0.0;

  printf( "    Areas of Circles\n\n" );
  printf( "    Radius          Area\n"
          "------------------------\n" );

  area = circularArea( radius );
  printf( "%10.1f    %10.2f\n", radius, area );

  radius = 5.0;
  area = circularArea( radius );
  printf( "%10.1f    %10.2f\n", radius, area );

  return 0;
}

// The function circularArea() calculates the area of a circle
// Parameter:    The radius of the circle
// Return value: The area of the circle

double circularArea( double r )   // Definition of circularArea() begins
{
  const double pi = 3.1415926536;  // Pi is a constant
  return  pi * r * r;
}
```

Output:

```
    Areas of Circles

    Radius          Area
------------------------
       1.0          3.14
       5.0         78.54
```

Note that the compiler requires a prior *declaration* of each function called. The prototype of circularArea() in the third line of Example 1-1 provides the information needed to compile a statement that calls this function. The prototypes of standard library functions are found in standard header files. Because the header file *stdio.h* contains the prototype of the printf() function, the *preprocessor directive* #include <stdio.h> declares the function indirectly by directing the compiler's preprocessor to insert the contents of that file. (See also "How the C Compiler Works" on page 19.)

You may arrange the functions defined in a program in any order. In Example 1-1, we could just as well have placed the function circularArea() before the function main(). If we had, then the prototype declaration of circularArea() would be superfluous, because the definition of the function is also a declaration.

Function definitions cannot be nested inside one another: you can define a local variable within a function block, but not a local function.

Source Files

The function definitions, global declarations, and preprocessing directives make up the source code of a C program. For small programs, the source code is written in a single source file. Larger C programs consist of several source files. Because the function definitions generally depend on preprocessor directives and global declarations, source files usually have the following internal structure:

1. Preprocessor directives
2. Global declarations
3. Function definitions

C supports modular programming by allowing you to organize a program in as many source and header files as desired, and to edit and compile them separately. Each source file generally contains functions that are logically related, such as the program's user interface functions. It is customary to label C source files with the filename suffix .c.

Examples 1-2 and 1-3 show the same program as Example 1-1, but divided into two source files.

Example 1-2. The first source file, containing the main() function

```
// circle.c: Prints the areas of circles.
// Uses circulararea.c for the math

#include <stdio.h>
double circularArea( double r );

int main()
{
  /* ... As in Example 1-1... */
}
```

Example 1-3. The second source file, containing the circularArea() function

```
// circulararea.c: Calculates the areas of circles.
// Called by main() in circle.c

double circularArea( double r )
{
  /* ... As in Example 1-1... */
}
```

When a program consists of several source files, you need to declare the same functions and global variables, and define the same macros and constants, in many of the files. These declarations and definitions thus form a sort of file header that is more or less constant throughout a program. For the sake of simplicity and consistency, you can write this information just once in a separate *header file*, and then reference the header file using an #include directive in each source code file. Header files are customarily identified by the filename suffix *.h*. A header file explicitly included in a C source file may in turn include other files.

Each C source file, together with all the header files included in it, makes up a *translation unit*. The compiler processes the contents of the translation unit sequentially, parsing the source code into tokens, its smallest semantic units, such as variable names and operators. See "Tokens" on page 21 for more detail.

Any number of whitespace characters can occur between two successive tokens, allowing you a great deal of freedom in formatting the source code. There are no rules for line breaks or indenting, and you may use spaces, tabs, and blank lines liberally to create "human-readable" source code. The preprocessor directives are slightly less flexible: a preprocessor directive must always appear on a line by itself, and no characters except spaces or tabs may precede the hash mark (#) that begins the line.

There are many different conventions and "house styles" for source code formatting. Most of them include the following common rules:

- Start a new line for each new declaration and statement.
- Use indentation to reflect the nested structure of block statements.

Comments

You should use comments generously in the source code to document your C programs. There are two ways to insert a comment in C: *block comments* begin with /* and end with */, and *line comments* begin with // and end with the next newline character.

You can use the /* and */ delimiters to begin and end comments within a line, and to enclose comments of several lines. For example, in the following function prototype, the ellipsis (...) signifies that the open() function has a third, optional parameter. The comment explains the usage of the optional parameter:

```
int open( const char *name, int mode, ... /* int permissions */ );
```

You can use // to insert comments that fill an entire line, or to write source code in a two-column format, with program code on the left and comments on the right:

```
const double pi = 3.1415926536;     // pi is constant
```

These line comments were officially added to the C language by the C99 standard, but most compilers already supported them even before C99. They are sometimes called "C++-style" comments, although they originated in C's forerunner, BCPL.

Inside the quotation marks that delimit a character constant or a string literal, the characters /* and // do not start a comment. For example, the following statement contains no comments:

```
printf( "Comments in C begin with /* or //.\n" );
```

The only thing that the preprocessor looks for in examining the characters in a comment is the end of the comment; thus it is not possible to nest block comments. However, you can insert /* and */ to comment out part of a program that contains line comments:

```
/* Temporarily removing two lines:
   const double pi = 3.1415926536;     // pi is constant
   area = pi * r * r                   // Calculate the area
   Temporarily removed up to here */
```

If you want to comment out part of a program that contains block comments, you can use a conditional preprocessor directive (described in Chapter 15):

```
#if 0
   const double pi = 3.1415926536;     /* pi is constant    */
   area = pi * r * r                   /* Calculate the area */
#endif
```

The preprocessor replaces each comment with a space. The character sequence min/*max*/Value thus becomes the two tokens min Value.

Character Sets

C makes a distinction between the environment in which the compiler translates the source files of a program (the *translation environment*) and the environment in which the compiled program is executed (the *execution environment*). Accordingly, C defines two character sets: the *source character set* is the set of characters that may be used in C source code, and the *execution character set* is the set of characters that can be interpreted by the running program. In many C implementations, the two character sets are identical. If they are not, then the compiler converts the characters in character constants and string literals in the source code into the corresponding elements of the execution character set.

Each of the two character sets includes both a *basic character set* and *extended characters*. The C language does not specify the extended characters, which are usually dependent on the local language. The extended characters together with the basic character set make up the *extended character set*.

The basic source and execution character sets both contain the following types of characters:

The letters of the Latin alphabet

A B C D E F G H I J K L M N O P Q R S T U V W X Y Z

a b c d e f g h i j k l m n o p q r s t u v w x y z

The decimal digits

0 1 2 3 4 5 6 7 8 9

The following 29 graphic characters

! " # % & ' ( ) * + , - . / : ; < = > ? [\ ] ^ _ { | } ~

The five whitespace characters

Space, horizontal tab, vertical tab, newline, and form feed

The basic execution character set also includes four nonprintable characters: the *null* character (which acts as the termination mark in a character string), *alert*, *backspace*, and *carriage return*. To represent these characters in character and string literals, type the corresponding *escape sequences* beginning with a backslash: \0 for the null character, \a for alert, \b for backspace, and \r for carriage return. See Chapter 3 for more details.

The actual numeric values of characters—the character codes—may vary from one C implementation to another. The language itself imposes only these conditions:

- Each character in the basic character set must be representable in one byte.

- The null character is a byte in which all bits are 0.

- The value of each decimal digit after 0 is greater by one than that of the preceding digit.

Wide Characters and Multibyte Characters

C was originally developed in an English-speaking environment where the dominant character set was the 7-bit ASCII code. Since then, the 8-bit byte has become the most common unit of character encoding, but software for international use generally has to be able to represent more different characters than can be coded in one byte. Furthermore, a variety of multibyte character encoding schemes have long been in use internationally to represent non-Latin alphabets and the nonalphabetic Chinese, Japanese, and Korean writing systems. In 1994, with the adoption of "Normative Addendum 1," ISO C standardized two ways of representing larger character sets:

- *Wide characters*, in which the same bit width is used for every character in a character set

- *Multibyte characters*, in which a given character can be represented by one or several bytes, and the character value of a given byte sequence can depend on its context in a string or stream

 Although C now provides abstract mechanisms to manipulate and convert the different kinds of encoding schemes, the language itself doesn't define or specify any encoding scheme, or any character set except the basic source and execution character sets described in the previous section. In other words, it is left up to individual implementations to specify how to encode wide characters, and what multibyte encoding schemes to support.

Wide characters

Since the 1994 addendum, C has provided not only the type char but also wchar_t, the *wide character* type. This type, defined in the header file *stddef.h*, is large enough to represent any element of the given implementation's extended character sets.

Although the C standard does not require support for Unicode character sets, many implementations use the Unicode transformation formats UTF-16 and UTF-32 (see *http://www.unicode.org/*) for wide characters. The Unicode standard is largely identical with the ISO/IEC 10646 standard, and is a superset of many previously existing character sets, including the 7-bit ASCII code. When the Unicode standard is implemented, the type wchar_t is at least 16 or 32 bits wide, and a value of type wchar_t represents one Unicode character. For example, the following definition initializes the variable wc with the Greek letter α:

```
wchar_t wc = '\x3b1';
```

The escape sequence beginning with \x indicates a character code in hexadecimal notation to be stored in the variable—in this case, the code for a lowercase alpha.

For better Unicode support, C11 introduced the additional wide-character types char16_t and char32_t, which are defined as unsigned integer types in the header file *uchar.h*. Characters of the type char16_t are encoded in UTF-16 in C implementations that define the macro __STDC_UTF_16__. Similarly, in implementations that define the macro __STDC_UTF_32__, characters of the type char32_t are encoded in UTF-32.

Multibyte characters

In multibyte character sets, each character is coded as a sequence of one or more bytes. Both the source and execution character sets may contain multibyte characters. If they do, then each character in the basic character set occupies only one byte, and no multibyte character except the null character may contain any byte in which all bits are 0. Multibyte characters can be used in character constants, string literals, identifiers, comments, and header filenames. Many multibyte character sets are designed to support a certain language, such as the Japanese Industrial Standard character set (JIS). The multibyte UTF-8 character set, defined by the Unicode Consortium, is capable of representing all Unicode characters. UTF-8 uses from one to four bytes to represent a character.

The key difference between multibyte characters and wide characters (that is, characters of the type wchar_t, char16_t, or char32_t) is that wide characters are all the same size, and multibyte characters are represented by varying numbers of bytes. This representation makes multibyte strings more complicated to process than strings of wide characters. For example, even though the character *A* can be represented in a single byte, finding it in a multibyte string requires more than a simple byte-by-byte comparison, because the same byte value in certain locations could be part of a different character. Multibyte characters are well suited for saving text in files, however (see Chapter 13). Furthermore, the encoding of multibyte characters is independent of the system architecture, while encoding of wide characters is dependent on the given system's byte order: that is, the bytes of a wide character may be in *big-endian* or *little-endian* order, depending on the system.

Conversion

C provides standard functions to obtain the wchar_t value of any multibyte character, and to convert any wide character to its multibyte representation. For example, if the C compiler uses the Unicode standards UTF-16 and UTF-8, then the following call to the function wctomb() (read: "wide character to multibyte") obtains the multibyte representation of the character α:

```
wchar_t wc = L'\x3B1';      // Greek lowercase alpha, α
char mbStr[10] = "";
int nBytes = 0;
nBytes = wctomb( mbStr, wc );
if( nBytes < 0)
    puts("Not a valid multibyte character in your locale.");
```

After a successful function call, the array mbStr contains the multibyte character, which in this example is the sequence "\xCE\xB1". The wctomb() function's return value, assigned here to the variable nBytes, is the number of bytes required to represent the multibyte character—namely, 2.

The standard library also provides conversion functions for char16_t and char32_t, the new wide-character types introduced in C11, such as the function c16rtomb(), which returns the multibyte character that corresponds to a given wide character of the type char16_t (see "Multibyte Characters" on page 333).

Universal Character Names

C also supports universal character names as a way to use the extended character set regardless of the implementation's encoding. You can specify any extended character by its *universal character name*, which is its Unicode value in the form:

    \u*XXXX*

or:

    \U*XXXXXXXX*

where *XXXX* or *XXXXXXXX* is a Unicode code point in hexadecimal notation. Use the lowercase u prefix followed by four hexadecimal digits, or the uppercase U followed by exactly eight hex digits. If the first four hexadecimal digits are zero, then the same universal character name can be written either as \u*XXXX* or as \U0000*XXXX*.

Universal character names are permissible in identifiers, character constants, and string literals. However, they must not be used to represent characters in the basic character set.

When you specify a character by its universal character name, the compiler stores it in the character set used by the implementation. For example, if the execution character set in a localized program is ISO 8859-7 (8-bit Greek), then the following definition initializes the variable alpha with the code\xE1:

    char alpha = '\u03B1';

However, if the execution character set is UTF-16, then you need to define the variable as a wide character:

    wchar_t alpha = '\u03B1'; // or char16_t alpha = u'\u03B1';

In this case, the character code value assigned to alpha is hexadecimal 3B1, the same as the universal character name.

Not all compilers support universal character names.

Digraphs and Trigraphs

C provides alternative representations for a number of punctuation marks that are not available on all keyboards. Six of these are the *digraphs*, or two-character tokens, which represent the characters shown in Table 1-1.

Table 1-1. Digraphs

Digraph	Equivalent
<:	[
:>	]
<%	{
%>	}
%:	#
%:%:	##

These sequences are not interpreted as digraphs if they occur within character constants or string literals. In all other positions, they behave exactly like the single-character tokens they represent. For example, the following code fragments are perfectly equivalent, and produce the same output. With digraphs:

```
int arr<::> = <% 10, 20, 30 %>;
printf( "The second array element is <%d>.\n", arr<:1:> );
```

Without digraphs:

```
int arr[] = { 10, 20, 30 };
printf( "The second array element is <%d>.\n", arr[1] );
```

Output:

```
The second array element is <20>.
```

C also provides *trigraphs*, three-character representations, all of them beginning with two question marks. The third character determines which punctuation mark a trigraph represents, as shown in Table 1-2.

Table 1-2. Trigraphs

Trigraph	Equivalent
??(	[
??)	]
??<	{
??>	}
??=	#
??/	\
??!	|
??'	^
??-	~

Trigraphs allow you to write any C program using only the characters defined in ISO/IEC 646, the 1991 standard corresponding to 7-bit ASCII. The compiler's preprocessor replaces the trigraphs with their single-character equivalents in the first phase of compilation. This means that the trigraphs, unlike digraphs, are translated into their single-character equivalents no matter where they occur, even in character constants, string literals, comments, and preprocessing directives. For example, the preprocessor interprets the following statement's second and third question marks as the beginning of a trigraph:

```
printf("Cancel???(y/n) ");
```

Thus, the line produces the following unintended preprocessor output:

```
printf("Cancel?[y/n) ");
```

If you need to use one of these three-character sequences and do not want it to be interpreted as a trigraph, you can write the question marks as escape sequences:

```
printf("Cancel\?\?\?(y/n) ");
```

If the character following any two question marks is not one of those shown in Table 1-2, then the sequence is not a trigraph, and remains unchanged.

 As another substitute for punctuation characters in addition to the digraphs and trigraphs, the header file *iso646.h* contains macros that define alternative representations of C's logical operators and bitwise operators, such as and for && and xor for ^. For details, see Chapter 16.

Identifiers

The term *identifier* refers to the names of variables, functions, macros, structures, and other objects defined in a C program. Identifiers can contain the following characters:

- The letters in the basic character set, a–z and A–Z (identifiers are case-sensitive)
- The underscore character, _
- The decimal digits 0–9, although the first character of an identifier must not be a digit
- Universal character names that represent the letters and digits of other languages

The permissible universal characters are defined in Annex D of the C standard, and correspond to the characters defined in the ISO/IEC TR 10176 standard, minus the basic character set.

Multibyte characters may also be permissible in identifiers. However, it is up to the given C implementation to determine exactly which multibyte characters are permitted and what universal character names they correspond to.

The following 44 keywords are *reserved* in C, each having a specific meaning to the compiler, and must not be used as identifiers:

auto	extern	short	while
break	float	signed	_Alignas
case	for	sizeof	_Alignof
char	goto	static	_Atomic
const	if	struct	_Bool
continue	inline	switch	_Complex
default	int	typedef	_Generic
do	long	union	_Imaginary
double	register	unsigned	_Noreturn
else	restrict	void	_Static_assert
enum	return	volatile	_Thread_local

The following examples are valid identifiers:

```
x dollar Break error_handler scale64
```

The following are not valid identifiers:

```
1st_rank switch y/n x-ray
```

If the compiler supports universal character names, then α is also an example of a valid identifier, and you can define a variable by that name:

```
double α = 0.5;
```

Your source code editor might save the character α in the source file as the universal character \u03B1.

When choosing identifiers in your programs, remember that many identifiers are already used by the C standard library. These include the names of standard library functions, which you cannot use for functions you define or for global variables. See Chapter 16 for details.

The C compiler provides the predefined identifier __func__ (note that there are four underscore characters), which you can use in any function to access a string constant containing the name of the function. This is useful for logging or for debugging output; for example:

```
#include <stdio.h>
int test_func( char *s )
{
  if( s == NULL) {
    fprintf( stderr,
          "%s: received null pointer argument\n", __func__ );
    return -1;
```

```
    }
    /* ... */
}
```

In this example, passing a null pointer to the function `test_func()` generates the following error message:

```
test_func: received null pointer argument
```

There is no limit on the length of identifiers. However, most compilers consider only a limited number of characters in identifiers to be significant. In other words, a compiler might fail to distinguish between two identifiers that start with a long identical sequence of characters. To conform to the C standard, a compiler must treat at least the first 31 characters as significant in the names of functions and global variables (that is, identifiers with external linkage), and at least the first 63 characters in all other identifiers.

Identifier Name Spaces

All identifiers fall into exactly one of the following four categories, which constitute separate *name spaces*:

- Label names
- Tags, which identify structure, union, and enumeration types
- Names of structure or union members (each structure or union constitutes a separate name space for its members)
- All other identifiers, which are called *ordinary identifiers*

Identifiers that belong to different name spaces may be the same without causing conflicts. In other words, you can use the same name to refer to different objects, if they are of different kinds. For example, the compiler is capable of distinguishing between a variable and a label with the same name. Similarly, you can give the same name to a structure type, an element in the structure, and a variable, as the following example shows:

```
struct pin { char pin[16];  /* ... */ };
_Bool check_pin( struct pin *pin )
{
  int len = strlen( pin->pin );
  /* ... */
}
```

The first line of the example defines a structure type identified by the tag `pin`, containing a character array named `pin` as one of its members. In the second line, the function parameter `pin` is a pointer to a structure of the type just defined. The expression `pin->pin` in the fourth line designates the member of the structure that the function's parameter points to. The context in which an identifier appears always determines its name space with no ambiguity. Nonetheless, it is generally a good

---

idea to make all identifiers in a program distinct, in order to spare human readers unnecessary confusion.

Identifier Scope

The *scope* of an identifier refers to that part of the translation unit in which the identifier is meaningful. Or to put it another way, the identifier's scope is that part of the program that can "see" that identifier. The type of scope is always determined by the location at which you declare the identifier (except for labels, which always have function scope). Four kinds of scope are possible:

File scope
> If you declare an identifier outside all blocks and parameter lists, then it has file scope. You can then use the identifier anywhere after the declaration and up to the end of the translation unit.

Block scope
> Except for labels, identifiers declared within a block have block scope. You can use such an identifier only from its declaration to the end of the smallest block containing that declaration. The smallest containing block is often, but not necessarily, the body of a function definition. Starting with C99, declarations do not have to be placed before all statements in a function block. The parameter names in the head of a function definition also have block scope, and are valid within the corresponding function block.

Function prototype scope
> The parameter names in a function prototype have function prototype scope. Because these parameter names are not significant outside the prototype itself, they are meaningful only as comments, and can also be omitted. See Chapter 7 for further information.

Function scope
> The scope of a label is always the function block in which the label occurs, even if it is placed within nested blocks. In other words, you can use a goto statement to jump to a label from any point within the same function that contains the label. (Jumping into nested blocks is not a good idea, though; see Chapter 6 for details.)

The scope of an identifier generally begins *after* its declaration. However, the type names—or tags—of structure, union, and enumeration types and the names of enumeration constants are an exception to this rule: their scope begins immediately after their appearance *in* the declaration so that they can be referenced again in the declaration itself. (Structures and unions are discussed in detail in Chapter 10; enumeration types are described in Chapter 2.) For example, in the following declaration of a structure type, the last member of the structure, next, is a pointer to the very structure type that is being declared:

```
struct Node { /* ... */
             struct Node *next; };          // Define a structure type
void printNode( const struct Node *ptrNode); // Declare a function

int printList( const struct Node *first )   // Begin a function
{                                           // definition
  struct Node *ptr = first;

  while( ptr != NULL ) {
    printNode( ptr );
    ptr = ptr->next;
  }
}
```

In this code snippet, the identifiers Node, next, printNode, and printList all have
file scope. The parameter ptrNode has function prototype scope, and the variables
first and ptr have block scope.

It is possible to use an identifier again in a new declaration nested within its existing
scope, even if the new identifier does not have a different name space. If you do so,
then the new declaration must have block or function prototype scope, and the
block or function prototype must be a true subset of the outer scope. In such cases,
the new declaration of the same identifier *hides* the outer declaration so that the
variable or function declared in the outer block is not *visible* in the inner scope. For
example, the following declarations are permissible:

```
double x;             // Declare a variable x with file scope
long calc( double x ); // Declare a new x with function prototype
                      // scope

int main()
{
  long x = calc( 2.5 ); // Declare a long variable x with block scope

  if( x < 0 )          // Here, x refers to the long variable
  { float x = 0.0F;    // Declare a new variable x with block scope
    /*...*/
  }
  x *= 2;              // Here, x refers to the long variable again
  /*...*/
}
```

In this example, the long variable x delcared in the main() function hides the global
variable x with type double. Thus, there is no direct way to access the double variable x from within main(). Furthermore, in the conditional block that depends on
the if statement, x refers to the newly declared float variable, which in turn hides
the long variable x.

How the C Compiler Works

Once you have written a source file using a text editor, you can invoke a C compiler to translate it into machine code. The compiler operates on a *translation unit* consisting of a source file and all the header files referenced by #include directives. If the compiler finds no errors in the translation unit, it generates an *object file* containing the corresponding machine code. Object files are usually identified by the filename suffix *.o* or *.obj*. In addition, the compiler may also generate an assembler listing (see Chapter 19).

Object files are also called *modules*. A library, such as the C standard library, contains compiled, rapidly accessible modules of the standard functions.

The compiler translates each translation unit of a C program—that is, each source file with any header files it includes—into a separate object file. The compiler then invokes the *linker*, which combines the object files and any library functions used in an *executable file*. Figure 1-1 illustrates the process of compiling and linking a program from several source files and libraries. The executable file also contains any information that the target operating system needs in order to load and start it.

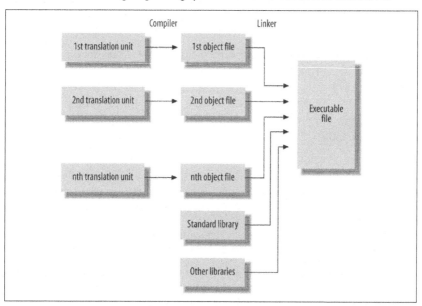

Figure 1-1. From source code to executable file

The C Compiler's Translation Phases

The compiling process takes place in eight logical steps. A given compiler may combine several of these steps as long as the results are not affected. The steps are:

1. Characters are read from the source file and converted, if necessary, into the characters of the source character set. The end-of-line indicators in the source file, if different from the newline character, are replaced. Likewise, any trigraph sequences are replaced with the single characters they represent. (Digraphs, however, are left alone; they are not converted into their single-character equivalents.)

2. Wherever a backslash is followed immediately by a newline character, the preprocessor deletes both. Because a line-end character ends a preprocessor directive, this processing step lets you place a backslash at the end of a line in order to continue a directive, such as a macro definition, on the next line.

Every source file, if not completely empty, must end with a newline character.

3. The source file is broken down into preprocessor tokens (see "Tokens" on page 21) and sequences of whitespace characters. Each comment is treated as one space.

4. The preprocessor directives are carried out and macro calls are expanded.

Steps 1 through 4 are also applied to any files inserted by #include directives. Once the compiler has carried out the preprocessor directives, it removes them from its working copy of the source code.

5. The characters and escape sequences in character constants and string literals are converted into the corresponding characters in the execution character set.

6. Adjacent string literals are concatenated into a single string.

7. The actual compiling takes place: the compiler analyzes the sequence of tokens and generates the corresponding machine code.

8. The linker resolves references to external objects and functions, and generates the executable file. If a module refers to external objects or functions that are not defined in any of the translation units, the linker takes them from the standard library or another specified library. External objects and functions must not be defined more than once in a program.

For most compilers, either the preprocessor is a separate program, or the compiler provides options to perform only the preprocessing (steps 1 through 4 in the preceding list). This setup allows you to verify that your preprocessor directives have the intended effects. For a more practically oriented look at the compiling process, see Chapter 19.

Tokens

A token is either a keyword, an identifier, a constant, a string literal, or a symbol. Symbols in C consist of one or more punctuation characters, and function as operators or digraphs, or have syntactic importance, like the semicolon that terminates a simple statement or the braces { } that enclose a block statement. For example, the following C statement consists of five tokens:

```
printf("Hello, world.\n");
```

The individual tokens are:

```
printf
(
"Hello, world.\n"
)
;
```

The tokens interpreted by the preprocessor are parsed in the third translation phase. These are only slightly different from the tokens that the compiler interprets in the seventh phase of translation:

- Within an #include directive, the preprocessor recognizes the additional tokens <*filename*> and "*filename*".

- During the preprocessing phase, character constants and string literals have not yet been converted from the source character set to the execution character set.

- Unlike the compiler proper, the preprocessor makes no distinction between integer constants and floating-point constants.

In parsing the source file into tokens, the compiler (or preprocessor) always applies the following principle: each successive non-whitespace character must be appended to the token being read, unless appending it would make a valid token invalid. This rule resolves any ambiguity in the following expression, for example:

```
a+++b
```

Because the first + cannot be part of an identifier or keyword starting with a, it begins a new token. The second + appended to the first forms a valid token—the increment operator—but a third + does not. Hence the expression must be parsed as:

```
a ++ + b
```

See Chapter 19 for more information on compiling C programs.

2

Types

Programs have to store and process different kinds of data, such as integers and floating-point numbers, in different ways. To this end, the compiler needs to know what kind of data a given value represents.

In C, the term *object* refers to a location in memory whose contents can represent values. Objects that have names are also called *variables*. An object's *type* determines how much space the object occupies in memory, and how its possible values are encoded. For example, the same pattern of bits can represent completely different integers depending on whether the data object is interpreted as *signed* (that is, either positive or negative) or *unsigned* (and hence unable to represent negative values).

Typology

The types in C can be classified as follows:

- Basic types
  - Standard and extended integer types
  - Real and complex floating-point types
- Enumerated types
- The type void
- Derived types
  - Pointer types
  - Array types
  - Structure types

- Union types
- Function types

The basic types and the enumerated types together make up the *arithmetic types*. The arithmetic types and the pointer types together are called the *scalar* types. Finally, array types and structure types are referred to collectively as the *aggregate types*. (Union types are not considered aggregate because only one of their members can store a value at any given time.)

A *function type* describes the interface to a function; that is, it specifies the type of the function's return value, and may also specify the types of all the parameters that are passed to the function when it is called.

All other types describe objects. This description may or may not include the object's storage size. If it does, the type is properly called an *object type*; if not, it is an *incomplete type*. An example of an incomplete type might be an externally defined array variable:

```
extern float fArr[ ];      // External declaration
```

This line declares fArr as an array whose elements have type float. However, because the array's size is not specified here, fArr's type is incomplete. As long as the global array fArr is defined with a specified size at another location in the program —in another source file, for example—this declaration is sufficient to let you use the array in its present scope. (For more details on external declarations, see Chapter 11.)

This chapter describes the basic types, enumerations, and the type void. The derived types are described in Chapters 7 through 10.

Some types are designated by a sequence of more than one keyword, such as unsigned short. In such cases, the keywords can be written in any order. However, there is a conventional keyword order, which we use in this book.

Integer Types

There are five signed integer types. Most of these types can be designated by several synonyms, which are listed in Table 2-1.

Table 2-1. Standard signed integer types

Type	Synonyms
signed char	
int	signed, signed int
short	short int, signed short, signed short int
long	long int, signed long, signed long int
long long (C99)	long long int, signed long long, signed long long int

For each of the five signed integer types in Table 2-1, there is also a corresponding unsigned type that occupies the same amount of memory, with the same *alignment*. In other words, if the compiler aligns signed int objects on even-numbered byte addresses, then unsigned int objects are also aligned on even addresses. These unsigned types are listed in Table 2-2.

Table 2-2. Unsigned standard integer types

Type	Synonyms
_Bool	bool (defined in *stdbool.h*)
unsigned char	
unsigned int	unsigned
unsigned short	unsigned short int
unsigned long	unsigned long int
unsigned long long	unsigned long long int

C99 introduced the unsigned integer type _Bool to represent Boolean truth values. The Boolean value *true* is coded as 1, and *false* is coded as 0. If you include the header file *stdbool.h* in a program, you can also use the identifiers bool, true, and false, which are familiar to C++ programmers. The macro bool is a synonym for the type _Bool, and true and false are symbolic constants equal to 1 and 0.

The type char is also one of the standard integer types. However, the one-word type name char is synonymous either with signed char or with unsigned char, depending on the compiler. Because this choice is left up to the implementation, char, signed char, and unsigned char are formally three different types.

 If your program relies on char being able to hold values less than zero or greater than 127, you should be using either signed char or unsigned char instead.

You can do arithmetic with character variables. It's up to you to decide whether your program interprets the number in a char variable as a character code or as something else. For example, the following short program treats the char value in ch as both an integer and a character, but at different times:

```
char ch = 'A';                  // A variable with type char
printf("The character %c has the character code %d.\n", ch, ch);
for ( ; ch <= 'Z'; ++ch )
  printf("%2c", ch);
```

In the printf() statement, ch is first treated as a character that gets displayed, and then as numeric code value of the character. Likewise, the for loop treats ch as an integer in the instruction ++ch, and as a character in the printf() function call. On systems that use the 7-bit ASCII code or an extension of it, the code produces the following output:

```
The character A has the character code 65.
 A B C D E F G H I J K L M N O P Q R S T U V W X Y Z
```

A value of type char always occupies one byte—in other words, sizeof(char) always yields 1—and a byte is at least eight bits wide. Every character in the basic character set can be represented in a char object as a positive value.

C defines only the *minimum* storage sizes of the other standard types: the size of type short is at least two bytes, long is at least four bytes, and long long is at least eight bytes. Furthermore, although the integer types may be larger than their minimum sizes, the sizes implemented must be in the order:

```
sizeof(short) ≤ sizeof(int) ≤ sizeof(long) ≤ sizeof(long long)
```

The type int is the integer type best adapted to the target system's architecture, with the size and bit format of a CPU register.

The internal representation of integer types is binary. Signed types may be represented in binary as *sign and magnitude*, as a *one's complement*, or as a *two's complement*. The most common representation is the two's complement. The non-negative values of a signed type are within the value range of the corresponding unsigned type, and the binary representation of a non-negative value is the same in both the signed and unsigned types. Table 2-3 shows the different interpretations of bit patterns as signed and unsigned integer types.

Table 2-3. Binary representations of signed and unsigned 16-bit integers

Binary	Decimal value as unsigned int	Decimal value as signed int, one's complement	Decimal value as signed int, two's complement
00000000 00000000	0	0	0
00000000 00000001	1	1	1
00000000 00000010	2	2	2
...			

Binary	Decimal value as unsigned int	Decimal value as signed int, one's complement	Decimal value as signed int, two's complement
01111111 11111111	32,767	32,767	32,767
10000000 00000000	32,768	-32,767	-32,768
10000000 00000001	32,769	-32,766	-32,767
...			
11111111 11111110	65,534	-1	-2
11111111 11111111	65,535	-0	-1

Table 2-4 lists the sizes and value ranges of the standard integer types.

Table 2-4. Common storage sizes and value ranges of standard integer types

Type	Storage size	Minimum value	Maximum value
char	(Same as either signed char or unsigned char)		
unsigned char	One byte	0	255
signed char	One byte	-128	127
int	Two bytes or four bytes	-32,768 or -2,147,483,648	32,767 or 2,147,483,647
unsigned int	Two bytes or four bytes	0	65,535 or 4,294,967,295
short	Two bytes	-32,768	32,767
unsigned short	Two bytes	0	65,535
long	Four bytes	-2,147,483,648	2,147,483,647
unsigned long	Four bytes	0	4,294,967,295
long long (C99)	Eight bytes	-9,223,372,036, 854,775,808	9,223,372,036, 854,775,807
unsigned long long (C99)	Eight bytes	0	18,446,744,073, 709,551,615

In the following example, each of the int variables iIndex and iLimit occupies four bytes on a 32-bit computer:

```
int iIndex,        // Define two int variables and
    iLimit = 1000; // initialize the second one.
```

To obtain the exact size of a type or variable, use the sizeof operator. The expression

```
sizeof(type)
```

yields the size of the type named, and

```
sizeof expression
```

yields the size of the given expression's type, as a number of bytes with the type size_t. The type size_t is defined in *stddef.h*, *stdio.h*, and other header files as an unsigned integer type (such as unsigned long, for example). If the operand is an expression, the size is that of the expression's type. In the previous example, the value of sizeof(int) would be the same as sizeof(iIndex)—namely, 4. The parentheses around the expression iIndex can be omitted because iIndex is an expression, not a type.

You can find the value ranges of the integer types for your C compiler in the header file *limits.h*, which defines macros such as INT_MIN, INT_MAX, UINT_MAX, and so on (see Chapter 16). The program in Example 2-1 uses these macros to display the minimum and maximum values for the types char and int.

Example 2-1. Value ranges of the types char and int

```
// limits.c: Display the value ranges of char and int.
// -------------------------------------------------------
#include <stdio.h>
#include <limits.h>      // Contains the macros CHAR_MIN, INT_MIN, etc.

int main()
{
  printf("Storage sizes and value ranges of the types char and int\n\n");
  printf("The type char is %s.\n\n", CHAR_MIN < 0 ? "signed" :"unsigned");

  printf(" Type   Size (in bytes)   Minimum         Maximum\n"
         "-----------------------------------------------------\n");
  printf(" char %8zu %20d %15d\n", sizeof(char), CHAR_MIN, CHAR_MAX );
  printf(" int  %8zu %20d %15d\n", sizeof(int), INT_MIN, INT_MAX );
  return 0;
}
```

In arithmetic operations with integers, overflows can occur. An overflow happens when the result of an operation is no longer within the range of values that the type being used can represent. In arithmetic with unsigned integer types, overflows are ignored. In mathematical terms, that means that the effective result of an unsigned integer operation is equal to the remainder of a division by *UTYPE_MAX* + 1, where *UTYPE_MAX* is the unsigned type's maximum representable value. For example, the following addition causes the variable to overflow:

```
    unsigned int ui = UINT_MAX;
    ui += 2;                        // Result: 1
```

C specifies this behavior only for the unsigned integer types. For all other types, the result of an overflow is undefined. For example, the overflow may be ignored, or it may raise a signal that aborts the program if it is not caught.

Integer Types Defined in Standard Headers

The headers of the standard library define numerous integer types for specific uses, such as the type wchar_t to represent wide characters. These types are typedef names—that is, synonyms for standard integer types (see "typedef Declarations" on page 185).

The types ptrdiff_t, size_t, and wchar_t are defined in the header *stddef.h* (and in other headers); the types char16_t and char32_t are defined in the header *uchar.h*. For special requirements, integer types with specifed bit widths, in signed and unsigned variants, are defined in the header *stdint.h*. These are described in the following subsection.

Furthermore, the header *stdint.h* also defines macros that supply the maximum and minimum representable values of all the integer types defined in the standard library. For example, SIZE_MAX equals the largest value you can store in a variable of the type size_t. For all details on the types listed here, and the corresponding macros, see Chapter 16.

Integer types with exact width (C99)

The width of an integer type is defined as the number of bits used to represent a value, including the sign bit. Typical widths are 8, 16, 32, and 64 bits. For example, the type int is at least 16 bits wide.

In C99, the header file *stdint.h* defines integer types to fulfill the need for known widths. These types are listed in Table 2-5. Those types whose names begin with u are unsigned. C99 implementations are not required to provide the types marked as "optional" in the table.

Table 2-5. Integer types with defined width

Type	Meaning	Implementation
int$N$_t uint$N$_t	An integer type whose width is exactly N bits	Optional
int_least$N$_t uint_least$N$_t	An integer type whose width is at least N bits	Required for $N = 8, 16, 32, 64$
int_fast$N$_t uint_fast$N$_t	The fastest type to process whose width is at least N bits	Required for $N = 8, 16, 32, 64$
intmax_t uintmax_t	The widest integer type implemented	Required
intptr_t uintptr_t	An integer type wide enough to store the value of a pointer	Optional

For example, int_least64_t and uint_least64_t are integer types with a width of at least 64 bits. If an optional signed type (without the prefix u) is defined, then the corresponding unsigned type (with the initial u) is required, and vice versa. The following example defines and initializes an array whose elements have the type int_fast32_t:

```
#define ARR_SIZE 100
int_fast32_t arr[ARR_SIZE];      // Define an array arr
                                 // with elements of type int_fast32_t
for ( int i = 0; i < ARR_SIZE; ++i )
    arr[i] = (int_fast32_t)i;    // Initialize each element
```

The types listed in Table 2-5 are usually defined as synonyms for existing standard types. For example, the *stdint.h* file supplied with one C compiler contains the line:

```
typedef signed char    int_fast8_t;
```

This declaration simply defines the new type int_fast8_t (the fastest 8-bit signed integer type) as being equivalent with signed char.

Furthermore, an implementation may also define extended integer types such as int24_t or uint_least128_t.

The signed int$N$_t types have a special feature: they must use the two's complement binary representation. As a result, their minimum value is -2^{N-1}, and their maximum value is $2^{N-1} - 1$.

The value ranges of the types defined in *stdint.h* are also easy to obtain: macros for the greatest and least representable values are defined in the same header file. The names of the macros are the uppercased type names, with the suffix _t (for *type*) replaced by _MAX or _MIN (see Chapter 16). For example, the following definition initializes the variable i64 with its smallest possible value:

```
int_least64_t i64 = INT_LEAST64_MIN;
```

The header file *inttypes.h* includes the header file *stdint.h*, and provides other features such as extended integer type specifiers for use in printf() and scanf() function calls (see Chapter 16).

Floating-Point Types

C also includes special numeric types that can represent nonintegers with a decimal point in any position. The standard *floating-point* types for calculations with real numbers are as follows:

float
> For variables with single precision

double
> For variables with double precision

long double
> For variables with extended precision

A floating-point value can be stored only with a limited precision, which is determined by the binary format used to represent it and the amount of memory used to store it. The precision is expressed as a number of significant digits. For example, a "precision of six decimal digits" or "six-digit precision" means that the type's binary representation is precise enough to store a real number of six decimal digits, so that its conversion back into a six-digit decimal number yields the original six digits. The position of the decimal point does not matter, and leading and trailing zeros are not counted in the six digits. The numbers 123,456,000 and 0.00123456 can both be stored in a type with six-digit precision.

In C, arithmetic operations with floating-point numbers are usually performed with double or greater precision. The floating-point precision used internally by the given implementation is indicated by the value of the macro FLT_EVAL_METHOD, defined in the header *float.h*. For example, if the macro FLT_EVAL_METHOD has the value 1, the following product is calculated using the double type:

```
float height = 1.2345, width = 2.3456;   // Float variables have
                                         // single precision.
double area = height * width;            // The actual calculation
                                         // is performed with
                                         // double precision.
```

If you assign the result to a float variable, the value is rounded as necessary. For more details on floating-point math, see "math.h" on page 300.

C defines only minimal requirements for the storage size and binary format of the floating-point types. However, the format commonly used is the one defined by the International Electrotechnical Commission (IEC) in the 1989 standard for binary floating-point arithmetic, IEC 60559. This standard is based in turn on the Institute of Electrical and Electronics Engineers' 1985 standard, IEEE 754. Compilers can indicate that they support the IEC floating-point standard by defining the macro __STDC_IEC_559__. Table 2-6 shows the value ranges and the precision of the real floating-point types in accordance with IEC 60559, using decimal notation.

Table 2-6. Real floating-point types

Type	Storage size	Value range	Smallest positive value	Precision
float	4 bytes	±3.4E+38	1.2E-38	6 digits
double	8 bytes	±1.7E+308	2.3E-308	15 digits
long double	10 bytes	±1.1E+4932	3.4E-4932	19 digits

The header file *float.h* defines macros that allow you to use these values and other details about the binary representation of real numbers in your programs. The macros FLT_MIN, FLT_MAX, and FLT_DIG indicate the value range and the precision of the float type. The corresponding macros for double and long double begin with the prefixes DBL_ and LDBL_. These macros, and the binary representation of floating-point numbers, are described in "float.h" on page 293.

The program in Example 2-2 starts by printing the typical values for the type float, and then illustrates the rounding error that results from storing a floating-point number in a float variable.

Example 2-2. Illustrating the precision of type float

```c
#include <stdio.h>
#include <float.h>

int main()
{
  puts("\nCharacteristics of the type float\n");

  printf("Storage size: %d bytes\n"
         "Smallest positive value: %E\n"
         "Greatest positive value: %E\n"
         "Precision: %d decimal digits\n",
         sizeof(float), FLT_MIN, FLT_MAX, FLT_DIG);

  puts("\nAn example of float precision:\n");
  double d_var = 12345.6;      // A variable of type double.
  float f_var = (float)d_var;   // Initializes the float
                               // variable with the value of d_var.
  printf("The floating-point number     "
         "%18.10f\n", d_var);
  printf("has been stored in a variable\n"
         "of type float as the value    "
         "%18.10f\n", f_var);
  printf("The rounding error is         "
         "%18.10f\n", d_var - f_var);

  return 0;
}
```

The last part of this program typically generates the following output:

```
The floating-point number     12345.6000000000
has been stored in a variable
of type float as the value    12345.5996093750
The rounding error is             0.0003906250
```

In this example, the nearest representable value to the decimal 12,345.6 is 12,345.5996093750. This may not look like a round number in decimal notation, but in the internal binary representation of the floating-point type, it *is* exactly representable, while 12,345.60 is not.

Complex Floating-Point Types

C99 supports mathematical calculations with complex numbers. The 1999 standard introduced complex floating-point types and extended the mathematical library to include complex arithmetic functions. These functions are declared in the header file *complex.h*, and include the trigonometric functions `csin()`, `ctan()`, and so on (see Chapter 16).

In the C11 standard, support for complex numbers is optional. The macro `__STDC_NO_COMPLEX__` can be defined to indicate that the implementation does not include the header file *complex.h*.

A complex number z can be represented in Cartesian coordinates as $z = x + y \times i$, where x and y are real numbers, and i is the *imaginary unit*, defined by the equation $i^2 = -1$. The number x is called the real part, and y the imaginary part, of z.

In C, a complex number is represented by a pair of floating-point values for the real and imaginary parts. Both parts have the same type, whether `float`, `double`, or `long double`. Accordingly, these are the three complex floating-point types:

- `float _Complex`
- `double _Complex`
- `long double _Complex`

Each of these types has the same size and alignment as an array of two `float`, `double`, or `long double` elements.

The header file *complex.h* defines the macros `complex` and `I`. The macro `complex` is a synonym for the keyword `_Complex`. The macro `I` represents the imaginary unit i, and has the type `const float _Complex`:

```
#include <complex.h>
// ...
double complex z = 1.0 + 2.0 * I;
z *= I;        // Rotate z through 90° counterclockwise around the origin
```

To compose a complex number from its real and imaginary parts, C11 also provides the macros `CMPLX`, `CMPLXF`, and `CMPLXL`. For example, the complex number `CMPLX(1.0, 2.0)` is equal to the number z defined in the preceding example, and has the type `double complex`. Similarly, the macros `CMPLXF` and `CMPLXL` yield a complex number of the type `float complex` and `long double complex`. An implementation may also include the following types to represent pure *imaginary* numbers: `float imaginary`, `double imaginary`, and `long double imaginary`.

Enumerated Types

Enumerations are integer types that you define in a program. The definition of an enumeration begins with the keyword `enum`, possibly followed by an identifier for the enumeration, and contains a list of the type's possible values, with a name for each value:

```
enum [identifier] { enumerator-list };
```

The following example defines the enumerated type `enum color`:

```
enum color { black, red, green, yellow, blue, white=7, gray };
```

The identifier `color` is the *tag* of this enumeration. The identifiers in the list—black, red, and so on—are the *enumeration constants*, and have the type `int`. You can use these constants anywhere within their scope—as `case` constants in a `switch` statement, for example.

Each enumeration constant of a given enumerated type represents a certain value, which is determined either implicitly by its position in the list, or explicitly by initialization with a constant expression. A constant without an initialization has the value 0 if it is the first constant in the list, or the value of the preceding constant plus one. Thus, in the previous example, the constants listed have the values 0, 1, 2, 3, 4, 7, 8.

Within an enumerated type's scope, you can use the type in declarations:

```
enum color bgColor = blue,      // Define two variables
           fgColor = yellow;    // of type enum color.
void setFgColor( enum color fgc ); // Declare a function with a
                                   // parameter of type enum color.
```

An enumerated type always corresponds to one of the standard integer types. Thus, your C programs may perform ordinary arithmetic operations with variables of enumerated types. The compiler may select the appropriate integer type depending on the defined values of the enumeration constants. In the previous example, the type `char` would be sufficient to represent all the values of the enumerated type `enum color`.

Different constants in an enumeration may have the same value:

```
enum { OFF, ON, STOP = 0, GO = 1, CLOSED = 0, OPEN = 1 };
```

As the preceding example also illustrates, the definition of an enumerated type does not necessarily have to include a tag. Omitting the tag makes sense if you only want to define constants and not declare any variables of the given type. Defining integer constants in this way is generally preferable to using a long list of `#define` directives, as the enumeration provides the compiler with the names of the constants as well as their numeric values. These names are a great advantage in a debugger's display, for example.

The Type void

The type specifier `void` indicates that no value is available. Consequently, you cannot declare variables or constants with this type. You can use the type `void` for the purposes described in the following sections.

void in Function Declarations

A function with no return value has the type void. For example, the standard function perror() is declared by the prototype:

```
void perror( const char * );
```

The keyword void in the parameter list of a function prototype indicates that the function has no parameters:

```
FILE *tmpfile( void );
```

As a result, the compiler issues an error message if you try to use a function call such as tmpfile("name.tmp"). If the function were declared without void in the parameter list, the C compiler would have no information about the function's parameters, and hence would be unable to determine whether the function call is correct.

Expressions of Type void

A void expression is one that has no value. For example, a call to a function with no return value is an expression of type void:

```
char filename[ ] = "memo.txt";
if ( fopen( filename, "r" ) == NULL )
    perror( filename );              // A void expression
```

The cast operation (void)*expression* explicitly discards the value of an expression, such as the return value of a function:

```
(void)printf("I don't need this function's return value!\n");
```

Pointers to void

A pointer of type void * represents the address of an object, but not its type. You can use such quasi-typeless pointers mainly to declare functions that can operate on various types of pointer arguments, or that return a "multipurpose" pointer. The standard memory management functions are a simple example:

```
void *malloc( size_t size );
void *realloc( void *ptr, size_t size );
void free( void *ptr );
```

As Example 2-3 illustrates, you can assign a void pointer value to another object pointer type, or vice versa, without explicit type conversion.

Example 2-3. Using the type void

```
// usingvoid.c: Demonstrates uses of the type void
// ------------------------------------------------------
#include <stdio.h>
#include <time.h>
#include <stdlib.h>  // Provides the following function prototypes:
```

```
                        // void srand( unsigned int seed );
                        // int rand( void );
                        // void *malloc( size_t size );
                        // void free( void *ptr );
                        // void exit( int status );

enum { ARR_LEN = 100 };

int main()
{
  int i,              // Obtain some storage space.
      *pNumbers = malloc(ARR_LEN * sizeof(int));

  if ( pNumbers == NULL )
  {
    fprintf(stderr, "Insufficient memory.\n");
    exit(1);
  }

  srand( (unsigned)time(NULL) );          // Initialize the
                                          // random number generator.

  for ( i=0; i < ARR_LEN; ++i )
    pNumbers[i] = rand() % 10000;         // Store some random numbers.

  printf("\n%d random numbers between 0 and 9999:\n", ARR_LEN );
  for ( i=0; i < ARR_LEN; ++i )          // Output loop:
  {
    printf("%6d", pNumbers[i]);          // Print one number per loop
    if ( i % 10 == 9 ) putchar('\n');    // iteration and a newline
  }                                       // after every 10 numbers.
  free( pNumbers );                       // Release the storage space.
  return 0;
}
```

The Alignment of Objects in Memory

Every complete object type imposes a certain *alignment* on objects of that type. In other words, the type specifies the kind of memory addresses at which objects of that type can be stored: all addresses, only even addresses, only addresses divisible by four, and so on. The alignment of a type is expressed as a number of bytes equal to the minimum distance between two objects of that type in storage. The specific values of the types' alignments can vary from one implementation to another, but they are always positive integer powers of 2: that is, 1, 2, 4, 8, and so on. An alignment with a greater value than another type's alignment is said to be *stricter* than the other.

C11 provides the operator _Alignof to determine a type's alignment, and the specifier _Alignas to specify the alignment in an object definition.

The _Alignof operator, like the sizeof operator, yields a constant value with the type size_t, an unsigned integer type defined in *stddef.h* and other header files. For example, the following expression yields the alignment of the type int, which is typically 4:

```
_Alignof(int)
```

An alignment value less than or equal to _Alignof(max_align_t) is called a *fundamental alignment*. All the fundamental types—that is, the basic types and pointer types—have a fundamental alignment. The type max_align_t is defined in the header *stddef.h*, and its alignment is supported in every context, including dynamic memory allocation, for example. In addition, the implementation may also support alignments greater than _Alignof(max_align_t), which are known as *extended alignments*.

When an object is defined with the specifier _Alignas, it can have a stricter alignment than its type requires. The argument of _Alignas can be a constant integer expression whose value is a valid alignment, or a type, as in the following examples:

```
_Alignas(4) short var;    // Defines var with the type short
                          // and four-byte alignment.
_Alignas(double) float x; // Defines x with the type float
                          // and the alignment of double.
```

The form _Alignas(type) is synonymous with _Alignas (_Alignof(type)). The header file *stdalign.h* defines alignof and alignas as synonyms for _Alignof and _Alignas. Thus, if your program includes *stdalign.h*, you can write alignas(int) instead of _Alignas(int).

3

Literals

In C source code, a *literal* is a token that denotes a fixed value, which may be an integer, a floating-point number, a character, or a string. A literal's type is determined by its value and its notation.

The literals discussed here are different from *compound literals*, which were introduced in the C99 standard. Compound literals are ordinary modifiable objects, similar to variables. For a full description of compound literals and the special operator used to create them, see Chapter 5.

Integer Constants

An *integer constant* can be expressed as an ordinary decimal numeral, or as a numeral in octal or hexadecimal notation. You must specify the intended notation by a prefix.

A *decimal constant* begins with a nonzero digit. For example, 255 is the decimal constant for the base-10 value 255.

A number that begins with a leading zero is interpreted as an *octal constant*. Octal (or base eight) notation uses only the digits from 0 to 7. For example, 047 is a valid octal constant representing $4 \times 8 + 7$, and is equivalent with the decimal constant 39. The decimal constant 255 is equal to the octal constant 0377.

A *hexadecimal constant* begins with the prefix 0x or 0X. The hexadecimal digits A to F can be upper- or lowercase. For example, 0xff, 0Xff, 0xFF, and 0XFF represent the same hexadecimal constant, which is equivalent to the decimal constant 255.

Because the integer constants you define will eventually be used in expressions and declarations, their type is important. The type of a constant is determined at the same time as its value is defined. Integer constants such as the examples just mentioned usually have the type int. However, if the value of an integer constant is outside the range of the type int, then it must have a bigger type. In this case, the compiler assigns it the first type in a hierarchy that is large enough to represent the value. For decimal constants, the type hierarchy is:

    int, long, long long

For octal and hexadecimal constants, the type hierarchy is:

    int, unsigned int, long, unsigned long, long long, unsigned long long

For example, on a 16-bit system, the decimal constant 50000 has the type long, as the greatest possible int value is 32,767, or $2^{15} - 1$.

You can also influence the types of constants in your programs explicitly by using suffixes. A constant with the suffix l or L has the type long (or a larger type if necessary, in accordance with the hierarchies just mentioned). Similarly, a constant with the suffix ll or LL has at least the type long long. The suffix u or U can be used to ensure that the constant has an unsigned type. The long and unsigned suffixes can be combined. Table 3-1 gives a few examples.

Table 3-1. Examples of constants with suffixes

Integer constant	Type
0x200	int
512U	unsigned int
0L	long
0Xf0fUL	unsigned long
0777LL	long long
0xAAAllu	unsigned long long

Floating-Point Constants

Floating-point constants can be written either in decimal or in hexadecimal notation. These notations are described in the next two sections.

Decimal Floating-Point Constants

An ordinary floating-point constant consists of a sequence of decimal digits containing a decimal point. You may also multiply the value by a power of 10, as in scientific notation: the power of 10 is represented simply by an exponent, introduced by the letter e or E. A floating-point constant that contains an exponent does not need to have a decimal point. Table 3-2 gives a few examples of decimal floating-point constants.

Table 3-2. Examples of decimal floating-point constants

Floating-point constant	Value
10.0	10
2.34E5	2.34×10^5
67e-12	67.0×10^{-12}

The decimal point can also be the first or last character. Thus, 10. and .234E6 are permissible numerals. However, the numeral 10 with no decimal point would be an integer constant, not a floating-point constant.

The default type of a floating-point constant is double. You can also append the suffix F or f to assign a constant the type float, or the suffix L or l to give a constant the type long double, as this example shows:

```
float  f_var = 123.456F;       // Initialize a float variable.

long double ld_var = f_var * 987E7L;  // Initialize a long double
                                      // variable with the product of
                                      // a multiplication performed
                                      // with long double precision.
```

Hexadecimal Floating-Point Constants

The C99 standard introduced *hexadecimal* floating-point constants, which have a key advantage over decimal floating-point numerals: if you specify a constant value in hexadecimal notation, it can be stored in the computer's binary floating-point format exactly, with no rounding error, whereas values that are "round numbers" in decimal notation—like 0.1—may be repeating fractions in binary, and have to be rounded for representation in the internal format. (For an example of rounding with floating-point numbers, see Example 2-2.)

A hexadecimal floating-point constant consists of the prefix 0x or 0X, a sequence of hexadecimal digits with an optional decimal point (which perhaps we ought to call a "hexadecimal point" in this case), and an exponent to base two. The exponent is a *decimal* numeral introduced by the letter p or P. For example, the constant 0xa.fP-10 is equal to the number $(10 + 15/16) \times 2^{-10}$ (not 2^{-16}) in decimal notation. Equivalent ways of writing the same constant value are 0xA.Fp-10, 0x5.78p-9, 0xAFp-14, and 0x.02BCp0. Each difference of 1 in the exponent multiplies or divides the hexadecimal fraction by a factor of 2, and each shift of the hexadecimal point by one place corresponds to a factor (or divisor) of 16, or 2^4.

In hexadecimal floating-point constants, you must include the exponent, even if its value is zero. This step is necessary in order to distinguish the type suffix F (after the exponent) from the hexadecimal digit F (to the left of the exponent). For example, if the exponent were not required, the constant 0x1.0F could represent either the number 1.0 with type float, or the number 1 + 15/256 with the default type double.

Like decimal floating-point constants, hexadecimal floating-point constants also have the default type double. Append the suffix F or f to assign a constant the type float, or the suffix L or l to give it the type long double.

Character Constants

A *character constant* consists of one or more characters enclosed in single quotation marks. Here are some examples:

```
'a'    'XY'    '0'    '*'
```

All the characters of the source character set are permissible in character constants, except the single quotation mark ', the backslash \, and the newline character. To represent these characters, you must use escape sequences:

```
'\''    '\\'    '\n'
```

In the fifth translation phase (see "How the C Compiler Works" on page 19), characters and escape sequences in character constants are converted into the corresponding characters of the execution character set. All the escape sequences that are permitted in character constants are described in "Escape Sequences" on page 44.

Wide-character constants are character constants defined with one of the prefixes L, u, or U. They have a different type and value range from character constants defined without a prefix.

Types and Values of Character Constants

Character constants that are not wide characters have the type int. If a character constant contains *one* character which can be represented in a single byte in the execution character set, then its value is the character code of that character. For example, the constant 'a' in ASCII or ISO 8859-1 encoding has the decimal value 97. In all other cases, and in particular if a character constant contains more than one character, the value of a character constant can vary from one compiler to another.

The following code fragment tests whether the character read is a digit between 1 and 5, inclusive:

```c
#include <stdio.h>
int c = 0;

/* ... */

c = getchar();                        // Read a character.
if ( c != EOF && c > '0' && c < '6' )  // Compare input to character
                                       // constants.
{
   /* This block is executed if the user entered a digit from 1 to 5. */
}
```

If the type char is signed, then the value of a character constant can also be negative, because the constant's value is the result of a type conversion of the character code from char to int. For example, ISO 8859-1 is a commonly used 8-bit character set, also known as the ISO Latin 1 or ANSI character set. In this character set, the currency symbol for pounds sterling, £, is coded as hexadecimal A3:

```
int c = '\xA3';                           // Symbol for pounds sterling
printf("Character: %c     Code: %d\n", c, c);
```

If the execution character set is ISO 8859-1, and the type char is signed, then the printf statement in the preceding example generates the following output:

```
Character: £     Code: -93
```

In a program that uses characters that are not representable in a single byte, you can use wide-character constants. A wide-character constant is written with one of the prefixes L, u, or U. The prefix determines the type of the character constant, as shown in Table 3-3.

Table 3-3. The types of character constants

Prefix	Examples	Type
none	'a' '\t'	int
L	L'a' L'\u0100'	wchar_t (defined in *stddef.h*)
u	u'a' u'\x3b3'	char16_t (defined in *uchar.h*)
U	U'a' U'\u27FA'	char32_t (defined in *uchar.h*)

The value of a wide-character constant that contains a *single* multibyte character which is representable in the execution character set is the code of the corresponding wide character. That is the value that would be returned for that multibyte character by the standard function mbtowc() ("multibyte to wide character"), or by mbrtoc16() or mbrtoc32(), depending on the type of the wide-character constant.

The Unicode types char16_t and char32_t, and the corresponding conversion functions, were introduced in the C11 standard. Characters of the type char16_t are encoded in UTF-16 if the macro __STDC_UTF_16__ is defined in the given implementation. Similarly, characters of the type char32_t are encoded in UTF-32 if the implementation defines the macro __STDC_UTF_32__.

The value of a character constant containing several characters, such as L'xy', is not specified. To ensure portability, make sure your programs do not depend on such a character constant having a specific value.

Escape Sequences

An escape sequence begins with a backslash \, and represents a single character. Escape sequences allow you to represent any character in character constants and string literals, including nonprintable characters and characters that otherwise have a special meaning, such as ' and ". Table 3-4 lists the escape sequences recognized in C.

Table 3-4. Escape sequences

Escape sequence	Character value	Action on output device
\'	A single quotation mark (')	Prints the character
\"	A double quotation mark (")	
\?	A question mark (?)	
\\	A backslash character (\)	
\a	Alert	Generates an audible or visible signal
\b	Backspace	Moves the active position back one character
\f	Form feed	Moves the active position to the beginning of the next page
\n	Newline	Moves the active position to the beginning of the next line
\r	Carriage return	Moves the active position to the beginning of the current line
\t	Horizontal tab	Moves the active position to the next horizontal tab stop
\v	Vertical tab	Moves the active position to the next vertical tab stop
\o, \oo, or \ooo (where o is an octal digit)	The character with the given octal code	Prints the character
\xh[h...] (where h is a hexadecimal digit)	The character with the given hexadecimal code	
\uhhhh \Uhhhhhhhh	The character with the given universal character name	

In the table, the *active position* refers to the position at which the output device prints the next output character, such as the position of the cursor on a console display. The behavior of the output device is not defined in the following cases: if the escape sequence \b (backspace) occurs at the beginning of a line; if \t (tab) occurs at the end of a line; or if \v (vertical tab) occurs at the end of a page.

As Table 3-4 shows, universal character names are also considered escape sequences. Universal character names allow you to specify any character in the extended character set, regardless of the encoding used. See "Universal Character Names" on page 12 for more information.

You can also specify any character code in the value range of the type unsigned char—or any wide-character code in the value range of wchar_t—using the *octal* and *hexadecimal escape sequences*, as shown in Table 3-5.

Table 3-5. Examples of octal and hexadecimal escape sequences

Octal	Hexadecimal	Description
'\0'	'\x0'	The null character
'\033' '\33'	'\x1B'	The control character ESC ("escape")
'\376'	'\xfe'	The character with the decimal code 254
'\417'	'\x10f'	Illegal, as the numeric value is beyond the range of the type unsigned char
L'\417'	L'\x10f'	That's better! It's now a wide-character constant; the type is wchar_t
-	L'\xF82'	Another wide-character constant
-	U'\x222B'	A wide-character constant with the type char32_t

There is no equivalent octal notation for the last two constants in the table because octal escape sequences cannot have more than three octal digits. For the same reason, the wide-character constant L'\3702' consists of two characters: L'\370' and L'2'.

String Literals

A *string literal* consists of a sequence of characters (and/or escape sequences) enclosed in double quotation marks. For example:

```
"Hello world!\n"
```

The individual characters of a string literal are governed by the same rules described for the values of characters in character constants. String literals may contain all the multibyte characters of the source character set. The only exceptions are the double quotation mark ", the backslash \, and the newline character, which must be represented by escape sequences. For example, each backslash character in Windows directory paths must be written as \\. The following printf statement first produces an alert tone, and then indicates a documentation directory in quotation marks, substituting the string literal addressed by the pointer argument doc_path for the conversion specification %s:

```
char doc_path[128] = ".\\share\\doc";    // That is, ".\share\doc"
printf("\aSee the documentation in the directory \"%s\"\n", doc_path);
```

A string literal is a static array of char that contains character codes followed by a string terminator, the null character \0 (see also Chapter 8). The empty string "" occupies exactly one byte in memory, which holds the terminating null character. Characters that cannot be represented in one byte are stored as multibyte characters.

As illustrated in the previous example, you can use a string literal to initialize a char array. A string literal can also be used to initialize a pointer to char:

```
char *pStr = "Hello, world!";      // pStr points to the first
                                   // character, 'H'
```

In such an initializer, the string literal represents the address of its first element, just as an array name would.

In Example 3-1, the array error_msg contains three pointers to char, each of which is assigned the address of the first character of a string literal.

Example 3-1. Sample function error_exit()

```
#include <stdlib.h>
#include <stdio.h>
void error_exit(unsigned int error_n)  // Print a last error message
{                                       // and exit the program.
  char * error_msg[] = { "Unknown error code.\n",
                         "Insufficient memory.\n",
                         "Illegal memory access.\n" };
  unsigned int arr_len = sizeof(error_msg)/sizeof(char *);

  if ( error_n >= arr_len )
    error_n = 0;
  fputs( error_msg[error_n], stderr );
  exit(1);
}
```

The C11 standard provides a new prefix, u8, which allows you to define a UTF-8 string literal. The multibyte characters in the char array defined by a UTF-8 string literal are encoded in UTF-8. A string literal of the form u8"…" is thus no different from a string literal without a prefix if the implementation's default encoding for multibyte characters is UTF-8.

Like wide-character constants, you can also specify string literals as strings of wide characters by using one of the prefixes L, u, or U. In this way, you define what is called a *wide-string literal*, which yields an array of wide characters ending with a character with the value 0. The prefix determines the array elements' type.

A wide-string literal is defined using the prefix L:

```
L"Here's a wide-string literal."
```

This expression defines a static null-terminated array of elements of the type wchar_t. The array is initialized by converting the multibyte characters in the string literal to wide characters in the same way as the standard function mbstowcs() ("multibyte string to wide-character string") would do.

The prefixes u and U, introduced in C11, yield a static array of wide characters of the type char16_t or char32_t. The multibyte characters in these wide-string literals are implicitly converted to wide characters by successive calls to the function mbrtoc16() or mbrtoc32().

If a multibyte character or an escape sequence in a string literal is not representable in the execution character set, the value of the string literal is not specified—that is, it depends on the compiler.

In the following example, \u03b1 is the universal name for the character α, and wprintf() is the wide-character version of the printf function, which formats and prints a string of wide characters:

```
double angle_alpha = 90.0/3;
wprintf( L"Angle \u03b1 measures %lf degrees.\n", angle_alpha );
```

The compiler's preprocessor concatenates any adjacent string literals—that is, those that are separated only by whitespace—into a single string. As the following example illustrates, this concatenation also makes it simple to break up a string into several lines for readability:

```
#define PRG_NAME "EasyLine"
char msg[ ] = "The installation of " PRG_NAME
              " is now complete.";
```

If any of the string literals involved has a prefix, then the resulting string is treated as a string literal with that prefix. Whether string literals with different prefixes can be concatenated depends on the compiler.

Another way to break a string literal into several lines is to end a line with a backslash, as in this example:

```
char info[ ] =
"This is a string literal broken up into\
  several source code lines.\nNow one more line:\n\
  that's enough, the string ends here.";
```

The string continues at the *beginning* of the next line: any spaces at the left margin, such as the space before several in the preceding example, are part of the string literal. Furthermore, the string literal defined here contains exactly two newline characters: one immediately before Now, and one immediately before that's; in other words, only the two that are explicitly written as \n.

The compiler interprets escape sequences before concatenating adjacent strings (see "The C Compiler's Translation Phases" on page 19). As a result, the following two string literals form one wide-character string that begins with the two characters '\xA7' and '2':

```
L"\xA7" L"2 et cetera"
```

However, if the string is written in one piece as L"\xA72 et cetera", then the first character in the string is the wide character '\xA72'.

Although C does not strictly prohibit modifying string literals, you should not attempt to do so. In the following example, the second statement is an attempt to replace the first character of a string:

```
char *p = "house";      // Initialize a pointer to char.
*p = 'm';               // This is *not* a good idea!
```

This statement is not portable, and causes a runtime error on some systems. For one thing, the compiler, treating the string literal as a constant, may place it in read-only memory, in which case the attempted write operation causes a fault. For another, if two or more identical string literals are used in the program, the compiler may store them at the same location, so that modifying one causes unexpected results when you access another.

However, if you use a string literal to initialize an *array variable*, you can then modify the contents of the array:

```
char s[] = "house";     // Initialize an array of char.
s[0] = 'm';             // Now the array contains the string "mouse".
```

In the same way, arrays whose elements have the type wchar_t, char16_t, or char32_t can be initialized using an appropriate wide-string literal.

4

Type Conversions

In C, operands of different types can be combined in one operation. For example, the following expressions are permissible:

```
double dVar = 2.5;    // Define dVar as a variable of type double.
dVar *= 3;            // Multiply dVar by an integer constant.
if ( dVar < 10L )     // Compare dVar with a long-integer constant.
   { /* ... */ }
```

When the operands have different types, the compiler tries to convert them to a uniform type before performing the operation. In certain cases, furthermore, you must insert type conversion instructions in your program. A type conversion yields the value of an expression in a new type, which can be either the type void (meaning that the value of the expression is discarded; see "Expressions of Type void" on page 35), or a scalar type—that is, an arithmetic type or a pointer. For example, a pointer to a structure can be converted into a different pointer type. However, an actual structure value cannot be converted into a different structure type.

The compiler provides *implicit* type conversions when operands have mismatched types, or when you call a function using an argument whose type does not match the function's corresponding parameter. Programs also perform implicit type conversion as necessary when initializing variables or otherwise assigning values to them. If the necessary conversion is not possible, the compiler issues an error message.

You can also convert values from one type to another *explicitly* using the *cast operator* (see Chapter 5):

```
(type_name) expression
```

In the following example, the cast operator causes the division of one integer variable by another to be performed as a floating-point operation:

```
int sum = 22, count = 5;
double mean = (double)sum / count;
```

Because the cast operator has precedence over division, the value of sum in this example is first converted to type double. The compiler must then implicitly convert the divisor, the value of count, to the same type before performing the division.

You should always use the cast operator whenever there is a possibility of losing information, as in a conversion from int to unsigned int, for example. Explicit casts avoid compiler warnings, and also signpost your program's type conversions for other programmers. For example, using an explicit cast to void when you discard the return value of a function serves as a reminder that you may be disregarding the function's error indications.

To illustrate the implicit type conversions that the compiler provides, however, the examples in this chapter use the cast operator only when strictly necessary.

Conversion of Arithmetic Types

Type conversions are always possible between any two arithmetic types, and the compiler performs them implicitly wherever necessary. The conversion preserves the value of an expression if the new type is capable of representing it. This is not always the case. For example, when you convert a negative value to an unsigned type, or convert a floating-point fraction from type double to the type int, the new type simply cannot represent the original value. In such cases, the compiler generally issues a warning.

Hierarchy of Types

When arithmetic operands have different types, the implicit type conversion is governed by the types' *conversion rank*. The types are ranked according to the following rules:

- Any two unsigned integer types have different conversion ranks. If one is wider than the other, then it has a higher rank.

- Each signed integer type has the same rank as the corresponding unsigned type. The type char has the same rank as signed char and unsigned char.

- The standard integer types are ranked in the order:

      _Bool < char < short < int < long < long long

- Any standard integer type has a higher rank than an extended integer type of the same width (extended integer types are described in "Integer types with exact width (C99)" on page 29).

- Every enumerated type has the same rank as its corresponding integer type (see "Enumerated Types" on page 33).

- The floating-point types are ranked in the following order:

  ```
  float < double < long double
  ```

- The lowest-ranked floating-point type, float, has a higher rank than any integer type.

- Every complex floating-point type has the same rank as the type of its real and imaginary parts.

Integer Promotion

In any expression, you can always use a value whose type ranks lower than int in place of an operand of type int or unsigned int. You can also use a bit-field as an integer operand (bit-fields are discussed in Chapter 10). In these cases, the compiler applies *integer promotion*: any operand whose type ranks lower than int is automatically converted to the type int, provided int is capable of representing all values of the operand's original type. If int is not sufficient, the operand is converted to unsigned int.

Integer promotion always preserves the value of the operand. Here are some examples:

```
char c = '?';
unsigned short var = 100;

if ( c < 'A' )        // The character constant 'A' has type int:
                      // the value of c is implicitly promoted
                      // to int for the comparison.

    var = var + 1;    // Before the addition, the value of var
                      // is promoted to int or unsigned int.
```

In the last of these statements, the compiler promotes the first addend, the value of var, to the type int or unsigned int before performing the addition. If int and short have the same width, which is likely on a 16-bit computer, then the signed type int is not wide enough to represent all possible values of the unsigned short variable var. In this case, the value of var is promoted to unsigned int. After the addition, the result is converted to unsigned short for assignment to var.

Usual Arithmetic Conversions

The *usual arithmetic conversions* are the implicit conversions that are automatically applied to operands of different arithmetic types for most operators. The purpose of the usual arithmetic conversions is to find a *common real type* for all of the operands and the result of the operation.

The usual arithmetic conversions are performed implicitly for the following operators:

Arithmetic operators with two operands

    *, /, %, +, and -

Relational and equality operators

    <, <=, >, >=, ==, and !=

The bitwise operators

    &, |, and ^

The ternary operator

    ?: (for the second and third operands)

With the exception of the relational and equality operators, the common real type obtained by the usual arithmetic conversions is generally the type of the result. However, if one or more of the operands has a complex floating-point type, then the result also has a complex floating-point type.

The usual arithmetic conversions are applied as follows:

1. If either operand has a floating-point type, then the operand with the lower conversion rank is converted to a type with the same rank as the other operand. Real types are converted only to real types, however, and complex types only to complex.

   In other words, if either operand has a complex floating-point type, the usual arithmetic conversion matches only the real type on which the actual type of the operand is based. Here are some examples:

   ```
   #include <complex.h>
   // ...
   short n = -10;
   double x = 0.5, y = 0.0;
   float _Complex f_z = 2.0F + 3.0F * I;
   double _Complex d_z = 0.0;

   y   = n * x;         // The value of n is converted to type double.
   d_z = f_z + x;       // Only the value of f_z is converted to
                        // double _Complex.
                        // The result of the operation also has
                        // type double _Complex.

   f_z = f_z / 3;       // The constant value 3 is converted to float.
   d_z = d_z - f_z;     // The value of f_z is converted to
                        // the type double _Complex.
   ```

2. If both operands are integers, integer promotion is first performed on both operands. If after integer promotion the operands still have different types, conversion continues as follows:

   • If one operand has an *unsigned* type *T* whose conversion rank is at least as high as that of the other operand's type, then the other operand is converted to type *T*.

- Otherwise, one operand has a *signed* type *T* whose conversion rank is higher than that of the other operand's type. The other operand is converted to type *T* only if type *T* is capable of representing all values of its previous type. If not, then both operands are converted to the unsigned type that corresponds to the signed type *T*.

The following lines of code contain some examples:

```
int i = -1;
unsigned int limit = 200U;
long n = 30L;

if ( i < limit )
    x = limit * n;
```

In this example, to evaluate the comparison in the if condition, the value of i, −1, must first be converted to the type unsigned int. The result is a large positive number. On a 32-bit system, that number is $2^{32} - 1$, and on any system it is greater than limit. Hence, the if condition is false.

In the last line of the example, the value of limit is converted to n's type, long, if the value range of long contains the whole value range of unsigned int. If not—for example, if both int and long are 32 bits wide—then both multiplicands are converted to unsigned long.

The usual arithmetic conversions preserve the operand's value, except in the following cases:

- When an integer of great magnitude is converted to a floating-point type, the target type's precision may not be sufficient to represent the number exactly.
- Negative values are outside the value range of unsigned types.

In these two cases, values that exceed the range or precision of the target type are converted as described in "The Results of Arithmetic Type Conversions" on page 54.

Other Implicit Type Conversions

The compiler also automatically converts arithmetic values in the following cases:

- In assignments and initializations, the value of the right operand is always converted to the type of the left operand.
- In function calls, the arguments are converted to the types of the corresponding parameters. If the parameters have not been declared, then the *default argument promotions* are applied: integer promotion is performed on integer arguments, and arguments of type float are promoted to double.

- In `return` statements, the value of the `return` expression is converted to the function's return type.

In a compound assignment, such as x += 2.5, the values of both operands are first subject to the usual arithmetic conversions, then the result of the arithmetic operation is converted, as for a simple assignment, to the type of the left operand. Most compilers issue a warning if the left operand's type may be unable to represent the right operand's value. Here are some examples:

```
#include <math.h>        // Declares the function double sqrt( double ).

int   i = 7;
float x = 0.5; // The constant value is converted from double to float.

i = x;          // The value of x is converted from float to int.

x += 2.5;       // Before the addition, the value of x is converted to
                // double. Afterward, the sum is converted to float for
                // assignment to x.

x = sqrt( i ); // Calculate the square root of i:
                // The argument is converted from int to double;
                // the return value is converted from double to
                // float for assignment to x.

long my_func()
{
  /* ... */
  return 0;     // The constant 0 is converted to long, the function's
                // return type.
}
```

The Results of Arithmetic Type Conversions

Because the different types have different purposes, representational characteristics, and limitations, converting a value from one type to another often involves the application of special rules to deal with such peculiarities. In general, the exact result of a type conversion depends primarily on the characteristics of the target type.

Conversions to _Bool

Any value of any scalar type can be converted to _Bool. The result is 0—i.e., false—if the scalar value is equal to 0; and 1, or true, if it is nonzero. Because a null pointer compares equal to zero, its value becomes false on conversion to _Bool.

Conversions to unsigned integer types other than _Bool

Integer values are always preserved if they are within the range of the new unsigned type—in other words, if they are between 0 and Utype_MAX, where Utype_MAX is the greatest value that can be represented by unsigned type.

For values outside the new unsigned type's range, the value after conversion is the value obtained by adding or subtracting (Utype_MAX + 1) as many times as necessary until the result is within the range of the new type. The following example illustrates the assignment of a negative value to an unsigned integer type:

```
#include <limits.h>        // Defines the macros USHRT_MAX,
                           // UINT_MAX, etc.
unsigned short  n = 1000;  // The value 1000 is within the
                           // range of unsigned short;
n = -1;                    // the value -1 must be converted.
```

To adjust a signed value of −1 to the variable's unsigned type, the program implicitly adds USHRT_MAX + 1 to it until a result within the type's range is obtained. Because −1 + (USHRT_MAX + 1) = USHRT_MAX, the final statement in the previous example is equivalent to n = USHRT_MAX;.

For positive integer values, subtracting (Utype_MAX + 1) as often as necessary to bring the value into the new type's range is the same as the remainder of a division by (Utype_MAX + 1), as the following example illustrates:

```
#include <limits.h>        // Defines the macros USHRT_MAX, UINT_MAX, etc.
unsigned short  n = 0;
n = 0xFEDCBA;              // The value is beyond the range of
                          // unsigned short.
```

If unsigned short is 16 bits wide, then its maximum value, USHRT_MAX, is hexadecimal FFFF. When the value FEDCBA is converted to unsigned short, the result is the same as the remainder of a division by hexadecimal 10000 (that's USHRT_MAX + 1), which is always FFFF or less. In this case, the value assigned to n is hexadecimal DCBA.

To convert a real floating-point number to an unsigned or signed integer type, the compiler discards the fractional part. If the remaining integer portion is outside the range of the new type, the result of the conversion is undefined. For example:

```
double x = 2.9;

unsigned long n = x;            // The fractional part of x is
                               // simply lost.

unsigned long m = round(x);     // If x is non-negative, this has the
                               // same effect as m = x + 0.5;
```

In the initialization of n in this example, the value of x is converted from double to unsigned long by discarding its fractional part, 0.9. The integer part, 2, is the value assigned to n. In the initialization of m, the C99 function round() rounds the value of x to the nearest integer value (whether higher or lower), and returns a value of type `double`. The fractional part of the resulting `double` value—3.0 in this case—is thus equal to zero before being discarded through type conversion for the assignment to `m`.

When a complex number is converted to an unsigned integer type, the imaginary part is first discarded. Then the resulting floating-point value is converted as described previously. For example:

```
#include <limits.h>      // Defines macros such as UINT_MAX.
#include <complex.h>      // Defines macros such as the imaginary
                          // constant I.

unsigned int  n = 0;
float _Complex  z = -1.7 + 2.0 * I;

n = z;                    // In this case, the effect is
                          // the same as n = -1;
                          // The resulting value of n is UINT_MAX.
```

The imaginary part of z is discarded, leaving the real floating-point value −1.7. Then the fractional part of the floating-point number is also discarded. The remaining integer value, −1, is converted to `unsigned int` by adding UINT_MAX + 1, so that the value ultimately assigned to n is equal to UINT_MAX.

Conversions to signed integer types

The problem of exceeding the target type's value range can also occur when a value is converted from an integer type, whether signed or unsigned, to a different, signed integer type; for example, when a value is converted from the type `long` or `unsigned int` to the type `int`. The result of such an overflow on conversion to a signed integer type, unlike conversions to unsigned integer types, is left up to the implementation.

Most compilers discard the highest bits of the original value's binary representation and interpret the lowest bits according to the new type. As the following example illustrates, under this conversion strategy the existing bit pattern of an `unsigned int` is interpreted as a signed `int` value:

```
#include <limits.h>      // Defines macros such as UINT_MAX
int i = UINT_MAX;        // Result: i = -1 (in two's complement
                         // representation)
```

However, depending on the compiler, such a conversion attempt may also result in a signal being raised to inform the program of the value range overflow.

When a real or complex floating-point number is converted to a signed integer type, the same rules apply as for conversion to an unsigned integer type, as described in the previous section.

Conversions to real floating-point types

Not all integer values can be exactly represented in floating-point types. For example, although the value range of the type float includes the range of the types long and long long, float is precise to only six decimal digits. Thus, some long values cannot be stored exactly in a float object. The result of such a conversion is the next lower or next higher representable value, as the following example illustrates:

```
long  l_var = 123456789L;
float f_var = l_var;          // Implicitly converts long value
                              // to float.

printf("The rounding error (f_var - l_var) is %f\n",
                              (double)f_var  - l_var);
```

Note that the subtraction in this example is performed with at least double precision. Typical output produced by this code is:

```
The rounding error (f_var - l_var;) is 3.000000
```

Any value in a floating-point type can be represented exactly in another floating-point type of greater precision. Thus, when a double value is converted to long double, or when a float value is converted to double or long double, the value is exactly preserved. In conversions from a more precise to a less precise type, however, the value being converted may be beyond the range of the new type. If the value exceeds the target type's range, the result of the conversion is undefined. If the value is within the target type's range, but not exactly representable in the target type's precision, then the result is the next smaller or next greater representable value. The program in Example 2-2 illustrates the rounding error produced by such a conversion to a less-precise floating-point type.

When a complex number is converted to a real floating-point type, the imaginary part is simply discarded, and the result is the complex number's real part, which may have to be further converted to the target type as described in this section.

Conversions to complex floating-point types

When an integer or a real floating-point number is converted to a complex type, the real part of the result is obtained by converting the value to the corresponding real floating-point type as described in the previous section. The imaginary part is zero.

When a complex number is converted to a different complex type, the real and imaginary parts are converted separately according to the rules for real floating-point types:

```
#include <complex.h>        // Defines macros such as the imaginary
                            // constant I
double _Complex dz = 2;
float _Complex fz = dz + I;
```

In the first of these two initializations, the integer constant 2 is implicitly converted to double _Complex for assignment to dz. The resulting value of dz is 2.0 + 0.0 × I.

In the initialization of fz, the two parts of the double _Complex value of dz are converted (after the addition) to float, so that the real part of fz is equal to 2.0F, and the imaginary part 1.0F.

Conversion of Nonarithmetic Types

Pointers and the names of arrays and functions are also subject to certain implicit and explicit type conversions. Structures and unions cannot be converted, although pointers to them can be converted to and from other pointer types.

Array and Function Designators

An array or function designator is any expression that has an array or function type. In most cases, the compiler implicitly converts an expression with an array type, such as the name of an array, into a pointer to the array's first element. The array expression is *not* converted into a pointer only in the following cases:

- When the array is the operand of the sizeof operator
- When the array is the operand of the address operator &
- When a string literal is used to initialize an array of char, wchar_t, char16_t, or char32_t

The following examples demonstrate the implicit conversion of array designators into pointers, using the conversion specification %p to print pointer values:

```
#include <stdio.h>

int *iPtr = 0;                      // A pointer to int, initialized with 0.
int iArray[] = { 0, 10, 20 };    // An array of int, initialized.

int array_length = sizeof(iArray) / sizeof(int); // The number of
                                                  // elements:
                                                  // in this case, 3.

printf("The array starts at the address %p.\n", iArray);

*iArray = 5;                         // Equivalent to iArray[0] = 5;

iPtr = iArray + array_length - 1; // Point to the last element of
                                  // iArray: equivalent to
                                  // iPtr = &iArray[array_length-1];

printf("The last element of the array is %d.\n", *iPtr);
```

In the initialization of array_length in this example, the expression sizeof(iArray) yields the size of the whole array, not the size of a pointer. However, the same identifier iArray is implicitly converted to a pointer in the other three statements in which it appears:

- As an argument in the first printf() call

- As the operand of the dereferencing operator *

- In the pointer arithmetic operations and assignment to iPtr (see also "Modifying and Comparing Pointers" on page 147)

The names of character arrays are used as pointers in string operations, as in this example:

```
#include <stdio.h>
#include <string.h>          // Declares size_t strlen( const char *s )

char msg[80] = "I'm a string literal."; // Initialize an array of char.
printf("The string is %d characters long.\n", strlen(msg));
                                     // Answer: 21.
printf("The array named msg is %d bytes long.\n", sizeof(msg));
                                     // Answer: 80.
```

In the function call strlen(msg) in this example, the array identifier msg is implicitly converted to a pointer to the array's first element with the function parameter's type, const char *. Internally, strlen() merely counts the characters beginning at that address until the first null character, the string terminator.

Similarly, any expression that designates a function, such as a function name, can also be implicitly converted into a pointer to the function. Again, this conversion does not apply when the expression is the operand of the address operator &. The sizeof operator cannot be used with an operand of function type. The following example illustrates the implicit conversion of function names to pointers (the program initializes an array of pointers to functions, then calls the functions in a loop):

```
#include <stdio.h>
void func0() { puts("This is the function func0(). "); }
void func1() { puts("This is the function func1(). "); }
/* ... */
void (*funcTable[2])(void) = { func0, func1 }; // Array of two pointers
                                        // to functions
                                        // returning void.
for ( int i = 0; i < 2; ++i )    // Use the loop counter as the array
    funcTable[i]();              // index.
```

Explicit Pointer Conversions

To convert a pointer from one pointer type to another, you must usually use an explicit cast. In some cases, the compiler provides an implicit conversion, as described in "Implicit Pointer Conversions" on page 61. Pointers can also be explicitly converted into integers, and vice versa.

Object pointers

You can explicitly convert an object pointer—that is, a pointer to a complete or incomplete object type—to any other object pointer type. In your program, you must ensure that your use of the converted pointer makes sense. Here is an example:

```
float  f_var = 1.5F;
long *l_ptr = (long *)&f_var;      // Initialize a pointer to long with
                                   // the address of f_var.
double *d_ptr = (double *)l_ptr;   // Initialize a pointer to double
                                   // with the same address.

// On a system where sizeof(float) equals sizeof(long):

printf( "The %zu bytes that represent %f, in hexadecimal: 0x%lX\n",
        sizeof(f_var), f_var, *l_ptr );

// Using a converted pointer in an assignment can cause trouble:

/*  *d_ptr = 2.5;  */    // Don't try this! f_var's location doesn't
                         // have space for a double value!
*(float *)d_ptr = 2.5;   // OK: stores a float value in that location.
```

If the object pointer after conversion does not have the alignment required by the new type, the results of using the pointer are undefined. In all other cases, converting the pointer value back into the original pointer type is guaranteed to yield an equivalent to the original pointer.

If you convert any type of object pointer into a pointer to any char type (char, signed char, or unsigned char), the result is a pointer to the first byte of the object. The first byte is considered here to be the byte with the lowest address, regardless of the system's byte order structure. The following example uses this feature to print a hexadecimal dump of a structure variable:

```
#include <stdio.h>
struct Data {
            short id;
            double val;
        };

struct Data myData = { 0x123, 77.7 };       // Initialize a
                                            // structure.

unsigned char *cp = (unsigned char *)&myData; // Pointer to the
                                            // first byte of
                                            // the structure.

printf( "%p: ", cp );                        // Print the starting
                                            // address.
```

```
for ( int i = 0; i < sizeof(myData); ++i )    // Print each byte
    printf( "%02X ", *(cp + i) );               // of the structure,
putchar( '\n' );                                // in hexadecimal.
```

This example produces output like the following:

```
0xbffffd70: 23 01 00 00 00 00 00 00 CD CC CC CC CC 6C 53 40
```

The output of the first two bytes, 23 01, shows that the code was executed on a little-endian system: the byte with the lowest address in the structure myData was the least significant byte of the short member id.

Function pointers

The type of a function always includes its return type, and may also include its parameter types. You can explicitly convert a pointer to a given function into a pointer to a function of a different type. In the following example, the typedef statement defines a name for the type "function that has one double parameter and returns a double value":

```
#include <math.h>                   // Declares sqrt() and pow().
typedef double (func_t)(double);    // Define a type named func_t.

func_t *pFunc = sqrt;               // A pointer to func_t, initialized
                                    // with the address of sqrt().

double y = pFunc( 2.0 );       // A correct function call by pointer.
printf( "The square root of 2 is %f.\n", y );

pFunc = (func_t *)pow;              // Change the pointer's value to
                                    // the address of pow().
/*  y = pFunc( 2.0 );  */           // Don't try this: pow() takes two
                                    // arguments.
```

In this example, the function pointer pFunc is assigned the addresses of functions that have different types. However, if the program uses the pointer to call a function with a definition that does not match the exact function pointer type, the program's behavior is undefined.

Implicit Pointer Conversions

The compiler converts certain types of pointers implicitly. Assignments, conditional expressions using the equality operators == and !=, and function calls involve implicit pointer conversion in three kinds of cases, which are described individually in the sections that follow. The three kinds of implicit pointer conversion are:

- Any object pointer type can be implicitly converted to a pointer to void, and vice versa.

- Any pointer to a given type can be implicitly converted into a pointer to a more qualified version of that type—that is, a type with one or more additional type qualifiers.

- A *null pointer constant* can be implicitly converted into any pointer type.

Pointers to void

Pointers to void—that is, pointers of the type void *—are used as "multipurpose" pointers to represent the address of any object, without regard for its type. For example, the malloc() function returns a pointer to void (see Example 2-3). Before you can access the memory block, the void pointer must always be converted into a pointer to an object.

Example 4-1 demonstrates more uses of pointers to void. The program sorts an array using the standard function qsort(), which is declared in the header file *stdlib.h* with the following prototype:

```
void qsort( void *array, size_t n, size_t element_size,
            int (*compare)(const void *, const void *) );
```

The qsort() function sorts the array in ascending order, beginning at the address *array*, using the quick-sort algorithm. The array is assumed to have *n* elements whose size is *element_size*.

The fourth parameter, *compare*, is a pointer to a function that qsort() calls to compare any two array elements. The addresses of the two elements to be compared are passed to this function in its pointer parameters. Usually this comparison function must be defined by the programmer. It must return a value that is less than, equal to, or greater than 0 to indicate whether the first element is less than, equal to, or greater than the second.

Example 4-1. A comparison function for qsort()

```
#include <stdlib.h>
#define ARR_LEN 20

/*
 * A function to compare any two float elements,
 * for use as a call-back function by qsort().
 * Arguments are passed by pointer.
 *
 * Returns: -1 if the first is less than the second;
 *           0 if the elements are equal;
 *           1 if the first is greater than the second.
 */
int  floatcmp( const void* p1, const void* p2 )
{
  float x = *(float *)p1,
        y = *(float *)p2;
```

```
  return (x < y) ? -1 : ((x == y) ? 0 : 1);
}

/*
 * The main() function sorts an array of float.
 */
int main()
{
  /* Allocate space for the array dynamically:  */
  float *pNumbers = malloc( ARR_LEN * sizeof(float) );

  /* ... Handle errors, initialize array elements ... */

  /* Sort the array: */
  qsort( pNumbers, ARR_LEN, sizeof(float), floatcmp );

  /* ... Work with the sorted array ... */

  return 0;
}
```

In Example 4-1, the malloc() function returns a void *, which is implicitly converted to float * in the assignment to pNumbers. In the call to qsort(), the first argument pNumbers is implicitly converted from float * to void *, and the function name floatcmp is implicitly interpreted as a function pointer. Finally, when the floatcmp() function is called by qsort(), it receives arguments of the type void *, the "universal" pointer type, and must convert them explicitly to float * before dereferencing them to initialize its float variables.

Pointers to qualified object types

The type qualifiers in C are const, volatile, and restrict (see Chapter 11 for details on these qualifiers). For example, the compiler implicitly converts any pointer to int into a pointer to const int where necessary. If you want to remove a qualification rather than adding one, however, you must use an explicit type conversion, as the following example illustrates:

```
int n = 77;
const int *ciPtr = 0;    // A pointer to const int.
                         // The pointer itself is not constant!

ciPtr = &n;              // Implicitly converts the address to the type
                         // const int *.

n = *ciPtr + 3;          // OK: this has the same effect as n = n + 3;

*ciPtr *= 2;             // Error: you can't change an object referenced by
                         // a pointer to const int.
```

```
*(int *)ciPtr *= 2;    // OK: Explicitly converts the pointer into a
                       // pointer to a nonconstant int.
```

The second to last statement in this example illustrates why pointers to const-qualified types are sometimes called *read-only pointers*: although you can modify the pointers' values, you can't use them to modify objects they point to.

Null pointer constants

A null pointer constant is an integer constant with the value 0, or a constant integer value of 0 cast as a pointer to void. The macro NULL is defined in the header files *stdlib.h*, *stdio.h*, and others as a null pointer constant. The following example illustrates the use of the macro NULL as a pointer constant to initialize pointers rather than an integer zero or a null character:

```
#include <stdlib.h>
long *lPtr = NULL;      // Initialize to NULL: pointer is not ready
                        // for use.

/* ... operations here may assign lPtr an object address ... */

if ( lPtr != NULL )
{
  /* ... use lPtr only if it has been changed from NULL ... */
}
```

When you convert a null pointer constant to another pointer type, the result is called a *null pointer*. The bit pattern of a null pointer is not necessarily zero. However, when you compare a null pointer to zero, to NULL, or to another null pointer, the result is always true. Conversely, comparing a null pointer to any valid pointer to an object or function always yields false.

Conversions Between Pointer and Integer Types

You can explicitly convert a pointer to an integer type, and vice versa. The result of such conversions depends on the compiler, and should be consistent with the addressing structure of the system on which the compiled executable runs. Conversions between pointer and integer types can be useful in system programming, and necessary when programs need to access specific physical addresses, such as ROM or memory-mapped I/O registers.

When you convert a pointer to an integer type whose range is not large enough to represent the pointer's value, the result is undefined. Conversely, converting an integer into a pointer type does not necessarily yield a valid pointer. The header file *stdint.h* may optionally define the integer types intptr_t (signed) and uintptr_t (unsigned). Any valid pointer can be converted to either of these types, and a subsequent conversion back into a pointer is guaranteed to yield the original pointer. You should therefore use one of these types, if *stdint.h* defines them, any time you need to perform conversions between pointers and integers.

Here are a few examples:

```
float x = 1.5F, *fPtr = &x;        // A float, and a pointer to it.

// Save the pointer's value as an integer:
unsigned long long adr_val = (unsigned long long)fPtr;

// Or, if stdint.h has been included and uintptr_t is defined:
uintptr_t adr_val = (uintptr_t)fPtr;

/*
 * On an Intel x86 PC in DOS, the BIOS data block begins at the
 * address 0x0040:0000. The first two-byte word at that address
 * contains the I/O address of the serial port COM1.
 * (Compile using DOS's "large" memory model.)
 */
unsigned short *biosPtr = (unsigned short *)0x400000L;
unsigned short com1_io = *biosPtr;  // The first word contains the
                                    // I/O address of COM1.
printf( "COM1 has the I/O base address %Xh.\n", com1_io );
```

The last three statements obtain information about the hardware configuration from the system data table, assuming the operating environment allows the program to access that memory area. In a DOS program compiled with the large memory model, pointers are 32 bits wide and consist of a segment address in the higher 16 bits and an offset in the lower 16 bits (often written in the form *segment:offset*). Thus, the pointer biosPtr in the prior example can be initialized with a long integer constant.

5

Expressions and Operators

An expression consists of a sequence of constants, identifiers, and operators that the program evaluates by performing the operations indicated. The expression's purpose in the program may be to obtain the resulting *value*, or to produce *side effects* of the evaluation, or both (see "Side Effects and Sequence Points" on page 70).

A single constant, string literal, or the identifier of an object or function is in itself an expression. Such a simple expression, or a more complex expression enclosed in parentheses, is called a *primary expression*. The C11 standard adds another kind of primary expression, the *generic selection*, which is described in the next section.

Every expression has a type. An expression's type is the type of the value that results when the expression is evaluated. If the expression yields no value, it has the type void. Some simple examples of expressions are listed in Table 5-1 (assume that a has been declared as a variable of type int, and z as a variable of type float _Complex).

Table 5-1. Example expressions

Expression	Type
'\n'	int
a + 1	int
a + 1.0	double
a < 77.7	int
"A string literal."	char *
abort()	void
sqrt(2.0)	double
z / sqrt(2.0)	double _Complex

As you can see from the last example in Table 5-1, compound expressions are formed by using an operator with expressions as its operands. The operands can themselves be primary or compound expressions. For example, you can use a function call as a factor in a multiplication. Likewise, the arguments in a function call can be expressions involving several operators, as in this example:

```
2.0 * sin( 3.14159 * fAngleDegrees/180.0 )
```

How Expressions Are Evaluated

Before we consider specific operators in detail, this section explains a few fundamental principles that will help you understand how C expressions are evaluated. The *precedence* and *associativity* of operators are obviously important in parsing compound expressions, but *generic selections*, *lvalues*, and *sequence points* are no less essential to understanding how a C program works.

Generic Selections (C11)

A *generic selection* is a primary expression that selects an expression from a list depending on the type of another expression. The selection takes place during compiling. This mechanism allows C developers to write type-generic macros like those provided for mathematical functions by the header *tgmath.h*, introduced in the C99 version of the standard. For example, *tgmath.h* provides six different square root functions, three for the real types float, double, and long double and three for the corresponding complex types. In a program that includes the header *tgmath.h*, the type-generic macro sqrt(*x*) can be used to automatically call whichever function fits the type of *x*.

A generic selection begins with the new keyword _Generic, followed by parentheses that enclose the controlling expression and a list of generic associations:

```
_Generic( expression, generic association 1
                [, generic association 2, ...] )
```

A generic association has the form

```
type name : expression
```

or

```
default : expression
```

The default association is optional and must not occur more than once in the list. The type names must designate distinct, mutually incompatible types. Incomplete types and types for variable-length arrays are not permitted.

The controlling expression *expression* is not evaluated, but its type is compared with the type names in the list of associations. If the controlling expression's type is compatible with one of the type names, then the compiler selects the expression associated with it in the list. If there is no compatible type name in the list, the expression from the `default` association is selected. If the list contains neither a compatible type nor a default association, the compiler issues an error message.

The type and value of a generic selection are those of the resulting expression, and only the resulting expression is evaluated at runtime. Here is a simple example:

```
_Generic( 1.0, int: "int", double: "double",
                default: "neither int nor double")
```

The result of this selection is the string literal `"double"`, because `1.0` has the type `double`. Generic selections are used primarily to define type-generic macros, as in the following example:

```
#define typeOf(x) _Generic((x), int: "int", double: "double", \
                default: "neither int nor double")
```

After this definition, the macro call `typeOf('A')` yields `"int"`, because a character constant in C has the type `int`. However, the value of `typeOf(var)` is the string `"neither int nor double"` if `var` has the type `unsigned int` or `const double`, as these types are not compatible with either of the two listed in the generic selection, `int` and `double`.

Another, more useful example of a type-generic macro written with a generic selection is shown in Chapter 15.

Lvalues

An *lvalue* is an expression that designates an object. The simplest example is the name of a variable. The initial "L" in the term originally meant "left": because an lvalue designates an object, it can appear on the left side of an assignment operator, as in *leftexpression* = *rightexpression*.[1] Other expressions—those that represent a value without designating an object—are called, by analogy, rvalues. An *rvalue* is an expression that can appear on the right side of an assignment operator, but not the left. Examples include constants and arithmetic expressions.

An lvalue can always be resolved to the corresponding object's address, unless the object is a bit-field or a variable declared with the *register* storage class (see "Storage Class Specifiers" on page 178). The operators that yield an lvalue include the subscript operator [] and the indirection operator *, as the examples in Table 5-2 illustrate (assume that `array` has been declared as an array and `ptr` as a pointer variable).

---

[1] The C standard acknowledges this etymology, but proposes that the L in *lvalue* be thought of as meaning "locator," because an lvalue always designates a *location* in memory. The standard steers clear of the term *rvalue*, preferring the phrase "not an lvalue."

Table 5-2. Pointer and array expressions may be lvalues

Expression	Lvalue?
array[1]	Yes; an array element is an object with a location
&array[1]	No; the location of the object is not an object with a location
ptr	Yes; the pointer variable is an object with a location
*ptr	Yes; what the pointer points to is also an object with a location
ptr+1	No; the addition yields a new address value, but not an object
*ptr+1	No; the addition yields a new arithmetic value, but not an object

An object may be declared as constant. If this is the case, you can't use it on the left side of an assignment, even though it is an lvalue, as the following example illustrates:

```
int a = 1;
const int b = 2, *ptr = &a;
b = 20;         // Error: b is declared as const int.
*ptr = 10;      // Error: ptr is declared as a pointer to const int.
```

In this example, the expressions a, b, ptr, and *ptr are all lvalues. However, b and *ptr are constant lvalues. Because ptr is declared as a pointer to const int, you cannot use it to modify the object it points to. For a full discussion of declarations, see Chapter 11.

The left operand of an assignment, as well as any operand of the increment and decrement operators, ++ and --, must be not only an lvalue but also a *modifiable lvalue*. A modifiable lvalue is an lvalue that is not declared as a const-qualified type (see "Type Qualifiers" on page 180), and that does not have an array type. If a modifiable lvalue designates an object with a structure or union type, none of its elements must be declared, directly or indirectly, as having a const-qualified type.

Side Effects and Sequence Points

In addition to yielding a value, the evaluation of an expression can result in other changes in the execution environment, called *side effects*. Examples of such changes include modifications of a variable's value, or of input or output streams.

During the execution of a program, there are determinate points at which all the side effects of a given expression have been completed, and no effects of the next expression have yet occurred. Such points in the program are called *sequence points*. Between two consecutive sequence points, partial expressions may be evaluated in any order. As a programmer, you must therefore remember not to modify any object more than once between two consecutive sequence points. Here is an example:

```
int i = 1;    // OK.
i = i++;      // Wrong: two modifications of i; behavior is undefined.
```

Because the assignment and increment operations in the last statement may take place in either order, the resulting value of i is undefined. Similarly, in the expression f()+g(), where f() and g() are two functions, C does not specify which function call is performed first. It is up to you, the programmer, to make sure that the results of such an expression are not dependent on the order of evaluation. Here's another example:

```
int i = 0, array[ ] = { 0, 10, 20 };
// ...
array[i] = array[++i];          // Wrong: behavior undefined.
array[i] = array[i + 1]; ++i;   // OK: modifications separated by a
                                // sequence point.
```

The most important sequence points occur at the following positions:

- After all the arguments in a function call have been evaluated, and before control passes to the statements in the function.

- At the end of an expression which is not part of a larger expression. Such *full expressions* include the expression in an expression statement (see "Expression Statements" on page 99), each of the three controlling expressions in a for statement, the condition of an if or while statement, the expression in a return statement, and initializers.

- After the evaluation of the first operand of each of the following operators:

&&
> Logical AND

||
> Logical OR

?:
> The conditional operator

,
> The comma operator

Thus, the expression ++i < 100 ? f(i++) : (i = 0) is permissible, as there is a sequence point between the first modification of i and whichever of the other two modifications is performed.

Operator Precedence and Associativity

An expression may contain several operators. In this case, the *precedence* of the operators determines which part of the expression is treated as the operand of each operator. For example, in keeping with the customary rules of arithmetic, the operators *, /, and % have higher precedence in an expression than the operators + and -. For example, the following expression:

```
a - b * c
```

is equivalent to a - (b * c). If you intend the operands to be grouped differently, you must use parentheses:

```
(a - b) * c
```

If two operators in an expression have the same precedence, then their *associativity* determines whether they are grouped with operands in order from left to right, or from right to left. For example, arithmetic operators are associated with operands from left to right, and assignment operators from right to left, as shown in Table 5-3. Table 5-4 lists the precedence and associativity of all the C operators, in order of precedence.

Table 5-3. Operator grouping

Expression	Associativity	Effective grouping
a / b % c	Left to right	(a / b) % c
a = b = c	Right to left	a = (b = c)

Table 5-4. Operator precedence and associativity

Precedence	Operators	Associativity
1.	Postfix operators: [] () . -> ++ -- (type name){list}	Left to right
2.	Unary operators: ++ -- ! ~ + - * & sizeof _Alignof	Right to left
3.	The cast operator: (type name)	Right to left
4.	Multiplicative operators: * / %	Left to right
5.	Additive operators: + -	Left to right
6.	Shift operators: << >>	Left to right
7.	Relational operators: < <= > >=	Left to right
8.	Equality operators: == !=	Left to right
9.	Bitwise AND: &	Left to right
10.	Bitwise exclusive OR: ^	Left to right
11.	Bitwise OR: |	Left to right
12.	Logical AND: &&	Left to right
13.	Logical OR: ||	Left to right
14.	The conditional operator: ? :	Right to left

Precedence	Operators	Associativity
15.	Assignment operators: = += -= *= /= %= &= ^= |= <<= >>=	Right to left
16.	The comma operator: ,	Left to right

The last of the highest-precedence operators in Table 5-4, (*type name*){*list*}, was added in C99. It is described in "Compound literals" on page 92.

A few of the operator tokens appear twice in the table. To start with, the increment and decrement operators, ++ and --, have a higher precedence when used as postfix operators (as in the expression x++) than the same tokens when used as prefix operators (as in ++x).

Furthermore, the tokens +,-, *, and & represent both *unary operators* —that is, operators that work on a single operand—and *binary operators*, or operators that connect two operands. For example, * with one operand is the indirection operator, and with two operands, it is the multiplication sign. In each of these cases, the unary operator has higher precedence than the binary operator. For example, the expression *ptr1 * *ptr2 is equivalent to (*ptr1) * (*ptr2).

Operators in Detail

This section describes in detail the individual operators, and indicates what kinds of operands are permissible. The descriptions are arranged according to the customary usage of the operators, beginning with the usual arithmetic and assignment operators.

Arithmetic Operators

Table 5-5 lists the arithmetic operators.

Table 5-5. Arithmetic operators

Operator	Meaning	Example	Result
*	Multiplication	x * y	The product of x and y
/	Division	x / y	The quotient of x by y
%	The modulo operation	x % y	The remainder of x divided by y
+	Addition	x + y	The sum of x and y
-	Subtraction	x - y	The difference of x and y
+ (unary)	Positive sign	+x	The value of x
- (unary)	Negative sign	-x	The arithmetic negation of x

The operands of the arithmetic operators are subject to the following rules:

- Only the % operator requires integer operands.
- The operands of all other operators may have any arithmetic type.

Furthermore, addition and subtraction operations may also be performed on pointers in the following cases:

- In an *addition*, one addend can be an object pointer while the other has an integer type.
- In a *subtraction*, either both operands can be pointers to objects of the same type (without regard to type qualifiers), or the *minuend* (the left operand) can be an object pointer, while the *subtrahend* (the right operand) has an integer type.

Standard arithmetic

The operands are subject to the *usual arithmetic conversions* (see "Conversion of Arithmetic Types" on page 50). The result of *division* with two integer operands is also an integer! To obtain the remainder of an integer division, use the modulo operation (the % operator). Implicit type conversion takes place in the evaluation of the following expressions, as shown in Table 5-6 (assume n is declared by short n = -5;).

Table 5-6. Implicit type conversions in arithmetic expressions

Expression	Implicit type conversion	The expression's type	The expression's value
-n	Integer promotion	int	5
n * -2L	Integer promotion: the value of n is promoted to long, because the constant -2L has the type long	long	10
8/n	Integer promotion	int	-1
8%n	Integer promotion	int	3
8.0/n	The value of n is converted to the type double, because 8.0 has the type double	double	-1.6
8.0%n	Error: the modulo operation (%) requires integer operands		

If both operands in a multiplication or a division have the same sign, the result is positive; otherwise, it is negative. However, the result of a modulo operation always has the same sign as the left operand. For this reason, the expression 8%n in Table 5-6 yields the value 3. If a program attempts to divide by zero, its behavior is undefined.

Pointer arithmetic

You can use the binary operators + and - to perform arithmetic operations on pointers. For example, you can modify a pointer to refer to another object a certain number of object sizes away from the object originally referenced. Such pointer arithmetic is generally useful only to refer to the elements of an array.

Adding an integer to or subtracting an integer from a pointer yields a pointer value with the same type as the pointer operand. The compiler automatically multiplies the integer by the size of the object referred to by the pointer type, as Example 5-1 illustrates.

Example 5-1. Pointer arithmetic

```
double dArr[5] = { 0.0, 1.1, 2.2, 3.3, 4.4 },  // Initialize an array and
       *dPtr = dArr;                            // a pointer to its first
                                                // element.
int i = 0;                    // An index variable.

dPtr = dPtr + 1;              // Advance dPtr to the second element.
dPtr = 2 + dPtr;              // Addends can be in either order.
                              // dPtr now points to dArr[3].

printf( "%.1f\n", *dPtr );      // Print the element referenced by dPtr.
printf( "%.1f\n", *(dPtr -1) ); // Print the element before that, without
                                // modifying the pointer dPtr.

i = dPtr - dArr;              // Result: the index of the
                             // array element that dPtr points to.
```

Figure 5-1 illustrates the effects of the two assignment expressions using the pointer dPtr.

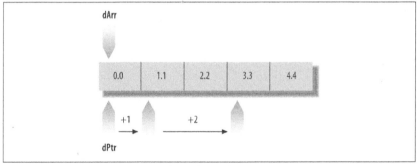

Figure 5-1. Using a pointer to move through the elements in an array

The statement dPtr = dPtr + 1; adds the size of one array element to the pointer, so that dPtr points to the next array element, dArr[1]. Because dPtr is declared as a pointer to double, its value is increased by sizeof(double).

The statement dPtr = dPtr + 1; in Example 5-1 has the same effect as any of the following statements (see "Assignment Operators" on page 76 and "Increment and Decrement Operators" on page 78):

```
dPtr += 1;
++dPtr;
dPtr++;
```

Subtracting one pointer from another yields an integer value with the type ptrdiff_t. The value is the number of objects that fit between the two pointer values. In the last statement in Example 5-1, the expression dPtr - dArr yields the value 3. This is also the index of the element that dPtr points to, because dArr represents the address of the first array element (with the index 0). The type ptrdiff_t is defined in the header file *stddef.h*, usually as int.

For more information on pointer arithmetic, see Chapter 9.

Assignment Operators

In an assignment operation, the left operand must be a *modifiable lvalue*; in other words, it must be an expression that designates an object whose value can be changed. In a *simple assignment* (that is, one performed using the operator =), the assignment operation stores the value of the right operand in this object.

There are also *compound assignments*, which combine an arithmetic or a bitwise operation in the same step with the assignment. Table 5-7 lists all the assignment operators.

Table 5-7. Assignment operators

Operator	Meaning	Example	Result
=	Simple assignment	x = y	Assign x the value of y
+= -= *= /= %= &= ^= |= <<= >>=	Compound assignment	x *= y	For each binary arithmetic or binary bitwise operator *op*, x *op*= y is equivalent to x = x *op* (y)

Simple assignment

The operands of a simple assignment must fulfill *one* of the following conditions:

- Both operands have arithmetic types.
- The left operand has the type _Bool and the right operand is a pointer.
- Both operands have the same structure or union type.
- Both operands are pointers to the same type, or the left operand is a pointer to a qualified version of the common type—that is, the type pointed to by the left

operand is declared with one or more additional type qualifiers (see Chapter 11).

- One operand is an object pointer and the other is a pointer to void (here again, the type pointed to by the left operand may have additional type qualifiers).

- The left operand is a pointer and the right is a null pointer constant.

If the two operands have different types, the value of the right operand is converted to the type of the left operand (see "The Results of Arithmetic Type Conversions" on page 54 and "Implicit Pointer Conversions" on page 61).

The modification of the left operand is a side effect of an *assignment expression*. The value of the entire assignment expression is the same as the value assigned to the left operand, and the assignment expression has the type of the left operand. However, unlike its left operand, the assignment expression itself is not an lvalue. If you use the value of an assignment expression in a larger expression, pay careful attention to implicit type conversions. Avoid errors such as that illustrated in the following example. This code is supposed to read characters from the standard input stream until the end-of-file is reached or an error occurs:

```
#include <stdio.h>
char c = 0;

/* ... */

while ( (c = getchar()) != EOF )
    { /* ... Process the character stored in c ... */ }
```

In the controlling expression of the while statement in this example, getchar() returns a value with type int, which is implicitly converted to char for assignment to c. Then the value of the entire assignment expression c = getchar(), which is the same char value, is promoted to int for comparison with the constant EOF, which is usually defined as -1 in the header file *stdio.h*. However, if the type char is equivalent to unsigned char, then the conversion to int always yields a non-negative value. In this case, the loop condition is always true.

As Table 5-4 shows, assignment operators have a low precedence, and are grouped with their operators from right to left. As a result, no parentheses are needed around the expression to the right of the assignment operator, and multiple assignments can be combined in one expression, as in this example:

```
double x = 0.5, y1, y2;     // Declarations
y1 = y2 = 10.0 * x;         // Equivalent to  y1 = (y2 = (10.0 * x));
```

This expression assigns the result of the multiplication to y1 and to y2.

Compound assignments

A compound assignment is performed by any of the following operators:

```
    *=  /= %= += -=  (arithmetic operation and assignment)
    <<= >>= &= ^= |=  (bitwise operation and assignment)
```

In evaluating a compound assignment expression, the program combines the two operands with the specified operation and assigns the result to the left operand. Here are two examples:

```
long var = 1234L ;
var *= 3;          // Triple the value of var.
var <<= 2;         // Shift the bit pattern in var two bit-positions
                   // to the left (i.e., multiply the value by four).
```

The only difference between a compound assignment x op= y and the corresponding expression x = x op (y) is that in the compound assignment, the left operand x is evaluated only once. In the following example, the left operand of the compound assignment operator is an expression with a side effect, so that the two expressions are not equivalent:

```
x[++i] *= 2;             // Increment i once, then double the indexed
                         // array element.
x[++i] = x[++i] * (2);   // Oops: you probably didn't want to
                         // increment i twice.
```

In the equivalent form x = x op (y), the parentheses around the right operand y are significant, as the following example illustrates:

```
double var1 = 2.5, var2 = 0.5;
var1 /= var2 + 1;        // Equivalent to var1 = var1 / (var2 + 1);
```

Without the parentheses, the expression var1 = var1 / var2 + 1 would yield a different result, because simple division, unlike the compound assignment, has higher precedence than addition.

The operands of a compound assignment can have any types that are permissible for the operands of the corresponding binary operator. The only additional restriction is that when you add a pointer to an integer, the pointer must be the left operand, as the result of the addition is a pointer. For example:

```
short *sPtr;
/* ... */
sPtr += 2;               // Equivalent to  sPtr = sPtr + 2;
                         // or  sPtr = 2 + sPtr;
```

Increment and Decrement Operators

Each of the tokens ++ and -- represents both a postfix and a prefix operator. Table 5-8 describes both forms of both operators.

Table 5-8. Increment and decrement operators

Operator	Meaning	Side effect	Value of the expression
Postfix: x++	Increment	Increases the value of x by one (like $x = x + 1$)	The value of x++ is the value that x had before it was incremented
Prefix: ++x			The value of ++x is the value that x has after it has been incremented
Postfix: x--	Decrement	Decreases the value of x by one (like $x = x - 1$)	The value of x-- is the value that x had before it was decremented
Prefix: --x			The value of --x is the value that x has after it has been decremented

These operators require a modifiable lvalue as their operand. More specifically, the operand must have a real arithmetic type (not a complex type), or an object pointer type. The expressions ++x and --x are equivalent to (x += 1) and (x -= 1).

The following examples demonstrate the use of the increment operators, along with the subscript operator [] and the indirection operator *:

```
char a[10] = "Jim";
int i = 0;
printf( "%c\n", a[i++] );      // Output: J
printf( "%c\n", a[++i] );      // Output: m
```

The character argument in the first printf() call is the character J from the array element a[0]. After the call, i has the value 1. Thus, in the next statement, the expression ++i yields the value 2, so that a[++i] is the character m.

The operator ++ can also be applied to the array element itself:

```
i = 0;
printf( "%c\n", a[i]++ );      // Output: J
printf( "%c\n", ++a[i] );      // Output: L
```

According to the operator precedences and associativity in Table 5-4, the expressions a[i]++ and ++a[i] are equivalent to (a[i])++ and ++(a[i]). Thus, each of these expressions increases the value of the array element a[0] by one, while leaving the index variable i unchanged. After the statements in this example, the value of i is still 0, and the character array contains the string "Lim", as the first element has been incremented twice.

The operators ++ and -- are often used in expressions with pointers that are dereferenced by the * operator. For example, the following while loop copies a string from the array a to a second char array, a2:

```
char a2[10], *p1 = a,  *p2 = a2;
// Copy string to a2:
while ( (*p2++ = *p1++) != '\0' )
    ;
```

Because the postfix operator ++ has precedence over the indirection operator * (see Table 5-4), the expression *p1++ is equivalent to *(p1++). In other words, the value of the expression *p1++ is the array element referenced by p1, and as a side effect, the value of p1 is one greater after the expression has been evaluated. When the end of the string is reached, the assignment *p2++ = *p1++ copies the terminator character '\0', and the loop ends, because the assignment expression yields the value '\0'.

By contrast, the expression (*p1)++ or ++(*p1) would increment the element referenced by p1, leaving the pointer's value unchanged. However, the parentheses in the expression ++(*p1) are unnecessary: this expression is equivalent to ++*p1 because the unary operators are associated with operands from right to left (see Table 5-4). For the same reason, the expression *++p1 is equivalent to *(++p1), and its value is the array element that p1 points to after p1 has been incremented.

Comparative Operators

The *comparative operators* , also called the *relational operators* and the *equality operators*, compare two operands and yield a value of type int. The value is 1 if the specified relation holds, and 0 if it does not. C defines the comparative operators listed in Table 5-9.

Table 5-9. Comparative operators

Operator	Meaning	Example	Result (1 = true, 0 = false)
<	Less than	x < y	1 if x is less than y; otherwise, 0
<=	Less than or equal to	x <= y	1 if x is less than or equal to y; otherwise, 0
>	Greater than	x > y	1 if x is greater than y; otherwise, 0
>=	Greater than or equal to	x >= y	1 if x is greater than or equal to y; otherwise, 0
==	Equal to	x == y	1 if x is equal to y; otherwise, 0
!=	Not equal to	x != y	1 if x is not equal to y; otherwise, 0

For all comparative operators, the operands must meet *one* of the following conditions:

- Both operands have real arithmetic types.
- Both operands are pointers to objects of the same type, which may be declared with different type qualifiers.

With the equality operators, == and !=, operands that meet any of the following conditions are also permitted:

- The two operands have any arithmetic types, including complex types.
- Both operands are pointers to functions of the same type.

- One operand is an object pointer, while the other is a pointer to void. The two may be declared with different type qualifiers (the operand that is not a pointer to void is implicitly converted to the type void* for the comparison).

- One operand is a pointer and the other is a null pointer constant. The null pointer constant is converted to the other operand's type for the comparison.

The operands of all comparison operators are subject to the *usual arithmetic conversions* (see "Conversion of Arithmetic Types" on page 50). Two complex numbers are considered equal if their real parts are equal and their imaginary parts are equal.

When you compare two object pointers, the result depends on the relative positions of the objects in memory. Elements of an array are objects with fixed relative positions: a pointer that references an element with a greater index is greater than any pointer that references an element with a lesser index. A pointer can also contain the address of the first memory location after the last element of an array. In this case, that pointer's value is greater than that of any pointer to an element of the array.

The function in Example 5-2 illustrates some expressions with pointers as operands.

Example 5-2. Operations with pointers

```
/* The function average() calculates the arithmetic mean of the
 * numbers passed to it in an array.
 * Arguments: An array of float, and its length.
 * Return value: The arithmetic mean of the array elements,
 * with type double.
 */
double average( const float *array, int length )
{
  double sum = 0.0;
  const float *end = array + length; // Points one past the last element.

  if ( length <= 0 )                 // The average of no elements is zero.
    return 0.0;
                                     // Accumulate the sum
  for ( const float *p = array; p < end; ++p )  // by walking a pointer
    sum += *p;                       // through the array.

  return sum/length;                 // The average of the element values.
}
```

Two pointers are equal if they point to the same location in memory, or if they are both null pointers. In particular, pointers to members of the same union are always equal because all members of a union begin at the same address. The rule for members of the same structure, however, is that a pointer to member2 is larger than a pointer to member1 if and only if member2 is declared after member1 in the structure type's definition.

The comparative operators have lower precedence than the arithmetic operators but higher precedence than the logical operators. As a result, the following two expressions are equivalent:

```
a < b && b < c + 1
(a < b) && (b < (c + 1))
```

Furthermore, the equality operators, == and !=, have lower precedence than the other comparative operators. Thus, the following two expressions are also equivalent:

```
a < b != b < c
(a < b) != (b < c)
```

This expression is true (that is, it yields the value 1) if and only if one of the two operand expressions, (a < b) and (b < c), is true and the other false.

Logical Operators

You can connect expressions using logical operators to form compound conditions, such as those often used in jump and loop statements to control the program flow. C uses the symbols described in Table 5-10 for the boolean operations AND, OR, and NOT.

Table 5-10. Logical operators

Operator	Meaning	Example	Result (1 = true, 0 = false)
&&	logical AND	x && y	1 if each of the operands x and y is not equal to zero; otherwise, 0
||	logical OR	x || y	0 if each of x and y is equal to zero; otherwise, 1
!	logical NOT	!x	1 if x is equal to zero; otherwise, 0

Like comparative expressions, logical expressions have the type int. The result has the value 1 if the logical expression is true, and the value 0 if it is false.

The operands may have any scalar type desired—in other words, any arithmetic or pointer type. Any operand with a value of 0 is interpreted as false; any value other than 0 is treated as true. Most often, the operands are comparative expressions, as in the following example. Assuming the variable deviation has the type double, all three of the expressions that follow are equivalent:

```
(deviation <  -0.2) || (deviation >  0.2)
 deviation <  -0.2  ||  deviation >  0.2
!(deviation >= -0.2  &&  deviation <= 0.2)
```

Each of these logical expressions yields the value 1, or true, whenever the value of the variable deviation is outside the interval [-0.2, 0.2]. The parentheses in the first expression are unnecessary because comparative operators have a higher precedence than the logical operators && and ||. However, the unary operator ! has a higher precedence. Furthermore, as Table 5-4 shows, the operator && has a higher precedence than ||. As a result, parentheses are necessary in the following expression:

```
( deviation < -0.2 || deviation > 0.2 ) && status == 1
```

Without the parentheses, that expression would be equivalent to this:

```
deviation < -0.2 || ( deviation > 0.2 && status == 1 )
```

These expressions yield different results if, for example, deviation is less than -0.2 and status is not equal to 1.

The operators && and || have an important peculiarity: their operands are evaluated in order from left to right, and if the value of the left operand is sufficient to determine the result of the operation, then the right operand is not evaluated at all. There is a sequence point after the evaluation of the left operand. The operator && evaluates the right operand only if the left operand yields a nonzero value; the operator || evaluates the right operand only if the left operand yields 0. The following example shows how programs can use these conditional-evaluation characteristics of the && and || operators:

```
double x;
_Bool get_x(double *x), check_x(double);    // Function prototype
                                            // declarations.
/* ... */
while ( get_x(&x) && check_x(x) )           // Read and test a number.
   { /* ... Process x ... */  }
```

In the controlling expression of the while loop, the function get_x(&x) is called first to read a floating-point number into the variable x. Assuming that get_x() returns a true value on success, the check_x() function is called only if there is a new value in x to be tested. If check_x() also returns true, then the loop body is executed to process x.

Bitwise Operators

For more compact data, C programs can store information in individual bits or groups of bits. File access permissions are a common example. The bitwise operators allow you to manipulate individual bits in a byte or in a larger data unit: you can clear, set, or invert any bit or group of bits. You can also shift the bit pattern of an integer to the left or right.

The bit pattern of an integer type consists of bit positions numbered from right to left, beginning with position 0 for the least significant bit. For example, consider the char value '*', which in ASCII encoding is equal to 42, or binary 101010:

Bit pattern	0	0	1	0	1	0	1	0
Bit positions	7	6	5	4	3	2	1	0

In this example, the value 101010 is shown in the context of an 8-bit byte; hence the two leading zeros.

Boolean bitwise operators

The operators listed in Table 5-11 perform Boolean operations on each bit position of their operands. The binary operators connect the bit in each position in one operand with the bit in the same position in the other operand. A bit that is set, or 1, is interpreted as true, and a bit that is cleared, or 0, is considered false.

In addition to the operators for boolean AND, OR, and NOT, there is also a bitwise exclusive-OR operator. These are all described in Table 5-11.

Table 5-11. Boolean bitwise operators

Operator	Meaning	Example	Result, for each bit position (1 = set, 0 = cleared)
&	Bitwise AND	x & y	1, if 1 in both x and y
			0, if 0 in x or y, or both
|	Bitwise OR	x | y	1, if 1 in x or y, or both
			0, if 0 in both x and y
^	Bitwise exclusive OR	x ^ y	1, if 1 either in x or in y, but not in both
			0, if either value in both x and y
~	Bitwise NOT (one's complement)	~x	1, if 0 in x
			0, if 1 in x

The operands of the bitwise operators must have integer types, and are subject to the usual arithmetic conversions. The resulting common type of the operands is the type of the result. Table 5-12 illustrates the effects of these operators.

Table 5-12. Effects of the bitwise operators

Expression (or declaration)	Bit pattern
int a = 6;	0 … 0 0 1 1 0
int b = 11;	0 … 0 1 0 1 1
a & b	0 … 0 0 0 1 0
a | b	0 … 0 1 1 1 1
a ^ b	0 … 0 1 1 0 1
~a	1 … 1 1 0 0 1

You can clear certain bits in an integer variable a by performing a bitwise AND with an integer in which only the bits to be cleared contain zeros, and assigning the result to the variable a. The bits that were set in the second operand—called a bit mask—have the same value in the result as they had in the first operand. For example, an AND with the bit mask 0xFF clears all bits except the lowest eight:

```
a &= 0xFF;        // Equivalent notation: a = a & 0xFF;
```

As this example illustrates, the compound assignment operator &= also performs the & operation. The compound assignments with the other binary bitwise operators work similarly.

The bitwise operators are also useful in making bit masks to use in further bit operations. For example, in the bit pattern of 0x20, only bit 5 is set. The expression ~0x20 therefore yields a bit mask in which all bits are set except bit 5:

```
a &= ~0x20;    // Clear bit 5 in a.
```

The bit mask ~0x20 is preferable to 0xFFFFFFDF because it is more portable: it gives the desired result regardless of the machine's word size. (It also makes the statement more readable for humans.)

You can also use the operators | (OR) and ^ (exclusive OR) to set and clear certain bits. Here is an example of each one:

```
int mask = 0xC;
a |= mask;     // Set bits 2 and 3 in a.
a ^= mask;     // Invert bits 2 and 3 in a.
```

A second inversion using the same bit mask reverses the first inversion. In other words, b^mask^mask yields the original value of b. This behavior can be used to swap the values of two integers without using a third, temporary variable:

```
a ^= b;        // Equivalent to a = a ^ b;
b ^= a;        // Assign b the original value of a.
a ^= b;        // Assign a the original value of b.
```

The first two expressions in this example are equivalent to b = b^(a^b) or b = (a^b)^b. The result is like b = a, with the side effect that a is also modified, and now equals a^b. At this point, the third expression has the effect of (using the original values of a and b) a = (a^b)^a, or a = b.

Shift operators

The shift operators transpose the bit pattern of the left operand by the number of bit positions indicated by the right operand. They are listed in Table 5-13.

Table 5-13. Shift operators

Operator	Meaning	Example	Result
<<	Shift left	x << y	Each bit value in x is moved y positions to the left
>>	Shift right	x >> y	Each bit value in x is moved y positions to the right

The operands of the shift operators must be integers. Before the actual bit-shift, the integer promotions are performed on both operands. The value of the right operand must not be negative, and must be less than the width of the left operand after inte-

ger promotion. If it does not meet these conditions, the program's behavior is undefined.

The result has the type of the left operand after integer promotion. The shift expressions in the following example have the type unsigned long.

```
unsigned long n = 0xB,    // Bit pattern:  0 ... 0 0 0 1 0 1 1
         result = 0;
result = n << 2;          //              0 ... 0 1 0 1 1 0 0
result = n >> 2;          //              0 ... 0 0 0 0 0 1 0
```

In a left shift, the bit positions that are vacated on the right are always cleared. Bit
values shifted beyond the leftmost bit position are lost. A left shift through y bit
positions is equivalent to multiplying the left operand by 2^y: if the left operand x has
an unsigned type, then the expression $x << y$ yields the value of $x \times 2^y$. Thus, in the
previous example, the expression n << 2 yields the value of n × 4, or 44.

On a right shift, the vacated bit positions on the left are cleared if the left operand
has an unsigned type, or if it has a signed type and a non-negative value. In this
case, the expression $x >> y$ yields the same value as the integer division $x/2^y$. If the
left operand has a negative value, then the fill value depends on the compiler: it may
be either zero or the value of the sign bit.

The shift operators are useful in generating certain bit masks. For example, the
expression 1 << 8 yields a word with only bit 8 set, and the expression ~(3<<4)
produces a bit pattern in which all bits are set except bits 4 and 5. The function
setBit() in Example 5-3 uses the bit operations to manipulate a bit mask.

Example 5-3. Using a shift operation to manipulate a bit mask

```
// Function setBit()
// Sets the bit at position p in the mask m.
// Uses CHAR_BIT, defined in limits.h, for the number of bits in a byte.
// Return value: The new mask with the bit set, or the original mask
//               if p is not a valid bit position.
unsigned int setBit( unsigned int mask, unsigned int p )
{
  if ( p >= CHAR_BIT * sizeof(int) )
    return mask;
  else
    return mask | (1 << p);
}
```

The shift operators have lower precedence than the arithmetic operators but higher
precedence than the comparative operators and the other bitwise operators. The
parentheses in the expression mask | (1 << p) in Example 5-3 are thus actually
unnecessary, but they make the code more readable.

Memory Addressing Operators

The five operators listed in Table 5-14 are used in addressing array elements and members of structures, and in using pointers to access objects and functions.

Table 5-14. Memory addressing operators

Operator	Meaning	Example	Result
&	Address of	&x	Pointer to x
*	Indirection operator	*p	The object or function that p points to
[ ]	Subscripting	x[y]	The element with the index y in the array x (or the element with the index x in the array y; the [ ] operator works either way)
.	Structure or union member designator	x.y	The member named y in the structure or union x
->	Structure or union member designator by reference	p->y	The member named y in the structure or union that p points to

The & and * operators

The *address operator* & yields the address of its operand. If the operand x has the type *T*, then the expression &x has the type "pointer to *T*."

The operand of the address operator must have an addressable location in memory. In other words, the operand must designate either a function or an object (i.e., an lvalue) that is not a bit-field, and has not been declared with the storage class `register` (see "Storage Class Specifiers" on page 178).

You need to obtain the addresses of objects and functions when you want to initialize pointers to them:

```
float x, *ptr;
ptr = &x;        // OK: Make ptr point to x.
ptr = &(x+1);    // Error: (x+1) is not an lvalue.
```

Conversely, when you have a pointer and want to access the object it references, use the *indirection operator* *, which is sometimes called the *dereferencing operator* (see "Using Pointers to Read and Modify Objects" on page 145 for more information). Its operand must have a pointer type. If ptr is a pointer, then *ptr designates the object or function that ptr points to. If ptr is an object pointer, then *ptr is an lvalue, and you can use it as the left operand of an assignment operator:

```
float x, *ptr = &x;
*ptr = 1.7;      // Assign the value 1.7 to the variable x
++(*ptr);        // and add 1 to it.
```

In the final statement of this example, the value of ptr remains unchanged. The value of x is now 2.7.

The behavior of the indirection operator * is undefined if the value of the pointer operand is not the address of an object or a function.

Like the other unary operators, the operators & and * have the second highest precedence. They are grouped with operands from right to left. The parentheses in the expression ++(*ptr) are thus superfluous.

The operators & and * are complementary: if x is an expression that designates an object or a function, then the expression *&x is equivalent to x. Conversely, in an expression of the form &*ptr, the operators cancel each other out so that the type and value of the expression are equivalent to ptr. However, &*ptr is never an lvalue, even if ptr is.

Elements of arrays

The *subscript operator* [] allows you to access individual elements of an array. It takes two operands. In the simplest case, one operand is an array name and the other operand designates an integer. In the following example, assume that myarray is the name of an array, and i is a variable with an integer type. The expression myarray[i] then designates element number i in the array, where the first element is element number zero (see Chapter 8).

The left operand of [] need not be an array name. One operand must be an expression whose type is "pointer to an object type"—an array name is a special case of such an expression—while the other operand must have an integer type. An expression of the form x[y] is always equivalent to (*((x)+(y))) (see also "Pointer arithmetic" on page 75 earlier in this chapter). Example 5-4 uses the subscript operator in initializing a dynamically generated array.

Example 5-4. Initializing an array

```
#include <stdlib.h>
#define ARRAY_SIZE 100
/* ... */
double *pArray = NULL; int i = 0;
pArray = malloc( ARRAY_SIZE * sizeof(double) ); // Generate the array
if ( pArray != NULL ) {
    for ( i = 0; i < ARRAY_SIZE; ++i )              // and initialize it.
       pArray[i] = (double)rand()/RAND_MAX;
/* ... */
}
```

In Example 5-4, the expression pArray[i] in the loop body is equivalent to *(pArray+i). The notation i[pArray] is also correct, and yields the same array element.

Members of structures and unions

The binary operators `.` and `->`, most often called the *dot operator* and the *arrow operator*, allow you to select a member of a structure or a union.

As Example 5-5 illustrates, the left operand of the dot operator `.` must have a structure or union type, and the right operand must be the name of a member of that type.

Example 5-5. The dot operator

```
struct Article { long number;       // The part number of an article
                 char name[32];     // The article's name
                 long price;        // The unit price in cents
                 /* ... */
               };
struct Article sw = { 102030L, "Heroes", 5995L };
sw.price = 4995L;                    // Change the price to 49.95
```

The result of the dot operator has the value and type of the selected member. If the left operand is an lvalue, then the operation also yields an lvalue. If the left operand has a qualified type (such as one declared with `const`), then the result is likewise qualified.

The left operand of the dot operator is not always an lvalue, as the following example shows:

```
struct Article getArticle();        // Function prototype
printf( "name: %s\n", getArticle().name );
```

The function `getArticle()` returns an object of type `struct Article`. As a result, `getArticle().name` is a valid expression, but not an lvalue, as the return value of a function is not an lvalue.

The operator `->` also selects a member of a structure or union, but its left operand must be a *pointer* to a structure or union type. The right operand is the name of a member of the structure or union. Example 5-6 illustrates the use of the `->` operator, again using the `Article` structure defined in Example 5-5.

Example 5-6. The arrow operator

```
struct Article *pArticle = &sw,     // A pointer to struct Article.
       const *pcArticle = &sw;      // A "read-only pointer" to struct
                                    // Article.
++(pArticle->number);               // Increment the part number.
if ( pcArticle->number == 102031L ) // Correct usage: read-only access.
  pcArticle->price += 50;           // Error: can't use a
                                    // const-qualified pointer
                                    // to modify the object.
```

The result of the arrow operator is always an lvalue. It has the type of the selected member, as well as any type qualifications of the pointer operand. In Example 5-6, pcArticle is a pointer to const struct Article. As a result, the expression pcArticle->price is constant.

Any expression that contains the arrow operator can be rewritten using the dot operator by dereferencing the pointer separately: an expression of the form p->m is equivalent to (*p).m. Conversely, the expression x.m is equivalent to (&x)->m, as long as x is an lvalue.

The operators . and ->, like [], have the highest precedence, and are grouped from left to right. Thus, the expression ++p->m, for example, is equivalent to ++(p->m), and the expression p->m++ is equivalent to (p->m)++. However, the parentheses in the expression (*p).m are necessary, as the dereferencing operator * has a lower precedence. The expression *p.m would be equivalent to *(p.m), and thus makes sense only if the member m is also a pointer.

To conclude this section, we can combine the subscript, dot, and arrow operators to work with an array whose elements are structures:

```
struct Article arrArticle[10];    // An array with ten elements
                                  // of type struct Article.
arrArticle[2].price = 990L;       // Set the price of the
                                  // array element arrArticle[2].
arrArticle->number = 10100L;      // Set the part number in the
                                  // array element arrArticle[0].
```

An array name, such as arrArticle in the example, is a constant pointer to the first array element. Hence arrArticle->number designates the member number in the first array element. To put it in more general terms: for any index i, the following three expressions are equivalent:

```
arrArticle[i].number
(arrArticle+i)->number
(*(arrArticle+i)).number
```

All of them designate the member number in the array element with the index i.

Other Operators

There are seven other operators in C that do not fall into any of the categories described in this chapter. Table 5-15 lists these operators in order of precedence.

Table 5-15. Other operators

Operator	Meaning	Example	Result
()	Function call	log(x)	Passes control to the specified function, with the specified arguments

Operator	Meaning	Example	Result
(type name){list}	Compound literal	(int [5]){ 1, 2 }	Defines an unnamed object that has the specified type and the values listed
sizeof	Storage size of an object or type, in bytes	sizeof x	The number of bytes occupied in memory by x
_Alignof	Alignment of an object type, in bytes	_Alignof(int)	The minimum distance between the locations of two such objects in memory
(type name)	Explicit type conversion, or "cast"	(short) x	The value of x converted to the type specified
?:	Conditional evaluation	x ? y : z	The value of y, if x is true (i.e., nonzero); otherwise, the value of z
,	Sequential evaluation	x,y	Evaluates first x, then y; the result of the expression is the value of y

Function calls

A function call is an expression of the form *fn_ptr(argument_list)*, where the operand *fn_ptr* is an expression with the type "pointer to a function." If the operand designates a function (as a function name does, for example), then it is automatically converted into a pointer to the function. A function call expression has the value and type of the function's return value. If the function has no return value, the function call has the type void.

Before you can call a function, you must make sure that it has been declared in the same translation unit. Usually a source file includes a header file containing the function declaration, as in this example:

```
#include <math.h>    // Contains the prototype
                      // double pow( double, double );
double x = 0.7, y = 0.0;
/* ... */
y = pow( x+1, 3.0 );    // Type: double
```

The parentheses enclose the comma-separated list of arguments passed to the function, which can also be an empty list. If the function declaration is in prototype form (as is usually the case), the compiler ensures that each argument is converted to the type of the corresponding parameter, as for an assignment. If this conversion fails, the compiler issues an error message:

```
pow( x, 3 );    // The integer constant 3 is converted to type double.
pow( x );       // Error: incorrect number of arguments.
```

The order in which the program evaluates the individual expressions that designate the function and its arguments is not defined. As a result, the behavior of a `printf` statement such as the following is undefined:

```
int i = 0;
printf( "%d %d\n", i, ++i );      // Behavior undefined
```

However, there is a sequence point after all of these expressions have been evaluated and before control passes to the function.

Like the other postfix operators, a function call has the highest precedence, and is grouped with operands from left to right. For example, suppose that `fn_table` is an array of pointers to functions that take no arguments and return a structure that contains a member named `price`. In this case, the following expression is a valid function call:

```
fn_table[i++]().price
```

The expression calls the function referenced by the pointer stored in `fn_table[i]`. The return value is a structure, and the dot operator selects the member `price` in that structure. The complete expression has the value of the member `price` in the return value of the function `fn_table[i]()`, and the side effect that `i` is incremented once.

Chapter 7 describes function calls in more detail, including recursive functions and functions that take a variable number of arguments.

Compound literals

Compound literals are an extension introduced in the C99 standard. This extension allows you to define literals with any object type desired. A *compound literal* consists of an object type in parentheses, followed by an initialization list in braces:

```
(type name ){ list of initializers }
```

The value of the expression is an unnamed object that has the specified type and the values listed. If you place a compound literal outside of all function blocks, then the initializers must be constant expressions, and the object has static storage duration. Otherwise, it has automatic storage duration, determined by the containing block.

Typical compound literals generate objects with array or structure types. Here are a few examples to illustrate their use:

```
float *fPtr = (float []){ -0.5, 0.0, +0.5 };
```

This declaration defines a pointer to a nameless array of three float elements:

```
#include "database.h"    // Contains prototypes and type definitions,
                         // including the structure Pair:
                         // struct Pair { long key; char value[32]; };

insertPair( &db, &(struct Pair){ 1000L, "New York JFK Airport" } );
```

This statement passes the address of a literal of type struct Pair to the function insertPair(). You can also store the address in a local variable first:

```
struct Pair p1 = { 1000L, "New York JFK Airport" };
insertPair( &db, &p1 );
```

To define a constant compound literal, use the type qualifier const:

```
(const char [ ]){"A constant string."}
```

If the previous expression appears outside of all functions, it defines a static array of char, like the following simple string literal:

```
"A constant string."
```

In fact, the compiler may store string literals and constant compound literals with the same type and contents at the same location in memory.

Despite their similar appearance, compound literals are not the same as cast expressions. The result of a cast expression has a scalar type or the type void, and is not an lvalue.

The sizeof operator

The sizeof operator yields the size of its operand in bytes. Programs need to know the size of objects mainly in order to reserve memory for them dynamically, or to store binary data in files.

The operand of the sizeof operator can be either an object type in parentheses or an expression that has an object type and is not a bit-field. The result has the type size_t, which is defined in *stddef.h* and other standard header files as an unsigned integer type.

For example, if i is an int variable and iPtr is a pointer to int, then each of the following expressions yields the size of int—on a 32-bit system, the value would be 4:

```
sizeof(int)  sizeof i  sizeof(i)  sizeof *iPtr  sizeof(*iPtr)
```

Note the difference to the following expressions, each of which yields the *size of a pointer* to int:

```
sizeof(int*)  sizeof &i  sizeof(&i)  sizeof iPtr  sizeof(iPtr)
```

Like *, &, and the other unary operators, sizeof has the second highest precedence, and is grouped from right to left. For this reason, no parentheses are necessary in the expression sizeof *iPtr.

For an operand with the type char, unsigned char, or signed char, the sizeof operator yields the value 1, because these types have the size of a byte. If the operand has a structure type, the result is the total size that the object occupies in memory, including any gaps that may occur due to the alignment of the structure members. In other words, the size of a structure is sometimes greater than the sum of its individual members' sizes. For example, if variables of the type short are aligned on even byte addresses, the following structure has the size sizeof(short) + 2:

```
struct gap { char version; short value; };
```

In the following example, the standard function memset() sets every byte in the structure to zero, including any gaps between members:

```
#include <string.h>
/* ... */
struct gap g;
memset( &g, 0, sizeof g );
```

If the operand of sizeof is an expression, it is not actually evaluated. The compiler determines the size of the operand by its type, and replaces the sizeof expression with the resulting constant. Variable-length arrays, introduced in the C99 standard, are an exception (see Chapter 8). Their size is determined at runtime, as Example 5-7 illustrates.

Example 5-7. Sizing variable-length arrays

```
void func( float a[ ], int n )
{
  float b[2*n];                  // A variable-length array of float.
  /* ... the value of n may change now ... */
  int m = sizeof(b) / sizeof(*b);  // Yields the number of elements
  /* ... */                        // in the array b.
}
```

Regardless of the current value of the variable n, the expression sizeof(b) yields the value of $2 \times n_0 \times$ sizeof(float), where n_0 is the value that n had at the beginning of the function block. The expression sizeof(*b) is equivalent to sizeof(b[0]), and in this case has the value of sizeof(float).

The parameter a in the function func() in Example 5-7 is a pointer, not an array. The expression sizeof(a) within the function would therefore yield the size of a pointer. See "Array and Function Designators" on page 58.

The _Alignof operator

The alignment of a type describes how objects of that type can be positioned in memory (see "The Alignment of Objects in Memory" on page 36). Alignment is expressed as an integer value. The operand of _Alignof is the name of a type in parentheses, and the resulting expression yields the type's alignment, as in the following example:

```
_Alignof(char*)    // The alignment of a char pointer
```

Because the alignment of types is determined by the compiler, _Alignof expressions, like sizeof expressions, are integer constants with the type size_t. If your program includes the header file *stdalign.h*, you can also use the synonym alignof in place of the keyword _Alignof. The _Alignof operator can only be applied to complete object types, not to function types or incomplete object types. If the operand is an array type, _Alignof yields the alignment of the array elements' type.

The conditional operator

The *conditional operator* is sometimes called the *ternary* or *trinary operator*, because it is the only one that has three operands:

```
condition ? expression 1 : expression 2
```

The operation first evaluates the condition. Then, depending on the result, it evaluates one or the other of the two alternative expressions.

There is a sequence point after the condition has been evaluated. If the result is not equal to 0 (in other words, if the condition is true), then only the second operand, expression 1, is evaluated, and the entire operation yields the value of expression 1. On the other hand, if condition does yield 0 (i.e., false), then only the third operand, expression 2, is evaluated, and the entire operation yields the value of expression 2. In this way, the conditional operator represents a conditional jump in the program flow, and is therefore an alternative to some if-else statements.

A common example is the following function, which finds the maximum of two numbers:

```
inline int iMax(int a, int b) { return a >= b ? a : b; }
```

The function iMax() can be rewritten using an if-else statement:

```
inline int iMax(int a, int b)
{ if ( a >= b ) return a;  else return b; }
```

The conditional operator has a very low precedence: only the assignment operators and the comma operator are lower. Thus, the following statement requires no parentheses:

```
distance = x < y ? y - x : x - y;
```

The first operand of the conditional operator, condition, must have a scalar type—that is, an arithmetic type or a pointer type. The second and third operands, expression 1 and expression 2, must fulfill one of the following cases:

- Both of the alternative expressions have arithmetic types, in which case the result of the complete operation has the type that results from performing the usual arithmetic conversions on these operands.

- Both of the alternative operands have the same structure or union type, or the type void. The result of the operation also has this type.

- Both of the alternative operands are pointers, and one of the following is true:

  — Both pointers have the same type. The result of the operation then has this type as well.

  — One operand is a null pointer constant. The result then has the type of the other operand.

  — One operand is an object pointer and the other is a pointer to void. The result then has the type void *.

The two pointers may point to differently qualified types. In this case, the result is a pointer to a type that has all of the type qualifiers of the two alternative operands. For example, suppose that the following pointers have been defined:

```
const int *cintPtr;        // Declare pointers
volatile int *vintPtr;
void *voidPtr;
```

The expressions in the following table then have the type indicated, regardless of the truth value of the variable flag:

Expression	Type
flag ? cintPtr : vintPtr	volatile const int*
flag ? cintPtr : NULL	const int*
flag ? cintPtr : voidPtr	const void*

The comma operator

The comma operator is a binary operator:

expression 1 , expression 2

The comma operator ensures sequential processing: first the left operand is evaluated, then the right operand. The result of the complete expression has the type and value of the right operand. The left operand is only evaluated for its side effects; its value is discarded. There is a sequence point after the evaluation of the left operand. For example:

```
x = 2.7, sqrt( 2*x )
```

In this expression, the assignment takes place first, before the sqrt() function is called. The value of the complete expression is the function's return value.

The comma operator has the lowest precedence of all operators. For this reason, the assignment x = 2.7 in the previous example does not need to be placed in parentheses. However, parentheses are necessary if you want to use the result of the comma operation in another assignment:

```
y = ( x = 2.7, sqrt( 2*x ));
```

This statement assigns the square root of 5.4 to y.

A comma in a list of initializers or function arguments is a list separator, not a comma operator. In such contexts, however, you can still use a comma operator by enclosing an expression in parentheses:

```
y = sqrt( (x=2.7, 2*x) );
```

This statement is equivalent to the one in the previous example. The comma operator allows you to group several expressions into one. This ability makes it useful for initializing or incrementing multiple variables in the head of a for loop, as in the following example:

```
int i;  float fArray[10], val;
for ( i=0, val=0.25;  i < 10;  ++i, val *= 2.0 )
   fArray[i] = val;
```

Constant Expressions

The compiler recognizes constant expressions in source code and replaces them with their values. The resulting constant value must be representable in the expression's type. You may use a constant expression wherever a simple constant is permitted.

Operators in constant expressions are subject to the same rules as in other expressions. Because constant expressions are evaluated at translation time, though, they cannot contain function calls or operations that modify variables, such as assignments.

Integer Constant Expressions

An *integer constant expression* is a constant expression with any integer type. These are the expressions you use to define the following items:

- The size of an array
- The value of an enumeration constant
- The size of a bit-field
- The alignment of an object in a definition using _Alignas (C11)
- The value of a case constant in a switch statement

For example, you may define an array as follows:

```
#define BLOCK_SIZE 512
char buffer[4*BLOCK_SIZE];
```

The following kinds of operands are permissible in an integer constant expression:

- Integer, character, and enumeration constants
- sizeof expressions and _Alignof expressions

However, the operand of `sizeof` in a constant expression must not be a variable-length array. You can also use floating-point constants if you cast them as an integer type.

Other Constant Expressions

You can also use constant expressions to initialize static and external objects. In these cases, the constant expressions can have any arithmetic or pointer type desired. You may use floating-point constants as operands in an *arithmetic constant expression*.

A constant with a pointer type, called an *address constant*, is usually a null pointer, an array or function name, or a value obtained by applying the address operator & to an object with static storage duration. However, you can also construct an address constant by casting an integer constant as a pointer type, or by pointer arithmetic. For example:

```
#define ARRAY_SIZE 200
static float fArray[ARRAY_SIZE];
static float *fPtr = fArray + ARRAY_SIZE - 1;  // Pointer to the last
                                               // array element
```

In composing an address constant, you can also use other operators, such as . and ->, as long as you do not actually dereference a pointer to access the *value* of an object. For example, the following declarations are permissible outside any function:

```
struct Person { char pin[32];
                char name[64];
                /* ... */
              };
struct Person boss;
const char *cPtr = &boss.name[0];    // or: ... = boss.name;
```

6

Statements

A *statement* specifies one or more actions to be performed such as assigning a value to a variable, passing control to a function, or jumping to another statement. The sum total of all the statements in a program determines what the program does.

Jumps and loops are statements that control the flow of the program. Except when those control statements result in jumps, statements are executed sequentially; that is, in the order in which they appear in the program.

Expression Statements

An expression statement is an expression followed by a semicolon:

```
[expression] ;
```

In an *expression statement*, the expression—whether an assignment or another operation—is evaluated for the sake of its side effects. Following are some typical expression statements :

```
y = x;                    // An assignment
sum = a + b;              // Calculation and assignment
++x;
printf("Hello, world\n"); // A function call
```

The type and value of the expression are irrelevant, and are discarded before the next statement is executed. For this reason, statements such as the following are syntactically correct, but not very useful:

```
100;
y < x;
```

If a statement is a function call and the return value of the function is not needed, it can be discarded explicitly by casting the function as void:

```
char name[32];
/* ... */
(void)strcpy( name, "Jim" );    // Explicitly discard
                                // the return value.
```

A statement can also consist of a semicolon alone; this is called a *null statement*. Null statements are necessary in cases where syntax requires a statement but the program should not perform any action. In the following example, a null statement forms the body of a for loop:

```
for ( i = 0; s[i] != '\0'; ++i ) // Loop conditions
    ;                            // A null statement
```

This code sets the variable i to the index of the first null character in the array s, using only the expressions in the head of the for loop.

Block Statements

A *compound statement*, called a *block* for short, groups a number of statements and declarations together between braces to form a single statement:

```
{ [list of declarations and statements] }
```

Unlike simple statements, block statements are not terminated by a semicolon. A block is used wherever the syntax calls for a single statement but the program's purpose requires several statements. For example, you can use a block statement in an if statement or when more than one statement needs to be repeated in a loop:

```
{   double result = 0.0, x = 0.0;    // Declarations
    static long status = 0;
    extern int limit;

    ++x;                              // Statements
    if ( status == 0 )
    {                                 // New block
        int i = 0;
        while ( status == 0 && i < limit )
        { /* ... */ }                 // Another block
    }
    else
    { /* ... */ }                     // And yet another block
}
```

The declarations in a block are usually placed at the beginning, before any statements. However, C99 allows declarations to be placed anywhere.

Names declared within a block have *block scope*; in other words, they are visible only from their declaration to the end of the block. Within that scope, such a declaration can also hide an object of the same name that was declared outside the block. The storage duration of automatic variables is likewise limited to the block in which they occur. This means that the storage space of a variable not declared as static or

---

extern is automatically freed at the end of its block statement. For a full discussion of scope and storage duration, see Chapter 11.

Loops

Use a *loop* to execute a group of statements, called the *loop body*, more than once. In C, you can introduce a loop using one of three *iteration statements*: while, do... while, and for.

In each of these statements, the number of iterations through the loop body is controlled by a condition, the *controlling expression*. This is an expression of a scalar type; that is, an arithmetic expression or a pointer. The loop condition is true if the value of the controlling expression is not equal to 0; otherwise, it is considered false.

The statements break and continue are used to jump out or back to the top of a loop before the end of an iteration. They are described in "Unconditional Jumps" on page 108.

while Statements

A while statement executes a statement repeatedly as long as the controlling expression is true:

```
while (expression ) statement
```

The while statement is a *top-driven* loop: first, the loop condition (i.e., the controlling expression) is evaluated. If it yields true, the loop body is executed, and then the controlling expression is evaluated again. If the condition is false, program execution continues with the statement that follows the loop body.

Syntactically, the loop body consists of one statement. If several statements are required, they are grouped in a block. Example 6-1 shows a simple while loop that reads in floating-point numbers from the console and accumulates a running total of them.

Example 6-1. A while loop

```
/* Read in numbers from the keyboard and
 * print out their average.
 * ----------------------------------- */
#include <stdio.h>
int main()
{
    double x = 0.0, sum = 0.0;
    int count = 0;

    printf( "\t--- Calculate Averages ---\n" );
    printf( "\nEnter some numbers:\n"
            "(Type a letter to end your input)\n" );
    while ( scanf( "%lf", &x ) == 1 )
```

```
    {
        sum += x;
        ++count;
    }
    if ( count == 0 )
        printf( "No input data!\n" );
    else
        printf( "The average of your numbers is %.2f\n", sum/count );
    return 0;
}
```

In Example 6-1, the controlling expression:

```
scanf( "%lf", &x ) == 1
```

is true as long as the user enters a decimal number. As soon as the function scanf()
is unable to convert the string input into a floating-point number—when the user
types the letter q, for example—scanf() returns the value 0 (or -1 for EOF, if the end
of the input stream was reached or an error occurred). The condition is then false,
and execution continues at the if statement that follows the loop body.

for Statements

Like the while statement, the for statement is a top-driven loop, but with more
loop logic contained within the statement itself:

```
for ( [expression1]; [expression2]; [expression3] )
    statement
```

The three actions that need to be executed in a typical loop are specified together at
the top of the loop body:

expression1 (initialization)
> Evaluated only once, before the first evaluation of the controlling expression, to
> perform any necessary initialization.

expression2 (controlling expression)
> Tested before each iteration. Loop execution ends when this expression evalu-
> ates to false.

expression3 (adjustment)
> An adjustment, such as the incrementation of a counter, performed *after* each
> loop iteration and before *expression2* is tested again.

Example 6-2 shows a for loop that initializes each element of an array.

Example 6-2. Using a for loop to initialize an array

```
#define ARR_LENGTH  1000
/* ... */
long arr[ARR_LENGTH];
```

```
int i;
for ( i = 0; i < ARR_LENGTH; ++i )
    arr[i] = 2*i;
```

Any of the three expressions in the head of the for loop can be omitted. This means that its shortest possible form is:

```
for ( ; ; )
```

A missing controlling expression is considered to be always true, and so defines an infinite loop.

The following form, with no initializer and no adjustment expression, is equivalent to while (*expression*):

```
for ( ;expression; )
```

In fact, every for statement can also be rewritten as a while statement, and vice versa. For example, the complete for loop in Example 6-2 is equivalent to the following while loop:

```
i = 0;                      // Initialize the counter
while ( i < ARR_LENGTH )    // The loop condition
{
    arr[i] = 2*i;
    ++i;                    // Increment the counter
}
```

for is generally preferable to while when the loop contains a counter or index variable that needs to be initialized and then adjusted after each iteration.

In ANSI C99, a declaration can also be used in place of *expression1*. In this case, the scope of the variable declared is limited to the for loop. For example:

```
for ( int i = 0; i < ARR_LENGTH; ++i )
    arr[i] = 2*i;
```

The variable i declared in this for loop, unlike that in Example 6-2, no longer exists after the end of the for loop.

The comma operator is often used in the head of a for loop in order to assign initial values to more than one variable in *expression1*, or to adjust several variables in *expression3*. For example, the function strReverse() shown here uses two index variables to reverse the order of the characters in a string:

```
void strReverse( char* str)
{
  char ch;
  for ( size_t i = 0, j = strlen(str)-1;  i < j;  ++i, --j )
    ch = str[i],  str[i] = str[j],  str[j] = ch;
}
```

The comma operator can be used to evaluate additional expressions in places where only one expression is permitted. See "Other Operators" on page 90 for a detailed description of the comma operator.

do...while Statements

The do...while statement is a *bottom-driven* loop:

```
do statement while ( expression );
```

The loop body statement is executed once before the controlling *expression* is evaluated for the first time. Unlike the while and for statements, do...while ensures that at least one iteration of the loop body is performed. If the controlling expression yields true, then another iteration follows. If false, the loop is finished.

In Example 6-3, the functions for reading and processing a command are called at least once. When the user exits the menu system, the function getCommand() returns the value of the constant END.

Example 6-3. do...while

```
// Read and carry out an incoming menu command.
// --------------------------------------------
int getCommand( void );
void performCommand( int cmd );
#define END 0
/* ... */
do
{
  int command = getCommand();  // Poll the menu system.
  performCommand( command );   // Execute the command received.
} while ( command != END );
```

Example 6-4 shows a version of the standard library function strcpy(), with just a simple statement rather than a block in the loop body. Because the loop condition is tested after the loop body, the copy operation includes the string terminator '\0'.

Example 6-4. A strcpy() function using do...while

```
// Copy string s2 to string s1.
// ----------------------------
char *strcpy( char* restrict s1, const char* restrict s2 )
{
  int i = 0;
  do
    s1[i] = s2[i];             // The loop body: copy each character
  while ( s2[i++] != '\0' );   // End the loop if we just copied a '\0'.
  return s1;
}
```

Nested Loops

A loop body can be any simple or block statement, and may include other loop statements. Note that a break or continue statement that occurs in a nested loop only jumps to the end or the beginning of the loop that immediately contains it (see "Unconditional Jumps" on page 108).

Example 6-5 is an implementation of the bubble-sort algorithm using nested loops. The inner loop in this algorithm inspects the entire array on each iteration, swapping neighboring elements that are out of order. The outer loop is reiterated until the inner loop finds no elements to swap. After each iteration of the inner loop, at least one element has been moved to its correct position. Hence the remaining length of the array to be sorted, len, can be reduced by one.

Example 6-5. Nested loops in the bubble-sort algorithm

```
// Sort an array of float in ascending order
// using the bubble-sort algorithm.
// ----------------------------------------
void bubbleSort( float arr[], int len ) // The array arr and
{                                        // its length len.
  int isSorted = 0;
  do
  {
    float temp;              // Holder for values being swapped.
    isSorted = 1;
    --len;
    for ( int i = 0;  i < len;  ++i )
      if ( arr[i] > arr[i+1] )
      {
        isSorted = 0;       // Not finished yet.
        temp = arr[i];      // Swap adjacent values.
        arr[i] = arr[i+1];
        arr[i+1] = temp;
      }
  } while ( !isSorted );
}
```

Note that the automatic variables temp, declared in the do...while loop, and i, declared in the head of the for loop, are created and destroyed again on each iteration of the outer loop.

Selection Statements

A *selection statement* can direct the flow of program execution along different paths depending on a given condition. There are two selection statements in C: if and switch.

if Statements

An if statement has the following form:

```
if (expression ) statement1 [ else statement2 ]
```

The else clause is optional. The *expression* is evaluated first, to determine which of the two statements is executed. This expression must have a scalar type. If its value is true—that is, not equal to 0—then *statement1* is executed. Otherwise, *statement2*, if present, is executed.

The following example uses if in a recursive function to test for the condition that ends its recursion:

```
// The recursive function power() calculates
// integer powers of floating-point numbers.
// -----------------------------------------
double power( double base, unsigned int exp )
{
    if ( exp == 0 ) return 1.0;
    else return base * power( base, exp-1 );
}
```

If several if statements are nested, then an else clause always belongs to the last if (on the same block nesting level) that does not yet have an else clause:

```
if ( n > 0 )
    if ( n % 2 == 0 )
        puts( "n is positive and even" );
    else                            // This is the alternative
        puts( "n is positive and odd" );   // to the *last* if
```

An else clause can be assigned to a different if by enclosing the last if statement that should not have an else clause in a block:

```
if ( n > 0 )
{
    if ( n % 2 == 0 )
        puts( "n is positive and even" );
}
else                            // This is the alternative
    puts( "n is negative or zero" );   // to the *first* if
```

To select one of more than two alternative statements, if statements can be cascaded in an else if chain. Each new if statement is simply nested in the else clause of the preceding if statement:

```
// Test measurements for tolerance.
// ------------------------------
double spec = 10.0, measured = 10.3, diff;
/* ... */
diff = measured - spec;

if ( diff >= 0.0 && diff < 0.5 )
```

```
      printf( "Upward deviation: %.2f\n", diff );
    else if ( diff < 0.0 && diff > -0.5 )
      printf( "Downward deviation: %.2f\n", diff );
    else
      printf( "Deviation out of tolerance!\n" );
```

The if conditions are evaluated one after another. As soon as one of these expression yields true, the corresponding statement is executed. Because the rest of the else if chain is cascaded under the corresponding else clause, it is alternative to the statement executed and hence skipped over. If none of the if conditions is true, then the last if statement's else clause is executed, if present.

switch Statements

A switch statement causes the flow of program execution to jump to one of several statements according to the value of an integer expression:

```
switch (expression ) statement
```

expression has an integer type, and statement is the switch body, which contains case labels and at most one default label. The expression is evaluated once and compared with constant expressions in the case labels. If the value of the expression matches one of the case constants, the program flow jumps to the statement following that case label. If none of the case constants match, the program continues at the default label, if there is one.

Example 6-6 uses a switch statement to process the user's selection from a menu.

Example 6-6. A switch statement

```
// Handle a command that the user selects from a menu.
// ---------------------------------------------------
// Declare other functions used:
int menu( void );              // Prints the menu and returns
                               // a character that the user types.
void action1( void ),
     action2( void );
/* ... */

switch ( menu() )              // Jump depending on the result of menu().
{
   case 'a':
   case 'A':  action1();       // Carry out action 1.
              break;           // Don't do any other "actions."

   case 'b':
   case 'B':  action2();       // Carry out action 2.
              break;           // Don't do the default "action."

   default:   putchar( '\a' ); // If no recognized command,
}                              // output an alert.
```

The syntax of the case and default labels is as follows:

```
case constant:  statement
default:        statement
```

constant is a constant expression with an integer type. Each case constant in a given switch statement must have a unique value. Any of the alternative statements may be indicated by more than one case label, though.

The default label is optional, and can be placed at any position in the switch body. If there is no default label, and the control expression of the switch statement does not match any of the case constants, then none of the statements in the body of the switch statement are executed. In this case, the program flow continues with the statement following the switch body.

The switch body is usually a block statement that begins with a case label. A statement placed before the first case label in the block would never be executed.

Labels in C merely identify potential destinations for jumps in the program flow. By themselves, they have no effect on the program. Thus, after the jump from the switch to the first matching case label, program execution continues sequentially, regardless of other labels. If the statements following subsequent case labels are to be skipped over, then the last statement to be executed must be followed by a break statement. The program flow then jumps to the end of the switch body.

If variables are declared within a switch statement, they should be enclosed in a nested block:

```
switch ( x )
{
  case C1: {  int temp = 10;       // Declare temp only for this "case"
              /* ... */
           }
           break;
  case C2:
           /* ... */
}
```

Integer promotion is applied to the switch expression. The case constants are then converted to match the resulting type of the switch expression.

You can always program a selection among alternative statements using an else if chain. If the selection depends on the value of one integer expression, however, then you can use a switch statement—and should, because it makes code more readable.

Unconditional Jumps

Jump statements interrupt the sequential execution of statements, so that execution continues at a different point in the program. A jump destroys automatic variables if the jump destination is outside their scope. There are four statements that cause unconditional jumps in C: break, continue, goto, and return.

The break Statement

The break statement can occur only in the body of a loop or a switch statement, and causes a jump to the first statement after the loop or switch statement in which it is immediately contained:

```
break;
```

Thus, the break statement can be used to end the execution of a loop statement at any position in the loop body. For example, the while loop in Example 6-7 may be ended either at the user's request (by entering a non-numeric string), or by a numeric value outside the range that the programmer wants to accept.

Example 6-7. The break statement

```
// Read user input of scores from 0 to 100
// and store them in an array.
// Return value: the number of values stored.
// ----------------------------------------
int getScores( short scores[ ], int len )
{
   int i = 0;
   puts( "Please enter scores between 0 and 100.\n"
         "Press <Q> and <Return> to quit.\n" );
   while ( i < len )
   {
      printf( "Score No. %2d: ", i+1 );
      if ( scanf( "%hd", &scores[i] ) != 1 )
         break;              // No number read: end the loop.
      if ( scores[i] < 0  ||  scores[i] > 100 )
      {
         printf( "%d: Value out of range.\n", scores[i] );
         break;              // Discard this value and end the loop.
      }
      ++i;
   }
   return i;                 // The number of values stored.
}
```

The continue Statement

The continue statement can be used only within the body of a loop, and causes the program flow to skip over the rest of the current iteration of the loop:

```
continue;
```

In a while or do...while loop, the program jumps to the next evaluation of the loop's controlling expression. In a for loop, the program jumps to the next evaluation of the third expression in the for statement, containing the operations that are performed after every loop iteration.

In Example 6-7, the second break statement terminates the data input loop as soon as an input value is outside the permissible range. To give the user another chance to enter a correct value, replace the second break with continue. Then the program jumps to the next iteration of the while loop, skipping over the statement that increments i:

```c
// Read in scores.
// -------------------------
int getScores( short scores[ ], int len )
{
    /* ... (as in Example 6-7) ... */
    while ( i < len )
    {
        /* ... (as in Example 6-7) ... */
        if ( scores[i] < 0 || scores[i] > 100 )
        {
            printf( "%d : Value out of range.\n", scores[i] );
            continue;           // Discard this value and read in another.
        }
        ++i;                    // Increment the number of values stored.
    }
    return i;                   // The number of values stored.
}
```

The goto Statement

The goto statement causes an unconditional jump to another statement in the same function. The destination of the jump is specified by the name of a label:

```c
goto label_name;
```

A *label* is a name followed by a colon:

```c
label_name: statement
```

Labels have a name space of their own, which means they can have the same names as variables or types without causing conflicts. Labels may be placed before any statement, and a statement can have several labels. Labels serve only as destinations of goto statements, and have no effect at all if the labeled statement is reached in the normal course of sequential execution. The following function uses a label after a return statement to mark the entry point to an error handling routine:

```c
// Handle errors within the function.
// ----------------------------------
#include <stdbool.h>          // Defines bool, true
                              // and false (C99).
#define MAX_ARR_LENGTH  1000
bool calculate( double arr[ ], int len, double* result )
{
    bool error = false;
    if ( len < 1 || len > MAX_ARR_LENGTH )
        goto error_exit;
```

```
for ( int i = 0; i < len; ++i )
{
  /* ... Some calculation that could result in
   * the error flag being set ...
   */
  if ( error )
    goto error_exit;
  /* ... Calculation continues; result is
   * assigned to the variable *result ...
   */
}
return true;                  // Flow arrives here if no error

error_exit:                   // The error handler
  *result = 0.0;
  return false;
}
```

You should never use a goto statement to jump into a block from outside it if the jump skips over declarations or statements that initialize variables. However, such a jump is illegal only if it leads into the scope of an array with variable length, skipping over the definition of the array (for more information about variable-length arrays, which were introduced with C99, see Chapter 8):

```
static const int maxSize = 1000;
double func( int n )
{
   double x = 0.0;
   if ( n > 0  &&  n < maxSize )
   {
      double arr[n];          // A variable-length array
      again:
      /* ... */
      if ( x == 0.0 )
         goto again;          // OK: the jump is entirely
   }                          // *within* the scope of arr.
   if ( x < 0.0 )
      goto again;             // Illegal: the jump leads
                              // *into* the scope of arr!
   return x;
}
```

Because code that makes heavy use of goto statements is hard to read, you should use them only when they offer a clear benefit, such as a quick exit from deeply nested loops. Any C program that uses goto statements can also be written without them!

The goto statement permits only *local* jumps; that is, jumps within a function. C also provides a feature to program non-local jumps to any point in the program, using the standard macro setjmp() and the standard function longjmp(). The macro setjmp() marks a location in the program by storing the necessary process information so that execution can be resumed at that point at another time by a call to the function longjmp(). For more information on these functions, see Part II.

The return Statement

The return statement ends execution of the current function and jumps back to where the function was called:

```
return [expression];
```

expression is evaluated and the result is given to the caller as the value of the function call. This *return value* is converted to the function's return type, if necessary.

A function can contain any number of return statements:

```
// Return the smaller of two integer arguments
int min( int a, int b )
{
    if  ( a < b ) return a;
    else          return b;
}
```

The contents of this function block can also be expressed by the following single statement:

```
return ( a < b ? a : b );
```

The parentheses do not affect the behavior of the return statement. However, complex return expressions are often enclosed in parentheses for the sake of readability.

A return statement with no *expression* can only be used in a function of type void. In fact, such functions do not need to have a return statement at all. If no return statement is encountered in a function, the program flow returns to the caller when the end of the function block is reached. Function calls are described in more detail in Chapter 7.

7

Functions

All the instructions of a C program are contained in *functions*. Each function performs a certain task. A special function name is main()—the function with this name is the first one to run when the program starts. All other functions are subroutines of the main() function (or otherwise dependent procedures, such as callback functions), and can have any names you wish.

Every function is defined exactly once. A program can declare and call a function as many times as necessary.

Function Definitions

The *definition* of a function consists of a *function head* (or the *declarator*), and a *function block*. The function head specifies the name of the function, the type of its return value, and the types and names of its parameters, if any. The statements in the function block specify what the function does. The general form of a function definition is as follows:

```
type name( parameter_declarations )   Function head
{
      /* declarations, statements */  Function block
}
```

In the function head, *name* is the function's name, while *type* consists of at least one type specifier, which defines the type of the function's return value. The return type may be void or any object type except array types. Furthermore, *type* may include one of the function specifiers inline or _Noreturn, and/or one of the storage class specifiers extern or static.

A function cannot return a function or an array. However, you can define a function that returns a pointer to a function or a pointer to an array.

The *parameter declarations* are contained in a comma-separated list of declarations of the function's parameters. If the function has no parameters, this list is either empty or contains merely the word void.

The type of a function specifies not only its return type but also the types of all its parameters. Example 7-1 is a simple function to calculate the volume of a cylinder.

Example 7-1. Function cylinderVolume()

```
// The cylinderVolume() function calculates the volume of a cylinder.
// Arguments:    Radius of the base circle; height of the cylinder.
// Return value: Volume of the cylinder.

extern double cylinderVolume( double r, double h )
{
   const double pi = 3.1415926536;     // pi is constant
   return  pi * r * r * h;
}
```

This function has the name cylinderVolume, and has two parameters, r and h, both with type double. It returns a value with the type double.

Functions and Storage Class Specifiers

The function in Example 7-1 is declared with the storage class specifier extern. This is not strictly necessary, as extern is the default storage class for functions. An ordinary function definition that does not contain a static or inline specifier can be placed in any source file of a program. Such a function can be called in all of the program's source files because its name is an external identifier (or in strict terms, an identifier with external linkage; see "Linkage of Identifiers" on page 187). You merely have to declare the function before its first use in a given translation unit (see "Function Declarations" on page 120). Furthermore, you can arrange functions in any order you wish within a source file. The only restriction is that you cannot define one function within another. C does not allow you to define "local functions" in this way.

You can hide a function from other source files. If you declare a function as static, its name identifies it only within the source file containing the function definition. Because the name of a static function is not an external identifier, you cannot use it in other source files. If you try to call such a function by its name in another source file, the linker will issue an error message, or the function call might refer to a different function with the same name elsewhere in the program.

The function printArray() in Example 7-2 might well be defined using static because it is a special-purpose helper function, providing formatted output of an array of float variables.

Example 7-2. Function printArray()

```c
// The static function printArray() prints the elements of an array
// of float to standard output, using printf() to format them.
// Arguments:    An array of float, and its length.
// Return value: None.

static void printArray( const float array[ ], int n )
{
  for ( int i=0; i < n; ++i )
  {
    printf( "%12.2f", array[i] );    // Field width: 12; decimal places: 2.
    if ( i % 5 == 4 ) putchar('\n'); // New line after every 5 numbers.
  }
  if ( n % 5 != 0 ) putchar('\n');   // New line at the end of the output.
}
```

If your program contains a call to the `printArray()` function before its definition, you must first declare it using the `static` keyword:

```c
static void printArray( const float [ ], int );

int main()
{
  float farray[123];
  /* ... */
  printArray( farray, 123 );
  /* ... */
}
```

K&R-Style Function Definitions

In the early Kernighan-Ritchie standard, the names of function parameters were separated from their type declarations. Function declarators contained only the names of the parameters, which were then declared by type between the function declarator and the function block. For example, the `cylinderVolume()` function from Example 7-1 would have been written as follows:

```c
double cylinderVolume( r, h )
double r, h;                         // Parameter declarations
{
    const double pi = 3.1415926536;  // pi is constant
    return  pi * r * r * h;
}
```

This notation, called a "K&R-style" or "old-style" function definition, is deprecated, although compilers still support it. In new C source code, use only the prototype notation for function definitions, as shown in Example 7-1.

Function Parameters

The parameters of a function are ordinary local variables. The program creates them and initializes them with the values of the corresponding arguments when a function call occurs. Their scope is the function block. A function can change the value of a parameter without affecting the value of the argument in the context of the function call. In Example 7-3, the factorial() function, which computes the factorial of a whole number, modifies its parameter n in the process.

Example 7-3. Function factorial()

```
// factorial() calculates n!, the factorial of a non-negative number n.
// For n > 0, n! is the product of all integers from 1 to n inclusive.
// 0! equals 1.
// Argument:     A whole number, with type unsigned int.
// Return value: The factorial of the argument, with type long double.

long double factorial( register unsigned int n )
{
  long double f = 1;
  while ( n > 1 )
    f *= n--;
  return f;
}
```

Although the factorial of an integer is always an integer, the function uses the type long double in order to accommodate very large results. As Example 7-3 illustrates, you can use the storage class specifier register in declaring function parameters. The register specifier is a request to the compiler to make a variable as quickly accessible as possible. (The compiler may ignore it.) No other storage class specifiers are permitted on function parameters.

Arrays as Function Parameters

If you need to pass an array as an argument to a function, you would generally declare the corresponding parameter in the following form:

> type name[ ]

Because array names are automatically converted to pointers when you use them as function arguments, this statement is equivalent to the declaration:

> type *name

When you use the array notation in declaring function parameters, any constant expression between the brackets ([ ]) is ignored. In the function block, the parameter name is a pointer variable, and can be modified. Thus, the function addArray() in Example 7-4 modifies its first two parameters as it adds pairs of elements in two arrays.

Example 7-4. Function addArray()

```
// addArray() adds each element of the second array to the corresponding
// element of the first (i.e., "array1 += array2", so to speak).
// Arguments:     Two arrays of float and their common length.
// Return value: None.

void addArray( register float a1[ ], register const float a2[ ], int len )
{
  register float *end = a1 + len;
  for ( ; a1 < end; ++a1, ++a2 )
    *a1 += *a2;
}
```

An equivalent definition of the addArray() function, using a different notation for the array parameters, would be:

```
void addArray( register float *a1, register const float *a2, int len )
{  /* Function body as earlier. */  }
```

An advantage of declaring the parameters with brackets ([ ]) is that human readers immediately recognize that the function treats the arguments as pointers to an array, and not just to an individual float variable. But the array-style notation also has two peculiarities in parameter declarations:

- In a parameter declaration—and only there—C99 allows you to place any of the type qualifiers const, volatile, and restrict inside the square brackets. This ability allows you to declare the parameter as a qualified pointer type.

- Furthermore, in C99 you can also place the storage class specifier static, together with a integer constant expression, inside the square brackets. This approach indicates that the number of elements in the array at the time of the function call must be at least equal to the value of the constant expression.

Here is an example that combines both of these possibilities:

```
int func( long array[const static 5] )
{ /* ... */ }
```

In the function defined here, the parameter array is a constant pointer to long, and so cannot be modified. It points to the first of at least five array elements.

C99 also lets you declare array parameters as *variable-length arrays* (see Chapter 8). To do so, place a nonconstant integer expression with a positive value between the square brackets. In this case, the array parameter is still a pointer to the first array element. The difference is that the array elements themselves can also have a variable length. In Example 7-5, the maximum() function's third parameter is a two-dimensional array of variable dimensions.

Example 7-5. Function maximum()

```
// The function maximum() obtains the greatest value in a
// two-dimensional matrix of double values.
// Arguments:   The number of rows, the number of columns, and the matrix.
// Return value: The value of the greatest element.

double maximum( int nrows, int ncols, double matrix[nrows][ncols] )
{
  double max = matrix[0][0];
  for ( int r = 0; r < nrows; ++r )
    for ( int c = 0; c < ncols; ++c )
      if ( max < matrix[r][c] )
        max = matrix[r][c];
  return max;
}
```

The parameter matrix is a pointer to an array with ncols elements.

The main() Function

C makes a distinction between two possible *execution environments*:

Freestanding

   A program in a *freestanding* environment runs without the support of an operating system, and therefore only has minimal capabilities of the standard
   library available to it (see Part II).

Hosted

   In a *hosted* environment, a C program runs under the control, and with the
   support, of an operating system. The full capabilities of the standard library are
   available.

In a freestanding environment, the name and type of the first function invoked
when the program starts is determined by the given implementation. Unless you
program embedded systems, your C programs generally run in a hosted environment. A program compiled for a hosted environment must define a function with
the name main, which is the first function invoked on program start. You can define
the main() function in one of the following two forms:

`int main( void ) { /* … */ }`

   A function with no parameters, returning int

`int main( int argc, char *argv[ ] ) { /* … */ }`

   A function with two parameters whose types are int and char **, returning
   int

These two approaches conform to the C standard. In addition, many C implementations support a third, nonstandard syntax as well:

```
int main( int argc, char *argv[ ], char *envp[ ] ) { /* … */ }
```
A function returning int, with three parameters, the first of which has the type int, while the other two have the type char **

In all cases, the main() function returns its final status to the operating system as an integer. A return value of 0 or EXIT_SUCCESS indicates that the program was successful; any nonzero return value, and in particular the value of EXIT_FAILURE, indicates that the program failed in some way. The constants EXIT_SUCCESS and EXIT_FAILURE are defined in the header file *stdlib.h*. The function block of main() need not contain a return statement. In the C99 and later standards, if the program flow reaches the closing brace } of main()'s function block, the status value returned to the execution environment is 0. Ending the main() function is equivalent to calling the standard library function exit(), whose argument becomes the return value of main().

The parameters argc and argv (which you may give other names if you wish) represent your program's command-line arguments. This is how they work:

- argc (short for *argument count*) is either 0 or the number of string tokens in the command line that started the program. The name of the program itself is included in this count.

- argv (short for *arguments vector*) is an array of pointers to char that point to the individual string tokens received on the command line:

    — The number of elements in this array is one more than the value of argc; the last element, argv[argc], is always a null pointer.

    — If argc is greater than 0, then the first string, argv[0], contains the name by which the program was invoked. If the execution environment does not supply the program name, the string is empty.

    — If argc is greater than 1, then the strings argv[1] through argv[argc - 1] contain the program's command-line arguments.

- envp (short for *environment pointer*) in the nonstandard, three-parameter version of main() is an array of pointers to the strings that make up the program's environment. Typically, these strings have the form *name=value*. In standard C, you can access the environment variables using the getenv() function.

The sample program in Example 7-6, *args.c*, prints its own name and command-line arguments as received from the operating system.

Example 7-6. The command line

```
#include <stdio.h>
int main( int argc, char *argv[ ] )
{
  if ( argc == 0 )
    puts( "No command line available." );
```

```
        else
        {                                       // Print the name of the program.
          printf( "The program now running: %s\n", argv[0] );
          if ( argc == 1 )
            puts( "No arguments received on the command line." );
          else
          {
            puts( "The command-line arguments:" );
            for ( int i = 1; i < argc; ++i )     // Print each argument on
                                                 // a separate line.
              puts( argv[i] );
          }
        }
}
```

Suppose we run the program on a Unix system by entering the following command:

```
$ ./args one two "and three"
```

The output is then as follows:

```
The program now running: ./args
The command-line arguments:
one
two
and three
```

Function Declarations

By declaring a function before using it, you inform the compiler of its type: in other words, a *declaration* describes a function's interface. A declaration must indicate at least the type of the function's return value, as the following example illustrates:

```
int rename();
```

This line declares rename() as a function that returns a value with type int. Because function names are external identifiers by default, that declaration is equivalent to this one:

```
extern int rename();
```

As it stands, this declaration does not include any information about the number and the types of the function's parameters. As a result, the compiler cannot test whether a given call to this function is correct. If you call the function with arguments that are different in number or type from the parameters in its definition, the result will be a critical runtime error. To prevent such errors, you should always declare a function's parameters as well. In other words, your declaration should be a *function prototype*. The prototype of the standard library function rename(), for example, which changes the name of a file, is as follows:

```
int rename( const char *oldname, const char *newname );
```

This function takes two arguments with type pointer to const char. In other words, the function uses the pointers only to read char objects. The arguments may thus be string literals.

The identifiers of the parameters in a prototype declaration are optional. If you include the names, their scope ends with the prototype itself. Because they have no meaning to the compiler, they are practically no more than comments telling programmers what each parameter's purpose is. In the prototype declaration of rename(), for example, the parameter names oldname and newname indicate that the old filename goes first and the new filename second in your rename() function calls. To the compiler, the prototype declaration would have exactly the same meaning without the parameter names:

```
int rename( const char *, const char * );
```

The prototypes of the standard library functions are contained in the standard header files. If you want to call the rename() function in your program, you can declare it by including the file *stdio.h* in your source code. Usually you will place the prototypes of functions you define yourself in a header file as well so that you can use them in any source file simply by adding the appropriate include directive.

Declaring Optional Parameters

C allows you to define functions so that you can call them with a *variable number of arguments* (for more information on writing such functions, see "Variable Numbers of Arguments" on page 127). The best-known example of such a function is printf(), which has the following prototype:

```
int printf( const char *format, ... );
```

As this example shows, the list of parameter types ends with an *ellipsis* (…) after the last comma. The ellipsis represents optional arguments. The first argument in a printf function call must be a pointer to char. This argument may be followed by others. The prototype contains no information about what number or types of optional arguments the function expects.

Declaring Variable-Length Array Parameters

When you declare a function parameter as a *variable-length array* elsewhere than in the head of the function definition, you can use the asterisk character (*) to represent the array-length specification. If you specify the array length using a nonconstant integer expression, the compiler will treat it the same as an asterisk. For example, all of the following declarations are permissible prototypes for the maximum() function defined in Example 7-5:

```
double maximum( int nrows, int ncols, double matrix[nrows][ncols] );
double maximum( int nrows, int ncols, double matrix[ ][ncols] );
double maximum( int nrows, int ncols, double matrix[*][*] );
double maximum( int nrows, int ncols, double matrix[ ][*] );
```

How Functions Are Executed

The instruction to execute a function—the function call—consists of the function's name and the operator ( ) (see "Other Operators" on page 90). For example, the following statement calls the function maximum( ) to compute the maximum of the matrix mat, which has r rows and c columns:

```
maximum( r, c, mat );
```

The program first allocates storage space for the parameters, and then copies the argument values to the corresponding locations. Then the program jumps to the beginning of the function, and execution of the function begins with first variable definition or statement in the function block.

If the program reaches a return statement or the closing brace (}) of the function block, execution of the function ends and the program jumps back to the calling function. If the program "falls off the end" of the function by reaching the closing brace, the value returned to the caller is undefined. For this reason, you must use a return statement to stop any function that does not have the type void. The value of the return expression is returned to the calling function (see "The return Statement" on page 112).

Pointers as Arguments and Return Values

C is inherently a *call by value* language, as the parameters of a function are local variables initialized with the argument values. This type of language has the advantage that any expression desired can be used as an argument as long as it has the appropriate type. On the other hand, the drawback is that copying large data objects to begin a function call can be expensive. Moreover, a function has no way to modify the originals—that is, the caller's variables—as it knows how to access only the local copy.

However, a function can directly access any variable visible to the caller if one of its arguments is that variable's *address*. In this way, C also provides *call by reference* functions. A simple example is the standard function scanf( ), which reads the standard input stream and places the results in variables referenced by pointer arguments that the caller provides:

```
int var;
scanf( "%d", &var );
```

This function call reads a string as a decimal numeral, converts it to an integer, and stores the value in the location of var.

In the following example, the initNode( ) function initializes a structure variable. The caller passes the structure's address as an argument.

```
#include <string.h>              // Prototypes of memset() and strcpy()
struct Node { long key;
              char name[32];
```

```
              /* ... more structure members ... */
              struct Node *next;
          };

void initNode( struct Node *pNode ) // Initialize the structure *pNode
{
  memset( pNode, 0, sizeof(*pNode) );
  strcpy( pNode->name, "XXXXX" );
}
```

Even if a function needs only to read and not to modify a variable, it still may be more efficient to pass the variable's address rather than its value. That's because passing by address avoids the need to copy the data; only the variable's address is pushed onto the stack. If the function does not modify such a variable, then you should declare the corresponding parameter as a *read-only pointer*, as in the following example:

```
void printNode( const struct Node *pNode );
{
  printf( "Key:  %ld\n", pNode->key );
  printf( "Name: %s\n",  pNode->name );
  /* ... */
}
```

You are also performing a "call by reference" whenever you call a function using an array name as an argument, because the array name is automatically converted into a pointer to the array's first element. The addArray() function defined in Example 7-4 has two such pointer parameters.

Often functions need to return a pointer type as well, as the mkNode() function does in the following example. This function dynamically creates a new Node object and gives its address to the caller:

```
#include <stdlib.h>
struct Node *mkNode()
{
  struct Node *pNode = malloc( sizeof(struct Node) );
  if ( pNode != NULL )
    initNode( pNode );
  return pNode;
}
```

The mkNode() function returns a null pointer if it fails to allocate storage for a new Node object. Functions that return a pointer usually use a null pointer to indicate a failure condition. For example, a search function may return the address of the desired object, or a null pointer if no such object is available.

Inline Functions

Ordinarily, calling a function causes the computer to save its current instruction address, jump to the function called and execute it, and then make the return jump to the saved address. With small functions that you need to call often, this can degrade the program's runtime behavior substantially. As a result, C99 has introduced the option of defining *inline* functions. The keyword inline is a request to the compiler to insert the function's machine code wherever the function is called in the program. The result is that the function is executed as efficiently as if you had inserted the statements from the function body in place of the function call in the source code.

To define a function as an inline function, use the function specifier inline in its definition. In Example 7-7, swapf() is defined as an inline function that exchanges the values of two float variables, and the function selection_sortf() calls the inline function swapf().

Example 7-7. Function swapf()

```
// The function swapf() exchanges the values of two float variables.
// Arguments:    Two pointers to float.
// Return value: None.

inline void swapf( float *p1, float *p2 ) // An inline function.
{
   float tmp = *p1; *p1 = *p2; *p2 = tmp;
}


// The function selection_sortf() uses the selection-sort
// algorithm to sort an array of float elements.
// Arguments:    An array of float, and its length.
// Return value: None.

void selection_sortf( float a[], int n )  // Sort an array a of length n.
{
  register int i, j, mini;                // Three index variables.
  for ( i = 0;  i < n - 1;  ++i )
  {
    mini = i;                 // Search for the minimum starting at index i.
    for ( j = i+1;  j < n;  ++j )
      if ( a[j] < a[mini] )
        mini = j;
    swapf( a+i, a+mini); // Swap the minimum with the element at index i.
  }
}
```

It is generally not a good idea to define a function containing loops, such as selection_sortf(), as inline. Example 7-7 uses inline instead to speed up the instructions inside a for loop.

The inline specifier is not imperative: the compiler may ignore it. Recursive functions, for example, are usually not compiled inline. It is up to the given compiler to determine when a function defined with inline is actually inserted inline.

Unlike other functions, you must repeat the definitions of inline functions in each translation unit in which you use them. The compiler must have the function definition at hand in order to insert the inline code. For this reason, function definitions with inline are customarily written in header files.

If all the declarations of a function in a given translation unit have the inline specifier but not the extern specifier, then the function has an *inline definition*. An inline definition is specific to the translation unit; it does not constitute an external definition, and therefore another translation unit may contain an external definition of the function. If there is an external definition in addition to the inline definition, then the compiler is free to choose which of the two function definitions to use.

If you use the storage class specifier, extern, outside all other functions in a declaration of a function that has been defined with inline, then the function's definition is external. For example, the following declaration, if placed in the same translation unit with the definition of swapf() in Example 7-7, would produce an external definition:

```
extern void swapf( float *p1, float *p2 );
```

Once the function swapf() has an external definition, other translation units only need to contain an ordinary declaration of the function in order to call it. However, calls to the function from other translation units will not be compiled inline.

Inline functions are ordinary functions except for the way they are called in machine code. Like ordinary functions, an inline function has a unique address. If macros are used in the statements of an inline function, the preprocessor expands them with their values as defined at the point where the function definition occurs in the source code. However, you should not define modifiable objects with static storage duration in an inline function that is not likewise declared as static.

Non-Returning Functions

Not all functions return control to their caller. Examples of functions that do not return include the standard functions abort(), exit(), _Exit(), quick_exit() and thread_exit(); these functions do not return because their purpose is to end the execution of a thread or of the whole program. Another example of a non-returning function is the standard function longjmp(), which does not end the program, but continues at the point defined by a prior call to the macro setjmp.

The function specifier _Noreturn is new in C11. It informs the compiler that the function in question does not return, so that the compiler can further optimize the code: on a call to a non-returning function, there is no need to push the return address or the contents of the CPU registers onto the stack. The compiler can also issue an "unreachable code" warning if there are other instructions in the same block after the non-returning function call.

The following example illustrates a user-defined function that does not return:

```
_Noreturn void myAbort()
{
    /* ... Instructions to clean up and save data ... */
    abort();
}
```

It is important that you only declare a function with _Noreturn if it absolutely cannot return. If a function declared with _Noreturn does return, the program's behavior is undefined, and the standard requires that the compiler issue a diagnostic message.

If your program includes the header file *stdnoreturn.h*, you can also use the synonym noreturn instead of the keyword _Noreturn.

Recursive Functions

A *recursive* function is one that calls itself, directly or indirectly. Indirect recursion means that a function calls another function (which may call a third function, and so on), which in turn calls the first function. Because a function cannot continue calling itself endlessly, recursive functions must always have an exit condition.

In Example 7-8, the recursive function binarySearch() implements the binary search algorithm to find a specified element in a sorted array. First, the function compares the search criterion with the middle element in the array. If they are the same, the function returns a pointer to the element found. If not, the function searches in whichever half of the array could contain the specified element by calling itself recursively. If the length of the array that remains to be searched reaches zero, then the specified element is not present, and the recursion is aborted.

Example 7-8. Function binarySearch()

```
// The binarySearch() function searches a sorted array.
// Arguments:   The value of the element to find;
//              the array of long to search; the array length.
// Return value: A pointer to the element found,
//              or NULL if the element is not present in the array.

long *binarySearch( long val, long array[ ], int n )
{
  int m = n/2;
  if ( n <= 0 )          return NULL;
  if ( val == array[m] ) return array + m;
  if ( val <  array[m] ) return binarySearch( val, array, m );
  else                   return binarySearch( val, array+m+1, n-m-1 );
}
```

For an array of n elements, the binary search algorithm performs at most $1+\log_2(n)$ comparisons. With a million elements, the maximum number of comparisons performed is 20, which means at most 20 recursions of the binarySearch() function.

Recursive functions depend on the fact that a function's automatic variables are created anew on each recursive call. These variables, and the caller's address for the return jump, are stored on the stack with each recursion of the function that begins. It is up to the programmer to make sure that there is enough space available on the stack. The `binarySearch()` function as defined in Example 7-8 does not place excessive demands on the stack size, though.

Recursive functions are a logical way to implement algorithms that are recursive by nature, such as the binary search technique or navigation in tree structures. However, even when recursive functions offer an elegant and compact solution to a problem, simple solutions using loops are often possible as well. For example, you could rewrite the binary search in Example 7-8 with a loop statement instead of a recursive function call. In such cases, the iterative solution is generally faster in execution than the recursive function.

Variable Numbers of Arguments

C allows you to define functions that you can call with a variable number of arguments. These are sometimes called *variadic* functions. Such functions require a fixed number of *mandatory* arguments, followed by a variable number of *optional* arguments. Each such function must have at least one mandatory argument. The types of the optional arguments can also vary. The number of optional arguments is either determined by the values of the mandatory arguments or by a special value that terminates the list of optional arguments.

The best-known examples of variadic functions in C are the standard library functions `printf()` and `scanf()`. Each of these two functions has one mandatory argument: the format string. The conversion specifiers in the format string determine the number and the types of the optional arguments.

For each mandatory argument, the function head shows an appropriate parameter, as in ordinary function declarations. These are followed in the parameter list by a comma and an ellipsis (…), which stands for the optional arguments.

Internally, variadic functions access any optional arguments through an object with the type `va_list`, which contains the argument information. An object of this type—also called an *argument pointer*—contains at least the position of one argument on the stack. The argument pointer can be advanced from one optional argument to the next, allowing a function to work through the list of optional arguments. The type `va_list` is defined in the header file *stdarg.h*.

When you write a function with a variable number of arguments, you must define an argument pointer with the type `va_list` in order to read the optional arguments. In the following description, the `va_list` object is named `argptr`. You can manipulate the argument pointer using four macros, which are defined in the header file *stdarg.h*:

```
void va_start(va_list argptr, lastparam);
```
The macro va_start initializes the argument pointer argptr with the position of the first optional argument. The macro's second argument must be the name of the function's last named parameter. You must call this macro before your function can use the optional arguments.

```
type va_arg(va_list argptr, type);
```
The macro va_arg expands to yield the optional argument currently referenced by argptr, and also advances argptr to reference the next argument in the list. The second argument of the macro va_arg is the type of the argument being read.

```
void va_end(va_list argptr);
```
When you have finished using an argument pointer, you should call the macro va_end. If you want to use one of the macros va_start or va_copy to reinitialize an argument pointer that you have already used, then you must call va_end first.

```
void va_copy(va_list dest, va_list src);
```
The macro va_copy initializes the argument pointer dest with the current value of src. You can then use the copy in dest to access the list of optional arguments again, starting from the position referenced by src.

The function in Example 7-9 demonstrates the use of these macros.

Example 7-9. Function add()

```
// The add() function computes the sum of the optional arguments.
// Arguments:   The mandatory first argument indicates the number of
//              optional arguments. The optional arguments are
//              of type double.
// Return value: The sum, with type double.

double add( int n, ... )
{
  int i = 0;
  double sum = 0.0;
  va_list argptr;
  va_start( argptr, n );                 // Initialize argptr; that is,
  for ( i = 0; i < n; ++i )              // for each optional argument,
    sum += va_arg( argptr, double );     // read an argument with type
                                         // double and accumulate in sum.
  va_end( argptr );
  return sum;
}
```

8

Arrays

An array contains objects of a given type, stored consecutively in a continuous memory block. The individual objects are called the *elements* of an array. The elements' type can be any object type. No other types are permissible: array elements may not have a function type or an incomplete type (see "Typology" on page 23).

An array is also an object itself, and its type is derived from its elements' type. More specifically, an array's type is determined by the type and number of elements in the array. If an array's elements have type *T*, then the array is called an "array of *T*." If the elements have type int, for example, then the array's type is "array of int." The type is an incomplete type, however, unless it also specifies the number of elements. If an array of int has 16 elements, then it has a complete object type, which is "array of 16 int elements."

Defining Arrays

The definition of an array determines its name, the type of its elements, and the number of elements in the array. An array definition without any explicit initialization has the following syntax:

```
type name[ number_of_elements ];
```

The number of elements, between square brackets ([ ]), must be an integer expression whose value is greater than zero. Here is an example:

```
char buffer[4*512];
```

This line defines an array with the name buffer, which consists of 2,048 elements of type char.

You can determine the size of the memory block that an array occupies using the sizeof operator. The array's size in memory is always equal to the size of one element times the number of elements in the array. Thus, for the array buffer in our example, the expression sizeof(buffer) yields the value of 2048 * sizeof(char); in other words, the array buffer occupies 2,048 bytes of memory because sizeof(char) always equals one.

In an array definition, you can specify the number of elements as a constant expression or, under certain conditions, as an expression involving variables. The resulting array is accordingly called a *fixed-length* or a *variable-length* array.

Fixed-Length Arrays

Most array definitions specify the number of array elements as a constant expression. An array so defined has a fixed length. Thus, the array buffer defined in the previous example is a fixed-length array.

Fixed-length arrays can have any storage class: you can define them outside all functions or within a block, and with or without the storage class specifier static. The only restriction is that no function parameter can be an array. An array argument passed to a function is always converted into a pointer to the first array element (see "Arrays as Function Parameters" on page 116).

The four array definitions in the following example are all valid:

```
int a[10];          // a has external linkage.
static int b[10];   // b has static storage duration and file scope.

void func()
{
  static int c[10]; // c has static storage duration and block scope.
  int d[10];        // d has automatic storage duration.
  /* ... */
}
```

Variable-Length Arrays

C99 also allows you to define an array using a nonconstant expression for the number of elements if the array has automatic storage duration—in other words, if the definition occurs within a block and does not have the specifier static. Such an array is then called a *variable-length array*.

Furthermore, the name of a variable-length array must be an *ordinary identifier* (see "Identifier Name Spaces" on page 16). Members of structures or unions cannot be variable-length arrays. In the following examples, only the definition of the array vla is a permissible definition:

```
void func( int n )
{
  int vla[2*n];       // OK: storage duration is automatic.
  static int e[n];    // Illegal: a variable length array cannot
                      //          have static storage duration.
  struct S { int f[n]; }; // Illegal: f is not an ordinary identifier.
```

```
    /* ... */
}
```

Like any other automatic variable, a variable-length array is created anew each time the program flow enters the block containing its definition. As a result, the array can have a different length at each such instantiation. Once created, however, even a variable-length array cannot change its length during its storage duration.

Storage for automatic objects is allocated on the stack, and is released when the program flow leaves the block. For this reason, variable-length array definitions are useful only for small, temporary arrays. To create larger arrays dynamically, you should generally allocate storage space explicitly using the standard functions, malloc() and calloc(). The storage duration of such arrays then ends with the end of the program or when you release the allocated memory by calling the function free() (see Chapter 12).

Accessing Array Elements

The *subscript operator*, [], provides an easy way to address the individual elements of an array by index. If myArray is the name of an array and i is an integer, then the expression myArray[i] designates the array element with the index i. Array elements are indexed beginning with 0. Thus, if len is the number of elements in an array, the last element of the array has the index len-1 (see "Memory Addressing Operators" on page 87).

The following code fragment defines the array myArray and assigns a value to each element.

```
#define A_SIZE 4
long myArray[A_SIZE];
for ( int i = 0;  i < A_SIZE;  ++i )
  myArray[i] = 2 * i;
```

The diagram in Figure 8-1 illustrates the result of this assignment loop.

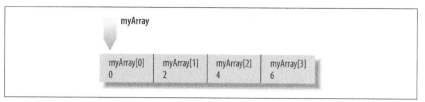

Figure 8-1. Values assigned to elements by index

An array index can be any integer expression desired. The subscript operator, [], does not bring any range checking with it; C gives priority to execution speed in this regard. It is up to you, the programmer, to ensure that an index does not exceed the range of permissible values. The following incorrect example assigns a value to a memory location outside the array:

```
long myArray[4];
myArray[4] = 8;          // Error: subscript must not exceed 3.
```

Such "off-by-one" errors can easily cause a program to crash (or, worse still, can cause silent data corruption), and are not always as easy to recognize as they are in this simple example.

Another way to address array elements, as an alternative to the subscript operator, is to use pointer arithmetic. After all, the name of an array is implicitly converted into a pointer to the first array element in all expressions except sizeof operations. For example, the expression myArray+i yields a pointer to the element with the index i, and the expression *(myArray+i) is equivalent to myArray[i] (see "Pointer arithmetic" on page 75).

The following loop statement uses a pointer instead of an index to step through the array myArray, and doubles the value of each element:

```
for ( long *p = myArray; p < myArray + A_SIZE; ++p )
    *p *= 2;
```

Initializing Arrays

If you do not explicitly initialize an array variable, the usual rules apply: if the array has automatic storage duration, then its elements have undefined values. Otherwise, all elements are initialized by default to the value 0. (If the elements are pointers, they are initialized to NULL.) For more details, see "Initialization" on page 190.

Writing Initialization Lists

To initialize an array explicitly when you define it, you must use an *initialization list*: this is a comma-separated list of *initializers*, or initial values for the individual array elements, enclosed in braces. Here is an example:

```
int a[4] = { 1, 2, 4, 8 };
```

This definition gives the elements of the array a the following initial values:

```
a[0] = 1,   a[1] = 2,   a[2] = 4,   a[3] = 8
```

When you initialize an array, observe the following rules:

- You cannot include an initialization in the definition of a variable-length array.
- If the array has static storage duration, then the array initializers must be constant expressions. If the array has automatic storage duration, then you can use variables in its initializers.
- You may omit the length of the array in its definition if you supply an initialization list. The array's length is then determined by the index of the last array element for which the list contains an initializer. For example, the definition of the array a in the previous example is equivalent to this:

```
int a[ ] = { 1, 2, 4, 8 };     // An array with four elements.
```

- If the definition of an array contains both a length specification and an initialization list, then the length is that specified by the expression between the square brackets. Any elements for which there is no initializer in the list are initialized to zero (or NULL, for pointers). If the list contains more initializers than the array has elements, the superfluous initializers are simply ignored.
- A superfluous comma after the last initializer is also ignored.

As a result of these rules, all of the following definitions are equivalent:

```
int a[4] = { 1, 2 };
int a[]  = { 1, 2, 0, 0 };
int a[]  = { 1, 2, 0, 0, };
int a[4] = { 1, 2, 0, 0, 5 };
```

In the final definition, the initializer 5 is ignored. Most compilers generate a warning when such a mismatch occurs.

Array initializers must have the same type as the array elements. If the array elements' type is a union, structure, or array type, then each initializer is generally another initialization list. Here is an example:

```
typedef struct { unsigned long pin;
                 char name[64];
                 /* ... */
               } Person;
Person team[6] = { { 1000, "Mary"}, { 2000, "Harry"} };
```

The other four elements of the array team are initialized to 0, or in this case, to { 0, "" }.

You can also initialize arrays of char, wchar_t, char16_t or char32_t with string literals (see "Strings" on page 134).

Initializing Specific Elements

C99 has introduced *element designators* to allow you to associate initializers with specific elements. To specify a certain element to initialize, place its index in square brackets. In other words, the general form of an element designator for array elements is:

```
[constant_expression]
```

The index must be an integer constant expression. In the following example, the element designator is [A_SIZE/2]:

```
#define A_SIZE 20
int a[A_SIZE] = { 1, 2, [A_SIZE/2] = 1, 2 };
```

This array definition initializes the elements a[0] and a[10] with the value 1, and the elements a[1] and a[11] with the value 2. All other elements of the array will be given the initial value 0. As this example illustrates, initializers without an element designator are associated with the element following the last one initialized.

If you define an array without specifying its length, the index in an element designator can have any non-negative integer value. As a result, the following definition creates an array of 1,001 elements:

```
int a[] = { [1000] = -1 };
```

All of the array's elements have the initial value of 0 except the last element, which is initialized to the value -1.

Strings

A *string* is a continuous sequence of characters terminated by '\0', the null character. The length of a string is considered to be the number of characters excluding the terminating null character. There is no string type in C, and consequently there are no operators that accept strings as operands.

Instead, strings are stored in arrays whose elements have the type char or a wide-character type—that is, one of the types wchar_t, char16_t, or char32_t. Strings of wide characters are also called *wide strings*. The C standard library provides numerous functions to perform basic operations on strings such as comparing, copying, and concatenating them. In addition to the traditional string functions, C11 has also introduced "secure" versions, which ensure that string operations do not exceed the bounds of an array (see "String Processing" on page 332).

You can initialize arrays of any character type using string literals. For example, the following two array definitions are equivalent:

```
char str1[30] = "Let's go";    // String length: 8; array length: 30.
```

```
char str1[30] = { 'L', 'e', 't', '\'', 's',' ', 'g', 'o', '\0' };
```

An array holding a string must always be at least one element longer than the string length to accommodate the terminating null character. The array str1 can store strings up to a maximum length of 29. It would be a mistake to define the array with a length of 8 rather than 30 because then it wouldn't contain the terminating null character.

If you define a character array without an explicit length and initialize it with a string literal, the array created is one element longer than the string length. Here is an example:

```
char str2[] = " to London!";   // String length: 11 (note leading space);
                               // array length: 12.
```

The following statement uses the standard function strcat() to append the string in str2 to the string in str1 (the array str1 must be large enough to hold all the characters in the concatenated string):

```
#include <string.h>

char str1[30] = "Let's go";
char str2[ ] = " to London!";
```

```
/* ... */

strcat( str1, str2 );
puts( str1 );
```

The output printed by the puts() call is the new content of the array str1:

```
Let's go to London!
```

The names str1 and str2 are pointers to the first character of the string stored in each array. Such a pointer is called a *pointer to a string*, or a *string pointer* for short. String manipulation functions such as strcat() and puts() receive the beginning addresses of strings as their arguments. Such functions generally process a string character by character until they reach the terminator, '\0'. The function in Example 8-1 is one possible implementation of the standard function strcat(). It uses pointers to step through the strings referenced by its arguments.

Example 8-1. Function strcat()

```
// The function strcat() appends a copy of the second string
// to the end of the first string.
// Arguments:    Pointers to the two strings.
// Return value: A pointer to the first string, now
//               concatenated with the second string.

char *strcat( char * restrict s1, const char * restrict s2 )
{
  char *rtnPtr = s1;
  while ( *s1 != '\0' )                 // Find the end of string s1.
    ++s1;
  while (( *s1++ = *s2++ ) != '\0' )    // The first character from s2
    ;                                   // replaces the terminator of s1.
  return rtnPtr;
}
```

The char array beginning at the address s1 must be at least as long as the sum of the two strings' lengths, plus one for the terminating null character. To test for this condition before calling strcat(), you might use the standard function strlen(), which returns the length of the string referenced by its argument:

```
if ( sizeof(str1) >= ( strlen( str1 ) + strlen( str2 ) + 1 ) )
  strcat( str1, str2 );
```

A wide-string literal is identified by one of the prefixes L, u, or U (see "String Literals" on page 45). Accordingly, the initialization of a wchar_t array looks like this:

```
#include <stddef.h>            // Definition of the type wchar_t
/* ... */
wchar_t dinner[] = L"chop suey";   // String length: 10;
                                   // array length: 11;
                                   // array size: 11 * sizeof(wchar_t)
```

Multidimensional Arrays

A *multidimensional* array in C is merely an array whose elements are themselves arrays. The elements of an *n*-dimensional array are (*n*-1)-dimensional arrays. For example, each element of a two-dimensional array is a one-dimensional array. The elements of a one-dimensional array, of course, do not have an array type.

A multidimensional array declaration has a pair of brackets for each dimension:

```
char screen[10][40][80];      // A three-dimensional array
```

The array screen consists of the 10 elements screen[0] to screen[9]. Each of these elements is a two-dimensional array consisting in turn of 40 one-dimensional arrays of 80 characters each. All in all, the array screen contains 32,000 elements of the type char.

To access a char element in the three-dimensional array screen, you must specify three indices. For example, the following statement writes the character Z in the last char element of the array:

```
screen[9][39][79] = 'Z';
```

Matrices

Two-dimensional arrays are also called *matrices*. Because they are so frequently used, they merit a closer look. It is often helpful to think of the elements of a matrix as being arranged in rows and columns. Thus, the matrix mat in the following definition has three rows and five columns:

```
float mat[3][5];
```

The three elements mat[0], mat[1], and mat[2] are the rows of the matrix mat. Each of these rows is an array of five float elements. Thus, the matrix contains a total of $3 \times 5 = 15$ float elements, as the following table illustrates:

	[0]	[1]	[2]	[3]	[4]
mat[0]	0.0	0.1	0.2	0.3	0.4
mat[1]	1.0	1.1	1.2	1.3	1.4
mat[2]	2.0	2.1	2.2	2.3	2.4

The values specified in the diagram can be assigned to the individual elements by a nested loop statement. The first index specifies a row, and the second index addresses a column in the row:

```
for ( int row = 0;  row < 3;  ++row )
  for ( int col = 0;  col < 5;  ++col )
    mat[row][col] = row + (float)col/10;
```

In memory, the three rows are stored consecutively, as they are the elements of the array mat. As a result, the float values in this matrix are all arranged consecutively in memory in ascending order.

Declaring Multidimensional Arrays

In an array declaration that is not a definition, the array type can be incomplete; you can declare an array without specifying its length. Such a declaration is a reference to an array that you must define with a specified length elsewhere in the program. However, you must always declare the complete type of an array's elements. For a multidimensional array declaration, only the first dimension can have an unspecified length. All other dimensions must have a magnitude. In declaring a two-dimensional matrix, for example, you must always specify the number of columns.

If the array mat in the previous example has external linkage, for example—that is, if its definition is placed outside all functions—then it can be used in another source file after the following declaration:

```
extern float mat[ ][5];      // External declaration
```

The external object so declared has an incomplete two-dimensional array type.

Initializing Multidimensional Arrays

You can initialize multidimensional arrays using an initialization list according to the rules described in "Initializing Arrays" on page 132. There are some peculiarities, however: you do not have to show all the braces for each dimension, and you may use multidimensional element designators.

To illustrate the possibilities, we will consider the array defined and initialized as follows:

```
int a3d[2][2][3] = { { { 1, 0, 0 }, { 4, 0, 0 } },
                     { { 7, 8, 0 }, { 0, 0, 0 } } };
```

This initialization list includes three levels of list-enclosing braces, and initializes the elements of the two-dimensional arrays a3d[0] and a3d[1] with the following values:

	[0]	[1]	[2]
a3d[0][0]	1	0	0
a3d[0][1]	4	0	0

	[0]	[1]	[2]
a3d[1][0]	7	8	0
a3d[1][1]	0	0	0

Because all elements that are not associated with an initializer are initialized by default to 0, the following definition has the same effect:

```
int a3d[ ][2][3] = { { { 1 }, { 4 } },  { { 7, 8 } } };
```

This initialization list also shows three levels of braces. You do not need to specify that the first dimension has a size of 2, as the outermost initialization list contains two initializers.

You can also omit some of the braces. If a given pair of braces contains more initializers than the number of elements in the corresponding array dimension, then the excess initializers are associated with the next array element in the storage sequence. Hence these two definitions are equivalent:

```
int a3d[2][2][3] = {  { 1, 0, 0, 4 }, { 7, 8 } };
int a3d[2][2][3] = { 1, 0, 0, 4, 0, 0, 7, 8 };
```

Finally, you can achieve the same initialization pattern using element designators as follows:

```
int a3d[2][2][3] = { 1, [0][1][0]=4, [1][0][0]=7, 8 };
```

Again, this definition is equivalent to the following:

```
int a3d[2][2][3] = { {1}, [0][1]={4}, [1][0]={7, 8} };
```

Using element designators is a good idea if only a few elements need to be initialized to a value other than 0.

Arrays as Arguments of Functions

When the name of an array appears as a function argument, the compiler implicitly converts it into a pointer to the array's first element. Accordingly, the corresponding parameter of the function is always a pointer to the same object type as the type of the array elements.

You can declare the parameter either in array form or in pointer form: *type* name[ ] or *type* *name. The strcat() function defined in Example 8-1 illustrates the pointer notation. For more details and examples, see "Arrays as Function Parameters" on page 116. Here, however, we'll take a closer look at the case of multidimensional arrays.

When you pass a multidimensional array as a function argument, the function receives a pointer to an array type. Because this array type is the type of the elements of the outermost array dimension, it must be a complete type. For this reason, you must specify all dimensions of the array elements in the corresponding function parameter declaration.

For example, the type of a matrix parameter is a pointer to a "row" array, and the length of the rows (i.e., the number of "columns") must be included in the declaration. More specifically, if NCOLS is the number of columns, then the parameter for a matrix of float elements can be declared as follows:

```
#define NCOLS 10                              // The number of columns.
/* ... */
void somefunction( float (*pMat)[NCOLS] ); // A pointer to a row array.
```

This declaration is equivalent to the following:

```
void somefunction( float pMat[ ][NCOLS] );
```

The parentheses in the parameter declaration float (*pMat)[NCOLS] are necessary in order to declare a pointer to an array of float. Without them, float *pMat[NCOLS] would declare the identifier pMat as an array whose elements have the type float*, or pointer to float. See "Complex Declarators" on page 182.

In C99, parameter declarations can contain variable-length arrays. Thus, in a declaration of a pointer to a matrix, the number of columns need not be constant but can be another parameter of the function. For example, you can declare a function as follows:

```
void someVLAfunction( int ncols, float pMat[][ncols] );
```

Example 7-5 shows a function that uses a variable-length matrix as a parameter.

If you use multidimensional arrays in your programs, it is a good idea to define a type name for the $(n-1)$-dimensional elements of an n-dimensional array. Such typedef names can make your programs more readable and your arrays easier to handle. For example, the following typedef statement defines a type for the row arrays of a matrix of float elements (see also "typedef Declarations" on page 185):

```
typedef float ROW_t[NCOLS];    // A type for the "row" arrays.
```

Example 8-2 illustrates the use of an array type name such as ROW_t. The function printRow() provides formatted output of a row array. The function printMatrix() prints all the rows in the matrix.

Example 8-2. Functions printRow() and printMatrix()

```
// Print one "row" array.
void printRow( const ROW_t pRow )
{
  for ( int c = 0; c < NCOLS; ++c )
    printf( "%6.2f", pRow[c] );
  putchar( '\n' );
}

// Print the whole matrix.
void printMatrix( const ROW_t *pMat, int nRows )
{
  for ( int r = 0; r < nRows; ++r )
    printRow( pMat[r] );                    // Print each row.
}
```

The parameters pRow and pMat are declared as pointers to const arrays because the functions do not modify the matrix. Because the number of rows is variable, it is passed to the function printMatrix() as a second argument.

The following code fragment defines and initializes an array of rows with type ROW_t, and then calls the function printMatrix():

```
ROW_t mat[] = { { 0.0F, 0.1F },
                { 1.0F, 1.1F, 1.2F },
                { 2.0F, 2.1F, 2.2F, 2.3F } };
int nRows = sizeof(mat) / sizeof(ROW_t);
printMatrix( mat, nRows );
```

9

Pointers

A *pointer* is a reference to a data object or a function. Pointers have many uses, such as defining "call-by-reference" functions and implementing dynamic data structures such as linked lists and trees, to name just two examples.

Very often the only efficient way to manage large volumes of data is to manipulate not the data itself but pointers to the data. For example, if you need to sort a large number of large records, it is often more efficient to sort a list of pointers to the records, rather than moving the records themselves around in memory. Similarly, if you need to pass a large record to a function, it's more economical to pass a pointer to the record than to pass the record contents, even if the function doesn't modify the contents.

Declaring Pointers

A *pointer* represents both the address and the type of an object or function. If an object or function has the type *T*, then a pointer to it has the derived type *pointer to T*. For example, if var is a float variable, then the expression &var—whose value is the address of the float variable—has the type *pointer to* float, or in C notation, the type float *. A pointer to any type *T* is also called a *T pointer* for short. Thus, the address operator in &var yields a float pointer.

Because var doesn't move around in memory, the expression &var is a constant pointer. However, C also allows you to define variables with pointer types. A pointer variable stores the address of another object or a function. We describe pointers to arrays and functions a little further on. To start out, the declaration of a pointer to an object that is not an array has the following syntax:

```
type * [type-qualifier-list] name [= initializer];
```

In declarations, the asterisk (*) means "pointer to." The identifier *name* is declared as an object with the type *type* *, or pointer to *type*. The optional type qualifier list may contain any combination of the type qualifiers const, volatile, and restrict. For details about qualified pointer types, see "Pointers and Type Qualifiers" on page 148.

Here is a simple example:

```
int *iPtr;        // Declare iPtr as a pointer to int.
```

The type int is the type of object that the pointer iPtr can point to. To make a pointer refer to a certain object, assign it the address of the object. For example, if iVar is an int variable, then the following assignment makes iPtr point to the variable iVar:

```
iPtr = &iVar;     // Let iPtr point to the variable iVar.
```

The general form of a declaration consists of a comma-separated list of declarators, each of which declares one identifier (see Chapter 11). In a pointer declaration, the asterisk (*) is part of an individual declarator. We can thus define and initialize the variables iVar and iPtr in one declaration, as follows:

```
int iVar = 77, *iPtr = &iVar; // Define an int variable and
                              // a pointer to it.
```

The second of these two declarations initializes the pointeriPtr with the address of the variable iVar, so that iPtr points to iVar.

Figure 9-1 illustrates one possible arrangement of the variables iVar and iPtr in memory. The addresses shown are purely fictitious examples. As Figure 9-1 shows, the value stored in the pointer iPtr is the address of the object iVar.

Variable:		iVar	iPtr	
Value in memory:	. . .	77	10000	. . .
Address:		10000	10004	

Figure 9-1. A pointer and another object in memory

It is often useful to output addresses for verification and debugging purposes. The printf() functions provide a format specifier for pointers: %p. The following statement prints the address and value of the variable iPtr:

```
printf("Value of iPtr (i.e. the address of iVar): %p\n"
       "Address of iPtr:                          %p\n", iPtr, &iPtr);
```

The size of a pointer in memory—given by the expression sizeof(iPtr), for example—is the same regardless of the type of object addressed. In other words, a char pointer takes up just as much space in memory as a pointer to a large structure. On 32-bit computers, pointers are usually four bytes long.

Null Pointers

A *null pointer* is what results when you convert a null pointer constant to a pointer type. A *null pointer constant* is an integer constant expression with the value of 0, or such an expression cast as the type void * (see "Null pointer constants" on page 64). The macro NULL is defined in *stdlib.h, stdio.h,* and other header files as a null pointer constant.

A null pointer is always unequal to any valid pointer to an object or function. For this reason, functions that return a pointer type usually use a null pointer to indicate a failure condition. One example is the standard function fopen(), which returns a null pointer if it fails to open a file in the specified mode:

```
#include <stdio.h>
/* ... */
FILE *fp = fopen( "demo.txt", "r" );
if ( fp == NULL )        // Also written as: if ( !fp )
{
    // Error: unable to open the file demo.txt for reading.
}
```

Null pointers are implicitly converted to other pointer types as necessary for assignment operations or for comparisons using == or !=. Hence, no cast operator is necessary in the previous example. (See also "Implicit Pointer Conversions" on page 61.)

void Pointers

A pointer to void, or *void pointer* for short, is a pointer with the type void *. As there are no objects with the type void, the type void * is used as the all-purpose pointer type. In other words, a void pointer can represent the address of any object—but not its type. To access an object in memory, you must always convert a void pointer into an appropriate object pointer.

To declare a function that can be called with different types of pointer arguments, you can declare the appropriate parameters as pointers to void. When you call such a function, the compiler implicitly converts an object pointer argument into a void pointer. A common example is the standard function memset(), which is declared in the header file *string.h* with the following prototype:

```
void *memset( void *s, int c, size_t n );
```

The memset() function assigns the value of c to each of the n bytes of memory in the block beginning at the address s. For example, the following function call assigns the value 0 to each byte in the structure variable record:

```
struct Data { /* ... */ } record;
memset( &record, 0, sizeof(record) );
```

The argument &record has the type struct Data *. In the function call, the argument is converted to the parameter's type, void *.

The compiler likewise converts void pointers into object pointers where necessary. For example, in the following statement, the malloc() function returns a void pointer whose value is the address of the allocated memory block. The assignment operation converts the void pointer into a pointer to int:

```
int *iPtr = malloc( 1000 * sizeof(int) );
```

For a more thorough illustration, see Example 2-3.

Initializing Pointers

Pointer variables with automatic storage duration start with an undefined value, unless their declaration contains an explicit initializer. All variables defined within any block have automatic storage duration unless they are defined with the storage class specifier static. All other pointers defined without an initializer have the initial value of a null pointer.

You can initialize a pointer with the following kinds of initializers:

- A null pointer constant
- A pointer to the same type, or to a less qualified version of the same type (see "Pointers and Type Qualifiers" on page 148)
- A void pointer, if the pointer being initialized is not a function pointer (here again, the pointer being initialized can be a pointer to a more qualified type)

Pointers that do not have automatic storage duration must be initialized with a constant expression such as the result of an address operation or the name of an array or function.

When you initialize a pointer, no implicit type conversion takes place except in the cases just listed. However, you can explicitly convert a pointer value to another pointer type. For example, to read any object byte by byte, you can convert its address into a char pointer to the first byte of the object:

```
double x = 1.5;
char *cPtr = &x;         // Error: type mismatch; no implicit conversion.
char *cPtr = (char *)&x; // OK: cPtr points to the first byte of x.
```

For more details and examples of pointer type conversions, see "Explicit Pointer Conversions" on page 59.

Operations with Pointers

This section describes the operations that can be performed using pointers. The most important of these operations is accessing the object or function that the pointer refers to. You can also compare pointers, and use them to iterate through a memory block. For a complete description of the individual operators in C with their precedence and permissible operands, see Chapter 5.

Using Pointers to Read and Modify Objects

The indirection operator * yields the location in memory whose address is stored in a pointer. If ptr is a pointer, then *ptr designates the object (or function) that ptr points to. Using the indirection operator is sometimes called *dereferencing* a pointer. The type of the pointer determines the type of object that is assumed to be at that location in memory. For example, when you access a given location using an int pointer, you read or write an object of type int.

Unlike the multiplication operator *, the indirection operator * is a unary operator; that is, it has only one operand. In Example 9-1, ptr points to the variable x. Hence, the expression *ptr is equivalent to the variable x itself.

Example 9-1. Dereferencing a pointer

```
double x, y, *ptr;     // Two double variables and a pointer to double.
ptr = &x;              // Let ptr point to x.
*ptr = 7.8;            // Assign the value 7.8 to the variable x.
*ptr *= 2.5;           // Multiply x by 2.5.
y = *ptr + 0.5;        // Assign y the result of the addition x + 0.5.
```

Do not confuse the asterisk (*) in a pointer declaration with the indirection operator. The syntax of the declaration can be seen as an illustration of how to use the pointer. Here is an example:

```
double *ptr;
```

As declared here, ptr has the type double * (read: "pointer to double"). Hence the expression *ptr would have the type double.

Of course, the indirection operator * must be used only with a pointer that contains a valid address. This usage requires careful programming! Without the assignment ptr = &x in Example 9-1, all of the statements containing *ptr would be senseless—dereferencing an undefined pointer value—and might cause the program to crash.

A pointer variable is itself an object in memory, which means that a pointer can point to it. To declare a pointer to a pointer, you must use two asterisks, as in the following example:

```
char c = 'A', *cPtr = &c, **cPtrPtr = &cPtr;
```

The expression *cPtrPtr now yields the char pointer cPtr, and the value of **cPtrPtr is the char variable c. Figure 9-2 illustrates these references.

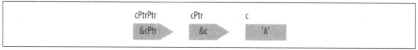

Figure 9-2. A pointer to a pointer

Pointers

Pointers to pointers are not restricted to the two-stage indirection illustrated here. You can define pointers with as many levels of indirection as you need. However, you cannot assign a pointer-to-a-pointer its value by mere repetitive application of the address operator:

```
char c = 'A', **cPtrPtr = &(&c);        // Wrong!
```

The second initialization in this example is illegal: the expression (&c) cannot be the operand of &, because it is not an lvalue. In other words, there is no pointer to char in this example for cPtrPtr to point to.

If you pass a pointer to a function by reference so that the function can modify its value, then the function's parameter is a pointer to a pointer. The following simple example is a function that dynamically creates a new record and stores its address in a pointer variable:

```
#include <stdlib.h>
// The record type:
typedef struct { long key; /* ... */ } Record;

_Bool newRecord( Record **ppRecord )
{
  *ppRecord = malloc( sizeof(Record) );
  if ( *ppRecord != NULL )
  {
    /* ... Initialize the new record's members ... */
    return 1;
  }
  else
    return 0;
}
```

The following statement is one possible way to call the newRecord() function:

```
Record *pRecord = NULL;
if ( newRecord( &pRecord) )
{
  /* ... pRecord now points to a new Record object ... */
}
```

The expression *pRecord yields the new record, and (*pRecord).key is the member key in that record. The parentheses in the expression (*pRecord).key are necessary because the dot operator (.) has higher precedence than the indirection operator (*).

Instead of this combination of operators and parentheses, you can also use the arrow operator -> to access structure or union members. If p is a pointer to a structure or union with a member m, then the expression p->m is equivalent to (*p).m. Thus, the following statement assigns a value to the member key in the structure that pRecord points to:

```
pRecord->key = 123456L;
```

Modifying and Comparing Pointers

Besides using assignments to make a pointer refer to a given object or function, you can also modify an object pointer using arithmetic operations. When you perform *pointer arithmetic*, the compiler automatically adapts the operation to the size of the objects referred to by the pointer type.

You can perform the following operations on pointers to objects:

- Adding an integer to, or subtracting an integer from, a pointer.
- Subtracting one pointer from another.
- Comparing two pointers.

When you subtract one pointer from another, the two pointers must have the same basic type, although you can disregard any type qualifiers. Furthermore, you may compare any pointer with a null pointer constant using the equality operators (== and !=), and you may compare any object pointer with a pointer to void.

The three pointer operations described here are generally useful only for pointers that refer to the elements of an array. To illustrate the effects of these operations, consider two pointers p1 and p2, which point to elements of an array a:

- If p1 points to the array element a[i], and n is an integer, then the expression p2 = p1 + n makes p2 point to the array element a[i+n] (assuming that i+n is an index within the array a).
- The subtraction p2 - p1 yields the number of array elements between the two pointers, with the type ptrdiff_t. The type ptrdiff_t is defined in the *stddef.h* header file, usually as int. After the assignment p2 = p1 + n, the expression p2 - p1 yields the value of n.
- The comparison p1 < p2 yields true if the element referenced by p2 has a greater index than the element referenced by p1. Otherwise, the comparison yields false.

Because the name of an array is implicitly converted into a pointer to the first array element wherever necessary, you can also substitute pointer arithmetic for array subscript notation:

- The expression a + i is a pointer to a[i], and the value of *(a+i) is the element a[i].
- The expression p1 - a yields the index i of the element referenced by p1.

In Example 9-2, the selection_sortf() function sorts an array of float elements using the selection-sort algorithm. This is the pointer version of the selec tion_sortf() function in Example 7-7; in other words, this function does the same job but uses pointers instead of indices. The helper function swapf() remains unchanged.

Example 9-2. Pointer version of the selection_sortf() function

```
// The swapf() function exchanges the values of two float variables.
// Arguments:  Two pointers to float.

inline void swapf( float *p1, float *p2 )
{
    float tmp = *p1;   *p1 = *p2;   *p2 = tmp;    // Swap *p1 and *p2.
}
// The function selection_sortf() uses the selection-sort
// algorithm to sort an array of float elements.
// Arguments: An array of float, and its length.

void selection_sortf( float a[], int n )   // Sort an array a of
                                           // n float elements.
{
  if ( n <= 1 ) return;                    // Nothing to sort.

  register float *last = a + n-1,          // A pointer to the last element.
                 *p,                       // A pointer to a selected element.
                 *minPtr;                  // A pointer to the current minimum.

  for (  ; a < last; ++a )                 // Walk pointer a through the array.
  {
    minPtr = a;                            // Find the smallest element
    for ( p = a+1;  p <= last;  ++p )      // between a and the last element.
      if ( *p < *minPtr )
        minPtr = p;
    swapf( a, minPtr );                    // Swap the smallest element
  }                                        // with the element at a.
}
```

The pointer version of such a function is generally more efficient than the index version because accessing the elements of the array a using an index i, as in the expression a[i] or *(a+i), involves adding the address a to the value i*sizeof(*element_type*) to obtain the address of the corresponding array element. The pointer version requires less arithmetic because the pointer is incremented instead of the index, and points to the required array element directly.

Pointers and Type Qualifiers

The declaration of a pointer may contain the type qualifiers const, volatile, and/or restrict. The const and volatile type qualifiers may qualify either the pointer type itself, or the type of object it points to. The difference is important. Those type qualifiers that occur in the pointer's declarator—that is, between the asterisk and the pointer's name—qualify the pointer itself. Here is an example:

```
short const volatile * restrict ptr;
```

In this declaration, the keyword restrict qualifies the pointer ptr. This pointer can refer to objects of type short that may be qualified with const or volatile, or both.

An object whose type is qualified with const is constant: the program cannot modify it after its definition. The type qualifier volatile is a hint to the compiler that the object so qualified may be modified not only by the present program, but also by other processes or events (see Chapter 11).

The most common use of qualifiers in pointer declarations is in pointers to constant objects, especially as function parameters. For this reason, the following description refers to the type qualifier const. The same rules govern the use of the volatile type qualifier with pointers.

Constant Pointers and Pointers to Constant Objects

When you define a constant pointer, you must also initialize it because you can't modify it later. As the following example illustrates, a constant pointer is not the same thing as a pointer to a constant object:

```
int var;                 // An object with type int.
int *const c_ptr = &var; // A constant pointer to int.
*c_ptr = 123;            // OK: we can modify the object referenced.
++c_ptr;                 // Error: we can't modify the pointer.
```

You can modify a pointer that points to an object that has a const-qualified type (also called a *pointer to* const). However, you can only use such a pointer to read the referenced object, not to modify it. For this reason, pointers to const are commonly called *read-only pointers*. The referenced object itself may or may not be constant. Here is an example:

```
int var;                        // An object with type int.
const int c_var = 100,          // A constant int object.
          *ptr_to_const;        // A pointer to const int: the pointer
                                // itself is not constant!
ptr_to_const = &c_var;          // OK: Let ptr_to_const point to c_var.
var = 2 * *ptr_to_const;        // OK. Equivalent to: var = 2 * c_var;
ptr_to_const = &var;            // OK: Let ptr_to_const point to var.
if ( c_var < *ptr_to_const )    // OK: "read-only" access.
  *ptr_to_const = 77;           // Error: we can't modify var using
                                // ptr_to_const, even though var is
                                // not constant.
```

Type specifiers and type qualifiers can be written in any order. Thus, the following is permissible:

```
int const c_var = 100, *ptr_to_const;
```

The assignment ptr_to_const = &var entails an implicit conversion: the int pointer value &var is automatically converted to the left operand's type, pointer to const int. For any operator that requires operands with like types, the compiler implicitly converts a pointer to a given type *T* into a more qualified version of the type *T*. If you want to convert a pointer into a pointer to a less-qualified type, you must use an explicit type conversion. The following code fragment uses the variables declared in the previous example:

```
int *ptr = &var;          // An int pointer that points to var.
*ptr = 77;                // OK: ptr is not a read-only pointer.
ptr_to_const = ptr;       // OK: implicitly converts ptr from "pointer to
                          // int" into "pointer to const int".
*ptr_to_const = 77;       // Error: can't modify a variable through a
                          // read-only pointer.
ptr = &c_var;             // Error: can't implicitly convert "pointer to
                          // const int" into "pointer to int".
ptr = (int *)&c_var;      // OK: Explicit pointer conversions are always
                          // possible.
*ptr = 200;               // Attempt to modify c_var: possible runtime
                          // error.
```

The final statement causes a runtime error if the compiler has placed the constant object c_var in a read-only section in memory.

You can also declare a constant pointer to const, as the parameter declaration in the following function prototype illustrates:

```
void func( const int * const c_ptr_to_const );
```

The function's parameter is a read-only pointer that is initialized when the function is called and remains constant within the function.

Restricted Pointers

C99 introduced the type qualifier restrict, which is applicable only to object pointers. A pointer qualified with restrict is called a *restricted pointer*. There is a special relationship between a restrict-qualified pointer and the object it points to: during the lifetime of the pointer, either the object is not modified or the object is not accessed except through the restrict-qualified pointer. Here is an example:

```
typedef struct { long key;                 // Define a structure type.
                 /* ... other members ... */
               } Data_t;
Data_t * restrict rPtr = malloc( sizeof(Data_t) ); // Allocate a
                                                   // structure.
```

This example illustrates one way to respect the relationship between the restricted pointer and its object: the return value of malloc()—the address of an anonymous Data_t object—is assigned only to the pointer rPtr, so the program won't access the object in any other way.

It is up to you, the programmer, to make sure that an object referenced by a restrict-qualified pointer is accessed only through that pointer. For example, if your program modifies an object through a restricted pointer, it must not access the object by name or through another pointer for as long as the restricted pointer exists.

The restrict type qualifier is a hint to the compiler that allows it to apply certain optimization techniques that might otherwise introduce inconsistencies. However, the restrict qualifier does not mandate any such optimization, and the compiler may ignore it. The program's outward behavior is the same in either case.

The restrict type qualifier is used in the prototypes of many standard library functions. For example, the memcpy() function is declared in the *string.h* header file as follows:

```
void *memcpy( void * restrict dest,     // Destination
              const void * restrict src,  // Source
              size_t n );                 // Number of bytes to copy
```

This function copies a memory block of n bytes, beginning at the address src, to the location beginning at dest. Because the pointer parameters are both restricted, you must make sure that the function will not use them to access the same objects; in other words, make sure that the source and destination blocks do not overlap. The following example contains one correct and one incorrect memcpy() call:

```
char a[200];
/* ... */
memcpy( a+100, a, 100 );   // OK: copy the first half of the array
                           // to the second half; no overlap.
memcpy( a+1, a, 199 );     // Error: move the whole array contents
                           // upward by one index; large overlap.
```

The second memcpy() call in this example violates the restrict condition, because the function must modify 198 locations that it accesses using both pointers.

The standard function memmove(), unlike memcpy(), allows the source and destination blocks to overlap. Accordingly, neither of its pointer parameters has the restrict qualifier:

```
void *memmove( void *dest, const void *src, size_t n );
```

Example 9-3 illustrates the second way to fulfill the restrict condition: the program may access the object pointed to using other names or pointers if it doesn't modify the object for as long as the restricted pointer exists. This simple function calculates the scalar product of two arrays.

Example 9-3. The function scalar_product()

```
// This function calculates the scalar product of two arrays.
// Arguments: Two arrays of double, and their length.
//            The two arrays need not be distinct.

double scalar_product( const double * restrict p1,
                       const double * restrict p2,
                       int n )
{
  double result = 0.0;
  for ( int i = 0; i < n; ++i )
    result += p1[i] * p2[i];
  return result;
}
```

Assuming an array named P with three double elements, you could call this function using the expression scalar_products(P, P, 3). The function accesses objects through two different restricted pointers, but as the const keyword in the first two parameter declarations indicates, it doesn't modify them.

Pointers to Arrays and Arrays of Pointers

Pointers occur in many C programs as references to arrays, and also as elements of arrays. A pointer to an array type is called an *array pointer* for short, and an array whose elements are pointers is called a *pointer array*.

Array Pointers

For the sake of example, the following description deals with an array of int. The same principles apply for any other array type, including multidimensional arrays.

To declare a pointer to an array type, you must use parentheses, as the following example illustrates:

```
int (* arrPtr)[10] = NULL; // A pointer to an array of
                           // ten elements with type int.
```

Without the parentheses, the declaration int * arrPtr[10]; would define arrPtr as an array of 10 pointers to int. Arrays of pointers are described in the next section.

In the example, the pointer to an array of 10 int elements is initialized with NULL. However, if we assign it the address of an appropriate array, then the expression *arrPtr yields the array, and (*arrPtr)[i] yields the array element with the index i. According to the rules for the subscript operator, the expression (*arrPtr)[i] is equivalent to *((*arrPtr)+1) (see "Memory Addressing Operators" on page 87). Hence, **arrPtr yields the first element of the array, with the index 0.

In order to demonstrate a few operations with the array pointer `arrPtr`, the following example uses it to address some elements of a two-dimensional array—that is, some rows of a matrix (see "Matrices" on page 136):

```
int matrix[3][10];      // Array of three rows, each with 10 columns.
                        // The array name is a pointer to the first
                        // element; i.e., the first row.
arrPtr = matrix;        // Let arrPtr point to the first row of
                        // the matrix.
(*arrPtr)[0] = 5;       // Assign the value 5 to the first element of
                        // the first row.
                        //
arrPtr[2][9] = 6;       // Assign the value 6 to the last element of
                        // the last row.
                        //
++arrPtr;               // Advance the pointer to the next row.
(*arrPtr)[0] = 7;       // Assign the value 7 to the first element
                        // of the second row.
```

After the initial assignment, `arrPtr` points to the first row of the matrix, just as the array name `matrix` does. At this point, you can use `arrPtr` in the same way as `matrix` to access the elements. For example, the assignment `(*arrPtr)[0] = 5` is equivalent to `arrPtr[0][0] = 5` or `matrix[0][0] = 5`.

However, unlike the array name `matrix`, the pointer name `arrPtr` does not represent a constant address, as the operation `++arrPtr` shows. The increment operation increases the address stored in an array pointer by the size of one array—in this case, one row of the matrix, or ten times the number of bytes in an `int` element.

If you want to pass a multidimensional array to a function, you must declare the corresponding function parameter as a pointer to an array type. For a full description and an example of this use of pointers, see "Arrays as Arguments of Functions" on page 138.

One more word of caution: if `a` is an array of ten `int` elements, then you cannot make the pointer from the previous example, `arrPtr`, point to the array `a` by this assignment:

```
arrPtr = a;     // Error: mismatched pointer types.
```

The reason is that an array name, such as `a`, is implicitly converted into a pointer to *the array's first element*, not a pointer to the whole array. The pointer to `int` is not implicitly converted into a pointer to an array of `int`. The assignment in the example requires an explicit type conversion, specifying the target type `int (*)[10]` in the cast operator:

```
arrPtr = (int (*)[10])a;     // OK
```

You can derive this notation for the array pointer type from the declaration of `arrPtr` by removing the identifier (see "Type Names" on page 184). However, for more readable and more flexible code, it is a good idea to define a simpler name for the type using typedef:

```
typedef int ARRAY_t[10];    // A type name for
                            // "array of ten int elements".
ARRAY_t a,                  // An array of this type,
        *arrPtr;            // and a pointer to this array type.
arrPtr = (ARRAY_t *)a;      // Let arrPtr point to a.
```

Pointer Arrays

Pointer arrays—that is, arrays whose elements have a pointer type—are often a handy alternative to two-dimensional arrays. Usually the pointers in such an array point to dynamically allocated memory blocks.

For example, if you need to process strings, you could store them in a two-dimensional array whose row size is large enough to hold the longest string that can occur:

```
#define ARRAY_LEN 100
#define STRLEN_MAX 256
char myStrings[ARRAY_LEN][STRLEN_MAX] =
{ // Several corollaries of Murphy's law:
  "If anything can go wrong, it will.",
  "Nothing is foolproof, because fools are so ingenious.",
  "Every solution breeds new problems."
};
```

However, this technique wastes memory, as only a small fraction of the 25,600 bytes devoted to the array is actually used. For one thing, a short string leaves most of a row empty; for another, memory is reserved for whole rows that may never be used. A simple solution in such cases is to use an array of pointers that reference the objects—in this case, the strings—and to allocate memory only for the pointer array and for objects that actually exist (unused array elements are null pointers):

```
#define ARRAY_LEN 100
char *myStrPtr[ARRAY_LEN] =    // Array of pointers to char
{ // Several corollaries of Murphy's law:
  "If anything can go wrong, it will.",
  "Nothing is foolproof, because fools are so ingenious.",
  "Every solution breeds new problems."
};
```

The diagram in Figure 9-3 illustrates how the objects are stored in memory.

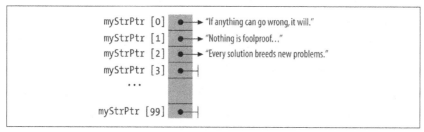

Figure 9-3. Pointer array

The pointers not yet used can be made to point to other strings at runtime. The necessary storage can be reserved dynamically in the usual way. The memory can also be released when it is no longer needed.

The program in Example 9-4 is a simple version of the filter utility *sort*. It reads text from the standard input stream, sorts the lines alphanumerically, and prints them to standard output. This routine does not move any strings; it merely sorts an array of pointers.

Example 9-4. A simple program to sort lines of text

```c
#include <stdio.h>
#include <stdlib.h>
#include <string.h>

char *getLine(void);              // Reads a line of text
int str_compare(const void *, const void *);

#define NLINES_MAX 1000           // Maximum number of text lines.
char *linePtr[NLINES_MAX];        // Array of pointers to char.

int main()
{
  // Read lines:
  int n = 0;                      // Number of lines read.
  for (  ; n < NLINES_MAX && (linePtr[n] = getLine()) != NULL; ++n )
    ;

  if ( !feof(stdin) )             // Handle errors.
  {
    if ( n == NLINES_MAX )
      fputs( "sorttext: too many lines.\n", stderr );
    else
      fputs( "sorttext: error reading from stdin.\n", stderr );
  }
  else                            // Sort and print.
  {
    qsort( linePtr, n, sizeof(char*), str_compare );    // Sort.
    for ( char **p = linePtr; p < linePtr+n; ++p )      // Print.
```

```
      puts(*p);
  }
  return 0;
}

// Reads a line of text from stdin; drops the terminating
// newline character.
// Return value: A pointer to the string read, or
//               NULL at end-of-file, or if an error occurred.
#define LEN_MAX 512                          // Maximum length of a line.

char *getLine()
{
  char buffer[LEN_MAX], *linePtr = NULL;
  if ( fgets( buffer, LEN_MAX, stdin ) != NULL )
  {
    size_t len = strlen( buffer );

    if ( buffer[len-1] == '\n' )             // Trim the newline character.
      buffer[len-1] = '\0';
    else
      ++len;

    if ( (linePtr = malloc( len )) != NULL ) // Get memory for the line.
      strcpy( linePtr, buffer );  // Copy the line to the allocated block.
  }
  return linePtr;
}

// Comparison function for use by qsort().
// Arguments: Pointers to two elements in the array being sorted:
//            here, two pointers to pointers to char (char **).
int str_compare( const void *p1, const void *p2 )
{
  return strcmp( *(char **)p1, *(char **)p2 );
}
```

The maximum number of lines that the program in Example 9-4 can sort is limited by the constant NLINES_MAX. However, we could remove this limitation by creating the array of pointers to text lines dynamically as well.

Pointers to Functions

There are a variety of uses for function pointers in C. For example, when you call a function, you might want to pass it not only the data for it to process but also pointers to subroutines that determine how it processes the data. We have just seen an example of this use: the standard function qsort(), used in Example 9-4, takes a pointer to a comparison function as one of its arguments in addition to the information about the array to be sorted. qsort() uses the pointer to call the specified function whenever it has to compare two array elements.

You can also store function pointers in arrays, and then call the functions using array index notation. For example, a keyboard driver might use a table of function pointers whose indices correspond to the key numbers. When the user presses a key, the program would jump to the corresponding function.

Like declarations of pointers to array types, function pointer declarations require parentheses. The examples that follow illustrate how to declare and use pointers to functions. This declaration defines a pointer to a function type with two parameters of type double and a return value of type double:

```
double (*funcPtr)(double, double);
```

The parentheses that enclose the asterisk and the identifier are important. Without them, the declaration double *funcPtr(double, double); would be the prototype of a function, not the definition of a pointer.

Wherever necessary, the name of a function is implicitly converted into a pointer to the function. Thus, the following statements assign the address of the standard function pow() to the pointer funcPtr, and then call the function using that pointer:

```
double result;
funcPtr = pow;              // Let funcPtr point to the function pow().
                            // The expression *funcPtr now yields the
                            // function pow().

result = (*funcPtr)( 1.5, 2.0 );  // Call the function referenced by
                                  // funcPtr.
result = funcPtr( 1.5, 2.0 );     // The same function call.
```

As the last line in this example shows, when you call a function using a pointer, you can omit the indirection operator because the left operand of the function call operator (i.e., the parentheses enclosing the argument list) has the type "pointer to function" (see "Function calls" on page 91).

The simple program in Example 9-5 prompts the user to enter two numbers, and then performs some simple calculations with them. The mathematical functions are called by pointers that are stored in the array funcTable.

Example 9-5. Simple use of function pointers

```
#include <stdio.h>
#include <stdlib.h>
#include <math.h>

double Add( double x, double y ) { return x + y; }
double Sub( double x, double y ) { return x - y; }
double Mul( double x, double y ) { return x * y; }
double Div( double x, double y ) { return x / y; }

// Array of 5 pointers to functions that take two double parameters
// and return a double:
```

```
double (*funcTable[5])(double, double)
        = { Add, Sub, Mul, Div, pow }; // Initializer list.

// An array of pointers to strings for output:
char *msgTable[5] = {"Sum", "Difference", "Product", "Quotient", "Power"};

int main()
{
  int i;                    // An index variable.
  double x = 0, y = 0;

  printf( "Enter two operands for some arithmetic:\n" );
  if ( scanf( "%lf %lf", &x, &y ) != 2 )
    printf( "Invalid input.\n" );

  for ( i = 0; i < 5; ++i )
    printf( "%10s: %6.2f\n", msgTable[i], funcTable[i](x, y) );

  return 0;
}
```

The expression funcTable[i](x,y) calls the function whose address is stored in the pointer funcTable[i]. The array name and subscript do not need to be enclosed in parentheses because the function call operator () and the subscript operator [] both have the highest precedence and left-to-right associativity (see Table 5-4).

Once again, complex types such as arrays of function pointers are easier to manage if you define simpler type names using typedef. For example, you could define the array funcTable as follows:

```
typedef double func_t( double, double );    // The functions' type is
                                            // now named func_t.
func_t *funcTable[5] = { Add, Sub, Mul, Div, pow };
```

This approach is certainly more readable than the array definition in Example 9-5.

10

Structures, Unions, and Bit-Fields

The pieces of information that describe the characteristics of objects, such as information on companies or customers, are generally grouped together in *records*. Records make it easy to organize, present, and store information about similar objects.

A record is composed of *fields* that contain the individual details, such as the name, address, and legal form of a company. In C, you determine the names and types of the fields in a record by defining a *structure type*. The fields are called the *members* of the structure.

A *union* is defined in the same way as a structure. Unlike the members of a structure, all the members of a union start at the same address. Hence you define a union type when you want to use the same location in memory for different types of objects.

In addition to the basic and derived types, the members of structures and unions can also include bit-fields. A *bit-field* is an integer variable composed of a specified number of bits. By defining bit-fields, you can break down an addressable memory unit into groups of individual bits that you can address by name.

Structures

A structure type is a type defined within the program that specifies the format of a record, including the names and types of its members, and the order in which they are stored. Once you have defined a structure type, you can use it like any other type in declaring objects, pointers to those objects, and arrays of such structure elements.

Defining Structure Types

The definition of a structure type begins with the keyword `struct`, and contains a list of declarations of the structure's members, in braces:

```
struct [tag_name] { member_declaration_list };
```

A structure must contain at least one member. The following example defines the type `struct Date`, which has three members of type `short`:

```
struct Date { short month, day, year; };
```

The identifier `Date` is this structure type's *tag*. The identifiers `year`, `month`, and `day` are the names of its members. The tags of structure types are a distinct name space: the compiler distinguishes them from variables or functions whose names are the same as a structure tag. Likewise, the names of structure members form a separate name space for each structure type. In this book, we have generally capitalized the first letter in the names of structure, union, and enumeration types: this is merely a common convention to help programmers distinguish such names from those of variables.

The members of a structure may have any desired complete type, including previously defined structure types. They must not be variable-length arrays, or pointers to such arrays.

The following structure type, `struct Song`, has five members to store five pieces of information about a music recording. The member `published` has the type `struct Date`, defined in the previous example:

```
struct Song { char title[64];
              char artist[32];
              char composer[32];
              short duration;         // Playing time in seconds.
              struct Date published;  // Date of publication.
            };
```

A structure type cannot contain itself as a member, as its definition is not complete until the closing brace (}). However, structure types can and often do contain pointers to their own type. Such *self-referential structures* are used in implementing linked lists and binary trees, for example. The following example defines a type for the members of a singly linked list:

```
struct Cell { struct Song song;    // This record's data.
              struct Cell *pNext;  // A pointer to the next record.
            };
```

If you use a structure type in several source files, you should place its definition in an included header file. Typically, the same header file will contain the prototypes of the functions that operate on structures of that type. Then you can use the structure type and the corresponding functions in any source file that includes the given header file.

Structure Objects and typedef Names

Within the scope of a structure type definition, you can declare objects of that type:

```
struct Song song1, song2, *pSong = &song1;
```

This example defines song1 and song2 as objects of type struct Song, and pSong as a pointer that points to the object song1. The keyword struct must be included whenever you use the structure type. You can also use typedef to define a one-word name for a structure type:

```
typedef struct Song Song_t;        // Song_t is now a synonym for
                                   // struct Song.
Song_t song1, song2, *pSong = &song1; // Two struct Song objects and a
                                   // struct Song pointer.
```

Objects with a structure type, such as song1 and song2 in our example, are called *structure objects* (or *structure variables*) for short.

You can also define a structure type without a tag. This approach is practical only if you define objects at the same time and don't need the type for anything else, or if you define the structure type in a typedef declaration so that it has a name after all. Here is an example:

```
typedef struct { struct Cell *pFirst, *pLast; } SongList_t;
```

This typedef declaration defines SongList_t as a name for the structure type whose members are two pointers to struct Cell named pFirst and pLast.

Incomplete Structure Types

You can define pointers to a structure type even when the structure type has not yet been defined. Thus, the definition of SongList_t in the previous example would be permissible and correct even if struct Cell had not yet been defined. In such a case, the definition of SongList_t would implicitly declare the name Cell as a structure tag. However, the type struct Cell would remain incomplete until explicitly defined. The pointers pFirst and pLast, whose type is struct Cell *, cannot be used to access objects until the type struct Cell is completely defined, with declarations of its structure members between braces.

The ability to declare pointers to incomplete structure types allows you to define structure types that refer to each other. Here is a simple example:

```
struct A { struct B *pB; /* ... other members of struct A ... */ };
struct B { struct A *pA; /* ... other members of struct B ... */ };
```

These declarations are correct and behave as expected, except in the following case: if they occur within a block, and the structure type struct B has already been defined in a larger scope, then the declaration of the member pB in structure A declares a pointer to the type already defined, and not to the type struct B defined after struct A. To preclude this interference from the outer scope, you can insert an "empty" declaration of struct B before the definition of struct A:

```
struct B;
struct A { struct B *pB; /* ... */ };
struct B { struct A *pA; /* ... */ };
```

This example declares B as a new structure tag that hides an existing structure tag from the larger scope, if there is one.

Accessing Structure Members

Two operators allow you to access the members of a structure object: the dot operator (.) and the arrow operator (->). Both of them are binary operators whose right operand is the name of a member.

The left operand of the dot operator is an expression that yields a structure object. Here are a few examples using the structure struct Song:

```
#include <string.h>          // Prototypes of string functions.
Song_t song1, song2,         // Two objects of type Song_t,
        *pSong = &song1;     // and a pointer to Song_t.

// Copy a string to the title of song1:
strcpy(song1.title, "Havana Club" );

// Likewise for the composer member:
strcpy( song1.composer, "Ottmar Liebert" );

song1.duration = 251;               // Playing time.

// The member published is itself a structure:
song1.published.year = 1998;        // Year of publication.

if ( (*pSong).duration > 180 )
  printf("The song %s is more than 3 minutes long.\n", (*pSong).title);
```

Because the pointer pSong points to the object song1, the expression *pSong denotes the object song1, and (*pSong).duration denotes the member duration in song1. The parentheses are necessary because the dot operator has a higher precedence than the indirection operator (see Table 5-4).

If you have a pointer to a structure, you can use the arrow operator -> to access the structure's members instead of the indirection and dot operators (* and .). In other words, an expression of the form p->m is equivalent to (*p).m. Thus, we might rewrite the if statement in the previous example using the arrow operator as follows:

```
if (pSong->duration > 180 )
  printf( "The song %s is more than 3 minutes long.\n", pSong->title );
```

You can use an assignment to copy the entire contents of a structure object to another object of the same type:

```
song2 = song1;
```

After this assignment, each member of song2 has the same value as the corresponding member of song1. Similarly, if a function parameter has a structure type, then the contents of the corresponding argument are copied to the parameter when you call the function. This approach can be rather inefficient unless the structure is small, as in Example 10-1.

Example 10-1. The function dateAsString()

```
// The function dateAsString() converts a date from a structure of type
// struct Date into a string of the form mm/dd/yyyy.
// Argument:    A date value of type struct Date.
// Return value: A pointer to a static buffer containing the date string.

const char *dateAsString( struct Date d )
{
  static char strDate[12];
  sprintf( strDate, "%02d/%02d/%04d", d.month, d.day, d.year );
  return strDate;
}
```

Larger structures are generally passed by reference. In Example 10-2, the function call copies only the address of a Song object, not the structure's contents. Furthermore, as the function does not modify the structure object, the parameter is a read-only pointer. Thus, you can also pass this function a pointer to a constant object.

Example 10-2. The function printSong()

```
// The printSong() function prints out the contents of a structure
// of type Song_t in a tabular format.
// Argument:    A pointer to the structure object to be printed.
// Return value: None.

void printSong( const Song_t *pSong )
{
  int m = pSong->duration / 60,        // Playing time in minutes
      s = pSong->duration % 60;        // and seconds.

  printf( "----------------------------------------\n"
          "Title:         %s\n"
          "Artist:        %s\n"
          "Composer:      %s\n"
          "Playing time:  %d:%02d\n"
          "Date:          %s\n",
          pSong->title, pSong->artist, pSong->composer, m, s,
          dateAsString( pSong->published ));
}
```

The song's playing time is printed in the format $m:ss$. The function dateAsString() converts the publication date from a structure to string format.

Initializing Structures

When you define structure objects without explicitly initializing them, the usual initialization rules apply: if the structure object has automatic storage class, then its members have indeterminate initial values. If, on the other hand, the structure object has static storage duration, then the initial value of its members is zero, or if they have pointer types, a null pointer (see "Initialization" on page 190).

To initialize a structure object explicitly when you define it, you must use an *initialization list*: this is a comma-separated list of *initializers*, or initial values for the individual structure members, enclosed in braces. The initializers are associated with the members in the order of their declarations: the first initializer is associated with the first member, the second initializer goes with the second member, and so forth. Of course, each initializer must have a type that matches (or can be implicitly converted into) the type of the corresponding member. Here is an example:

```
Song_t mySong = { "What It Is",
                  "Aubrey Haynie; Mark Knopfler",
                  "Mark Knopfler",
                  297,
                  { 9, 26, 2000 }
                };
```

This list contains an initializer for each member. Because the member published has a structure type, its initializer is another initialization list.

You may also specify fewer initializers than the number of members in the structure. In this case, any remaining members are initialized to zero.

```
Song_t yourSong = { "El Macho" };
```

After this definition, all members of yourSong have the value zero, except for the first member. The char arrays contain empty strings, and the member published contains the invalid date { 0, 0, 0 }.

The initializers may be nonconstant expressions if the structure object has automatic storage class. You can also initialize a new, automatic structure variable with an existing object of the same type:

```
Song_t yourSong = mySong;        // Valid initialization within a block
```

Initializing Specific Members

The C99 standard allows you to explicitly associate an initializer with a certain member. To do so, you must prefix a *member designator* with an equal sign to the initializer. The general form of a designator for the structure member *member* is:

```
.member                  // Member designator
```

The declaration in the following example initializes a Song_t object using the member designators .title and .composer:

```
Song_t aSong = { .title = "I've Just Seen a Face",
                 .composer = "John Lennon; Paul McCartney",
                 127
               };
```

The member designator `.title` is actually superfluous here because `title` is the first member of the structure. An initializer with no designator is associated with the first member, if it is the first initializer, or with the member that follows the last member initialized. Thus, in the previous example, the value `127` initializes the member `duration`. All other members of the structure have the initial value 0.

Structure Members in Memory

The members of a structure object are stored in memory in the order in which they are declared in the structure type's definition. The address of the first member is identical with the address of the structure object itself. The address of each member declared after the first one is greater than those of members declared earlier.

Sometimes it is useful to obtain the offset of a member from the beginning address of the structure. This offset, as a number of bytes, is given by the macro `offsetof`, defined in the header file *stddef.h*. The macro's arguments are the structure type and the name of the member:

```
offsetof(structure_type, member )
```

The result has the type `size_t`. As an example, if `pSong` is a pointer to a `Song_t` structure, then we can initialize the pointer `ptr` with the address of the first character in the member `composer`:

```
char *ptr = (char *)pSong + offsetof( Song_t, composer );
```

The compiler may align the members of a structure on certain kinds of addresses, such as 32-bit boundaries, to ensure fast access to the members. This step results in gaps, or unused bytes between the members. The compiler may also add extra bytes, commonly called *padding*, to the structure after the last member. As a result, the size of a structure can be greater than the sum of its members' sizes. You should always use the `sizeof` operator to obtain a structure's size, and the `offsetof` macro to obtain the positions of its members.

You can control the compiler's alignment of structure members—to avoid gaps between members, for example—by means of compiler options, such as the `-fpack-struct` flag for GCC, or the `/Zp1` command-line option or the pragma `pack(1)` for Visual C/C++. However, you should use these options only if your program places special requirements on the alignment of structure elements (for conformance to hardware interfaces, for example).

Programs need to determine the sizes of structures when allocating memory for objects, or when writing the contents of structure objects to a binary file. In the following example, `fp` is the `FILE` pointer to a file opened for writing binary data:

```
#include <stdio.h>              // Prototype of fwrite().

/* ... */

if ( fwrite( &aSong, sizeof(aSong), 1, fp ) < 1 )
    fprintf( stderr, "Error writing \"%s\".\n", aSong.title );
```

If the function call is successful, fwrite() writes one data object of size sizeof(aSong), beginning at the address &aSong, to the file opened with the FILE pointer fp.

Flexible Structure Members

C99 allows the last member of a structure with more than one member to have an incomplete array type—that is, the last member may be declared as an array of unspecified length. Such a structure member is called a *flexible array member*. In the following example, array is the name of a flexible member:

```
typedef struct { int len; float array[]; } DynArray_t;
```

There are only two cases in which the compiler gives special treatment to a flexible member:

- The size of a structure that ends in a flexible array member is equal to the offset of the flexible member. In other words, the flexible member is not counted in calculating the size of the structure (although any padding that precedes the flexible member is counted). For example, the expressions sizeof(DynArray_t) and offsetof(DynArray_t, array) yield the same value.

- When you access the flexible member using the dot or arrow operator (. or ->), you the programmer must make sure that the object in memory is large enough to contain the flexible member's value. You can do this by allocating the necessary memory dynamically. Here is an example:

    ```
    DynArray_t *daPtr = malloc(sizeof(DynArray_t) + 10*sizeof(float));
    ```

    This initialization reserves space for ten elements in the flexible array member. Now you can perform the following operations:

    ```
    daPtr->len = 10;
    for ( int i = 0; i < daPtr->len; ++i )
        daPtr->array[i] = 1.0F/(i+1);
    ```

    Because you have allocated space for only ten array elements in the flexible member, the following assignment is not permitted:

    ```
    daPtr->array[10] = 0.1F          // Invalid array index.
    ```

Although some implementations of the C standard library are aimed at making programs safer from such array index errors, you should avoid them by careful

---

programming. In all other operations, the flexible member of the structure is ignored, as in this structure assignment, for example:

```
DynArray_t da1;
da1 = *daPtr;
```

This assignment copies only the member len of the object addressed by daPtr, not the elements of the object's array member. In fact, the left operand, da1, doesn't even have storage space for the array. But even when the left operand of the assignment has sufficient space available, the flexible member is still ignored.

C99 also doesn't allow you to initialize a flexible structure member:

```
DynArray_t da1 = { 100 },                      // OK.
           da2 = { 3, { 1.0F, 0.5F, 0.25F } }; // Error.
```

Nonetheless, many compilers support language extensions that allow you to initialize a flexible structure member and generate an object of sufficient size to contain those elements that you initialize explicitly.

Pointers as Structure Members

To include data items that can vary in size in a structure, it is a good idea to use a pointer rather than including the actual data object in the structure. The pointer then addresses the data in a separate object for which you allocate the necessary storage space dynamically. Moreover, this indirect approach allows a structure to have more than one variable-length "member."

Pointers as structure members are also very useful in implementing dynamic data structures. The structure types SongList_t and Cell_t that we defined earlier in this chapter for the head and items of a list are an example:

```
// Structures for a list head and list items:

typedef struct { struct Cell *pFirst, *pLast; } SongList_t;

typedef struct Cell { struct Song song;    // The record data.
                      struct Cell *pNext;   // A pointer to the next
                                            // record.
                    } Cell_t;
```

Figure 10-1 illustrates the structure of a singly linked list made of these structures.

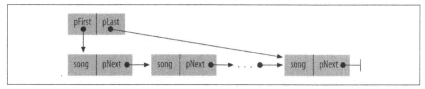

Figure 10-1. A singly linked list

Special attention is required when manipulating such structures. For example, it generally makes little sense to copy structure objects with pointer members, or to save them in files. Usually, the data referenced needs to be copied or saved, and the pointer to it does not. For example, if you want to initialize a new list, named your List, with the existing list myList, you probably don't want to do this:

```
SongList_t yourList = myList;
```

Such an initialization simply makes a copy of the pointers in myList without creating any new objects for yourList. To copy the list itself, you have to duplicate each object in it. The function cloneSongList(), defined in Example 10-3, does just that:

```
SongList_t yourList = cloneSongList( &myList );
```

The function cloneSongList() creates a new object for each item linked to myList, copies the item's contents to the new object, and links the new object to the new list. cloneSongList() calls appendSong() to do the actual creating and linking. If an error occurs, such as insufficient memory to duplicate all the list items, then clone SongList() releases the memory allocated up to that point and returns an empty list. The function clearSongList() destroys all the items in a list.

Example 10-3. The functions cloneSongList(), appendSong(), and clearSongList()

```
// The function cloneSongList() duplicates a linked list.
// Argument:     A pointer to the list head of the list to be cloned.
// Return value: The new list. If insufficient memory is available to
//               duplicate the entire list, the new list is empty.
#include "songs.h"    // Contains type definitions (Song_t, etc.) and
                      // function prototypes for song-list operations.

SongList_t cloneSongList( const SongList_t *pList )
{
  SongList_t newSL = { NULL, NULL };  // A new, empty list.

  Cell_t *pCell = pList->pFirst;      // We start with the first list item.
  while ( pCell != NULL && appendSong( &newSL, &pCell->song ))
    pCell = pCell->pNext;

  if ( pCell != NULL )              // If we didn't finish the last item,
    clearSongList( &newSL );        // discard any items cloned.

  return newSL;                     // In either case, return the list head.
}

// The function appendSong() dynamically allocates a new list item, copies
// the given song data to the new object, and appends it to the list.
// Arguments:   A pointer to a Song_t object to be copied, and a pointer
//              to a list to add the copy to.
// Return value: True if successful; otherwise, false.
```

```
bool appendSong( SongList_t *pList, const Song_t *pSong )
{
    Cell_t *pCell = calloc( 1, sizeof(Cell_t) );   // Create a new list item.

    if ( pCell == NULL )
        return false;                      // Failure: no memory.

    pCell->song  = *pSong;                 // Copy data to the new item.
    pCell->pNext = NULL;

    if ( pList->pFirst == NULL )           // If the list is still empty,
        pList->pFirst = pList->pLast = pCell;   // link a first (and last) item.
    else
    {                                      // If not,
        pList->pLast->pNext = pCell;       // insert a new last item.
        pList->pLast = pCell;
    }

    return true;                           // Success.
}

// The function clearSongList() destroys all the items in a list.
// Argument:   A pointer to the list head.

void clearSongList( SongList_t *pList )
{
    Cell_t *pCell, *pNextCell;
    for ( pCell = pList->pFirst; pCell != NULL; pCell = pNextCell )
    {
        pNextCell = pCell->pNext;
        free( pCell );              // Release the memory allocated for each item.
    }
    pList->pFirst = pList->pLast = NULL;
}
```

Before the function `clearSongList()` frees each item, it has to save the pointer to the item that follows; you can't read a structure object member after the object has been destroyed. The header file *songs.h* included in Example 10-3 is the place to put all the type definitions and function prototypes needed to implement and use the song list, including declarations of the functions defined in the example itself. The header *songs.h* must also include the header file *stdbool.h* because the `appendSong()` function uses the identifiers `bool`, `true`, and `false`.

Unions

Unlike structure members, which all have distinct locations in the structure, the members of a *union* all share the same location in memory; that is, all members of a union start at the same address. Thus, you can define a union with many members, but only one member can contain a value at any given time. Unions are an easy way for programmers to use a location in memory in different ways.

Defining Union Types

The definition of a union is formally the same as that of a structure, except for the keyword union in place of struct:

```
union [tag_name] { member_declaration_list };
```

The following example defines a union type named Data which has the three members i, x, and str:

```
union Data { int i; double x; char str[16]; };
```

An object of this type can store an integer, a floating-point number, or a short string. This declaration defines var as an object of type union Data, and myData as an array of 100 elements of type union Data (a union is at least as big as its largest member):

```
union Data var, myData[100];
```

To obtain the size of a union, use the sizeof operator. Using our example, sizeof(var) yields the value 16, and sizeof(myData) yields 1,600.

As Figure 10-2 illustrates, all the members of a union begin at the same address in memory.

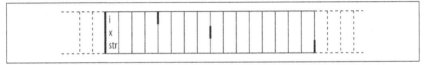

Figure 10-2. An object of the type union Data in memory

To illustrate how unions are different from structures, consider an object of the type struct Record with members i, x, and str, defined as follows:

```
struct Record { int i; double x; char str[16]; };
```

As Figure 10-3 shows, each member of a structure object has a separate location in memory.

Figure 10-3. An object of the type struct Record in memory

You can access the members of a union in the same ways as structure members. The only difference is that when you change the value of a union member, you modify all the members of the union. Here are a few examples using the union objects var and myData:

```
var.x = 3.21;
var.x += 0.5;
strcpy( var.str, "Jim" );          // Occupies the place of var.x.
myData[0].i = 50;
for ( int i = 0; i < 50; ++i )
  myData[i].i = 2 * i;
```

As for structures, the members of each union type form a name space unto themselves. Hence, in the last of these statements, the index variable i and the union member i identify two distinct objects.

You, the programmer, are responsible for making sure that the momentary contents of a union object are interpreted correctly. The different types of the union's members allow you to interpret the same collection of byte values in different ways. For example, the following loop uses a union to illustrate the storage of a double value in memory:

```
var.x = 1.25;

for ( int i = sizeof(double) - 1; i >= 0; --i )
  printf( "%02X ", (unsigned char)var.str[i] );
```

This loop begins with the highest byte of var.x, and generates the following output:

```
3F F4 00 00 00 00 00 00
```

Initializing Unions

Like structures, union objects are initialized by an *initialization list*. For a union, though, the list can only contain one *initializer*. As for structures, C99 allows the use of a member designator in the initializer to indicate which member of the union is being initialized. Furthermore, if the initializer has no member designator, then it is associated with the first member of the union. A union object with automatic storage class can also be initialized with an existing object of the same type. Here are some examples:

```
union Data var1 = { 77 },
           var2 = { .str = "Mary" },
           var3 = var1,
           myData[100] = { {.x= 0.5}, { 1 }, var2 };
```

The array elements of myData for which no initializer is specified are implicitly initialized to the value 0.

Anonymous Structures and Unions

Anonymous structures and unions are a new feature of the C11 standard that permits still greater flexibility in defining structure and union types. A structure or union is called *anonymous* if it is defined as an unnamed member of a structure or union type and has no tag name. In the following example, the second member of the union type WordByte is an anonymous structure type:

```
union WordByte
{
    short w;
    struct { char b0, b1 };        // Anonymous structure
};
```

The members of an anonymous structure or union are treated as members of the structure or union type that contains the anonymous type.

```
union WordByte wb = { 256 };
char lowByte = wb.b0;
```

This rule is applied recursively if the containing structure or union is also anonymous. The following example shows members in a nested anonymous type:

```
struct Demo
{
    union                        // Anonymous union
    { struct { long  a, b; };    // Anonymous structure
        struct { float x, y; } fl;  // Named member, not anonymous
    }
} dObj;
```

After this definition, the assignment dObj.a = 100; would be correct. However, you could not directly address x and y as members of dObj; they must be identified as members of dObj.fl:

```
dObj.a = 100;           // Right
dObj.y = 1.0;           // Wrong!
dObj.fl.y = 1.0;        // Right
```

Bit-Fields

Members of structures or unions can also be bit-fields. A *bit-field* is an integer variable that consists of a specified number of bits. If you declare several small bit-fields in succession, the compiler packs them into a single machine word. This permits very compact storage of small units of information. Of course, you can also manipulate individual bits using the bitwise operators, but bit-fields offer the advantage of handling bits by name, like any other structure or union member.

The declaration of a bit-field has the form:

type [*member_name*] : *width* ;

The parts of this syntax are as follows:

type
    An integer type that determines how the bit-field's value is interpreted. The type may be _Bool, int, signed int, unsigned int, or another type defined by the given implementation. The type may also include type qualifiers.

Bit-fields with type signed int are interpreted as signed; bit-fields whose type is unsigned int are interpreted as unsigned. Bit-fields of type int may be signed or unsigned, depending on the compiler.

member_name

The name of the bit-field, which is optional. If you declare a bit-field with no name, though, there is no way to access it. Nameless bit-fields can serve only as padding to align subsequent bit-fields to a certain position in a machine word.

width

The number of bits in the bit-field. The width must be a constant integer expression whose value is non-negative, and must be less than or equal to the bit width of the specified type.

Nameless bit-fields can have zero width. In this case, the next bit-field declared is aligned at the beginning of a new addressable storage unit.

When you declare a bit-field in a structure or union, the compiler allocates an addressable unit of memory that is large enough to accommodate it. Usually, the storage unit allocated is a machine word whose size is that of the type int. If the following bit-field fits in the rest of the same storage unit, then it is defined as being adjacent to the previous bit-field. If the next bit-field does not fit in the remaining bits of the same unit, then the compiler allocates another storage unit, and may place the next bit-field at the start of new unit, or wrap it across the end of one storage unit and the beginning of the next.

The following example redefines the structure type struct Date so that the members month and day occupy only as many bits as necessary. To demonstrate a bit-field of type _Bool, we have also added a flag for daylight saving time. This code assumes that the target machine uses words of at least 32 bits:

```
struct Date {
    unsigned int month : 4;     // 1 is January; 12 is December.
    unsigned int day   : 5;     // The day of the month (1 to 31).
    signed int   year  : 22;    // (-2097152 to +2097151)
    _Bool        isDST : 1;     // True if daylight saving time is in effect.
};
```

A bit-field of n bits can have 2^n distinct values. The structure member month now has a value range from 0 to 15; the member day has the value range from 0 to 31; and the value range of the member year is from -2097152 to +2097151. We can initialize an object of type struct Date in the normal way, using an initialization list:

```
struct Date birthday = { 5, 17, 1982 };
```

The object birthday occupies the same amount of storage space as a 32-bit int object. Unlike other structure members, bit-fields generally do not occupy an addressable location in memory. You cannot apply the address operator (&) or the offsetof macro to a bit-field.

In all other respects, however, you can treat bit-fields the same as other structure or union members; use the dot and arrow operators to access them, and perform arithmetic with them as with int or unsigned int variables. As a result, the new definition of the Date structure using bit-fields does not necessitate any changes in the dateAsString() function:

```
const char *dateAsString( struct Date d )
{
  static char strDate[12];
  sprintf( strDate, "%02d/%02d/%04d", d.month, d.day, d.year );
  return strDate;
}
```

The following statement calls the dateAsString() function for the object birthday, and prints the result using the standard function puts():

```
puts( dateAsString( birthday ));
```

11

Declarations

A *declaration* determines the significance and properties of one or more identifiers. _Static_assert declarations, introduced in C11, are an exception: these *static assertions* do not declare identifiers, but only instruct the compiler to test whether a constant expression is nonzero. Static assertions are only classed as declarations because of their syntax.

In other declarations, the identifiers you declare can be the names of objects, functions, types, or other things, such as enumeration constants. Identifiers of objects and functions can have various types and scopes. The compiler needs to know all of these characteristics of an identifier before you can use it in an expression. For this reason, each translation unit must contain a declaration of each identifier used in it.

Labels used as the destination of goto statements may be placed before any statement. These identifiers are declared implicitly where they occur. All other identifiers require explicit declaration before their first use, either outside of all functions or at the beginning of a block. Beginning with C99, declarations may also appear after statements within a block.

After you have declared an identifier, you can use it in expressions until the end of its scope. The identifiers of objects and functions can have *file* or *block scope* (see "Identifier Scope" on page 17).

There are several different kinds of declarations:

- Declarations that only declare a structure, union, or enumeration tag, or the members of an enumeration (that is, the enumeration constants)
- Declarations that declare one or more object or function identifiers

- `typedef` declarations, which declare new names for existing types
- `_Static_assert` declarations, which instruct the compiler to test an assertion without declaring an identifier (C11)

Declarations of enumerated, structure, and union types are described in Chapters 2 and 10. This chapter deals mainly with object, function, and `typedef` declarations.

Object and Function Declarations

These declarations contain a *declarator list* with one or more declarators. Each declarator declares an identifier for an object or a function. The general form of this kind of declaration is:

```
[storage_class_specifier] type declarator [, declarator [, ...]];
```

The parts of this syntax are as follows:

storage_class_specifier
> No more than one of the storage class specifiers `extern`, `static`, `_Thread_local`, `auto`, or `register`, or the specifier `_Thread_local` in conjunction with `extern` or `static`. The exact meanings of the storage class specifiers, and restrictions on their use, are described in "Storage Class Specifiers" on page 178.

type
> At least a type specifier, possibly with type qualifiers. The type specifier may be any of these:
>
> - A basic type
> - The type `void`
> - An enumerated, structure, or union type
> - A name defined by a previous `typedef` declaration
>
> In a function declaration, *type* may also include one of the type specifiers `inline` or `_Noreturn`.
>
> In an object declaration, *type* may also contain one or more of the type qualifiers `const`, `volatile`, and `restrict`. In C11 implementations that support atomic objects, an object declaration may declare the object as atomic by using the type qualifier `_Atomic`, or by using a type specifier of the form `_Atomic(type_name)`. The various type qualifiers are described with examples in "Type Qualifiers" on page 180.
>
> The C11 keyword `_Alignas` allows you to influence the alignment of objects you declare. For more on the alignment of objects, see "The Alignment of Objects in Memory" on page 36.

declarator

The declarator list is a comma-separated list containing at least one declarator. A declarator names the identifier that is being declared. If the declarator defines an object, it may also include an initializer for the identifier. There are four different kinds of declarators:

Function declarator

The identifier is declared as a function name if it is immediately followed by a left parenthesis (().

Array declarator

The identifier is declared as an array name if it is immediately followed by a left bracket ([).

Pointer declarator

The identifier is the name of a pointer if it is preceded by an asterisk (*)—possibly with interposed type qualifiers—and if the declarator is neither a function nor an array declarator.

Other

Otherwise, the identifier designates an object of the specified type.

A declarator in parentheses is equivalent to the same declarator without the parentheses, and the rules listed here assume that declarations contain no unnecessary parentheses. However, you can use parentheses intentionally in declarations to control the associations between the syntax elements described. We will discuss this in detail in "Complex Declarators" on page 182.

Examples

Let us examine some examples of object and function declarations. We discuss declarations of `typedef` names in "typedef Declarations" on page 185.

In the following example, the declarator list in the first line contains two declarators, one of which includes an initializer. The line declares two objects, iVar1 and iVar2, both with type int. iVar2 begins its existence with the value 10:

```
int iVar1, iVar2 = 10;
static char msg[] = "Hello, world!";
```

The second line in this example defines and initializes an array of char named msg with static storage duration (we discuss storage duration in "Storage Class Specifiers" on page 178).

Next, you see the declaration of an external variable named status with the qualified type volatile short:

```
extern volatile short status;
```

The next declaration defines an anonymous enumerated type with the enumeration constants OFF and ON, as well as the variable toggle with this type. The declaration initializes toggle with the value ON:

```
enum { OFF, ON } toggle = ON;
```

The following example defines the structure type struct CharColor, whose members are the bit-fields fg, bg, and bl. It also defines the variable attribute with this type, and initializes the members of attribute with the values 12, 1, and 0.

```
struct CharColor { unsigned fg:4, bg:3, bl:1; } attribute = {12, 1, 0};
```

The second line of the next example defines an array named clientArray with 100 elements of type struct Client, and a pointer to struct Client named clientPtr, initialized with the address of the first element in clientArray:

```
struct Client { char name[64], pin[16]; /* ... */ };
struct Client clientArray[100], *clientPtr = clientArray;
```

Next you see a declaration of a float variable, x, and an array, flPtrArray, whose 10 elements have the type pointer to float. The first of these pointers, flPtrArray[0], is initialized with &x; the remaining array elements are initialized as null pointers:

```
float x, *flPtrArray[10] = { &x };
```

The following line declares the function func1() with the return value type int. This declaration offers no information about the number and types of the function's parameters, if any:

```
int func1();
```

We'll move on to the declaration of a static function named func2(), whose only parameter has the type pointer to double, and which also returns a pointer to double:

```
static double *func2( double * );
```

Last, we define the inline function printAmount(), with two parameters, returning int:

```
inline int printAmount( double amount, int width )
{ return printf( "%*.2lf", width, amount ); }
```

Storage Class Specifiers

A *storage class specifier* in a declaration modifies the linkage of the identifier (or identifiers) declared, and the storage duration of the corresponding objects. (The concepts of linkage and storage duration are explained individually in later sections of this chapter.)

A frequent source of confusion in regard to C is the fact that linkage (which is a property of identifiers) and storage duration (which is a property of objects) are both influenced in declarations by the same set of keywords—the storage class specifiers. As we explain in the upcoming sections of this chapter, the storage duration of an object can be automatic, static, or allocated, and the linkage of an identifer can be external, internal, or none. Expressions such as "static linkage" or "external storage" in the context of C declarations are meaningless except as warning signs of incipient confusion. Remember: objects have storage duration, not linkage; and identifiers have linkage, not storage duration.

No more than one storage class specifier may appear in a declaration. Function identifiers may be accompanied only by the storage class specifier `extern` or `static`. Function parameters may take only the storage class specifier `register`. The five storage class specifiers have the following meanings:

auto

> Objects declared with the `auto` specifier have automatic storage duration. This specifier is permissible only in object declarations within a function. In ANSI C, objects declared within a function have automatic storage duration by default, and the `auto` specifier is archaic.

register

> You can use the specifier `register` when declaring objects with automatic storage duration. The `register` keyword is a hint to the compiler that the object should be made as quickly accessible as possible—ideally, by storing it in a CPU register. However, the compiler may treat some or all objects declared with `register` the same as ordinary objects with automatic storage duration. In any case, programs must not use the address operator on objects declared with the `register` specifier.

static

> A function identifier declared with the specifier `static` has internal linkage. In other words, such an identifier cannot be used in another translation unit to access the function.

> An object identifier declared with `static` has either no linkage or internal linkage, depending on whether the object's definition is inside a function or outside all functions. Objects declared with `static` always have static storage duration. Thus, the specifier `static` allows you to define local objects—that is, objects with block scope—that have static storage duration.

extern

> Function and object identifiers declared with the `extern` specifier have external linkage. You can use them anywhere in the entire program. External objects have static storage duration.

_Thread_local

The specifier _Thread_local declares the given object as *thread-local*, which means that each thread has its own separate instance of the object. Only objects can be declared as thread-local, not functions. If you declare a thread-local object within a function, the declaration must also have either the extern or the static specifier. In expressions, the identifier of a thread-local object always refers to the local instance of the object belonging to the thread in which the expression is being evaluated. For an example, see "Using Thread-Local Objects" on page 257.

Type Qualifiers

You can modify types in a declaration by including the type qualifiers const, volatile, restrict, and _Atomic. A declaration may contain any number of type qualifiers in any order. A type qualifier list may even contain the same type qualifier several times, or the same qualifier may be applied repeatedly through qualified typedef names. The compiler ignores such repetitions of any qualifier, treating them as if the qualifier were present only once.

The individual type qualifiers have the following meanings:

const

An object whose type is qualified with const is constant; the program cannot modify it after its definition.

volatile

An object whose type is qualified with volatile may be modified by other processes or events. The volatile keyword instructs the compiler to reread the object's value each time it is used, even if the program itself has not changed it since the previous access. This is most commonly used in programming for hardware interfaces, where a value can be changed by external events.

restrict

The restrict qualifier is applicable only to object pointer types. The type qualifier restrict was introduced in C99, and is a hint to the compiler that the object referenced by a given pointer, if it is modified at all, will not be accessed in any other way except using that pointer, whether directly or indirectly. This feature allows the compiler to apply certain optimization techniques that would not be possible without such a restriction. The compiler may ignore the restrict qualifier without affecting the result of the program.

_Atomic

An object declared with the type qualifier _Atomic is an *atomic object*. Arrays cannot be atomic. Support for atomic objects is optional: C11 implementations may define the macro __STDC_NO_ATOMICS__ to indicate that programs cannot declare atomic objects. For more information about atomic objects, see "Atomic Objects" on page 247.

The compiler may store objects qualified as const but not volatile, in a read-only segment of memory. It may also happen that the compiler allocates no storage for such an object if the program does not use its address.

Objects qualified with both const and volatile, such as the object ticks in the following example, cannot be modified by the program itself but may be modified by something else, such as a clock chip's interrupt handler:

```
extern const volatile int ticks;
```

Here are some more examples of declarations using qualified types:

```
const int limit = 10000;                  // A constant int object.
typedef struct { double x, y, r; } Circle; // A structure type.
const Circle unit_circle = { 0, 0, 1 };   // A constant Circle object.
const float v[] = { 1.0F, 0.5F, 0.25F };  // An array of constant
                                          // float elements.
volatile short * restrict vsPtr;          // A restricted pointer to
                                          // volatile short.
```

With pointer types, the type qualifiers to the right of the asterisk qualify the pointer itself, and those to the left of the asterisk qualify the type of object it points to. In the last example, the pointer vsPtr is qualified with restrict, and the object it points to is qualified with volatile. For more details, including more about restricted pointers, see "Pointers and Type Qualifiers" on page 148.

Declarations and Definitions

You can declare an identifier as often as you want, but only one declaration within its scope can be a definition. Placing the definitions of objects and functions with external linkage in header files is a common way of introducing duplicate definitions and is therefore not a good idea.

An identifier's declaration is a *definition* in the following cases:

- A function declaration is a definition if it contains the function block. Here is an example:

```
int iMax( int a, int b );   // This is a declaration, not a
                            // definition.
int iMax( int a, int b )    // This is the function's definition.
{ return ( a >= b ? a : b ); }
```

- An object declaration is a definition if it allocates storage for the object. Declarations that include initializers are always definitions. Furthermore, all declarations within function blocks are definitions unless they contain the storage class specifier extern. Here are some examples:

```
int a = 10;            // Definition of a.
extern double b[];     // Declaration of the array b, which is
                       // defined elsewhere in the program.
void func()
{
```

```
        extern char c;          // Declaration of c, not a definition.
        static short d;         // Definition of d.
        float e;                // Definition of e.
        /* ... */
    }
```

If you declare an object outside of all functions, without an initializer and without the storage class specifier extern, the declaration is a *tentative definition*. Here are some examples:

```
    int i, v[];                 // Tentative definitions of i, v and j.
    static int j;
```

A tentative definition of an identifier remains a simple declaration if the translation unit contains another definition for the same identifier. If not, then the compiler behaves as if the tentative definition had included an initializer with the value zero, making it a definition. Thus, the int variables i and j in the previous example, whose identifiers are declared without initializers, are implicitly initialized with the value 0, and the int array v has one element, with the initial value 0.

Complex Declarators

The symbols (), [ ], and * in a declarator specify that the identifier has a function, array, or pointer type. A *complex declarator* may contain multiple occurrences of any or all of these symbols. This section explains how to interpret such declarators.

The basic symbols in a declarator have the following meanings:

()

    A function whose return value has the type...

[ ]

    An array whose elements have the type...

*

    A pointer to the type...

In declarators, these symbols have the same priority and associativity as the corresponding operators would have in an expression. Furthermore, as in expressions, you can use additional parentheses to modify the order in which they are interpreted. Here is an example:

```
    int *abc[10];       // An array of 10 elements whose
                        // type is pointer to int.
    int (*abc)[10];     // A pointer to a array of 10
                        // elements whose type is int.
```

In a declarator that involves a function type, the parentheses that indicate a function may contain the parameter declarations. The following example declares a pointer to a function type:

```
int (*fPtr)(double x);      // fPtr is a pointer to a function that has
                            // one double parameter and returns int.
```

The declarator must include declarations of the function parameters if it is part of the function definition.

When interpreting a complex declarator, always begin with the identifier. Starting from there, repeat the following steps in order until you have interpreted all the symbols in the declarator:

1. If a left parenthesis (() or bracket ([) appears immediately to the *right*, then interpret the pair of parentheses or brackets.

2. Otherwise, if an asterisk (*) appears to the *left*, interpret the asterisk.

Here is an example:

```
extern char *(* fTab[])(void);
```

Table 11-1 interprets this example bit by bit. The third column is meant to be read from the top row down, as a sentence.

Table 11-1. Interpretation of extern char *(* fTab[ ])(void);

Step	Symbols interpreted	Meaning (read this column from the top down, as a sentence)
1. Start with the identifier.	fTab	fTab is...
2. Brackets to the right.	fTab[]	an array whose elements have the type...
3. Asterisk to the left.	(* fTab[])	pointer to...
4. Function parentheses (and parameter list) to the right.	(* fTab[])(void)	a function, with no parameters, whose return value has the type...
5. Asterisk to the left.	*(* fTab[])(void)	pointer to...
6. No more asterisks, parentheses, or brackets: read the type name.	char *(* fTab[])(void)	char.

fTab has an incomplete array type because the declaration does not specify the array length. Before you can use the array, you must define it elsewhere in the program with a specific length.

The parentheses around *fTab[] are necessary. Without them, fTab would be declared as an array whose elements are functions—which is impossible.

The next example shows the declaration of a function identifier, followed by its interpretation:

```
float (* func())[3][10];
```

The identifier func is...
a function whose return value has the type...
pointer to...
an array of three elements of type...
array of ten elements of type...
float.

In other words, the function func returns a pointer to a two-dimensional array of 3 rows and 10 columns. Here again, the parentheses around * func() are necessary, as without them the function would be declared as returning an array—which is impossible.

Type Names

To convert a value explicitly from one type to another using the cast operator, you must specify the new type by name. For example, in the cast expression (char *)ptr, the type name is char * (read: "char pointer" or "pointer to char"). When you use a type name as the operand of sizeof, it appears the same way, in parentheses. Function prototype declarations also designate a function's parameters by their type names, even if the parameters themselves have no names.

The syntax of a type name is like that of an object or function declaration, but with no identifier (and no storage class specifier). Here are two simple examples to start with:

unsigned char
    The type unsigned char

unsigned char *
    The type "pointer to unsigned char"

In the examples that follow, the type names are more complex. Each type name contains at least one asterisk (*) for "pointer to," as well as parentheses or brackets. To interpret a complex type name, start with the first pair of brackets or parentheses that you find to the right of the last asterisk. (If you were parsing a declarator with an identifier rather than a type name, the identifier would be immediately to the left of those brackets or parentheses.) If the type name includes a function type, then the parameter declarations must be interpreted separately:

float *[]
    The type "array of pointers to float." The number of elements in the array is undetermined.

float (*)[10]
    The type "pointer to an array of ten elements whose type is float."

```
double *(double *)
```
   The type "function whose only parameter has the type pointer to double, and which also returns a pointer to double."

```
double (*)()
```
   The type "pointer to a function whose return value has the type double." The number and types of the function's parameters are not specified.

```
int *(*(*)[10])(void)
```
   The type "pointer to an array of ten elements whose type is pointer to a function with no parameters which returns a pointer to int."

typedef Declarations

The easy way to use types with complex names, such as those described in the previous section, is to declare simple synonyms for them. You can do this using typedef declarations.

A typedef declaration starts with the keyword typedef, followed by the normal syntax of an object or function declaration, except that no storage class or _Alignas specifiers and no initializers are permitted.

Each declarator in a typedef declaration defines an identifier as a synonym for the specified type. The identifier is then called a *typedef name* for that type. Without the keyword typedef, the same syntax would declare an object or function of the given type. Here are some examples:

```
typedef unsigned int UINT, UINT_FUNC();
typedef struct Point { double x, y; } Point_t;
typedef float Matrix_t[3][10];
```

In the scope of these declarations, UINT is synonymous with unsigned int, and Point_t is synonymous with the structure type struct Point. You can use the typedef names in declarations, as the following examples show:

```
UINT ui = 10, *uiPtr = &ui;
```

The variable ui has the type unsigned int, and uiPtr is a pointer to unsigned int.

```
UINT_FUNC *funcPtr;
```

The pointer funcPtr can refer to a function whose return value has the type unsigned int. The function's parameters are not specified:

```
Matrix_t *func( float * );
```

The function func() has one parameter, whose type is pointer to float, and returns a pointer to the type Matrix_t.

Example 11-1 uses the typedef name of one structure type, Point_t, in the typedef definition of a second structure type.

Example 11-1. typedef declarations

```
typedef struct Point { double x, y; } Point_t;
typedef struct { Point_t top_left; Point_t bottom_right; } Rectangle_t;
```

Ordinarily, you would use a header file to hold the definitions of any typedef names that you need to use in multiple source files. However, you must make an exception in the case of typedef declarations for types that contain a variable-length array. Variable-length arrays can only be declared within a block, and the actual length of the array is calculated anew each time the flow of program execution reaches the typedef declaration. Here is an example:

```
int func( int size )
{
  typedef float VLA[size]; // A typedef name for the type "array of
                           // float whose length is the value of size."
  size *= 2;
  VLA temp;                 // An array of float whose length is the
                           // value that size had
                           // in the typedef declaration.
  /* ... */
}
```

The length of the array temp in this example depends on the value that size had when the typedef declaration was reached, not the value that size has when the array definition is reached.

One advantage of typedef declarations is that they help to make programs more easily portable. Types that are necessarily different on different system architectures, for example, can be called by uniform typedef names. typedef names are also helpful in writing human-readable code. As an example, consider the prototype of the standard library function qsort():

```
void qsort( void *base, size_t count, size_t size,
            int (*compare)( const void *, const void * ));
```

We can make this prototype much more readable by using a typedef name for the comparison function's type:

```
typedef int CmpFn( const void *, const void * );
void qsort( void *base, size_t count, size_t size, CmpFn *compare );
```

_Static_assert Declarations

The _Static_assert declaration, introduced in C11, is a special case among declarations. It is only an instruction to the compiler to test an assertion, and does not declare an identifier at all. A static assertion has the following syntax:

```
_Static_assert( constant_expression , string_literal );
```

The assertion to be tested, *constant_expression*, must be a constant expression with an integer type (see "Integer Constants" on page 39). If the expression is true—

that is, if its value is not 0—the _Static_assert declaration has no effect. If the evaluation of the expression yields the value 0, however, the compiler generates a error message containing the specified string literal. The string literal should contain only characters of the basic source character set, as extended characters are not necessarily displayed. In the following example, a static assertion ensures that objects of the type int are bigger than two bytes:

```
_Static_assert( sizeof(int) > 2 , "16-bit code not supported");
```

If the type int is only two bytes wide, the compiler's error message may look like this:

```
demo.c(10): fatal error:
Static assertion failed: "16-bit code not supported".
```

If you include the header *assert.h* in your program, you can also use the synonym static_assert in place of the keyword _Static_assert.

The new capability of testing an assertion at compile time is an addition to the two related techniques:

- The macro assert, described in Chapter 18, which tests an assertion during the program's execution
- The preprocessor directive #error, described in Chapter 15, which makes the preprocessor exit with an error message on a condition specified using an #if directive

Linkage of Identifiers

An identifier that is declared in several translation units, or several times in the same translation unit, may refer to the same object or function in each instance. The extent of an identifier's identity in and among translation units is determined by the identifier's *linkage*. The term reflects the fact that identifiers in separate source files need to be linked if they are to refer to a common object.

Identifiers in C have either *external, internal,* or *no linkage.* The linkage is determined by the declaration's position and storage class specifier, if any. Only object and function identifiers can have external or internal linkage.

External Linkage

An identifier with external linkage represents the same function or object throughout the program. The compiler presents such identifiers to the linker, which resolves them with other occurrences in other translation units and libraries.

Function and object identifiers declared with the storage class specifier extern have external linkage, with one exception: if an identifier has already been declared with internal linkage, a second declaration within the scope of the first cannot change the identifier's linkage to external.

The compiler treats function declarations without a storage class specifier as if they included the specifier extern. Similarly, any object identifiers that you declare outside all functions and without a storage class specifier have external linkage.

Internal Linkage

An identifier with internal linkage represents the same object or function within a given translation unit. The identifier is not presented to the linker. As a result, you cannot use the identifier in another translation unit to refer to the same object or function.

A function or object identifier has internal linkage if it is declared outside all functions and with the storage class specifier static.

Identifiers with internal linkage do not conflict with similar identifiers in other translation units. If you declare an identifier with internal linkage in a given translation unit, you cannot also declare and use an external identifier with the same spelling in that translation unit.

No Linkage

All identifiers that have neither external nor internal linkage have no linkage. Each declaration of such an identifier therefore introduces a new entity. Identifiers with no linkage include the following:

- Identifiers that are not names of variables or functions, such as label names, structure tags, and typedef names
- Function parameters
- Object identifiers that are declared within a function and without the storage class specifier extern

Here are a few examples:

```
int func1( void );       // func1 has external linkage.
int a;                   // a has external linkage.
extern int b = 1;        // b has external linkage.
static int c;            // c has internal linkage.

static void func2( int d ) // func2 has internal linkage; d has no
                         // linkage.
{
  extern int a;          // This a is the same as that above, with
                         // external linkage.
  int b = 2;             // This b has no linkage, and hides the
                         // external b declared above.
  extern int c;          // This c is the same as that above, and
                         // retains internal linkage.
  static int e;          // e has no linkage.
  /* ... */
}
```

As this example illustrates, an identifier with external or internal linkage is not always visible. The identifier b with no linkage, declared in the function func2(), hides the identifier b with external linkage until the end of the function block (see "Identifier Scope" on page 17).

Storage Duration of Objects

During the execution of the program, each object exists as a location in memory for a certain period, called its *lifetime*. There is no way to access an object before or after its lifetime. For example, the value of a pointer becomes invalid when the object that it references reaches the end of its lifetime.

In C, the lifetime of an object is determined by its *storage duration*. Objects in C have one of four kinds of storage duration: *static*, *thread*, *automatic*, or *allocated*. The C standard does not specify how objects must be physically stored in any given system architecture, but typically, objects with static or thread storage duration are located in a data segment of the program, and objects with automatic storage duration are located on the stack. Allocated storage is memory that the program obtains at runtime by calling the malloc(), calloc(), and realloc() functions. Dynamic storage allocation is described in Chapter 12.

Static Storage Duration

Objects that are defined outside all functions, or within a function and with the storage class specifier static, have static storage duration. These include all objects whose identifiers have internal or external linkage.

All objects with static storage duration are generated and initialized before execution of the program begins. Their lifetime spans the program's entire runtime.

Thread Storage Duration

Objects defined with the storage class specifier _Thread_local are called *thread-local* objects and have thread storage duration. The storage duration of a thread-local object is the entire runtime of the thread for which it is created. Each thread has its own separate instance of a thread-local object, which is initialized when the thread starts.

Automatic Storage Duration

Objects defined within a function and with no storage class specifier (or with the unnecessary specifier auto) have automatic storage duration. Function parameters also have automatic storage duration. Objects with automatic storage duration are generally called *automatic variables* for short.

The lifetime of an automatic object is delimited by the braces ({}) that begin and end the block in which the object is defined. Variable-length arrays are an exception: their lifetime begins at the point of declaration, and ends with the identifier's scope—that is, at the end of the block containing the declaration, or when a jump occurs to a point before the declaration.

Each time the flow of program execution enters a block, new instances of any automatic objects defined in the block are generated (and initialized, if the declaration includes an initializer). This fact is important in recursive functions, for example.

Initialization

You can explicitly specify an object's initial value by including an initializer in its definition. An object defined without an initializer either has an undetermined initial value, or is implicitly initialized by the compiler.

Implicit Initialization

Objects with automatic storage duration have an undetermined initial value if their definition does not include an initializer. Function parameters, which also have automatic storage duration, are initialized with the argument values when the function call occurs. All other objects have static storage duration, and are implicitly initialized with the default value 0, unless their definition includes an explicit initializer. Or, to put it more exactly:

- Objects with an arithmetic type have the default initial value 0.
- The default initial value of pointer objects is a null pointer (see "Initializing Pointers" on page 144).

The compiler applies these rules recursively in initializing array elements, structure members, and the first members of unions.

Explicit Initialization

An initializer in an object definition specifies the object's initial value explicitly. The initializer is appended to the declarator for the object's identifier with an equals sign (=). The initializer can be either a single expression or a list of initializer expressions enclosed in braces.

For objects with a scalar type, the initializer is a single expression:

```
#include <string.h>                  // Prototypes of string functions.
double var = 77, *dPtr = &var;
int (*funcPtr)( const char*, const char* ) = strcmp;
```

The initializers here are 77 for the variable var, and &var for the pointer dPtr. The function pointer funcPtr is initialized with the address of the standard library function strcmp().

As in an assignment operation, the initializer must be an expression that can be implicitly converted to the object's type. In the previous example, the constant value 77, with type int, is implicitly converted to the type double.

Objects with an array, structure, or union type are initialized with a comma-separated list containing initializers for their individual elements or members:

```
short a[4] = { 1, 2, 2*2, 2*2*2 };
Rectangle_t rect1 = { { -1, 1 }, { 1, -1 } };
```

The type Rectangle_t used here is the typedef name of the structure we defined in Example 11-1, whose members are structures with the type Point_t.

The initializers for objects with static storage duration must be constant expressions, as in the previous examples. Automatic objects are not subject to this restriction. You can also initialize an automatic structure or union object with an existing object of the same type:

```
#include <string.h>           // Prototypes of string functions.
/* ... */
void  func( const char *str )
{
  size_t len = strlen( str );  // Call a function to initialize len.
  Rectangle_t rect2 = rect1;   // Refers to rect1 from the previous
                               // example.
  /* ... */
}
```

More details on initializing arrays, structures, and unions, including the initialization of strings and the use of element designators, are presented in "Initializing Arrays" on page 132, "Initializing Structures" on page 164, and "Initializing Unions" on page 171.

Objects declared with the type qualifier const ordinarily must have an initializer, as you can't assign them the desired value later. However, a declaration that is not a definition, such as the declaration of an external identifier, must not include an initializer. Furthermore, you cannot initialize a variable-length array.

```
void func( void )
{
  extern int n;              // Declaration of n, not a definition.
  char buf[n];               // buf is a variable-length array.
  /* ... */
}
```

The declarations of the objects n and buf cannot include initializers.

12

Dynamic Memory Management

When you're writing a program, you often don't know how much data it will have to process, or you can anticipate that the amount of data to process will vary widely. In these cases, efficient resource use demands that you allocate memory only as you actually need it at runtime, and release it again as soon as possible. This is the principle of dynamic memory management, which also has the advantage that a program doesn't need to be rewritten in order to process larger amounts of data on a system with more available memory.

This chapter describes dynamic memory management in C, and demonstrates the most important functions involved using a general-purpose binary tree implementation as an example.

The standard library provides the following four functions for dynamic memory management:

`malloc()`, `calloc()`
    Allocate a new block of memory.

`realloc()`
    Resize an allocated memory block.

`free()`
    Release allocated memory.

All of these functions are declared in the header file *stdlib.h*. The size of an object in memory is specified as a number of bytes. Various header files, including *stdlib.h*, define the type `size_t` specifically to hold information of this kind. The `sizeof` operator, for example, yields a number of bytes with the type `size_t`.

Allocating Memory Dynamically

The two functions for allocating memory, `malloc()` and `calloc()`, have slightly different parameters:

`void *malloc( size_t `*`size`*` );`

    The `malloc()` function reserves a contiguous memory block whose size in bytes is at least *size*. When a program obtains a memory block through `malloc()`, its contents are undetermined.

`void *calloc( size_t `*`count`*`, size_t `*`size`*` );`

    The `calloc()` function reserves a block of memory whose size in bytes is at least *count* × *size*. In other words, the block is large enough to hold an array of *count* elements, each of which takes up *size* bytes. Furthermore, `calloc()` initializes every byte of the memory with the value 0.

Both functions return a pointer to `void`, also called a *typeless pointer*. The pointer's value is the address of the first byte in the memory block allocated, or a null pointer if the memory requested is not available.

When a program assigns the `void` pointer to a pointer variable of a different type, the compiler implicitly performs the appropriate type conversion. Some programmers prefer to use an explicit type conversion, however.[1] When you access locations in the allocated memory block, the type of the pointer you use determines how the contents of the location are interpreted.

Here are some examples:

```
#include <stdlib.h>                      // Provides function prototypes.
typedef struct { long key;
                 /* ... more members ... */
               } Record;                 // A structure type.

float *myFunc( size_t n )
{
  // Reserve storage for an object of type double.
  double *dPtr = malloc( sizeof(double) );
  if ( dPtr == NULL )                    // Insufficient memory.
  {
    /* ... Handle the error ... */
    return NULL;
  }
  else                                   // Got the memory: use it.
  {
    *dPtr = 0.07;
    /* ... */
  }
```

---

1 Perhaps in part for historic reasons: in early C dialects, `malloc()` returned a pointer to `char`.

```
// Get storage for two objects of type Record.
Record *rPtr;
if  ( ( rPtr = malloc( 2 * sizeof(Record) ) ) == NULL )
{
   /* ... Handle the insufficient-memory error ... */
   return NULL;
}
// Get storage for an array of n elements of type float.
float *fPtr = malloc( n * sizeof(float) );
if ( fPtr == NULL )
  {
   /* ... Handle the error ... */
   return NULL;
  }
/* ... */
  return fPtr;
}
```

It is often useful to initialize every byte of the allocated memory block to zero, which ensures that not only the members of a structure object have the default value zero but also any padding between the members. In such cases, the calloc() function is preferable to malloc(), although it may be slower, depending on the implementation. The size of the block to be allocated is expressed differently with the calloc() function. We can rewrite the statements in the previous example as follows:

```
// Get storage for an object of type double.
double *dPtr = calloc( 1, sizeof(double) );

// Get storage for two objects of type Record.
Record *rPtr;
if  ( ( rPtr = calloc( 2, sizeof(Record) ) ) == NULL )
{ /* ... Handle the insufficient-memory error ... */  }

// Get storage for an array of n elements of type float.
float *fPtr = calloc( n, sizeof(float));
```

Characteristics of Allocated Memory

A successful memory allocation call yields a pointer to the beginning of a memory block. "The beginning" means that the pointer's value is equal to the lowest byte address in the block. The allocated block is aligned so that any type of object can be stored at that address.

An allocated memory block stays reserved for your program until you explicitly release it by calling free() or realloc(). In other words, the storage duration of the block extends from its allocation to its release, or to end of the program.

The arrangement of memory blocks allocated by successive calls to malloc(), calloc(), and/or realloc() is unspecified.

It is also unspecified whether a request for a block of size zero results in a null pointer or an ordinary pointer value. In any case, however, there is no way to use a pointer to a block of zero bytes, except perhaps as an argument to `realloc()` or `free()`.

Resizing and Releasing Memory

When you no longer need a dynamically allocated memory block, you should give it back to the operating system. You can do this by calling the function `free()`. Alternatively, you can increase or decrease the size of an allocated memory block by calling the function `realloc()`. The prototypes of these functions are as follows:

`void free( void *ptr );`
> The `free()` function releases the dynamically allocated memory block that begins at the address in `ptr`. A null pointer value for the `ptr` argument is permitted, and such a call has no effect.

`void *realloc( void *ptr, size_t size );`
> The `realloc()` function releases the memory block addressed by `ptr` and allocates a new block of `size` bytes, returning its address. The new block may start at the same address as the old one.
>
> `realloc()` also preserves the contents of the original memory block—up to the size of whichever block is smaller. If the new block doesn't begin where the original one did, then `realloc()` copies the contents to the new memory block. If the new memory block is larger than the original, then the values of the additional bytes are unspecified.
>
> It is permissible to pass a null pointer to `realloc()` as the argument `ptr`. If you do, then `realloc()` behaves similarly to `malloc()`, and reserves a new memory block of the specified size.
>
> The `realloc()` function returns a null pointer if it is unable to allocate a memory block of the size requested. In this case, it does not release the original memory block or alter its contents.

The pointer argument that you pass to either of the functions `free()` and `realloc()`—if it is not a null pointer—must be the starting address of a dynamically allocated memory block that has not yet been freed. In other words, you may pass these functions only a null pointer or a pointer value obtained from a prior call to `malloc()`, `calloc()`, or `realloc()`. If the pointer argument passed to `free()` or `realloc()` has any other value, or if you try to free a memory block that has already been freed, the program's behavior is undefined.

The memory management functions keep internal records of the size of each allocated memory block. This is why the functions `free()` and `realloc()` require only the starting address of the block to be released, and not its size. There is no way to test whether a call to the free() function is successful, because it has no return value.

The function getLine() in Example 12-1 is another variant of the function defined with the same name in Example 9-4. It reads a line of text from standard input and stores it in a dynamically allocated buffer. The maximum length of the line to be stored is one of the function's parameters. The function releases any memory it doesn't need. The return value is a pointer to the line read.

Example 12-1. The getLine() function

```
// Read a line of text from stdin into a dynamically allocated buffer.
// Replace the newline character with a string terminator.
//
// Arguments:    The maximum line length to read.
// Return value: A pointer to the string read, or
//               NULL if end-of-file was read or if an error occurred.

char *getLine( unsigned int len_max )
{
  char *linePtr = malloc( len_max+1 ); // Reserve storage for "worst case."
  if ( linePtr != NULL )
  {
    // Read a line of text and replace the newline characters with
    // a string terminator:
    int c = EOF;
    unsigned int i = 0;
    while ( i < len_max && ( c = getchar() ) != '\n' && c != EOF )
      linePtr[i++] = (char)c;
    linePtr[i] = '\0';

    if ( c == EOF && i == 0 )       // If end-of-file before any
    {                               // characters were read,
      free( linePtr );              // release the whole buffer.
      linePtr = NULL;
    }
    else                            // Otherwise, release the unused portion.
      linePtr = realloc( linePtr, i+1 );   // i is the string length.
  }
  return linePtr;
}
```

The following code shows how you might call the getLine() function:

```
    char *line;
    if (( line = getLine(128) ) != NULL )  // If we can read a line,
    {
      /* ... */                            // process the line,
      free( line );                        // then release the buffer.
    }
```

An All-Purpose Binary Tree

Dynamic memory management is fundamental to the implementation of dynamic data structures such as linked lists and trees. In Chapter 10, we presented a simple linked list (see Figure 10-1). The advantage of linked lists over arrays is that new elements can be inserted and existing members removed quickly. However, they also have the drawback that you have to search through the list in sequential order to find a specific item.

A *binary search tree* (BST), on the other hand, makes linked data elements more quickly accessible. The data items must have a key value that can be used to compare and sort them. A binary search tree combines the flexibility of a linked list with the advantage of a sorted array, in which you can find a desired data item using the binary search algorithm.

Characteristics

A binary tree consists of a number of nodes that contain the data to be stored (or pointers to the data), and the following structural characteristics:

- Each node has up to two direct child nodes.
- There is exactly one node, called the *root* of the tree, that has no parent node. All other nodes have exactly one parent.
- Nodes in a binary tree are placed according to this rule: the value of a node is greater than or equal to the values of any descendant in its left branch, and less than or equal to the value of any descendant in its right branch.

Figure 12-1 illustrates the structure of a binary tree.

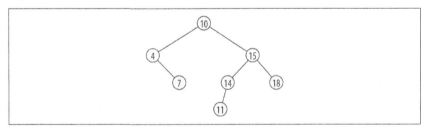

Figure 12-1. A binary tree

A *leaf* is a node that has no children. Each node of the tree is also considered as the root of a *subtree*, which consists of the node and all its descendants.

An important property of a binary tree is its *height*. The height is the length of the longest *path* from the root to any leaf. A path is a succession of linked nodes that form the connection between a given pair of nodes. The length of a path is the number of nodes in the path, not counting the first node. It follows from these definitions that a tree consisting only of its root node has a height of 0, and the height of the tree in Figure 12-1 is 3.

Implementation

The example that follows is an implementation of the principal functions for a binary search tree, and uses dynamic memory management. This tree is intended to be usable for data of any kind. For this reason, the structure type of the nodes includes a flexible member to store the data, and a member indicating the size of the data:

```
typedef struct Node { struct Node *left,    // Pointers to the left and
                                  *right;    // right child nodes.
                      size_t size;           // Size of the data payload.
                      char data[];           // The data itself.
                    } Node_t;
```

The pointers left and right are null pointers if the node has no left or right child.

As the user of our implementation, you must provide two auxiliary functions. The first of these is a function to obtain a key that corresponds to the data value passed to it, and the second compares two keys. The first function has the following type:

```
typedef const void *GetKeyFunc_t( const void *dData );
```

The second function has a type like that of the comparison function used by the standard function bsearch():

```
typedef int CmpFunc_t( const void *pKey1, const void *pKey2 );
```

The arguments passed on calling the comparison function are pointers to the two keys that you want to compare. The function's return value is less than zero, if the first key is less than the second; or equal to zero, if the two keys are equal; or greater than zero, if the first key is greater than the second. The key may be the same as the data itself. In this case, you need to provide only a comparison function.

Next, we define a structure type to represent a tree. This structure has three members: a pointer to the root of the tree; a pointer to the function to calculate a key, with the type GetKeyFunc_t; and a pointer to the comparison function, with the type CmpFunc_t:

```
typedef struct { struct Node  *pRoot;    // Pointer to the root.
                 CmpFunc_t     *cmp;      // Compares two keys.
                 GetKeyFunc_t *getKey;    // Converts data into a key
               } BST_t;                   // value.
```

The pointer pRoot is a null pointer while the tree is empty.

The elementary operations for a binary search tree are performed by functions that insert, find, and delete nodes, and functions to traverse the tree in various ways, performing a programmer-specified operation on each element if desired.

The prototypes of these functions, and the typedef declarations of GetKeyFunc_t, CmpFunc_t, and BST_t, are placed in the header file *BSTree.h*. To use this binary tree implementation, you must include this header file in the program's source code.

The function prototypes in *BSTree.h* are:

```
BST_t *newBST( CmpFunc_t *cmp, GetKeyFunc_t *getKey );
```
This function dynamically generates a new object with the type BST_t, and returns a pointer to it.

```
_Bool BST_insert( BST_t *pBST, const void *pData, size_t size );
```
BST_insert() dynamically generates a new node, copies the data referenced by pData to the node, and inserts the node in the specified tree.

```
const void *BST_search( BST_t *pBST, const void *pKey );
```
The BST_search() function searches the tree and returns a pointer to the data item that matches the key referenced by the pKey argument.

```
_Bool BST_erase( BST_t *pBST, const void *pKey );
```
This function deletes the first node whose data contents match the key referenced by pKey.

```
void BST_clear( BST_t *pBST );
```
BST_clear() deletes all nodes in the tree, leaving the tree empty.

```
int BST_inorder( BST_t *pBST, _Bool (*action)( void *pData ));
int BST_rev_inorder( BST_t *pBST, _Bool (*action)( void *pData ));
int BST_preorder( BST_t *pBST, _Bool (*action)( void *pData ));
int BST_postorder( BST_t *pBST, _Bool (*action)( void *pData ));
```
Each of these functions traverses the tree in a certain order, and calls the function referenced by action to manipulate the data contents of each node. If the action modifies the node's data, then at least the key value must remain unchanged to preserve the tree's sorting order.

The function definitions, along with some recursive helper functions, are placed in the source file *BSTree.c*. The helper functions are declared with the static specifier because they are for internal use only, and not part of the search tree's "public" interface. The file *BSTree.c* also contains the definition of the nodes' structure type. As the programmer, you do not need to deal with the contents of this file, and may be content to use a binary object file compiled for the given system, adding it to the command line when linking the program.

Generating an Empty Tree

When you create a new binary search tree, you specify how a comparison between two data items is performed. For this purpose, the newBST() function takes as its arguments a pointer to a function that compares two keys, and a pointer to a function that calculates a key from an actual data item. The second argument can be a null pointer if the data itself serves as the key for comparison. The return value is a pointer to a new object with the type BST_t:

```c
const void *defaultGetKey( const void *pData ) { return pData; }

BST_t *newBST( CmpFunc_t *cmp, GetKeyFunc_t *getKey )
{
  BST_t *pBST = NULL;
  if ( cmp != NULL )
    pBST = malloc( sizeof(BST_t) );
  if ( pBST != NULL )
  {
    pBST->pRoot = NULL;
    pBST->cmp = cmp;
    pBST->getKey = (getKey != NULL) ? getKey : defaultGetKey;
  }
  return pBST;
}
```

The pointer to BST_t returned by newBST() is the first argument to all the other binary-tree functions. This argument specifies the tree on which you want to perform a given operation.

Inserting New Data

To copy a data item to a new leaf node in the tree, pass the data to the BST_insert() function. The function inserts the new leaf at a position that is consistent with the binary tree's sorting condition. The recursive algorithm involved is simple: if the current subtree is empty—that is, if the pointer to its root node is a null pointer— then insert the new node as the root by making the parent point to it. If the subtree is not empty, continue with the left subtree if the new data is less than the current node's data; otherwise, continue with the right subtree. The recursive helper function insert() applies this algorithm.

The insert() function takes an additional argument, which is a pointer to a pointer to the root node of a subtree. Because this argument is a pointer to a pointer, the function can modify it in order to link a new node to its parent. BST_insert() returns true if it succeeds in inserting the new data; otherwise, false.

```c
static _Bool insert( BST_t *pBST, Node_t **ppNode, const void *pData,
                     size_t size );

_Bool BST_insert( BST_t *pBST, const void *pData, size_t size )
{
  if ( pBST == NULL || pData == NULL || size == 0 )
    return false;
  return insert( pBST, &(pBST->pRoot), pData, size );
}

static _Bool insert( BST_t *pBST, Node_t **ppNode, const void *pData,
                     size_t size )
```

```
{
  Node_t *pNode = *ppNode;       // Pointer to the root node of the
                                 // subtree to insert the new node in.
  if ( pNode == NULL )
  {                              // There's a place for a new leaf here.
    pNode = malloc( sizeof(Node_t) + size );
    if ( pNode != NULL )
    {
      pNode->left = pNode->right = NULL;   // Initialize the new node's
                                           // members.
      memcpy( pNode->data, pData, size );
      *ppNode = pNode;                     // Insert the new node.
      return true;
    }
    else
      return false;
  }
  else                           // Continue looking for a place ...
  {
    const void *key1 = pBST->getKey( pData ),
               *key2 = pBST->getKey( pNode->data );
    if ( pBST->cmp( key1, key2 ) < 0 )     // ... in the left subtree,
      return insert( pBST, &(pNode->left), pData, size );
    else                                   // or in the right subtree.
      return insert( pBST, &(pNode->right), pData, size );
  }
}
```

Finding Data in the Tree

The function BST_search() uses the binary search algorithm to find a data item that matches a given key. If a given node's data does not match the key, the search continues in the node's left subtree if the key is less than that of the node's data, or in the right subtree if the key is greater. The return value is a pointer to the data item from the first node that matches the key, or a null pointer if no match was found.

The search operation uses the recursive helper function search(). Like insert(), search() takes as its second parameter a pointer to the root node of the subtree to be searched:

```
static const void *search( BST_t *pBST, const Node_t *pNode,
                           const void *pKey );

const void *BST_search( BST_t *pBST, const void *pKey )
{
  if  ( pBST == NULL || pKey == NULL ) return NULL;
  return search( pBST, pBST->pRoot, pKey );  // Start at the root
                                             // of the tree.
}

static const void *search( BST_t *pBST, const Node_t *pNode,
                           const void *pKey )
```

```
{
  if ( pNode == NULL )
    return NULL;                         // No subtree to search;
                                         // no match found.
  else
  {                                      // Compare data:
    int cmp_res = pBST->cmp( pKey, pBST->getKey(pNode->data) );

    if ( cmp_res == 0 )                  // Found a match.
      return pNode->data;
    else if ( cmp_res < 0 )              // Continue the search
      return search( pBST, pNode->left, pKey ); // in the left subtree,
    else
      return search( pBST, pNode->right, pKey ); // or in the right
                                         // subtree.
  }
}
```

Removing Data from the Tree

The BST_erase() function searches for a node that matches the specified key, and deletes it if found. Deleting means removing the node from the tree structure and releasing the memory it occupies. The function returns false if it fails to find a matching node to delete, or true if successful.

The actual searching and deleting is performed by means of the recursive helper function erase(). The node needs to be removed from the tree in such a way that the tree's sorting condition is not violated. A node that has no more than one child can be removed simply by linking its child, if any, to its parent. If the node to be removed has two children, though, the operation is more complicated: you have to replace the node you are removing with the node from the right subtree that has the smallest data value. This is never a node with two children. For example, to remove the root node from the tree in Figure 12-1, we would replace it with the node that has the value 11. This removal algorithm is not the only possible one, but it has the advantage of not increasing the tree's height.

The recursive helper function detachMin() plucks the minimum node from a specified subtree, and returns a pointer to the node:

```
static Node_t *detachMin( Node_t **ppNode )
{
  Node_t *pNode = *ppNode;              // A pointer to the current node.
  if ( pNode == NULL )
    return NULL;                        // pNode is an empty subtree.
  else if ( pNode->left != NULL )
    return detachMin( &(pNode->left) ); // The minimum is in the left
                                        // subtree.
  else
  {                                     // pNode points to the minimum node.
    *ppNode = pNode->right;             // Attach the right child to the parent.
    return pNode;
```

```
      }
    }
```

Now we can use this function in the definition of erase() and BST_erase():

```
    static _Bool erase( BST_t *pBST, Node_t **ppNode, const void *pKey );

    _Bool BST_erase( BST_t *pBST, const void *pKey )
    {
      if ( pBST == NULL || pKey == NULL ) return false;
      return erase( pBST, &(pBST->pRoot), pKey );      // Start at the root
                                                       // of the tree.
    }

    static _Bool erase( BST_t *pBST, Node_t **ppNode, const void *pKey )
    {
      Node_t *pNode = *ppNode;               // Pointer to the current node.
      if ( pNode == NULL )
        return false;                        // No match found.

                                             // Compare data:
      int cmp_res = pBST->cmp( pKey, pBST->getKey(pNode->data) );

      if ( cmp_res < 0 )                              // Continue the search
        return  erase( pBST, &(pNode->left), pKey);   // in the left subtree,
      else if ( cmp_res > 0 )
        return erase( pBST, &(pNode->right), pKey);   // or in the right
                                                      // subtree.
      else                                   // Found the node to be deleted.
      {
        if ( pNode->left == NULL )     // If no more than one child,
          *ppNode = pNode->right;      // attach the child to the parent.
        else if ( pNode->right == NULL )
          *ppNode = pNode->left;
        else                           // Two children: replace the node with
        {                              // the minimum from the right subtree.
          Node_t *pMin = detachMin( &(pNode->right) );
          *ppNode = pMin;         // Graft it onto the deleted node's parent.
          pMin->left  = pNode->left; // Graft the deleted node's children.
          pMin->right = pNode->right;
        }
        free( pNode );               // Release the deleted node's storage.
        return true;
      }
    }
```

A function in Example 12-2, BST_clear(), deletes all the nodes of a tree. The recursive helper function clear() deletes first the descendants of the node referenced by its argument and then the node itself.

Example 12-2. The BST_clear() and clear() functions

```c
static void clear( Node_t *pNode );

void BST_clear( BST_t *pBST )
{
  if ( pBST != NULL)
  {
    clear( pBST->pRoot );
    pBST->pRoot = NULL;
  }
}

static void clear( Node_t *pNode )
{
  if ( pNode != NULL )
  {
    clear( pNode->left );
    clear( pNode->right );
    free( pNode );
  }
}
```

Traversing a Tree

There are several recursive schemes for traversing a binary tree. They are often designated by abbreviations in which L stands for a given node's left subtree, R for its right subtree, and N for the node itself:

In-order or LNR traversal
    First traverse the node's left subtree, then visit the node itself, then traverse the right subtree.

Pre-order or NLR traversal
    First visit the node itself, then traverse its left subtree, then its right subtree.

Post-order or LRN traversal
    First traverse the node's left subtree, then the right subtree, then visit the node itself.

An *in-order* traversal visits all the nodes in their sorting order, from least to greatest. If you print each node's data as you visit it, the output appears sorted.

It's not always advantageous to process the data items in their sorting order, though. For example, if you want to store the data items in a file and later insert them in a new tree as you read them from the file, you might prefer to traverse the tree in *pre-order*. Then reading each data item in the file and inserting it will reproduce the original tree structure. And the clear() function in Example 12-2 uses a *post-order* traversal to avoid destroying any node before its children.

Each of the traversal functions takes as its second argument a pointer to an "action" function that it calls for each node visited. The action function takes as its argument a pointer to the current node's data, and returns true to indicate success and false on failure. This functioning enables the tree-traversal functions to return the number of times the action was performed successfully.

The following example contains the definition of the BST_inorder() function, and its recursive helper function inorder() (the other traversal functions are similar):

```c
static int inorder( Node_t *pNode, _Bool (*action)(void *pData) );

int BST_inorder( BST_t *pBST, _Bool (*action)(void *pData) )
{
  if ( pBST == NULL || action ==  NULL )
    return 0;
  else
    return inorder( pBST->pRoot, action );
}

static int inorder( Node_t *pNode, _Bool (*action)(void *pData) )
{
  int count = 0;
  if ( pNode == NULL )
    return 0;

  count = inorder( pNode->left, action );      // L: Traverse the left
                                               // subtree.
  if ( action( pNode->data ))                  // N: Visit the current
    ++count;                                   // node itself.
  count += inorder( pNode-> right, action );   // R: Traverse the right
                                               // subtree.

  return count;
}
```

A Sample Application

To illustrate one use of a binary search tree, the filter program in Example 12-3, *sortlines*, presents a simple variant of the Unix utility *sort*. It reads text line by line from the standard input stream, and prints the lines in sorted order to standard output. A typical command line to invoke the program might be:

```
sortlines < demo.txt
```

This command prints the contents of the file *demo.txt* to the console.

Example 12-3. The sortlines program

```c
// This program reads each line of text into a node of a binary tree,
// and then prints the text in sorted order.

#include <stdio.h>
#include <string.h>
#include <stdlib.h>
#include "BSTree.h"               // Prototypes of the BST functions.

#define LEN_MAX 1000              // Maximum length of a line.
char buffer[LEN_MAX];

// Action to perform for each line:
_Bool printStr( void *str ) { return printf( "%s", str ) >= 0; }

int main()
{
  BST_t *pStrTree = newBST( (CmpFunc_t*)strcmp, NULL );
  int n;

  while ( fgets( buffer, LEN_MAX, stdin ) != NULL )    // Read each line.
  {
    size_t len = strlen( buffer );                     // Length incl.
                                                       // newline character.
    if ( !BST_insert( pStrTree, buffer, len+1 ))       // Insert the line in
      break;                                           // the tree.
  }
  if ( !feof(stdin) )
  {                                                    // If unable to read
                                                       // the entire text:
    fprintf( stderr, "sortlines: "
            "Error reading or storing text input.\n" );
    exit( EXIT_FAILURE );
  }
  n = BST_inorder( pStrTree, printStr );               // Print each line,
                                                       // in sorted order.
  fprintf( stderr, "\nsortlines: Printed %d lines.\n", n );

  BST_clear( pStrTree );                               // Discard all nodes.
  return 0;
}
```

The loop that reads input lines breaks prematurely if a read error occurs, or if there is insufficient memory to insert a new node in the tree. In such cases, the program exits with an error message.

An in-order traversal visits every node of the tree in sorted order. The return value of BST_inorder() is the number of lines successfully printed. *sortlines* prints the error and success information to the standard error stream, so that it is separate from the actual data output. Redirecting standard output to a file or a pipe affects the sorted text but not these messages.

The `BST_clear()` function call is technically superfluous, as all of the program's dynamically allocated memory is automatically released when the program exits.

The binary search tree presented in this chapter can be used for any kind of data. Most applications require the `BST_search()` and `BST_erase()` functions in addition to those used in Example 12-3. Furthermore, more complex programs will no doubt require functions not presented here, such as one to keep the tree's left and right branches balanced.

13

Input and Output

Programs must be able to write data to files or to physical output devices such as displays or printers, and to read in data from files or input devices such as a keyboard. The C standard library provides numerous functions for these purposes. This chapter presents a survey of the part of the standard library that is devoted to input and output, which is often referred to as the *I/O library*. Further details on the individual functions can be found in Chapter 18. Apart from these library functions, the C language itself contains no input or output support at all.

All of the basic functions, macros, and types for input and output are declared in the header file *stdio.h*. The corresponding input and output function declarations for wide characters of the type wchar_t are contained in the header file *wchar.h*.

As alternatives to the traditional standard I/O functions, C11 introduces many new functions that permit more secure programming, in particular by checking the bounds of arrays when copying data. These alternative functions have names that end with the suffix _s (such as scanf_s(), for example).

Support for these "secure" functions is optional. The macro __STDC_LIB_EXT1__ is defined in implementations that provide them (see "Functions with Bounds-Checking" on page 287).

Streams

From the point of view of a C program, all kinds of files and devices for input and output are uniformly represented as logical data *streams* regardless of whether the program reads or writes a character or byte at a time, or text lines, or data blocks of a given size. Streams in C can be either *text* or *binary streams*, although on some systems even this difference is nil. Opening a file by means of the function `fopen()` (or `tmpfile()`) creates a new stream, which then exists until closed by the `fclose()` function. C leaves file management up to the execution environment—in other words, the system on which the program runs. Thus, a stream is a channel by which data can flow from the execution environment to the program, or from the program to its environment. Devices, such as consoles, are addressed in the same way as files.

Every stream has a lock that the I/O library's functions use for synchronization when several threads access the same stream. All stream I/O functions first obtain exclusive access to a stream before performing read or write operations, or querying and moving the stream's file position indicator. Once the operation has been performed, the stream is released again for access by other threads. Exclusive stream access prevents "data races" and concurrent I/O operations. For more information about multithreaded programs, see Chapter 14.

Text Streams

A text stream transports the characters of a text that is divided into *lines*. A line of text consists of a sequence of characters ending in a newline character. A line of text can also be empty, meaning that it consists of a newline character only. The last line transported may or may not have to end with a newline character, depending on the implementation.

The internal representation of text in a C program is the same regardless of the system on which the program is running. Text input and output on a given system may involve removing, adding, or altering certain characters. For example, on systems that are not Unix-based, end-of-line indicators ordinarily have to be converted into newline characters when reading text files, as on Windows systems, for instance, where the end-of-line indicator is a sequence of two control characters, \r (carriage return) and \n (newline). Similarly, the control character ^Z (character code 26) in a text stream on Windows indicates the end of the stream.

As the programmer, you generally do not have to worry about the necessary adaptations, because they are performed automatically by the I/O functions in the standard library. However, if you want to be sure that an input function call yields exactly the same text that was written by a previous output function call, your text should contain only the newline and horizontal tab control characters, in addition to printable characters. Furthermore, the last line should end with a newline character, and no line should end with a space immediately before the newline character.

Binary Streams

A binary stream is a sequence of bytes that are transmitted without modification. That is, the I/O functions do not involve any interpretation of control characters when operating on binary streams. Data written to a file through a binary stream can always be read back unchanged on the same system. However, in certain implementations there may be extra zero-valued bytes appended at the end of the stream.

Binary streams are normally used to write binary data—for example, database records—without converting it to text. If a program reads the contents of a text file through a binary stream, then the text appears in the program in its stored form, with all the control characters used on the given system.

 On common Unix systems, there is no difference between text streams and binary streams.

Files

A file represents a sequence of bytes. The fopen() function associates a file with a stream and initializes an object of the type FILE, which contains all the information necessary to control the stream. Such information includes a pointer to the buffer used; a file position indicator, which specifies a position to access in the file; and flags to indicate error and end-of-file conditions.

Each of the functions that open files—namely, fopen(), freopen(), and tmpfile() —returns a pointer to a FILE object for the stream associated with the file being opened. Once you have opened a file, you can call functions to transfer data and to manipulate the stream. Such functions have a pointer to a FILE object—commonly called a FILE pointer—as one of their arguments. The FILE pointer specifies the stream on which the operation is carried out.

The I/O library also contains functions that operate on the file system, and take the name of a file as one of their parameters. These functions do not require the file to be opened first. They include the following:

- The remove() function deletes a file (or an empty directory). The string argument is the file's name. If the file has more than one name, then remove() only deletes the specified name, not the file itself. The data may remain accessible in some other way, but not under the deleted filename.

- The rename() function changes the name of a file (or directory). The function's two string arguments are the old and new names, in that order. The remove() and rename() functions both have the return type int, and return zero on success, or a nonzero value on failure. The following statement changes the name of the file *songs.dat* to *mysongs.dat*:

```
if ( rename( "songs.dat", "mysongs.dat" ) != 0 )
    fprintf( stderr, "Error renaming \"songs.dat\".\n" );
```

Conditions that can cause the rename() function to fail include the following: no file exists with the old name; the program does not have the necessary access privileges; or the file is open. The rules for forming permissible filenames depend on the implementation.

File Position

Like the elements of a char array, each character in an ordinary file has a definite position in the file. The *file position indicator* in the object representing the stream determines the position of the next character to be read or written.

When you open a file for reading or writing, the file position indicator points to the beginning of the file so that the next character accessed has the position 0. If you open the file in "append" mode, the file position indicator may point to the end of the file. Each read or write operation increases the indicator by the number of characters read from the file or written to the file. This behavior makes it simple to process the contents of a file sequentially. Random access within the file is achieved by using functions that change the file position indicator, fseek(), fsetpos(), and rewind(), which are discussed in detail in"Random File Access" on page 235.

Of course, not all files support changing access positions. Sequential I/O devices such as terminals and printers do not, for example.

Buffers

In working with files, it is generally not efficient to read or write individual characters. For this reason, a stream has a buffer in which it collects characters, which are transferred as a block to or from the file. Sometimes you don't want buffering, however. For example, after an error has occurred, you might want to write data to a file as directly as possible.

Streams are buffered in one of three ways:

Fully buffered
  The characters in the buffer are normally transferred only when the buffer is full.

Line-buffered
  The characters in the buffer are normally transferred only when a newline character is written to the buffer, or when the buffer is full. A stream's buffer is also written to the file when the program requests input through an unbuffered stream, or when an input request on a line-buffered stream causes characters to be read from the host environment.

Unbuffered
  Characters are transferred as promptly as possible.

You can also explicitly transfer the characters in the stream's output buffer to the associated file by calling the fflush() function. The buffer is also flushed when you close a stream, and normal program termination flushes the buffers of all the program's streams.

When you open an ordinary file by calling fopen(), the new stream is fully buffered. Opening interactive devices is different, however: such device files are associated on opening with a line-buffered stream. After you have opened a file, and

---

before you perform the first input or output operation on it, you can change the buffering mode using the setbuf() or setvbuf() function.

The Standard Streams

Three standard text streams are available to every C program on starting. These streams do not have to be explicitly opened. Table 13-1 lists them by the names of their respective FILE pointers.

Table 13-1. The standard streams

FILE pointer	Common name	Buffering mode
stdin	Standard input	Line-buffered
stdout	Standard output	Line-buffered
stderr	Standard error output	Unbuffered

stdin is usually associated with the keyboard, and stdout and stderr with the console display. These associations can be modified by redirection. Redirection is performed either by the program calling the freopen() function, or by the environment in which the program is executed.

Opening and Closing Files

To write to a new file or modify the contents of an existing file, you must first open the file. When you open a file, you must specify an *access mode* indicating whether you plan to read, to write, or some combination of the two. When you have finished using a file, close it to release resources.

Opening a File

The standard library provides the function fopen() to open a file (for special cases, the freopen() and tmpfile() functions also open files):

```
FILE *fopen( const char * restrict filename,
             const char * restrict mode );
```

This function opens the file whose name is specified by the string *filename*. The filename may contain a directory part, and must not be longer than the maximum length specified by the value of the macro FILENAME_MAX. The second argument, *mode*, is also a string, and specifies the access mode. The possible access modes are described in the next section. The fopen() function associates the file with a new stream:

```
FILE *freopen( const char * restrictfilename,
               const char * restrict mode,
               FILE * restrict stream );
```

This function redirects a stream. Like `fopen()`, `freopen()` opens the specified file in the specified mode. However, rather than creating a new stream, `freopen()` associates the file with the existing stream specified by the third argument. The file previously associated with that stream is closed. The most common use of `freopen()` is to redirect the standard streams, `stdin`, `stdout`, and `stderr`.

```
FILE *tmpfile( void );
```

The `tmpfile()` function creates a new temporary file whose name is distinct from all other existing files, and opens the file for binary writing and reading (as if the mode string `"wb+"` were used in an `fopen()` call). If the program is terminated normally, the file is automatically deleted.

All three file-opening functions, `fopen()`, `freopen()` and `tmpfile()`, return a pointer to the opened stream if successful, or a null pointer to indicate failure.

 If a file is opened for writing, the program should have *exclusive* access to the file to prevent simultaneous write operations by other programs. The traditional standard functions do not guarantee exclusive file access, but three of the new "secure" functions introduced by C11, `fopen_s()`, `freopen_s()` and `tmpfile_s()`, do provide exclusive access, if the operating system supports it.

Access Modes

The access mode specified by the second argument to `fopen()` or `freopen()` determines what input and output operations the new stream permits. The permissible values of the mode string are restricted. The first character in the mode string is always r for "read," w for "write," or a for "append," and in the simplest case, the string contains just that one character. However, the mode string may also contain one or both of the characters + and b (in either order: +b has the same effect as b+).

A plus sign (+) in the mode string means that both read and write operations are permitted. However, a program must not alternate immediately between reading and writing. After a write operation, you must call the `fflush()` function or a positioning function (`fseek()`, `fsetpos()`, or `rewind()`) before performing a read operation. After a read operation, you must call a positioning function before performing a write operation.

A b in the mode string causes the file to be opened in binary mode—that is, the new stream associated with the file is a binary stream. If there is no b in the mode string, the new stream is a text stream.

If the mode string begins with r, the file must already exist in the file system. If the mode string begins with w, then the file will be created if it does not already exist. If it does exist, its previous contents will be lost, because the fopen() function truncates it to zero length in "write" mode.

C11 introduces the capability to open a file in *exclusive* write mode, if the operating system supports it. To specify exclusive access, you can use the suffix x in a mode string that begins with w, such as wx or w+bx. The file-opening function then fails—returning a null pointer—if the file already exists or cannot be created. Otherwise, the file is created and opened for exclusive access.

A mode string beginning with a (for append) also causes the file to be created if it does not already exist. If the file does exist, however, its contents are preserved, because all write operations are automatically performed at the end of the file. Here is a brief example:

```
#include <stdio.h>
#include <stdbool.h>
_Bool isReadWriteable( const char *filename )
{
  FILE *fp = fopen( filename, "r+" );  // Open a file to read and write.

  if ( fp != NULL )                      // Did fopen() succeed?
  {
    fclose(fp);                   // Yes: close the file; no error handling.
    return true;
  }
  else                        // No.
    return false;
}
```

This example also illustrates how to close a file using the fclose() function.

Closing a File

To close a file, use the fclose() function. The prototype of this function is:

```
int fclose( FILE *fp );
```

The function flushes any data still pending in the buffer to the file, closes the file, and releases any memory used for the stream's input and output buffers. The fclose() function returns zero on success, or EOF if an error occurs.

When the program exits, all open files are closed automatically. Nonetheless, you should always close any file that you have finished processing. Otherwise, you risk losing data in the case of an abnormal program termination. Furthermore, there is a limit to the number of files that a program may have open at one time; the number of open files allowed is greater than or equal to the value of the constant FOPEN_MAX.

Reading and Writing

This section describes the functions that actually retrieve data from or send data to a stream. First, there is another detail to consider: an open stream can be used either for byte characters or for wide characters.

Byte-Oriented and Wide-Oriented Streams

In addition to the type char, C also provides a type for wide characters, named wchar_t. This type is wide enough to represent any character in the extended character sets that the implementation supports (see "Wide Characters and Multibyte Characters" on page 9). Accordingly, there are two complete sets of functions for input and output of characters and strings: the *byte-character I/O functions* and the *wide-character I/O functions*. Functions in the second set operate on characters with the type wchar_t. Each stream has an *orientation* that determines which set of functions is appropriate.

Immediately after you open a file, the orientation of the stream associated with it is undetermined. If the first file access is performed by a byte-character I/O function, then from that point on the stream is *byte-oriented*. If the first access is by a wide-character function, then the stream is *wide-oriented*. The orientation of the standard streams, stdin, stdout, and stderr, is likewise undetermined when the program starts.

You can call the function fwide() at any time to ascertain a stream's orientation. Before the first I/O operation, fwide() can also set a new stream's orientation. To change a stream's orientation once it has been determined, you must first reopen the stream by calling the freopen() function.

The wide characters written to a wide-oriented stream are stored as multibyte characters in the file associated with the stream. The read and write functions implicitly perform the necessary conversion between wide characters of type wchar_t and the multibyte character encoding. This conversion may be stateful. In other words, the value of a given byte in the multibyte encoding may depend on control characters that precede it, which alter the *shift state* or *conversion state* of the character sequence. For this reason, each wide-oriented stream has an associated object with the type mbstate_t, which stores the current multibyte conversion state. The functions fgetpos() and fsetpos(), which get and set the value of the file position indicator, also save and restore the conversion state for the given file position.

Error Handling

The I/O functions can use a number of mechanisms to indicate to the caller when they incur errors, including return values, error and EOF flags in the FILE object, and the global error variable errno. To read which mechanisms are used by a given function, see the individual function descriptions in Chapter 18. This section describes the I/O error-handling mechanisms in general.

Return values and status flags

The I/O functions generally indicate any errors that occur by their return value. In addition, they also set an error flag in the FILE object that controls the stream if an error in reading or writing occurs. To query this flag, you can call the ferror() function. Here is an example:

```
(void)fputc( '*', fp );          // Write an asterisk to the stream fp.
if ( ferror(fp) )
    fprintf( stderr, "Error writing.\n" );
```

Furthermore, read functions set the stream's EOF flag on reaching the end of the file. You can query this flag by calling the feof() function. A number of read functions return the value of the macro EOF if you attempt to read beyond the last character in the file. (Wide-character functions return the value WEOF.) A return value of EOF or WEOF can also indicate an error, however. To distinguish between the two cases, you must call ferror() or feof(), as the following example illustrates:

```
int i, c;
char buffer[1024];
/* ... Open a file to read using the stream fp ... */
i = 0;
while ( i < 1024 &&                  // While there is space in the buffer
        (c = fgetc( fp )) != EOF) // ... and the stream can deliver
    buffer[i++] = (char)c;           // characters.
if ( i < 1024 && ! feof(fp) )
    fprintf( stderr, "Error reading.\n" );
```

The if statement in this example prints an error message if fgetc() returns EOF and the EOF flag is not set.

The error variable errno

Several standard library functions support more specific error handling by setting the global error variable errno to a value that indicates the kind of error that has occurred. Stream handling functions that set the errno variable include ftell(), fgetpos(), and fsetpos(). Depending on the implementation, other functions may also set the errno variable. errno is declared in the header *errno.h* with the type int (see Chapter 16). *errno.h* also defines macros for the possible values of errno.

The perror() function prints a system-specific error message for the current value of errno to the stderr stream:

```
long pos = ftell(fp);        // Get the current file position.
if ( pos < 0L )              // ftell() returns -1L if an error occurs.
    perror( "ftell()" );
```

The perror() function prints its string argument followed by a colon, the error message, and a newline character. The error message is the same as the string that strerror() would return if called with the given value of errno as its argument. In the previous example, the perror() function as implemented in the GCC compiler prints the following output to indicate an invalid FILE pointer argument:

```
ftell(): Bad file descriptor
```

The error variable errno is also set by functions that convert between wide characters and multibyte characters in reading from or writing to a wide-oriented stream. Such conversions are performed internally by calls to the wcrtomb() and mbrtowc() functions. When these functions are unable to supply a valid conversion, they return the value of -1 cast to size_t, and set errno to the value of EILSEQ (for "illegal sequence").

Unformatted I/O

The standard library provides functions to read and write unformatted data in the form of individual characters, strings, or blocks of any given size. This section describes these functions, listing the prototypes of both the byte-character and the wide-character functions. The type wint_t is an integer type capable of representing at least all the values in the range of wchar_t, and the additional value WEOF. The macro WEOF has the type wint_t and a value that is distinct from all the character codes in the extended character set.

Unlike EOF, the value of WEOF is not necessarily negative.

Reading characters

Use the following functions to read characters from a file:

```
int fgetc( FILE *fp );
int getc( FILE *fp );
int getchar( void );
wint_t fgetwc( FILE *fp );
wint_t getwc( FILE *fp );
wint_t getwchar( void );
```

The fgetc() function reads a character from the input stream referenced by fp. The return value is the character read, or EOF if an error occurred. The macro getc() has the same effect as the function fgetc(). The macro is commonly used because it is faster than a function call. However, if the argument fp is an expression with side effects (see Chapter 5), then you should use the function instead because a macro may evaluate its argument more than once. The macro getchar() reads a character from standard input. It is equivalent to getc(stdin).

fgetwc(), getwc(), and getwchar() are the corresponding functions and macros for wide-oriented streams. These functions set the global variable errno to the value EILSEQ if an error occurs in converting a multibyte character to a wide character.

Putting a character back

Use one of the following functions to push a character back into the stream from whence it came:

```
int ungetc( intc, FILE *fp );
wint_t ungetwc( wint_t c, FILE *fp );
```

ungetc() and ungetwc() push the last character read, c, back onto the input stream referenced by fp. Subsequent read operations then read the characters put back, in LIFO (last in, first out) order—that is, the last character put back is the first one to be read. You can always put back at least one character, but repeated attempts might or might not succeed. The functions return EOF (or WEOF) on failure, or the character pushed onto the stream on success.

Writing characters

The following functions allow you to write individual characters to a stream:

```
int fputc( intc, FILE *fp );
int putc( int c, FILE *fp);
int putchar( int c );
wint_t fputwc( wchar_t wc, FILE *fp );
wint_t putwc( wchar_t wc, FILE *fp );
wint_t putwchar( wchar_t wc );
```

The function fputc() writes the character value of the argument c to the output stream referenced by fp. The return value is the character written, or EOF if an error occurred. The macro putc() has the same effect as the function fputc(). If either of its arguments is an expression with side effects (see Chapter 5), then you should use the function instead because a macro might evaluate its arguments more than once. The macro putchar() writes the specified character to the standard output stream.

fputwc(), putwc(), and putwchar() are the corresponding functions and macros for wide-oriented streams. These functions set the global variable errno to the value EILSEQ if an error occurs in converting the wide character to a multibyte character.

The following example copies the contents of a file opened for reading, referenced by fpIn, to a file opened for writing, referenced by fpOut (both streams are byte-oriented):

```
_Bool error = 0;
int c;
rewind( fpIn );      // Set the file position indicator to the beginning
                     // of the file, and clear the error and EOF flags.
while (( c = getc( fpIn )) != EOF )  // Read one character at a time.
```

```
    if ( putc( c, fpOut ) == EOF )      // Write each character to the
    {                                    // output stream.
      error = 1; break;                  // A write error.
    }
  if ( ferror( fpIn ))                   // A read error.
    error = 1;
```

Reading strings

The following functions allow you to read a string from a stream:

```
char *fgets( char *buf, int n, FILE *fp );
wchar_t *fgetws( wchar_t *buf, int n, FILE *fp);
char *gets( char *buf);                         // Obsolete
char *gets_s(char *buf, size_t n);              // C11
```

The functions fgets() and fgetws() read up to $n - 1$ characters from the input stream referenced by *fp* into the buffer addressed by *buf*, appending a null character to terminate the string. If the functions encounter a newline character or the end of the file before they have read the maximum number of characters, then only the characters read up to that point are read into the buffer. The newline character '\n' (or, in a wide-oriented stream, L'\n') is also stored in the buffer if read.

gets() reads a line of text from standard input into the buffer addressed by *buf*. The newline character that ends the line is replaced by the null character that terminates the string in the buffer. fgets() is a preferable alternative to gets(), as gets() offers no way to limit the number of characters read. The C11 standard retires the function gets() and adds a further alternative to gets(), the new function gets_s(), in implementations that support bounds-checking interfaces.

All four functions return the value of their argument *buf*, or a null pointer if an error occurred, or if there were no more characters to be read before the end of the file.

Writing strings

Use the following functions to write a null-terminated string to a stream:

```
int fputs( const char *s, FILE *fp );
int puts( const char *s );
int fputws( const wchar_t *s, FILE *fp );
```

The three puts functions have some features in common as well as certain differences:

- fputs() and fputws() write the string *s* to the output stream referenced by *fp*. The null character that terminates the string is not written to the output stream.

- puts() writes the string *s* to the standard output stream, followed by a newline character. There is no wide-character function that corresponds to puts().

- All three functions return EOF (not WEOF) if an error occurred, or a non-negative value to indicate success.

The function in the following example prints all the lines of a file that contain a specified string.

```
// Write to stdout all the lines containing the specified search
// string in the file opened for reading as fpIn.
// Return value: The number of lines containing the search string,
//               or -1 on error.
// -----------------------------------------------------------------
#include <stdio.h>
#include <string.h>
int searchFile( FILE*fpIn, const char *keyword )
{
  #define MAX_LINE 256
  char line[MAX_LINE] = "";
  int count = 0;

  if ( fpIn == NULL || keyword == NULL )
    return -1;
  else
    rewind( fpIn );

  while ( fgets( line, MAX_LINE, fpIn ) != NULL )
    if ( strstr( line, keyword ) != NULL )
    {
      ++count;
      fputs( line, stdout );
    }

  if ( !feof( fpIn ) )
    return -1;
  else
    return count;
}
```

Reading and writing blocks

The fread() function reads up to *n* objects whose size is *size* from the stream referenced by *fp*, and stores them in the array addressed by *buffer*:

```
size_t fread( void *buffer, size_t size, size_t n, FILE *fp );
```

The function's return value is the number of objects transferred. A return value less than the argument *n* indicates that the end of the file was reached while reading, or that an error occurred.

The fwrite() function sends *n* objects whose size is *size* from the array addressed by *buffer* to the output stream referenced by *fp*:

```
size_t fwrite( const void *buffer, size_t size, size_t n, FILE *fp );
```

Again, the return value is the number of objects written. A return value less than the argument *n* indicates that an error occurred.

Because the fread() and fwrite() functions do not deal with characters or strings as such, there are no corresponding functions for wide-oriented streams. On systems that distinguish between text and binary streams, the fread() and fwrite() functions should be used only with binary streams.

The function in the following example assumes that records have been saved in the file *records.dat* by means of the fwrite() function. A key value of 0 indicates that a record has been marked as deleted. In copying records to a new file, the program skips over records whose key is 0:

```
// Copy records to a new file, filtering out those with the key 0.
// ----------------------------------------------------------------
#include <stdio.h>
#include <stdlib.h>

#define ARRAY_LEN 100       // Maximum number of records in the buffer.
// A structure type for the records:
typedef struct { long key;
                 char name[32];
                 /* ... other fields in the record ... */ } Record_t;

char inFile[ ]  = "records.dat",              // Filenames.
     outFile[ ] = "packed.dat";

// Terminate the program with an error message:
static inline void error_exit( int status, const char *error_msg )
{
  fputs( error_msg, stderr );
  exit( status );
}

int main()
{
  FILE *fpIn, *fpOut;
  Record_t record, *pArray;
  unsigned int i;

  if (( fpIn = fopen( inFile, "rb" )) == NULL )        // Open to read.
    error_exit( 1, "Error on opening input file." );

  else if (( fpOut = fopen( outFile, "wb" )) == NULL ) // Open to write.
    error_exit( 2, "Error on opening output file." );

  else                                            // Create the buffer.
```

```
    if ((pArray = malloc( ARRAY_LEN * sizeof(Record_t) )) == NULL )
      error_exit( 3, "Insufficient memory." );

    i = 0;                              // Read one record at a time:
    while ( fread( &record, sizeof(Record_t), 1, fpIn ) == 1 )
    {
      if ( record.key != 0L )          // If not marked as deleted ...
      {                                // ... then copy the record:
        pArray[i++] = record;
        if ( i == ARRAY_LEN )          // Buffer full?
        {                              // Yes: write to file.
          if ( fwrite( pArray, sizeof(Record_t), i, fpOut) < i )
            break;
          i = 0;
        }
      }
    }
    if ( i > 0 && !ferror(fpOut) )     // Write the remaining records.
      fwrite( pArray, sizeof(Record_t), i, fpOut );

    if ( ferror(fpOut) )                         // Handle errors.
      error_exit( 4, "Error on writing to output file." );
    else if ( ferror(fpIn) )
      error_exit( 5, "Error on reading input file." );

    return 0;
  }
```

Formatted Output

C provides formatted data output by means of the printf() family of functions. This section illustrates commonly used formatting options with appropriate examples. A complete, tabular description of output formatting options is included in Part II; see the discussion of the printf() function in Chapter 18.

The printf() function family

The printf() function and its various related functions all share the same capabilities of formatting data output as specified by an argument called the *format string*. However, the various functions have different output destinations and ways of receiving the data intended for output. The printf() functions for byte-oriented streams are:

int printf(const char * restrict *format*, ...);
   Writes to the standard output stream, stdout.

int fprintf(FILE * restrict *fp*, const char * restrict *format*, ...);
   Writes to the output stream specified by *fp*. The printf() function can be considered to be a special case of fprintf().

```
int sprintf( char * restrict buf,
             const char * restrict format, ... );
```
Writes the formatted output to the char array addressed by *buf*, and appends a terminating null character.

```
int snprintf( char * restrict buf, size_t n,
              const char * restrict format, ... );
```
Like sprintf(), but never writes more than *n* bytes to the output buffer.

The ellipsis (...) in these function prototypes stands for more arguments, which are optional. Another subset of the printf() functions takes a pointer to an argument list, rather than accepting a variable number of arguments directly in the function call. The names of these functions begin with a v for "variable argument list":

```
int vprintf( const char * restrictformat, va_list argptr );
int vfprintf( FILE * restrict fp, const char * restrict format,
              va_list argptr );
int vsprintf( char * restrict buf, const char * restrict format,
              va_list argptr );
int vsnprintf( char * restrict buffer, size_t n,
               const char * restrict format, va_list argptr );
```

To use the variable argument list functions, you must include *stdarg.h* in addition to *stdio.h*.

There are counterparts to all of these functions for output to wide-oriented streams. The wide-character printf() functions have names containing wprintf instead of printf, as in vfwprintf() and swprintf(), for example. There is one exception: there is no snwprintf(). Instead, swprintf() corresponds to the function snprintf(), with a parameter for the maximum output length.

The C11 standard provides a new "secure" alternative to each of these functions. The names of these new functions end in the suffix _s (for example, fprintf_s()). The new functions test whether any pointer arguments they receive are null pointers.

The format string

One argument passed to every printf() function is a format string. This is a definition of the data output format, and contains some combination of ordinary characters and *conversion specifications*. Each conversion specification defines how the function should convert and format one of the optional arguments for output. The printf() function writes the format string to the output destination, replacing each conversion specification in the process with the formatted value of the corresponding optional argument.

A conversion specification begins with a percent sign % and ends with a letter, called the *conversion specifier*. (To include a percent sign in the output, there is a special

---

conversion specification: %%. `printf()` converts this sequence into a single percent sign.)

 The syntax of a conversion *specification* ends with the conversion *specifier*. Throughout the rest of this section, we use both these terms frequently in talking about the format strings used in `printf()` and `scanf()` function calls.

The conversion specifier determines the type of conversion to be performed, and must match the corresponding optional argument. Here is an example:

```
int score = 120;
char player[ ] = "Mary";
printf( "%s has %d points.\n", player, score );
```

The format string in this `printf()` call contains two conversion specifications: %s and %d. Accordingly, two optional arguments have been specified: a string, matching the conversion specifier s (for "string"), and an `int`, matching the conversion specifier d (for "decimal"). The function call in the example writes the following line to standard output:

```
Mary has 120 points.
```

All conversion specifications (with the exception of %%) have the following general format:

```
%[flags][field_width][.precision][length_modifier]specifier
```

The parts of this syntax that are indicated in square brackets are all optional, but any of them that you include must be placed in the order shown here. The permissible conversion specifications for each argument type are described in the sections that follow. Any conversion specification can include a *field width*. The *precision* does not apply to all conversion types, however, and its significance is different depending on the specifier.

Field widths

The field width option is especially useful in formatting tabular output. If included, the *field width* must be a positive decimal integer (or an asterisk, as described momentarily). It specifies the minimum number of characters in the output of the corresponding data item. The default behavior is to position the converted data *right-justified* in the field, padding it with spaces to the left. If the flags include a minus sign (-), then the information is *left-justified*, and the excess field width padded with space characters to the right.

The following example first prints a line numbering the character positions to illustrate the effect of the field width option:

```
printf("1234567890123456\n");              // Character positions.
printf( "%-10s %s\n", "Player", "Score" ); // Table headers.
printf( "%-10s %4d\n", "John", 120 );      // Field widths: 10; 4.
printf( "%-10s %4d\n", "Mary", 77 );
```

These statements produce a little table:

```
1234567890123456
Player     Score
John        120
Mary         77
```

If the output conversion results in more characters than the specified width of the field, then the field is expanded as necessary to print the complete data output.

If a field is right-justified, it can be padded with leading zeros instead of spaces. To do so, include a 0 (that's the digit zero) in the conversion specification's flags. The following example prints a date in the format *mm-dd-yyyy*:

```
int month = 5, day = 1, year = 1987;
printf( "Date of birth: %02d-%02d-%04d\n", month, day, year );
```

This printf() call produces the following output:

```
Date of birth: 05-01-1987
```

You can also use a variable to specify the field width. To do so, insert an asterisk (*) as the field width in the conversion specification, and include an additional optional argument in the printf() call. This argument must have the type int, and must appear immediately before the argument to be converted for output. Here is an example:

```
char str[ ] = "Variable field width";
int width = 30;
printf( "%-*s!\n", width, str );
```

The printf statement in this example prints the string str at the left end of a field whose width is determined by the variable width. The results are as follows:

```
Variable field width          !
```

Notice the trailing spaces preceding the bang (!) character in the output. Those spaces are not present in the string used to initialize str[ ]. The spaces are generated by virtue of the fact that the printf statement specifies a 30-character width for the string.

Printing characters and strings

The printf() conversion specifier for strings is s, as you have already seen in the previous examples. The specifier for individual characters is c (for char). They are summarized in Table 13-2.

Table 13-2. Conversion specifiers for printing characters and strings

Specifier	Argument types	Representation
c	int	A single character
s	Pointer to any char type	The string addressed by the pointer argument

The following example prints a separator character between the elements in a list of team members:

```
char *team[ ] = { "Vivian", "Tim", "Frank", "Sally" };
char separator = ';';
for ( int i = 0;  i < sizeof(team)/sizeof(char *); ++i )
  printf( "%10s%c ", team[i], separator );
putchar( '\n' );
```

The argument represented by the specification %c can also have a narrower type than int, such as char. Integer promotion automatically converts such an argument to int. The printf() function then converts the int arguments to unsigned char, and prints the corresponding character.

For string output, you can also specify the maximum number of characters of the string that may be printed. This is a special use of the precision option in the conversion specification, which consists of a dot followed by a decimal integer. Here is an example:

```
char msg[] = "Every solution breeds new problems.";
printf( "%.14s\n", msg );     // Precision: 14.
printf( "%20.14s\n", msg );   // Field width is 20; precision is 14.
printf( "%.8s\n", msg+6 );    // Print the string starting at the 7th
                              // character in msg, with precision 8.
```

These statements produce the following output:

```
Every solution
      Every solution
solution
```

Printing integers

The printf() functions can convert integer values into decimal, octal, or hexadecimal notation. The conversion specifiers listed in Table 13-3 are provided for this purpose.

Table 13-3. Conversion specifiers for printing integers

Specifier	Argument types	Representation
d, i	`int`	Decimal
u	`unsigned int`	Decimal
o	`unsigned int`	Octal
x	`unsigned int`	Hexadecimal with lowercase a, b, c, d, e, f
X	`unsigned int`	Hexadecimal with uppercase A, B, C, D, E, F

The following example illustrates different conversions of the same integer value:

```
printf( "%4d %4o %4x %4X\n", 63, 63, 63, 63 );
```

This `printf()` call produces the following output:

```
  63   77   3f   3F
```

The specifiers u, o, x, and X interpret the corresponding argument as an unsigned integer. If the argument's type is `int` and its value negative, the converted output is the positive number that corresponds to the argument's bit pattern when interpreted as an `unsigned int`:

```
printf( "%d   %u   %X\n", -1, -1, -1 );
```

If `int` is 32 bits wide, this statement yields the following output:

```
-1   4294967295   FFFFFFFF
```

Because the arguments are subject to integer promotion, the same conversion specifiers can be used to format `short` and `unsigned short` arguments. For arguments with the type `long` or `unsigned long`, you must prefix the length modifier l (a lowercase L) to the d, i, u, o, x, and X specifiers. Similarly, the length modifier for arguments with the type `long long` or `unsigned long long` is ll (two lowercase Ls). Here is an example:

```
long bignumber = 100000L;
unsigned long long hugenumber = 100000ULL * 1000000ULL;
printf( "%ld   %llX\n", bignumber, hugenumber );
```

These statements produce the following output:

```
100000   2540BE400
```

Printing floating-point numbers

Table 13-4 shows the `printf()` conversion specifiers to format floating-point numbers in various ways.

Table 13-4. Conversion specifiers for printing floating-point numbers

Specifier	Argument types	Representation
f	double	Decimal floating-point number
e, E	double	Exponential notation, decimal
g, G	double	Floating-point or exponential notation, whichever is shorter
a, A	double	Exponential notation, hexadecimal

The most commonly used specifiers are f and e (or E). The following example illustrates how they work:

```
double x = 12.34;
printf( "%f  %e  %E\n", x, x, x );
```

This printf() call generates following output line:

```
12.340000  1.234000e+01  1.234000E+01
```

The e that appears in the exponential notation in the output is lowercase or uppercase, depending on whether you use e or E for the conversion specifier. Furthermore, as the example illustrates, the default output shows precision to six decimal places. The precision option in the conversion specification modifies this behavior:

```
double value = 8.765;
printf( "Value: %.2f\n", value );          // Precision is 2: output to
                                           // two decimal places.
printf( "Integer value:\n"
        " Rounded:     %5.0f\n"            // Field width 5; precision 0.
        " Truncated:   %5d\n", value, (int)value );
```

These printf() calls produce the following output:

```
Value: 8.77
Integer value:
  Rounded:     9
  Truncated:   8
```

As this example illustrates, printf() rounds floating-point numbers up or down in converting them for output. If you specify a precision of 0, the decimal point itself is suppressed. If you simply want to truncate the fractional part of the value, you can cast the floating-point number as an integer type.

The specifiers described can also be used with float arguments, because they are automatically promoted to double. To print arguments of type long double, however, you must insert the length modifier L before the conversion specifier, as in this example:

```
#include <math.h>
long double xxl = expl(1000);
printf( "e to the power of 1000 is %.2Le\n", xxl );
```

Formatted Input

To read in data from a formatted source, C provides the scanf() family of functions. Like the printf() functions, the scanf() functions take as one of their arguments a format string that controls the conversion between the I/O format and the
program's internal data. This section highlights the differences between the uses of
format strings and conversion specifications in the scanf() and printf() functions.

The scanf() function family

The various scanf() functions all process the characters in the input source in the
same way. They differ in the kinds of data sources they read, however, and in the
ways in which they receive their arguments. The scanf() functions for byte-
oriented streams are:

int scanf(const char * restrict *format*, ...);
    Reads from the standard input stream, stdin.

int fscanf(FILE * restrict *fp*, const char * restrict *format*, ...);
    Reads from the input stream referenced by *fp*.

int sscanf(const char * restrict *src*,
            const char * restrict *format*, ...);
    Reads from the char array addressed by *src*.

The ellipsis (...) stands for more arguments, which are optional. The optional arguments are pointers to the variables in which the scanf() function stores the results
of its conversions.

Like the printf() functions, the scanf() family also includes variants that take a
pointer to an argument list, rather than accepting a variable number of arguments
directly in the function call. The names of these functions begin with the letter v for
"variable argument list": vscanf(), vfscanf(), and vsscanf(). To use the variable
argument list functions, you must include *stdarg.h* in addition to *stdio.h*.

There are counterparts to all of these functions for reading wide-oriented streams.
The names of the wide-character functions contain the sequence wscanf in place of
scanf, as in wscanf() and vfwscanf(), for example.

The C11 standard provides a new "secure" alternative to each of the scanf() functions. The names of these new functions end in the suffix _s, as in fscanf_s(), for
example. The new functions test whether the array bounds would be exceeded
before reading a string into an array.

The format string

The format string for the scanf() functions contains both ordinary characters and conversion specifications that define how to interpret and convert the sequences of characters read. Most of the conversion specifiers for the scanf() functions are similar to those defined for the printf() functions. However, conversion specifications in the scanf() functions have no flags and no precision options. The general syntax of conversion specifications for the scanf() functions is as follows:

%[*][*field_width*][*length_modifier*]*specifier*

For each conversion specification in the format string, one or more characters are read from the input source and converted in accordance with the conversion specifier. The result is stored in the object addressed by the corresponding pointer argument. Here is an example:

```
int age = 0;
char name[64] = "";
printf( "Please enter your first name and your age:\n" );
scanf( "%s%d", name, &age );
```

Suppose that the user enters the following line when prompted:

Bob 27\n

The scanf() call writes the string Bob into the char array name, and the value 27 in the int variable age.

All conversion specifications, except those with the specifier c, skip over leading whitespace characters. In the previous example, the user could type any number of space, tab, or newline characters before the first word, Bob, or between Bob and 27, without affecting the results.

The sequence of characters read for a given conversion specification ends when scanf() reads any whitespace character, or any character that cannot be interpreted under that conversion specification. Such a character is pushed back onto the input stream so that processing for the next conversion specification begins with that character. In the previous example, suppose the user enters this line:

Bob 27years\n

Then on reaching the character y, which cannot be part of a decimal numeral, scanf() stops reading characters for the conversion specification %d. After the function call, the characters years\n would remain in the input stream's buffer.

If, after skipping over any whitespace, scanf() doesn't find a character that matches the current conversion specification, an error occurs and the scanf() function stops processing the input. We'll show you how to detect such errors in a moment.

Often the format string in a scanf() function call contains only conversion specifications. If not, all other characters in the format string, except whitespace characters, must literally match characters in corresponding positions in the input source.

Otherwise, the scanf() function quits processing and pushes the mismatched character back on to the input stream.

One or more consecutive whitespace characters in the format string matches any number of consecutive whitespace characters in the input stream. In other words, for any whitespace in the format string, scanf() reads past all whitespace characters in the data source up to the first non-whitespace character. Knowing this, what's the matter with the following scanf() call?

```
scanf( "%s%d\n", name, &age );      // Problem?
```

Suppose that the user enters the following line:

```
Bob 27\n
```

In this case, scanf() doesn't return after reading the newline character but instead continues reading more input—until a non-whitespace character comes along.

Sometimes you will want to read past any sequence of characters that matches a certain conversion specification without storing the result. You can achieve exactly this effect by inserting an asterisk (*) immediately after the percent sign (%) in the conversion specification. Do not include a pointer argument for a conversion specification with an asterisk.

The return value of a scanf() function is the number of data items successfully converted and stored. If everything goes well, the return value matches the number of conversion specifications, not counting any that contain an asterisk. The scanf() functions return the value of EOF if a read error occurs or they reach the end of the input source before converting any data items. Here is an example:

```
if ( scanf( "%s%d", name, &age ) < 2 )
  fprintf( stderr, "Bad input.\n" );
else
{ /* ... Test the values stored ... */ }
```

Field widths

The field width is a positive decimal integer that specifies the *maximum* number of characters that scanf() reads for the given conversion specification. For string input, this item can be used to prevent buffer overflows:

```
char city[32];
printf( "Your city: " );
if ( scanf( "%31s", city ) < 1 )  // Never read in more than 31
                                  // characters!
  fprintf( stderr, "Error reading from standard input.\ n" );
else
/* ... */
```

Unlike printf(), which exceeds the specified field width whenever the output is longer than that number of characters, scanf() with the s conversion specifier never writes more characters to a buffer than the number specified by the field width.

Reading characters and strings

The conversion specifications %c and %1c read the next character in the input stream, even if it is a whitespace character. By specifying a field width, you can read that exact number of characters, including whitespace characters, as long as the end of the input stream does not intervene. When you read more than one character in this way, the corresponding pointer argument must point to a char array that is large enough to hold all the characters read. The scanf() function with the c conversion specifer does not append a terminating null character. Here is an example:

```
scanf( "%*5c" );
```

This scanf() call reads and discards the next five characters in the input source.

The conversion specification %s always reads just one word, as a whitespace character ends the sequence read. To read entire text lines, you can use the fgets() function.

The following example reads the contents of a text file word by word. Here we assume that the file pointer fp is associated with a text file that has been opened for reading:

```
char word[128];
while ( fscanf( fp, "%127s", word ) == 1 )
{
    /* ... process the word read ... */
}
```

In addition to the conversion specifier s, you can also read strings using the "scan-set" specifier, which consists of an unordered set of characters between square brackets ([scanset]). The scanf() function then reads all characters, and saves them as a string (with a terminating null character), until it reaches a character that does not match any of those in the scanset. Here is an example:

```
char strNumber[32];
scanf( "%[0123456789]", strNumber );
```

If the user enters 345X67, then scanf() stores the string 345\0 in the array strNumber. The character X and all subsequent characters remain in the input buffer.

To invert the scanset—that is, to match all characters *except* those between the square brackets—insert a caret (^) immediately after the opening bracket. The following scanf() call reads all characters, including whitespace, up to a punctuation character that terminates a sentence, and then reads the punctuation character itself:

```
char ch, sentence[512];
scanf( "%511[^.!?]%c", sentence, &ch );
```

The following `scanf()` call can be used to read and discard all characters up to the end of the current line:

```
scanf( "%*[^\n]%*c" );
```

Reading integers

Like the `printf()` functions, the `scanf()` functions offer the following conversion specifiers for integers: d, i, u, o, x, and X. These allow you to read and convert decimal, octal, and hexadecimal notation to `int` or `unsigned int` variables. Here is an example:

```
// Read a non-negative decimal integer:
unsigned int value = 0;
if ( scanf( "%u", &value ) < 1 )
  fprintf( stderr, "Unable to read an integer.\n" );
else
  /* ... */
```

For the specifier i in the `scanf()` functions, the base of the numeral read is not predefined. Instead, it is determined by the prefix of the numeric character sequence read, in the same way as for integer constants in C source code (see "Integer Constants" on page 39). If the character sequence does not begin with a zero, then it is interpreted as a decimal numeral. If it does begin with a zero and the second character is not x or X, then the sequence is interpreted as an octal numeral. A sequence that begins with 0x or 0X is read as a hexadecimal numeral.

To assign the integer read to a `short`, `char`, `long`, or `long long` variable (or to a variable of a corresponding unsigned type), you must insert a length modifier before the conversion specifier: h for `short`, hh for `char`, l for `long`, or ll for `long long`. In the following example, the `FILE` pointer fp refers to a file opened for reading:

```
unsigned long position = 0;
if (fscanf( fp, "%lX", &position) < 1 )  // Read a hexadecimal integer.
  /* ... Handle error: unable to read a numeral ... */
```

Reading floating-point numbers

To process floating-point numerals, the `scanf()` functions use the same conversion specifiers as `printf()`: f, e, E, g, and G. Furthermore, C99 has added the specifiers a and A. All of these specifiers interpret the character sequence read in the same way. The character sequences that can be interpreted as floating-point numerals are the same as the valid floating-point constants in C; see "Floating-Point Constants" on page 40. `scanf()` can also convert integer numerals and store them in floating-point variables.

All of these specifiers convert the numeral read into a floating-point value with the type `float`. If you want to convert and store the value read as a variable of type, double or `long double`, you must insert a length modifier: either `l` (a lowercase L) for `double`, or `L` for `long double`. Here is an example:

```
float x = 0.0F;
double xx = 0.0;
// Read in two floating-point numbers; convert one to float and the
// other to double:
if ( scanf( "%f %lf", &x, &xx ) < 2 )
   /* ... */
```

If this `scanf()` call receives the input sequence 12.3 7\n, then it stores the value 12.3 in the `float` variable x, and the value 7.0 in the `double` variable xx.

Random File Access

Random file access refers to the ability to read or modify information directly at any given position in a file. You do this by getting and setting a file position indicator, which represents the current access position in the file associated with a given stream.

Obtaining the Current File Position

The following functions return the current file access position. Use one of these functions when you need to note a position in the file to return to it later:

`long ftell( FILE *fp );`

> `ftell()` returns the file position of the stream specified by *fp*. For a binary stream, this is the same as the number of characters in the file before this given position—that is, the offset of the current character from the beginning of the file. `ftell()` returns -1 if an error occurs.

`int fgetpos( FILE * restrict fp, fpos_t * restrict ppos );`

> `fgetpos()` writes the file position indicator for the stream designated by *fp* to an object of type `fpos_t`, addressed by *ppos*. If *fp* is a wide-oriented stream, then the indicator saved by `fgetpos()` also includes the stream's current conversion state (see "Byte-Oriented and Wide-Oriented Streams" on page 216). `fgetpos()` returns a nonzero value to indicate that an error occurred. A return value of zero indicates success.

The following example records the positions of all lines in the text file *messages.txt* that begin with the character #:

```
#define ARRAY_LEN 1000
long arrPos[ARRAY_LEN] = { 0L };
FILE *fp = fopen( "messages.txt", "r" );
if ( fp != NULL)
{
  int i = 0, c1 = '\n', c2;
  while ( i < ARRAY_LEN  && ( c2 = getc(fp) ) != EOF )
    {
```

```
    if ( c1 == '\n'  &&  c2 == '#' )
        arrPos[i++] = ftell( fp ) - 1;
    c1 = c2;
  }
  /* ... */
}
```

Setting the File Access Position

The following functions modify the file position indicator:

`int fsetpos( FILE *fp, const fpos_t *ppos );`

Sets both the file position indicator and the conversion state to the values stored in the object referenced by *ppos*. These values must have been obtained by a call to the fgetpos() function. If successful, fsetpos() returns 0 and clears the stream's EOF flag. A nonzero return value indicates an error.

`int fseek( FILE *fp, long offset, int origin );`

Sets the file position indicator to a position specified by the value of *offset* and by a reference point indicated by the *origin* argument. The *offset* argument indicates a position relative to one of three possible reference points, which are identified by macro values. Table 13-5 lists these macros, as well as the numeric values that were used for *origin* before ANSI C defined them. The value of *offset* can be negative. The resulting file position must be greater than or equal to zero, however.

Table 13-5. The origin parameter in fseek()

Macro name	Traditional value of origin	Offset is relative to
SEEK_SET	0	The beginning of the file
SEEK_CUR	1	The current file position
SEEK_END	2	The end of the file

When working with text streams—on systems that distinguish between text and binary streams—you should always use a value obtained by calling the ftell() function for the *offset* argument, and let *origin* have the value SEEK_SET. The function pairs ftell()-fseek() and fgetpos()-fsetpos() are not mutually compatible, because the fpos_t object used by fgetpos() and fsetpos() to indicate a file position may not have an arithmetic type.

If successful, fseek() clears the stream's EOF flag and returns zero. A nonzero return value indicates an error. rewind() sets the file position indicator to the beginning of the file and clears the stream's EOF and error flags:

`void rewind( FILE *fp );`

Except for the error flag, the call rewind(*fp*) is equivalent to:

```
(void)fseek(fp, 0L, SEEK_SET )
```

If the file has been opened for reading and writing, you can perform either a read or a write operation after a successful call to fseek(), fsetpos(), or rewind().

The following example uses an index table to store the positions of records in the file. This approach permits direct access to a record that needs to be updated:

```c
// setNewName(): Finds a keyword in an index table
// and updates the corresponding record in the file.
// The file containing the records must be opened in
// "update mode"; i.e., with the mode string "r+b".
// Arguments: - A FILE pointer to the open data file;
//            - The key;
//            - The new name.
// Return value: A pointer to the updated record,
//               or NULL if no such record was found.
// -----------------------------------------------------------------
#include <stdio.h>
#include <string.h>
#include "Record.h"   // Defines the types Record_t, IndexEntry_t:
                      // typedef struct { long key; char name[32];
                      //                  /* ... */ } Record_t;
                      // typedef struct { long key, pos; } IndexEntry_t;

extern IndexEntry_t indexTab[];    // The index table.
extern int indexLen;               // The number of table entries.

Record_t *setNewName( FILE *fp, long key, const char *newname )
{
  static Record_t record;
  int i;
  for ( i = 0; i < indexLen; ++i )
  {
    if ( key == indexTab[i].key )
      break;                       // Found the specified key.
  }
  if ( i == indexLen )
    return NULL;                   // No match found.
  // Set the file position to the record:
  if (fseek( fp, indexTab[i].pos, SEEK_SET ) != 0 )
    return NULL;                   // Positioning failed.
  // Read the record:
  if ( fread( &record, sizeof(Record_t), 1, fp ) != 1 )
    return NULL;                   // Error on reading.

  if ( key != record.key )         // Test the key.
    return NULL;
  else
  {                                // Update the record:
    size_t size = sizeof(record.name);
    strncpy( record.name, newname, size-1 );
```

```
      record.name[size-1] = '\0';

   if ( fseek( fp, indexTab[i].pos, SEEK_SET ) != 0 )
      return NULL;                      // Error setting file position.
   if ( fwrite( &record, sizeof(Record_t), 1, fp ) != 1 )
      return NULL;                      // Error writing to file.

   return &record;
   }
}
```

The second fseek() call before the write operation could also be replaced with the following, moving the file pointer relative to its previous position:

```
if (fseek( fp, -(long)sizeof(Record_t), SEEK_CUR ) != 0 )
      return NULL;                      // Error setting file position.
```

14

Multithreading

C programs often perform several tasks simultaneously. For example, a program may:

- Execute procedures that accomplish intermediate tasks in parallel and so improve performance
- Process user input while carrying on time-consuming data communication or real-time operations "in the background"

Different tasks are performed simultaneously by the *concurrent execution* of parts of the program. Especially on modern multiprocessor systems—including multicore processors, of course—it is increasingly important for programs to take advantage of concurrency to use the system's resources efficiently.

Until recently, C developers have had to depend on features of the operating system or appropriate libraries to implement concurrent execution. Now, however, the new C11 standard makes concurrency in C programming portable. C11 supports *multithreaded execution*, or multiple parallel paths of control flow within a process, and provides the same degree of concurrency as all modern operating systems. To this end, C11 defines an appropriate *memory model* and supports *atomic operations*. Support for multithreading and atomic operations are optional under the C11 standard, however. An implementation that conforms to C11 must simply define the macros __STDC_NO_THREADS__ and __STDC_NO_ATOMICS__ if it does not provide the corresponding features.

You may have already worked with the POSIX threads extension to C (called *pthreads* for short); that is, the library that implements multithreading in accordance with the Portable Operating System Interface for UNIX (POSIX) standard,

IEEE 1003.1c. If so, you will find that the C11 threads programming interface is similar in most respects to the POSIX standard.

Threads

When you start a program, the operating system creates a new process in which the program is executed. A process consists of one or more *threads*. Each thread is a partial process that executes a sequence of instructions independently of other parts of the process. When the process begins, its main thread is active. From then on, any running thread can launch other threads. All threads that have been started but not yet ended are terminated when the process terminates—for example, by executing a return statement in the main() function or by calling the exit() function.

The system's scheduler allocates the available CPU time to all runnable threads equally. Usually the scheduler is preemptive: that means it interrupts the thread being executed by a central processing unit (CPU) at brief intervals and assigns the CPU a different thread for a time. As a result, threads appear to the user to be executed in parallel, even on a single-processor system. Truly simultaneous execution of several threads is only possible on a multiprocessor system, however.

Every process has its own address space in memory, and has other exclusive resources, such as open files. All the threads of a process inherit its resources. Most significantly, several threads in one process share the same address space. That makes task-switching within a process much simpler for the scheduler than switching to a different process.

However, each thread also has resources of its own that are necessary for task-switching between threads: these include stack memory and CPU registers. These allow each thread to process its own local data without interference between threads. In addition, a thread may also have thread-specific permanent memory (see "Thread-Local Objects and Thread-Specific Storage" on page 256).

Because the threads of a given process use the same address space, they share their global and static data. That means, however, that two different threads can access the same memory locations concurrently. This situation is called a *data race* in the C standard, or a *race condition* in popular parlance. To prevent inconsistencies in shared data, the programmer must explicitly *synchronize* different threads' writing operations or reading and writing operations if they use the same locations in memory.

Creating Threads

The macro definitions and the declarations of types and functions to support multithreading are declared in the header *threads.h*. All of the identifiers that are directly related to threads begin with the prefix thrd_. For example, thrd_t is the type of an object that identifies a thread.

The function that creates and starts executing a new thread is called `thrd_create()`. One of its arguments names the function to be executed in the new thread. The complete prototype of `thrd_create()` is:

```
int thrd_create(thrd_t *thr, thrd_start_t func, void *arg);
```

The parameter `func` is a pointer to the function that the thread will execute, and the void pointer `arg` is used to pass an argument to that function. In other words, the new thread will perform the function call `func(arg)`. The type of the `func` argument, `thrd_start_t`, is defined as `int (*)(void*)` (that is, a pointer to a function that takes a void pointer as its argument and returns an `int`), so the function that the thread carries out returns a value of the type `int`. The program can subsequently obtain this return value—waiting for the thread to finish if necessary—by calling the function `thread_join()`.

If it succeeds in starting a thread, the function `thread_create()` writes the identification of the new thread in the object pointed to by the argument *thr*, and returns the value of the macro `thread_success`.

In most cases, other operations later in the program depend on the results of the thread's execution and can only be performed when it has finished. The function `thread_join()` is used to ensure that a thread has finished. Its prototype is:

```
int thrd_join(thrd_t thr, int *result);
```

The thread that calls `thread_join()` blocks—that is, it stops at that point in the program as long as necessary—until the thread identified by `thr` finishes. Then `thread_join()` writes the return value of that thread's function in the `int` variable that the pointer `result` refers to (unless `result` is a null pointer). Finally, `thread_join()` releases any resources that belong to the thread.

If the program's logic does not require it to wait for a thread to end, it should call the function:

```
int thrd_detach(thrd_t thr);
```

Then all of the thread's resources will be released when the thread finishes. Once a thread has been detached, there is no way for the program to wait for it to end, nor to obtain the return value of the thread function. A program can call either `thread_join()` or `thread_detach()` no more than once for each thread created.

The program in Example 14-1 illustrates a way of processing an array using parallel operations. Separate threads first process parts of the array, and then their results are joined together. The program merely calculates the sum of a sequence of numbers.

The function `sum()` first determines the maximum size of a block of array elements from the number of threads to be created, and then calls the recursive helper function `parallel_sum()`.

The parallel_sum() function divides the array into two halves and gives one half to a new thread to work on, and then calls itself to process the other half. As the example illustrates, several arguments needed by a thread function are generally grouped in a structure.

Example 14-1. Calculating the sum of array elements in several parallel threads

```c
#include <stdbool.h>
#include <threads.h>

#define MAX_THREADS 8      // 1, 2, 4, 8 ... Maximum number
                           // of threads to create.
#define MIN_BLOCK_SIZE 100 // Minimum size of an array block.

typedef struct            // Arguments for the parallel_sum() function.
{
    float *start;         // Start and length of the
    int len;              // array block passed to parallel_sum().
    int block_size;       // Size of the smallest blocks.
    double sum;           // The result.
} Sum_arg;

int parallel_sum(void *arg);      // Prototype of the thread function.

// -----------------------------------------------------------------
// Calculate the sum of array elements and write it to *sumPtr.
// sum() calls the function parallel_sum() for parallel processing.
// Return value: true if no error occurs; otherwise, false.
bool sum(float arr[], int len, double* sumPtr)
{
    int block_size = len / MAX_THREADS;
    if (block_size < MIN_BLOCK_SIZE) block_size = len;

    Sum_arg args = { arr, len, block_size, 0.0 };
    if (parallel_sum(&args))
    { *sumPtr = args.sum;   return true; }
    else
       return false;
}
// -----------------------------------------------------------------
// Recursive helper function to divide the work among several threads.
int parallel_sum(void *arg)
{
    Sum_arg *argp = (Sum_arg*)arg;      // A pointer to the arguments.

    if (argp->len <= argp->block_size) // If length <= block_size,
    {                                  // add up the elements.
        for (int i = 0; i < argp->len; ++i)
            argp->sum += argp->start[i];
        return 1;
```

```
        }
        else                          // If length > block_size,
        {                             // divide the array.
            int mid = argp->len / 2;
            Sum_arg arg2 = { argp->start+mid, argp->len-mid,
                        argp->block_size, 0};   // Specifies second half
            argp->len = mid;                    // Length of first half


            thrd_t th;              // Process first half in a new thread.
            int res = 0;
            if (thrd_create(&th, parallel_sum, arg) != thrd_success)
                return 0;           // Couldn't spawn a thread

            if (!parallel_sum(&arg2)) // Process second half by recursion
                                      // in the current thread.
            {
                thrd_detach(th); return 0;   // Recursive call failed
            }
            thrd_join(th, &res);
            if (!res)
                return 0;   // Sibling thread reported failure

            argp->sum += arg2.sum;
            return 1;
        }
    }
}
```

Other Thread Functions

In addition to the thread_create(), thread_join() and thread_detach() functions described in the previous section, C11 provides five more functions for thread
control:

thrd_t thrd_current(void);
> This function returns the identification of the thread in which it is called.

int thrd_equal(thrd_t *thr0*, thrd_t *thr1*);
> Returns 0 if and only if the two thread identifiers refer to different threads.

int thrd_sleep(const struct timespec *duration*,
                struct timespec *remaining*);
> Blocks the calling thread for the period specified by duration. The function
> returns earlier only if it receives a signal that is not being ignored (see "Signals"
> on page 339). In that case, the function saves the remaining countdown time in
> the object pointed to by remaining, provided remaining is not a null pointer.
> The pointers duration and remaining must not point to the same object.

The structure argument `timespec` has two members for storing seconds and nanoseconds:

```
time_t tv_sec;    // Seconds >= 0
long   tv_nsec;   // 0 <= nanoseconds <= 999999999
```

The order of the members in the structure is not specified. In the following example, the calling thread waits for at least 100 milliseconds unless interrupted by a signal:

```
struct timespec duration = {0};
duration.tv_nsec = 100*1E6;   // 1 millisecond
                              // = 1,000,000 nanoseconds
thrd_sleep(&duration,NULL);   // Sleep for 100 milliseconds.
```

The function `thrd_sleep()` returns 0 if the countdown has expired, or -1 if it was interrupted by a signal. Other negative return values indicate errors.

```
void thrd_yield(void);
```
This function advises the operating system's scheduler to interrupt the calling thread and give CPU time to another thread.

```
_Noreturn void thrd_exit(int result);
```
Ends the calling thread with the result `result`. Any function executed in the thread may call `thrd_exit()`. This function call is equivalent to the statement `return result;` in the thread function. Exiting the last remaining thread causes the program to exit normally; that is, as if the `exit()` function were called with the argument `EXIT_SUCCESS`.

Accessing Shared Data

If several threads access the same data and at least one of them modifies it, then all access to the shared data must be synchronized in order to prevent data races. Otherwise, a thread that reads shared data could interrupt another thread that is in the middle of modifying the same data, and would then read inconsistent values. Moreover, because the system may schedule the threads differently each time a program is executed, such errors only manifest themselves intermittently in running programs and are difficult to reproduce in testing. As the program in Example 14-2 illustrates, a data race can occur even in such a simple operation as incrementing a counter.

Example 14-2. Concurrent memory access without synchronization

```
#include <stdio.h>
#include <threads.h>

#define COUNT 10000000L

long counter = 0;
void incFunc(void) {  for (long i = 0; i < COUNT; ++i)  ++counter; }
```

```
void decFunc(void) {  for (long i = 0; i < COUNT; ++i)  --counter; }

int main(void)
{
    clock_t cl = clock();
    thrd_t th1, th2;
    if (thrd_create(&th1, (thrd_start_t)incFunc, NULL) != thrd_success
      || thrd_create(&th2, (thrd_start_t)decFunc, NULL) != thrd_success)
    {
        fprintf(stderr,"Error creating thread\n"); return -1;
    }
    thrd_join(th1, NULL);
    thrd_join(th2, NULL);

    printf("Counter: %ld \t", counter);
    printf("CPU time: %ld ms\n", (clock()-cl)*1000L/CLOCKS_PER_SEC);
    return 0;
}
```

The counter should be 0 when the program ends. However, without synchronization, that is not the case: the final counter value is different each time the program runs. Here is a typical output sample:

```
Counter: -714573        CPU time: 59 ms
```

To permit synchronization, the C library provides *mutex operations* and *atomic operations*.

Mutual Exclusion

The technique of *mutual exclusion*, or *mutex* for short, is used to prevent several threads from accessing shared resources at the same time. The name mutex is given to an object used to control exclusive access authorization. Together with *condition variables*, mutexes permit extensive control of synchronized access. For example, they allow you to specify the order in which data access operations must occur.

In C programs, a mutex is represented by an object of the type mtx_t that can be locked by only one thread at a time, while other threads must wait until it is unlocked. All of the declarations pertaining to operations on mutexes are contained in the header *threads.h*. The most important mutex functions are:

int mtx_init(mtx_t *mtx, int mutextype);

> Creates a mutex with the properties specified by mutextype. If it succeeds in creating a new mutex, the function mtx_init() writes the ID of the new mutex in the object pointed to by the argument mtx, and returns the value of the macro thrd_success.

The argument mutextype can have one of the following four values:

```
mtx_plain
mtx_timed
```

```
mtx_plain | mtx_recursive
mtx_timed | mtx_recursive
```

The value mtx_plain requests a simple mutex that supports neither timeouts nor recursion; the other values specify timeout and/or recursion support.

`void mtx_destroy(mtx_t *mtx);`

Destroys the mutex pointed to by mtx, releasing all its resources.

`int mtx_lock(mtx_t *mtx);`

Blocks the calling thread until it obtains the mutex specified by mtx. The calling thread must not already hold the mutex unless the mutex supports recursion. If the call succeeds in obtaining the mutex, it returns the value of thrd_success. Otherwise, it returns thrd_error.

`int mtx_unlock(mtx_t *mtx);`

Releases the mutex referred to by mtx. The caller must hold the mutex before calling mtx_unlock(). If the call succeeds in releasing the mutex, it returns the value of thrd_success. Otherwise, it returns thrd_error.

The complementary functions mtx_lock() and mtx_unlock() are called at the beginning and end of a *critical section* of code which only one thread at a time must execute. Two alternatives to mtx_lock() are the functions mtx_trylock(), which obtains the mutex if it happens to be free but doesn't block if it is not, and mtx_timedlock(), which only blocks until a specified time. All of these functions indicate by their return value whether the call succeeded in obtaining the mutex.

The program in Example 14-3 is a modification of Example 14-2 and shows how to use a mutex to eliminate the data race for the variable counter.

Example 14-3. Adding a mutex to the program in Example 14-2

```c
#include <stdio.h>
#include <threads.h>

#define COUNT 10000000L

long counter = 0;
mtx_t mtx;                       // A mutex for access to counter

void incFunc(void)
{
    for (long i = 0; i < COUNT; ++i)
    { mtx_lock(&mtx);  ++counter;  mtx_unlock(&mtx); }
}
void decFunc(void)
{
    for (long i = 0; i < COUNT; ++i)
    { mtx_lock(&mtx);  --counter;  mtx_unlock(&mtx); }
}
```

```
int main(void)
{
    if (mtx_init(&mtx, mtx_plain) != thrd_success)
    {
        fprintf(stderr, "Error initializing the mutex.\n");
        return -1;
    }
    //
    // As in Example 14-2: start threads, wait for them to finish,
    // print output.
    //
    mtx_destroy(&mtx);
    return 0;
}
```

The functions incFunc() and decFunc() can no longer access counter concurrently, as only one of them can lock the mutex at a time. (Error checking has been omitted for the sake of readability.) Now the counter has the correct value, 0, at the end of the program. Here is a typical output sample:

```
Counter: 0        CPU time: 650 ms
```

Synchronization works, but at a price. The higher CPU time shows that the program now takes about ten times as long to run. The reason is that synchronization by locking a mutex is a much more complex operation than incrementing and decrementing a variable. Better performance can be achieved using atomic objects in cases where they obviate the need for a mutex lock.

Atomic Objects

An *atomic object* is an object that can be read or modified by means of *atomic operations*; that is, by operations that cannot be interrupted by a concurrent thread. You can declare an atomic object using the type qualifier _Atomic, introduced in C11 (unless the implementation defines the macro __STDC_NO_ATOMICS__). For example, the counter variable in the program in Example 14-2 can be made atomic by declaring it as follows:

```
_Atomic long counter = ATOMIC_VAR_INIT(0L);
```

This declaration defines the atomic long variable counter and initializes it with the value 0. The macro ATOMIC_VAR_INIT and all the other macros, types, and declarations for using atomic objects are found in the header *stdatomic.h*. In particular, *stdatomic.h* defines abbreviations for atomic types corresponding to all the integer types. For example, the type atomic_uchar is equivalent to _Atomic unsigned char.

The syntax _Atomic(*T*) can also be used to specify the atomic type corresponding to a given non-atomic type *T*. Array and function types cannot be atomic, however. An atomic type may have a different size and alignment from those of the corresponding non-atomic type.

Atomic Operations

Reading or writing an atomic object is an *atomic operation*; that is, an operation that cannot be interrupted. That means that different threads can access an atomic object concurrently without causing a race condition. For every atomic object, all modifications of the object are performed in a definite global order, which is called its *modification order*.

An atomic object with a structure or union type should only be read or written as a whole: for safe access to individual members, the atomic structure or union should first be copied to an equivalent non-atomic object.

Note that the initialization of an atomic object, whether using the macro ATOMIC_VAR_INIT or by the generic function atomic_init(), is not an atomic operation.

Atomic operations are typically carried out as *read-modify-write operations*. For example, the postfix increment and decrement operators ++ and --, when applied to an atomic object, are atomic read-modify-write operations. Likewise, the compound assignment operators, such as +=, work atomically when their left operand is an atomic object. The program in Example 14-2 can be made to deliver the correct final counter value 0, without any other changes, by declaring the variable counter as atomic. The program's timekeeping shows that the version with an atomic counter variable is more than twice as fast as the version using a mutex in Example 14-3.

In addition to the operators already mentioned, there are a number of functions to perform atomic operations, including atomic_store(), atomic_exchange(), and atomic_compare_exchange_strong(). You will find an overview of this group of functions in Chapter 17, and a detailed description of each one in Chapter 18.

An atomic type has the *lock-free* property if atomic access to an object of this type can be realized without using lock and unlock operations. Only the type atomic_flag, a structure type that can represent the two states "set" and "cleared", is guaranteed to have the lock-free property. The macro ATOMIC_FLAG_INIT initializes an atomic_flag object in the "cleared" state, as in the following declaration, for example:

```
atomic_flag done = ATOMIC_FLAG_INIT;
```

To perform the customary flag operations on an atomic_flag object, C11 provides the functions atomic_flag_test_and_set() and atomic_flag_clear(). The integer atomic types are usually also lock-free. To determine whether a given type is actually lock-free, a program can check the value of a macro of the form ATOMIC_*type*_LOCK_FREE, where *type* is a capitalized abbreviation for a specific integer type, such as BOOL, INT, or LLONG. The corresponding macro for pointer types is `ATOMIC_POINTER_LOCK_FREE`. All of these macros yield values of 0, 1, or 2. The value 0 means that the type is never lock-free; 1 means it is lock-free for certain objects; and 2 means it is always lock-free. Alternatively, you can find out whether a given atomic object is lock-free by calling the generic function:

```
_Bool atomic_is_lock_free(const volatile A *obj);
```

The placeholder *A* in the function's parameter declaration stands for any atomic type. The argument `obj` is thus a pointer to any given atomic object.

Memory Ordering

In optimizing program code, compilers and processors are free to rearrange the order of any instructions that are not interdependent. For example, the two assignment statements a = 0; b = 1; can be executed in either order. In a multithreading environment, however, such optimizations can lead to errors, because dependencies between memory operations in different threads are ordinarily not visible to the compiler or processor.

Using atomic objects prevents such reordering by default. Preventing an optimization may mean sacrificing speed, however. Experienced programmers can improve performance by explicitly using atomic operations with lower memory-ordering requirements. For each function that performs an atomic operation (such as `atomic_store()`, for example), there is also a version that takes an additional argument of the type `memory_order`. These functions have names that end in `_explicit`, such as `atomic_store_explicit()`.

The `memory_order` type is an enumeration that defines the following constants to specify the given memory ordering requirements:

`memory_order_relaxed`
: The caller specifies that there are no memory order requirements, so that the compiler is free to change the order of operations.

`memory_order_release`
: Write access to an atomic object *A* performs a *release operation*. The effect of the release operation is that all the preceding memory access operations in the given thread are visible to another thread that performs an acquire operation on *A*.

`memory_order_acquire`
: A read operation on an atomic object performs an *acquire operation*. That ensures that subsequent memory access operations are not rearranged to occur before this function call.

`memory_order_consume`
> A *consume operation* is less restrictive than an acquire operation: it prevents the reordering only of subsequent memory access operations that depend directly on the atomic variable read.

`memory_order_acq_rel`
> Performs both an acquire and a release operation.

`memory_order_seq_cst`
> The request for *sequential consistency* includes the acquire and release operations of `memory_order_acq_rel`. In addition, it also specifies that all operations that are so qualified are performed in an absolute order that conforms to the modification order of the atomic objects involved. Sequential consistency is the default memory order requirement that is applied to all atomic operations if no lower requirement is explicitly specified.

In the program in Example 14-2, modified to declare `counter` as atomic, the incrementation and decrementation of the counter are performed independently of other operations so that no memory order specifications are necessary. In other words, in place of the statement

```
++counter;              // Implies memory_order_seq_cst
```

the following statement is sufficient, and allows the compiler to perform more optimization:

```
atomic_fetch_add_explicit( &counter, 1, memory_order_relaxed );
```

Release and acquire operations are an efficient way to establish a *happens-before* relation between instructions. In other words, as the following example illustrates, the _explicit functions ensure that a given operation B is only executed after another thread has completed an operation A:

```
struct Data *dp = NULL, data;
atomic_intptr_t aptr = ATOMIC_VAR_INIT(0);

// Thread 1:
   data = ...;                          // Operation A
   atomic_store_explicit( &aptr, (intptr_t)&data,
                          memory_order_release );

// Thread 2:
   dp = (struct Data*)atomic_load_explicit( &aptr,
                                    memory_order_acquire );
   if( dp != NULL)
     // Process the data at *dp
                                        // Operation B
   else
     // Data at *dp not available yet.
```

Synchronization using a mutex also implies an acquire operation when the mutex is locked, and a release operation when it is unlocked. That means that if a thread T1 uses a mutex to protect an operation A, and another thread T2 uses the same mutex to protect an operation B, then operation A will be executed completely before operation B if T1 locks the mutex first. Conversely, if T2 locks the mutex first, then all the modifications performed by operation B will be visible to thread T1 when T1 executes operation A.

Fences

The memory order requirements for an atomic operation can also be specified separately from an atomic operation. This technique is called establishing a *fence* or *memory barrier*. To set a fence, C11 provides the function:

```
void atomic_thread_fence(memory_order order);
```

If the argument's value is memory_order_release, the function establishes a *release fence*. In this case, the atomic write operations must occur after the release fence.

The atomic_thread_fence() function establishes an *acquire fence* if its argument's value is memory_order_acquire or memory_order_consume. The atomic read operations must occur before the acquire fence.

If the argument's value is memory_order_relaxed, the function has no effect. The argument values memory_order_acq_rel and memory_order_seq_cst specify a release and acquire fence.

Fences permit a greater degree of memory-order optimization. In our previous example, an acquire operation in the if branch is sufficient to synchronize the thread operations:

```
// Thread 2:
dp = (struct Data*)atomic_load_explicit( &aptr,
                                memory_order_relaxed );
if( dp != NULL)
{
    atomic_thread_fence(memory_order_acquire);
    // Operation B:
    // Process the data at *dp.
}
else
    // Data at *dp not available yet.
```

Communication Between Threads: Condition Variables

The C11 standard provides *condition variables* for communication between threads. Threads can use condition variables to wait for a notification from another thread indicating that a certain condition is fulfilled. Such a notification may mean that certain data are ready for processing, for example.

A condition variable is represented by an object of the type cnd_t, and is used in conjunction with a mutex. The general procedure is as follows: The thread obtains the mutex and tests the condition. If the condition is not fulfilled, the thread waits on the condition variable—releasing the mutex—until another thread wakes it up. Then the thread obtains the mutex and tests the condition again. This procedure is repeated until the condition is fulfilled.

The functions for working with condition variables, declared in the header *threads.h*, are as follows:

`int cnd_init(cnd_t *cond);`
  Initializes the condition variable pointed to by cond.

`void cnd_destroy(cnd_t *cond);`
  Frees all the resources used by the specified condition variable.

`int cnd_signal(cnd_t *cond);`
  Wakes up one of any number of threads that are waiting for the specified condition variable.

`int cnd_broadcast(cnd_t *cond);`
  Wakes up all the threads waiting for the specified condition variable.

`int cnd_wait(cnd_t *cond, mtx_t *mtx);`
  Blocks the calling thread and releases the specified mutex. A thread must hold the mutex before calling cnd_wait(). If another thread unblocks the caller by sending a signal—that is, by specifying the same condition variable as the argument to a cnd_signal() or cnd_broadcast() call—then the thread that has called cnd_wait() obtains the mutex again before cnd_wait() returns.

`int cnd_timedwait(cnd_t *restrict cond, mtx_t *restrict mtx,`
`              const struct timespec *restrict ts);`
  Like cnd_wait(), cnd_timedwait() blocks the thread that calls it, but only until the time specified by the argument ts. A struct timespec object representing the current time can be obtained by calling the function time spec_get().

All of the condition variable functions except cnd_destroy() return the value of thrd_error if they incur an error, and otherwise thrd_success. The function cnd_timedwait() can also return the value of thrd_timedout if it returns when the time limit has been reached.

The program in Examples 14-4 and 14-5 illustrates the use of condition variables in the common "producer-consumer" model. The program starts a new thread for each producer and for each consumer. A producer puts a new product—in our case, an int value—in a ring buffer, provided the buffer is not full, and signals waiting consumers that a product is available. Each consumer takes products from the buffer, if available, and signals the fact to waiting producers.

Only one thread can modify the ring buffer at any given time. Thread synchronization therefore takes place in the functions bufPut(), which inserts an element in the buffer, and bufGet(), which removes an element from it. There are two condition variables: a producer waits on one of them if the buffer is full, and a consumer waits on the other if the buffer is empty. All the necessary elements of the buffer are contained in the structure `Buffer`. The `bufInit()` function initializes a `Buffer` object with a specified size, and the `bufDestroy()` function destroys it.

Example 14-4. A ring buffer for the producer-consumer model

```
/* buffer.h
 * Declarations for a thread-safe buffer.
 */
#include <stdbool.h>
#include <threads.h>

typedef struct Buffer
{
    int *data;              // Pointer to the array of data.
    size_t size, count;     // Maximum and current numbers of elements.
    size_t tip, tail;       // tip = index of the next free spot.
    mtx_t mtx;              // A mutex and
    cnd_t cndPut, cndGet;   // two condition variables.
} Buffer;

bool bufInit( Buffer *bufPtr, size_t size );
void bufDestroy(Buffer *bufPtr);

bool bufPut(Buffer *bufPtr, int data);
bool bufGet(Buffer *bufPtr, int *dataPtr, int sec);

/* -------------------------------------------------------------
 * buffer.c
 * Definitions of functions operating on Buffer.
 */
#include "buffer.h"
#include <stdlib.h>           // For malloc() and free()

bool bufInit( Buffer *bufPtr, size_t size)
{
    if ((bufPtr->data = malloc( size * sizeof(int))) == NULL)
        return false;
    bufPtr->size = size;
    bufPtr->count = 0;
    bufPtr->tip = bufPtr->tail = 0;
    return    mtx_init( &bufPtr->mtx, mtx_plain) == thrd_success
           && cnd_init( &bufPtr->cndPut) == thrd_success
           && cnd_init( &bufPtr->cndGet) == thrd_success;
}

void bufDestroy(Buffer *bufPtr)
{
    cnd_destroy( &bufPtr->cndGet );
    cnd_destroy( &bufPtr->cndPut );
```

```
    mtx_destroy( &bufPtr->mtx );
    free( bufPtr->data );
}

// Insert a new element in the buffer:
bool bufPut(Buffer *bufPtr, int data)
{
    mtx_lock( &bufPtr->mtx );

    while (bufPtr->count == bufPtr->size)
        if (cnd_wait( &bufPtr->cndPut, &bufPtr->mtx ) != thrd_success)
            return false;

    bufPtr->data[bufPtr->tip] = data;
    bufPtr->tip = (bufPtr->tip + 1) % bufPtr->size;
    ++bufPtr->count;

    mtx_unlock( &bufPtr->mtx );
    cnd_signal( &bufPtr->cndGet );

    return true;
}

// Remove an element from the buffer. If the buffer is empty,
// wait no more than sec seconds.
bool bufGet(Buffer *bufPtr, int *dataPtr, int sec)
{
    struct timespec ts;
    timespec_get( &ts, TIME_UTC );    // The current time
    ts.tv_sec  += sec;                // + sec seconds delay.

    mtx_lock( &bufPtr->mtx );

    while ( bufPtr->count == 0 )
        if (cnd_timedwait(&bufPtr->cndGet,
                          &bufPtr->mtx, &ts) != thrd_success)
            return false;

    *dataPtr = bufPtr->data[bufPtr->tail];
    bufPtr->tail = (bufPtr->tail + 1) % bufPtr->size;
    --bufPtr->count;

    mtx_unlock( &bufPtr->mtx );
    cnd_signal( &bufPtr->cndPut );

    return true;
}
```

The corresponding main() function, shown in Example 14-5, creates a buffer and starts several producer and consumer threads, giving each of them an identification number and a pointer to the buffer. Each producer thread creates a certain number of "products" and then quits with a return statement. A consumer thread returns if it is unable to get a product to consume within a certain delay.

Example 14-5. Starting the producer and consumer threads

```c
// producer_consumer.c
#include "buffer.h"
#include <stdio.h>
#include <stdlib.h>

#define NP 2                        // Number of producers
#define NC 3                        // Number of consumers

int producer(void *);               // The thread functions.
int consumer(void *);

struct Arg { int id; Buffer *bufPtr; };  // Arguments for the
                                         // thread functions.
_Noreturn void errorExit(const char* msg)
{
    fprintf(stderr, "%s\n", msg); exit(0xff);
}

int main(void)
{
    printf("Producer-Consumer Demo\n\n");
    Buffer buf;                         // Create a buffer for
    bufInit( &buf, 5 );                 // five products.

    thrd_t prod[NP], cons[NC];          // The threads and
    struct Arg prodArg[NP], consArg[NC]; // their arguments.
    int i = 0, res = 0;

    for ( i = 0; i < NP; ++i )          // Start the producers.
    {
        prodArg[i].id = i+1, prodArg[i].bufPtr = &buf;
        if (thrd_create( &prod[i], producer, &prodArg[i] ) != thrd_success)
            errorExit("Thread error.");
    }

    for ( i = 0; i < NC; ++i )          // Start the consumers.
    {
        consArg[i].id = i+1, consArg[i].bufPtr = &buf;
        if ( thrd_create( &cons[i], consumer, &consArg[i] ) != thrd_success)
            errorExit("Thread error.");
    }

    for ( i = 0; i < NP; ++i )    // Wait for the threads to finish.
        thrd_join(prod[i], &res),
        printf("\nProducer %d ended with result %d.\n", prodArg[i].id, res);
```

```
    for ( i = 0; i < NC; ++i )
        thrd_join(cons[i], &res),
        printf("Consumer %d ended with result %d.\n", consArg[i].id, res);

    bufDestroy( &buf );
    return 0;
}

int producer(void *arg)        // The producers' thread function.
{
    struct Arg *argPtr = (struct Arg *)arg;
    int id = argPtr->id;
    Buffer *bufPtr = argPtr->bufPtr;

    int count = 0;
    for (int i = 0; i < 10; ++i)
    {
        int data = 10*id + i;
        if (bufPut( bufPtr, data ))
            printf("Producer %d produced %d\n", id, data), ++count;
        else
        { fprintf( stderr,
                "Producer %d: error storing %d\n", id, data);
          return -id;
        }
    }
    return count;
}

int consumer(void *arg)        // The consumers' thread function.
{
    struct Arg *argPtr = (struct Arg *)arg;
    int id = argPtr->id;
    Buffer *bufPtr = argPtr->bufPtr;

    int count = 0;
    int data = 0;
    while (bufGet( bufPtr, &data, 2 ))
    {
        ++count;
        printf("Consumer %d consumed %d\n", id, data);
    }
    return count;
}
```

Thread-Local Objects and Thread-Specific Storage

Thread-local objects and *thread-specific storage* are two techniques by which each thread can maintain separate data while using global identifiers for its variables.

They allow functions that are executed in a given thread to share data without incurring conflicts, even when other threads are executing the same functions.

Using Thread-Local Objects

A global or static object whose declaration contains the new storage class specifier _Thread_local is a *thread-local* object. That means that each thread possesses its own instance of the object, which is created and initialized when the thread starts. The object's storage duration lasts as long as the thread runs. In expressions, the object's name always refers to the local instance of the object that belongs to the thread evaluating the expression.

The specifier _Thread_local can be used together with one of the specifiers static or extern. The header *threads.h* defines thread_local as a synonym for _Thread_local. In Example 14-6, the main thread and the newly started thread each have an instance of the thread-local variable var.

Example 14-6. Using a thread-local object

```
#include <stdio.h>
#include <threads.h>

thread_local int var = 10;

void print_var(void){ printf("var = %d\n", var); }
int func(void *);          // Thread function

int main(int argc, char *argv[])
{
    thrd_t th1;
    if ( thrd_create( &th1, func, NULL ) != thrd_success ){
      fprintf(stderr,"Error creating thread.\n"); return 0xff;
    }
    print_var();           // Output: var = 10
    thrd_join(th1, NULL);
    return 0;
}

int func(void *arg)        // Thread function
{
    var += 10;             // Thread-local variable
    print_var();           // Output: var = 20
    return 0;
}
```

Using Thread-Specific Storage

The technique of thread-specific storage is much more flexible than thread-local objects. The individual threads can use different amounts of storage, for example. They can dynamically allocate memory, and free it again by calling a destructor function. At the same time, the individual threads' distinct memory blocks can be accessed using the same identifiers.

This flexibility is achieved by initially creating a global key that represents a pointer to thread-specific storage. The individual threads can then load this pointer with the location of their thread-specific storage. The key is an object of the type tss_t. The header *threads.h* contains this type definition and the declarations of four functions for managing thread-specific storage (abbreviated TSS):

`int tss_create(tss_t *key, tss_dtor_t dtor);`
> Generates a new TSS pointer with the destructor dtor and sets the object pointed to by key to a value that uniquely identifies the pointer. The type tss_dtor_t is a function pointer, defined as void (*)(void*) (that is, a pointer to a function that takes one void pointer argument and has no return value). The value of dtor may be a null pointer.

`void tss_delete(tss_t key);`
> Frees all the resources used by the TSS key *key*.

`int tss_set(tss_t key, void *val);`
> Sets the TSS pointer identified by key, for the thread that calls tss_set(), to the memory block addressed by val.

`void *tss_get(tss_t key);`
> Returns a pointer to the memory block that the calling thread has set by calling tss_set(). If an error occurs, tss_get() returns NULL.

The functions tss_create() and tss_set() return thrd_error if they incur an error; otherwise, thrd_success.

The program in Example 14-7 stores the name of a thread in dynamically allocated thread-specific memory.

Example 14-7. Using thread-specific storage

```
#include <threads.h>
#include <stdio.h>
#include <stdlib.h>
#include <string.h>

tss_t key;        // Global key for a TSS pointer

int thFunc(void *arg);       // Thread function
void destructor(void *data);  // Destructor function

int main(void)
{
    thrd_t th1, th2;
    int result1 = 0, result2 = 0;
```

```
      // Create the TSS key:
      if (tss_create(&key, destructor) != thrd_success)
        return -1;

      // Create threads:
      if (thrd_create(&th1, thFunc, "Thread_1") != thrd_success
          || thrd_create(&th2, thFunc, "Thread_2") != thrd_success)
        return -2;

      thrd_join(th1, &result1);   thrd_join(th2, &result2);
      if ( result1 != 0 || result2 != 0 )
        fputs("Thread error\n", stderr);
      else
        puts("Threads finished without error.");

      tss_delete(key);   // Free all resources of the TSS pointer.
      return 0;
}

void print(void)      // Display thread-specific storage.
{
  printf( "print: %s\n", (char*)tss_get(key) );
}

int thFunc( void *arg )
{
    char *name = (char*)arg;
    size_t size = strlen(name)+1;

    // Set thread-specific storage:
    if ( tss_set(key, malloc(size)) != thrd_success )
        return -1;
    // Store data:
    strcpy((char*)tss_get(key), name);
    print();
    return 0;
}

void destructor(void *data)
{
  printf("Destructor for %s\n", (char*)data);
  free(data);               // Release memory.
}
```

15

Preprocessing Directives

In "How the C Compiler Works" on page 19, we outlined the eight steps in translation from C source to an executable program. In the first four of those steps, the C preprocessor prepares the source code for the actual compiler. The result is a modified source in which comments have been deleted and *preprocessing directives* have been replaced with the results of their execution.

This chapter describes the C preprocessing directives. Among these are directives to insert the contents of other source files; to identify sections of code to be compiled only under certain conditions; and to define macros, which are identifiers that the preprocessor replaces with another text.

Each preprocessor directive appears on a line by itself, beginning with the character #. Only space and tab characters may precede the # character on a line. A directive ends with the first newline character that follows its beginning. The shortest preprocessor directive is the *null directive*. This directive consists of a line that contains nothing but the character #, and possibly comments or whitespace characters. Null directives have no effect: the preprocessor removes them from the source file.

If a directive doesn't fit on one text line, you can end the line with a backslash (\) and continue the directive on the next line. Here is an example:

```
#define MacroName  A long, \
long macro replacement value
```

The backslash must be the last character before the newline character. The preprocessor concatenates the lines by removing each backslash-and-newline pair that it encounters. Because the preprocessor also replaces each comment with a space, the backslash no longer has the same effect if you put a comment between the backslash and the newline character.

Spaces and tab characters may appear between the # character that introduces a directive and the directive name. (In the previous example, the directive name is define.)

You can verify the results of the C preprocessor, either by running the preprocessor as a separate program or by using a compiler option to perform only the preprocessing steps.

Inserting the Contents of Header Files

An #include directive instructs the preprocessor to insert the contents of a specified file in the place of the directive. There are two ways to specify the file to be inserted:

```
#include  <filename>
#include  "filename"
```

Use the first form, with angle brackets, when you include standard library header files or additional header files provided by the implementation. Here is an example:

```
#include <math.h>      // Prototypes of mathematical functions,
                       // with related types and macros.
```

Use the second form, with double quotation marks, to include source files specific to your programs. Files inserted by #include directives typically have names ending in *.h*, and contain function prototypes, macro definitions, and type definitions. These definitions can then be used in any program source file after the corresponding #include directive. Here is an example:

```
#include "myproject.h"   // Function prototypes, type definitions
                         // and macros used in my project.
```

You may use macros in an #include directive. If you do use a macro, the macro's replacement must result in a correct #include directive. Example 15-1 demonstrates such #include directives.

Example 15-1. Macros in #include directives

```
#ifdef _DEBUG_
  #define MY_HEADER "myProject_dbg.h"
#else
  #define MY_HEADER "myProject.h"
#endif
#include MY_HEADER
```

If the macro _DEBUG_ is defined when this segment is preprocessed, then the preprocessor inserts the contents of *myProject_dbg.h*. If not, it inserts *myProject.h*. The #ifdef, #else, and #endif directives are described in detail in "Conditional Compiling" on page 272.

How the Preprocessor Finds Header Files

It is up to the given C implementation to define where the preprocessor searches for files specified in #include directives. Whether filenames are case-sensitive is also implementation-dependent. For files specified between angle brackets (<*file name*>), the preprocessor usually searches in certain system directories, such as */usr/local/include* and */usr/include* on Unix systems, for example.

For files specified in quotation marks ("*filename*"), the preprocessor usually looks in the current directory first, which is typically the directory containing the program's other source files. If such a file is not found in the current directory, the preprocessor searches the system *include* directories as well. A *filename* may contain a directory path. If so, the preprocessor looks for the file only in the specified directory.

You can always specify your own search path for #include directives, either by using an appropriate command-line option in running the compiler, or by adding search paths to the contents of an environment variable, often named INCLUDE. Consult your compiler's documentation.

Nested #include Directives

#include directives can be nested; that is, a source file inserted by an #include directive may in turn contain #include directives. The preprocessor permits at least 15 levels of nested includes.

Because header files sometimes include one another, it can easily happen that the same file is included more than once. For example, suppose the file *myProject.h* contains the line:

```
#include <stdio.h>
```

Then a source file that contains the following #include directives would include the file *stdio.h* twice, once directly and once indirectly:

```
#include <stdio.h>
#include "myProject.h"
```

However, you can easily guard the contents of a header file against multiple inclusions using the directives for conditional compiling (explained in "Conditional Compiling" on page 272). Example 15-2 demonstrates this usage.

Preprocessing

Example 15-2. Preventing multiple inclusions

```
#ifndef INCFILE_H_
#define INCFILE_H_

/* ... The actual contents of the header file incfile.h are here ... */

#endif   /* INCFILE_H_ */
```

At the first occurrence of a directive to include the file *incfile.h*, the macro INCFILE_H_ is not yet defined. The preprocessor therefore inserts the contents of the block between #ifndef and #endif—including the definition of the macro INCFILE_H_. On subsequent insertions of *incfile.h*, the #ifndef condition is false, and the preprocessor discards the block up to #endif.

Defining and Using Macros

You can define macros in C using the preprocessor directive #define. This directive allows you to give a name to any text you want, such as a constant or a statement. Wherever the macro's name appears in the source code after its definition, the preprocessor replaces it with that text.

A common use of macros is to define a name for a numeric constant:

```
#define ARRAY_SIZE 100
double data[ARRAY_SIZE];
```

These two lines define the macro name ARRAY_SIZE for the number 100, and then use the macro in a definition of the array data. Writing macro names in all capitals is a widely used convention that helps to distinguish them from variable names. This simple example also illustrates how macros can make a C program more flexible. It's safe to assume that the length of an array like data will be used in several places in the program—to control for loops that iterate through the elements of the array, for example. In each instance, use the macro name instead of a number. Then, if a program maintainer ever needs to modify the size of the array, it needs to be changed in only one place: in the #define directive.

In the third translation step, the preprocessor parses the source file as a sequence of preprocessor tokens and whitespace characters (see "The C Compiler's Translation Phases" on page 19 in Chapter 1). If any token is a macro name, the preprocessor *expands* the macro; that is, it replaces the macro name with the text it has been defined to represent. Macro names that occur in string literals are not expanded, because a string literal is itself a single preprocessor token.

Preprocessor directives cannot be created by macro expansion. Even if a macro expansion results in a formally valid directive, the preprocessor doesn't execute it.

You can define macros with or without parameters.

Macros Without Parameters

A macro definition with no parameters has the form:

```
#define macro_name replacement_text
```

Whitespace characters before and after `replacement_text` are not part of the replacement text. The `replacement_text` can also be empty. Here are some examples:

```
#define TITLE  "*** Examples of Macros Without Parameters ***"
#define BUFFER_SIZE  (4 * 512)
#define RANDOM  (-1.0 + 2.0*(double)rand() / RAND_MAX)
```

The standard function `rand()` returns a pseudorandom integer in the interval $[0, \text{RAND\_MAX}$. The prototype of `rand()` and the definition of the macro RAND_MAX are contained in the standard header file *stdlib.h*.

The following statements illustrate one possible use of the preceding macros:

```
#include <stdio.h>
#include <stdlib.h>
/* ... */
// Display the title:
puts( TITLE );

// Set the stream fp to "fully buffered" mode, with a buffer of
// BUFFER_SIZE bytes.
// The macro _IOFBF is defined in stdio.h as 0.
static char myBuffer[BUFFER_SIZE];
setvbuf( fp, myBuffer, _IOFBF, BUFFER_SIZE );

// Fill the array data with ARRAY_SIZE random numbers in the range
// [-10.0, +10.0]:
for ( int i = 0; i < ARRAY_SIZE; ++i )
   data[i] = 10.0 * RANDOM;
```

Replacing each macro with its replacement text, the preprocessor produces the following statements:

```
puts( "*** Examples of Macros Without Parameters ***" );

static char myBuffer[(4 * 512)];
setvbuf( fp, myBuffer, 0, (4 * 512) );

for ( int i = 0; i < 100; ++i )
   data[i] = 10.0 * (-1.0 + 2.0*(double)rand() / 2147483647);
```

In this example, the implementation-dependent value of the macro RAND_MAX is 2,147,483,647. With a different compiler, the value of RAND_MAX may be different.

If you write a macro containing an expression with operators, you should always enclose the expression in parentheses to avoid unexpected effects of operator precedence when you use the macro. For example, the outer parentheses in the macro RANDOM ensure that the expression 10.0 * RANDOM yields the desired result. Without them, macro replacement would produce this expression instead:

```
10.0 * -1.0 + 2.0*(double)rand() / 2147483647
```

This expression yields a random number in the interval [-10.0, -8.0].

Macros with Parameters

You can also define macros with parameters. When the preprocessor expands such a macro, it incorporates arguments you specify for each use of the macro in the replacement text. Macros with parameters are often called *function-like macros*.

You can define a macro with parameters in either of the following ways:

```
#define macro_name( [parameter_list] ) replacement_text
#define macro_name( [parameter_list ,] ... ) replacement_text
```

The *parameter_list* is a comma-separated list of identifiers for the macro's parameters. When you use such a macro, the comma-separated argument list must contain as many arguments as there are parameters in the macro definition. (However, C99 allows you to use "empty arguments," as we will explain in a moment.) The ellipsis (...) stands for one or more additional arguments.

When defining a macro, you must make sure there are no whitespace characters between the macro name and the left parenthesis ((). If there is any space after the name, then the directive defines a macro without parameters whose replacement text begins with the left parenthesis.

The standard library usually includes macros, defined in *stdio.h*, to implement the well-known functions getchar() and putchar(). Their expansion values can vary from one implementation to another, but in any case, their definitions are similar to the following:

```
#define getchar()    getc(stdin)
#define putchar(x)   putc(x, stdout)
```

When you "call" a function-like macro, the preprocessor replaces each occurrence of a parameter in the replacement text with the corresponding argument. C99 allows you to leave blank the place of any argument in a macro call. In this case, the corresponding parameter is replaced with nothing; that is, it is deleted from the replacement text. However, this use of "empty arguments" is not yet supported by all compilers.

If an argument contains macros, these are ordinarily expanded before the argument is substituted into the replacement text. Arguments for parameters which are operands of the # or ## operators are treated specially. For details, see the subsequent subsections "The stringify operator" on page 268 and "The token-pasting

---

operator" on page 269. Here are some examples of function-like macros and their expansions:

```
#include <stdio.h>            // Contains the definition of putchar().
#define DELIMITER ':'
#define SUB(a,b)  (a-b)
putchar( DELIMITER );
putchar( str[i] );
int var = SUB( ,10);
```

If putchar(x) is defined as putc(x, stdout), then the preprocessor expands the last three lines as follows:

```
putc(':', stdout);
putc(str[i], stdout);
int var = (-10);
```

As the following example illustrates, you should generally enclose the parameters in parentheses wherever they occur in the replacement text. This ensures correct evaluation in case any argument is an expression:

```
#define DISTANCE( x, y )  ((x)>=(y) ? (x)-(y) : (y)-(x))
d = DISTANCE( a, b+0.5 );
```

This macro call expands to the following:

```
d = ((a)>=(b+0.5) ? (a)-(b+0.5) : (b+0.5)-(a));
```

Without the parentheses around the parameters x and y, the expansion would contain the expression a-b+0.5 instead of (a)-(b+0.5).

Variable numbers of arguments

The C99 standard lets you define macros with an ellipsis (…) at the end of the parameter list to represent optional arguments. You can then invoke such a macro with a variable number of arguments.

When you invoke a macro with optional arguments, the preprocessor groups all of the optional arguments, including the commas that separate them, into one argument. In the replacement text, the identifier __VA_ARGS__ represents this group of optional arguments. The identifier __VA_ARGS__ can be used only in the replacement text of a macro definition. __VA_ARGS__ behaves the same as any other macro parameter, except that it is replaced by all the remaining arguments in the argument list, rather than just one argument. Here is an example of a macro that takes a variable number of arguments:

```
// Assume we have opened a log file to write with file pointer fp_log.
//
#define printLog(...)  fprintf( fp_log, __VA_ARGS__ )
// Using the printLog macro:
printLog( "%s: intVar = %d\n", __func__, intVar );
```

The preprocessor replaces the macro call in the last line of this example with the following:

```
fprintf( fp_log, "%s: intVar = %d\n", __func__, intVar );
```

The predefined identifier __func__, used in any function, represents a string containing the name of that function (see "Identifiers" on page 14). Thus, the macro call in this example writes the current function name and the contents of the variable intVar to the log file.

The stringify operator

The unary operator # is commonly called the *stringify operator* (or sometimes the *stringizing* operator) because it converts a macro argument into a string. The operand of # must be a parameter in a macro replacement text. When a parameter name appears in the replacement text with a prefixed # character, the preprocessor places the corresponding argument in double quotation marks, forming a string literal. All characters in the argument value itself remain unchanged, with the following exceptions:

- Any sequence of whitespace characters between tokens in the argument value is replaced with a single space character.
- A backslash character (\) is prefixed to each double quotation mark character (") in the argument.
- A backslash character is also prefixed to each existing backslash that occurs in a character constant or string literal in the argument, unless the existing backslash character introduces a universal character name (see "Universal Character Names" on page 12 in Chapter 1).

The following example illustrates how you might use the # operator to make a single macro argument work both as a string and as an arithmetic expression in the replacement text:

```
#define printDBL( exp ) printf( #exp " = %f ", exp )
printDBL( 4 * atan(1.0));       // atan() is declared in math.h.
```

The macro call in the last line expands to this statement:

```
printf( "4 * atan(1.0)" " = %f ", 4 * atan(1.0));
```

Because the compiler merges adjacent string literals, this code is equivalent to the following:

```
printf( "4 * atan(1.0) = %f ", 4 * atan(1.0));
```

That statement would generate the following console output:

```
4 * atan(1.0) = 3.141593
```

The invocation of the showArgs macro in the following example illustrates how the # operator modifies whitespace characters, double quotation marks, and backslashes in macro arguments:

```
#define showArgs(...)  puts(#__VA_ARGS__)
showArgs( one\n,       "2\n", three );
```

The preprocessor replaces this macro with the following text:

```
puts("one\n, \"2\\n\", three");
```

This statement produces the following output:

```
one
, "2\n", three
```

The token-pasting operator

The operator ## is a binary operator, and can appear in the replacement text of any macro. It joins its left and right operands together into a single token, and for this reason is commonly called the *token-pasting operator*. If the resulting text also contains a macro name, the preprocessor performs macro replacement on it. Whitespace characters that occur before and after the ## operator are removed along with the operator itself.

Usually, at least one of the operands is a macro parameter. In this case, the argument value is first substituted for the parameter, but the macro expansion itself is postponed until after token-pasting. Here is an example:

```
#define TEXT_A "Hello, world!"
#define msg(x) puts( TEXT_ ## x )
msg(A);
```

Regardless of whether the identifier A has been defined as a macro name, the preprocessor first substitutes the argument A for the parameter x, and then performs the token-pasting operation. The result of these two steps is the following line:

```
puts( TEXT_A );
```

Now, because TEXT_A is a macro name, the subsequent macro replacement yields this statement:

```
puts( "Hello, world!" );
```

If a macro parameter is an operand of the ## operator and a given macro invocation contains no argument for that parameter, then the preprocessor uses a placeholder to represent the empty string substituted for the parameter. The result of token pasting between such a placeholder and any token is that token. Token-pasting between two placeholders results in one placeholder. When all the token-pasting operations have been carried out, the preprocessor removes any remaining placeholders. Here is an example of a macro call with an empty argument:

```
   msg();
```

This call expands to the following line:

```
   puts( TEXT_ );
```

If TEXT_ is not an identifier representing a string, the compiler will issue an error message.

The order of evaluation of the stringify and token-pasting operators # and ## is not specified. If the order matters, you can influence it by breaking a macro up into several macros.

Using Macros Within Macros

After argument substitution and execution of the # and ## operations, the preprocessor examines the resulting replacement text and expands any macros it contains. No macro can be expanded recursively, though; if the preprocessor encounters the name of any macro in the replacement text of the same macro, or in the replacement text of any other macro nested in it, that macro name is not expanded.

Similarly, even if expanding a macro yields a valid preprocessing directive, that directive is not executed. However, the preprocessor does process any _Pragma operators that occur in a completely expanded macro replacement (see "The _Pragma Operator" on page 276).

The following sample program prints a table of function values:

```
// fn_tbl.c: Display values of a function in tabular form.
//           This program uses nested macros.
// ----------------------------------------------------------------
#include <stdio.h>
#include <math.h>        // Prototypes of the cos() and exp() functions.

#define PI          3.141593
#define STEP        (PI/8)
#define AMPLITUDE   1.0
#define ATTENUATION 0.1              // Attenuation in wave propagation.
#define DF(x)       exp(-ATTENUATION*(x))
#define FUNC(x)     (DF(x) * AMPLITUDE * cos(x))  // Attenuated
                                                  // oscillation.
// For the function display:
#define STR(s)  #s
#define XSTR(s) STR(s)       // Expand the macros in s, then stringify.

int main()
{
  double x = 0.0;

  printf( "\nFUNC(x) = %s\n", XSTR(FUNC(x)) );   // Print the function.

  printf("\n %10s %25s\n", "x", STR(y = FUNC(x)) );   // Table header.
  printf("-------------------------------------------\n");
```

```
    for ( ; x < 2*PI + STEP/2;  x += STEP )
      printf( "%15f %20f\n", x, FUNC(x) );

    return 0;
}
```

This example prints the following table:

```
FUNC(x) = (exp(-0.1*(x)) * 1.0 * cos(x))

            x                 y = FUNC(x)
    - - - - - - - - - - - - - - - - - - - - - - - -
        0.000000               1.000000
        0.392699               0.888302
...
        5.890487               0.512619
        6.283186               0.533488
```

Macro Scope and Redefinition

You cannot use a second #define directive to redefine an identifier that is currently defined as a macro, unless the new replacement text is identical to the existing macro definition. If the macro has parameters, the new parameter names must also be identical to the old ones.

To change the meaning of a macro, you must first cancel its current definition using the following directive:

```
#undef macro_name
```

After that point, the identifier *macro_name* is available for use in a new macro definition. If the specified identifier is not the name of a macro, the preprocessor ignores the #undef directive.

The names of several functions in the standard library are also defined as macros. For these functions, you can use the #undef directive if you want to make sure your program calls one of those functions and not the macro of the same name. You don't need to specify a parameter list with the #undef directive, even when the macro you are undefining has parameters. Here is an example:

```
#include <ctype.h>
#undef isdigit          // Remove any macro definition with this name.
/* ... */
if ( isdigit(c) )       // Call the function isdigit().
/* ... */
```

The scope of a macro ends with the first #undef directive with its name, or if there is no #undef directive for that macro, then with the end of the translation unit in which it is defined.

Type-generic Macros

The C11 standard introduces the *generic selection*, which works somewhat like a switch statement for data types. A generic selection is equivalent to an expression selected from a list of possibilities depending on the type of another expression. (The exact mechanism is described in "Generic Selections (C11)" on page 68.) This means that C programmers now have a way to define their own type-generic macros like those provided by C99 for mathematical functions in the header *tgmath.h*.

A generic selection begins with the new keyword _Generic. The following example illustrates a possible implementation of the type-generic macro log10(*x*) from *tgmath.h*:

```
#define log10(X) _Generic((X), \
    long double: log10l, \
    float:      log10f, \
    default:    log10  \
    )(X)
```

The compiler selects one of the expressions log10l, log10f, or log10 depending on the type of the expression *X*. If the macro is called with an argument *arg* whose type is double or an integer type, the result of the generic selection is the default expression, so that the macro call ultimately results in the expression log10(*arg*).

Conditional Compiling

The *conditional compiling* directives instruct the preprocessor to retain or omit parts of the source code depending on specified conditions. You can use conditional compiling to adapt a program to different target systems, for example, without having to manage a variety of source files.

A conditional section begins with one of the directives #if, #ifdef, or #ifndef, and ends with the directive #endif. Any number of #elif directives, and at most one #else directive, may occur within the conditional section. A conditional section that begins with #if has the following form:

```
#if expression1
  [ group1 ]
[#elif expression2
  [ group2 ]]
...
[#elif expression(n)
  [ group(n) ]]
[#else
  [ group(n+1) ]]
#endif
```

The preprocessor evaluates the conditional expressions in sequence until it finds one whose value is nonzero, or "true." The preprocessor retains the text in the corresponding group for further processing. If none of the expressions is true, and the

---

conditional section contains an #else directive, then the text in the #else directive's group is retained.

The token groups *group1*, *group2*, and so on consist of any C source code, and may include more preprocessing directives, including nested conditional compiling directives. Groups that the preprocessor does not retain for further processing are removed from the program at the end of the preprocessor phase.

The #if and #elif Directives

The expression that forms the condition of an #if or #elif directive must be an integer constant preprocessor expression. This is different from an ordinary integer constant expression (see "Constant Expressions" on page 97) in these respects:

- You may not use the cast operator in an #if or #elif expression.

- You may use the preprocessor operator defined (see "The defined Operator" on page 273).

- After the preprocessor has expanded all macros and evaluated all defined expressions, it replaces all other identifiers or keywords in the expression with the character 0.

- All signed values in the expression have the type intmax_t, and all unsigned values have the type uintmax_t. Character constants are subject to these rules as well. The types intmax_t and uintmax_t are defined in the header file *stdint.h*.

- The preprocessor converts characters and escape sequences in character constants and string literals into the corresponding characters in the execution character set. Whether character constants have the same value in a preprocessor expression as in later phases of compiling is up to the given implementation, however.

The defined Operator

The unary operator defined can occur in the condition of an #if or #elif directive. Its form is one of the following:

```
defined identifier
defined (identifier)
```

These preprocessor expressions yield the value 1 if the specified identifier is a macro name—that is, if it has been defined in a #define directive and its definition hasn't been canceled by an #undef directive. For any other identifier, the defined operator yields the value 0.

The advantage of the defined operation over the #ifdef and #ifndef directives is that you can use its value in a larger preprocessor expression. Here is an example:

```
#if defined( __unix__ ) && defined( __GNUC__ )
/* ... */
#endif
```

Most compilers provide predefined macros, like those used in this example, to identify the target system and the compiler. Thus, on a Unix system, the macro __unix__ is usually defined, and the macro __GNUC__ is defined if the compiler being used is GCC. Similarly, the Microsoft Visual C compiler on Windows automatically defines the macros _WIN32 and _MSC_VER.

The #ifdef and #ifndef Directives

You can also test whether a given macro is defined using the #ifdef and #ifndef directives. Their syntax is:

```
#ifdef identifier
#ifndef identifier
```

These are equivalent to the following #if directives:

```
#if defined identifier
#if !defined identifier
```

The conditional code following the #ifndef identifier is retained if identifier is not a macro name. Examples 15-1 and 15-2 illustrate possible uses of these directives.

Defining Line Numbers

The compiler includes line numbers and source filenames in warnings, error messages, and information provided to debugging tools. You can use the #line directive in the source file itself to change the compiler's filename and line numbering information. The #line directive has the following syntax:

```
#line line_number ["filename"]
```

The next line after a #line directive has the number specified by line_number. If the directive also includes the optional string literal "filename", then the compiler uses the contents of that string as the name of the current source file.

The line_number must be a decimal constant greater than zero. Here is an example:

```
#line 1200 "primary.c"
```

The line containing the #line directive may also contain macros. If so, the preprocessor expands them before executing the #line directive. The #line directive must then be formally correct after macro expansion.

Programs can access the current line number and filename settings as values of the standard predefined macros __LINE__ and __FILE__:

```
printf( "This message was printed by line %d in the file %s.\n",
        __LINE__, __FILE__ );
```

The #line directive is typically used by programs that generate C source code as their output. By placing the corresponding input file line numbers in #line directives, such programs can make the C compiler's error messages refer to the pertinent lines in the original source.

Generating Error Messages

The #error directive makes the preprocessor issue an error message, regardless of any actual formal error. Its syntax is:

```
#error [text]
```

If the optional *text* is present, it is included in the preprocessor's error message. The compiler then stops processing the source file and exits as it would on encountering a fatal error. The *text* can be any sequence of preprocessor tokens. Any macros contained in it are not expanded. It is a good idea to use a string literal here to avoid problems with punctuation characters, such as single quotation marks.

The following example tests whether the standard macro __STDC__ is defined, and generates an error message if it is not:

```
#ifndef __STDC__
    #error  "This compiler does not conform to the ANSI C standard."
#endif
```

The #pragma Directive

The #pragma directive is a standard way to provide additional information to the compiler. This directive has the following form:

```
#pragma [tokens]
```

If the first token after #pragma is STDC, then the directive is a standard pragma. If not, then the effect of the #pragma directive is implementation-dependent. For the sake of portability, you should use #pragma directives sparingly.

If the preprocessor recognizes the specified tokens, it performs whatever action they stand for, or passes information on to the compiler. If the preprocessor doesn't recognize the tokens, it must ignore the #pragma directive.

Recent versions of the GNU C compiler and Microsoft's Visual C compiler both recognize the pragma pack(n), for example, which instructs the compiler to align structure members on certain byte boundaries. The following example uses pack(1) to specify that each structure member be aligned on a byte boundary:

```
#if defined( __GNUC__ ) || defined( _MSC_VER )
  #pragma pack(1)                          // Byte-aligned: no padding.
#endif
```

Single-byte alignment ensures that there are no gaps between the members of a structure. The argument *n* in a pack pragma is usually a small power of two. For example, pack(2) aligns structure members on even-numbered byte addresses, and pack(4) on four-byte boundaries. pack() with no arguments resets the alignment to the implementation's default value.

C99 introduced the following three standard pragmas:

```
#pragma  STDC  FP_CONTRACT    on_off_switch
#pragma  STDC  FENV_ACCESS    on_off_switch
#pragma  STDC  CX_LIMITED_RANGE  on_off_switch
```

The value of the *on_off_switch* must be ON, OFF, or DEFAULT. The effects of these pragmas are discussed in "Mathematical Functions" on page 323.

The _Pragma Operator

You cannot construct a #pragma directive (or any other preprocessor directive) by means of a macro expansion. For cases where you would want to do that, C99 has also introduced the preprocessor operator _Pragma, which you can use with macros. Its syntax is as follows:

```
_Pragma (string_literal )
```

Here is how the _Pragma operator works. First, the *string_literal* operand is "destringized," or converted into a sequence of preprocessor tokens, in this way: the quotation marks enclosing the string are removed; each sequence of a backslash followed by a double quotation mark (\") is replaced by a quotation mark alone ("); and each sequence of two backslash characters (\\) is replaced with a single backslash (\). Then the preprocessor interprets the resulting sequence of tokens as if it were the text of a #pragma directive.

The following line defines a helper macro, STR, which you can use to rewrite any #pragma directive using the _Pragma operator:

```
#define  STR(s)  #s              // This # is the "stringify" operator.
```

With this definition, the following two lines are equivalent:

```
#pragma tokens
_Pragma ( STR(tokens) )
```

The following example uses the _Pragma operator in a macro:

```
#define ALIGNMENT(n) _Pragma( STR(pack(n)) )
ALIGNMENT(2)
```

Macro replacement changes the ALIGNMENT(2) macro call to the following:

```
_Pragma( "pack(2)" )
```

The preprocessor then processes the line as it would the following directive:

```
#pragma pack(2)
```

Predefined Macros

Every compiler that conforms to the ISO C standard must define the following seven macros. Each of these macro names begins and ends with two underscore characters:

__DATE__

  The replacement text is a string literal containing the compilation date in the format "Mmm dd yyyy" (example: "Mar 19 2006"). If the day of the month is less than 10, the tens place contains an additional space character.

__FILE__

  A string literal containing the name of the current source file.

__LINE__

  An integer constant whose value is the number of the line in the current source file that contains the __LINE__ macro reference, counting from the beginning of the file.

__TIME__

  A string literal that contains the time of compilation, in the format "hh:mm:ss" (example: "08:00:59").

__STDC__

  The integer constant 1, indicating that the compiler conforms to the ISO C standard.

__STDC_HOSTED__

  The integer constant 1 if the current implementation is a hosted implementation; otherwise, the constant 0.

__STDC_VERSION__

  The long integer constant 199901L if the compiler supports the C99 standard of January 1999, or 201112L if the compiler supports the C11 standard of December 2011.

The values of the __FILE__ and __LINE__ macros can be influenced by the #line directive. The values of all the other predefined macros remains constant throughout the compilation process.

The value of the constant __STDC_VERSION__ will be adjusted with each future revision of the international C standard.

Beginning with the C99 standard, C programs are executed either in a hosted or in a freestanding environment. Most C programs are executed in a hosted environment, which means that the C program runs under the control and with the support of an operating system. In this case, the constant __STDC_HOSTED__ has the value 1, and the full standard library is available.

A program in a *freestanding* environment runs without the support of an operating system, and therefore only minimal standard library resources are available to it (see "Execution Environments" on page 284).

Conditionally Defined Macros

Unlike the macros listed previously, the following standard macros are predefined only under certain conditions. If any of these macros is defined, it indicates that the implementation supports a certain IEC or ISO standard:

__STDC_IEC_559__
> This constant is defined with the value 1 if the implementation's real floating-point arithmetic conforms to the IEC 60559 standard.

__STDC_IEC_559_COMPLEX__
> This constant is defined with the value 1 if the implementation's complex floating-point arithmetic also conforms to the IEC 60559 standard.

__STDC_ISO_10646__
> This long integer constant represents a date in the form yyyymmL (example: 199712L). This constant is defined if the encoding of wide characters with the type wchar_t conforms to the Unicode standard ISO/IEC 10646, including all supplements and corrections up to the year and month indicated by the macro's value.

The C11 standard adds the following optional macros:

__STDC_MB_MIGHT_NEQ_WC__
> This constant is defined with the value 1 if a character in the basic character set, when encoded in a wchar_t object, is not necessarily equal to its encoding in the corresponding character constant.

__STDC_UTF_16__
> This constant is defined with the value 1 if characters of the type char16_t are encoded in UTF-16. If the type uses a different encoding, the macro is not defined.

__STDC_UTF_32__
> This constant is defined with the value 1 if characters of the type char32_t are encoded in UTF-32. If the type uses a different encoding, the macro is not defined.

__STDC_ANALYZABLE__

This constant is defined with the value 1 if the implementation supports the analysis of runtime errors as specified in Annex L of the C11 standard.

__STDC_LIB_EXT1__

This constant is defined with the value 201112L if the implementation supports the new functions with bounds-checking specified in Annex K of the C11 standard. The names of these new function end in _s.

__STDC_NO_ATOMICS__

This constant is defined with the value 1 if the implementation does not include the types and functions for atomic memory access operations (that is, the header *stdatomic.h* is absent).

__STDC_NO_COMPLEX__

This constant is defined with the value 1 if the implementation does not support arithmetic with complex numbers (that is, the header *complex.h* is absent).

__STDC_NO_THREADS__

This constant is defined with the value 1 if the implementation does not support multithreading (that is, the header *threads.h* is absent).

__STDC_NO_VLA__

This constant is defined with the value 1 if the implementation does not support variable-length arrays.

You must not use any of the predefined macro names described in this section in a #define or #undef directive. Finally, the macro name __cplusplus is reserved for C++ compilers, and must not be defined when you compile a C source file.

Preprocessing

Standard Library

16

The Standard Headers

Each standard library function is declared in one or more of the *standard headers*. These headers also contain all the macro and type definitions that the C standard provides. This chapter describes the contents and use of the standard headers.

Each of the standard headers contains a set of related function declarations, macros, and type definitions. For example, mathematical functions are declared in the header *math.h*. The standard headers are also called *header files*, as the contents of each header are usually stored in a file. Strictly speaking, however, the standard does not require the headers to be organized in files.

The C standard defines the following 29 headers (those marked with an asterisk were added in C11):

assert.h	*inttypes.h*	*signal.h*	*stdint.h*	*threads.h**
complex.h	*iso646.h*	*stdalign.h**	*stdio.h*	*time.h*
ctype.h	*limits.h*	*stdarg.h*	*stdlib.h*	*uchar.h**
errno.h	*locale.h*	*stdatomic.h**	*stdnoreturn.h**	*wchar.h*
fenv.h	*math.h*	*stdbool.h*	*string.h*	*wctype.h*
float.h	*setjmp.h*	*stddef.h*	*tgmath.h*	

The headers *complex.h*, *stdatomic.h*, and *threads.h* are optional components. There are standard macros that a C11 implementation can define to indicate that it does not include these options. If the macro __STDC_NO_COMPLEX__, __STDC_NO_ATOMICS__, or __STDC_NO_THREADS__ is defined as equal to 1, the implementation does not include the corresponding optional header.

Using the Standard Headers

You can add the contents of a standard header to a source file by inserting an #include directive, which must be placed outside all functions (see "Inserting the Contents of Header Files" on page 262). You can include the standard headers as many times as you want, and in any order. However, before the #include directive for any header, your program must not define any macro with the same name as an identifier in that header. To make sure that your programs respect this condition, always include the required standard headers at the beginning of your source files, before any header files of your own.

Execution Environments

C programs run in one of two execution environments: hosted or freestanding. Most common programs run in a *hosted* environment; that is, under the control and with the support of an operating system. In a hosted environment, the full capabilities of the standard library are available. Furthermore, programs compiled for a hosted environment must define a function named main(), which is the first function invoked on program start.

A program designed for a *freestanding* environment runs without the support of an operating system. In a freestanding environment, the name and type of the first function invoked when a program starts is determined by the given implementation. Programs for a freestanding environment cannot use complex floating-point types, and may be limited to the following headers:

float.h	*stdalign.h*	*stddef.h*
iso646.h	*stdarg.h*	*stdint.h*
limits.h	*stdbool.h*	*stdnoreturn.h*

Specific implementations may also provide additional standard library resources.

Function and Macro Calls

All standard library functions have external linkage. You may use standard library functions without including the corresponding header by declaring them in your own code. However, if a standard function requires a type defined in the header, then you must include the header.

The standard library functions are not guaranteed to be reentrant—that is, two calls to a standard library function may not safely be in execution concurrently in one process. One reason for this rule is that several of the functions use and modify static or thread-local variables, for example.

As a result, you can't generally call standard library functions in signal handling routines. Signals are asynchronous, which means that a program may receive a signal at any time, even while it's executing a standard library function. If that happens, and the handler for that signal calls the same standard function, then the function must be reentrant. It is up to individual implementations to determine which functions are reentrant, or whether to provide a reentrant version of the whole standard library.

Most of the standard library functions—with a few explicitly specified exceptions—are *thread-safe*, meaning they can be safely executed by several threads "simultaneously." In other words, the standard functions must be so implemented that any objects they use internally are not subject to data races when called in more than one thread. In particular, they must not use static objects without ensuring synchronization. However, you the programmer are responsible for coordinating different threads' access to any objects referred to directly or indirectly by a function's arguments.

Each stream has a corresponding lock which the functions in the I/O library use to obtain exclusive access to the stream before performing an operation. In this way, the standard library functions prevent data races when several threads access a given stream.

As the programmer, you are responsible for calling functions and function-like macros with valid arguments. Wrong arguments can cause severe runtime errors. Typical mistakes to avoid include the following:

- Argument values outside the domain of the function, as in the following call:

  ```
  double x = -1.0, y = sqrt(x);
  ```

- Pointer arguments that do not point to an object or a function, as in this function call with an uninitialized pointer argument:

  ```
  char *msg; strcpy( msg, "error" );
  ```

- Arguments whose type does not match that expected by a function with a variable number of arguments. In the following example, the conversion specifier %f calls for a float pointer argument, but &x is a pointer to double:

  ```
  double x;    scanf( "%f", &x );
  ```

- Array address arguments that point to an array that isn't large enough to accommodate data written by the function. Here is an example:

  ```
  char name[] = "Hi ";    strcat( name, "Alice" );
  ```

Macros in the standard library make full use of parentheses so that you can use them in expressions in the same way as individual identifiers. Furthermore, each

Standard
Headers

function-like macro in the standard library uses its arguments only once.[1] This means that you can call these macros in the same way as ordinary functions, even using expressions with side effects as arguments. Here is an example:

```
int c = 'A';
while ( c <= 'Z' ) putchar( c++ );    // Output: 'ABC ... XYZ'
```

The functions in the standard library may be implemented both as macros and as functions. In such cases, the same header file contains both a function prototype and a macro definition for a given function name. As a result, each use of the function name after you include the header file invokes the macro. The following example calls the macro or function toupper() to convert a lowercase letter to uppercase:

```
#include <ctype.h>
/* ... */
  c = toupper(c);    // Invokes the macro toupper(), if there is one.
```

However, if you specifically want to call a function and not a macro with the same name, you can use the #undef directive to cancel the macro definition:

```
#include <ctype.h>
#undef toupper       // Remove any macro definition with this name.
/* ... */
  c = toupper(c)     // Calls the function toupper().
```

You can also call a function rather than a macro with the same name by setting the name in parentheses:

```
#include <ctype.h>
/* ... */
  c = (toupper)(c)   // Calls the function toupper().
```

Finally, you can omit the header containing the macro definition, and declare the function explicitly in your source file:

```
extern int toupper(int);
/* ... */
  c = toupper(c)     // Calls the function toupper().
```

---

1 The C11 standard contradicts itself on this point. In describing the use of library functions, it says, "Any invocation of a library function that is implemented as a macro shall expand to code that evaluates each of its arguments exactly once, fully protected by parentheses where necessary, so it is generally safe to use arbitrary expressions as arguments," but in its descriptions of the functions putc(), putwc(), getc(), and getwc(), the standard contains warnings like this one: "The putc function is equivalent to fputc, except that if it is implemented as a macro, it *may evaluate stream more than once*, so that argument should never be an expression with side effects."

Reserved Identifiers

When choosing identifiers to use in your programs, you must be aware that certain identifiers are reserved for the standard library. Reserved identifiers include the following:

- All identifiers that begin with an underscore followed by a second underscore or an uppercase letter are always reserved. Thus, you cannot use identifiers such as __x or _Max, even for local variables or labels.

- All other identifiers that begin with an underscore are reserved as identifiers with file scope. Thus, you cannot use an identifier such as _a_ as the name of a function or a global variable, although you can use it for a parameter, a local variable, or a label. The identifiers of structure or union members can also begin with an underscore, as long as the second character is not another underscore or an uppercase letter.

- Identifiers declared with external linkage in the standard headers are reserved as identifiers with external linkage. Such identifiers include function names, as well as the names of global variables such as errno. Although you cannot declare these identifiers with external linkage as names for your own functions or objects, you may use them for other purposes. For example, in a source file that does not include *string.h*, you may define a static function named strcpy().

- The identifiers of all macros defined in any header you include are reserved.

- Identifiers declared with file scope in the standard headers are reserved within their respective name spaces. Once you include a header in a source file, you cannot use any identifier that is declared with file scope in that header for another purpose in the same name space (see "Identifier Name Spaces" on page 16) or as a macro name.

Although some of the conditions listed here have "loopholes" that allow you to reuse identifiers in a certain name space or with static linkage, overloading identifiers can cause confusion, and it's generally safest to avoid the identifiers declared in the standard headers completely. In the following sections, we also list identifiers that have been reserved for future extensions of the C standard. The last three rules in the previous list apply to such reserved identifiers as well.

Functions with Bounds-Checking

Many traditional functions in the C standard library copy strings to arrays that are provided by the programmer as pointer arguments. There is no way for these functions to test whether the given destination array is large enough to accommodate the result. The programmer alone is responsible for ensuring that no data is written past the end of an array, where it could modify adjacent objects in memory. This is a significant threat to the reliability and security of a program, and can cause it to crash.

To alleviate this problem, Appendix K of the C11 standard, "Bounds-checking Interfaces," introduces many new functions as secure alternatives to the traditional standard C functions. These alternative functions, also called the secure functions, take an additional argument which specifies the size of the destination array. The secure functions use this information to ensure that the results they produce do not exceed the array's bounds. The names of the secure functions end with the suffix _s (s for "secure"), as in strcpy_s(), for example. Unlike the traditional function strcpy(), the function strcpy_s() only copies a string if the specified destination vector is large enough to accommodate it.

Availability

Support for the bounds-checking functions is optional. They are available only in implementations that define the macro __STDC_LIB_EXT1__.

If these functions are provided, their declarations and the accompanying type and macro definitions are included in the same headers that provide the corresponding traditional functions. For example, the header *stdio.h* then contains the declaration of scanf_s() in addition to scanf(), and *string.h* contains the declaration of strcpy_s() alongside strcpy(). To make the declarations of the secure functions visible to the compiler, however, your program must define the macro __STDC_WANT_LIB_EXT1__ as equal to 1 before including the corresponding headers, for example, by using the lines:

```
#define __STDC_WANT_LIB_EXT1__ 1
#include <stdio.h>
```

To prevent name conflicts with functions defined in your program or in other libraries it uses, you can ensure that the secure functions are not visible by defining the macro __STDC_WANT_LIB_EXT1__ as equal to 0. If __STDC_WANT_LIB_EXT1__ is not defined before the program includes a standard header, the corresponding secure functions may or may not be available, depending on the given compiler.

Runtime Constraints

The parameter that specifies the size of an array in a bounds-checking function has the type rsize_t. This type is defined in the header *stddef.h* as equal to size_t. However, rsize_t places a special restriction on the value of a variable: a variable of the type rsize_t must not be assigned a value greater than that of the macro RSIZE_MAX. Passing an array length argument greater than RSIZE_MAX to a bounds-checking function causes an error. This constraint can detect errors that arise through the conversion of negative numbers to unsigned types, as such conversions result in very large positive numbers.

The secure functions perform other tests in addition to bounds-checking. For example, they test whether pointers passed as arguments are non-null. All the conditions that must be fulfilled for a function to execute successfully are called the function's *runtime constraints*.

If a secure function's runtime constraints are violated, the destination objects remain unchanged, and the function calls a *runtime constraint handler*, passing it a return value and an error message. The handler can end the program by calling abort(), or return to the secure function which called it. A program may replace the default runtime constraint handler with another standard handler or with a function of its own by calling the function set_constraint_handler_s(). For details, see the description of the function set_constraint_handler_s() in Chapter 18.

The return value of a secure function indicates whether an error has occurred. Many of the secure functions have a return value of the type errno_t. This type is defined in the header *errno.h* as int. These secure functions return the value 0 after a successful call, and a nonzero value if an error has occured.

Contents of the Standard Headers

The following subsections list the standard headers in alphabetical order, with brief descriptions of their contents, including all the types and macros defined in them.

The standard functions are described in the next two chapters: Chapter 17 summarizes the functions that the standard library provides for each area of application— the mathematical functions, string manipulation functions, functions for time and date operations, and so on. Chapter 18 then provides a detailed description of each function individually, in alphabetical order, with examples illustrating their use.

assert.h

This header defines the function-like macro assert(), which tests whether the value of an expression is nonzero in the running program. If you define the macro NDEBUG before including *assert.h* , then calls to assert() have no effect.

In C11, the header *assert.h* defines the macro static_assert as a synonym for the keyword _Static_assert. A _Static_assert declaration tests a constant expression for a nonzero value at compile time (see "_Static_assert Declarations" on page 186).

complex.h

C99 supports arithmetic with complex numbers by introducing complex floating-point types and including appropriate functions in the math library. The header file *complex.h* contains the prototypes of the complex math functions and defines the related macros. For a brief description of complex numbers and their representation in C, see "Complex Floating-Point Types" on page 32.

Under the C11 standard, support for complex numbers is optional. The header *complex.h* is absent if the macro __STDC_NO_COMPLEX__ is defined.

The names of the mathematical functions for complex numbers all begin with the letter c. For example, csin() is the complex sine function, and cexp() the complex exponential function. You can find a complete list of these functions in "Mathematical Functions" on page 323. In addition, the following function names are reserved for future extensions:

```
cerf()    cerfc()    cexp2()    cexpm1()    clog10()    clog1p()
clog2()   clgamma()  ctgamma()
```

The same names with the suffixes f (for float _Complex) and l (for long double _Complex) are also reserved.

The header file *complex.h* defines the following macros:

complex
> This is a synonym for the keyword _Complex.

_Complex_I
> This macro represents an expression of type const float _Complex whose value is the imaginary unit, *i*.

I
> This macro is a synonym for _Complex_I (or for _Imaginary_I, if defined), and likewise represents the imaginary unit, *i*.

A C11 implementation may also include types to represent pure *imaginary numbers*. If and only if a given C implementation includes such types, it defines the two following macros:

imaginary
> This is a synonym for the keyword _Imaginary.

_Imaginary_I
> This macro represents an expression of type const float _Imaginary whose value is the imaginary unit, *i*. If _Imaginary_I is defined, the macro I is defined as a synonym for it.

C11 also provides the function-like macros CMPLX, CMPXF, and CMPLXL to compose a complex number from its real and imaginary parts.

ctype.h

This header contains the declarations of functions to classify and convert single characters. These include the following functions, which are usually also implemented as macros:

```
isalnum()  isalpha()  isblank()  iscntrl()  isdigit()  isgraph()
islower()  isprint()  ispunct()  isspace()  isupper()  isxdigit()
tolower()  toupper()
```

These functions or macros take an argument of type int, whose value must be between 0 and 255, inclusive, or EOF. The macro EOF is defined in *stdio.h*. The classification of characters, and hence the behavior of these functions (except isdigit() and isxdigit()), is dependent on the current locale.

All names that begin with is or to followed by a lowercase letter are reserved for future extensions.

errno.h

The header *errno.h* defines the macro errno as representing a thread-local error variable of the type int. Various functions in the standard library set errno to a specified positive value to indicate the type of error encountered during execution. For each function that uses errno, its possible values are indicated in the function's description in Chapter 18.

The identifier errno is not necessarily declared as a global variable. It may be a macro that represents a modifiable lvalue with the type int. For example, if _errno() is a function that returns a pointer to int, then errno could be defined as follows:

```
#define errno  (* _errno())
```

When the program starts, errno in the initial thread has the value zero. The initial value of errno in any other thread is undetermined. Because no standard function sets the value of errno to zero, a program that uses errno to detect errors should set the value of errno to zero before calling a standard library function.

The header *errno.h* also defines an appropriate macro constant for each possible value of errno. The names of these macros begin with E, and include at least these three:

EDOM
> Domain error; the function is mathematically not defined for the given value of the argument.

EILSEQ
> Illegal sequence. For example, a multibyte character conversion function may have encountered a sequence of bytes that cannot be interpreted as a multibyte character in the encoding used.

ERANGE
> Range error; the function's mathematical result is not representable by its return type.

All macro names that begin with E followed by a digit or an uppercase letter are reserved for future extensions.

C11 implementations that support the new bounds-checking, "secure" functions also define the type errno_t in the header *errno.h* as a synonym for int.

fenv.h

C99 introduced the *floating-point environment*, which provides system variables to allow programs to deal flexibly with floating-point exceptions and control modes. (See also "Mathematical Functions" on page 323.) The header *fenv.h* contains all the declarations that may be used in accessing the floating-point environment, although implementations are not required to support floating-point exceptions or control modes.

Macro and type definitions for the floating-point environment

The header *fenv.h* contains the following definitions to manipulate the floating-point environment:

fenv_t
> A type capable of representing the floating-point environment as a whole.

FE_DFL_ENV
> An object of the type const fenv_t *; points to the default floating-point environment, which is in effect when the program starts.

Macro and type definitions for floating-point exceptions

Implementations that support floating-point exceptions also define an integer macro corresponding to the status flag for each kind of exception that can occur. Standard names for these macros are:

FE_DIVBYZERO, FE_INEXACT, FE_INVALID, FE_OVERFLOW, FE_UNDERFLOW
> These macros allow you to select one or more kinds of exceptions when accessing the status flags. You can also combine several such macros using the bitwise OR operator (|) to obtain a value that represents several kinds of exceptions.

FE_ALL_EXCEPT
> This macro represents the bitwise OR of all the exception macros defined in the given implementation.

If a given implementation does not support one or more of the exceptions indicated by these macros, then the corresponding macro is not defined. Furthermore, implementations may also define other exception macros, with names that begin with FE_ followed by an uppercase letter.

In addition to the macros listed previously, implementations that support floating-point exceptions also define a type for the floating-point exception status flags:

```
fexcept_t
```
This type represents all of the floating-point exception status flags, including all the information that the given implementation provides about exceptions. Such information may include the address of the instruction that raised the exception, for example. This type is used by the functions `fegetexceptflag()` and `fesetexceptflag()`.

Macro definitions for rounding modes

Implementations may allow programs to query or set the way floating-point results are rounded. If so, the header *fenv.h* defines the following macros as distinct integer constants:

```
FE_DOWNWARD    FE_TOWARDZERO
FE_TONEAREST   FE_UPWARD
```

A given implementation might not define all of these macros if it does not support the corresponding rounding direction, and might also define macro names for other rounding modes that it does support. The function `fegetround()` returns the current rounding mode—that is, the value of the corresponding macro name; and `fesetround()` sets the rounding mode as specified by its argument.

float.h

The header file *float.h* defines macros that describe the value range, the precision, and other properties of the types `float`, `double`, and `long double`.

Normalized representation of floating-point numbers

The values of the macros in *float.h* refer to the following normalized representation of a floating-point number x:

$$x = s \times 0.d_1 d_2 ... d_p \times b^e$$

The symbols in this representation have the following meanings and conditions:

s

The sign of x; $s = 1$ or $s = -1$

d_i

A base b digit in the significand (also called the *mantissa*) of x ($0.d_1 d_2 ... d_p$ in the general representation); $d_1 > 0$ if $x \neq 0$

p

The number of digits in the significand (or to be more precise, in the fraction part)

b

The base of the exponent; $b > 1$

e

The integer exponent; $e_{min} \leq e \leq e_{max}$

The floating-point types may also be able to represent other values besides normalized floating-point numbers, such as the following kinds of values:

- Subnormal floating-point numbers, or those for which $x \neq 0$, $e = e_{min}$, and $d_1 = 0$.
- Non-normalized floating-point numbers, for which $x \neq 0$, $e > e_{min}$, and $d_1 = 0$.
- Infinities; that is, values that represent $+\infty$ or $-\infty$.
- NaNs, or values that do not represent valid floating-point numbers. NaN stands for "not a number."

NaNs can be either *quiet* or *signaling* NaNs. When a signaling NaN occurs in the evaluation of an arithmetic expression, it sets the exception flag FE_INVALID in the floating-point environment. Quiet NaNs do not set the exception flag.

Rounding mode and evaluation method

The following two macros defined in the header *float.h* provide details about how floating-point arithmetic is performed:

FLT_ROUNDS

This macro represents the currently active rounding direction, and is the only macro defined in *float.h* whose value can change during runtime. It can have the following values:

-1 Undetermined

0   Toward zero

1   Toward the nearest representable value

2   Toward the next greater value

3   Toward the next smaller value

Other values may stand for implementation-defined rounding modes. If the implementation supports different rounding modes, you can change the active rounding mode by calling the function fesetround().

FLT_EVAL_METHOD

The macro FLT_EVAL_METHOD has one of several possible values, but does not change during the program's runtime. This macro indicates the floating-point format used internally for operations on floating-point numbers. The internal format may have greater precision and a broader value range than the operands' type. The possible values of FLT_EVAL_METHOD have the following meanings:

-1 Undetermined

0 Arithmetic operations are performed with the precision of the operands' type.

1 Operations on float or double values are executed in double precision, and operations on long double are executed in long double precision.

2 All operations are performed internally in long double precision.

Precision and value range

For a given base, the precision with which numbers are represented is determined by the number of digits in the significand, and the value range is indicated by the least and greatest values of the exponent. These values are provided, for each real floating-point type, by the following macros. The macro names with the prefix FLT_ represent characteristics of the type float; those with the prefix DBL_ refer to double; and those with LDBL_ refer to long double. The value of FLT_RADIX applies to all three floating-point types.

FLT_RADIX

The *radix* or base (*b*) of the exponential representation of floating point numbers; usually 2

FLT_MANT_DIG, DBL_MANT_DIG, LDBL_MANT_DIG

The number of digits in the significand or mantissa (p)

FLT_MIN_EXP, DBL_MIN_EXP, LDBL_MIN_EXP

The smallest negative exponent to the base FLT_RADIX (e_{min})

FLT_MAX_EXP, DBL_MAX_EXP, LDBL_MAX_EXP

The largest positive exponent to the base FLT_RADIX (e_{max})

In practice, it is useful to have the precision and the value range of a floating-point type in decimal notation. Macros for these characteristics are listed in Table 16-1. The values in the second column represent the C standard's minimum requirements. The values in the third column are the requirements of the IEC 60559 standard for floating-point numbers with single and double precision. In most C implementations, the types float and double have these IEC 60559 characteristics.

Table 16-1. Macros for the range and precision of floating-point types in decimal notation

Macro	ISO 9899	IEC 60559	Meaning
FLT_DIG	6	6	The precision as a number of decimal
DBL_DIG	10	15	digits. A decimal floating-point number of
LDBL_DIG	10		this many digits, stored in binary representation, always yields the same value to this many digits when converted back to decimal notation.
DECIMAL_DIG	10	17	The number of decimal digits necessary to represent any number of the largest floating-point type supported so that it can be converted to decimal notation and back to binary representation without its value changing.
FLT_MIN_10_EXP	-37	-37	The smallest negative exponent to base 10,
DBL_MIN_10_EXP	-37	-307	n, such that 10^n is within the positive
LDBL_MIN_10_EXP	-37		range of the type.
FLT_MAX_10_EXP	+37	+38	The greatest exponent to base 10, n, such
DBL_MAX_10_EXP	+37	+308	that 10^n is within the range of the type.
LDBL_MAX_10_EXP	+37		
FLT_MIN	1E-37	1.17549435E-38F	The smallest representable positive
DBL_MIN	1E-37	2.2250738585072014E-308	floating-point number.
LDBL_MIN	1E-37		
FLT_MAX	1E+37	3.40282347E+38F	The greatest representable finite floating-
DBL_MAX	1E+37	1.7976931348623157E+308	point number.
LDBL_MAX	1E+37		
FLT_EPSILON	1E-5	1.19209290E-07F	The positive difference between 1 and the
DBL_EPSILON	1E-9	2.2204460492503131E-16	smallest representable number greater
LDBL_EPSILON	1E-9		than 1.

inttypes.h

The header *inttypes.h* includes the header *stdint.h*, and contains extensions to it. The header *stdint.h* defines integer types with specified bit widths, including the types intmax_t and uintmax_t, which represent the widest integer types implemented. (See also "Integer Types Defined in Standard Headers" on page 29.)

Types

The header *inttypes.h* defines the following structure type:

imaxdiv_t
    This is a structure type of two members named quot and rem, whose type is intmax_t. The function imaxdiv() divides one number of type intmax_t by

another, and stores the quotient and remainder in an object of type struct imaxdiv_t.

Functions

In addition to imaxdiv(), the header *inttypes.h* also declares the function imax abs(), which returns the absolute value of an integer of the type intmax_t, and four functions to convert strings into integers with the type intmax_t or uintmax_t.

Macros

Furthermore, *inttypes.h* defines macros for string literals that you can use as type specifiers in format string arguments to the printf and scanf functions. The header contains macros to specify each of the types defined in *stdint.h*.

The names of the type specifier macros for the printf family of functions begin with the prefix PRI, followed by a conversion specifier (d, i, o, x, or X) and a sequence of uppercase letters that refers to a type name. For example, the macro names with the conversion specifier d are:

```
PRIdN  PRIdLEASTN  PRIdFASTN  PRIdMAX  PRIdPTR
```

The letter *N* at the end of the first three macro names listed here is a placeholder for a decimal number indicating the bit width of a given type. Commonly implemented values are 8, 16, 32, and 64.

Other PRI... macro names are analogous to the five just listed, but have different conversion specifiers in place of the letter d, such as i, o, x, or X. The following example uses a variable with the type int_fast32_t:

```
#include <inttypes.h>
int_fast32_t  i32Var;
/* ... */
  printf( "The value of i32Var, in hexadecimal notation: "
          "%10" PRIxFAST32 "\n", i32Var);
```

The preprocessor concatenates the string literals "%10" and PRIxFAST32 to form the full conversion specification. The resulting output of i32Var has a field width of 10 characters.

The names of the conversion specifier macros for the scanf family of functions begins with the prefix SCN. The remaining characters are the same as the corresponding PRI... macros, except that there is no conversion specifier X for scanf(). For example, the macro names with the conversion specifier d are:

```
SCNdN  SCNdLEASTN  SCNdFASTN  SCNdMAX  SCNdPTR
```

Again, the letter *N* at the end of the first three macro names as listed here is a placeholder for a decimal number indicating the bit width of a given type. Commonly implemented values are 8, 16, 32, and 64.

iso646.h

The header *iso646.h* defines the eleven macros listed in Table 16-2, which you can use as synonyms for C's logical and bitwise operators.

Table 16-2. ISO 646 operator names

Macro	Meaning
and	&&
or	||
not	!
bitand	&
bitor	|
xor	^
compl	~
and_eq	&=
or_eq	|=
xor_eq	^=
not_eq	!=

limits.h

The header *limits.h* contains macros to represent the least and greatest representable value of each integer type. These macros are listed in Table 16-3. The numeric values in the table represent the minimum requirements of the C standard.

Table 16-3. Value ranges of the integer types

Type	Minimum	Maximum	Maximum value of the unsigned type
char	CHAR_MIN	CHAR_MAX	UCHAR_MAX $2^8 - 1$
signed char	SCHAR_MIN $-(2^7 - 1)$	SCHAR_MAX $2^7 - 1$	
short	SHRT_MIN $-(2^{15} - 1)$	SHRT_MAX $2^{15} - 1$	USHRT_MAX $2^{16} - 1$
int	INT_MIN $-(2^{15} - 1)$	INT_MAX $2^{15} - 1$	UINT_MAX $2^{16} - 1$
long	LONG_MIN $-(2^{31} - 1)$	LONG_MAX $2^{31} - 1$	ULONG_MAX $2^{32} - 1$
long long	LLONG_MIN $-(2^{63} - 1)$	LLONG_MAX $2^{63} - 1$	ULLONG_MAX $2^{64} - 1$

The range of the type char depends on whether char is signed or unsigned. If char is signed, then CHAR_MIN is equal to SCHAR_MIN and CHAR_MAX equal to SCHAR_MAX. If char is unsigned, then CHAR_MIN is zero and CHAR_MAX is equal to UCHAR_MAX.

The header *limits.h* also defines the following two macros:

CHAR_BIT
> The number of bits in a byte, which must be at least 8.

MB_LEN_MAX
> The maximum number of bytes in a multibyte character, which must be at least 1.

The value of the macro CHAR_BIT determines the value of UCHAR_MAX: UCHAR_MAX is equal to $2^{CHAR\_BIT} - 1$.

The value of MB_LEN_MAX is greater than or equal to the value of MB_CUR_MAX, which is defined in the header *stdlib.h*. MB_CUR_MAX represents the maximum number of bytes in a multibyte character in the current locale. More specifically, the value depends on the locale setting for the LC_CTYPE category (see the description of set locale() in Chapter 18 for details). If the current locale uses a stateful multibyte encoding, then both MB_LEN_MAX and MB_CUR_MAX include the number of bytes necessary for a state-shift sequence before the actual multibyte character.

locale.h

The standard library supports the development of C programs that are able to adapt to local cultural conventions. For example, programs may use locale-specific character sets or formats for currency information.

The header *locale.h* declares two functions, the type struct lconv, the macro NULL for the null pointer constant, and macros whose names begin with LC_ for the locale information categories.

The function setlocale() allows you to query or set the current locale. The information that makes up the locale is divided into categories, which you can query and set individually. The following integer macros are defined to designate these categories:

LC_ALL	LC_COLLATE	LC_CTYPE
LC_MONETARY	LC_NUMERIC	LC_TIME

The function setlocale() takes one of these macros as its first argument, and operates on the corresponding locale category. The meanings of the macros are described under the setlocale() function in Chapter 18. Implementations may also define additional macros whose names start with LC_ followed by an uppercase letter.

The second function declared in *locale.h* is localeconv(), which supplies information about the conventions of the current locale by filling the members of a structure of the type struct lconv. localeconv() returns a pointer to the structure. The structure contains members to describe the local formatting of numerals, monetary amounts, and date and time information. For details, see the description of locale conv() in Chapter 18.

math.h

The header *math.h* declares the mathematical functions for real floating-point numbers, and the related macros and types.

The mathematical functions for integer types are declared in *stdlib.h*, and those for complex numbers in *complex.h*. In addition, the header *tgmath.h* defines the *type-generic macros*, which allow you to call mathematical functions by uniform names regardless of the arguments' type. For a summary of the mathematical functions in the standard library, see "Mathematical Functions" on page 323.

The types float_t and double_t

The header *math.h* defines the two types float_t and double_t. These types represent the floating-point precision used internally by the given implementation in evaluating arithmetic expressions of the types float and double. (If you use operands of the type float_t or double_t in your programs, they will not need to be converted before arithmetic operations, as float and double may.) The value of the macro FLT_EVAL_METHOD, defined in the header *float.h*, indicates which basic types correspond to float_t and double_t. The possible values of FLT_EVAL_METHOD are explained in Table 16-4.

Table 16-4. The types float_t and double_t

FLT_EVAL_METHOD	float_t	double_t
0	float	double
1	double	double
2	long double	long double

Any other value of FLT_EVAL_METHOD indicates that the evaluation of floating-point expressions is implementation-defined.

Classification macros

In addition to normalized floating-point numbers, the floating-point types can also represent other values, such as infinities and NaNs (see "Normalized representation of floating-point numbers" on page 293). C99 specifies five classes of floating-point values, and defines an integer macro to designate each of these categories. The five macros are:

```
FP_ZERO  FP_NORMAL  FP_SUBNORMAL  FP_INFINITE  FP_NAN
```

Implementations may also define additional categories, and corresponding macros whose names begin with FP_ followed by an uppercase letter.

math.h defines the following function-like macros to classify floating-point values:

fpclassify()

This macro expands to the value of the FP_... macro that designates the category of its floating-point argument.

isfinite(), isinf(), isnan(), isnormal(), signbit()

These function-like macros test whether their argument belongs to a specific category.

Other macros in math.h

The header *math.h* also defines the following macros:

HUGE_VAL, HUGE_VALF, HUGE_VALL

HUGE_VAL represents a large positive value with the type double. Mathematical functions that return double can return the value of HUGE_VAL, with the appropriate sign, when the result exceeds the finite value range of double. The value of HUGE_VAL may also represent a positive infinity, if the implementation supports such a value.

HUGE_VALF and HUGE_VALL are analogous to HUGE_VAL, but have the types float and long double.

INFINITY

This macro's value is constant expression of type float that represents a positive or unsigned infinity, if such a value is representable in the given implementation. If not, then INFINITY represents a constant expression of type float that yields an overflow when evaluated, so that the compiler generates an error message when processing it.

NAN

NaN stands for "not a number." The macro NAN is a constant of type float whose value is not a valid floating-point number. It is defined only if the implementation supports quiet NaNs—that is, if a NaN can occur without raising a floating-point exception.

FP_FAST_FMA, FP_FAST_FMAF, FP_FAST_FMAL

FMA stands for "fused multiply-and-add." The macro FP_FAST_FMA is defined if the function call fma(x,y,z) can be evaluated at least as fast as the mathematically equivalent expression x*y+z, for x, y, and z of type double. This is typically the case if the fma() function makes use of a special FMA machine operation.

The macros FP_FAST_FMAF and FP_FAST_FMAL are analogous to FP_FAST_FMA, but refer to the types float and long double.

`FP_ILOGB0, FP_ILOGBNAN`

These macros represent the respective values returned by the function call `ilogb(x)` when the argument *x* is zero or NaN. `FP_ILOGB0` is equal either to `INT_MIN` or to `-INT_MAX`, and `FP_ILOGBNAN` equals either `INT_MIN` or `INT_MAX`.

`MATH_ERRNO, MATH_ERREXCEPT, math_errhandling`

`MATH_ERRNO` is the constant 1 and `MATH_ERREXCEPT` is the constant 2. These values are represented by distinct bits, and hence can be used as bit masks in querying the value of `math_errhandling`. The identifier `math_errhandling` is either a macro or an external variable with the type `int`. Its value is constant throughout runtime, and you can query it in your programs to determine whether the mathematical functions indicate errors by raising exceptions or by providing an error code, or both. If the expression `math_errhandling` & `MATH_ERRNO` is not equal to zero, then the program can read the global error variable `errno` to identify domain and range errors in math function calls. Similarly, if `math_errhandling` & `MATH_ERREXCEPT` is nonzero, then the math functions indicate errors using the floating-point environment's exception flags. For more details, see "Error Handling" on page 329.

If a given implementation supports programs that use floating-point exceptions, then the header *fenv.h* must define at least the macros `FE_DIVBYZERO`, `FE_INVALID`, and `FE_OVERFLOW`.

setjmp.h

The header *setjmp.h* declares the function `longjmp()`, and defines the array type `jmp_buf` and the function-like macro `setjmp()`.

Calling `setjmp()` saves the current execution environment, including at least the momentary register and stack values, in a variable whose type is `jmp_buf`. In this way, the `setjmp()` call bookmarks a point in the program, which you can then jump back to at any time by calling the companion function `longjmp()`. In effect, `setjmp()` and `longjmp()` allow you to program a nonlocal "goto."

signal.h

The header *signal.h* declares the functions `raise()` and `signal()`, as well as related macros and the following integer type:

`sig_atomic_t`

You can use the type `sig_atomic_t` to define objects that are accessible in an atomic operation. Such objects are suitable for use in hardware interrupt signal handlers, for example. The value range of this type is described by the values of the macros `SIG_ATOMIC_MIN` and `SIG_ATOMIC_MAX`, which are defined in the header *stdint.h*.

A *signal handler* is a function that is automatically executed when the program receives a given signal from the operating environment. You can use the function signal() in your programs to install functions of your own as signal handlers.

Each type of signal that programs can receive is identified by a signal number. Accordingly, *signal.h* defines macros of type int to designate the signal types. The required signal type macros are:

```
SIGABRT  SIGILL  SIGSEGV
SIGFPE   SIGINT  SIGTERM
```

The meanings of these signal types are described along with the signal() function in Chapter 18. Implementations may also define other signals. The names of the corresponding macros begin with SIG or SIG_, followed by an uppercase letter.

The first argument to the function signal() is a signal number. The second is the address of a signal handler function, or one of the following macros:

SIG_DFL, SIG_IGN
> These macros are constant expressions whose values cannot be equal to the address of any declarable function. SIG_DFL installs the implementation's default signal handler for the given signal type. If you call signal() with SIG_IGN as the second argument, the program ignores signals of the given type, if the implementation allows programs to ignore them.

SIG_ERR
> This macro represents the value returned by the signal() function if an error occurs.

stdalign.h

The header *stdalign.h* is new in C11, and defines the following four macros:

alignas
> This is a synonym for the specifier _Alignas. When an object is defined with the specifier _Alignas, it can have a stricter alignment than its type requires.

alignof
> This is a synonym for the operator _Alignof, which obtains the alignment of a type.

__alignas_is_defined, __alignof_is_defined
> These macros are equal to the integer constant 1.

For more information on the alignment of objects, see "The Alignment of Objects in Memory" on page 36.

stdarg.h

The header *stdarg.h* defines one type and four macros for use in accessing the optional arguments of functions that support them (see "Variable Numbers of Arguments" on page 127):

va_list
> Functions with variable numbers of arguments use an object of the type va_list to access their optional arguments. Such an object is commonly called an *argument pointer*, as it serves as a reference to a list of optional arguments.

The following function-like macros operate on objects of the type va_list:

va_start()
> Sets the argument pointer to the first optional argument in the list.

va_arg()
> Returns the current argument and sets the argument pointer to the next one in the list.

va_copy()
> Copies the va_list object in its current state.

va_end()
> Cleans up after the use of a va_list object. A function with a variable number of arguments must contain a va_end() macro call corresponding to each invocation of va_start() or va_copy().

The macros va_copy() and va_end() may also be implemented as functions.

stdatomic.h

The header *stdatomic.h* is new in C11. It contains function declarations and definitions of various types and macros for atomic operations on data that is shared by several threads. For explanations and examples of atomic operations, see "Accessing Shared Data" on page 244.

Support for atomic operations is optional: C11 implementations that define the macro __STDC_NO_ATOMICS__ need not provide the header *stdatomic.h*.

The names of the functions declared begin with the prefix atomic_, as in atomic_store(). All function names that begin with the prefix atomic_ followed by a lowercase letter are reserved for future extensions. Type names that begin with atomic_ or memory_ followed by a lowercase letter are likewise reserved, as are macro names that begin with ATOMIC_ followed by an uppercase letter.

Types defined in stdatomic.h

atomic_flag

A structure type that is capable of representing the states "set" and "clear," and is atomically accessible without using a lock.

memory_order

An enumerated type that defines the following constants used for specifying the memory-ordering constraints of atomic operations:

memory_order_relaxed memory_order_release memory_order_acquire
memory_order_consume memory_order_acq_rel memory_order_seq_cst

For a description of these enumeration constants with examples, see "Memory Ordering" on page 249. An argument of the type memory_order is used with the atomic functions whose names end with the suffix _explicit, such as atomic_store_explicit(), and with the function atomic_thread_fence().

The header *stdatomic.h* also defines the type names listed in Table 16-5, which are synonyms for the integer atomic types named in the right column.

Table 16-5. Integer atomic types

Atomic type name	Type
atomic_bool	_Atomic _Bool
atomic_char	_Atomic char
atomic_schar	_Atomic signed char
atomic_uchar	_Atomic unsigned char
atomic_short	_Atomic short
atomic_ushort	_Atomic unsigned short
atomic_int	_Atomic int
atomic_uint	_Atomic unsigned int
atomic_long	_Atomic long
atomic_ulong	_Atomic unsigned long
atomic_llong	_Atomic long long
atomic_ullong	_Atomic unsigned long long
atomic_char16_t	_Atomic char16_t
atomic_char32_t	_Atomic char32_t
atomic_wchar_t	_Atomic wchar_t
atomic_int_least8_t	_Atomic int_least8_t
atomic_uint_least8_t	_Atomic uint_least8_t
atomic_int_least16_t	_Atomic int_least16_t
atomic_uint_least16_t	_Atomic uint_least16_t

Atomic type name	Type
atomic_int_least32_t	_Atomic int_least32_t
atomic_uint_least32_t	_Atomic uint_least32_t
atomic_int_least64_t	_Atomic int_least64_t
atomic_uint_least64_t	_Atomic uint_least64_t
atomic_int_fast8_t	_Atomic int_fast8_t
atomic_uint_fast8_t	_Atomic uint_fast8_t
atomic_int_fast16_t	_Atomic int_fast16_t
atomic_uint_fast16_t	_Atomic uint_fast16_t
atomic_int_fast32_t	_Atomic int_fast32_t
atomic_uint_fast32_t	_Atomic uint_fast32_t
atomic_int_fast64_t	_Atomic int_fast64_t
atomic_uint_fast64_t	_Atomic uint_fast64_t
atomic_intptr_t	_Atomic intptr_t
atomic_uintptr_t	_Atomic uintptr_t
atomic_size_t	_Atomic size_t
atomic_ptrdiff_t	_Atomic ptrdiff_t
atomic_intmax_t	_Atomic intmax_t
atomic_uintmax_t	_Atomic uintmax_t

Macros Defined in stdatomic.h

The values of the following macros indicate whether the corresponding atomic types (signed and unsigned) are "lock free"—in other words, whether they permit atomic access without the use of a lock.

```
ATOMIC_BOOL_LOCK_FREE        ATOMIC_SHORT_LOCK_FREE
ATOMIC_CHAR_LOCK_FREE        ATOMIC_INT_LOCK_FREE
ATOMIC_CHAR16_T_LOCK_FREE    ATOMIC_LONG_LOCK_FREE
ATOMIC_CHAR32_T_LOCK_FREE    ATOMIC_LLONG_LOCK_FREE
ATOMIC_WCHAR_T_LOCK_FREE     ATOMIC_POINTER_LOCK_FREE
```

All of these macros have values of 0, 1, or 2. The value 0 means that the type is never lock-free, 1 means it is lock-free for certain objects, and 2 means it is always lock-free.

In addition to the LOCK_FREE macros, *stdatomic.h* also defines three other macros:

ATOMIC_FLAG_INIT
> This macro is an initializer used to initialize an object of the type `atomic_flag` to the "clear" state.

ATOMIC_VAR_INIT(*value*)
> This function-like macro expands to an initializer which can be used to initialize an atomic object that is capable of storing the argument's value.

Atomic objects can also be initialized using the generic function `atomic_init()`. In any case, the initialization of an atomic object is not an atomic operation. Like nonatomic objects, atomic objects with static or thread-local storage duration which are not explicitly initialized have the initial value 0.

kill_dependency(*y*)
> This function-like macro breaks a dependency chain that was started by a consume operation—that is, by an atomic load operation with the memory order specification `memory_order_consume`. The macro's return value is the value of the argument *y*, and is no longer a part of a dependency chain. This allows the compiler to apply further optimization.

stdbool.h

The header *stdbool.h* defines the following four macros:

bool
> A synonym for the type `_Bool`

true
> The constant 1

false
> The constant 0

__bool_true_false_are_defined
> The constant 1

stddef.h

The header *stddef.h* defines three types and two macros for use in all kinds of programs. The three types are:

ptrdiff_t
> A signed integer type that represents the difference between two pointers.

size_t
> An unsigned integer type used to represent the result of `sizeof` operations; also defined in *stdlib.h*, *wchar.h*, *stdio.h*, and *string.h*.

`wchar_t`
> An integer type that is wide enough to store any code in the largest extended character set that the implementation supports; also defined in *stdlib.h* and *wchar.h*.

Macros that specify the least and greatest representable values of these three types are defined in the header *stdint.h* .

In C11 implementations, one or two other types are also defined in *stddef.h*:

`max_align_t`
> In C11, this is an object type with the largest possible alignment that the implementation supports in all contexts. It may be a type with an alignment of 8 or 16, for example.

`rsize_t`
> This type is equivalent with `size_t`, and is defined only if the C11 implementation supports the secure standard functions with bounds-checking. If `rsize_t` is defined, then the macro `RSIZE_MAX` is also defined in the header *stdint.h*, typically with a value less than that of `SIZE_MAX`. In standard functions with a parameter of the type `rsize_t`, passing a value greater than `RSIZE_MAX` violates a runtime constraint.

The two macros defined in *stddef.h* are:

`NULL`
> This macro represents a null pointer constant, which is an integer constant expression with the value 0, or such an expression cast as the type `void *`. The macro `NULL` is also defined in the headers *stdio.h*, *stdlib.h*, *string.h*, *time.h*, and *wchar.h*.

`offsetof( structure_type, member )`
> This macro yields an integer constant with type `size_t` whose value is the number of bytes between the beginning of the structure and the beginning of its member *member*. The member must not be a bit-field.

stdint.h

The header *stdint.h* defines integer types with specific bit widths, and macros that indicate the value ranges of these and other types. For example, you can use the `int64_t` type, defined in *stdint.h*, to define a signed, 64-bit integer.

Value ranges of the integer types with specific widths

If a signed type of a given specific width is defined, then the corresponding unsigned type is also defined, and vice versa. Unsigned types have names that start with u (such as `uint64_t`, for example), which is followed by the name of the corresponding signed type (such as `int64_t`).

For each type defined in *stdint.h*, macros are also defined to designate the type's least and greatest representable values. Table 16-6 lists the names of these macros, with the standard's requirements for their values. The word "exactly" in the table indicates that the standard specifies an exact value rather than a maximum or minimum. Otherwise, the standard allows the implementation to exceed the ranges given in the table. The letter N before an underscore in the type names as listed here is a placeholder for a decimal number indicating the bit width of a given type. Commonly implemented values are 8, 16, 32, and 64.

Table 16-6. Value ranges of the integer types with specific widths

Type	Minimum	Maximum	Maximum value of the unsigned type
int$N$_t	INTN_MIN	INTN_MAX	UINTN_MAX
	Exactly $-(2^{N-1})$	Exactly $2^{N-1} - 1$	Exactly $2^N - 1$
int_least$N$_t	INT_LEASTN_MIN	INT_LEASTN_MAX	UINT_LEASTN_MAX
	$-(2^{N-1} - 1)$	$2^{N-1} - 1$	$2^N - 1$
int_fast$N$_t	INT_FASTN_MIN	INT_FASTN_MAX	UINT_FASTN_MAX
	$-(2^{N-1} - 1)$	$2^{N-1} - 1$	$2^N - 1$
intmax_t	INTMAX_MIN	INTMAX_MAX	UINTMAX_MAX
	$-(2^{63} - 1)$	$2^{63} - 1$	$2^{64} - 1$
intptr_t	INTPTR_MIN	INTPTR_MAX	UINTPTR_MAX
	$-(2^{15} - 1)$	$2^{15} - 1$	$2^{16} - 1$

For the meanings of the fixed-width integer type names, and the C standard's requirements as to which of them must be defined, see "Integer Types Defined in Standard Headers" on page 29.

Value ranges of other integer types

The header *stdint.h* also contains macros to document the value ranges of types defined in other headers. These types are listed in Table 16-7. The numbers in the table represent the minimum requirements of the C standard. The types sig_atomic_t, wchar_t, and wint_t may be defined as signed or unsigned.

Table 16-7. Value ranges of other integer types

Type	Minimum	Maximum
ptrdiff_t	PTRDIFF_MIN	PTRDIFF_MAX
	−65535	+65535
sig_atomic_t	SIG_ATOMIC_MIN	SIG_ATOMIC_MAX
	If signed: ≤ -127	If signed: ≥ 127
	If unsigned: 0	If unsigned: ≥ 255
size_t	N/A	SIZE_MAX
		65535

Type	Minimum	Maximum
rsize_t	N/A	RSIZE_MAX ≤ SIZE_MAX
wchar_t	WCHAR_MIN If signed: ≤ −127 If unsigned: 0	WCHAR_MAX If signed: ≥ 127 If unsigned: ≥ 255
wint_t	WINT_MIN If signed: ≤ −32767 If unsigned: 0	WINT_MAX If signed: ≥ 32767 If unsigned: ≥ 65535

The types ptrdiff_t, size_t, rsize_t and wchar_t are described in "stddef.h" on page 307. The type rsize_t, and hence the corresponding macro RSIZE_MAX, are only defined if the implementation supports the bounds-checking, "secure" functions. The type sig_atomic_t is described in "signal.h" on page 302, and wint_t is described in "wchar.h" on page 318.

Macros for integer constants

For each decimal number *N* for which the *stdint.h* header defines a type int_least *N*_t (an integer type that is at least *N* bits wide), the header also defines two function-like macros to generate values with the type int_least*N*_t. Arguments to these macros must be constants in decimal, octal, or hexadecimal notation, and must be within the value range of the intended type (see "Integer Constants" on page 39). The macros are:

INT*N*_C(*value*), UINT*N*_C(*value*)
> Expands to a signed or unsigned integer constant with the specified *value* and the type int_least*N*_t or uint_least*N*_t, which is at least *N* bits wide. For example, if uint_least32_t is defined as a synonym for the type unsigned long, then the macro call UINT32_C(123) may expand to the constant 123UL.

The following macros are defined for the types intmax_t and uintmax_t:

INTMAX_C(*value*), UINTMAX_C(*value*)
> These macros expand to a constant with the specified *value* and the type intmax_t or uintmax_t.

stdio.h

The header *stdio.h* contains the declarations of all the basic functions for input and output, as well as related macro and type definitions. The declarations for wide-character I/O functions—that is, for input and output of characters with the type wchar_t—are contained in the header file *wchar.h* (see also Chapter 13).

In addition to size_t, which is discussed in "stddef.h" on page 307, *stdio.h* defines the following two types:

FILE

An object of the type FILE contains all the information necessary for controlling an I/O stream. This information includes a pointer to the stream's buffer, a file access position indicator, and flags to indicate error and end-of-file conditions.

fpos_t

Objects of this type, which is the return type of the fgetpos() function, are able to store all the information pertaining to a file access position. You can use the fsetpos() function to resume file processing at the position described by an fpos_t object.

In C11 implementations that support the bounds-checking, "secure" functions, the header *stdio.h* also declares the types errno_t (see "errno.h" on page 291) and rsize_t (see "stddef.h" on page 307).

The header *stdio.h* defines the macro NULL (described in "stddef.h" on page 307) as well as the following 12 macros, all of which represent integer constant expressions:

_IOFBF, _IOLBF, _IONBF

These constants are used as arguments to the setvbuf() function, and specify I/O buffering modes. The names stand for "fully buffered," "line buffered," and "not buffered."

BUFSIZ

This is the size of the buffer activated by the setbuf() function, in bytes.

EOF

"End of file." A negative value (usually -1) with type int. Various functions return the constant EOF to indicate an attempt to read at the end of a file, or to indicate an error.

FILENAME_MAX

This constant indicates how big a char array must be to store the longest filename supported by the fopen() function.

FOPEN_MAX

Programs are allowed to have at least this number of files open simultaneously.

L_tmpnam

This constant indicates how big a char array must be to store a filename generated by the tmpnam() function.

SEEK_SET, SEEK_CUR, SEEK_END

These constants are used as the third argument to the fseek() function.

TMP_MAX
>   The maximum number of unique filenames that the tmpnam() function can
>   generate. This number is at least 25.

C11 implementations that support the new bounds-checking, "secure" functions
also define the following macros:

L_tmpnam_s, TMP_MAX_S
>   The meanings of these macros in the context of the function tmpnam_s() are
>   analogous to those of the macros L_tmpnam and TMP_MAX, described in the pre-
>   ceding list, for the function tmpnam().

The header *stdio.h* also declares three objects:

stdin, stdout, stderr
>   These are the standard I/O streams. They are pointers to the FILE objects asso-
>   ciated with the "standard input," "standard output," and "standard error output"
>   streams.

stdlib.h

The header *stdlib.h* declares general utility functions for the following purposes:

- Conversion of numeral strings into binary numeric values
- Random number generation
- Memory management
- Communication with the operating system
- Searching and sorting
- Integer arithmetic
- Conversion of multibyte characters to wide characters and vice versa

stdlib.h also defines the types size_t and wchar_t, which are described in "stddef.h"
on page 307, as well as the following three types:

div_t, ldiv_t, lldiv_t
>   These are structure types used to hold the results of the integer division func-
>   tions div(), ldiv(), and lldiv(). These types are structures of two members,
>   quot and rem, which have the type int, long, or long long.

In C11 implementations that support the bounds-checking, "secure" functions, the
header *stdlib.h* also declares the types errno_t (see "errno.h" on page 291), and
rsize_t (see "stddef.h" on page 307), and the following type:

constraint_handler_t
>   This is the function-pointer type of the constraint handler argument passed to
>   the function set_constraint_handler_s(). The last handler function passed

---

in this way to the `set_constraint_handler_s()` function is called when a run-time constraint is violated during a call to a "secure" function.

The header *stdlib.h* defines the macro `NULL` (see "stddef.h" on page 307) as well as the following four macros:

`EXIT_FAILURE, EXIT_SUCCESS`
> Integer constants that you can pass as arguments to the functions `exit()` and `_Exit()` to report your program's exit status to the operating environment.

`MB_CUR_MAX`
> A nonzero integer expression with the type `size_t`. This is the maximum number of bytes in a multibyte character under the current locale setting for the locale category `LC_CTYPE`. This value must be less than or equal to `MB_LEN_MAX`, defined in *limits.h*.

`RAND_MAX`
> An integer constant that indicates the greatest possible value that can be returned by the function `rand()`.

stdnoreturn.h

The header *stdnoreturn.h* is new in C11 and defines only one macro, `noreturn`, as a synonym for the keyword `_Noreturn`.

string.h

The header *string.h* declares the string manipulation functions, along with other functions that operate on byte arrays. The names of these functions begin with `str`, as in `strcpy()`, for example, or with `mem`, as in `memcpy()`. Function names beginning with `str`, `mem`, or `wcs` followed by a lowercase letter are reserved for future extensions.

The header *string.h* also defines the type `size_t` and the macro `NULL`, described in "stddef.h" on page 307.

 In C11 implementations that support the bounds-checking, "secure" functions, the header *string.h* also declares the types `errno_t` (described in "errno.h" on page 291) and `rsize_t` (described in "stddef.h" on page 307).

tgmath.h

The header *tgmath.h* includes the headers *math.h* and *complex.h*, and defines the *type-generic macros*. These macros allow you to call different variants of mathematical functions by a uniform name, regardless of the arguments' type.

The mathematical functions in the standard library are defined with parameters of specific real or complex floating-point types. Their names indicate types other than double by the prefix c for _Complex, or by the suffixes f for float and l for long double. The type-generic macros are overloaded names for these functions that you can use with arguments of any arithmetic type. These macros detect the arguments' type and call the appropriate math function.

The header *tgmath.h* defines type-generic macros for all the mathematical functions with floating-point parameters except modf(), modff(), and modfl(). If a given function is defined for both real and complex or only for real floating-point types, then the corresponding type-generic macro has the same name as the function version for arguments of the type double—that is, the base name of the function with no c prefix and no f or l suffix. For an example, assume the following declarations:

```
#include <tgmath.h>
float  f = 0.5F;
double d = 1.5;
double _Complex z1 = -1;
long double _Complex z2 = I;
```

Each of the macro calls in Table 16-8 then expands to the function call shown in the right column.

Table 16-8. Expansion of type-generic macros

Type-generic macro call	Expansion
sqrt(f)	sqrtf(f)
sqrt(d)	sqrt(d)
sqrt(z1)	csqrt(z1)
sqrt(z2)	csqrtl(z2)

Arguments with integer types are automatically converted to double. If you use arguments of different types in invoking a type-generic macro with two parameters, such as pow(), the macro calls the function version for the argument type with the higher rank (see "Hierarchy of Types" on page 50). If any argument has a complex floating-point type, the macro calls the function for complex numbers.

Several functions are defined only for complex floating-point types. The type-generic macros for these functions have names that start with c, but with no f or l suffix:

    carg() cimag() conj() cproj() creal()

If you invoke one of these macros with a real argument, it calls the function for the complex type that corresponds to the argument's real floating-point type.

threads.h

The header *threads.h*, which was introduced in C11, declares the functions for multithreading support, and defines the accompanying types and macros. The header *threads.h* also includes the header *time.h*. For details and examples on multithreaded programming using C11 features, see Chapter 14.

Multithreading support is optional in C11: implementations that define the macro __STDC_NO_THREADS__ need not provide the header *threads.h*.

The functions and types defined in *threads.h* are related to threads, mutex objects, condition variables and thread-specific storage. Accordingly, the names of the functions and types begin with one of the prefixes thrd_, mtx_, cnd_ and tss_. Other names beginning with any of these prefixes, followed by a lowercase letter, are reserved for future extensions.

Types Defined in threads.h

thrd_t
> The type of an object that represents a thread.

thrd_start_t
> The type int (*)(void*) (that is, a pointer to a function that takes one void-pointer argument and returns an integer). This is the function pointer type passed as an argument to the function thrd_create() to specify the function that a new thread will execute.

mtx_t
> The type of an object that represents a mutex.

cnd_t
> The type of an object that represents a condition variable.

tss_t
> The type of an object that represents a pointer to thread-specific storage.

tss_dtor_t
> The type void (*)(void*) (that is, a pointer to a function that takes one void-pointer argument and has no return value). This is the function-pointer type of the argument passed to the function tss_create() to specify the destructor function for the thread-specific storage requested.

once_flag
> The type of a flag used by the function call_once().

Enumeration constants defined in threads.h

The header *threads.h* defines the following enumeration constants for the return value of the thread functions:

thrd_success
> Indicates that the function succeeded in performing the requested operation.

thrd_error
> Indicates that an error occurred during the execution of the function.

thrd_busy
> Indicates that the function failed because a required resource is still in use.

thrd_nomem
> Indicates that the function was unable to allocate sufficient memory.

thrd_timeout
> Indicates that the time limit specified in the function call expired before the function was able to obtain the required resource.

Three constants are defined for use as an argument to the function mtx_init() to specify the properties of the new mutex to be created. The three constants are used to form one of four argument values as follows:

mtx_plain
> Create a simple mutex without support for recursion or timeouts.

mtx_timed
> Create a mutex that supports timeouts.

mtx_plain|mtx_recursive
> Create a mutex that supports recursion.

mtx_timed|mtx_recursive
> Create a mutex that supports timeouts and recursion.

Macros defined in threads.h

The *threads.h* header defines the following three macros:

thread_local
> This is a synonym for the keyword _Thread_local.

ONCE_FLAG_INIT
> This macro represents an initializer for objects of the type once_flag.

TSS_DTOR_ITERATIONS
> A constant integer expression that specifies the maximum number of times a thread-specific storage destructor will be called on thread termination.

time.h

The header *time.h* declares the standard functions, macros, and types for manipulating date and time information (by the Gregorian calendar). These functions are listed in "Date and Time" on page 337.

The types declared in *time.h* are `size_t` (see *stddef.h* in this chapter) and the following three types:

`clock_t`
> This is the arithmetic type returned by the function `clock()` (usually defined as `unsigned long`).

`time_t`
> This is an arithmetic type returned by the functions `timer()` and `mktime()` (usually defined as `long`).

`struct tm`
> The members of this structure represent a date or a time, broken down into seconds, minutes, hours, the day of the month, and so on. The functions `gmtime()` and `localtime()` return a pointer to `struct tm`. The structure's members are described under the `gmtime()` function in Chapter 18.

 In C11 implementations that support the bounds-checking, "secure" functions, the header *time.h* also declares the types `errno_t` (see "errno.h" on page 291) and `rsize_t` (see "stddef.h" on page 307).

The header *time.h* defines the macro `NULL` (see *stddef.h*) and the following macro:

`CLOCKS_PER_SEC`
> This is a constant expression with the type `clock_t`. You can divide the return value of the `clock()` function by `CLOCKS_PER_SEC` to obtain your program's CPU use in seconds.

uchar.h

In C11, the new header *uchar.h* declares types and functions for processing Unicode characters. The types declared are `size_t` (see "stddef.h" on page 307), `mbstate_t` (see "wchar.h" on page 318), and the following two new types:

`char16_t`
> An unsigned integer type for 16-bit characters. This type is the same as `uint_least16_t`. Implementations that define the macro `__STDC_UTF_16__` use UTF-16 encoding for characters of the type `char16_t`. The macro is not defined if a different encoding is used.

char32_t

> An unsigned integer type for 32-bit characters. This type is the same as uint_least32_t. Implementations that define the macro __STDC_UTF_32__ use UTF-32 encoding for characters of the type char32_t. The macro is not defined if a different encoding is used.

The types uint_least16_t and uint_least32_t are described in "stdint.h" on page 308. The header *uchar.h* declares the following four functions for converting 16-bit or 32-bit Unicode characters to multibyte characters and vice versa: mbrtoc16(), c16rtomb(), mbrtoc32(), and c32rtomb().

Functions and types for processing wide characters of the type wchar_t are declared in the header *wchar.h*.

wchar.h

The headers *stdio.h*, *stdlib.h*, *string.h*, and *time.h* all declare functions for processing byte-character strings—that is, strings of characters with the type char. The header *wchar.h* declares similar functions for *wide strings*: strings of wide characters, which have the type wchar_t. The names of these functions generally contain an additional w, as in wprintf(), for example, or start with wcs instead of str, as in wcscpy(), which is the name of the wide-string version of the strcpy() function.

Furthermore, the header *wchar.h* declares more functions for converting multibyte characters to wide characters and vice versa, in addition to those declared in *stdlib.h*. *wchar.h* declares functions for the following kinds of purposes:

- Wide and multibyte character I/O
- Conversion of wide-string numerals
- Copying, concatenating, and comparing wide strings and wide-character arrays
- Formatting date and time information in wide strings
- Conversion of multibyte characters to wide characters and vice versa

The types defined in *wchar.h* are size_t and wchar_t (explained in "stddef.h" on page 307); struct tm (see *time.h*); and the following two types:

mbstate_t

> Objects of this type store the parsing state information involved in the conversion of a multibyte string to a wide-character string, or vice versa.

wint_t

> An integer type whose bit width is at least that of int. wint_t must be wide enough to represent the value range of wchar_t and the value of the macro WEOF. The types wint_t and wchar_t may be identical.

In C11 implementations that support the bounds-checking, "secure" functions, the header *wchar.h* also declares the types errno_t (see "errno.h" on page 291) and rsize_t (see "stddef.h" on page 307).

The header *wchar.h* defines the macro NULL (see "stddef.h" on page 307), the macros WCHAR_MIN and WCHAR_MAX (see "stdint.h" on page 308), and the following macro:

WEOF
> The macro WEOF has the type wint_t and a value that is distinct from all the character codes in the extended character set. Unlike EOF, its value may be positive. Various functions return the constant WEOF to indicate an attempt to read at the end of a file, or to indicate an error.

wctype.h

The header *wctype.h* declares functions to classify and convert wide characters. These functions are analogous to those for byte characters declared in the header *ctype.h*. In addition, *wctype.h* declares *extensible* wide-character classification and conversion functions.

The types defined in *wctype.h* are wint_t (described in "wchar.h" on page 318) and the following two types:

wctrans_t
> This is a scalar type to represent locale-specific mapping rules. You can obtain a value of this type by calling the wctrans() function, and use it as an argument to the function towctrans() to perform a locale-specific wide-character conversion.

wctype_t
> This is a scalar type to represent locale-specific character categories. You can obtain a value of this type by calling the wctype() function, and pass it as an argument to the function iswctype() to determine whether a given wide character belongs to the given category.

The header *wctype.h* also defines the macro WEOF, described in "wchar.h" on page 318.

17

Functions at a Glance

This chapter lists the functions in the standard library according to their respective areas of application, describing shared features of the functions and their relationships to one another. This compilation might help you to find the right function for your purposes while programming.

The individual functions are described in detail in Chapter 18, which explains them in alphabetical order, with examples.

The alternative functions with bounds-checking introduced in C11, also called the *secure functions*, are listed in Tables 17-1 and 17-2. The names of these functions end with the suffix _s (s for "secure"), as in scanf_s(). Note that C implementations are not required to support the secure functions. For more information on using the secure functions, see "Functions with Bounds-Checking" on page 287.

Input and Output

We have dealt with this topic in detail in Chapter 13, which contains sections on I/O streams, sequential and random file access, formatted I/O, and error handling. A tabular list of the I/O functions will therefore suffice here. Table 17-1 lists general file access functions declared in the header *stdio.h*.

Table 17-1. General file access functions

Purpose	Functions
Rename a file, delete a file	`rename()`, `remove()`
Create and/or open a file	`fopen()`, `freopen()`, `tmpfile()` `fopen_s()`, `freopen_s()`, `tmpfile_s()`
Close a file	`fclose()`
Generate a unique filename	`tmpnam()`, `tmpnam_s()`
Query or clear file access flags	`feof()`, `ferror()`, `clearerr()`
Query the current file access position	`ftell()`, `fgetpos()`
Change the current file access position	`rewind()`, `fseek()`, `fsetpos()`
Write buffer contents to file	`fflush()`
Control file buffering	`setbuf()`, `setvbuf()`

There are two complete sets of functions for input and output of characters and strings: the *byte-character* and the *wide-character* I/O functions (see "Byte-Oriented and Wide-Oriented Streams" on page 216 for more information). The wide-character functions operate on characters with the type `wchar_t`, and are declared in the header *wchar.h*. Table 17-2 lists both sets.

Table 17-2. File I/O functions

Purpose	Functions in stdio.h	Functions in wchar.h
Get/set stream orientation		`fwide()`
Write characters	`fputc()`, `putc()`, `putchar()`	`fputwc()`, `putwc()`, `putwchar()`
Read characters	`fgetc()`, `getc()`, `getchar()`	`fgetwc()`, `getwc()`, `getwchar()`
Put back characters read	`ungetc()`	`ungetwc()`
Write lines	`fputs()`, `puts()`	`fputws()`
Read lines	`fgets()`, `gets()`, `gets_s()`	`fgetws()`
Write blocks	`fwrite()`	
Read blocks	`fread()`	

Write formatted strings	`printf()`, `vprintf()`
	`fprintf()`, `vfprintf()`
	`sprintf()`, `vsprintf()`
	`snprintf()`, `vsnprintf()`
		`wprintf()`, `vwprintf()`
		`fwprintf()`, `vfwprintf()`
		`swprintf()`, `vswprintf()`

Read formatted strings	`scanf()`, `vscanf()`
	`fscanf()`, `vfscanf()`
	`sscanf()`, `vsscanf()`
		`wscanf()`, `vwscanf()`
		`fwscanf()`, `vfwscanf()`
		`swscanf()`, `vswscanf()`

For each function in the printf and scanf families, there is a secure alternative function whose name ends in the suffix _s.

Mathematical Functions

The standard library provides many mathematical functions. Most of them operate on real or complex floating-point numbers. However, there are also several functions with integer types, such as the functions to generate random numbers.

The functions to convert numeral strings into arithmetic types are listed in "String Processing" on page 332. The remaining math functions are described in the following subsections.

Mathematical Functions for Integer Types

The math functions for the integer types are declared in the header *stdlib.h*. Two of these functions, abs() and div(), are declared in three variants to operate on the three signed integer types int, long, and long long. As Table 17-3 shows, the functions for the type long have names beginning with the letter l; those for long long begin with ll. Furthermore, the header *inttypes.h* declares function variants for the type intmax_t, with names that begin with imax.

Table 17-3. Integer arithmetic functions

Purpose	Functions declared in stdlib.h	Functions declared in stdint.h
Absolute value	abs(), labs(), llabs()	imaxabs()
Division	div(), ldiv(), lldiv()	imaxdiv()
Random numbers	rand(), srand()	

Floating-Point Functions

The functions for real floating-point types are declared in the header *math.h*, and those for complex floating-point types are declared in *complex.h*. Table 17-4 lists the functions that are available for both real and complex floating-point types. The complex versions of these functions have names that start with the prefix c. Table 17-5 lists the functions that are only defined for the real types; and Table 17-6 lists the functions that are specific to complex types.

For the sake of readability, Tables 17-4 through 17-6 show only the names of the functions for the types double and double _Complex. Each of these functions also exists in variants for the types float (or float _Complex) and long double (or long double _Complex). The names of these variants end in the suffix f for float or l for long double. For example, the functions sin() and csin() listed in Table 17-4 also exist in the variants sinf(), sinl(), csinf(), and csinl() (but see also "Type-generic macros" on page 325).

Table 17-4. Functions for real and complex floating-point types

Mathematical function	C functions in math.h	C functions in complex.h
Trigonometry	sin(), cos(), tan() asin(), acos(), atan()	csin(), ccos(), ctan() casin(), cacos(), catan()
Hyperbolic trigonometry	sinh(), cosh(), tanh() asinh(), acosh(), atanh()	casinh(), cacosh(), catanh() csinh(), ccosh(), ctanh()
Exponential function	exp()	cexp()
Natural logarithm	log()	clog()
Powers, square root	pow(), sqrt()	cpow(), csqrt()
Absolute value	fabs()	cabs()

Table 17-5. Functions for real floating-point types

Mathematical function	C function
Arctangent of a quotient	atan2()
Exponential functions	exp2(), expm1(), frexp(), ldexp(), scalbn(), scalbln()
Logarithmic functions	log10(), log2(), log1p(), logb(), ilogb()
Roots	cbrt(), hypot()
Error functions for normal distributions	erf(), erfc()
Gamma function	tgamma(), lgamma()
Remainder	fmod(), remainder(), remquo()
Separate integer and fractional parts	modf()
Next integer	ceil(), floor()
Next representable number	nextafter(), nexttoward()
Rounding functions	trunc(), round(), lround(), llround(), nearbyint(), rint(), lrint(), llrint()
Positive difference	fdim()
Multiply and add	fma()
Minimum and maximum	fmin(), fmax()
Assign one number's sign to another	copysign()
Generate a NaN	nan()

Table 17-6. Functions for complex floating-point types

Mathematical function	C function
Isolate real and imaginary parts	`creal()`, `cimag()`
Argument (the angle in polar coordinates)	`carg()`
Conjugate	`conj()`
Project onto the Riemann sphere	`cproj()`

Function-Like Macros

The standard headers *math.h* and *tgmath.h* define a number of function-like macros that can be invoked with arguments of different floating-point types. Variable argument types in C are supported only in macros, not in function calls.

Type-generic macros

Each floating-point math function exists in three or six different versions: one for each of the three real types, or for each of the three complex types, or for both real and complex types. The header *tgmath.h* defines the *type-generic* macros, which allow you to call any version of a given function under a uniform name. The compiler detects the appropriate function from the arguments' type. Thus, you do not need to edit the math function calls in your programs when you change an argument's type from double to long double, for example. The type-generic macros are described in "tgmath.h" on page 313.

Categories of floating-point values

C99 defines five kinds of values for the real floating-point types, with distinct integer macros to designate them (see the section on *math.h* in Chapter 16):

```
FP_ZERO  FP_NORMAL  FP_SUBNORMAL  FP_INFINITE  FP_NAN
```

These classification macros, and the function-like macros listed in Table 17-7, are defined in the header *math.h*. The argument of each of the function-like macros must be an expression with a real floating-point type.

Table 17-7. Function-like macros to classify floating-point values

Purpose	Function-like macros
Get the category of a floating-point value	`fpclassify()`
Test whether a floating-point value belongs to a certain category	`isfinite()`, `isinf()`, `isnan()`, `isnormal()`, `signbit()`

For example, the following two tests are equivalent:

```
if ( fpclassify( x ) == FP_INFINITE )  /* ... */ ;
if ( isinf( x ) )                       /* ... */ ;
```

Comparison macros

Any two real, finite floating-point numbers can be compared. In other words, one is always *less than*, *equal to*, or *greater than* the other. However, if one or both operands of a comparative operator is a NaN—a floating-point value that is not a number—for example, then the operands are not comparable. In this case, the operation yields the value 0, or "false," and may raise the floating-point exception FE_INVALID.

In practice, you may want to avoid risking an exception when comparing floating-point objects. For this reason, the header *math.h* defines the function-like macros listed in Table 17-8. These macros yield the same results as the corresponding expressions with comparative operators, but perform a "quiet" comparison; that is, they never raise exceptions, but simply return false if the operands are not comparable. The two arguments of each macro must be expressions with real floating-point types.

Table 17-8. Function-like macros to compare floating-point values

Comparison	Function-like macro
$(x) > (y)$	isgreater(x, y)
$(x) >= (y)$	isgreaterequal($x, y\_$)
$(x) < (y)$	isless(x, y)
$(x) <= (y)$	islessequal(x, y)
$((x) < (y) \mid\mid (x) > (y))$	islessgreater(x, y)[a]
Test for comparability	isunordered(x, y)

[a] Unlike the corresponding operator expression, the function-like macro islessgreater() evaluates its arguments only once.

Pragmas for Arithmetic Operations

The following two standard pragmas influence the way in which arithmetic expressions are compiled:

```
#pragma STDC FP_CONTRACT    on_off_switch
#pragma STDC CX_LIMITED_RANGE  on_off_switch
```

The value of *on_off_switch* must be ON, OFF, or DEFAULT. If switched ON, the first of these pragmas, FP_CONTRACT, allows the compiler to *contract* floating-point expressions with several C operators into fewer machine operations, if possible. Contracted expressions are faster in execution. However, because they also eliminate rounding errors, they may not yield precisely the same results as uncontracted expressions. Furthermore, an uncontracted expression may raise floating-point exceptions that are not raised by the corresponding contracted expression. It is up to the compiler to determine how contractions are performed, and whether expressions are contracted by default.

The second pragma, CX_LIMITED_RANGE, affects the multiplication, division, and absolute values of complex numbers. These operations can cause problems if their operands are infinite, or if they result in invalid overflows or underflows. When switched ON, the pragma CX_LIMITED_RANGE instructs the compiler that it is safe to use simple arithmetic methods for these three operations, as only finite operands will be used, and no overflows or underflows need to be handled. By default, this pragma is switched OFF.

In source code, these pragma directives can be placed outside all functions, or at the beginning of a block, before any declarations or statements. The pragmas take effect from the point where they occur in the source code. If a pragma directive is placed outside all functions, its effect ends with the next directive that invokes the same pragma, or at the end of the translation unit. If the pragma directive is placed within a block, its effect ends with the next directive that invokes the same pragma in a nested block, or at the end of the containing block. At the end of a block, the compiler behavior returns to the state that was in effect at the beginning of the block.

The Floating-Point Environment

The *floating-point environment* consists of system variables for floating-point status flags and control modes. Status flags are set by operations that raise *floating-point exceptions*, such as division by zero. Control modes are features of floating-point arithmetic behavior that programs can set, such as the way in which results are rounded to representable values. Support for floating-point exceptions and control modes is optional.

All of the declarations involved in accessing the floating-point environment are contained in the header *fenv.h* (see Chapter 16).

Programs that access the floating-point environment should inform the compiler beforehand by means of the following standard pragma:

```
#pragma STDC FENV_ACCESS ON
```

This directive prevents the compiler from applying optimizations, such as changes in the order in which expressions are evaluated, that might interfere with querying status flags or applying control modes.

FENV_ACCESS can be applied in the same ways as FP_CONTRACT and CX_LIMITED_RANGE: outside all functions, or locally within a block (see the preceding section). It is up to the compiler whether the default state of FENV_ACCESS is ON or OFF.

Accessing status flags

The functions in Table 17-9 allow you to access the exception status flags. One argument to these functions indicates the kind or kinds of exceptions to operate on. The following integer macros are defined in the header *fenv.h* to designate the individual exception types:

```
FE_DIVBYZERO  FE_INEXACT  FE_INVALID  FE_OVERFLOW  FE_UNDERFLOW
```

Each of these macros is defined only if the implementation supports the corresponding exception. The macro `FE_ALL_EXCEPT` designates all the supported exception types.

Table 17-9. Functions giving access to the floating-point exceptions

Purpose	Function
Test floating-point exceptions	fetestexcept()
Clear floating-point exceptions	feclearexcept()
Raise floating-point exceptions	feraiseexcept()
Save floating-point exceptions	fegetexceptflag()
Restore floating-point exceptions	fesetexceptflag()

Rounding modes

The floating-point environment also includes the rounding mode currently in effect for floating-point operations. The header *fenv.h* defines a distinct integer macro for each supported rounding mode. Each of the following macros is defined only if the implementation supports the corresponding rounding direction:

```
FE_DOWNWARD  FE_TONEAREST  FE_TOWARDZERO  FE_UPWARD
```

Implementations may also define other rounding modes and macro names for them. The values of these macros are used as return values or as argument values by the functions listed in Table 17-10.

Table 17-10. Rounding mode functions

Purpose	Function
Get the current rounding mode	fegetround()
Set a new rounding mode	fesetround()

Saving the whole floating-point environment

The functions listed in Table 17-11 operate on the floating-point environment as a whole, allowing you to save and restore the floating-point environment's state.

Table 17-11. Functions that operate on the whole floating-point environment

Purpose	Function
Save the floating-point environment	fegetenv()
Restore the floating-point environment	fesetenv()
Save the floating-point environment and switch to *nonstop* processing	feholdexcept()[a]
Restore a saved environment and raise any exceptions that are currently set	feupdateenv()

[a] In the nonstop processing mode activated by a call to feholdexcept(), floating-point exceptions do not interrupt program execution.

Error Handling

C99 defines the behavior of the functions declared in *math.h* in cases of invalid arguments or mathematical results that are out of range. The value of the macro math_errhandling, which is constant throughout a program's runtime, indicates whether the program can handle errors using the global error variable errno, or the exception flags in the floating-point environment, or both.

Domain errors

A *domain error* occurs when a function is mathematically not defined for a given argument value. For example, the real square root function sqrt() is not defined for negative argument values. The domain of each function in *math.h* is indicated in the description of the function in Chapter 18.

In the case of a domain error, functions return a value determined by the implementation. In addition, if the expression math_errhandling & MATH_ERRNO is not equal to zero—in other words, if the expression is true—then a function incurring a domain error sets the error variable errno to the value of EDOM. If the expression math_errhandling & MATH_ERREXCEPT is true, then the function raises the floating-point exception FE_INVALID.

Range errors

A *range error* occurs if the mathematical result of a function is not representable in the function's return type without a substantial rounding error. An *overflow* occurs if the range error is due to a mathematical result whose magnitude is finite, but too large to be represented by the function's return type. If the default rounding mode is in effect when an overflow occurs, or if the exact result is infinity, then the function returns the value of HUGE_VAL (or HUGE_VALF or HUGE_VALL, if the function's type is float or long double) with the appropriate sign. In addition, if the expression math_errhandling & MATH_ERRNO is true, then the function sets the error variable errno to the value of ERANGE. If the expression math_errhandling &

MATH_ERREXCEPT is true, then an overflow raises the exception FE_OVERFLOW if the mathematical result is finite, or FE_DIVBYZERO if it is infinite.

An *underflow* occurs when a range error is due to a mathematical result whose magnitude is nonzero, but too small to be represented by the function's return type. When an underflow occurs, the function returns a value that is defined by the implementation but less than or equal to the value of DBL_MIN (or FLT_MIN, or LDBL_MIN, depending on the function's type). The implementation also determines whether the function sets the error variable errno to the value of ERANGE if the expression math_errhandling & MATH_ERRNO is true. Furthermore, the implementation defines whether an underflow raises the exception FE_UNDERFLOW if the expression math_errhandling & MATH_ERREXCEPT is true.

Character Classification and Conversion

The standard library provides a number of functions to classify characters and to perform conversions on them. The header *ctype.h* declares such functions for byte characters, with character codes from 0 to 255. The header *wctype.h* declares similar functions for wide characters, which have the type wchar_t. These functions are commonly implemented as macros.

The results of these functions, except for isdigit() and isxdigit(), depends on the current locale setting for the locale category LC_CTYPE. You can query or change the locale using the setlocale() function.

Character Classification

The functions listed in Table 17-12 test whether a character belongs to a certain category. Their return value is nonzero, or true, if the argument is a character code in the given category.

Table 17-12. Character classification functions

Category	Functions in ctype.h	Functions in wctype.h
Letters	isalpha()	iswalpha()
Lowercase letters	islower()	iswlower()
Uppercase letters	isupper()	iswupper()
Decimal digits	isdigit()	iswdigit()
Hexadecimal digits	isxdigit()	iswxdigit()
Letters and decimal digits	isalnum()	iswalnum()
Printable characters (including whitespace)	isprint()	iswprint()
Printable, non-whitespace characters	isgraph()	iswgraph()
Whitespace characters	isspace()	iswspace()
Whitespace characters that separate words in a line of text	isblank()	iswblank()

Category	Functions in ctype.h	Functions in wctype.h
Punctuation marks	ispunct()	iswpunct()
Control characters	iscntrl()	iswcntrl()

The functions isgraph() and iswgraph() behave differently if the execution character set contains other byte-coded, printable, whitespace characters (that is, whitespace characters that are not control characters) in addition to the space character (' '). In that case, iswgraph() returns false for all such printable whitespace characters, while isgraph() returns false only for the space character (' ').

The header *wctype.h* also declares the two additional functions listed in Table 17-13 to test wide characters. These are called the *extensible* classification functions, which you can use to test whether a wide-character value belongs to an implementation-defined category designated by a string.

Table 17-13. Extensible character classification functions

Purpose	Function
Map a string argument that designates a character class to a scalar value that can be used as the second argument to iswctype()	wctype()
Test whether a wide character belongs to the class designated by the second argument	iswctype()

The two functions in Table 17-13 can be used to perform at least the same tests as the functions listed in Table 17-12. The strings that designate the character classes recognized by wctype() are formed from the name of the corresponding test functions, minus the prefix isw. For example, the string "alpha", like the function name iswalpha(), designates the category "letters." Thus, for a wide-character value *wc*, the following tests are equivalent:

```
iswalpha(wc )
iswctype( wc, wctype("alpha") )
```

Implementations may also define other such strings to designate locale-specific character classes.

Case Mapping

The functions listed in Table 17-14 yield the uppercase letter that corresponds to a given lowercase letter, and vice versa. All other argument values are returned unchanged.

Table 17-14. Character conversion functions

Conversion	Functions in ctype.h	Functions in wctype.h
Upper- to lowercase	tolower()	towlower()
Lower- to uppercase	toupper()	towupper()

Here again, as in the previous section, the header *wctype.h* declares two additional *extensible functions* to convert wide characters. These are described in Table 17-15. Each kind of character conversion supported by the given implementation is designated by a string.

Table 17-15. Extensible character conversion functions

Purpose	Function
Map a string argument that designates a character conversion to a scalar value that can be used as the second argument to `towctrans()`	`wctrans()`
Perform the conversion designated by the second argument on a given wide character	`towctrans()`

The two functions in Table 17-15 can be used to perform at least the same conversions as the functions listed in Table 17-14. The strings that designate those conversions are "tolower" and "toupper". Thus, for a wide-character wc, the following two calls have the same result:

```
towupper( wc );
towctrans( wc, wctrans("toupper") );
```

Implementations may also define other strings to designate locale-specific character conversions.

String Processing

A *string* is a continuous sequence of characters terminated by '\0', the string terminator character. The length of a string is considered to be the number of characters before the string terminator. Strings can be either *byte strings*, which consist of byte characters, or *wide strings*, which consist of wide characters. Byte strings are stored in arrays of char, and wide strings are stored in arrays whose elements have one of the wide-character types: wchar_t, char16_t, or char32_t.

C does not have a basic type for strings, and hence has no operators to concatenate, compare, or assign values to strings. Instead, the standard library provides numerous functions, listed in Table 17-16, to perform these and other operations with strings. The header *string.h* declares the functions for conventional strings of char. The names of these functions begin with str. The header *wchar.h* declares the corresponding functions for strings of wide characters, with names beginning with wcs.

Like any other array, a string that occurs in an expression is implicitly converted into a pointer to its first element. Thus, when you pass a string as an argument to a function, the function receives only a pointer to the first character, and can determine the length of the string only by the position of the string terminator character.

Table 17-16. String-processing functions

Purpose	Functions in string.h	Functions in wchar.h
Find the length of a string	strlen(), strnlen_s()	wcslen(), wcsnlen_s()
Copy a string	strcpy(), strncpy(), strcpy_s(), strncpy_s()	wcscpy(), wcsncpy(), wcscpy_s(), wcsncpy_s()
Concatenate strings	strcat(), strncat(), strcat_s(), strncat_s()	wcscat(), wcsncat(), wcscat_s(), wcsncat_s()
Compare strings	strcmp(), strncmp(), strcoll()	wcscmp(), wcsncmp(), wcscoll()
Transform a string so that a comparison of two transformed strings using strcmp() yields the same result as a comparison of the original strings using the locale-sensitive function strcoll()	strxfrm()	wcsxfrm()
In a string, find:		
... the first or last occurrence of a given character	strchr(), strrchr()	wcschr(), wcsrchr()
... the first occurrence of another string	strstr()	wcsstr()
... the first occurrence of any of a given set of characters	strcspn(), strpbrk()	wcscspn(), wcspbrk()
... the first character that is not a member of a given set	strspn()	wcsspn()
Parse a string into tokens	strtok(), strtok_s()	wcstok(), wcstok_s()

Multibyte Characters

In *multibyte character sets*, each character is coded as a sequence of one or more bytes (see "Wide Characters and Multibyte Characters" on page 9). While each wide character is represented by one object of the type wchar_t, char16_t, or char32_t, the number of bytes necessary to represent a given character in a multibyte encoding is variable. However, the number of bytes that represent a multibyte character, including any necessary state-shift sequences, is never more than the value of the macro MB_CUR_MAX, which is defined in the header *stdlib.h*.

Standard library functions allow you to obtain the character code of the wide character corresponding to any multibyte character, and the multibyte representation of any wide character. Some multibyte encoding schemes are *stateful*; the interpretation of a given multibyte sequence may depend on its position with respect to control characters, called *shift sequences*, that are used in the multibyte stream or string. In such cases, the conversion of a multibyte character to a wide character, or the conversion of a multibyte string into a wide string, depends on the current *shift state* at the point where the first multibyte character is read. For the same reason, converting a wide character to a multibyte character, or a wide string to a multibyte string, may entail inserting appropriate shift sequences in the output. An example of a multibyte-encoding that uses shift sequences is BOCU-1, a MIME-compatible, compressed Unicode encoding that takes up less space than UTF-8. UTF-8 itself, on the other hand, does not use shift sequences.

Conversions between wide and multibyte characters or strings may be necessary when you read or write characters from a *wide-oriented stream* (see "Byte-Oriented and Wide-Oriented Streams" on page 216).

Table 17-17 lists all of the standard library functions for handling multibyte characters.

Table 17-17. Multibyte character functions

Purpose	Functions in stdlib.h	Functions in wchar.h	Functions in uchar.h
Find the length of a multibyte character	mblen()	mbrlen()	
Find the wide character corresponding to a given multibyte character	mbtowc()	mbrtowc()	mbrtoc16(), mbrtoc32()
Find the multibyte character corresponding to a given wide character	wctomb(), wctomb_s()	wcrtomb(), wcrtomb_s()	c16rtomb(), c32rtomb()
Convert a multibyte string into a wide string	mbstowcs(), mbstowcs_s()	mbsrtowcs(), mbsrtowcs_s()	
Convert a wide string into a multibyte string	wcstombs(), wcstombs_s()	wcsrtombs(), wcsrtombs_s()	
Convert between byte characters and wide characters		btowc(), wctob()	
Test for the initial shift state		mbsinit()	

The letter r in the names of functions declared in *wchar.h* stands for "restartable." The restartable functions—in contrast to those declared in *stdlib.h*, without the r in their names—take an additional argument, which is a pointer to an object that stores the shift state of the multibyte character or string argument.

Converting Between Numbers and Strings

The standard library provides a variety of functions to interpret a numeral string and return a numeric value. These functions are listed in Table 17-18. The numeral conversion functions differ both in their target types and in the string types they interpret. The functions for char strings are declared in the header *stdlib.h*, and those for wide strings in *wchar.h*. Furthermore, C99 introduced four functions to convert a string into a number of the widest available signed or unsigned integer type, intmax_t or uintmax_t. These four functions are declared in *inttypes.h*.

Table 17-18. Conversion of numeral strings

Conversion	Functions in stdlib.h	Functions in wchar.h	Functions in inttypes.h
String to int	atoi()		
String to long	atol(), strtol()	wcstol()	
String to unsigned long	strtoul()	wcstoul()	
String to long long	atoll(), strtoll()	wcstoll()	
String to unsigned long long	strtoull()	wcstoull()	
String to intmax_t			strtoimax(), wcstoimax()
String to uintmax_t			strtoumax(), wcstoumax()
String to float	strtof()	wcstof()	
String to double	atof(), strtod()	wcstod()	
String to long double	strtold()	wcstold()	

The functions strtol(), strtoll(), and strtod() can be more practical to use than the corresponding functions atol(), atoll(), and atof(), as they return the position of the next character in the source string after the character sequence that was interpreted as a numeral.

In addition to the functions listed in Table 17-18, you can also perform string-to-number conversions using one of the sscanf() functions with an appropriate format string. Similarly, you can use the sprintf() functions to perform the reverse conversion, generating a numeral string from a numeric argument. These functions are declared in the header *stdio.h*. Once again, the corresponding functions for wide strings are declared in the header *wchar.h*. Both sets of functions are listed in Table 17-19.

Table 17-19. Conversions between strings and numbers using format strings

Conversion	Functions in stdio.h	Functions in wchar.h
String to number	sscanf(), vsscanf()	swscanf(), vswscanf()
Number to string	sprintf(), snprintf(), vsprintf(), vsnprintf()	swprintf(), vswprintf()

For each of these functions, there is a secure alternative function whose name ends in the suffix _s.

Searching and Sorting

Table 17-20 lists the standard library's four general searching and sorting functions, which are declared in the header *stdlib.h*. The functions to search the contents of a string are listed in "String Processing" on page 332.

Table 17-20. Searching and sorting functions

Purpose	Function
Sort an array	qsort(), qsort_s()
Search a sorted array	bsearch(), bsearch_s()

These functions feature an abstract interface that allows you to use them for arrays of any element type. One parameter of the qsort() and qsort_s() functions is a pointer to a call-back function that qsort() and qsort_s() can use to compare pairs of array elements. Usually you will need to define this function yourself. The bsearch() and bsearch_s() functions, which find the array element designated by a "key" argument, use the same technique, calling a user-defined function to compare array elements with the specified key.

The bsearch() and bsearch_s() functions use the binary search algorithm, and therefore require that the array be sorted beforehand. Although the names of the qsort() and qsort_s() functions suggest that they implement the quick-sort algorithm, the standard does not specify which sorting algorithm they use.

Memory Block Handling

The functions listed in Table 17-21 initialize, copy, search, and compare blocks of memory. The functions declared in the header *string.h* access a memory block byte by byte, and those declared in *wchar.h* read and write units of the type wchar_t. Accordingly, the size parameter of each function indicates the size of a memory block as a number of bytes, or as a number of wide characters.

Table 17-21. Functions to manipulate blocks of memory

Purpose	Functions in string.h	Functions in wchar.h
Copy a memory block, where source and destination do not overlap	`memcpy()`, `memcpy_s()`	`wmemcpy()`, `wmemcpy_s()`
Copy a memory block, where source and destination may overlap	`memmove()`, `memmove_s()`	`wmemmove()`, `wmemmove_s()`
Compare two memory blocks	`memcmp()`	`wmemcmp()`
Find the first occurrence of a given character	`memchr()`	`wmemchr()`
Fill the memory block with a given character value	`memset()`, `memset_s()`	`wmemset()`, `wmemset_s()`

Dynamic Memory Management

Many programs, including those that work with dynamic data structures, for example, depend on the ability to allocate and release blocks of memory at runtime. C programs can do that by means of the four dynamic memory management functions declared in the header *stdlib.h*, which are listed in Table 17-22. The use of these functions is described in detail in Chapter 12.

Table 17-22. Dynamic memory management functions

Purpose	Function
Allocate a block of memory	`malloc()`
Allocate a memory block and fill it with null bytes	`calloc()`
Resize an allocated memory block	`realloc()`
Release a memory block	`free()`

Date and Time

The header *time.h* declares the standard library functions to obtain the current date and time, to obtain the process's running time, to perform certain conversions on date and time information, and to format it for output. A key function is `time()`, which yields the current calendar time in the form of an arithmetic value of the type `time_t`. This is usually encoded as the number of seconds elapsed since a specified moment in the past, called the *epoch*. The Unix epoch is 00:00:00 o'clock on January 1, 1970, UTC (Coordinated Universal Time, formerly called Greenwich Mean Time or GMT).

There are also standard functions to convert a calendar time value with the type `time_t` into a string or a structure of type `struct tm`. The structure type has members of type int for the second, minute, hour, day, month, year, day of the week, day of the year, and a daylight saving time flag (see the description of the gmtime() function in Chapter 18). Table 17-23 lists all the date and time functions.

Table 17-23. Date and time functions

Purpose	Function
Get the amount of CPU time used	clock()
Get the current calendar time	time()
Get the difference between two calendar times	difftime()
Convert calendar time to struct tm	gmtime(), gmtime_s()
Convert calendar time to struct tm with local time values	localtime(), localtime_s()
Normalize the values of a struct tm object and return the calendar time with type time_t	mktime()
Convert calendar time to a string	ctime(), ctime_s(), asctime(), asctime_s(), strftime(), wcsftime()

The extremely flexible strftime() function uses a format string (in a similar way as the printf() functions) and the LC_TIME locale category to generate a date and time string. You can query or change the locale using the setlocale() function. The function wcsftime() is the wide-string version of strftime(), and is declared in the header *wchar.h* rather than *time.h*.

The diagram in Figure 17-1 offers an organized summary of the available date and time functions.

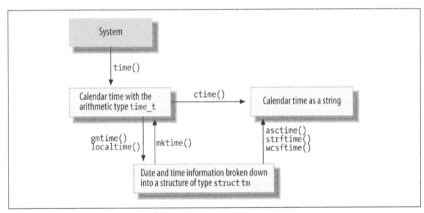

Figure 17-1. Date and time functions

Process Control

A *process* is a program that is being executed. Each process has a number of attributes, such as its open files. The exact attributes of processes are dependent on the given system. The standard library's process control features can be divided into two kinds: those for communication with the operating system, and those concerned with signals.

Communication with the Operating System

The functions in Table 17-24 are declared in the header *stdlib.h*, and allow programs to communicate with the operating system.

Table 17-24. Functions for communication with the operating system

Purpose	Function
Query the value of an environment variable	`getenv()`, `getenv_s()`
Execute a system command	`system()`
Register a function to be executed when the program exits	`atexit()`, `at_quick_exit()`
Exit the program normally	`exit()`, `_Exit()`, `quick_exit()`
Exit the program abruptly	`abort()`

In Unix and Windows, one attribute of a process is the *environment*, which consists of a list of strings of the form *name=value*. Usually, a process inherits an environment generated by its parent process. The `getenv()` function is one way for a program to receive control information, such as the names of directories containing files to use.

In contrast to `exit()`, the `_Exit()` function ignores all signals, and does not call any functions registered by `atexit()`. The `quick_exit()` function, introduced in C99, first calls all the functions that have been registered by calls to the `at_quick_exit()` function, and then terminates the program by calling `_Exit()`. The `abort()` function causes an abnormal program termination by raising the SIGABRT signal.

Signals

An operating system sends various signals to processes to notify them of unusual events. Such events typically include severe errors, such as illegal memory access, or hardware interrupts such as timer alarms. Signals may also be caused by a user at the console, however, or by the program itself calling the `raise()` function.

Each program may determine for itself how to react to specific signals. A program can choose to ignore signals, let the default signal handler deal with them, or install its own *signal handler* function. A signal handler is a function that is executed automatically when the program receives a given type of signal.

The two C functions that deal with signals are declared, along with macros to designate the signal types, in the header *signal.h*. The functions are listed in Table 17-25.

Table 17-25. Signal functions

Purpose	Function
Set the response to a given signal type	`signal()`
Send a signal to the calling process	`raise()`

Internationalization

The standard library supports the development of C programs that are able to adapt to local cultural conventions. For example, programs may use locale-specific character sets or formats for currency information.

All programs start in the default locale, named `"C"`, which contains no country or language-specific information. During runtime, programs can change their locale or query information about the current locale. The information that makes up a locale is divided into categories, which you can query and set individually.

The functions that operate on the current locale are declared, along with the related types and macros, in the header *locale.h*. They are listed in Table 17-26.

Table 17-26. Locale functions

Purpose	Function
Query or set the locale for a specified category of information	`setlocale()`
Get information about the local formatting conventions for numeric and monetary strings	`localeconv()`

Many functions make use of locale-specific information. The standard library function descriptions in Chapter 18 point out whenever a given function accesses locale settings. Such functions include the following:

- Character classification and case mapping functions
- Locale-sensitive string comparison (`strcoll()` and `wcscoll()`)
- Date and time formatting (`strftime()` and `wcsftime()`)
- Conversion of numeral strings
- Conversions between multibyte and wide characters

Nonlocal Jumps

The goto statement in C can be used to jump only within a function. For greater freedom, the header *setjmp.h* declares a pair of functions that permit jumps to any point in a program. Table 17-27 lists these functions.

Table 17-27. Nonlocal jump functions

Purpose	Function
Save the current execution context as a jump target for the longjmp( ) function	setjmp( )
Jump to a program context saved by a call to the setjmp( ) function	longjmp( )

When you call the function-like macro setjmp( ), it stores a value in its argument with the type jmp_buf that acts as a bookmark to that point in the program. The jmp_buf object holds all the necessary parts of the current execution state (including registers and stack). When you pass a jmp_buf object to longjmp( ), longjmp( ) restores the saved state, and the program continues at the point following the earlier setjmp( ) call. The longjmp( ) call must not occur after the function that called setjmp( ) returns. Furthermore, if any variables with automatic storage duration in the function that called setjmp( ) were modified after the setjmp( ) call (and were not declared as volatile), then their values after the longjmp( ) call are indeterminate.

The return value of setjmp( ) indicates whether the program has reached that point after the original setjmp( ) call, or through a longjmp( ) call: setjmp( ) itself returns 0. If setjmp( ) appears to return any other value, then that point in the program was reached by calling longjmp( ). If the second argument in the longjmp( ) call—that is, the requested return value—is 0, it is replaced with 1 as the apparent return value after the corresponding setjmp( ) call.

Multithreading (C11)

The features provided by the C11 standard for programming multithreaded applications in C are described in detail in Chapter 14. The tables in this section simply present a summary of the C multithreading library. Note that support for multithreading and atomic operations is optional. An implementation that conforms to C11 must simply define the macros __STDC_NO_THREADS__ and __STDC_NO_ATOMICS__ if it does not provide the corresponding features.

Thread Functions

The threads library provides functions for the following kinds of tasks:

- Managing threads
- Synchronizing thread execution using mutex objects

- Using condition variables for communication between threads
- Thread-specific storage

Accordingly, the names of the multithreading functions begin with one of the prefixes thrd_, mtx_, cnd_, or tss_. The only exception is the function call_once() (see Table 17-28). All of these functions are declared in the header *threads.h*.

Table 17-28. Initialization function

Purpose	Function
Call a function exactly once	call_once()

call_once() guarantees that only the first call to the function specified by the argument will be executed. This is useful in initializing data to be shared among several threads, for example.

The functions listed in Table 17-29 perform operations on a program's threads of execution, such as starting and stopping them.

Table 17-29. Functions for managing threads

Purpose	Function
Create and start a new thread to execute a specified function	thrd_create()
Get the ID of the thread performing this function call	thrd_current()
Test whether two thread IDs refer to the same thread	thrd_equal()
Suspend execution of the current thread for a specified time	thrd_sleep()
Advise the system to let other threads run	thrd_yield()
Terminate the current thread	thrd_exit()
Wait for another thread to terminate	thrd_join()
Disown a thread	thrd_detach()

C provides the functions listed in Table 17-30 to synchronize different threads' work using mutexes.

Table 17-30. Mutex functions

Purpose	Function
Create and initialize a mutex	mtx_init()
Lock a mutex; block until it becomes available	mtx_lock()
Lock a mutex only if it becomes available within a specified time	mtx_timedlock()
Lock a mutex only if it is available now	mtx_trylock()
Destroy a specified mutex	mtx_destroy()

Condition variables are used for communication between a program's various threads, as when one thread needs to notify others that certain data are available, for example. Table 17-31 lists all the functions provided for working with condition variables.

Table 17-31. Functions for condition variables

Purpose	Function
Initialize a condition variable	cnd_init()
Wake up one of the threads waiting for a condition variable	cnd_signal()
Wake up all the threads waiting for a condition variable	cnd_broadcast()
Wait for a condition variable until woken up by another thread	cnd_wait()
Wait a limited time for a condition variable	cnd_timedwait()
Destroy a condition variable	cnd_destroy()

The four functions listed in Table 17-32 operate on thread-specific storage (TSS). Multiple threads use a global key that represents each thread's pointer to a thread-specific memory block.

Table 17-32. Functions for thread-specific storage

Purpose	Function
Create a TSS key and optionally specify a destructor to be called when a thread exits	tss_create()
Set the memory block for the current thread to access using a given key	tss_set()
Get the pointer to the current thread's memory block for the given key	tss_get()
Release the resources used by a TSS key	tss_delete()

Atomic Operations

The function declarations and the definitions of types and macros for atomic operations are contained in the header *stdatomic.h*.

The macro ATOMIC_VAR_INIT can be used to initialize atomic objects. The macros of the form _ATOMIC_*type*_LOCK_FREE indicate whether an atomic object with the corresponding integer type *type* has the "lock-free" property. (For details, see "stdatomic.h" on page 304.). The generic functions listed in Table 17-33 can also be used as an alternative to these macros.

Table 17-33. Functions for initializing atomic objects and determining whether atomic objects are lock-free

Purpose	Function
Initialize an atomic object	`atomic_init()`
Test whether an atomic object is lock-free	`atomic_is_lock_free()`

Reading or writing an atomic object is an atomic operation. "Read-modify-write" operations, like those performed by the increment and decrement operators (++ and --), and by the compound assignment operators (+= etc.) when the left operand is an atomic object, are also atomic operations. Initializing an atomic object is not an atomic operation, however.

Besides the operators named, the standard library provides a number of functions to perform atomic operations, such as `atomic_load()`. By default, atomic operations are performed with the strictest memory-ordering constraint: *sequential consistency*. To perform atomic operations with lower memory-ordering constraints, another version of each atomic operation function takes an additional argument to explicitly specify a memory-ordering constraint. The latter functions have names that end in `_explicit`, such as `atomic_load_explicit()`. For details on these functions, see "Memory Ordering" on page 249.

The generic functions listed in Table 17-34 can be used with objects of all the atomic types that are defined in *stdatomic.h*. For a complete list of these types, see "stdatomic.h" on page 304.

Table 17-34. Generic functions for atomic operations

Purpose	Function
Get the value of an atomic object	`atomic_load()`, `atomic_load_explicit()`
Write a value to an atomic object	`atomic_store()`, `atomic_store_explicit()`
Get the existing value and write a new value	`atomic_exchange()`, `atomic_exchange_explicit()`
Compare the value of an atomic object with an expected value; if equal, write a new value to the object	`atomic_compare_exchange_strong()`, `atomic_compare_exchange_strong_explicit()`, `atomic_compare_exchange_weak()`, `atomic_compare_exchange_weak_explicit()`

Purpose	Function
Replace the value of an integer atomic object with the result of an arithmetic operation or a bit operation; unlike the corresponding compound assignments, these functions return the object's original value before the operation	`atomic_fetch_add()`, `atomic_fetch_add_explicit()`, `atomic_fetch_sub()`, `atomic_fetch_sub_explicit()`, `atomic_fetch_or()`, `atomic_fetch_or_explicit()`, `atomic_fetch_xor()`, `atomic_fetch_xor_explicit()`, `atomic_fetch_and()`, `atomic_fetch_and_explicit()`

Objects of the type `atomic_flag` are guaranteed to be lock-free. The functions listed in Table 17-35 provide the usual flag-operations for `atomic_flag` objects.

Table 17-35. Functions for `atomic_flag` objects

Purpose	Function
Clear an atomic flag	`atomic_flag_clear()`, `atomic_flag_clear_explicit()`
Set an atomic flag and return its prior state	`atomic_flag_test_and_set()`, `atomic_flag_test_and_set_explicit()`

Memory fences specify the memory-ordering constraint that must be observed in the synchronization of atomic write and read operations (see "Fences" on page 251 for more information).

Table 17-36. Functions for memory fences

Purpose	Function
Insert an acquire, release, or acquire-and-release fence	`atomic_thread_fence()`
Insert a fence that applies ordering constraints only between the operations in a thread and in a signal handler executed in that thread	`atomic_signal_fence()`

Debugging

Using the macro `assert()` is a simple way to find logical mistakes during program development. This macro is defined in the header *assert.h*. It simply tests its scalar argument for a nonzero value. If the argument's value is zero, `assert()` prints an error message that lists the argument expression, function, filename, and line number, and then calls `abort()` to stop the program. In the following example, the `assert()` calls perform some plausibility checks on the argument to be passed to `free()`:

```
#include <stdlib.h>
#include <assert.h>

char *buffers[64] = { NULL };    // An array of pointers
int i;

/* ... allocate some memory buffers; work with them ... */

   assert( i >= 0 && i < 64 );       // Index out of range?
   assert( buffers[i] != NULL );     // Was the pointer used at all?
   free( buffers[i] );
```

Rather than trying to free a nonexistent buffer, this code aborts the program (here compiled as *assert.c*) with the following diagnostic output:

```
assert: assert.c:14: main: Assertion 'buffers[i] != ((void *)0)' failed.
Aborted
```

When you have finished testing, you can disable all `assert()` calls by defining the macro `NDEBUG` before the `#include` directive for *assert.h*. The macro does not need to have a replacement value. For example:

```
#define NDEBUG
#include <assert.h>
/* ... */
```

C11 has introduced the capability to test the assertion of an integer constant expression during compiling. This is done using `_Static_assert` declarations. For details and an example, see "_Static_assert Declarations" on page 186.

Error Messages

Various standard library functions set the global variable `errno` to a value indicating the type of error encountered during execution (see "errno.h" on page 291). The functions in Table 17-37 generate an appropriate error message for the current value of `errno`.

Table 17-37. Error message functions

Purpose	Function	Header
Print an appropriate error message on `stderr` for the current value of `errno`	`perror()`	*stdio.h*
Return a pointer to the appropriate error message for a given error number	`strerror()`	*string.h*
Copy the error message corresponding to a given `errno` value to an array	`strerror_s()`	*string.h*
Find the length of the error message corresponding to a given `errno` value	`strerrorlen_s()`	*string.h*

The function perror() prints the string passed to it as an argument, followed by a colon and the error message that corresponds to the value of errno. This error message is the one that strerror() would return if called with the same value of errno as its argument. Here is an example:

```
if ( remove("test1") != 0)  // If we can't delete the file ...
    perror( "Couldn't delete 'test1'" );
```

This perror() call produces the same output as the following statement:

```
fprintf( stderr, "Couldn't delete 'test1': %s\n", strerror( errno ) );
```

In this example, if the file test1 does not exist, a program compiled with GCC prints the following message:

```
Couldn't delete 'test1': No such file or directory
```

The error message whose address is provided by the function strerror() may be replaced on a subsequent strerror() call. To avoid data races, multithreaded programs should therefore use the alternative function strerror_s(), which copies the error message to an array provided by the caller.

18

Standard Library Functions

This chapter describes in alphabetical order the functions available in the standard ANSI C libraries. Most of the functions described here were included in the 1989 ANSI standard or in the 1995 "Normative Addendum" and are currently supported by all major compilers. The ISO/IEC 9899:1999 standard ("C99") introduced several new functions, which are also widely supported by today's compilers. The same cannot be said of the new, mostly optional features, such as multithreading and bounds-checking functions, introduced by the new ISO/IEC standard 9899:2011. The new functions introduced in that standard are labeled "C11" in this chapter.

Each description includes the function's purpose and return value, the function prototype, the header file in which the function is declared, and a brief example. For the sake of brevity, the examples do not always show a main() function or the #include directives that indicate the header file with the function's declaration. When using the functions described in this chapter, remember that you must provide a declaration of each standard function used in your program by including the appropriate header file. Also, any filename may also contain a relative or absolute directory path. For more information about errors and exceptions that can occur in standard function calls, see the sections on the standard headers *math.h*, *fenv.h*, and *errno.h* in Chapter 16.

In C11 implementations that support the "secure" alternative functions—that is, the bounds-checking functions with names ending in _s—the following rule applies: before the include directive that includes the header containing the declaration of the desired function, the macro __STDC_WANT_LIB_EXT1__ must be defined as equal to 1. For more information on using the secure functions, see "Functions with Bounds-Checking" on page 287.

Ends program execution without calling atexit() functions or signal handlers.

```
#include <stdlib.h>
_Noreturn void _Exit( int status );
```

The _Exit() function terminates the program normally but without calling any cleanup functions that you have installed using atexit() or at_quick_exit(), or signal handlers you have installed using signal(). _Exit() returns a status value to the operating system in the same way as the exit() function does.

Whether _Exit() flushes the program's file buffers or removes its temporary files may vary from one implementation to another.

Example

```
int main (int argc, char *argv[])
{
  if (argc < 3)
  {
    fprintf(stderr, "Missing required arguments.\n");
    _Exit(-1);
  }
  /* ... */
}
```

See Also

abort(), exit(), atexit(), quick_exit(), at_quick_exit(), raise()

abort

Ends program execution immediately.

```
#include <stdlib.h>
_Noreturn void abort( void );
```

The abort() function terminates execution of a program by raising the SIGABRT signal.

For a "clean" program termination, use the exit() function. The abort() function does not flush the buffers of open files or call any cleanup functions that you have installed using atexit() or at_quick_exit(). The abort() function generally prints a message on the stderr stream such as:

```
Abnormal program termination
```

In Unix, aborting a program also produces a core dump.

Example

```
struct record { long id;
                int data[256];
                struct record *next;
```

```
                };
/* ... */
struct record *new = (struct record *)malloc( sizeof(struct record) );
if ( new == NULL )              // Check whether malloc failed!
{
    fprintf( stderr, "%s: out of memory!\n", __func__ );
    abort();
}
else /* ... */
```

See Also

_Exit(), exit(), atexit(), quick_exit(), at_quick_exit(), raise()

abort_handler_s   C11

Handles errors occurring in secure function calls.

```
#include <stdlib.h>
void abort_handler_s( const char * restrict msg, void * restrict ptr,
                      errno_t error);
```

If the function abort_handler_s() is passed as an argument to the function
set_constraint_handler_s(), it is installed as a runtime error handler so that
abort_handler_s() is called if one of the secure functions (with names ending in
_s) violates its runtime constraints. A runtime constraint is violated if the function
call contains an invalid pointer argument, or if the bounds of an array are exceeded
during the execution of the function.

If such an error occurs, the function abort_handler_s() outputs a message to
stderr containing the string passed in the parameter *msg* (usually the name of the
function which incurred the error). Then the abort_handler_s() function terminates the program by calling abort().

Example

```
char name[15]= "NN";

set_constraint_handler_s(abort_handler_s);
strcpy_s( name, sizeof(name), "Abraham Lincoln");
```

Because the array name is too small for the string being copied, this code snippet
results in an error message like the following:

```
Runtime-constraint: Range error
abort -- terminating
```

See Also

ignore_handler_s(), set_constraint_handler_s()

abs

Gives the absolute value of an integer.

```c
#include <stdlib.h>
int abs( int n );
long labs( long n );
long long llabs( long long n );
```

The abs() functions return the absolute value of the integer argument *n*; if *n* is greater than or equal to 0, the return value is equal to *n*. If *n* is less than 0, the function returns -*n*.

Example

```c
int amount = -1234;
char currencysym[2] = "$";
char sign[2]        = "-";
div_t dollarsandcents = { 0, 0 };

if ( amount >= 0 )
  sign[0] = '\0';

dollarsandcents = div(abs( amount ), 100 );

printf( "The balance is %s%s%d.%2d\n", sign, currencysym,
        dollarsandcents.quot, dollarsandcents.rem );
```

This code produces the following output:

```
The balance is -$12.34
```

See Also

The C99 absolute value function imaxabs(), declared in the header file *inttypes.h* for the type intmax_t; the absolute value functions for real numbers, fabs(), fabsf(), and fabsl(); the absolute value functions for complex numbers, cabs(), cabsf(), and cabsl()

acos

Calculates the inverse cosine of a number.

```c
#include <math.h>
double acos( double x );
float acosf( float x );          (C99)
long double acosl( long double x );     (C99)
```

acos() implements the inverse cosine function, commonly called *arc cosine*. The argument *x* must be between −1 and 1, inclusive: $-1 \leq x \leq 1$. If *x* is outside the function's domain—that is, greater than 1 or less than −1—the function incurs a domain error.

The return value is given in radians, and is thus in the range $0 \leq acos(x) \leq \pi$.

Example

```
/*
 * Calculate the pitch of a roof given
 * the sloping width from eaves to ridge and
 * the horizontal width of the floor below it.
 */
#define PI 3.141593
#define DEG_PER_RAD (180.0/PI)

double floor_width = 30.0;
double roof_width = 34.6;

double roof_pitch = acos( floor_width / roof_width ) * DEG_PER_RAD ;
printf( "The pitch of the roof is %2.0f degrees.\n", roof_pitch );
```

This code produces the following output:

```
The pitch of the roof is 30 degrees.
```

See Also

The arc cosine functions for complex numbers: cacos(), cacosf(), and cacosl()

acosh   C99

Calculates the inverse hyperbolic cosine of a number.

```
#include <math.h>
double acosh( double x );
float acoshf( float x );
long double acoshl( long double x );
```

The acosh() functions return the non-negative number whose hyperbolic cosine is equal to the argument x. Because the hyperbolic cosine of any number is greater than or equal to 1, acosh() incurs a domain error if the argument is less than 1.

Example

```
double x, y1, y2;

puts("acosh(x) is equal to log( x + sqrt(x*x - 1))\n");
puts("Enter some numbers greater than or equal to 1.0"
     "\n(type any letter to quit):");
while ( scanf("%lf", &x) == 1)
{
  errno = 0;
  y1 = acosh(x);
  if ( errno == EDOM)
  {
    perror("acosh");    break;
  }
  y2 = log( x + sqrt( x*x - 1));
```

```
    printf("x = %f;  acosh(x) = %f;  log(x + sqrt(x*x-1)) = %f\n",
         x, y1, y2);
}
```

This code produces the following output:

```
Enter some numbers greater than or equal to 1.0
(type any letter to quit):
1.5
x = 1.500000;  acosh(x) = 0.962424;  log(x + sqrt(x*x-1)) = 0.962424
0.5
acosh: Numerical argument out of domain
```

See Also

Other hyperbolic trigonometry functions for real numbers: asinh(), atanh(), sinh(), cosh(), and tanh(); the hyperbolic cosine and inverse hyperbolic cosine functions for complex numbers: ccosh() and cacosh()

asctime

Converts a date-and-time structure to string form.

```
#include <time.h>
char *asctime( struct tm *systime );
```

The single argument of the asctime() function is a pointer to a structure of type struct tm, in which a date and time is represented by elements for the year, month, day, hour, and so on. The structure is described under mktime() in this chapter. The asctime() function returns a pointer to a static string of 26 bytes containing the date and time in a timestamp format:

```
"Wed Apr 13 07:23:20 2005\n"
```

The day of the week and the month are abbreviated with the first three letters of their English names, with no period. If the day of the month is a single digit, an additional space fills the place of its tens digit. If the hour is less than ten, it is represented with a leading zero. The function strftime() permits more flexible date and time output using a format string.

Example

```
time_t now;
time( &now );          /* Get the time (seconds since 1/1/70) */
printf( "Date: %.24s GMT\n", asctime( gmtime( &now ) ));
```

Typical output:

```
Date: Sun Aug 28 14:22:05 2005 GMT
```

See Also

localtime(), localtime_s(), gmtime(), gmtime_s(), ctime(), ctime_s(), diff time(), mktime(), strftime(), time(). The localtime(), localtime_s(), gmtime(), and gmtime_s() functions are the most common ways of filling in the values in the tm structure. The function call `ctime(&seconds)` is equivalent to the call `asctime(localtime(&seconds))`.

asctime_s C11

Converts a date-and-time structure to string form with bounds-checking.

```
#include <time.h>
errno_t asctime_s(char *s, rsize_t maxsize,
                const struct tm *tmPtr);
```

The function `asctime_s()`, like `asctime()`, converts the contents of the structure pointed to by its *tmPtr* argument into a date-and-time string of 26 bytes in a time-stamp format: `"Thu Oct 7 09:33:02 2014\n"`

Unlike the function `asctime()`, `asctime_s()` does not use an internal, static string buffer. Instead it copies the result to the address passed in the argument *s*, whose length, given by *maxsize*, must be at least 26 bytes. This makes the function `asctime_s()` safe for use in multithreading environments.

The function has the following runtime constraints: the pointers *s* and *tmPtr* must not be null pointers, and the value of *maxsize* must be between 26 and RSIZE_MAX. Furthermore, the members of the struct tm object pointed to by *tmPtr* must contain valid, normalized values. The member tm_year must represent a year between 0 and 9999. The tm structure is described in the section on `gmtime()` in this chapter.

The function `asctime_s()` returns 0 if no error occurs. Otherwise, it returns a non-zero error code, and writes the string terminator character `'\0'` to *s*[0], if the values of *s* and *maxsize* permit.

Example

```
time_t now;
struct tm timeStruct;
char timeStr[26];

time(&now);                          // Date and time as an integer.
localtime_s(&now, &timeStruct);      // Convert to a structure.
if( asctime_s( timeStr, sizeof(timeStr), &timeStruct) == 0)
    printf("Date and time: %s", timeStr);
```

Typical output:

```
Date and time: Thu Jan 29 08:30:09 2015
```

See Also

`asctime()`, `localtime()`, `localtime_s()`, `gmtime()`, `gmtime_s()`, `ctime()`, `ctime_s()`, `difftime()`, `mktime()`, `strftime()`, `time()`. The functions local time(), `localtime_s()`, `gmtime()`, and `gmtime_s()` can be called to fill in the members of an object of the type struct tm.

asin

Calculates the inverse sine of a number.

```
#include <math.h>
double asin( double x );
float asinf( float x );          (C99)
long double asinl( long double x );          (C99)
```

asin() implements the inverse sine function, commonly called *arc sine*. The argument *x* must be between -1 and 1, inclusive: $-1 \le x \le 1$. If *x* is outside the function's domain—that is, if *x* is greater than 1 or less than −1—the function incurs a domain error.

The return value is given in radians, and is thus in the range $-\pi/2 \le \text{asin}(x) \le \pi/2$.

Example

```
/*
 * Calculate the altitude of the sun (its angle upward from the horizon)
 * given the height of a vertical object and the length of the object's
 * shadow.
 */
#define PI 3.141593
#define DEG_PER_RAD (180.0/PI)

float height = 2.20F;
float length = 1.23F;
float altitude = asinf( height / sqrtf( height*height + length*length));
printf( "The sun's altitude is %2.0f\xB0.\n", altitude * DEG_PER_RAD);
```

This code produces the following output:

```
The sun's altitude is 61°.
```

See Also

Arcsine functions for complex numbers: `casin()`, `casinf()`, and `casinl()`

asinh   C99

Calculates the inverse hyperbolic sine of a number.

```
#include <math.h>
double asinh( double x );
float asinhf( float x );
long double asinhl( long double x );
```

The asinh() functions return the number whose hyperbolic sine is equal to the argument *x*.

Example

```
puts("    x          asinh(x)        log( x + sqrt(x*x+1))\n"
     "-------------------------------------------------------");
```

```
for ( double x = -2.0; x < 2.1; x += 0.5)
    printf("%6.2f %15f %20f\n", x, asinh(x), log( x + sqrt(x*x+1)));
```

This code produces the following output:

```
    x          asinh(x)        log( x + sqrt(x*x+1))
--------------------------------------------------------
  -2.00       -1.443635          -1.443635
  -1.50       -1.194763          -1.194763
  -1.00       -0.881374          -0.881374
  -0.50       -0.481212          -0.481212
   0.00        0.000000           0.000000
   0.50        0.481212           0.481212
   1.00        0.881374           0.881374
   1.50        1.194763           1.194763
   2.00        1.443635           1.443635
```

See Also

Other hyperbolic trigonometry functions for real numbers: acosh(), atanh(), sinh(), cosh(), and tanh(); the hyperbolic sine and inverse hyperbolic sine functions for complex numbers: csinh() and casinh()

assert

Tests an expression.

```
#include <assert.h>
void assert( int expression );
```

The assert() macro evaluates a given expression and aborts the program if the result is 0 (that is, false). In this case, assert() also prints a message on stderr, indicating the name of the program, and the source file, line number, and function in which the failing assert() call occurs:

```
program: file:line: function: Assertion 'expression' failed.
```

If the value of *expression* is true (that is, nonzero), assert() does nothing and the program continues.

Use assert() during development to guard against logical errors in your program. When debugging is complete, you can instruct the preprocessor to suppress all assert() calls by defining the symbolic constant NDEBUG before you include *assert.h*.

Example

```
int units_in_stock = 10;
int units_shipped = 9;
/* ... */
    units_shipped++;
    units_in_stock--;
/* ... */
    units_in_stock -= units_shipped;
    assert(units_in_stock >= 0);
```

This code produces the following output:

```
inventory: inventory.c:110: main: Assertion 'units_in_stock >= 0' failed.
Aborted.
```

See Also

exit(), _Exit(), quick_exit(), at_quick_exit(), raise(), abort()

at_quick_exit   C99

Registers a function to be called on program termination by quick_exit().

```
#include <stdlib.h>
int at_quick_exit( void (*func)( void ));
```

The function at_quick_exit() registers the function specified by the argument *func* following the same rules as the atexit() function. The functions so registered are called only if the program is terminated by quick_exit(), not on normal program termination. If you want a function to be executed in either case, you must register it using both atexit() and at_quick_exit().

The argument *func* is a pointer to a function with no parameters and the return type void. The function at_quick_exit() can be called several times to register multiple functions. The number of possible calls is at least 32. If the program is ended by a call to quick_exit(), all the functions so registered are called in last-in, first-out order: that is, in the opposite order in which they were registered.

The function at_quick_exit() returns zero to indicate that the specified function was successfully registered.

Example

```
void nexit(void) { puts("Program terminated normally."); }
void qexit(void) { puts("Programm terminated by \"quick_exit()\"."); }

int main(void)
{
    int a = -1;
    atexit( nexit);
    at_quick_exit( qexit);

    if( a < 0)
        quick_exit(EXIT_FAILURE);

    return 0;
}
```

This example would generate the following console output:

```
Program terminated by "quick_exit()".
```

See Also

quick_exit(), exit(), atexit(), _Exit(), abort()

atan

Calculates the inverse tangent of a number.

```c
#include <math.h>
double atan( double x );
float atanf( float x );          (C99)
long double atanl( long double x );          (C99)
```

`atan()` implements the inverse tangent function, commonly called *arc tangent*.

The return value is given in radians, and is thus in the range $-\pi/2 \leq \text{atan}(x) \leq \pi/2$.

Example

```c
#ifdef PI
  printf("The symbol PI was already defined.\n");
  long double pi = (long double) PI;
#else
  long double pi = 4.0L * atanl( 1.0L );   // Because tan(pi/4) = 1
#endif
  printf( "Assume pi equals %.17Lf.\n", pi);
```

This code produces the following output:

```
Assume pi equals 3.14159265358979324.
```

See Also

The arc tangent functions for complex numbers: `catan()`, `catanf()`, and `catanl()`

atan2

Calculates the inverse tangent of a quotient.

```c
#include <math.h>
double atan2( double y, double x );
float atan2f( float y, float x );          (C99)
long double atan2l( long double y, long double x );          (C99)
```

The `atan2()` function divides the first argument by the second and returns the arc tangent of the result, or $\arctan(y/x)$.

The return value is given in radians, and is in the range $-\pi \leq \text{atan2}(y,x) \leq \pi$. The signs of x and y determine the quadrant of the result:

$x > 0, y > 0$:

$0 \leq \text{atan2}(\,y,x) \leq \pi/2$

$x < 0, y > 0$:

$\pi/2 \leq \text{atan2}(\,y,x) \leq \pi$

$x < 0, y < 0$:

$-\pi \leq \text{atan2}(\,y,x) \leq -\pi/2$

x > 0, y < 0:

$$-\pi/2 \le \text{atan2}(\,y,x\,) \le 0$$

If both arguments are zero, then the function may incur a domain error.

Example

```
/*
 * Calculate an acute angle of a right triangle, given
 * the adjacent and opposite sides.
 */
#define PI 3.141593
#define DEG_PER_RAD (180.0/PI)

double adjacent = 3.0;
double opposite = 4.0;
double angle = atan2( opposite, adjacent ) * DEG_PER_RAD;

printf( "The acute angles of a 3-4-5 right triangle are %4.2f\xB0 "
        "and %4.2f\xB0.\n", angle, 90.0 - angle );
```

This code produces the following output:

```
The acute angles of a 3-4-5 right triangle are 53.13° and 36.87°.
```

See Also

The arc tangent function for a single argument: atan()

atanh   C99

Calculates the inverse hyperbolic tangent of a number.

```
#include <math.h>
double atanh( double x );
float atanhf( float x );
long double atanhl( long double x );
```

The atanh() functions return the number whose hyperbolic tangent is equal to their argument *x*. Because the hyperbolic tangent of any number is between -1 and +1, atanh() incurs a domain error if the absolute value of the argument is greater than 1. Furthermore, a range error may result if the absolute value of the argument is equal to 1.

Example

```
double x[ ] = { -1.0, -0.5, 0.0, 0.5, 0.99, 1.0, 1.01 };

puts("               x                    atanh(x) \n"
     "    ----------------------------------------------");
for ( int i = 0; i < sizeof(x) / sizeof(x[0]); ++i )
{
  errno = 0;
  printf("%+15.2f %+20.10f\n", x[i], atanh(x[i]) );
  if ( errno)
```

```
    perror("atanh");
}
```

This code produces the following output:

```
        x              atanh(x)
    - - - - - - - - - - - - - - - - - - - - - - - - - - -
        -1.00              -inf
atanh: Numerical argument out of domain
        -0.50          -0.5493061443
        +0.00          +0.0000000000
        +0.50          +0.5493061443
        +0.99          +2.6466524124
        +1.00              +inf
atanh: Numerical argument out of domain
        +1.01              +nan
atanh: Numerical argument out of domain
```

See Also

Other hyperbolic trigonometry functions for real numbers: asinh(), acosh(), sinh(), cosh(), and tanh(); the hyperbolic tangent and inverse hyperbolic tangent functions for complex numbers: ctanh() and catanh()

atexit

Registers a function to be called when the program exits.

```
#include <stdlib.h>
int atexit( void (*func)( void ));
```

The argument of the atexit() function is a pointer to a function that has no parameters and the return type void. If the atexit() call is successful, your program will call the function referenced by this pointer if and when it exits normally; that is, if the program is terminated by a return statement in main() or by a call to exit(). The atexit() call returns 0 to indicate that the specified function has been registered successfully.

You may call atexit() up to 32 times in a program. If you register more than one function in this way, they will be called in LIFO order: the last function registered will be the first one called when your program exists.

Example

```
int main()
{
  void f1(void), f2(void);

  printf("Registering the \"at-exit\" functions f1 and f2:");

  if ( atexit(f1) || atexit(f2) )
    printf(" failed.\n");
  else
    printf(" done.\n");
```

```
    printf("Exiting now.\n");
    exit(0);              // Equivalent to return 0;
}
void f1(void)
{ printf("Running the \"at-exit\" function f1().\n"); }
void f2(void)
{ printf("Running the \"at-exit\" function f2().\n"); }
```

This code produces the following output:

```
Registering the "at-exit" functions f1 and f2: done.
Exiting now.
Running the "at-exit" function f2().
Running the "at-exit" function f1().
```

See Also

_Exit(), exit(), quick_exit(), at_quick_exit(), abort()

atof

Converts a string to a floating-point number.

```
#include <stdlib.h>
double atof( const char *s );
```

The atof() function converts a string of characters representing a numeral into a floating-point number of type double. The string must be in a customary floating-point numeral format, including scientific notation (e.g., 0.0314 or 3.14e-2). The conversion ignores any leading whitespace (space, tab, and newline) characters. A minus sign may be prefixed to the mantissa or exponent to make it negative; a plus sign in either position is permissible.

Any character in the string that cannot be interpreted as part of a floating-point numeral has the effect of terminating the input string, and atof() converts only the partial string to the left of that character. If the string cannot be interpreted as a numeral at all, atof() returns 0.

Example

```
char string[ ] = " -1.02857e+2 \260C";  // symbol for degrees Celsius
double z;

z = atof(string);
printf( "\"%s\" becomes  %.2f\n", string, z );
```

This code produces the following output:

```
" -1.02857e+2 °C" becomes -102.86
```

See Also

strtod(), atoi(), atol(), atoll(), strtol(), strtoll()

atoi

Converts a string to an integer.

```
#include <stdlib.h>
int atoi( const char *s );
long atol( const char *s );
long long atoll( const char *s );        (C99)
```

The atoi() function converts a string of characters representing a numeral into a number of type int. Similarly, atol() returns a long integer, and in C99, the atoll() function converts a string into an integer of type long long.

The conversion ignores any leading whitespace characters (spaces, tabs, newlines). A leading plus sign is permissible; a minus sign makes the return value negative. Any character that cannot be interpreted as part of an integer, such as a decimal point or exponent sign, has the effect of terminating the numeral input so that atoi() converts only the partial string to the left of that character. If, under these conditions, the string still does not appear to represent a numeral, then atoi() returns 0.

Example

```
char *s = " -135792468.00 Balance on Dec. 31";
printf("\"%s\" becomes %ld\n", s, atol(s));
```

These statements produce the output:

```
" -135792468.00 Balance on Dec. 31" becomes -135792468
```

See Also

strtol() and strtoll(); atof() and strtod()

atol, atoll

See atoi().

atomic_compare_exchange_strong,
atomic_compare_exchange_strong_explicit,
atomic_compare_exchange_weak,
atomic_compare_exchange_weak_explicit   C11

Exchanges the value of an atomic object after a successful comparison.

```
#include <stdatomic.h>
_Bool atomic_compare_exchange_strong( volatile A *object,
    C *expected, C desired);
_Bool atomic_compare_exchange_strong_explicit( volatile A *object,
    C *expected, C desired,
    memory_order success, memory_order failure);
```

```
_Bool atomic_compare_exchange_weak( volatile A *object,
    C *expected, C desired);
_Bool atomic_compare_exchange_weak_explicit( volatile A *object,
    C *expected, C desired,
    memory_order success, memory_order failure);
```

In these prototypes, A stands for any atomic type defined in *stdatomic.h*, and C stands for the corresponding non-atomic type. Each of these functions first compares the value of the atomic object pointed to by the argument *object* with the value of the object pointed to by *expected*. If the values are equal, the value of the argument *desired* is written to the atomic object. If they are not equal, the value of the atomic object is copied to the address specified by *expected*. The operations are carried out as atomic read-modify-write operations. The return value of all the functions is the result of the initial comparison; that is, true if the compared values are equal, and false if they are not equal.

The explicit versions of the functions apply the memory-ordering requirement specified by *success* if the compared values are equal, and the memory ordering specified by *failure* if they are not equal. The argument *failure* must not be memory_order_release or memory_order_acq_rel, and must not be stricter than the memory-ordering requirement specified by *success*.

The weak versions of the functions can also fail when the compared values are equal, in which case they behave as if the values were not equal. They must therefore be called inside a loop. When the compare-and-exchange operation is executed in a loop, the weak function versions offer better performance on some computers than the strong versions.

The weak versions permit efficient implementation of the compare-and-exchange operation on a broader range of computers, including those with Advanced RISC Machine (ARM) architecture, which provides "load-locked store-conditional" CPU instructions.

Example

This example illustrates a possible implementation of the *= operator for objects of the type atomic_long. This corresponds to the code sequence indicated in the footnote to Section 6.5.16.2 of the C11 standard.

```
long mulwith( volatile atomic_long *alPtr, long val)
{
    long old = *alPtr, new;

    do { new = old * val; }
    while (!atomic_compare_exchange_weak(alPtr, &old, new));

    return new;
}
```

See Also

atomic_exchange(),   atomic_exchange_explicit(),   atomic_store(),
atomic_store_explicit()

atomic_exchange, atomic_exchange_explicit   C11

Exchange the value of an atomic object.

```
#include <stdatomic.h>
C atomic_exchange( volatile A *object, C desired);
C atomic_exchange_explicit( volatile A *object, C desired,
                            memory_order order);
```

In these prototypes, A stands for any atomic type defined in *stdatomic.h*, and C stands for the corresponding non-atomic type. These generic functions replace the value of the atomic object referenced by *object* with the value of the object *desired*, and return the previous value of the atomic object. The explicit version applies the memory-ordering requirement specified by *order*. These operations are carried out as atomic read-modify-write operations.

Example

Implements a spin-lock mutex using atomic_exchange().

```
atomic_bool lock = ATOMIC_VAR_INIT(false);  // false if not locked;
                                            // true if locked.
void func(char *msg)
{
   static int count;                        // Initial value is 0.
   while( atomic_exchange(&lock, true))     // Spin until we lock.
      ;
   ++count;                                 // Critical section ...
   printf("%3u. %s\n", count, msg);
   lock = false;                            // Release the lock.
}

#define NUM_THREADS 20
int main()
{
   struct { thrd_t th; char msg[32]; } th_arr[NUM_THREADS];

   for( int i = 0; i < NUM_THREADS; ++i)
   {
      sprintf( th_arr[i].msg,"Thread %2u", i);
      if( thrd_create( &th_arr[i].th, (thrd_start_t)func,
                  (void*)th_arr[i].msg) != thrd_success)
         return EXIT_FAILURE;
   }
   for( int i = 0; i < NUM_THREADS; ++i)
      thrd_join( th_arr[i].th, NULL);
   return EXIT_SUCCESS;
}
```

Library Functions

Sample output:

```
1. Thread  0
2. Thread 12
3. Thread  9
... (17 more lines)
```

See Also

atomic_compare_exchange_strong(),   atomic_compare_exchange_weak(),
atomic_load(), atomic_store(), atomic_flag_test_and_set()

atomic_fetch_*op*, atomic_fetch_*op*_explicit   C11

Replaces the value of an atomic object with the result of an operation.

```
#include <stdatomic.h>
C atomic_fetch_op( volatile A *object, M operand);
C atomic_fetch_op_explicit( volatile A *object, M operand,
                            memory_order order);
```

The placeholder *op* in these function names stands for one of five abbreviations, shown in Table 18-1, indicating the operation to be performed.

In these prototypes, A stands for any atomic type defined in *stdatomic.h* except the type atomic_bool, and C stands for the corresponding non-atomic type. M is the type ptrdiff_t if A is an atomic pointer type; otherwise, M is the same type as C.

Table 18-1. Compound atomic-fetch operations

op	Operation
add	Addition (+)
sub	Subtraction (-)
or	Bitwise OR (|)
xor	Bitwise exclusive OR (^)
and	Bitwise AND (&)

These generic functions atomically replace the value of the atomic object referenced by *object* with the result of the operation **object op operand*. For example, the function atomic_fetch_add() adds the value of *operand* to the atomic object. The atomic_fetch_*op*() functions are thus similar to the corresponding compound assignments, *op*=, except that the atomic_fetch_*op*() functions return the previous value of the atomic object, not its new value after the operation.

For atomic signed integer types, the arithmetic operations use two's-complement representation with silent overflow. None of the operations have undefined results. Operations on pointers can result in invalid addresses, however.

The operations are carried out as atomic read-modify-write operations, with the usual strict memory ordering, memory_order_seq_cst. The explicit version applies the memory-ordering requirement specified by *order*.

Example

This code implements a semaphore using atomic_fence_sub() and atomic_fence_add().

```c
#define MAX_READERS 5      // Number of data-reading threads.

// Semaphore counts the number of idle resources (here: readers),
// or -1 if locked by writer. Busy readers == MAX_READERS - count.
atomic_int count = ATOMIC_VAR_INIT(MAX_READERS);

int data = 0;              // Valid data are positive.

// 1 millisecond = 1,000,000 nanoseconds
const struct timespec ms = { .tv_nsec = 1000*1000 };

void reader(int* idPtr)
{
    int id = *idPtr;
    while(1)
    {
        // Check semaphore; decrement and read if count > 0.
        while( atomic_fetch_sub(&count, 1) <= 0)
        { atomic_fetch_add(&count, 1);  thrd_yield(); }

        if( data > 0)               // Read valid data.
            printf("Reader %d is reading %d\n", id, data);
        if( data < 0)               // End marker: stop looping.
            break;

        atomic_fetch_add(&count, 1); // Release our reader slot.
        thrd_sleep(&ms,NULL);        // Simulate data processing.
    }
}

void writer(void) // Writes positive values; ends with a negative value.
{
    const int N = 20;                  // Number of data values to write.
    for(int n = 0; n <= N; ++n)
    {
        int d = n < N ? 10+n : -1;     // Prepare data or end marker.
        // When no readers are busy, lock the semaphore (count = -1):
        while( atomic_fetch_sub(&count,MAX_READERS+1) != MAX_READERS)
            atomic_fetch_add(&count, MAX_READERS+1);
        printf("Writer is writing %d\n", d),  // Critical section.
        data = d;
        atomic_fetch_add(&count, MAX_READERS+1); // Release the
                                                 // semaphores.
        thrd_sleep(&ms,NULL);          // Simulate data production.
```

```
        }
    }

    int main(void)
    {
        thrd_t wth;
        struct { thrd_t th; int id; } th_arr[MAX_READERS];

        // Writer thread:
        if( thrd_create( &wth,(thrd_start_t)writer, NULL) != thrd_success)
            return EXIT_FAILURE;

        // Reader threads:
        for( int i = 0; i < MAX_READERS; ++i)
        {
            th_arr[i].id = i;
            if( thrd_create( &th_arr[i].th, (thrd_start_t)reader,
                             &th_arr[i].id) != thrd_success)
                return EXIT_FAILURE;
        }

        thrd_join( wth, NULL);
        for( int i = 0; i < MAX_READERS; ++i)
            thrd_join( th_arr[i].th, NULL);
        return EXIT_SUCCESS;
    }
```

See Also

atomic_load(), atomic_store(), atomic_flag_test_and_set(), atomic_com
pare_exchange_strong(), atomic_compare_exchange_weak()

atomic_flag_clear, atomic_flag_clear_explicit   C11

Clears a flag atomically.

```
    #include <stdatomic.h>
    void atomic_flag_clear( volatile atomic_flag *obj);
    void atomic_flag_clear_explicit( volatile atomic_flag *obj,
                                     memory_order order);
```

These functions atomically clear the flag pointed to by *obj*—that is, they set the flag
to false. The explicit version applies the memory-ordering requirement specified
by *order*. This argument must not be memory_order_acquire or
memory_order_acq_rel.

Example

See the example for atomic_flag_test_and_set() in this chapter.

See Also

atomic_flag_test_and_set()

atomic_flag_test_and_set, atomic_flag_test_and_set_explicit   C11

Sets a flag atomically.

```
#include <stdatomic.h>
_Bool atomic_flag_test_and_set( volatile atomic_flag *obj);
_Bool atomic_flag_test_and_set_explicit( volatile atomic_flag *obj,
                                         memory_order order);
```

These functions atomically set the flag pointed to by *obj* to true, and return the flag's previous value. These operations are carried out as atomic read-modify-write operations. The explicit version applies the memory-ordering requirement specified by *order*.

Example

A spin-lock using atomic_flag_test_and_set().

```
atomic_flag lock = ATOMIC_FLAG_INIT;     // false if not locked;
                                         // true if locked.
void th_func(char *msg)
{
    static int count;                    // Initial value is 0

    while( atomic_flag_test_and_set(&lock))  // Spin until we lock.
        ;
    ++count;                             // Critical section ...
    printf("%3u. %s\n", count, msg);
    atomic_flag_clear(&lock);            // Release lock.
}
```

See Also

atomic_flag_clear()

atomic_init   C11

Initializes an atomic object.

```
#include <stdatomic.h>
void atomic_init( volatile A *obj, C value);
```

In these prototypes, *A* stands for any atomic type defined in *stdatomic.h*, and *C* stands for the corresponding non-atomic type. This generic function initializes the atomic object referenced by *obj* to the value of *value*. The initialization includes all the operations necessary to provide atomic access to the object. The initialization itself is not an atomic operation, however! The function has no return value.

Example

```
atomic_long count;
atomic_init(&count, 0L);
```

The macro ATOMIC_VAR_INIT and the function call_once()

atomic_is_lock_free   C11

Tests whether an atomic object is lock-free.

```
#include <stdatomic.h>
_Bool atomic_is_lock_free( const volatile A *obj);
```

The generic function atomic_is_lock_free() indicates whether the atomic object pointed to by *obj* is lock-free. The function returns a value not equal to 0 (i.e., true) if the atomic object is lock-free, and 0 (false) if it is not.

An atomic object is lock-free if it can be implemented without using a mutex or another locking mechanism—that is, atomic operations are performed on the object simply by means of atomic CPU instructions. If an atomic object is lock-free, that does not imply that other atomic objects of the same type are also lock-free. A different lock-free status may be caused by different alignment of the objects, for example.

Example

```
_Atomic(int_least64_t) avar64 = ATOMIC_VAR_INIT(0);
if( atomic_is_lock_free(&avar64))
{ /* ... avar64 is lock-free; use without a mutex  ... */ }
```

See Also

The macros ATOMIC_*type*_LOCK_FREE in the header *stdatomic.h*.

atomic_load, atomic_load_explicit   C11

Reads the value of an atomic object.

```
#include <stdatomic.h>
C atomic_load( volatile A *obj);
C atomic_load_explicit( volatile A *obj, memory_order order);
```

In these prototypes, A stands for any atomic type defined in *stdatomic.h*, and C stands for the corresponding non-atomic type. These generic functions return the value of the atomic object referenced by *obj*. The explicit version applies the memory-ordering requirement specified by *order*, which must not be memory_order_release or memory_order_acq_rel.

Example

```
struct Data { double x; } data[10];      // Shared data
atomic_int ai = ATOMIC_VAR_INIT(0);
...
// In first thread:
   for( int i = 0; i < 10; ++i)          // Operation A
       data[i].x = 0.5 *i;
```

```
    atomic_store_explicit(&ai,10, memory_order_release);
...
// In second thread:
    int n = atomic_load_explicit(&ai, memory_order_acquire);
    if( n > 0)
    {
        for( int i = 0; i < n; ++i)       // Operation B
            printf("%8.2lf", data[i].x);
        putchar('\n');
    }
    else
        printf("\nData not yet available.\n");
```

See Also

atomic_store(), atomic_exchange(), atomic_compare_exchange_strong(), atomic_compare_exchange_weak(), atomic_flag_test_and_set()

atomic_signal_fence   C11

Sets a memory fence for synchronization with a signal handler.

```
#include <stdatomic.h>
void atomic_signal_fence( memory_order order);
```

The function atomic_signal_fence(), like atomic_thread_fence(), creates a memory fence. However, the specified ordering requirements for the synchronization of read and write operations are applied only between a thread and a signal handler executed in that thread.

Example

```
static_assert(ATOMIC_INT_LOCK_FREE == 2,
             "atomic_int must be lock-free in the signal handler.");

atomic_int guide = ATOMIC_VAR_INIT(0),
           data  = ATOMIC_VAR_INIT(0);

void SIGTERM_handler(int sig)
{
    if( atomic_load_explicit( &guide, memory_order_relaxed) == 1)
    {
        atomic_signal_fence(memory_order_acquire);
        int d = atomic_load_explicit( &data, memory_order_relaxed);
        assert(d == 100);           // Condition fulfilled!
    // ...
    }
    _Exit(0);
}

int main(void)
{
    if( signal(SIGTERM, SIGTERM_handler) == SIG_ERR)
```

```
              perror("signal"), exit(1);
    // ...
        atomic_store_explicit( &data, 100, memory_order_relaxed);
        atomic_signal_fence( memory_order_release);
        atomic_store_explicit( &guide, 1, memory_order_relaxed);
    // ...
        return 0;
    }
```

See Also

`atomic_thread_fence()`, `signal()`

atomic_store, atomic_store_explicit   C11

Writes a value to an atomic object.

```
#include <stdatomic.h>
void atomic_store( volatile A *obj, C desired);
void atomic_store_explicit( volatile A *obj, C desired,
                            memory_order order);
```

In these prototypes, A stands for any atomic type defined in *stdatomic.h*, and C
stands for the corresponding non-atomic type. These generic functions replace the
value of the atomic object referenced by *obj* with the value of *desired*. The
`explicit` version applies the memory-ordering requirement specified by *order*,
which may be `memory_order_relaxed`, `memory_order_release`, or `mem
ory_order_seq_cst`.

Example

See the example for `atomic_load()` in this chapter.

See Also

`atomic_load()`,   `atomic_exchange()`,   `atomic_compare_exchange_strong()`,
`atomic_compare_exchange_weak()`, `atomic_flag_test_and_set()`

atomic_thread_fence   C11

Sets a memory fence for synchronization with other threads.

```
#include <stdatomic.h>
void atomic_thread_fence( memory_order order);
```

The function `atomic_thread_fence()` creates a memory fence for the synchronization of read and write access to objects that are shared among several threads. A
fence specifies memory-ordering requirements but does not perform an atomic
operation.

The resulting fence is a *release fence* if the argument is `memory_order_release`, and
an *acquire fence* if the argument is `memory_order_acquire` or `memory_order_con
sume`. If the argument is `memory_order_acq_rel` or `memory_order_seq_cst`, the

fence established is a release-and-acquire fence. The function has no effect when called with the argument memory_order_relaxed.

The basic pattern for synchronization between threads by means of fences is as follows:

Thread 1

1. Performs an operation A.

2. Sets a release fence.

3. Writes to an atomic variable *M*, without any memory-ordering requirements (in other words, with the semantics of memory_order_relaxed).

Thread 2

1. Reads the atomic variable *M* without any memory-ordering requirements.

2. Sets an acquire fence.

3. Performs an operation B.

If Thread 1 writes to the atomic variable *M* before Thread 2 reads the value of *M*, the fences guarantee that operation A is completed before operation B begins.

Example

Here's a variation on the example for atomic_load() in this chapter, but using an acquire fence.

```
struct Data { double x; } data[10];        // Shared data.
atomic_int ai = ATOMIC_VAR_INIT(0);
...
// In first thread:
   for( int i = 0; i < 10; ++i)             // Operation A.
      data[i].x = 0.5 *i;
// atomic_fetch_add_explicit(&ai,10, memory_order_release);
// Replacing above line with:
   atomic_thread_fence(memory_order_release);
   atomic_fetch_add_explicit(&ai,10, memory_order_relaxed);
...
// In second thread:
   int n1 = 0;
   // ...
   int n2 = atomic_load_explicit(&ai, memory_order_relaxed);
   if( n2 > n1)
   {
       atomic_thread_fence(memory_order_acquire);
       for( int i = n1; i < n2; ++i)        // Operation B.
          printf("%8.2lf", data[i].x);      // Process the data.
       putchar('\n');
       n1 = n2;
   }
```

```
    else                                    // No fence necessary.
        printf("\nNo new data available.\n");
```

See Also

```
atomic_signal_fence()
```

bsearch

Searches an array for a specified key.

```
#include <stdlib.h>
void *bsearch(const void *key, const void *array, size_t n, size_t size,
        int (*compare)(const void *, const void *));
```

The bsearch() function uses the binary search algorithm to find an element that
matches *key* in a sorted array of *n* elements of size *size*. (The type size_t is defined
in *stdlib.h*, usually as unsigned int.) The last argument, *compare*, gives bsearch() a
pointer to a function that it calls to compare the search key with any array element.
This function must return a value that indicates whether its first argument, the
search key, is less than, equal to, or greater than its second argument, an array element to test. For a detailed description of such comparison functions, see qsort()
in this chapter.

You should generally use qsort() before bsearch() because the array must be sorted before searching. This step is necessary because the binary search algorithm
tests whether the search key is higher or lower than the middle element in the array,
then eliminates half of the array, tests the middle of the result, eliminates half again,
and so forth. If you define the comparison function for bsearch() with identical
types for its two arguments, then qsort() can use the same comparison function.

The bsearch() function returns a pointer to the first array element found that
matches the search key. If several elements in the array match the key, which one of
them the return value points to is undetermined. If no matching element is found,
bsearch() returns a null pointer.

Example

```
#include <stdio.h>
#include <stdlib.h>

typedef struct  { unsigned long id;
                  int data;
                } record ;

int main()
{
  //Declare comparison function:
  int id_cmp(const void *s1, const void *s2);

  record recordset[] = { {3, 5}, {5, -5}, {4, 10}, {2,  2}, {1, -17} };
  record querykey;
  record *found = NULL;
```

```
int recordcount = sizeof( recordset ) / sizeof ( record );

printf( "Query record number: ");
scanf( "%lu", &querykey.id );

printf( "\nRecords before sorting:\n\n"
        "%8s %8s %8s\n", "Index", "ID", "Data" );

for ( int i = 0; i < recordcount ; i++ )
  printf( "%8d %8u %8d\n", i, recordset[i].id, recordset[i].data );

qsort( recordset, recordcount, sizeof( record ), id_cmp );

printf( "\nRecords after sorting:\n\n"
        "%8s %8s %8s\n", "Index", "ID", "Data" );
for ( int i = 0; i < recordcount ; i++ )
  printf( "%8d %8u %8d\n", i, recordset[i].id, recordset[i].data );

found = (record *) bsearch( &querykey, recordset, recordcount,
                            sizeof( record ), id_cmp  );
if ( found == NULL )
  printf( "No record with the ID %lu found.\n", querykey.id );
else
  printf( "The data value in record %lu is %d.\n",
          querykey.id, found->data );

} // End of main().

int id_cmp(const void *s1, const void *s2)
/* Compares records by ID, not data content. */
{
  record *p1 = (record *)s1;
  record *p2 = (record *)s2;

  if      ( p1->id <  p2->id ) return -1;
  else if ( p1->id == p2->id ) return  0;
  else return 1;
}
```

This example produces the following output:

```
Query record number: 4

Records before sorting:

   Index       ID     Data
       0        3        5
       1        5       -5
       2        4       10
       3        2        2
       4        1      -17
```

```
Records after sorting:
     Index       ID    Data
        0        1     -17
        1        2       2
        2        3       5
        3        4      10
        4        5      -5
  The data value in record 4 is 10.
```

See Also

bsearch_s(), qsort()

bsearch_s   C11

Searches a sorted array for a member that matches a specified key.

```
#include <stdlib.h>
void *bsearch_s( const void *key, const void *array, rsize_t n,
    rsize_t size,
    int (*compare)(const void *k, const void *el, void *context),
    void *context);
```

The function bsearch_s(), like bsearch(), searches the sorted array *array* for an element that matches the search key *key*. The array consists of *n* elements, and the size of each element is *size*. The type rsize_t is equivalent with size_t.

The bsearch_s() function tests the following runtime constraints: the values of *n* and *size* must not be greater than RSIZE_MAX, and if *n* is not 0, then *key*, *array*, and *compare* must not be null pointers.

The bsearch_s() function passes the value of the parameter *context* to the function *compare*. That makes the use of a comparison function more flexible at runtime. For example, context may be used to determine the sorting order of characters. It is permissible to pass a null pointer to bsearch_s() as the *context* argument.

The bsearch_s() function calls the comparison function *compare* to compare the search key *key* with an array element. The return value of *compare* must be less than 0 if the search key is smaller than the array element, 0 if they are equal, and greater than 0 if the search key is greater than the array element.

The function bsearch_s() returns the address of an array element that matches the search key. If several elements in the array match the key, it is undetermined which one of them the return value points to. If the array contains no matching element, or if a violation of the runtime constraints occurs, bsearch_s() returns NULL.

Example

```
typedef struct  { unsigned long id;
                  const char* value;
                } record;
```

```
int main(void)
{
    // Declaration of the comparison function:
    int cmp(const void *r1, const void *r2, void *ct);

    record data[] = { {1789,"George"}, {1809,"James"},
                      {1797,"John"}, {1801,"Thomas"} };
    size_t datacount = sizeof(data) / sizeof(data[0]);
    record querykey = { .id=1801 };
    record *found = NULL;

    // Sort the array:
    qsort_s( data, datacount, sizeof(data[0]), cmp, NULL );
    // Search the array:
    found = bsearch_s( &querykey, data, datacount, sizeof(data[0]),
                       cmp, NULL );
    if( found == NULL )
        printf( "No record with the ID %lu found.\n", querykey.id );
    else
        printf( "The record %lu contains the value %s.\n",
                querykey.id, found->value );
} // End of main().

int cmp(const void *r1, const void *r2, void *ct)
// Compares the IDs of the records, not their data values.
// The context parameter ct is not used here.
{
    const record *p1 = (const record *)r1;
    const record *p2 = (const record *)r2;

    if      ( p1->id <  p2->id ) return -1;
    else if ( p1->id == p2->id ) return  0;
    else return 1;
}
```

See Also

bsearch(), qsort(), qsort_s()

btowc

Converts a byte character into a wide character.

```
#include <stdio.h>
#include <wchar.h>
wint_t btowc( int c );
```

The btowc() function returns the corresponding wide character for its byte character argument, if possible. A return value of WEOF indicates that the argument's value is EOF, or that the argument does not represent a valid byte character representation in the initial shift state of a multibyte stream.

Example

```
/* Build a table of wide characters for the first 128 byte values */
wchar_t low_table[128];

for ( int i = 0; i < 128 ; i++ )
  low_table[ i ] = (wchar_t)btowc( i );
```

See Also

wctob(), mbtowc(), wctomb()

c16rtomb   C11

Converts a 16-bit Unicode character into a multibyte character.

```
#include <uchar.h>
size_t c16rtomb( char * restrict dst, char16_t c16,
                 mbstate_t * restrict ps );
```

The function c16rtomb() determines the multibyte representation corresponding to
the wide character *c16* and stores that result, including any necessary shift sequences, in the char array beginning at the address *dst*. The number of bytes written to
the array is at most MB_CUR_MAX. The third argument, *ps*, points to an object that
contains the current shift state, which is taken into account in converting the character. The function c16rtomb() also updates the shift state referenced by *ps*, so that
it represents the appropriate shift state for the next character conversion.

If *c16* is a null character, c16rtomb() writes a zero byte to the array, preceded by a
shift sequence if necessary to restore the shift state to the initial state. In this case,
the state variable referenced by *ps* is updated to represent the initial shift state.

If the argument *dst* is a null pointer, the function call is equivalent to

```
c16rtomb( buf, L'\0', ps)
```

where buf is an internal buffer.

The function c16rtomb() returns the number of bytes written to the destination
array. If *c16* is not a valid wide character, c16rtomb() then returns the value
(size_t)(-1), and sets the error variable errno to the value of EILSEQ. In that case,
the status of the conversion is undetermined.

Example

```
char16_t c16Str[] = u"Grüße";
char mbChar[MB_CUR_MAX];
mbstate_t mbstate = {0};

if( setlocale(LC_ALL, "en_US.UTF-8") == NULL)
    fputs("Unable to set the locale.\n", stderr);

for( int i = 0; c16Str[i] != 0; ++i)
{
```

```
        size_t nBytes = c16rtomb( mbChar, c16Str[i], &mbstate );
        printf("0x%04X %lc  Multibyte: [", c16Str[i], c16Str[i]);
        for( size_t j=0; j < nBytes; ++j)
            printf(" 0x%02X", (unsigned char)mbChar[j]);
        puts(" ]");
    }
```

Examples from the output of this code:

```
0x0047 G  Multibyte: [ 0x47 ]
0x0072 r  Multibyte: [ 0x72 ]
0x00FC ü  Multibyte: [ 0xC3 0xBC ]
0x00DF ß  Multibyte: [ 0xC3 0x9F ]
0x0065 e  Multibyte: [ 0x65 ]
```

See Also

mbrtoc16(), c32rtomb(), mbrtoc32(), wctomb(), wcrtomb(), wcstombs(),
wcsrtombs()

c32rtomb   C11

Converts a 32-bit Unicode character into a multibyte character.

```
#include <uchar.h>
size_t c32rtomb( char * restrict dst, char32_t c32,
                 mbstate_t * restrict ps );
```

The function c32rtomb(), like c16rtomb(), converts a wide character to the appropriate multibyte representation, except that its wide-character parameter has the
type char32_t.

Example

See the example for c16rtomb() in this chapter (note that, for 32-bit characters, you
would use the format specifier 0x%08X in the first printf() statement).

See Also

mbrtoc32(), c16rtomb(), mbrtoc16(), wctomb(), wcrtomb(), wcstombs(),
wcsrtombs()

cabs   C99

Obtains the absolute value of a complex number.

```
#include <complex.h>
double cabs( double complex z );
float cabsf( float complex z );
long double cabsl( long double complex z );
```

For a complex number $z = x + y \times i$, where x and y are real numbers, cabs(z) is
equal to the square root of $x^2 + y^2$, or hypot(x,y). The result is a non-negative real
number.

Example

The absolute value of a complex number is its absolute distance from the origin in the complex plane—in other words, a positive real number, as this example demonstrates:

```
double complex z[4];
z[0] = 3.0 + 4.0 * I;
z[1] = conj( z[0] );
z[2] =  z[0] * I;
z[3] = -( z[0] );

for (int i = 0; i < 4 ; i++ )
  {
    double a = creal(z[i]);
    double b = cimag(z[i]);
    printf ( "The absolute value of (%4.2f %+4.2f x I) is ", a, b );

    double absolute_z = cabs(z[i]);
    printf ( "%4.2f.\n", absolute_z );
  }
```

The output of the sample code is as follows:

```
The absolute value of (3.00 +4.00 x I) is 5.00.
The absolute value of (3.00 -4.00 x I) is 5.00.
The absolute value of (-4.00 +3.00 x I) is 5.00.
The absolute value of (-3.00 -4.00 x I) is 5.00.
```

See Also

cimag(), creal(), carg(), conj(), cproj()

cacos   C99

Calculates the inverse cosine of a complex number.

```
#include <complex.h>
double complex cacos( double complex z );
float complex cacosf( float complex z );
long double complex cacosl( long double complex z );
```

The cacos() functions accept a complex number as their argument and return a complex number, but otherwise work the same as acos().

Example

```
double complex v, z ;
double a = 0.0, b = 0.0;

puts("Calculate the arc cosine of a complex number, cacos(z)\n");
puts("Enter the real and imaginary parts of a complex number:");
if ( scanf("%lf %lf", &a, &b) == 2)
{
  z = a + b * I;
```

```
printf( "z = %.2f %+.2f*I.\n", creal(z), cimag(z) );

v = cacos(z);
printf( "The cacos(z) function yields %.2f %+.2f*I.\n",
        creal(v), cimag(v) );
printf("The inverse function, ccos(cacos(z)), yields %.2f %+.2f*I.\n",
        creal( ccos(v)), cimag( ccos(v)) );
}
else
   printf("Invalid input. \n");
```

See Also

ccos(), csin(), ctan(), cacos(), casin(), catan()

cacosh   C99

Calculates the inverse hyperbolic cosine of a complex number.

```
#include <complex.h>
double complex cacosh( double complex z );
float complex cacoshf( float complex z );
long double complex cacoshl( long double complex z );
```

The cacosh() functions return the complex number whose hyperbolic cosine is equal to the argument z. The real part of the return value is non-negative; the imaginary part is in the interval $[-\pi i, +\pi i]$.

Example

```
double complex v, z ;
double a = 0.0, b = 0.0;

puts("Calculate the inverse hyperbolic cosine of a complex number,"
     " cacosh(z)\n");
puts("Enter the real and imaginary parts of a complex number:");
if ( scanf("%lf %lf", &a, &b) == 2)
{
  z = a + b * I;
  printf( "z = %.2f %+.2f*I.\n", creal(z), cimag(z) );

  v = cacosh(z);
  printf( "The cacosh(z) function yields %.2f %+.2f*I.\n",
          creal(v), cimag(v) );
  printf( "The inverse function, ccosh(cacosh(z)),"
          " yields %.2f %+.2f*I.\n",
          creal( ccosh(v)), cimag( ccosh(v)) );
}
else
   printf("Invalid input.\n");
```

Other hyperbolic trigonometry functions for complex numbers: casinh(), catanh(), csinh(), ccosh(), and ctanh(); the hyperbolic cosine and inverse hyperbolic cosine functions for real numbers: cosh() and acosh()

call_once   C11

Ensures that a function is called exactly once.

```
#include <threads.h>
void call_once(once_flag *flag, void (*func)(void));
```

The function call_once() guarantees that the function passed to it as the argument *func* is called only once. That is, only the first call to call_once() causes it to call *func*. The function call_once() is controlled by a flag of the type once_flag pointed to by the argument *flag*. Subsequent calls to call_once() with the same flag pointer argument do not result in a call to the function *func* specified in the second argument.

Example

```
once_flag flag = ONCE_FLAG_INIT;

void doOnce(void) { puts("Function doOnce()."); }

int th_func(void * arg)
{
    puts((char*)arg);
    call_once(&flag, doOnce);
    return 0;
}

int main()
{
    thrd_t th1, th2, th3;

    if (   thrd_create(&th1, th_func, "Thread 1") != thrd_success
        || thrd_create(&th2, th_func, "Thread 2") != thrd_success
        || thrd_create(&th3, th_func, "Thread 3") != thrd_success )
    {
        fprintf(stderr,"Error creating thread.\n");   return 0xff;
    }
    puts("Hello ...");

    thrd_join(th1, NULL);
    thrd_join(th2, NULL);
    thrd_join(th3, NULL);
    return 0;
}
```

Possible output of this program:

```
Thread 1
Thread 2
Hello ...
Function doOnce().
Thread 3
```

See Also

thrd_create(), atomic_init()

calloc

Allocates memory for an array.

```
#include <stdlib.h>
void *calloc( size_t n, size_t size );
```

The calloc() function obtains a block of memory from the operating system that is large enough to hold an array of *n* elements of size *size*.

If successful, calloc() returns a void pointer to the beginning of the memory block obtained. void pointers are converted automatically to another pointer on assignment, so that you do not need to use an explicit cast, although you may want do so for the sake of clarity. If no memory block of the requested size is available, the function returns a null pointer. Unlike malloc(), calloc() initializes every byte of the block allocated with the value 0.

Example

```
size_t n;
int *p;
printf("\nHow many integers do you want to enter? ");
scanf("%u", &n);
p = (int *)calloc(n, sizeof(int)); /* Allocate some memory */
if (p == NULL)
  printf("\nInsufficient memory.");
else
  /* read integers into array elements ... */
```

See Also

malloc(), realloc(), free(), memset()

carg   C99

Calculates the argument of a complex number.

```
#include <complex.h>
double carg( double complex z );
float cargf( float complex z );
long double cargl( long double complex z );
```

The carg() function determines the *argument* of a complex number, or the angle it forms with the origin and the positive part of the real axis. A complex number is defined in polar coordinates by its argument and *modulus* (or radius), which is the same as the absolute value of the complex number, given by cabs(). The return value of carg() is in radians, and within the range [-π, π]. For a complex number z = x + y × i, where x and y are real numbers, carg(z) is equal to atan2(y, x).

Example

```
/* Convert a complex number from Cartesian to polar coordinates. */
double complex z = -4.4 + 3.3 * I;
double radius = cabs( z );
double argument = carg( z );

double x = creal( z );
double y = cimag( z );

printf( "Cartesian (x, y): (%4.1f, %4.1f)\n", x, y );
printf( "Polar (r, theta): (%4.1f, %4.1f)\n", radius, argument );
```

This code produces the following output:

```
Cartesian (x, y): (-4.4,  3.3)
Polar (r, theta): ( 5.5,  2.5)
```

See Also

cabs(), cimag(), creal(), carg(), conj(), cproj()

casin   C99

Calculates the inverse sine of a complex number.

```
#include <complex.h>
double complex casin( double complex z );
float complex casinf( float complex z );
long double complex casinl( long double complex z );
```

The casin() functions accept a complex number as their argument and return a complex number, but otherwise work the same as asin(). The real part of the return value is in the interval [-π/2, π/2].

Example

```
puts("Results of the casin() function for integer values:");
float complex z = 0;
for ( int n = -3; n <= 3; ++n)
{
  z = casinf(n);
  printf(" casin(%+d) = %+.2f %+.2f*I\n", n, crealf(z), cimagf(z) );
}
```

This code produces the following output:

```
Results of the casin() function for integer values:
  casin(-3) = -1.57 +1.76*I
  casin(-2) = -1.57 +1.32*I
  casin(-1) = -1.57 -0.00*I
  casin(+0) = +0.00 +0.00*I
  casin(+1) = +1.57 -0.00*I
  casin(+2) = +1.57 +1.32*I
  casin(+3) = +1.57 +1.76*I
```

See Also

ccos(), csin(), ctan(), cacos(), casin(), catan()

casinh

Calculates the inverse hyperbolic sine of a number.

```
#include <complex.h>
double complex casinh( double complex z );
float complex casinhf( float complex z );
long double complex casinhl( long double complex z );
```

The casinh() functions return the complex number whose hyperbolic sine is equal to their argument z.

Example

```
double complex v, w, z ;
double a = 0.0, b = 0.0;

puts("Enter the real and imaginary parts of a complex number:");
if ( scanf("%lf %lf", &a, &b) == 2)
{
  z = a + b * I;
  printf( "z = %.2f %+.2f*I.\n", creal(z), cimag(z) );

  v = casin(z);
  w = casinh(z);
  printf( "z is the sine of %.2f %+.2f*I\n",  creal(v), cimag(v) );
  printf( "and the hyperbolic sine of %.2f %+.2f*I.\n",
          creal(w), cimag(w) );
}
else
  printf("Invalid input. \n");
```

See Also

cacosh(), catanh(), ccosh(), csinh(), ctanh(); the hyperbolic trigonometry functions for real numbers: acosh(), atanh(), sinh(), cosh(), and tanh()

Calculates the inverse tangent of a complex number.

```
#include <complex.h>
double complex catan( double complex z );
float complex catanf( float complex z );
long double complex catanl( double long complex z );
```

The catan() functions accept a complex number as their argument and return a complex number, but otherwise work the same as atan().

Example

```
double complex v, w, z ;
double a = 0.0, b = 0.0;

puts("Enter the real and imaginary parts of a complex number:");
if ( scanf("%lf %lf", &a, &b) == 2)
{
  z = a + b * I;
  printf( "z = %.2f %+.2f*I.\n", creal(z), cimag(z) );

  v = catan(z);
  w = catanh(z);
  printf( "z is the tangent of %.2f %+.2f*I\n",  creal(v), cimag(v) );
  printf( "and the hyperbolic tangent of %.2f %+.2f*I.\n",
          creal(w), cimag(w) );
}
else
  printf("Invalid input. \n");
```

This code produces output like the following:

```
Enter the real and imaginary parts of a complex number:30 30
z = 30.00 +30.00*I.
z is the tangent of 1.55 +0.02*I
and the hyperbolic tangent of 0.02 +1.55*I.
```

See Also

ccos(), csin(), ctan(), cacos(), casin()

Calculates the inverse hyperbolic tangent of a complex number.

```
#include <complex.h>
double complex catanh( double complex z );
float complex catanhf( float complex z );
long double complex catanhl( double long complex z );
```

The catanh() functions return the number whose hyperbolic tangent is equal to their argument *z*. The imaginary part of the return value is in the interval [-π/2 × *i*, π/2 × *i*].

Example

See the example for catan() in this chapter.

See Also

Other hyperbolic trigonometry functions for complex numbers: casinh(), cacosh(), csinh(), ccosh(), and ctanh(); the hyperbolic tangent and inverse hyperbolic tangent functions for real numbers: tanh() and atanh()

cbrt   C99

Calculates the cube root of a number.

```
#include <math.h>
double cbrt( double x );
float cbrtf( float x );
long double cbrtl( long double x );
```

The cbrt() functions return the cube root of their argument x.

Example

```
#define KM_PER_AU (149597870.691) // An astronomical unit is the mean
                                  // distance between Earth and Sun:
                                  // about 150 million km.
#define DY_PER_YR (365.24)

double dist_au, dist_km, period_dy, period_yr;

printf("How long is a solar year on your planet (in Earth days)?\n");
scanf( "%lf", &period_dy );

period_yr = period_dy / DY_PER_YR;
dist_au = cbrt( period_yr * period_yr );    // by Kepler's Third Law
dist_km = dist_au * KM_PER_AU;

printf("Then your planet must be about %.0lf km from the Sun.\n",
                                        dist_km );
```

See Also

sqrt(), hypot(), pow()

Calculates the cosine of a complex number.

```
#include <complex.h>
double complex ccos( double complex z );
float complex ccosf( float complex z );
long double complex ccosl( long double complex z );
```

The ccos() function returns the cosine of its complex number argument z, which is equal to $(e^{iz} + e^{-iz})/2$.

Example

```
/* Demonstrate the exponential definition
 * of the complex cosine function.
 */
double complex z = 2.2 + 3.3 * I;
double complex c, d;

c = ccos( z );
d = 0.5 * ( cexp( z * I ) + cexp( - z * I ));

printf("The ccos() function returns %.2f %+.2f × I.\n",
        creal(c), cimag(c) );
printf("Using the cexp() function, the result is %.2f %+.2f × I.\n",
        creal(d), cimag(d) );
```

This code produces the following output:

```
The ccos() function returns -7.99 -10.95 × I.
Using the cexp() function, the result is -7.99 -10.95 × I.
```

See Also

csin(), ctan(), cacos(), casin(), catan(), cexp()

Calculates the hyperbolic cosine of a complex number.

```
#include <complex.h>
double complex ccosh( double complex z );
float complex ccoshf( float complex z );
long double complex ccoshl( long double complex z );
```

The hyperbolic cosine of a complex number z is equal to $(\exp(z) + \exp(-z)) / 2$. The ccosh functions return the hyperbolic cosine of their complex argument.

Example

```
double complex v, w, z = 1.2 - 3.4 * I;

v = ccosh( z );
w = 0.5 * ( cexp(z) + cexp(-z) );
```

```
printf( "The ccosh() function returns %.2f %+.2f*I.\n",
        creal(v), cimag(v) );
printf( "Using the cexp() function, the result is %.2f %+.2f*I.\n",
        creal(w), cimag(w) );
```

This code produces the following output:

```
The ccosh() function returns -1.75 +0.39*I.
Using the cexp() function, the result is -1.75 +0.39*I.
```

See Also

csinh(), ctanh(), cacosh(), casinh(), catanh()

ceil

Rounds a real number up to an integer value.

```
#include <math.h>
double ceil( double x );
float ceilf( float x );            (C99)
long double ceill( long double x );      (C99)
```

The ceil() function returns the smallest integer that is greater than or equal to its argument. However, the function does not have an integer *type*; it returns an integer *value*, but with a floating-point type.

Example

```
/* Amount due = unit price * count * VAT, rounded up to the next cent */
div_t total = { 0, 0 };
int count = 17;
int price = 9999;          // 9999 cents is $99.99
double vat_rate = 0.055;   // Value-added tax of 5.5%

total = div( (int)ceil( (count * price) * (1 + vat_rate)), 100);

printf("Total due: $%d.%2d\n", total.quot, total.rem);
```

This code produces the following output:

```
Total due: $1793.33
```

See Also

floor(), floorf(), and floorl(), round(), roundf(), and roundl(); the C99
rounding functions that return floating-point types: trunc(), rint(), nearbyint(),
nextafter(), nexttoward(); the C99 rounding functions that return integer types:
lrint(), lround(), llrint(), llround(); the fesetround() and fegetround()
functions, which operate on the C99 floating-point environment

Calculates the natural exponential of a complex number.

```
#include <complex.h>
double complex cexp( double complex z );
float complex cexpf( float complex z );
long double complex cexpl( long double complex z );
```

The return value of the cexp() function is e raised to the power of the function's argument, or e^z, where e is Euler's number, 2.718281.... Furthermore, in complex mathematics, $e^{zi} = \cos(z) + \sin(z) \times i$ for any complex number z.

 The natural exponential function cexp() is the inverse of the natural logarithm, clog().

Example

```
// Demonstrate Euler's theorem in the form
// e^(I*z) = cos(z) + I * sin(z)

double complex z = 2.2 + 3.3 * I;
double complex c, d;

c = cexp( z * I );
d = ccos( z ) + csin( z ) * I ;

printf( "cexp( z*I ) yields %.2f %+.2f × I.\n",
        creal(c), cimag(c) );
printf( "ccos( z ) + csin( z ) * I yields %.2f %+.2f × I.\n",
        creal(d), cimag(d) );
```

This code produces the following output:

```
cexp( z*I ) yields -0.02 +0.03 × I.
ccos( z ) + csin( z ) * I yields -0.02 +0.03 × I.
```

See Also

ccos(), csin(), clog(), cpow(), csqrt()

Obtains the imaginary part of a complex number.

```
#include <complex.h>
double cimag( double complex z );
float cimagf( float complex z );
long double cimagl( long double complex z );
```

A complex number is represented as two floating-point numbers, one quantifying the real part and one quantifying the imaginary part. The cimag() function returns the floating-point number that represents the imaginary part of the complex argument.

Example

```
double complex z = 4.5 - 6.7 * I;

printf( "The complex variable z is equal to %.2f %+.2f × I.\n",
        creal(z),cimag(z) );
```

This code produces the following output:

```
The complex variable z is equal to 4.50 -6.70 × I.
```

See Also

cabs(), creal(), carg(), conj(), cproj()

clearerr

Clears the file error and EOF flags.

```
#include <stdio.h>
void clearerr(FILE *fp);
```

The clearerr() function is useful in handling errors in file I/O routines. It clears the end-of-file (EOF) and error flags associated with a specified FILE pointer.

Example

```
FILE *fp;
int c;
if ((fp = fopen("infile.dat", "r")) == NULL)
  fprintf(stderr, "Couldn't open input file.\n");
else
{
  c = fgetc(fp);   // fgetc() returns a character on success;
  if (c == EOF)    // EOF means either an error or end-of-file.
  {
    if ( feof(fp))
      fprintf(stderr, "End of input file reached.\n");
    else if ( ferror(fp))
      fprintf(stderr, "Error on reading from input file.\n");
    clearerr(fp);  // Same function clears both conditions.
  }
  else
  { /* ... */ }    // Process the character that we read.
}
```

See Also

feof(), ferror(), rewind()

clock

Obtains the CPU time used by the process.

```
#include <time.h>
clock_t clock( void );
```

If you want to know how much CPU time your program has used, call the clock()
function. The function's return type, clock_t, is defined in *time.h* as long. If the
function returns -1, then the CPU time is not available. Note that the value of
clock() does not reflect actual elapsed time, as it doesn't include any time the system may have spent on other tasks.

The basic unit of CPU time, called a "tick," varies from one system to another. To
convert the result of the clock() call into seconds, divide it by the constant
CLOCKS_PER_SEC, which is also defined in *time.h*.

Example

```
#include <stdio.h>
#include <time.h>
time_t start, stop;
clock_t ticks; long count;

int main()
{
  time(&start);
  for (count = 0; count <= 50000000; ++count)
  {
    if (count % 1000000 != 0) continue;    // measure only full millions
    ticks = clock();
    printf("Performed %ld million integer divisions; "
           "used %0.2f seconds of CPU time.\n", count / 1000000,
           (double)ticks/CLOCKS_PER_SEC);
  }
  time(&stop);
  printf("Finished in about %.0f seconds.\n", difftime(stop, start));
  return 0;
}
```

This program produces 51 lines of output, ending with something like this:

```
Performed 50 million integer divisions; used 2.51 seconds of CPU time.
Finished in about 6 seconds.
```

See Also

time(), difftime()

Calculates the natural logarithm of a complex number.

```
#include <complex.h>
double complex clog( double complex z );
float complex clogf( float complex z );
long double complex clogl( long double complex z );
```

The clog() functions calculate the natural logarithm—that is, the logarithm to base e—of their complex argument. The imaginary part of the return value is in the interval $[-\pi i, +\pi i]$.

Example

```
double complex z = clog( -1.0 );      // z = 0.0 + 3.1415926 * I
```

See Also

cexp( ), cpow( )

cnd_broadcast   C11

Wakes up all threads waiting for a condition variable.

```
#include <threads.h>
int cnd_broadcast(cnd_t *cond);
```

The function cnd_broadcast() wakes up all the threads waiting for the condition variable referenced by its pointer argument *cond*. The return value is thrd_success if no error occurs; otherwise, thrd_error. If there is no thread waiting on the condition variable *cond*, the function does nothing, and returns thrd_success.

Example

```
// Wake up three threads waiting for one condition variable using
// cnd_signal() and cnd_broadcast().
#include <stdio.h>
#include <threads.h>
#include <stdatomic.h>

cnd_t cv;
mtx_t mtx;           // Mutex for the condition variable cv
atomic_bool go = ATOMIC_VAR_INIT(0);         // Initially false

int th_func(void * arg)                       // Thread function
{
    mtx_lock(&mtx);
    printf("%s waiting ... \n", (char*)arg );

    while( !go)
        if( cnd_wait(&cv, &mtx) != thrd_success)
            return -1;
```

```
        printf("%s finished.\n", (char*)arg);
        mtx_unlock(&mtx);
        return 0;
    }

    int main(void)
    {
        thrd_t th1, th2, th3;

        if( cnd_init(&cv) != thrd_success
            || mtx_init(&mtx, mtx_plain) != thrd_success)
        {
            fputs("Initialization error.\n", stderr); return 1;
        }

        if(    thrd_create(&th1, th_func, "Thread 1") != thrd_success
            || thrd_create(&th2, th_func, "Thread 2") != thrd_success
            || thrd_create(&th3, th_func, "Thread 3") != thrd_success)
        {
            fputs("Thread error.\n", stderr); return 2;
        }

        struct timespec duration = { .tv_sec = 1 };
        thrd_sleep( &duration, NULL);        // Wait 1 second.

        go = 1;
        puts("cnd_signal ...");
        if ( cnd_signal(&cv) != thrd_success)
        {   fputs("Signal error.\n", stderr); return 3;   }

        thrd_sleep( &duration, NULL);        // Wait 1 second.
        puts("cnd_broadcast ...");
        if ( cnd_broadcast(&cv) != thrd_success)
        {   fputs("Broadcast error.\n", stderr); return 4;   }

        thrd_join(th1, NULL);  thrd_join(th2, NULL);  thrd_join(th3, NULL);

        cnd_destroy( &cv);
        mtx_destroy( &mtx);
        return 0;
    }
```

Possible output of this program:

```
Thread 1 waiting ...
Thread 2 waiting ...
Thread 3 waiting ...
cnd_signal ...
Thread 1 finished.
cnd_broadcast ...
```

```
Thread 3 finished.
Thread 2 finished.
```

See Also

cnd_signal(), cnd_wait(), cnd_timedwait()

cnd_destroy   C11

Destroys a condition variable.

```
#include <threads.h>
void cnd_destroy(cnd_t *cond);
```

The function cnd_destroy() frees all the resources used by the condition variable
referenced by its pointer argument *cond*. There must be no threads waiting for the
condition variable when cnd_destroy() is called.

Example

```
cnd_t cv;            // A condition variable.

int func()
{
    if( cnd_init(&cv) != thrd_success)
    {
        fputs("Initialization error.\n", stderr); return -1;
    }
// ...   Use the condition variable ...

    cnd_destroy( &cv);
    return 0;
}
```

See Also

cnd_init(), cnd_wait(), cnd_signal()

cnd_init   C11

Creates a condition variable.

```
#include <threads.h>
int cnd_init(cnd_t *cond);
```

The cnd_init() function creates a new condition variable and initializes the variable referenced by its pointer argument *cond* to a unique identifier value for the new
condition variable. If no error occurs, cnd_init() returns thrd_success. If there is
not enough memory available to create the condition variable, the function returns
thrd_nomem. Other errors produce the return value thrd_error.

Example

See the examples for cnd_destroy() and cnd_broadcast() in this chapter.

cnd_destroy(), cnd_wait(), cnd_signal()

cnd_signal   C11

Wakes up one thread waiting for a condition variable.

```
#include <threads.h>
int cnd_signal(cnd_t *cond);
```

The function cnd_signal() wakes up one of the threads that are waiting for the condition variable referenced by its pointer argument *cond*. The return value is thrd_success if no error occurs; otherwise, thrd_error. If there is no thread waiting for the condition variable *cond, the function does nothing, and returns thrd_success.

Example

See the example for cnd_broadcast() in this chapter, and Example 14-4 in Chapter 14.

See Also

cnd_broadcast(), cnd_wait(), cnd_timedwait()

cnd_timedwait   C11

Blocks the thread on a condition variable for a limited time.

```
#include <threads.h>
int cnd_timedwait(cnd_t *restrict cond, mtx_t *restrict mtx,
                  const struct timespec *restrict ts);
```

The calling thread must hold the mutex referenced by the *mtx* argument. The function cnd_timedwait() releases the mutex and blocks the thread on the condition variable referenced by the pointer argument *cond*. The function sleeps until another thread wakes it up by calling cnd_signal() or cnd_broadcast() with the same condition variable argument, or until the time specified by the argument *ts*. Before the cnd_timedwait() function returns, it obtains the mutex again for the calling thread.

The parameter *ts* specifies a point in Coordinated Universal Time, or UTC (also called Greenwich Mean Time). The current time in UTC can be obtained using the function timespec_get().

The return value is thrd_success if no error occurs, thrd_timedout if the time limit elapsed, or thrd_error if an error occurred.

Example

```
cnd_t cv;
mtx_t mtx;                          // Mutex for the condition variable cv
atomic_bool go = ATOMIC_VAR_INIT(0);         // Initially false.

int th_func(void * millisec)                 // Thread function.
{
    int res = thrd_success;
    struct timespec ts;
    timespec_get( &ts, TIME_UTC);            // The current time
    ts.tv_nsec  += *(long*)millisec * 1E6;   // + millions of ns.

    mtx_lock(&mtx);
    puts("Waiting ...");
    while( !go && res == thrd_success)
        res = cnd_timedwait(&cv, &mtx, &ts);
    switch( res )
    {
        case thrd_success:
            puts("Working ... done.");  break;
        case thrd_timedout:
            puts("Timed out.");    break;
        default:
            puts("cnd_timedwait: error.");
    };
    mtx_unlock(&mtx);
    return res;
}

int main(void)
{
    thrd_t th1, th2;
    long tm_limit1 = 100, tm_limit2 = 500;   // In milliseconds.

    if( cnd_init(&cv) != thrd_success
        || mtx_init(&mtx, mtx_plain) != thrd_success)
    {
        fputs("Initialization error.\n", stderr); return 1;
    }

    if(    thrd_create(&th1, th_func, &tm_limit1) != thrd_success
        || thrd_create(&th2, th_func, &tm_limit2) != thrd_success)
    {
        fputs("Thread error.\n", stderr); return 2;
    }

    struct timespec dura = { 0 };
    dura.tv_nsec = 200 *1E6;         // 200 million nanoseconds.
    thrd_sleep( &dura, NULL);        // Wait 200 milliseconds.

    go = 1;
```

```
puts("Sending broadcast ...");
cnd_broadcast(&cv);

thrd_join(th1, NULL);  thrd_join(th2, NULL);
cnd_destroy( &cv);
mtx_destroy( &mtx);
return 0;
}
```

Typical output:

```
Waiting ...
Waiting ...
Timed out.
Sending broadcast ...
Working ... done.
```

See Also

cnd_wait(), cnd_signal(), cnd_broadcast(), timespec_get()

cnd_wait   C11

Blocks the thread on a condition variable.

```
#include <threads.h>
int cnd_wait(cnd_t *cond, mtx_t *mtx);
```

The calling thread must hold the mutex referenced by the *mtx* argument. The function cnd_wait() releases the mutex and blocks the thread on the condition variable
referenced by the pointer argument *cond*. The function sleeps until another wakes it
up by calling cnd_signal() or cnd_broadcast() with the same condition variable
argument. Before the cnd_wait() function returns, it obtains the mutex again for
the calling thread.

The return value is thrd_success if no error occurs; otherwise, thrd_error.

Example

See the example for cnd_broadcast() in this chapter.

See Also

cnd_timedwait(), cnd_signal(), cnd_broadcast()

conj   C99

Obtains the conjugate of a complex number.

```
#include <complex.h>
double complex conj( double complex z );
float complex conjf( float complex z );
long double complex conjl( long double complex z );
```

The conj() function returns the complex conjugate of its complex argument. The conjugate of a complex number *x + yi*, where *x* and *y* are the real and imaginary parts, is defined as *x − yi*. Accordingly, the conj() function calculates the conjugate by changing the sign of the imaginary part.

Example

See the example for cabs() in this chapter.

See Also

cabs(), cimag(), creal(), carg(), conj(), cproj()

copysign   C99

Makes the sign of a number match that of another number.

```
#include <math.h>
double copysign( double x, double y );
float copysignf( float x, float y );
long double copysignl( long double x, long double y );
```

The copysign() function returns a value with the magnitude of its first argument and the sign of its second argument.

Example

```
/* Test for signed zero values */
double x = copysign(0.0, -1.0);
double y = copysign(0.0, +1.0);

printf( "x is %+.1f; y is %+.1f.\n", x, y);
printf( "%+.1f is %sequal to %+.1f.\n",
        x, ( x == y ) ? "" : "not ", y);
```

This code produces the following output:

```
x is -0.0; y is +0.0.
-0.0 is equal to +0.0.
```

See Also

abs(), fabs(), fdim(), fmax(), fmin()

cos

Calculates the cosine of an angle.

```
#include <math.h>
double cos( double x );
float cosf( float x );              (C99)
long double cosl( long double x );         (C99)
```

The cos() function returns the cosine of its argument, which is an angle measure in radians. The return value is in the range $-1 \leq \cos(x) \leq 1$.

Example

```
/*
 * Calculate the sloping width of a roof
 * given the horizontal width
 * and the angle from the horizontal.
 */
#define PI 3.141593
#define DEG_PER_RAD (180.0/PI)

double roof_pitch = 20.0;            // In degrees
double floor_width = 30.0;           // In feet, say.
double roof_width = 1.0 / cos(roof_pitch / DEG_PER_RAD) * floor_width;

printf( "The sloping width of the roof is %4.2f ft.\n", roof_width );
```

This code produces the following output:

```
The sloping width of the roof is 31.93 ft.
```

See Also

sin(), tan(), acos(), ccos()

cosh

Calculates the hyperbolic cosine of a number.

```
#include <math.h>
double cosh( double x );
float coshf( float x );           (C99)
long double coshl( long double x );        (C99)
```

The hyperbolic cosine of any number x equals $(e^x + e^{-x})/2$ and is always greater than or equal to 1. If the result of cosh() is too great for the double type, the function incurs a range error.

Example

```
double x, sum = 1.0;
unsigned max_n;
printf("Cosh(x) is the sum as n goes from 0 to infinity "
       "of x^(2*n) / (2*n)!\n");
    // That's x raised to the power of 2*n, divided by 2*n factorial.
printf("Enter x and a maximum for n (separated by a space): ");
if (scanf(" %lf %u", &x, &max_n) < 2)
{
    printf("Couldn't read two numbers.\n");
    return -1;
}
printf("cosh(%.2f) = %.4f;\n", x, cosh(x));
for ( unsigned n = 1 ; n <= max_n ; n++ )
{
    unsigned factor = 2 * n;          // Calculate (2*n)!
    unsigned divisor = factor;
```

```
while ( factor > 1 )
{
    factor--;
    divisor *= factor;
}
sum += pow(x, 2 * n) / divisor;    // Accumulate the series
}
printf("Approximation by series of %u terms = %.4f.\n", max_n+1, sum);
```

With the numbers 1.72 and 3 as input, the program produces the following output:

```
cosh(1.72) = 2.8818;
Approximation by series of 4 terms = 2.8798.
```

See Also

The C99 inverse hyperbolic cosine function, acosh(); the hyperbolic cosine and inverse hyperbolic cosine functions for complex numbers, ccosh(), cacosh(); the example for sinh()

cpow   C99

Raises a complex number to a complex power.

```
#include <complex.h>
double complex cpow( double complex x, double complex y );
float complex cpowf( float complex x, float complex y );
long double complex cpowl( long double complex x,
                          long double complex y );
```

The cpow() function raises its first complex argument x to the power of the second argument, y. In other words, it returns the value of x^y.

The cpow() function has a branch cut along the negative real axis to yield a unique result.

Example

```
double complex z = 0.0 + 2.7 * I;
double complex w = 2.7 + 0.0 * I;

double complex c = cpow(w, z);    // Raise e to the power of i*2.7

printf("%.2f %+.2f × I raised to the power of %.2f %+.2f × I \n"
       "is %.2f %+.2f × I.\n",
       creal(w), cimag(w), creal(z), cimag(z), creal(c), cimag(c));
```

This code produces the following output:

```
2.70 +0.00 × I raised to the power of 0.00 +2.70 × I
is -0.90 +0.44 × I.
```

See Also

The corresponding function for real numbers, pow(); the complex math functions cexp(), clog(), cpow(), csqrt()

Calculates the projection of a complex number on the Riemann sphere.

```
#include <complex.h>
double complex cproj( double complex z );
float complex cprojf( float complex z );
long double complex cprojl( long double complex z );
```

The Riemann sphere is a surface that represents the entire complex plane and one point for infinity. The cproj() function yields the representation of a complex number on the Riemann sphere. The value of cproj(*z*) is equal to *z*, except in cases where the real or complex part of *z* is infinite. In all such cases, the real part of the result is infinity, and the imaginary part is zero with the sign of the imaginary part of the argument *z*.

Example

```
double complex z = -INFINITY - 2.7 * I;

double complex c = cproj(z);
printf("%.2f %+.2f * I is projected to %.2f %+.2f * I.\n",
        creal(z), cimag(z), creal(c), cimag(c));
```

This code produces the following output:

```
-inf -2.70 * I is projected to inf -0.00 * I.
```

See Also

cabs(), cimag(), creal(), carg(), conj()

Obtains the real part of a complex number.

```
#include <complex.h>
double creal( double complex z );
float crealf( float complex z );
long double creall( long double complex z );
```

A complex number is represented as two floating-point numbers, one quantifying the real part and one quantifying the imaginary part. The creal() function returns the floating-point number that represents the real part of the complex argument.

Example

```
double complex z = 4.5 - 6.7 * I;

printf( "The complex variable z is equal to %.2f %+.2f × I.\n",
                                            creal(z), cimag(z) );
```

This code produces the following output:

```
The complex variable z is equal to 4.50 -6.70 × I.
```

---

cimag(), cabs(), carg(), conj(), cproj()

csin

Calculates the sine of a complex number.

```
#include <complex.h>
double complex csin( double complex z );
float complex csinf( float complex z );
long double complex csinl( long double complex z );
```

The csin() function returns the sine of its complex number argument z, which is equal to $(e^{iz} - e^{-iz})/2 \times i$.

Example

```
// Demonstrate the exponential definition of the complex sine function.
double complex z = 4.3 - 2.1 * I;
double complex c, d;

c = csin( z );
d = ( cexp( z * I ) - cexp( - z * I )) / (2 * I);

printf("The csin() function returns %.2f %+.2f × I.\n",
        creal(c), cimag(c) );
printf("Using the cexp() function, the result is %.2f %+.2f × I.\n",
        creal(d), cimag(d) );
```

This code produces the following output:

```
The csin() function returns -3.80 +1.61 × I.
Using the cexp() function, the result is -3.80 +1.61 × I.
```

See Also

ccos(), ctan(), cacos(), casin(), catan()

csinh

Calculates the hyperbolic sine of a complex number.

```
#include <complex.h>
double complex csinh( double complex z );
float complex csinhf( float complex z );
long double complex csinhl( long double complex z );
```

The hyperbolic sine of a complex number z is equal to $(\exp(z) - \exp(-z)) / 2$. The csinh functions return the hyperbolic sine of their complex argument.

Example

```
double complex v, w, z = -1.2 + 3.4 * I;

v = csinh( z );
w = 0.5 * ( cexp(z) - cexp(-z) );

printf( "The csinh() function returns %.2f %+.2f*I.\n",
        creal(v), cimag(v) );
printf( "Using the cexp() function, the result is %.2f %+.2f*I.\n",
        creal(w), cimag(w) );
```

This code produces the following output:

```
The csinh() function returns 1.46 -0.46*I.
Using the cexp() function, the result is 1.46 -0.46*I.
```

See Also

ccosh(), ctanh(), cacosh(), casinh(), catanh()

---

csqrt   C99

Calculates the square root of a complex number.

```
#include <complex.h>
double complex csqrt( double complex z );
float complex csqrtf( float complex z );
long double complex csqrtl( long double complex z );
```

The csqrt() function returns the complex square root of its complex number argument.

Example

```
double complex z = 1.35 - 2.46 * I;
double complex c, d;

c = csqrt( z );
d = c * c;

printf("If the square root of %.2f %+.2f x I equals %.2f %+.2f x I,"
       "\n", creal(z), cimag(z), creal(c), cimag(c) );
printf("then %.2f %+.2f x I squared should equal %.2f %+.2f x I.\n",
       creal(c), cimag(c), creal(d), cimag(d) );
```

This code produces the following output:

```
If the square root of 1.35 -2.46 x I equals 1.44 -0.85 x I,
then 1.44 -0.85 x I squared should equal 1.35 -2.46 x I.
```

See Also

cexp(), clog(), cpow(), csqrt()

ctan

Calculates the tangent of a complex number.

```
#include <complex.h>
double complex ctan( double complex z );
float complex ctanf( float complex z );
long double complex ctanl( long double complex z );
```

The ctan() function returns the tangent of its complex number argument z, which is equal to $\sin(z) / \cos(z)$.

Example

```
double complex z = - 0.53 + 0.62 * I;
double complex c, d;

c = ctan( z );
d = csin( z ) / ccos( z );

printf("The ctan() function returns %.2f %+.2f × I.\n",
       creal(c), cimag(c) );
printf("Using the csin() and ccos() functions yields %.2f %+.2f × I.\n",
       creal(d), cimag(d) );
```

This code produces the following output:

```
The ctan() function returns -0.37 +0.67 × I.
Using the csin() and ccos() functions yields -0.37 +0.67 × I.
```

See Also

csin(), ccos(), cacos(), casin(), catan()

ctanh

Calculates the hyperbolic tangent of a complex number.

```
#include <complex.h>
double complex ctanh( double complex z );
float complex ctanhf( float complex z );
long double complex ctanhl( long double complex z );
```

The hyperbolic tangent of a complex number z is equal to $\sinh(z) / \cosh(z)$. The ctanh functions return the hyperbolic tangent of their complex argument.

Example

```
double complex v, w, z =  -0.5 + 1.23 * I;

v = ctanh( z );
w = csinh( z ) / ccosh( z );

printf("The ctanh() function returns %.2f %+.2f*I.\n",
                                creal(v), cimag(v) );
```

```
printf("Using the csinh() and ccosh() functions yields %.2f %+.2f*I.\n",
        creal(w), cimag(w) );
```

This code produces the following output:

```
The ctanh() function returns -1.53 +0.82*I.
Using the csinh() and ccosh() functions yields -1.53 +0.82*I.
```

See Also

ccosh(), csinh(), cacosh(), casinh(), catanh()

ctime

Converts an integer time value into a date-and-time string.

```
#include <time.h>
char *ctime( const time_t *seconds );
```

The argument passed to the ctime() function is a pointer to a number interpreted as a number of seconds elapsed since the epoch (on Unix systems, January 1, 1970).

The function converts this value into a human-readable character string showing the local date and time, and returns a pointer to that string. The string is exactly 26 bytes long, including the terminating null character, and has the following format:

```
Thu Apr 28 15:50:56 2005\n
```

The argument's type, time_t, is defined in *time.h*, usually as a long or unsigned long integer.

The function call ctime(&*seconds*) is equivalent to asctime(localtime(&*seconds*)). A common way to obtain the argument value passed to ctime() is by calling the time() function, which returns the current time in seconds.

Example

```
void logerror(int errorcode)
{
  time_t eventtime;

  time(&eventtime);
  fprintf( stderr, "%s: Error number %d occurred.\n",
          ctime(&eventtime), errorcode );
}
```

This code produces output like the following:

```
Wed Sep  9 14:58:03 2015
: Error number 23 occurred.
```

The output contains a line break because the string produced by ctime() ends in a newline character.

asctime(), asctime_s(), difftime(), gmtime(), gmtime_s(), localtime(), local time_s(), mktime(), strftime(), time()

ctime_s   C11

Converts an integer time value into a date-and-time string.

```
#include <time.h>
errno_t ctime_s(char *s, rsize_t maxsize, const time_t *timer);
```

Like the function ctime(), the function ctime_s() converts the integer calendar time addressed by the pointer *timer* into a string showing the local date and time. The parameter *timer* is in UTC, or Greenwich Mean Time. The output string is exactly 26 bytes long, including the null terminator character, and has the following timestamp format:

```
Thu Jan 29 09:30:01 2015
```

Unlike ctime(), the ctime_s() function does not return a pointer to a static string but instead copies the output string to the address specified by the *s* argument. This makes the function ctime_s() safe for use in multithreading environments. The length of the buffer at *s*, specified by *maxsize*, must be at least 26 bytes. A call to the function ctime_s() is equivalent to the following asctime_s() call:

```
asctime_s( s, maxsize, localtime_s(timer, &tmStruct))
```

where tmStruct has the type struct tm.

The function ctime_s() tests the following runtime constraints: the pointer arguments *s* and *timer* must not be null pointers, and the value of *maxsize* must be between 26 and RSIZE_MAX.

The ctime_s() function returns zero if no error occurs. Otherwise, it returns a nonzero error code, and writes the string terminator character '\0' to s[0], if the values of *s* and *maxsize* permit.

Example

```
#define __STDC_WANT_LIB_EXT1__   1
#include <time.h>
// ...

    time_t now = 0;
    char timeStr[26];

    time(&now);                    // Date and time as an integer.
    if(ctime_s( timeStr, sizeof(timeStr), &now) == 0)
        printf("Date and time: %s", timeStr);
```

Typical output for this code is:

```
Date and time: Sun May 17 14:40:04 2015
```

ctime(), asctime(), asctime_s(), localtime(), localtime_s(), gmtime(), gmtime_s(), difftime(), mktime(), strftime(), time()

difftime

Calculates the difference between two arithmetic time values.

```
#include <time.h>
double difftime( time_t time2, time_t time1 );
```

The difftime() function returns the difference between two time values, *time2 – time1*, as a number of seconds. While difftime() has the return type double, its arguments have the type time_t. The time_t type is usually, but not necessarily, defined as an integer type such as long or unsigned long.

A common way to obtain the argument values passed to difftime() is by successive calls to the time() function, which returns the current time as a single arithmetic value.

Example

See the sample program for clock() in this chapter.

See Also

asctime(), ctime(), gmtime(), localtime(), mktime(), strftime(), time()

div

Performs integer division, returning quotient and remainder.

```
#include <stdlib.h>
div_t div(int dividend, int divisor );
ldiv_t ldiv( long dividend, long divisor );
lldiv_t lldiv( long long dividend, long long divisor );        (C99)
```

The div() functions divide an integer *dividend* by an integer *divisor*, and return the integer part of the quotient along with the remainder in a structure of two integer members named quot and rem. div() obtains the quotient and remainder in a single machine operation, replacing both the / and % operations. The header file *stdlib.h* defines this structure for the various integer types as follows:

```
typedef struct { int quot; int rem; } div_t;
typedef struct { long int quot; long int rem; } ldiv_t;
typedef struct { long long int quot; long long int rem; } lldiv_t;
```

Example

```
int people, apples;
div_t  share;

for ( apples = -3 ; apples < 6 ; apples += 3 )
{
```

```
if ( apples == 0 )
  continue;                        // Don't bother dividing up nothing.
for ( people = -2 ; people < 4 ; people += 2 )
{
  if ( people == 0 )
    continue;                      // Don't try to divide by zero.
  share = div( apples, people );

  printf( "If there are %+i of us and %+i apples, "
          "we each get %+i with %+i left over.\n",
          people, apples, share.quot, share.rem );
  }
}
```

As the output of the preceding code illustrates, any nonzero remainder has the same sign as the dividend:

```
If there are -2 of us and -3 apples, we each get +1 with -1 left over.
If there are +2 of us and -3 apples, we each get -1 with -1 left over.
If there are -2 of us and +3 apples, we each get -1 with +1 left over.
If there are +2 of us and +3 apples, we each get +1 with +1 left over.
```

See Also

imaxdiv(), remainder()

erf   C99

Calculates the error function of a floating-point number.

```
#include <math.h>
double erf( double x );
float erff( float x );
long double erfl( long double x );
```

The function erf(), called the *error function*, is associated with the Gaussian function or normal distribution. If the measured values of a given random variable conform to a normal distribution with the standard deviation σ, then the probability that a single measurement has an error within ± a is erf(a / (σ × √2)).

The return value of erf(x) is

$$erf(x) = \frac{2}{\sqrt{\pi}} \cdot \int_0^x e^{-t^2} dt$$

The function erfc() is the complementary error function, defined as erfc(x) = 1 − erf(x).

Example

```
/*
 * Given a normal distribution with mean 0 and standard deviation 1,
 * calculate the probability that the random variable is within the
 * range [0, 1.125]
 */
double sigma = 1.0;          // The standard deviation
double bound = 1.125;
double probability;          // probability that mean <= value <= bound

probability = 0.5 *erf( bound / (sigma * sqrt(2.0)) );
```

See Also

erfc()

erfc   C99

Calculates the complementary error function of a floating-point number.

```
#include <math.h>
double erfc( double x );
float erfcf( float x );
long double erfcl( long double x );
```

The function erfc() is the complementary error function, defined as erfc(x) = 1 − erf(x).

See Also

erf()

exit

Terminates the program normally.

```
#include <stdlib.h>
_Noreturn void exit( int status );
```

The exit() function ends the program and returns a value to the operating environment to indicate the program's final status. Control never returns from the exit() function.

Before terminating the program, exit() calls any functions that have been registered by the atexit() function (in LIFO order), closes any open files, and deletes any files created by the tmpfile() function. Functions registered by at_quick_exit() are not called.

The header *stdlib.h* defines two macros for use as arguments to exit(): EXIT_SUCCESS and EXIT_FAILURE. If the argument is equal to one of these values, the program returns a corresponding system-specific value to the operating system to indicate success or failure. An argument value of 0 is treated the same as

EXIT_SUCCESS. For other argument values, the value returned to the host environment is determined by the implementation.

Example

```
FILE *f_in, *f_out;

enum { X_OK = 0, X_ARGS, X_NOIN, X_NOOUT };

if ( argc != 3 ) {
  fprintf( stderr, "Usage: program input-file output-file\n");
  exit( X_ARGS );
}

f_in  = fopen(argv[1], "r");
if ( f_in == NULL ) {
  fprintf( stderr, "Unable to open input file.\n");
  exit( X_NOIN );
}
f_out = fopen(argv[2], "a+");
if ( f_out == NULL ) {
  fprintf( stderr, "Unable to open output file.\n");
  exit( X_NOOUT );
}

/* ... read, process, write, close files ... */

exit( X_OK );
```

See Also

_Exit(), atexit(), abort()

exp

Calculates the natural exponential of a number.

```
#include <math.h>
double exp( double x );
float expf( float x );
long double expl( long double x );
```

The return value of the exp() function is e raised to the power of the function's argument, or e^x, where e is Euler's number, 2.718281.... If the result is beyond the range of the function's type, a range error occurs.

The natural exponential function exp() is the inverse of the natural logarithm function, log().

Example

```
/* Amount owed = principal * e^(interest_rate * time) */
int principal = 10000;     // Initial debt is ten thousand dollars.
int balance = 0;
double rate = 0.055;       // Interest rate is 5.5% annually.
double time = 1.5;         // Period is eighteen months.

balance = principal * exp( rate * time );
printf("Invest %d dollars at %.1f%% compound interest, and "
       "in %.1f years you'll have %d dollars.\n",
       principal, rate*100.0, time, balance );
```

This code produces the following output:

```
Invest 10000 dollars at 5.5% compound interest, and in 1.5 years
you'll have 10859 dollars.
```

See Also

The C99 exponential functions exp2() and expm1(); the exponential functions for complex numbers, cexp(), cexpf(), and cexpl(); the general exponential function pow()

exp2   C99

Calculates the base 2 exponential of a number.

```
#include <math.h>
double exp2( double x );
float exp2f( float x );
long double exp2l( long double x );
```

The return value of the exp2() function is 2 raised to the power of the function's argument, or 2^x. If the result is beyond the range of the function's type, a range error occurs.

The base 2 exponential function exp2() is the inverse of the base 2 logarithm function, log2().

Example

```
// The famous grains-of-rice-on-a-chessboard problem.
// The sultan loses a chess game. The wager was one grain for square 1
// on the chessboard, then double the last number for each successive
// square. How much rice in all?

int squares = 64;
long double gramspergrain = 0.0025L;     // A grain of rice weighs 25 mg.
long double sum = 0.0L;
```

```
for ( int i = 0; i < squares; i++ )
    sum += gramspergrain * exp2l( (long double)i );

printf( "The sultan's wager costs him %.3Lf metric tons of rice.\n",
        sum / 1000000.0L );            // A million grams per ton.
```

This code produces the following output:

```
The sultan's wager costs him 46116860184.274 metric tons of rice.
```

See Also

exp(), expm1(), log(), log1p(), log2(), log10()

expm1 C99

Calculates the natural exponential of a number, minus one.

```
#include <math.h>
double expm1( double x );
float expm1f( float x );
long double expm1l( long double x );
```

The return value of the expm1() function is one less than e raised to the power of
the function's argument, or e^x, where e is Euler's number, 2.718281.... The expm1()
function is designed to yield a more accurate result than the expression exp(x)-1,
especially when the value of the argument is close to zero. If the result is beyond the
range of the function's type, a range error occurs.

Example

```
/* let y = (-e^(-2x) - 1 ) / (e^(-2x) + 1), for certain values of x */

double w, x, y;
if (( x > 1.0E-12 ) && ( x < 1.0 ))
{
  w = expm1( -(x+x) );
  y = - w / ( w + 2.0 );
}
else
  /* ... handle other values of x ... */
```

See Also

exp(), log1p(), log()

fabs

Obtains the absolute value of a number.

```
#include <math.h>
double fabs( double x );
float fabsf( float x );
long double fabsl( long double x );
```

Library
Functions

Standard Library Functions | 413

The fabs() function returns the absolute value of its floating-point argument x; if x is greater than or equal to 0, the return value is equal to x. If x is less than 0, the function returns $-x$.

Example

```
float x = 4.0F * atanf( 1.0F );
long double y = 4.0L * atanl( 1.0L );

if ( x == y )
  printf( "x and y are exactly equal.\n" );
else if ( fabs( x - y ) < 0.0001 * fabsl( y ) )
  printf( "x and y are approximately equal:\n"
          "x is %.8f; y is %.8Lf.\n", x, y );
```

This code produces the following output:

```
x and y are approximately equal:
x is 3.14159274; y is 3.14159265.
```

See Also

The absolute value functions for integer types, abs(), labs(), llabs(), and imax abs(); the absolute value functions for complex numbers, cabs(), cabsf(), cabsl(); the C99 functions fdim() and copysign(); the functions fmax() and fmin()

fclose

Closes a file or stream.

```
#include <stdio.h>
int fclose( FILE *fp );
```

The fclose() function closes the file associated with a given FILE pointer, and releases the memory occupied by its I/O buffer. If the file was opened for writing, fclose() flushes the contents of the file buffer to the file.

The fclose() function returns 0 on success. If fclose() fails, it returns the value EOF.

Example

```
/* Print a file to the console, line by line. */
FILE *fp_infile;
char linebuffer[512];

if (( fp_infile= fopen("input.dat", "r")) == NULL )
{
  fprintf(stderr, "Couldn't open input file.\n");
  return -1;
}

while ( fgets( linebuffer, sizeof(linebuffer), fp_infile ) != NULL )
  fputs( linebuffer, stdout );
```

```
if ( ! feof(fp_infile) )    // This means "if not end of file"
  fprintf( stderr, "Error reading from input file.\n" );

if ( fclose(fp_infile) != 0 )
{
  fprintf(stderr, "Error closing input file.\n");
  return -2;
}
```

See Also

fflush(), fopen(), setbuf()

fdim   C99

Obtains the positive difference between two numbers.

```
#include <math.h>
double fdim( double x, double y );
float fdimf( float x, float y );
long double fdiml( long double x, long double y );
```

The fdim() function return $x - y$ or 0, whichever is greater. If the implementation
has signed zero values, the zero returned by fdim() is positive.

Example

```
/* Make sure an argument is within the domain of asin() */

double sign, argument, result;
/* ... */

sign = copysign( 1.0, argument );      // Save the sign ...
argument = copysign( argument, 1.0 );  // then use only positive values
argument = 1.0 - fdim( 1.0, argument ); // Trim excess beyond 1.0
result = asin( copysign(argument, sign) );  // Restore sign and
                                            // call asin()
```

See Also

copysign(), fabs(), fmax(), fmin()

feclearexcept   C99

Clears status flags in the floating-point environment.

```
#include <fenv.h>
int feclearexcept( int excepts );
```

The feclearexcept() function clears the floating-point exceptions specified by its
argument. The value of the argument is the bitwise OR of one or more of the integer
constant macros described under feraiseexcept() in this chapter.

The function returns 0 if successful; a nonzero return value indicates that an error occurred.

Example

```
double x, y, result;
int exceptions;

#pragma STDC FENV_ACCESS ON
feclearexcept( FE_ALL_EXCEPT );
result = somefunction( x, y );   // This function may raise exceptions!
exceptions = fetestexcept( FE_INEXACT | FE_UNDERFLOW );

if ( exceptions & FE_UNDERFLOW )
{
  /* ... handle the underflow ... */
}
else if ( exceptions & FE_INEXACT )
{
  /* ... handle the inexact result ... */
}
```

See Also

feraiseexcept(), feholdexcept(), fetestexcept()

fegetenv   C99

Stores a copy of the current floating-point environment.

```
#include <fenv.h>
int fegetenv( fenv_t *envp );
```

The fegetenv() function saves the current state of the floating-point environment in the object referenced by the pointer argument. The function returns 0 if successful; a nonzero return value indicates that an error occurred.

The object type that represents the floating-point environment, fenv_t, is defined in *fenv.h*. It contains at least two kinds of information: *floating-point status* flags, which are set to indicate specific floating-point processing exceptions, and a *floating-point control mode*, which can be used to influence the behavior of floating-point arithmetic, such as the direction of rounding.

Example

The fegetenv() and fesetenv() functions can be used to provide continuity of the floating-point environment between different locations in a program:

```
static fenv_t  fpenv;    // Global environment variables.
static jmp_buf env;
/* ... */

#pragma STDC FENV_ACCESS ON
fegetenv(&fpenv);          // Store a copy of the floating-point
                           // environment
```

```
if ( setjmp(env) == 0 )   // setjmp() returns 0 when actually called
{
  /* ... Proceed normally; floating-point environment unchanged ... */
}
else                    // Nonzero return value means longjmp() occurred
{
  fesetenv(&fpenv);     // Restore floating-point environment
                        // to known state
  /* ... */
}
```

See Also

fegetexceptflag(), feholdexcept(), fesetenv(), feupdateenv(), feclearex
cept(), feraiseexcept(), fetestexcept()

fegetexceptflag   C99

Stores the floating-point environment's exception status flags.

```
#include <fenv.h>
int fegetexceptflag( fexcept_t *flagp, int excepts );
```

The fegetexceptflag() function saves the current state of specified status flags in
the floating-point environment, which indicate specific floating-point processing
exceptions, in the object referenced by the pointer argument. The object type that
represents the floating-point status flags, fexcept_t, is defined in *fenv.h*. Unlike the
integer argument that represents the floating-point exception status flags in this and
other functions that manipulate the floating-point environment, the object with
type fexcept_t cannot be directly modified by user programs.

The integer argument is a bitwise OR of the values of macros defined in *fenv.h* to
represent the floating-point exception flags. The macros are listed under feraiseex
cept() in this chapter. fegetexceptflag() stores the state of those flags that correspond to the values that are set in this mask.

The function returns 0 if successful; a nonzero return value indicates that an error
occurred.

Example

```
/* Temporarily store the state of the FE_INEXACT, FE_UNDERFLOW
 * and FE_OVERFLOW flags
 */
fexcept_t fpexcepts;

#pragma STDC FENV_ACCESS ON
/* Save state: */
fegetexceptflag( &fpexcepts, FE_INEXACT | FE_UNDERFLOW | FE_OVERFLOW );

feclearexcept( FE_INEXACT | FE_UNDERFLOW | FE_OVERFLOW );
```

```
/* ... Perform calculations that might raise those exceptions ... */

/* ... Handle (or ignore) the exceptions our calculations raised ... */

/* Restore state as saved: */
fesetexceptflag( &fpexcepts, FE_INEXACT | FE_UNDERFLOW | FE_OVERFLOW );
```
See Also

fesetexceptflag(), feraiseexcept(), feclearexcept(), fetestexcept()

fegetround   C99

Determines the current rounding direction in the floating-point environment.

```
#include <fenv.h>
int fegetround( void );
```

The fegetround() function obtains the current rounding direction. The integer
return value is negative if the rounding direction is undetermined, or equal to one
of the following macros, defined in *fenv.h* as integer constants, if the function is successful:

FE_DOWNWARD
> Round down to the next lower integer.

FE_UPWARD
> Round up to the next greater integer.

FE_TONEAREST
> Round up or down toward whichever integer is nearest.

FE_TOWARDZERO
> Round positive values downward and negative values upward.

Example

See the examples for fmod() and fesetround() in this chapter.

See Also

fesetround(), fegetenv(), fegetexceptflag()

feholdexcept   C99

Saves the current floating-point environment and switches to nonstop mode.

```
#include <fenv.h>
int feholdexcept( fenv_t *envp );
```

Like fegetenv(), the feholdexcept() function saves the current floating-point
environment in the object pointed to by the pointer argument. However,
feholdexcept() also clears the floating-point status flags and switches the floating-

point environment to a *nonstop mode*, meaning that after any floating-point exception, normal execution continues uninterrupted by signals or traps. The function returns 0 if it succeeds in switching to nonstop floating-point processing; otherwise, the return value is nonzero.

Example

```
/*
 * Compute the hypotenuse of a right triangle, avoiding intermediate
 * overflow or underflow.
 *
 * (This example ignores the case of one argument having
 * great magnitude and the other small, causing both overflow
 * and underflow!)
 */
double hypotenuse(double sidea, double sideb)
{
#pragma STDC FENV_ACCESS ON
  double  sum, scale, ascaled, bscaled, invscale;
  fenv_t fpenv;
  int    fpeflags;

  if ( signbit( sidea ) ) sidea = fabs( sidea );
  if ( signbit( sideb ) ) sideb = fabs( sideb );

  feholdexcept(&fpenv);   // Save previous environment,
                          // clear exceptions,
                          // switch to nonstop processing.
  invscale = 1.0;
  sum = sidea * sidea + sideb * sideb;    // First try whether a^2 + b^2
                                          // causes any exceptions.

  fpeflags = fetestexcept(FE_UNDERFLOW | FE_OVERFLOW);   // Did it?
  if ( fpeflags & FE_OVERFLOW && sidea > 1.0 && sideb > 1.0 )
  {
    /* a^2 + b^2 caused an overflow. Scale the triangle down. */
    feclearexcept(FE_OVERFLOW);
    scale = scalbn(1.0, (DBL_MIN_EXP /2 ));
    invscale = 1.0 / scale;
    ascaled = scale * sidea;
    bscaled = scale * sideb;
    sum = ascaled * ascaled + bscaled * bscaled;
  }
  else if (fpeflags & FE_UNDERFLOW && sidea < 1.0 && sideb < 1.0 )
  {
    /* a^2 + b^2 caused an underflow. Scale the triangle up. */
    feclearexcept(FE_UNDERFLOW);
    scale = scalbn(1.0, (DBL_MAX_EXP /2 ));
    invscale = 1.0 / scale;
    ascaled = scale * sidea;
    bscaled = scale * sideb;
    sum = ascaled * ascaled + bscaled * bscaled;
  }
```

```
    feupdateenv(&fpenv);          // restore the caller's environment, and
                                  // raise any new exceptions

    /* c = (1/scale) * sqrt((a * scale)^2 + (b * scale)^2): */
    return invscale * sqrt(sum);
}
```

See Also

fegetenv(), fesetenv(), feupdateenv(), feclearexcept(), feraiseexcept(), fegetexceptflag(), fesetexceptflag(), fetestexcept()

feof

Tests whether the file position is at the end.

```
#include <stdio.h>
int feof( FILE *fp );
```

The feof() macro tests whether the file position indicator of a given file is at the end of the file.

The feof() macro's argument is a FILE pointer. One attribute of the file or stream referenced by this pointer is the end-of-file flag, that indicates whether the program has attempted to read past the end of the file. The feof() macro tests the end-of-file flag and returns a nonzero value if the flag is set. If not, feof() returns 0.

Example

See the examples for clearerr() and fclose() in this chapter.

See Also

rewind(), fseek(), clearerr(), ferror()

feraiseexcept   C99

Raises floating-point exceptions.

```
#include <fenv.h>
int feraiseexcept( int excepts );
```

The feraiseexcept() function raises the floating-point exceptions represented by its argument. Unlike the fesetexceptflag() function, feraiseexcept() invokes any traps that have been enabled for the given exceptions.

The argument is a bitwise OR of the values of the following macros, defined in *fenv.h* to represent the floating-point exception flags:

FE_DIVBYZERO
    This exception occurs when a nonzero, noninfinite number is divided by zero.

FE_INEXACT

This exception indicates that true result of an operation cannot be represented with the available precision, and has been rounded in the current rounding direction.

FE_INVALID

This exception flag is set when the program attempts an operation which has no defined result, such as dividing zero by zero or subtracting infinity from infinity. Some systems may also set FE_INVALID whenever an overflow or underflow exception is raised.

FE_OVERFLOW

The result of an operation exceeds the range of representable values.

FE_UNDERFLOW

The result of an operation is nonzero, but too small in magnitude to be represented.

Each of these macros is defined if and only if the system supports the corresponding floating-point exception. Furthermore, the macro FE_ALL_EXCEPT is the bitwise OR of all of the macros that are supported.

If feraiseexcept() raises the FE_INEXACT exception in conjunction with FE_UNDER FLOW or FE_OVERFLOW, then the underflow or overflow exception is raised first. Otherwise, multiple exceptions are raised in an unspecified order.

The function returns 0 if successful; a nonzero return value indicates that an error occurred.

Example

Although user programs rarely need to raise a floating-point exception by artificial means, the following example illustrates how to do so:

```
int result, except_set, except_test;

#pragma STDC FENV_ACCESS ON
feclearexcept (FE_ALL_EXCEPT);
except_set = FE_OVERFLOW;
result = feraiseexcept( except_set );
if ( result != 0 )
{
  printf( "feraisexcept() failed (%d)\n", result );
  exit( result );
}
except_test = fetestexcept( except_set );
if ( except_test != except_set )
  printf( "Tried to raise flags %X, but only raised flags %X.\n",
          except_set, except_test );
```

feclearexcept(), feholdexcept(), fetestexcept(), fegetexceptflag(), fesetex ceptflag()

ferror

Tests whether a file access error has occurred.

```
#include <stdio.h>
int ferror( FILE *fp );
```

The ferror() function—often implemented as a macro—tests whether an error has been registered in reading or writing a given file.

ferror()'s argument is a FILE pointer. One attribute of the file or stream referenced by this pointer is an error flag which indicates that an error has occurred during a read or write operation. The ferror() function or macro tests the error flag and returns a nonzero value if the flag is set. If not, ferror() returns 0.

Example

See the examples for clearerr() and fclose() in this chapter.

See Also

rewind(), clearerr(), feof()

fesetenv   C99

Sets the floating-point environment to a previously saved state.

```
#include <fenv.h>
int fesetenv( const fenv_t *envp );
```

The fesetenv() function reinstates the floating-point environment from an object obtained by a prior call to fegetenv() or feholdexcept(), or a macro such as FE_DFL_ENV, which is defined as a pointer to an object of type fenv_t representing the default floating-point environment. Although a call to fesetenv() may result in floating-point exception flags being set, the function does not raise the corresponding exceptions. The function returns 0 if successful; a nonzero return value indicates that an error occurred.

Example

See the example for fegetenv() in this chapter.

See Also

fegetenv(), feholdexcept(), fegetexceptflag(), fesetexceptflag(), feupda teenv(), feclearexcept(), feraiseexcept(), fetestexcept()

fesetexceptflag C99

Reinstates the floating-point environment's exception status flags.

```
#include <fenv.h>
int fesetexceptflag( const fexcept_t *flagp, int excepts );
```

The `fesetexceptflag()` function resets the exception status flags in the floating-point environment to a state that was saved by a prior call to `fegetexceptflag()`. The object type that represents the floating-point status flags, `fexcept_t`, is defined in *fenv.h*.

The second argument is a bitwise OR of the values of macros defined in *fenv.h* to represent the floating-point exception flags. The macros are listed under `feraiseex cept()` in this chapter. `fesetexceptflag()` sets those flags that correspond to the values that are set in this mask.

All of the flags specified in the mask argument must be represented in the status flags object passed to `fesetexceptflag()` as the first argument. Thus, in the `fegetexceptflag()` call used to save the flags, the second argument must have specified at least all of the flags to be set by the call to `fesetexceptflag()`.

The function returns 0 if successful (or if the value of the integer argument was zero). A nonzero return value indicates that an error occurred.

Example

See the example for `fegetexceptflag()` in this chapter.

See Also

`fegetexceptflag()`, `feraiseexcept()`, `feclearexcept()`, `fetestexcept()`, `fege tenv()`, `feholdexcept()`, `fesetenv()`, `feupdateenv()`

fesetround C99

Sets the rounding direction in the floating-point environment.

```
#include <fenv.h>
int fesetround( int round );
```

The `fesetround()` function sets the current rounding direction in the program's floating-point environment to the direction indicated by its argument. On success, the function returns 0. If the argument's value does not correspond to a rounding direction, the current rounding direction is not changed.

Recognized values of the argument are given by macros in the following list, defined in *fenv.h* as integer constants. A given implementation may not define all of these macros if it does not support the corresponding rounding direction, and may also define macro names for other rounding modes that it does support.

FE_DOWNWARD

    Round down to the next lower integer.

FE_UPWARD

    Round up to the next greater integer.

FE_TONEAREST

    Round up or down toward whichever integer is nearest.

FE_TOWARDZERO

    Round positive values downward and negative values upward.

The function returns zero if successful; a nonzero return value indicates that an error occurred.

Example

```
/*
 * Save, set, and restore the rounding direction.
 * Report an error and abort if setting the rounding direction fails.
 */
#pragma STDC FENV_ACCESS ON
int prev_rounding_dir;
int result;
prev_rounding_dir = fegetround();
result = fesetround( FE_TOWARDZERO );

/* ... perform a calculation that requires rounding toward 0 ... */

fesetround( prev_rounding_dir );
#pragma STDC FENV_ACCESS OFF
```

See also the example for fmod() in this chapter.

See Also

fegetround(), round(), lround(), llround(), nearbyint(), rint(), lrint(), llrint()

fetestexcept   C99

Tests the status flags in the floating-point environment against a bit mask.

```
#include <fenv.h>
int fetestexcept( int excepts );
```

The fetestexcept() function takes as its argument a bitwise OR of the values of macros defined in *fenv.h* to represent the floating-point exception flags. The macros are listed under feraiseexcept() in this chapter.

fetestexcept() returns the bitwise AND of the values representing the exception flags that were set in the argument and the exception flags that are currently set in the floating-point environment.

Example

See the examples for feclearexcept() and feholdexcept() in this chapter.

See Also

feclearexcept(), feraiseexcept(), feholdexcept(), fesetexceptflag(), feupdateenv(), fegetenv(), fesetenv()

feupdateenv $\hspace{6cm}$ C99

Sets the floating-point environment to a previously saved state, but preserves exceptions.

```
#include <fenv.h>
void feupdateenv( const fenv_t *envp );
```

The feupdateenv() function internally saves the current floating-point exception status flags before installing the floating-point environment stored in the object referenced by its pointer argument. Then the function raises floating-point exceptions that were set in the saved status flags.

The argument must be a pointer to an object obtained by a prior call to fegetenv() or feholdexcept(), or a macro such as FE_DFL_ENV, which is defined as a pointer to an object of type fenv_t representing the default floating-point environment.

The function returns 0 if successful; a nonzero return value indicates that an error occurred.

Example

See the example for feholdexcept() in this chapter.

See Also

fegetexceptflag(), feraiseexcept(), feclearexcept(), fetestexcept(), fegetenv(), feholdexcept(), fesetenv(), feupdateenv()

fflush

Clears a file buffer.

```
#include <stdio.h>
int fflush( FILE *fp );
```

The fflush() function empties the I/O buffer of the open file specified by the FILE pointer argument. If the file was opened for writing, or if it was opened for reading and writing and the last operation on it was not a read operation, fflush() writes the contents of the file. If the file is only opened for reading, the behavior of fflush() is not specified by the standard. Most implementations simply clear the input buffer. The function returns 0 if successful, or EOF if an error occurs in writing to the file.

The argument passed to fflush() may be a null pointer. In this case, fflush() flushes the output buffers of all the program's open streams. The fflush() function does not close the file, and has no effect at all on unbuffered files (see "Files" on page 211 for more information on unbuffered input and output).

Example

In the following example, the program *fflush.c* writes two lines of text to a file. If the macro FLUSH is defined, the program flushes the file output buffer to disk after each line. If not, only the first output line is explicitly flushed. Then the program raises a signal to simulate a fatal error so that we can observe the effect with and without the second fflush() call.

```
/* fflush.c: Tests the effect of flushing output file buffers. */
FILE *fp;

#ifdef FLUSH
char filename[ ] = "twice.txt";
#else
char filename[ ] = "once.txt";
#endif /* FLUSH */

fp = fopen( filename, "w" );
if ( fp == NULL )
  fprintf( stderr, "Failed to open file '%s' to write.\n", filename );

fputs( "Going once ...\n", fp );
fflush( fp );                // Flush the output unconditionally

fputs( "Going twice ...\n", fp );

#ifdef FLUSH
fflush( fp );                // Now flush only if compiled with '-DFLUSH'
#endif

raise( SIGKILL );           // End the program abruptly.

fputs( "Gone.\n", fp );     // These three lines will never be executed.
fclose( fp );
exit( 0 );
```

When we compile and test the program, the output looks like this:

```
$cc -DFLUSH -o fflushtwice fflush.c
$ ./fflushtwice
Killed
$ cc -o fflushonce fflush.c
$ ./fflushonce
Killed
$ ls -l
-rw-r--r--   1 tony    tony         781 Jul 22 12:36 fflush.c
-rwxr-xr-x   1 tony    tony       12715 Jul 22 12:38 fflushonce
-rwxr-xr-x   1 tony    tony       12747 Jul 22 12:37 fflushtwice
```

```
-rw-r--r--    1 tony     tony          15 Jul 22 12:38 once.txt
-rw-r--r--    1 tony     tony          31 Jul 22 12:37 twice.txt
```

The two cc commands have created two different executables, named *fflushonce* and *fflushtwice*, and each version of the program has run and killed itself in the process of generating an output file. The contents of the two output files, *once.txt* and *twice.txt*, are different:

```
$cat twice.txt
Going once ...
Going twice ...
$ cat once.txt
Going once ...
$
```

When the fputs() call returned, the output string was still in the file buffer, waiting for the operating system to write it to disk. Without the second fflush() call, the intervening "kill" signal caused the system to abort the program, closing all its files, before the disk write occurred.

See Also

setbuf(), setvbuf()

fgetc

Reads a character from a file.

```
#include <stdio.h>
int fgetc( FILE *fp );
```

The fgetc() function reads the character at the current file position in the specified file, and increments the file position.

The return value of fgetc() has the type int. If the file position is at the end of the file, or if the end-of-file flag was already set, fgetc() returns EOF and sets the end-of-file flag. If you convert the function's return value to char, you might no longer be able to distinguish a value of EOF from a valid character such as '\xFF'.

Example

```
FILE *fp;
int c;
char buffer[1024];
int i = 0;

/* ... Open input file ... */

while ( i < 1023 )
{
  c = fgetc( fp );       // Returns a character on success;
  if (c == EOF)          // EOF means either an error or end-of-file.
  {
    if (feof( fp ))
```

```
      fprintf( stderr, "End of input.\n" );
    else if ( ferror( fp ))
      fprintf( stderr, "Input error.\n" );
    clearerr( fp );       // Clear the file's error or EOF flag.
    break;
  }
  else
  {
    buffer[i++] = (char) c;  // Use value as char *after* checking
                             // for EOF.
  }
}
buffer[i] = '\0';          // Terminate string.
```

See Also

getc(), getchar(), putc(), fputc(), fgets(), fgetwc(), getwc()

fgetpos

Obtains the current read/write position in a file.

```
#include <stdio.h>
int fgetpos( FILE * restrict fp, fpos_t * restrict ppos );
```

The fgetpos() function determines the current value of the file position indicator in an open file, and places the value in the variable referenced by the pointer argument *ppos*. You can use this value in subsequent calls to fsetpos() to restore the file position.

If the FILE pointer argument refers to a multibyte stream, then the fgetpos() function also obtains the stream's multibyte parsing state. In this case, the type fpos_t is defined as a structure to hold both the file position information and the parsing state.

The fgetpos() function returns 0 if successful. If an error occurs, fgetpos() returns a nonzero return value and sets the errno variable to indicate the type of error.

Example

```
FILE *datafile; fpos_t bookmark;

if ((datafile = fopen(".testfile", "r+")) == NULL)
{
  fprintf( stderr, "Unable to open file %s.\n",".testfile" );
  return 1;
}

if ( fgetpos( datafile, &bookmark ))    // Save initial position
  perror( "Saving file position" );
else
{
  /* ... Read data, modify data ... */
```

```
    if ( fsetpos( datafile, &bookmark ))      // Back to initial position
        perror( "Restoring file position" );

    /* ... write data back at the original position in the file ... */
}
```

See Also

fsetpos( ), fseek( ), ftell( ), rewind( )

fgets

Reads a string from a file.

```
#include <stdio.h>
char *fgets( char * restrict buffer, int n, FILE * restrict fp );
```

The fgets( ) function reads a sequence of up to *n* − 1 characters from the file referenced by the FILE pointer argument, and writes it to the buffer indicated by the
char pointer argument, appending the string terminator character '\0'. If a newline character ('\n') is read, reading stops and the string written to the buffer is terminated after the newline character.

The fgets( ) function returns the pointer to the string buffer if anything was written to it, or a null pointer if an error occurred or if the file position indicator was at
the end of the file.

Example

```
FILE *titlefile;
char title[256];
int counter = 0;

if ((titlefile = fopen("titles.txt", "r")) == NULL)
    perror( "Opening title file" );
else
{
    while ( fgets( title, 256, titlefile ) != NULL )
    {
        title[ strlen(title) -1 ] = '\0';    // Trim off newline character.
        printf( "%3d: \"%s\"\n", ++counter, title );
    }
    /* fgets() returned NULL: either EOF or an error occurred. */
    if ( feof(titlefile) )
        printf("Total: %d titles.\n", counter);
}
```

If the working directory contains an appropriate text file, the program produces
output like this:

```
    1: "The Amazing Maurice"
    2: "La condition humaine"
    3: "Die Eroberung der Maschinen"
 Total: 3 titles.
```

See Also

fputs( ), puts( ), fgetc( ), fgetws( ), fputws( )

fgetwc

Reads a wide character from a file.

```
#include <stdio.h>
#include <wchar.h>
wint_t fgetwc( FILE *fp );
```

The fgetwc( ) function reads the wide character at the current file position in the specified file and increments the file position.

The return value of fgetwc( ) has the type wint_t. If the file position is at the end of the file, or if the end-of-file flag was already set, fgetwc( ) returns WEOF and sets the end-of-file flag. If a wide-character encoding error occurs, fgetwc( ) sets the errno variable to EILSEQ ("illegal sequence") and returns WEOF. Use feof( ) and ferror( ) to distinguish errors from end-of-file conditions.

Example

```
char file_in[ ]  = "local_in.txt",
     file_out[ ] = "local_out.txt";
FILE *fp_in_wide, *fp_out_wide;
wint_t wc;

if ( setlocale( LC_CTYPE, "" ) == NULL)
  fwprintf( stderr,
          L"Sorry, couldn't change to the system's native locale.\n"),
  exit(1);

if (( fp_in_wide = fopen( file_in, "r" )) == NULL )
  fprintf( stderr, "Error opening the file %s\n", file_in), exit(2);

if (( fp_out_wide = fopen( file_out, "w" )) == NULL )
  fprintf( stderr, "Error opening the file %s\n", file_out), exit(3);

fwide( fp_in_wide, 1);      // Not strictly necessary, since first
fwide( fp_out_wide, 1);     // file access also sets wide or byte mode.

while (( wc = fgetwc( fp_in_wide )) != WEOF )
{
  // ... process each wide character read ...

  if ( fputwc( (wchar_t)wc, fp_out_wide) == WEOF)
    break;
}
```

```
if ( ferror( fp_in_wide))
  fprintf( stderr, "Error reading the file %s\n", file_in);
if ( ferror( fp_out_wide))
  fprintf( stderr, "Error writing to the file %s\n", file_out);
```

See Also

getwc( ), getwchar( ), fputwc( ), putwc( ), fgetc( )

fgetws

Reads a wide-character string from a file.

```
#include <stdio.h>
#include <wchar.h>
wchar_t *fgetws( wchar_t * restrict buffer, int n, FILE * restrict fp );
```

The fgetws() function reads a sequence of up to $n - 1$ wide characters from the file referenced by the FILE pointer argument, and writes it to the wchar_t array addressed by the pointer argument *buffer*, appending the string terminator character L'\0'. If a newline character (L'\n') is read, reading stops and the string written to the buffer is terminated after the newline character.

The fgetws() function returns the pointer to the wide-string buffer if anything was written to it, or a null pointer if an error occurred or if the file position indicator was at the end of the file.

Example

```
FILE *fp_in_wide;
wchar_t buffer[4096];
wchar_t *line = buffer;

if (( fp_in_wide = fopen( "local.doc", "r" )) == NULL )
  perror( "Opening input file" );
fwide( fp_in_wide );

line = fgetws( buffer, sizeof(buffer), fp_in_wide );
if ( line == NULL )
  perror( "Reading from input file" );
```

See Also

fputws( ), putwc( ), fgetwc( ), fgets( ), fputs( )

floor

Rounds a real number down to an integer value.

```
#include <math.h>
double floor( double x );
float floorf( float x );          (C99)
long double floorl( long double x );          (C99)
```

The floor() function returns the greatest integer that is less than or equal to its argument. However, the function does not have an integer *type*; it returns an integer *value*, but with a floating-point type.

Example

```
/* Scale a point by independent x and y factors */
struct point { int x, y; };

int width_orig = 1024, height_orig = 768;
int width_new = 800, height_new = 600;

struct point scale( struct point orig )
{
  struct point new;
  new.x = (int)floor(orig.x * (double)width_new  / (double)width_orig);
  new.y = (int)floor(orig.y * (double)height_new / (double)height_orig);
  return new;
}
```

See Also

ceil(), round(); the C99 rounding functions that return floating-point types, trunc(), rint(), nearbyint(), nextafter(), and nexttoward(); the C99 rounding functions that return integer types, lrint(), lround(), llrint(), and llround(); the fesetround() and fegetround() functions, which operate on the C99 floating-point environment

fma   C99

Multiplies two numbers and adds a third number to their product.

```
#include <math.h>
double fma( double x, double y, double z );
float fmaf( float x, float y, float z );
long double fmal( long double x, long double y, long double z );
```

The name of the fma() function stands for "fused multiply-add." fma() multiplies its first two floating-point arguments, and then adds the third argument to the result. The advantage over the expression $(x * y) + z$, with two separate arithmetic operations, is that fma() avoids the error that would be incurred by intermediate rounding, as well as intermediate overflows or underflows that might otherwise be caused by the separate multiplication.

If the implementation defines the macro FP_FAST_FMA in *math.h*, that indicates that the fma() function is about as fast to execute as, or faster than, the expression $(x * y) + z$. This is typically the case if the fma() function makes use of a special FMA machine operation. The corresponding macros FP_FAST_FMAF and FP_FAST_FMAL provide the same information about the float and long double versions.

Example

```
double x, y, z;

x = nextafter( 3.0, 4.0 ); // Smallest possible double value
                           // greater than 3
y = 1.0/3.0;
z = -1.0;

printf( "x = %.15G\n"
        "y = %.15G\n"
        "z = %.15G\n", x, y, z );

#ifdef FP_FAST_FMA

printf( "fma( x, y, z) = %.15G\n", fma( x, y, z) );

#else     // i.e., not def FP_FAST_FMA

double product = x * y;

printf( "x times y = %.15G\n", product );
printf( "%.15G + z = %.15G\n", product, product + z );

#endif    // def FP_FAST_FMA
```

fmax C99

Determines the greater of two floating-point numbers.

```
#include <math.h>
double fmax( double x, double y );
float fmaxf( float x, float y );
long double fmaxl( long double x , long double y );
```

The fmax() functions return the value of the greater argument.

Example

```
// Let big equal the second-greatest-possible double value ...
const double big = nextafter( DBL_MAX, 0.0 );
// ... and small the second-least possible-double value:
const double small = nextafter( DBL_MIN, 0.0 );

double a, b, c;

/* ... */

if ( fmin( fmin( a, b ), c ) <= small )
  printf( "At least one value is too small.\n" );
if ( fmax( fmax( a, b ), c ) >= big )
  printf( "At least one value is too great.\n" );
```

See Also

fabs(), fmin()

fmin   C99

Determines the lesser of two floating-point numbers.

```
#include <math.h>
double fmin( double x, double y );
float fminf( float x, float y );
long double fminl( long double x , long double y );
```

The fmin() functions return the value of the lesser argument.

Example

See the example for fmax().

See Also

fabs(), fmax()

fmod

Performs the modulo operation.

```
#include <math.h>
double fmod( double x, double y );
float fmodf( float x, float y );        (C99)
long double fmodl( long double x, long double y );    (C99)
```

The fmod() function returns the remainder of the floating-point division of x by y, called "x modulo y." The remainder is equal to x minus the product of y and the largest integer quotient whose absolute value is not greater than that of y. This quotient is negative (or 0) if x and y have opposite signs, and the return value has the same sign as x. If the argument y is zero, fmod() may incur a domain error, or return 0.

Example

```
double people = -2.25, apples = 3.3, eachgets = 0.0, someleft = 0.0;
int saverounding = fegetround();      // Save previous setting

fesetround(FE_TOWARDZERO);

eachgets = rint( apples / people );
someleft = fmod( apples, people );

printf( "If there are %+.2f of us and %+.2f apples, \n"
        "each of us gets %+.2f, with %+.2f left over.\n",
        people, apples, eachgets, someleft );

fesetround( saverounding );           // Restore previous setting
```

This code produces the following output:

```
If there are -2.25 of us and +3.30 apples,
each of us gets -1.00, with +1.05 left over.
```

See Also

The C99 functions remainder() and remquo()

fopen

Opens a file.

```
#include <stdio.h>
FILE *fopen( const char * restrict name, const char * restrict mode );
```

The fopen() function opens the file with the specified name. The second argument is a character string that specifies the requested access mode. The possible values of the mode string argument are shown in Table 18-2.

fopen() returns the FILE pointer for you to use in subsequent input or output operations on the file, or a null pointer if the function fails to open the file with the requested access mode.

Table 18-2. File access modes

Mode string	Access mode	Notes
"r" "r+"	Read Read and write	The file must already exist
"w" "w+"	Write Write and read	If the file does not exist, fopen() creates it; if it does exist, fopen() erases its contents on opening
"a" "a+"	Append Append and read	If the file does not exist, fopen() creates it

When a file is first opened, the file position indicator points to the first byte in the file. If a file is opened with the mode string "a" or "a+", then the file position indicator is automatically placed at the end of the file before each write operation so that existing data in the file cannot be written over.

If the mode string includes a plus sign, then the mode allows both input and output, and you must synchronize the file position indicator between reading from and writing to the file. Do this by calling fflush() or a file-positioning function—fseek(), fsetpos(), or rewind()—after writing and before reading, and by calling a file-positioning function after reading and before writing (unless it's certain that you have read to the end of the file).

The mode string may also include b as the second or third letter (that is, "ab+" is the same as "a+b", for example), which indicates a binary file, as opposed to a text file. The exact significance of this distinction depends on the given system.

The C11 standard allows you to create a file *exclusively*: this means that the fopen()
call fails if the file already exists. To do so, append an "x" to the file mode strings that
begin with "w", forming, for example, the mode string "wx" or "w+bx".

Example

```
FILE *in, *out;
int c;

if ( argc != 3 )
  fprintf( stderr, "Usage: program input-file output-file\n"), exit(1);

// If "-" appears in place of input filename, use stdin:
in = (strcmp(argv[1], "-") == 0) ? stdin  : fopen(argv[1], "r");
if ( in == NULL )
  { perror( "Opening input file" ); return -1; }

// If "-" appears in place of output filename, use stdout:
out = (strcmp(argv[2], "-") == 0) ? stdout : fopen(argv[2], "a+");
if ( out == NULL )
  { perror( "Opening output file" ); return -1; }

while (( c = fgetc( in )) != EOF)
  if ( fputc(c, out) == EOF )
    break;

if ( !feof( in ))
  perror( "Error while copying" );
fclose(in), fclose(out);
```

See Also

fopen_s(), fclose(), fflush(), freopen(), setbuf()

fopen_s   C11

Opens a file.

```
#include <stdio.h>
errno_t fopen_s( FILE * restrict * restrict streamPtr,
        const char * restrict name, const char * restrict mode );
```

The function fopen_s(), like fopen(), opens a file with the specified name and
access mode. For the possible values of the mode string argument, see the description of the fopen() function in this chapter. The new FILE pointer is given to the
caller, not as the return value but in the variable addressed by the first argument of
fopen_s(). The type of the parameter streamPtr is therefore a pointer to a FILE
pointer.

If the operating system supports opening files for exclusive write access, fopen_s()
does so to prevent simultaneous write operations to the file. The fopen_s() function assigns access privileges to the file so that no other user can open it, provided

the operating system supports such access restrictions. To assign a new file the system's default access privileges, as fopen() does, prefix the letter "u" to the mode string, forming a string such as "uwx" or "ua+", for example.

Before opening the file, the function fopen_s() tests the following runtime constraints: the pointer arguments *streamPtr*, *name*, and *mode* must not be null pointers.

If the file has been opened successfully, fopen_s() returns zero, and writes the new FILE pointer to the variable addressed by *streamPtr*. If unsuccessful, the function returns a nonzero value and places a null pointer in the variable addressed by *streamPtr*, provided *streamPtr* is not a null pointer itself.

Example

```
#define __STDC_WANT_LIB_EXT1__ 1
#include <stdio.h>
// ...

    FILE *fp;   errno_t err;   char filename[] = "new.txt";

    // Open a new file for writing and reading:
    err = fopen_s( &fp, filename, "w+x");
    if( err != 0)
    {
        fprintf(stderr, "Unable to create the file \"%s\".\n", filename);
        exit(err);
    }
    // ... The file is open.
```

See Also

fopen(), fclose(), freopen(), freopen_s(), setbuf()

fpclassify   C99

Obtains a classification of a real floating-point number.

```
#include <math.h>
int fpclassify( x );
```

The fpclassify() macro determines whether its argument is a normal floating-point number, or one of several special categories of values, including NaN (not a number), infinity, subnormal floating-point values, zero, and possibly other implementation-specific categories.

To determine what category the argument belongs to, compare the return value of fpclassify() with the values of the following number classification macros, defined in *math.h*:

FP_INFINITE

FP_NAN

```
FP_NORMAL
FP_SUBNORMAL
FP_ZERO
```

These five macros expand to distinct integer values.

Example

```
double minimum( double a, double b )
{
  register int aclass = fpclassify( a );
  register int bclass = fpclassify( b );

  if ( aclass == FP_NAN || bclass == FP_NAN )
    return NAN;

  if ( aclass == FP_INFINITE )        // -Inf is less than anything;
    return ( signbit( a ) ? a : b );  // +inf is greater than anything.

  if ( bclass == FP_INFINITE )
    return ( signbit( b ) ? b : a );

  return ( a < b ? a : b );
}
```

See Also

isfinite(), isinf(), isnan(), isnormal(), signbit()

fprintf, fprintf_s

Writes formatted output to an open file.

```
#include <stdio.h>
int fprintf( FILE * restrict fp, const char * restrict format, ... );
int fprintf_s( FILE * restrict fp,
               const char * restrict format, ... );        (C11)
```

The functions fprintf() and fprintf_s() are similar to printf() and printf_s() except that they write their output to the stream specified by *fp* instead of stdout.

Example

```
FILE *fp_log;
time_t sec;

fp_log = fopen("example.log", "a");
if ( fp != NULL)
{
  time(&sec);
  fprintf( fp_log, "%.24s Opened log file.\n", ctime( &sec ) );
}
```

This code appends a line like the following to the file *example.log*:

```
Wed Dec  9 21:10:43 2015 Opened log file.
```

printf(), sprintf(), snprintf(), declared in *stdio.h*; vprintf(), vfprintf(), vsprintf(), vsnprintf(), declared in *stdio.h* and *stdarg.h*; the wide-character functions wprintf(), fwprintf(), swprintf(), declared in *stdio.h* and *wchar.h*; vwprint(), vfwprint(), and vswprint(), declared in *stdio.h*, *wchar.*h, and *stdarg.h*; the scanf() input functions. Argument conversion in the printf() family of functions is described under printf() in this chapter.

For each of these functions there is also a corresponding "secure" function, if the implementation supports the C11 bounds-checking functions (i.e., if the macro __STDC_LIB_EXT1__ is defined)

fputc

Writes a character to a file.

```
#include <stdio.h>
int fputc( int c, FILE *fp );
```

The fputc() function writes one character to the current file position of the specified FILE pointer. The return value is the character written, or EOF if an error occurred.

Example

```
#define CYCLES 10000
#define DOTS 4

printf("Performing %d modulo operations ", CYCLES );
for (int count = 0; count < CYCLES; ++count)
{
    if ( count % ( CYCLES / DOTS ) != 0) continue;
    fputc( '.', stdout );              // Mark every nth cycle
}
printf( " done.\n" );
```

This code produces the following output:

```
Performing 10000 modulo operations .... done.
```

See Also

putc(), fgetc(), fputwc()

fputs

Writes a string to a file.

```
#include <stdio.h>
int fputs( const char * restrict string, FILE * restrict fp );
```

The fputs() function writes a string to the file specified by the FILE pointer argument. The string is written without the terminator character ('\0'). If successful, fputs() returns a value greater than or equal to zero. A return value of EOF indicates that an error occurred.

Example

See the examples for fclose() and fflush() in this chapter.

See Also

fgets(), fputws()

fputwc

Writes a wide character to a file.

```
#include <wchar.h>
wint_t fputwc( wchar_t wc, FILE *fp );
```

The fputwc() function writes a wide character to the current file position of the specified FILE pointer. The return value is the character written, or WEOF if an error occurred. Because the external file associated with a wide-oriented stream is considered to be a sequence of multibyte characters, fputwc() implicitly performs a wide-to-multibyte character conversion. If an encoding error occurs in the process, fputwc() sets the errno variable to the value of EILSEQ ("illegal byte sequence").

Example

See the example for fgetwc() in this chapter.

See Also

fputc(), fgetwc(), putwc(), putwchar()

fputws

Writes a string of wide characters to a file.

```
#include <wchar.h>
int fputws( const wchar_t * restrict ws, FILE * restrict fp );
```

The fputws() function writes a string of wide characters to the file specified by the FILE pointer argument. The string is written without the terminator character (L'\0'). If successful, fputws() returns a value greater than or equal to zero. A return value of EOF indicates that an error occurred.

Example

```
FILE *fpw;
char fname_wide[] = "widetest.txt";
int widemodeflag = 1;
int result;

wchar_t widestring[] =
                L"How many umlauts are there in Fahrvergnügen?\n";
```

```
if ((fpw = fopen(fname_wide, "a")) == NULL)
  { perror( "Opening output file" ); return -1; }

// Set file to wide-character orientation:
widemodeflag = fwide(fpw, widemodeflag);
if ( widemodeflag <= 0 )
{
  fprintf(stderr, "Unable to set output file %s to wide characters\n",
          fname_wide);
  (void)fclose(fpw);
  return -1;
}

// Write wide-character string to the file:
result = fputws( widestring, fpw );
```

See Also

fgets(), fputs(), fgetws(), fwprintf()

fread

Reads a number of objects from a file.

```
#include <stdio.h>
size_t fread( void * restrict buffer, size_t size, size_t n,
              FILE * restrict fp );
```

The fread() function reads up to *n* data objects of size *size* from the specified file, and stores them in the memory block pointed to by the *buffer* argument. You must make sure that the available size of the memory block in bytes is at least *n* times *size*. Furthermore, on systems that distinguish between text and binary file access modes, the file should be opened in binary mode.

The fread() function returns the number of data objects read. If this number is less than the requested number, then either the end of the file was reached or an error occurred.

Example

```
typedef struct {
  char name[64];
  /* ... more members ... */
} item;

#define CACHESIZE 32            // Size as a number of array elements.

FILE *fp;
int readcount = 0;
item itemcache[CACHESIZE];      // An array of "items".

if (( fp = fopen( "items.dat", "r+" )) == NULL )
  { perror( "Opening data file" ); return -1; }
```

```
/* Read up to CACHESIZE "item" records from the file.*/

readcount = fread( itemcache, sizeof (item), CACHESIZE, fp );
```
See Also

fwrite(), feof(), ferror()

free

Releases allocated memory.

```
#include <stdlib.h>
void free( void *ptr );
```

After you have finished using a memory block that you allocated by calling mal
loc(), calloc() or realloc(), the free() function releases it to the system for
recycling. The pointer argument must be the exact address furnished by the allocating function; otherwise, the behavior is undefined. If the argument is a null pointer,
free() does nothing. In any case, free() has no return value.

Example

```
char *ptr;

/* Obtain a block of 4096 bytes ... */
ptr = calloc(4096, sizeof(char));

if ( ptr == NULL )
  fprintf( stderr, "Insufficient memory.\n" ), abort();
else
{
/* ... use the memory block ... */
  strncpy( ptr, "Imagine this is a long string.\n", 4095 );
  fputs( stdout, ptr );
/* ... and release it. */
  free( ptr );
}
```
See Also

malloc(), calloc(), realloc()

freopen

Changes the file associated with an existing file pointer.

```
#include <stdio.h>
FILE *freopen( const char * restrict name, const char * restrict mode,
               FILE * restrict fp );
```

The freopen() function closes the file associated with the FILE pointer argument
and opens the file with the specified name, associating it with the same FILE pointer
as the file just closed. That FILE pointer is the function's return value. If an error

occurs, freopen() returns a null pointer, and the FILE pointer passed to the function is closed.

The new access mode is specified by the second character string argument, in the same way described under fopen(). The filename *name* can be a null pointer. In that case, the stream remains associated with the original file, and only the access mode is changed as specified by *mode*.

The most common use of freopen() is to redirect the standard I/O streams stdin, stdout, and stderr.

Example

```
time_t sec;
char fname[ ] = "test.dat";
if ( freopen( fname, "w", stdout ) == NULL )
  fprintf( stderr, "Unable to redirect stdout.\n" );
else
{
  time(&sec);
  printf( "%.24s: This file opened as stdout.\n", ctime(&sec) );
}
```

See Also

freopen_s(), fopen(), fopen_s(), fclose(), fflush(), setbuf()

freopen_s
C11

Changes the file associated with an existing file pointer.

```
#include <stdio.h>
errno_t freopen_s( FILE * restrict * restrict fpPtr,
                   const char * restrict name,
                   const char * restrict mode,
                   FILE * restrict fp );
```

The function freopen_s(), like freopen(), closes the file associated with the FILE pointer argument *fp* and opens the file with the specified name and access mode, associating it with the same FILE pointer as the file just closed. If *name* is a null pointer, freopen_s() opens the original file again with the specified new access mode.

Unlike freopen(), the freopen_s() function opens the file subject to the rules described in the section on fopen_s() in this chapter. Furthermore, instead of returning the FILE pointer *fp*, freopen_s() copies it to the variable addressed by its first argument, *fpPtr*. Before doing anything, freopen_s() tests the following run-time constraints: the pointer arguments *fpPtr*, *mode*, and *fp* must not be null pointers.

If it succeeds in opening the file, freopen_s() returns zero and places the value of *fp* in the variable addressed by *fpPtr*. If unsuccessful, the function returns a nonzero value and places a null pointer in the variable addressed by *fpPtr*, provided *fpPtr* is not a null pointer itself.

Example

```
#define __STDC_WANT_LIB_EXT1__ 1
#include <stdio.h>
// ...

    char filename[] = "redirect.txt";
    FILE *fp;
    // Redirect standard output to the file redirect.txt:
    errno_t err = freopen_s( &fp, filename, "w", stdout);
    if( err != 0)
    { fprintf( stderr, "Unable to redirect stdout to %s\n",
               filename);
        exit(err);
    }
    printf("This text is being written to the file %s.\n", filename);
    fclose(stdout);
```

See Also

freopen(), fopen_s(), fopen(), fclose()

frexp

Splits a real number into a mantissa and exponent.

```
#include <math.h>
double frexp( double x, int *exp );
float frexpf( float x, int *exp );              (C99)
long double frexpl( long double x, int *exp );      (C99)
```

The frexp() function expresses a floating-point number x as a normalized fraction f and an integer exponent e to base 2. In other words, if the mantissa f is the return value of the function call frexp(x, &e), then $x = f \times 2^e$ and $0.5 \le |f| < 1$, where $|f|$ is the absolute value of f.

The normalized fraction is the return value of the frexp() function. The function places the other part of its "answer," the exponent, in the location addressed by the pointer argument. If the floating-point argument x is equal to 0, then the function stores the value 0 at the exponent location and returns 0.

Example

```
double fourthrt( double x )
{
    int exponent, exp_mod_4;
    double mantissa = frexp( x, &exponent );

    exp_mod_4 = exponent % 4;
    exponent -= ( exp_mod_4 );      // Get an exponent that's
                                    // divisible by four ...
    for ( int i = abs( exp_mod_4 ); i > 0; i-- )
```

```
    {
      if ( exp_mod_4 > 0 )          // ... and compensate in the mantissa.
        mantissa *= 2.0;
      else
        mantissa /= 2.0;
    }
    return ldexp( sqrt( sqrt( mantissa )), exponent / 4 );
  }
```

See Also

The ldexp() function, which performs the reverse calculation.

fscanf, fscanf_s

Reads formatted data from an open file.

```
#include <stdio.h>
int fscanf( FILE * restrict fp, const char * restrict format, ... );
int fscanf_s( FILE * restrict fp,
             const char * restrict format, ... );      (C11)
```

The functions fscanf() and fscanf_s() are like the functions scanf() and scanf_s(), except that they read from the stream specified by their argument *fp* instead of stdin.

Like scanf(), the fscanf() functions return the number of data items converted and stored in variables. If an input error occurs or the function reads to the end of the file before any data can be converted, the return value is EOF. The fscanf_s() function also returns EOF if a violation of its runtime constraints occurs.

Example

The example code reads information about a user from a file, which we will suppose contains a line of colon-separated strings like this:

```
tony:x:1002:31:Tony Crawford,,,:/home/tony:/bin/bash
```

Here is the code:

```
struct pwrecord {        // Structure for contents of passwd fields.
  unsigned int uid;
  unsigned int gid;
  char   user[32];
  char   pw  [32];
  char   realname[128];
  char   home    [128];
  char   shell   [128];
};

/* ... */

FILE *fp;
int results = 0;
struct pwrecord record;
```

```
struct pwrecord *recptr = &record;
char   gecos[256] = "";

/* ... Open the password file to read ... */

record = (struct pwrecord) { UINT_MAX, UINT_MAX, "", "", "", "", "" };

/* 1. Read login name, password, UID and GID. */
results = fscanf( fp, "%31[^:]:%31[^:]:%u:%u:",
                   recptr->user, recptr->pw,
                   &recptr->uid, &recptr->gid );
```

This function call reads the first part of the input string, tony:x:1002:31:, and copies the two strings "tony" and "x" and assigns two unsigned int values, 1002 and 31, to the corresponding structure members. The return value is 4. The remainder of the code is then as follows:

```
if ( results < 4 )
{
  fprintf( stderr, "Unable to parse line.\n" );
  fscanf( fp, "%*[^\n]\n" );          // Read and discard rest of line.
}

/* 2. Read the "gecos" field, which may contain nothing, or just the
 *    real name, or comma-separated sub-fields.
 */
results = fscanf( fp, "%255[^:]:", gecos );
if ( results < 1 )
  strcpy( recptr->realname,  "[No real name available]" );
else
  sscanf( gecos, "%127[^,]", recptr->realname ); // Truncate at
                                                 // first comma.

/* 3. Read two more fields before the end of the line. */

results = fscanf( fp, "%127[^:]:%127[^\n]\n",
                   recptr->home, recptr->shell );
if ( results < 2 )
{
  fprintf( stderr, "Unable to parse line.\n" );
  fscanf( fp, "%*[^\n]\n" );          // Read and discard rest of line.
}
printf( "The user account %s with UID %u belongs to %s.\n",
         recptr->user, recptr->uid, recptr->realname );
```

For our sample input line, the printf() call produces the following output:

```
The user account tony with UID 1002 belongs to Tony Crawford.
```

If the implementation supports the secure functions, the function fscanf_s() can also be used as an alternative to fscanf(). The first fscanf_s() call in the preceding example would then be as follows:

```
/* 1. Read login name, password, UID and GID. */
results = fscanf_s( fp, "%31[^:]:%31[^:]:%u:%u:",
                    recptr->user, sizeof(recptr->user),
                    recptr->pw, sizeof(recptr->pw),
                    &recptr->uid, &recptr->gid );
```

See Also

scanf(), sscanf(), vscanf(), vfscanf(), and vsscanf(); wscanf(), fwscanf(), swscanf(), vwscanf(), vfwscanf(), and vswscanf()

For each of these functions, there is also a corresponding "secure" function, if the implementation supports the C11 bounds-checking functions (i.e., if the macro __STDC_LIB_EXT1__ is defined)

fseek

Moves the access position in a file.

```
#include <stdio.h>
int fseek( FILE *fp, long offset, int origin );
```

The fseek() function moves the file position indicator for the file specified by the FILE pointer argument. The new position is *offset* bytes from the position selected by the value of the *origin* argument, which may indicate the beginning of the file, the previous position, or the end of the file. Table 18-3 lists the permitted values for *origin*.

Table 18-3. Values for fseek()'s origin argument

Value of origin	Macro name	Offset is relative to
0	SEEK_SET	The beginning of the file
1	SEEK_CUR	The current position
2	SEEK_END	The end of the file

You can use a negative *offset* value to move the file access position backward, but the position indicator cannot be moved backward past the beginning of the file. However, it is possible to move the position indicator forward past the end of the file. If you then perform a write operation at the new position, the file's contents between its previous end and the new data are undefined.

The fseek() function returns 0 if successful, or -1 if an error occurs.

Example

```
typedef struct {  long id;
                  double value;
              } record;
FILE *fp;
record cur_rec = (record) { 0, 0.0 };
int reclength_file = sizeof(record);
```

```
long seek_id = 123L;

if ((fp = fopen("records", "r")) == NULL)
  perror( "Unable to open records file" );
else do
{
  if ( 1 > fread( &cur_rec.id, sizeof (long), 1, fp ))
    fprintf( stderr, "Record with ID %ld not found\n", seek_id );
  else      // Skip rest of record
    if ( fseek( fp, reclength_file - sizeof(long), 1 ))
      perror( "fseek failed" );
} while ( cur_rec.id != seek_id );
```

See Also

fgetpos(), fsetpos(), ftell(), rewind()

fsetpos

Sets a file position indicator to a previously recorded position.

```
#include <stdio.h>
int fsetpos( FILE *fp, const fpos_t *ppos );
```

The fsetpos() function sets the file position indicator for the file specified by the FILE pointer argument. The *ppos* argument, a pointer to the value of the new position, typically points to a value obtained by calling the fgetpos() function.

The function returns 0 if successful. If an error occurs, fsetpos() returns a nonzero value and sets the errno variable to an appropriate positive value.

The type fpos_t is defined in *stdio.h*, and may or may not be an integer type.

Example

See the example for fgetpos() in this chapter.

See Also

fgetpos(), fseek(), ftell(), rewind()

ftell

Obtains the current file access position.

```
#include <stdio.h>
long ftell( FILE *fp );
```

The ftell() function returns the current access position in the file controlled by the FILE pointer argument. If the function fails to obtain the file position, it returns the value -1 and sets the errno variable to an appropriate positive value.

To save the access position in a multibyte stream, use the `fget pos()` function, which also saves the stream's multibyte parsing state.

Example

This example searches in a file, whose name is the second command-line argument, for a string, which the user can specify in the first command-line argument.

```c
#define MAX_LINE 256

FILE *fp;
long lOffset = 0L;
char sLine[MAX_LINE] = "";
char *result = NULL;
int lineno = 0;
/* ... */
if ((fp = fopen(argv[2], "r")) == NULL)
{
  fprintf(stderr, "Unable to open file %s\n", argv[2]);
  exit( -1 );
}
do
{
  lOffset = ftell( fp );     // Bookmark the beginning of
                             // the line we're about to read.
  if ( -1L == lOffset )
    fprintf( stderr, "Unable to obtain offset in %s\n", argv[2] );
  else
    lineno++;

  if ( ! fgets(sLine,MAX_LINE,fp )) // Read next line from file.
    break;
} while ( strstr( sLine, argv[1] ) == NULL ); // Test for argument
                                              // in sLine.
/* Dropped out of loop: Found search keyword or EOF */
if ( feof(fp) || ferror(fp) )
{
  fprintf( stderr,"Unable to find \"%s\" in %s\n", argv[1], argv[2] );
  rewind(fp);
}
else
{
  printf( "%s (%d): %s\n", argv[2], lineno, sLine );
  fseek( fp, lOffset, 0 );   // Set file pointer at beginning of
                             // the line containing the keyword
}
```

The following example runs this program on its own source file, searching for a line containing the word "the". As you can see, the first occurrence of "the" is in line 22. The program finds that line and displays it:

```
tony@luna:~/ch18$ ./ftell the ftell.c
ftell.c (22):        lOffset = ftell(fp);    // Bookmark the beginning of
```

See Also

fgetpos(), fsetpos(), fseek(), rewind()

fwide

Determines whether a stream is byte-character- or wide-character-oriented.

```
#include <stdio.h>
#include <wchar.h>
int fwide( FILE *fp, int mode );
```

The fwide() function either gets or sets the character type orientation of a file, depending on the value of the *mode* argument:

mode > 0
> The fwide() function attempts to change the file to wide-character orientation.

mode < 0
> The function attempts to change the file to byte-character orientation.

mode = 0
> The function does not alter the orientation of the stream.

In all three cases, the return value of fwide() indicates the stream's orientation *after* the function call in the same way:

Greater than 0
> After the fwide() function call, the file has wide-character orientation.

Less than 0
> The file now has byte-character orientation.

Equal to 0
> The file has no orientation.

The normal usage of fwide() is to call it once immediately after opening a file to set it to wide-character orientation. Once you have determined the file's orientation, fwide() does not change it on subsequent calls. If you do not call fwide() for a given file, its orientation is determined by whether the first read or write operation is byte-oriented or wide-oriented. You can remove a file's byte or wide-character orientation by calling freopen(). For more information, see "Byte-Oriented and Wide-Oriented Streams" on page 216.

Example

See the example for fputws() in this chapter.

See Also

The many functions for working with streams of wide characters, listed in Table 17-2.

fwprintf, fwprintf_s

Writes formatted output in a wide-character string to a file.

```
#include <stdio.h>
#include <wchar.h>
int fwprintf( FILE * restrict fp, const wchar_t * restrict format, ... );
int fwprintf_s( FILE * restrict fp,
              const wchar_t * restrict format, ...);      (C11)
```

The functions fwprintf() and fwprintf_s() are like fprintf() and fprintf_s(), except that their format string argument and their output are strings of wide characters.

Example

```
wchar_t name_local[ ]   = L"Ka\u0142u\u017Cny";
char    name_portable[ ]= "Kaluzny";
char    locale[ ]       = "pl_PL.UTF-8";
char *  newlocale;

newlocale = setlocale( LC_ALL, locale );
if ( newlocale == NULL )
  fprintf( stderr, "Sorry, couldn't change the locale to %s.\n"
           "The current locale is %s.\n",
           locale, setlocale( LC_ALL, NULL ));

fwprintf( stdout,
          L"Customer's name: %ls (Single-byte transliteration: %s)\n",
          name_local, name_portable );
```

If the specified Polish locale is available, this example produces the output:

```
Customer's name: Kałużny (Single-byte transliteration: Kaluzny)
```

See Also

The byte-character output functions in the printf() family; the wide-character output functions fputwc(), fputwc(), putwc(), putwchar(), wprintf(), vfwprintf() and vwprintf(); the wide-character input functions fgetwc(), fgetws(), getwc(), getwchar(), fwscanf(), wscanf(), vfwscanf() and vwscanf()

For each of these functions, there is also a corresponding "secure" function, if the implementation supports the C11 bounds-checking functions (i.e., if the macro __STDC_LIB_EXT1__ is defined)

fwscanf, fwscanf_s

Reads a formatted data string of wide characters from a file.

```
#include <stdio.h>
#include <wchar.h>
int fwscanf( FILE * restrict fp, const wchar_t * restrict format, ... );
int fwscanf_s( FILE * restrict fp,
               const wchar_t * restrict format, ... );    (C11)
```

The functions fwscanf() and fwscanf_s() are like the functions wscanf() and wscanf_s(), except that they read from the stream specified by their argument *fp* instead of stdin.

Like wscanf(), the fwscanf() functions return the number of data items converted and stored in variables. If an input error occurs or the function reads to the end of the file before any data can be converted, the return value is EOF. The fwscanf_s() function also returns EOF if a violation of its runtime constraints occurs.

Example

See the example for wscanf() in this chapter.

See Also

wscanf(), swscanf(), wcstod(), wcstol(), wcstoul(), scanf(), fscanf(); the wide-character output functions fwprintf(), wprintf(), vfwprint(), and vwprint()

For each of these functions, there is also a corresponding "secure" function, if the implementation supports the C11 bounds-checking functions (i.e., if the macro __STDC_LIB_EXT1__ is defined)

fwrite

Writes a number of objects of a given size to a file.

```
#include <stdio.h>
size_t fwrite( const void * restrict buffer, size_t size, size_t n,
               FILE * restrict fp );
```

The fwrite() function writes up to *n* data objects of the specified size from the buffer addressed by the pointer argument *buffer* to the file referenced by the FILE pointer *fp*. Furthermore, on systems that distinguish between text and binary file access modes, the file should be opened in binary mode.

The function returns the number of data objects that were actually written to the file. This value is 0 if either the object size *size* or the number of objects *n* was 0, and may be less than the argument *n* if a write error occurred.

Example

```
typedef struct {
  char name[64];
```

```
/* ... more structure members ... */
} item;

#define CACHESIZE 32          // Size as a number of array elements.

FILE *fp;
int writecount = 0;
item itemcache[CACHESIZE];    // An array of "items".

/* ... Edit the items in the array ... */

if (( fp = fopen( "items.dat", "w" )) == NULL )
  { perror ( "Opening data file" ); return -1; }

/* Write up to CACHESIZE "item" records to the file.*/

writecount = fwrite( itemcache, sizeof (item), CACHESIZE, fp );
```

See Also

The corresponding input function fread(); the string output functions fputs() and fprintf()

getc

Reads a character from a file.

```
#include <stdio.h>
int getc( FILE *fp );
```

The getc() function is the same as fgetc(), except that it may be implemented as a macro and may evaluate its argument more than once. If the argument is an expression with side effects, use fgetc() instead.

getc() returns the character read. A return value of EOF indicates an error or an attempt to read past the end of the file. In these cases, the function sets the file's error or end-of-file flag as appropriate.

Example

```
FILE *inputs[16];
int nextchar, i = 0;

/* ... open 16 input streams ... */

do {
  nextchar = getc( inputs[i++] );     // Warning: getc() is a macro!
  /* ... process the character ... */
} while (i < 16);
```

The do...while statement in this example skips over some files in the array if getc() evaluates its argument more than once. Here is a safer version, without side effects in the argument to getc():

```
for ( i = 0; i < 16; i++ ) {
  nextchar = getc( inputs[i] );
  /* ... process the character ... */
}
```

See Also

fgetc(), getchar(), fputc(), putc(), putchar(), ungetc(); the functions to read and write wide characters, getwc(), fgetwc(), getwchar(), putwc(), fputwc(), putwchar(), and ungetwc()

getchar

Reads a character from the standard input stream.

```
#include <stdio.h>
int getchar( void );
```

The function call getchar() is equivalent to getc(stdin). Like getc(), getchar() may be implemented as a macro. As it has no arguments, however, unforeseen side effects are unlikely.

getchar() returns the character read. A return value of EOF indicates an error or an attempt to read past the end of the input stream. In these cases, the function sets the error or end-of-file flag for stdin as appropriate.

Example

```
char file_name[256};
int answer;

/* ... */

fprintf( stderr, "Are you sure you want to replace the file \"%s\"?\n",
         file_name );
answer = tolower(getchar());
if ( answer != 'y' )
  exit( -1 );
```

See Also

fgetc(), fputc(), getchar(), putc(), putchar(), ungetc(); the functions to read and write wide characters, getwc(), fgetwc(), getwchar(), putwc(), fputwc(), putwchar(), and ungetwc()

getenv

Obtains the string value of a specified environment variable.

```
#include <stdlib.h>
char *getenv( const char *name );
```

The getenv() function searches the environment variables at runtime for an entry with the specified name, and returns a pointer to the variable's value. If there is no environment variable with the specified name, getenv() returns a null pointer.

Your program must not modify the string addressed by the pointer returned, and the string at that address may be replaced by subsequent calls to getenv(). The function getenv() is not guaranteed to be thread-safe.

Furthermore, C itself does not define a function to set or modify environment variables, or any list of variable names that you can expect to exist; these features, if available at all, are system-specific.

Example

```
#define MAXPATH 1024;
char sPath[MAXPATH] = "";
char *pTmp;

if (( pTmp = getenv( "PATH" )) != NULL )
  strncpy( sPath, pTmp, MAXPATH - 1 );        // Save a copy for our use.
else
  fprintf( stderr, "No PATH variable set.\n") ;
```

See Also

getenv_s(), system()

getenv_s   C11

Obtains the string value and the length of a specified environment variable.

```
#include <stdlib.h>
errno_t getenv_s( size_t * restrict len,
                  char * restrict value, rsize_t maxsize,
                  const char * restrict name););
```

The function getenv_s(), like getenv(), searches the environment variables at runtime for an entry with the specified name. If the variable exists, getenv_s() performs the following operations:

- Writes the length of the environment variable's value string to the variable addressed by the pointer argument *len*, provided *len* is not a null pointer

- Copies the value of the environment variable to the char array addressed by the *value* argument, provided the length of the environment variable's value is less than *maxsize*

If the environment variable *name* is not defined, then zero is written to the variable that *len* points to, and the string terminator '\0' is written to *value*[0], provided that *len* is not a null pointer and *maxsize* is greater than zero.

The function getenv_s() tests the following runtime constraints: the pointer argument *name* must not be a null pointer, and *maxsize* must be less than or equal to RSIZE_MAX. If *maxsize* is greater than zero, *value* must not be a null pointer. If a runtime constraint is violated, getenv_s() does not search the list of environment variables but stores the value zero in the object that *len* points to, provided *len* is not a null pointer.

The function getenv_s() returns zero if the environment variable *name* exists and its value string was copied to the address in *value*. Otherwise, the function returns a nonzero value. The function is not guaranteed to be thread-safe.

Example

```
#define __STDC_WANT_LIB_EXT1__ 1
#include <stdlib.h>
// ...
  char envStr[512];
  size_t len;
  if( getenv_s( &len, envStr, sizeof(envStr),"PATH") == 0)
    printf("PATH variable (%u characters): \n%s\n", len, envStr);
  else if( len > 0)
    printf("The PATH variable (%u characters) is more than "
           "%u bytes long.\n", len, sizeof(envStr));
  else
    printf("PATH variable not found.\n");
```

See Also

getenv(), set_constraint_handler_s(), system()

gets

Reads a line of text from standard input.

```
#include <stdio.h>
char *gets( char *buffer );
```

The gets() function reads characters from the standard input stream until it reads a newline character or reaches the end of the stream. The characters read are stored as a string in the buffer addressed by the pointer argument. A string terminator character '\0' is appended after the last character read (not counting the newline character, which is discarded).

If successful, the function returns the value of its argument. If an error occurs, or if the end of the file is reached before any characters can be read in, gets() returns a null pointer.

The gets() function provides no way to limit the input length, and if the stdin stream happens to deliver a long input line, gets() will attempt to store characters past the end of the available buffer. Such buffer overflows are a potential security risk. Use fgets() instead, which has a parameter to control the maximum input length.

The C11 standard retires the function gets(), replacing it with the function gets_s(), which has an additional parameter for the size of the input buffer.

Example

```
char buffer[1024];

/* Replaced gets() with fgets() to avoid potential buffer overflow
 * OLD:  while ( gets( buffer ) != NULL )
 * NEW: below
 */
while ( fgets( buffer, sizeof(buffer), stdin ) != NULL )
{
  /* ... process the line; remember that fgets(), unlike gets(),
     retains the newline character at the end of the string ... */
}
```

See Also

gets_s(), fgets(), fgetws(); the corresponding string output functions, puts(), fputs(), fputws()

gets_s   C11

Reads a line of text from standard input.

```
#include <stdio.h>
char *gets_s( char *buffer, rsize_t n);
```

The secure function gets_s() reads characters from the standard input stream (stdin) until it reads a newline character or reaches the end of the stream. The characters read are stored as a string in the buffer addressed by the pointer argument. A string terminator character '\0' is appended after the last character read (not counting the newline character, which is discarded). The second argument specifies the size of the available buffer. Hence the line to be read may contain at most $n - 1$ characters.

The function has the following runtime constraints: the pointer argument *buffer* must not be a null pointer, and n must be greater than zero and less than or equal to RSIZE_MAX. Furthermore, the line to be read must not be more than $n - 1$ characters long. In other words, a newline character or the end of the stream must occur before the nth character read.

If a read error or a violation of the runtime constraints occurs, the function writes a string terminator character to *buffer*[0], provided *buffer* is not a null pointer and RSIZE_MAX is greater than zero. In case of such an error, the entire line read is discarded: gets_s() reads and discards all characters until it reads a newline character or reaches the end of the stream, or a read error occurs.

If successful, the gets_s() function returns the value of its pointer argument *buffer*. If an error occurs, or if the end of the stream is reached before any characters can be read in, gets_s() returns a null pointer.

 An alternative to gets_s() to process lines of any length correctly is the function fgets(), which does not discard any characters read. fgets() also stores newline characters ('\n') that it reads.

Example

```
#define __STDC_WANT_LIB_EXT1__ 1
#include <stdio.h>
// ...

    char text[100];
    puts("Enter a line of text:");
    if( gets_s(text, sizeof(text)) == NULL)
        fputs("Unable to read the text.\n", stderr);
    else
        printf("Your text:\n%s\n", text);
```

See Also

gets(), fgets(), fgetws(); the corresponding string output functions, puts(), fputs(), fputws()

getwc

Reads a wide character from a file.

```
#include <stdio.h>
#include <wchar.h>
wint_t getwc( FILE *fp );
```

The getwc() function is the wide-character counterpart to getc(): it may be implemented as a macro, and may evaluate its argument more than once, causing unforeseen side effects. Use fgetwc() instead.

getwc() returns the character read. A return value of WEOF indicates an error or an attempt to read past the end of the input stream. In these cases, the function sets the error or end-of-file flag for stdin as appropriate.

Example

```
wint_t wc;

if ( setlocale( LC_CTYPE, "" ) == NULL)
{
  fwprintf( stderr,
           L"Sorry, couldn't change to the system's native locale.\n");
  return 1;
}
while ( (wc = getwc( stdin)) != WEOF )
{
  wc = towupper(wc);
  putwc( (wchar_t)wc, stdout);
}
```

See Also

The function fgetwc(); the corresponding output functions putwc() and fputwc(); the byte-character functions getc() and getchar(); the byte-character output functions putc(), putchar(), and fputc()

getwchar

Reads a wide character from the standard input stream.

```
#include <wchar.h>
wint_t getwchar( void );
```

The getwchar() function is the wide-character counterpart to getchar(); it is equivalent to getwc(stdin) and returns the wide character read. Like getwc(), getwchar() may be implemented as a macro, but because it has no arguments, unforeseen side effects are not likely. A return value of WEOF indicates an error or an attempt to read past the end of the stream. In these cases, the function sets the stdin stream's error or end-of-file flag as appropriate.

Example

```
wint_t wc;

if ( setlocale( LC_CTYPE, "" ) == NULL)
{
  fwprintf( stderr,
           L"Sorry, couldn't change to the system's native locale.\n");
  return 1;
}
while ( (wc = getwchar()) != WEOF ) // or:  (wc = getwc( stdin))
{
  wc = towupper(wc);
  putwchar((wchar_t)wc);           // or:  putwc( (wchar_t)wc, stdout);
}
```

fgetwc(); the byte-character functions getc() and getchar(); the output functions fputwc() and putwchar()

gmtime

Converts a time value into a year, month, day, hour, minute, second, etc.

```
#include <time.h>
struct tm *gmtime( const time_t *timer );
```

The gmtime() function converts a numeric time value (usually a number of seconds since January 1, 1970, but not necessarily) into the equivalent date-and-time structure in Coordinated Universal Time (UTC, formerly called Greenwich Mean Time; hence the function's name). To obtain similar values for the local time, use the function localtime().

The function's argument is not the number of seconds itself but a pointer to that value. The function returns a pointer to a static struct tm object that contains the results. If an error occurs, the function returns a null pointer.

Both in the structure type struct tm and the arithmetic type time_t are defined in the header *time.h*. The tm structure is defined as follows:

```
struct tm {
    int tm_sec;      /* Seconds since the full minute: 0 to 60 */
    int tm_min;      /* Minutes since the full hour:   0 to 59 */
    int tm_hour;     /* Hours since midnight:          0 to 23 */
    int tm_mday;     /* Day of the month:       1 to  31 */
    int tm_mon;      /* Months since January: 0 to  11 */
    int tm_year;     /* Years since 1900              */
    int tm_wday;     /* Days since Sunday:      0 to   6 */
    int tm_yday;     /* Days since Jan. 1:      0 to 365 */
    int tm_isdst;    /* Flag for daylight saving time:
                        greater than 0 if time is DST;
                        equal to 0 if time is not DST;
                        less than 0 if unknown.        */
};
```

The argument most often passed to gmtime() is the current time, obtained as a number with type time_t by calling the function time(). The type time_t is usually defined as long, long long, or unsigned long.

Example

The following program prints a string showing the offset of the local time zone from UTC:

```
time_t     rawtime;
struct tm  utc_tm, local_tm, *ptr_tm;
char       buffer[1024] = "";

time( &rawtime );                    // Get current time as an integer.
```

```
ptr_tm = gmtime( &rawtime );          // Convert to UTC in a struct tm.
memcpy( &utc_tm, ptr_tm, sizeof(struct tm) );   // Save a local copy.
ptr_tm = localtime( &rawtime );       // Do the same for local time zone.
memcpy( &local_tm, ptr_tm, sizeof(struct tm) );

if ( strftime( buffer, sizeof(buffer),
               "It's %A, %B %d, %Y, %R o'clock, UTC.", &utc_tm ) )
  puts( buffer );
if ( strftime( buffer, sizeof(buffer),
               "Here it's %A, %B %d, %Y, %R o'clock, UTC %z.",
               &local_tm ) )
  puts( buffer );
```

This code produces output like the following:

```
It's Tuesday, March 24, 2015, 22:26 o'clock, UTC.
Here it's Wednesday, March 25, 2015, 00:26 o'clock, UTC +0200.
```

See Also

gmtime_s(), localtime(), localtime_s(), strftime(), time()

gmtime_s   C11

Converts an integer time value into a year, month, day, hour, minute, second, etc.

```
#include <time.h>
struct tm *gmtime_s( const time_t * restrict timer ,
                     struct tm * restrict result);
```

The function gmtime_s(), like gmtime(), converts a numeric time value (usually a
number of seconds since January 1, 1970, but not necessarily) into the equivalent
date-and-time structure in Coordinated Universal Time (UTC; also called Greenwich Mean Time). The results are stored in an object of the type struct tm. This
structure is described in the section on gmtime() in this chapter.

Unlike gmtime(), gmtime_s() does not use an internal, static struct tm object, but
places the results in the struct tm addressed by its second argument. As a result,
the gmtime_s() function is thread-safe.

The function first tests its runtime constraints: the pointer arguments timer and
result must not be null pointers. If a runtime constraint is violated or if the value
of timer cannot be converted into a UTC calendar time, gmtime_s() returns a null
pointer. If no error occurs, the return value is the pointer result.

Example

```
#define __STDC_WANT_LIB_EXT1__ 1
#include <time.h>
// ...

    time_t now;    struct tm tmStruct;    char timeStr[26];

    time(&now);                          // Current time as an integer.
```

```
if( gmtime_s(&now, &tmStruct) != NULL          // Convert to UTC.
    && asctime_s( timeStr, sizeof(timeStr), &tmStruct) == 0)
    printf("The current universal time (UTC): %s\n", timeStr);
```

Typical output:

```
The current universal time (UTC): Sun May 17 14:58:09 2015
```

See Also

gmtime(), localtime(), localtime_s(), strftime(), time()

hypot   C99

Calculates a hypotenuse by the Pythagorean formula.

```
#include <math.h>
double hypot( double x, double y );
float hypotf( float x, float y );
long double hypotl( long double x, long double y );
```

The hypot() functions compute the square root of the sum of the squares of their arguments, while avoiding intermediate overflows. If the result exceeds the function's return type, a range error may occur.

Example

```
double x, y, h;              // Three sides of a triangle

printf( "How many kilometers do you want to go westward? " );
scanf( "%lf", &x );

printf( "And how many southward? " );
scanf( "%lf", &y );

errno = 0;
h = hypot( x, y );

if ( errno )
  perror( __FILE__ );
else
  printf( "Then you'll be %4.2lf km from where you started.\n", h );
```

If the user answers the prompts with 3.33 and 4.44, the program prints this output:

```
Then you'll be 5.55 km from where you started.
```

See Also

sqrt(), cbrt(), csqrt()

Does nothing in response to runtime errors in secure functions.

```
#include <stdlib.h>
void ignore_handler_s( const char * restrict msg, void * restrict ptr,
                       errno_t error);
```

If the function ignore_handler_s() is passed as an argument to the function set_constraint_handler_s(), it is installed as a runtime error handler so that ignore_handler_s() is called if one of the secure functions (with names ending in _s) violates its runtime constraints.

The function ignore_handler_s() takes no action on such errors, but simply returns control to the secure function in which the error occurred. That function then returns a value to its caller to indicate that an error occurred. Such return values are described in the section on each secure function in this chapter. The secure functions usually indicate errors by returning a null pointer or a nonzero value of the type errno_t.

To install a runtime error handler other than ignore_handler_s(), you can also pass the standard function abort_handler_s() or your own handler function to set_constraint_handler_s().

Example

```
// Handle runtime constraint violations using only
// the return value of secure functions.
#define __STDC_WANT_LIB_EXT1__ 1
#include <stdlib.h>
// ...

    char message[20] = "Hello, ",
         name[20];
    set_constraint_handler_s(ignore_handler_s);

    printf("Please enter your name: ");
    if( gets_s( name, sizeof(name)) == NULL)
    { /* Error: user entered more than 19 characters.*/ }
    else if( strcat_s( message, sizeof(message), name) != 0)
    { /* Error: message array is too small.*/ }
    else
        puts( message);
```

See Also

abort_handler_s(), set_constraint_handler_s()

Returns the exponent of a floating-point number as an integer.

```
#include <math.h>
int ilogb( double x )
int ilogbf( float x )
int ilogbl( long double x )
```

The ilogb() functions return the exponent of their floating-point argument as a signed integer. If the argument is not normalized, ilogb() returns the exponent of its normalized value.

If the argument is 0, ilogb() returns the value of the macro FP_ILOGB0 (defined in *math.h*), and may incur a range error. If the argument is infinite, the return value is equal to INT_MAX. If the floating-point argument is NaN ("not a number"), ilogb() returns the value of the macro FP_ILOGBNAN.

Example

```
int exponent = 0;
double x = -1.509812734e200;

while ( exponent < INT_MAX )
{
  exponent = ilogb( x );
  printf( "The exponent of %g is %d.\n", x, exponent );

  if ( x < 0.0 && x * x > 1.0 )
    x /= 1e34;
  else
    x += 1.1, x *= 2.2e34 ;
}
```

This code produces some 15 output lines, including these samples:

```
The exponent of -1.50981e+200 is 664.
The exponent of -1.50981e+30 is 100.
The exponent of -0.000150981 is -13.
The exponent of 2.41967e+34 is 114.
The exponent of inf is 2147483647.
```

See Also

logb(), log(), log10(), log1p(), exp(), pow()

Gives the absolute value of a number of the longest available integer type.

```
#include <inttypes.h>
intmax_t imaxabs( intmax_t n )
```

The imaxabs() function is the same as either labs() or llabs(), depending on how many bits wide the system's largest integer type is. Accordingly, the type intmax_t is the same as either long or long long.

Example

```
intmax_t quantity1 = 9182734;
intmax_t quantity2 = 1438756;

printf( "The difference between the two quantities is %ji.\n",
        imaxabs( quantity2 - quantity1 ));
```

See Also

abs(), labs(), llabs(), fabs()

imaxdiv   C99

Performs integer division, returning quotient and remainder.

```
#include <inttypes.h>
imaxdiv_t imaxdiv( intmax_t dividend, intmax_t divisor );
```

The imaxdiv() function is the same as either ldiv() or lldiv(), depending on how many bits wide the system's largest integer type is. Accordingly, the structure type of the return value, imaxdiv_t, is the same as either ldiv_t or lldiv_t.

Example

```
intmax_t people = 110284, apples = 9043291;
imaxdiv_t  share;

if ( people == 0 )                  // Avoid dividing by zero.
   { printf( "There's no one here to take the apples.\n" ); return -1; }
else
  share = imaxdiv( apples, people );

printf( "If there are %ji of us and %ji apples,\n"
        "each of us gets %ji, with %ji left over.\n",
        people, apples, share.quot, share.rem );
```

This example prints the following output:

```
If there are 110284 of us and 9091817 apples,
each of us gets 82, with 3 left over.
```

See Also

The description under div() in this chapter; the floating-point functions remainder() and remquo()

isalnum

Ascertains whether a given character is alphanumeric.

```
#include <ctype.h>
int isalnum( int c );
```

The function isalnum() tests whether its character argument is alphanumeric; that is, whether the character is either a letter of the alphabet or a digit. In other words, isalnum() is true for all characters for which either isalpha() or isdigit() is true.

Which characters are considered alphabetic or numeric depends on the current locale setting for the localization category LC_CTYPE, which you can query or change using the setlocale() function. (See the note on character classes and locales in the section on isalpha().)

If the character is alphanumeric, isalnum() returns a nonzero value (that is, true); if not, the function returns 0 (false).

Example

See the example for isprint() in this chapter.

See Also

isalpha(), isblank(), iscntrl(), isdigit(), isgraph(), islower(), isprint(), ispunct(), isspace(), isupper(), isxdigit(); the corresponding C99 function for wide characters, iswalnum(); setlocale()

isalpha

Ascertains whether a given character is a letter of the alphabet.

```
#include <ctype.h>
int isalpha( int c );
```

The function isalpha() tests whether its character argument is a letter of the alphabet. If the character is alphabetic, isalpha() returns a nonzero value (that is, true); if not, the function returns 0 (false).

Which characters are considered alphabetic depends on the current locale setting for the localization category LC_CTYPE, which you can query or change using the setlocale() function.

In the C locale, which is the default locale setting, the alphabetic characters are those for which isupper() or islower() returns true. These are the 26 lowercase and 26 uppercase letters of the Latin alphabet, which are the letters in the basic source and execution character sets (see "Character Sets" on page 8).

Accented characters, umlauts, and the like are considered alphabetic only in certain locales. Moreover, other locales may have characters that are alphabetic but neither uppercase nor lowercase, or both uppercase and lowercase.

In all locales, the isalpha() classification is mutually exclusive with iscntrl(), isdigit(), ispunct(), and isspace().

Example

See the example for isprint() in this chapter.

See Also

The corresponding C99 function for wide characters, iswalpha(); isalnum(), isblank(), iscntrl(), isdigit(), isgraph(), islower(), isprint(), ispunct(), isspace(), isupper(), isxdigit(), setlocale()

isblank   C99

Ascertains whether a given character is a space or tab character.

```
#include <ctype.h>
int isblank( int c );
```

The function isblank() is a recent addition to the C character type functions. It returns a nonzero value (that is, true) if its character argument is either a space or a tab character. If not, the function returns 0 (false).

Example

This program trims trailing blank characters from the user's input:

```
#define MAX_STRING 80

char raw_name[MAX_STRING];
int i;

printf( "Enter your name, please: " );
fgets( raw_name, sizeof(raw_name), stdin );

/* Trim trailing blanks: */

i = ( strlen(raw_name) - 1 );   // Index the last character.
while ( i >= 0 )                // Index must not go
{                               // below first character.
  if (  raw_name[i] == '\n' )
    raw_name[i] = '\0';         // Chomp off the newline character.
  else if ( isblank( raw_name[i] ) )
    raw_name[i] = '\0';         // Lop off trailing spaces and tabs.
  else
    break;                      // Real data found; stop truncating.
  --i;                          // Count down.
}
```

See also the example for isprint() in this chapter.

See Also

The corresponding C99 function for wide characters, iswblank(); isalnum(), isal
pha(), iscntrl(), isdigit(), isgraph(), islower(), isprint(), ispunct(),
isspace(), isupper(), isxdigit()

iscntrl

Ascertains whether a given character is a control character.

```
#include <ctype.h>
int iscntrl( int c );
```

The function iscntrl() tests whether its character argument is a control character.
For the ASCII character set, these are the character codes from 0 through 31 and
127. The function may yield different results depending on the current locale setting
for the localization category LC_CTYPE, which you can query or change using the
setlocale() function.

If the argument is a control character, iscntrl() returns a nonzero value (that is,
true); if not, the function returns 0 (false).

Example

See the example for isprint() in this chapter.

See Also

The corresponding C99 function for wide characters, iswcntrl(); isalnum(), isal
pha(), isblank(), isdigit(), isgraph(), islower(), isprint(), ispunct(),
isspace(), isupper(), isxdigit(), setlocale()

isdigit

Ascertains whether a given character is a decimal digit.

```
#include <ctype.h>
int isdigit( int c );
```

The function isdigit() tests whether its character argument is a digit. isdigit()
returns a nonzero value (that is, true) for the 10 characters between '0' (not to be
confused with the null character, '\0') and '9' inclusive. Otherwise, the function
returns 0 (false).

Example

See the example for isprint() in this chapter.

See Also

The corresponding C99 function for wide characters, iswdigit(); isalnum(), isal
pha(), isblank(), iscntrl(), isgraph(), islower(), isprint(), ispunct(),
isspace(), isupper(), isxdigit(), setlocale()

Tests whether a given floating-point value is a finite number.

```
#include <math.h>
int isfinite( float x );
int isfinite( double x );
int isfinite( long double x );
```

The macro isfinite() yields a nonzero value (that is, true) if its argument is not an infinite number and not a NaN. Otherwise, isfinite() yields 0. The argument must be a real floating-point type. The rule that floating-point types are promoted to at least double precision for mathematical calculations does not apply here; the argument's properties are determined based on its representation in its actual semantic type.

Example

```
double vsum( int n, ... )
// n is the number of arguments in the list
{
  va_list argptr;
  double sum = 0.0, next = 0.0;
  va_start( argptr, n );
  while ( n-- )
  {
    next = va_arg( argptr, double );
    sum += next;
    if ( isfinite( sum ) == 0 )
      break;                    // If sum reaches infinity, stop adding.
  }
  va_end( argptr );
  return sum;
}
```

See Also

fpclassify(), isinf(), isnan(), isnormal(), signbit()

isgraph

Ascertains whether a given character is graphic.

```
#include <ctype.h>
int isgraph( int c );
```

The function isgraph() tests whether its character argument is a graphic character; that is, whether the value represents a printing character other than the space character. (In other words, the space character is considered printable but not graphic.) If the character is graphic, isgraph() returns a nonzero value (that is, true); if not, the function returns 0 (false).

Whether a given character code represents a graphic character depends on the current locale setting for the category LC_CTYPE, which you can query or change using the setlocale() function.

Example

See the example for isprint() in this chapter.

See Also

The corresponding C99 function for wide characters, iswgraph(); isalnum(), isalpha(), isblank(), iscntrl(), isdigit(), islower(), isprint(), ispunct(), isspace(), isupper(), isxdigit(), setlocale()

isgreater, isgreaterequal   C99

Compares two floating-point values without risking an exception.

```
#include <math.h>
int isgreater( x, y );
int isgreaterequal( x, y );
```

The macro isgreater() tests whether the argument *x* is greater than the argument *y*, but without risking an exception. Both operands must have real floating-point types. The result of isgreater() is the same as the result of the operation (*x*) > (*y*), but that operation could raise an "invalid operand" exception if either operand is NaN ("not a number"), in which case neither is greater than, equal to, or less than the other.

The macro isgreater() returns a nonzero value (that is, true) if the first argument is greater than the second; otherwise, it returns 0. The macro isgreaterequal() functions similarly, but corresponds to the relation (*x*) >= (*y*), returning true if the first argument is greater than or equal to the second; otherwise, 0.

Example

```
/* Can a, b, and c be three sides of a triangle? */
double a, b, c, temp;
/* First get the longest "side" in a. */
if ( isgreater( a, b ) )
    temp = a; a = b; b = temp;
if ( isgreater( a, c ) )
    temp = a; a = c; c = temp;
/* Then see if a is longer than the sum of the other two sides: */
if ( isgreaterequal( a, b + c ) )
    printf( "The three numbers %.2lf, %.2lf, and %.2lf "
            "are not sides of a triangle.\n", a, b, c );
```

See Also

isless(), islessequal(), islessgreater(), isunordered()

isinf   C99

Tests whether a given floating-point value is an infinity.

```
#include <math.h>
int isinf( float x );
int isinf( double x );
int isinf( long double x );
```

The macro isinf() yields a nonzero value (that is, true) if its argument is a positive or negative infinity. Otherwise, isinf() yields 0. The argument must be a real floating-point type. The rule that floating-point types are promoted to at least double precision for mathematical calculations does not apply here; the argument's properties are determined based on its representation in its actual semantic type.

Example

This function takes a shortcut if it encounters an infinite addend:

```
double vsum( int n, va_list argptr )
{
  double sum = 0.0, next = 0.0;
  va_start( argptr, n );

  for ( int i = 0; i < n; i ++ )
  {
    next = va_arg( argptr, double );
    if ( isinf( next ) )
      return next;
    sum += next;
  }
  va_end( argptr );
  return sum;
}
```

See Also

fpclassify(), isfinite(), isnan(), isnormal(), signbit()

isless, islessequal, islessgreater   C99

Compares two floating-point values without risking an exception.

```
#include <math.h>
int isless( x, y );
int islessequal( x, y );
int islessgreater( x, y );
```

The macro isless() tests whether the argument x is less than the argument y, but without risking an exception. Both operands must have real floating-point types. The result of isless() is the same as the result of the operation (x) < (y), but that operation could raise an "invalid operand" exception if either operand is NaN ("not a number"), in which case neither is greater than, equal to, or less than the other.

The macro isless() returns a nonzero value (that is, true) if the first argument is less than the second; otherwise, it returns 0. The macro islessequal() functions similarly but corresponds to the relation (x) <= (y), returning true if the first argument is less than or equal to the second; otherwise, 0.

The macro islessgreater() is also similar but corresponds to the expression (x) < (y) || (x) > (y), returning true if the first argument is less than or greater than the second; otherwise, 0.

Example

```
double minimum( double a, double b )
{
  if ( islessgreater( a, b ) )
    return ( isless( a, b ) ? a : b );
  if ( a == b )
    return a;
  feraiseexcept( FE_INVALID );
  return NAN;
}
```

See Also

isgreater(), isgreaterequal(), isunordered()

islower

Ascertains whether a given character is a lowercase letter.

```
#include <ctype.h>
int islower( int c );
```

The function islower() tests whether its character argument is a lowercase letter. Which characters are letters and which letters are lowercase both depend on the current locale setting for the category LC_CTYPE, which you can query or change using the setlocale(). (See the note on character classes and locales in the section on isalpha().)

If the character is a lowercase letter, islower() returns a nonzero value (that is, true); if not, the function returns 0 (false).

In the default locale C, the truth values of isupper() and islower() are mutually exclusive for the alphabetic characters. However, other locales may have alphabetic characters for which both isupper() and islower() return true, or characters that are alphabetic but neither uppercase nor lowercase.

Example

See the example for isprint() in this chapter.

isupper(), tolower(), toupper(); the corresponding C99 function for wide characters, iswlower(); isalnum(), isalpha(), isblank(), iscntrl(), isdigit(), isgraph(), isprint(), ispunct(), isspace(), isxdigit(), setlocale()

isnan   C99

Tests whether a given floating-point value is "not a number."

```
#include <math.h>
int isnan( float x );
int isnan( double x );
int isnan( long double x );
```

The macro isnan() yields a nonzero value (that is, true) if its argument is a NaN, or "not a number" (see "float.h" on page 293). Otherwise, isnan() yields 0. The argument must be a real floating-point type. The rule that floating-point types are promoted to at least double precision for mathematical calculations does not apply here; the argument's properties are determined based on its representation in its actual semantic type.

Example

```
double dMax( double a, double b )
{
    // NaN overrides all comparison:
    if ( isnan( a ) ) return a;
    if ( isnan( b ) ) return b;
    // Anything is greater than -inf:
    if ( isinf( a ) && signbit( a ) ) return b;
    if ( isinf( b ) && signbit( b ) ) return a;

    return ( a > b ? a : b );
}
```

See Also

fpclassify(), isfinite(), isinf(), isnormal(), signbit()

isnormal   C99

Tests whether a given floating-point value is normalized.

```
#include <math.h>
int isnormal( float x );
int isnormal( double x );
int isnormal( long double x );
```

The macro isnormal() yields a nonzero value (that is, true) if its argument's value is a normalized floating-point number. Otherwise, isnormal() yields 0. The argument must be a real floating-point type. The rule that floating-point types are promoted to at least double precision for mathematical calculations does not apply here; the argument's properties are determined based on its representation in its actual semantic type.

Example

```
double maximum( double a, double b )
{
  if ( isnormal( a ) && isnormal( b ) )      // Handle normal case first.
    return ( a >= b ) ? a : b ;

  else if ( isnan( a ) || isnan( b ) )
  {
    /* ... */
```

See Also

fpclassify(), isfinite(), isinf(), isnan(), signbit()

isprint

Ascertains whether a given character is printable.

```
#include <ctype.h>
int isprint( int c );
```

The isprint() function tests whether its argument is a printing character. If the argument is a printing character, isprint() returns a nonzero value (that is, true); if not, the function returns 0 (false).

"Printing" means only that the character occupies printing space on the output medium, not that it fills the space with a glyph. Thus, the space is a printing character (isprint(' ') returns true), even though it does not leave a mark (isgraph(' ') returns false).

Which character codes represent printable characters depends on the current locale setting for the category LC_CTYPE, which you can query or change using the setlocale() function. In the default locale C, the printable characters are the alphanumeric characters, the punctuation characters, and the space character; the corresponding character codes are those from 32 through 126.

Example

```
unsigned int c;

printf("\nThe current locale for the 'is ...' functions is '%s'.\n",
       setlocale(LC_CTYPE, NULL));

printf("Here is a table of the 'is ...' values for the characters"
       " from 0 to 127 in this locale:\n\n");

for ( c = 0; c < 128; c++ ) // Loop iteration for each table row.
{
  if ( c % 24 == 0 )         // Repeat table header every 24 rows.
```

```
{
    printf("Code char alnum alpha blank cntrl digit graph lower"
           " print punct space\n");
    printf("-------------------------------------------------"
           "----------------\n");
}
printf( "%4u %4c %3c %5c %5c %5c %5c %5c %5c %5c %5c %5c\n",
        c,                                // Print numeric character code.
        ( isprint( c ) ? c : ' ' ),       // Print the glyph, or a space
                                          // if it's not printable.
        ( isalnum( c ) ? 'X' : '-' ),     // In a column for each category,
        ( isalpha( c ) ? 'X' : '-' ),     // print X for yes or - for no.
        ( isblank( c ) ? 'X' : '-' ),
        ( iscntrl( c ) ? 'X' : '-' ),
        ( isdigit( c ) ? 'X' : '-' ),
        ( isgraph( c ) ? 'X' : '-' ),
        ( islower( c ) ? 'X' : '-' ),
        ( isprint( c ) ? 'X' : '-' ),
        ( ispunct( c ) ? 'X' : '-' ),
        ( isspace( c ) ? 'X' : '-' ) );
} // end of loop for each character value
```

The following selected lines from the table produced by this program include at least one member and one nonmember of each category:

```
Code char alnum alpha blank cntrl digit graph lower print punct space
----------------------------------------------------------------------
  31           -     -     X     -     -     -     -     -     -     -
  32           -     -     X     -     -     -     -     X     -     X
  33    !      -     -     -     -     -     X     -     X     X     -

  48    0      X     -     -     -     X     X     -     X     -     -

  65    A      X     X     -     -     -     X     -     X     -     -

 122    z      X     X     -     -     -     X     X     X     -     -
```

See Also

isgraph(); the corresponding C99 function for wide characters, iswprint(); isal
num(), isalpha(), isblank(), iscntrl(), isdigit(), islower(), ispunct(),
isspace(), isupper(), isxdigit()

ispunct

Ascertains whether a given character is a punctuation mark.

```
#include <ctype.h>
int ispunct( int c );
```

The function ispunct() tests whether its character argument is a punctuation mark. If the character is a punctuation mark, ispunct() returns a nonzero value (that is, true); if not, the function returns 0 (false).

The punctuation characters are dependent on the current locale setting for the category LC_CTYPE, which you can query or change using the setlocale() function. In the default locale C, the punctuation characters are all of the graphic characters (those for which isgraph() is true), except the alphanumeric characters (those for which isalnum() is true).

Example

See the example for isprint() in this chapter.

See Also

The corresponding C99 function for wide characters, iswpunct(); isalnum(), isalpha(), isblank(), iscntrl(), isdigit(), isgraph(), islower(), isprint(), isspace(), isupper(), isxdigit()

isspace

Ascertains whether a given character produces space.

```
#include <ctype.h>
int isspace( int c );
```

The function isspace() tests whether its character argument produces whitespace rather than a glyph when printed—such as a space, tabulator, newline, or the like. If the argument is a whitespace character, isspace() returns a nonzero value (that is, true); if not, the function returns 0 (false).

Which characters fall into the whitespace class depends on the current locale setting for the category LC_CTYPE, which you can query or change using the setlocale() function. In the default locale C, the isspace() function returns true for the characters in Table 18-4.

Table 18-4. Whitespace characters in the default locale, C

Character	ASCII name	Decimal value
'\t'	Horizontal tabulator	9
'\n'	Line feed	10
'\v'	Vertical tabulator	11
'\f'	Form feed	12
'\r'	Carriage return	13
' '	Space	32

Example

```
char buffer[1024];
char *ptr = buffer;

while ( fgets( buffer, sizeof(buffer), stdin ) != NULL )
{
```

```
    ptr = buffer;
    while ( isspace( *ptr ))            // Skip over leading whitespace.
        ptr++;
    printf( "The line read: %s\n", ptr );
}
```

See also the example for isprint() in this chapter.

See Also

The C99 function isblank(), which returns true for the space and horizontal tab characters; the corresponding C99 functions for wide characters, iswspace() and iswblank(); isalnum(), isalpha(), iscntrl(), isdigit(), isgraph(), islower(), isprint(), ispunct(), isxdigit()

isunordered C99

Tests whether two floating-point values can be numerically ordered.

```
#include <math.h>
int isunordered(x, y )
```

The macro isunordered() tests whether any ordered relation exists between two floating-point values, without risking an "invalid operand" exception in case either of them is NaN ("not a number"). Both operands must have real floating-point types. Two floating-point values are be said to be ordered if one is either less than, equal to, or greater than the other. If either or both of them are NaN, then they are unordered. isunordered() returns a nonzero value (that is, true) if there is no ordered relation between the two arguments.

Example

```
double maximum( double a, double b )
{
    if ( isinf( a ) )          // +Inf > anything; -Inf < anything
        return ( signbit( a ) ? b : a );

    if ( isinf( b ) )
        return ( signbit( b ) ? a : b );

    if ( isunordered( a, b ) )
    {
        feraiseexcept( FE_INVALID );
        return NAN;
    }
    return ( a > b ? a : b );
}
```

See Also

isgreater(), isgreaterequal(), isless(), islessequal(), islessgreater()

isupper

Ascertains whether a given character is an uppercase letter.

```
#include <ctype.h>
int isupper( int c );
```

The function isupper() tests whether its character argument is a capital letter. If the character is an uppercase letter, isupper() returns a nonzero value (that is, true); if not, the function returns 0 (false).

Which characters are letters and which letters are uppercase both depend on the current locale setting for the category LC_CTYPE, which you can query or change using the setlocale() function.(See the note on character classes and locales in the section on isalpha().)

In the default locale C, the truth values of isupper() and islower() are mutually exclusive for the alphabetic characters. However, other locales may have alphabetic characters for which both isupper() and islower() return true, or characters that are alphabetic but neither uppercase nor lowercase.

Example

See the examples for setlocale() and isprint() in this chapter.

See Also

islower(), tolower(), toupper(); the corresponding C99 function for wide characters, iswupper(); isalnum(), isalpha(), isblank(), iscntrl(), isdigit(), isgraph(), isprint(), ispunct(), isspace(), isxdigit(), setlocale()

iswalnum

Ascertains whether a given wide character is alphanumeric.

```
#include <wctype.h>
int iswalnum( wint_t wc );
```

The iswalnum() function is the wide-character version of the isalnum() character classification function. It tests whether its character argument is alphanumeric; that is, whether the character is either a letter of the alphabet or a digit. If the character is alphanumeric, iswalnum() returns a nonzero value (that is, true); if not, the function returns 0 (false).

Which characters are considered alphabetic or numeric depends on the current locale setting for the localization category LC_CTYPE, which you can query or change using the setlocale() function. (See the note on character classes and locales in the section on isalpha().)

In general, iswalnum() is true for all characters for which either iswalpha() or iswdigit() is true.

Example

```
wint_t wc;
int i, dummy;

setlocale( LC_CTYPE, "" );

wprintf( L"\nThe current locale for the 'is ...' functions is '%s'.\n",
        setlocale( LC_CTYPE, NULL ) );
wprintf( L"These are the alphanumeric wide characters"
        " in this locale:\n\n" );

for ( wc = 0, i = 0; wc < 1024; wc++ )
  if ( iswalnum( wc ) )
    {
      if ( i % 25 == 0 )
        {
          wprintf( L"... more ...\n" );
          dummy = getchar();              // Wait before printing more
          wprintf( L"Wide character    Code\n" );
          wprintf( L"---------------------\n" );
        }
      wprintf(   L"%5lc           %4lu\n", wc, wc );
      i++;
    }
wprintf( L"---------------------\n" );
return 0;
```

Here are samples from the output of this code. Which characters can be displayed correctly on the screen depends on the font used:

```
The current locale for the 'is ...' functions is 'de_DE.UTF-8'.
These are the alphanumeric wide characters in this locale:

Wide character    Code
---------------------
        0           48
        1           49
        2           50
...
        þ          254
        ÿ          255
        Ā          256
        ā          257
        Ă          258
        ă          259
        Ą          260
        ą          261
```

See Also

iswalpha() and iswdigit(); the corresponding function for byte characters, isalnum(); iswblank(), iswcntrl(), iswgraph(), iswlower(), iswprint(), iswpunct(), iswspace(), iswupper(), iswxdigit(), setlocale(); the extensible wide-character classification function iswctype()

iswalpha

Ascertains whether a given wide character is a letter of the alphabet.

```
#include <wctype.h>
int iswalpha( wint_t wc );
```

The iswalpha() function is the wide-character version of the isalpha() character classification function. It tests whether its character argument is a letter of the alphabet. If the character is alphabetic, iswalpha() returns a nonzero value (that is, true); if not, the function returns 0 (false).

 Which characters are considered alphabetic depends on the current locale setting for the localization category LC_CTYPE, which you can query or change using the setlocale() function. In all locales, the iswalpha() classification is mutually exclusive with iswcntrl(), iswdigit(), iswpunct() and iswspace().

Accented characters, umlauts, and the like are considered alphabetic only in certain locales. Moreover, other locales may have wide characters that are alphabetic but neither uppercase nor lowercase, or both uppercase and lowercase.

Example

```
wint_t wc;

if ( setlocale( LC_CTYPE, "" ) == NULL)
{
  fwprintf( stderr,
          L"Sorry, couldn't change to the system's native locale.\n");
  return 1;
}
wprintf( L"The current locale for the 'isw ...' functions is '%s'.\n",
        setlocale(LC_CTYPE, NULL));

wprintf( L"Here is a table of the 'isw ...' values for the characters "
        L"from 128 to 255 in this locale:\n\n");

for ( wc = 128; wc < 255; ++wc ) // Loop iteration for each table row.
{
  if ( (wc-128) % 24 == 0 )      // Repeat table header every 24 rows.
  {
    wprintf(L"Code char alnum alpha blank cntrl digit graph lower"
            L" print punct space\n");
    wprintf(L"-------------------------------------------------"
            L"-----------------\n");
```

```
    }
    wprintf(L"%4u %4lc %3c %5c %5c %5c %5c %5c %5c %5c %5c %5c %5c %5c\n",
        wc,                                // Print numeric character code.
        ( iswprint( wc ) ? wc  : ' ' ),    // Print the glyph, or a space
                                           // if it's not printable.
        ( iswalnum( wc ) ? 'X' : '-' ),    // In a column for each
        ( iswalpha( wc ) ? 'X' : '-' ),    // category, print X for
        ( iswblank( wc ) ? 'X' : '-' ),    // yes or - for no.
        ( iswcntrl( wc ) ? 'X' : '-' ),
        ( iswdigit( wc ) ? 'X' : '-' ),
        ( iswgraph( wc ) ? 'X' : '-' ),
        ( iswlower( wc ) ? 'X' : '-' ),
        ( iswprint( wc ) ? 'X' : '-' ),
        ( iswpunct( wc ) ? 'X' : '-' ),
        ( iswspace( wc ) ? 'X' : '-' ) );
    } // end of loop for each character value
```

The following selected lines from the table produced by this program illustrate members of various categories:

```
Code char alnum alpha blank cntrl digit graph lower print punct space
-----------------------------------------------------------------------
128         -     -     X     -     -     -     -     -     -     -
162   ¢     -     -     -     -     -     X     -     X     X     -
163   £     -     -     -     -     -     X     -     X     X     -
169   ©     -     -     -     -     -     X     -     X     X     -
170   ª     X     X     -     -     -     X     -     X     -     -
171   «     -     -     -     -     -     X     -     X     X     -
180   ´     -     -     -     -     -     X     -     X     X     -
181   µ     X     X     -     -     -     X     X     X     -     -
182   ¶     -     -     -     -     -     X     -     X     X     -
185   ¹     -     -     -     -     -     X     -     X     X     -
186   º     X     X     -     -     -     X     -     X     -     -
191   ¿     -     -     -     -     -     X     -     X     X     -
192   À     X     X     -     -     -     X     -     X     -     -
```

See Also

The corresponding function for byte characters, isalpha(); iswalnum(), iswblank(), iswcntrl(), iswdigit(), iswgraph(), iswlower(), iswprint(), iswpunct(), iswspace(), iswupper(), iswxdigit(), setlocale(); the extensible wide-character classification function iswctype()

iswblank   C99

Ascertains whether a given wide character is a space or tab character.

```
#include <wctype.h>
int iswblank( wint_t wc );
```

The iswblank() function is the wide-character version of the isblank() character classification function. It tests whether its wide-character argument is either a space or a tab character. In the default locale C, iswblank() returns a nonzero value (that is, true) only for the argument values L' ' (space) and L'\t' (horizontal tab); these are called the standard blank wide characters. In other locales, iswblank() may also be true for other wide characters for which iswspace() also returns true.

Example

See the example for iswalpha() in this chapter.

See Also

The corresponding function for byte characters, isblank(); iswalnum(), iswalpha(), iswcntrl(), iswdigit(), iswgraph(), iswlower(), iswprint(), iswpunct(), iswspace(), iswupper(), iswxdigit(), setlocale(); the extensible wide-character classification function iswctype()

iswcntrl

Ascertains whether a given wide character is a control character.

```
#include <wctype.h>
int iswcntrl( wint_t wc );
```

The iswcntrl() function is the wide-character version of the iscntrl() character classification function. It tests whether its wide-character argument is a control character. If the argument is a control character, iswcntrl() returns a nonzero value (that is, true); if not, the function returns 0 (false).

The function may yield different results depending on the current locale setting for the localization category LC_CTYPE, which you can query or change using the setlocale() function.

Example

See the example for iswalpha() in this chapter.

See Also

The corresponding function for byte characters, iscntrl(); iswalnum(), iswalpha(), iswblank(), iswdigit(), iswgraph(), iswlower(), iswprint(), iswpunct(), iswspace(), iswupper(), iswxdigit(), setlocale(); the extensible wide-character classification function iswctype()

iswctype

Ascertains whether a given wide character fits a given description.

```
#include <wctype.h>
int iswctype( wint_t wc, wctype_t description );
```

The iswctype() function tests whether the wide character passed as its first argument falls in the category indicated by the second argument. The value of the second argument, with the special-purpose type wctype_t, is obtained by calling the function wctype() with a string argument that names a property of characters in the current locale. In the default locale, C, characters can have the properties listed in Table 18-5.

Table 18-5. Wide-character properties

Character property	iswctype() call	Equivalent single function call
"alnum"	iswctype(wc, wctype("alnum"))	iswalnum(wc)
"alpha"	iswctype(wc, wctype("alpha"))	iswalpha(wc)
"blank"	iswctype(wc, wctype("blank"))	iswblank(wc)
"cntrl"	iswctype(wc, wctype("cntrl"))	iswcntrl(wc)
"digit"	iswctype(wc, wctype("digit"))	iswdigit(wc)
"graph"	iswctype(wc, wctype("graph"))	iswgraph(wc)
"lower"	iswctype(wc, wctype("lower"))	iswlower(wc)
"print"	iswctype(wc, wctype("print"))	iswprint(wc)
"punct"	iswctype(wc, wctype("punct"))	iswpunct(wc)
"space"	iswctype(wc, wctype("space"))	iswspace(wc)
"upper"	iswctype(wc, wctype("upper"))	iswupper(wc)
"xdigit"	iswctype(wc, wctype("xdigit"))	iswxdigit(wc)

If the wide-character argument has the property indicated, iswctype() returns a nonzero value (that is, true); if not, the function returns 0 (false). Thus, the call iswctype(wc, wctype("upper")) is equivalent to iswupper(wc).

The result of an iswctype() function call depends on the current locale setting for the localization category LC_CTYPE, which you can query or change using the setlocale() function. Furthermore, additional property strings are defined in other locales. For example, in a Japanese locale, the call iswctype(wc, wctype("jkanji")) can be used to distinguish kanji from katakana or hiragana characters. You must not change the LC_CTYPE setting between the calls to wctype() and iswctype().

Example

```
wint_t wc = L'ß';

setlocale( LC_CTYPE, "de_DE.UTF-8" );
if ( iswctype( wc, wctype( "alpha" )) )
{
  if ( iswctype( wc, wctype( "lower" ) ))
    wprintf( L"The character %lc is lowercase.\n", wc );
  if ( iswctype( wc, wctype( "upper" ) ))
    wprintf( L"The character %lc is uppercase.\n", wc );
}
```

wctype(), iswalnum(), iswalpha(), iswblank(), iswcntrl(), iswdigit(), iswgraph(), iswlower(), iswprint(), iswpunct(), iswspace(), iswupper(), iswxdigit()

iswdigit

Ascertains whether a given wide character is a decimal digit.

```
#include <wctype.h>
int iswdigit( wint_t wc );
```

The iswdigit() function is the wide-character version of the isdigit() character classification function. It tests whether its wide-character argument corresponds to a digit character.

The digit wide characters are L'0' (not to be confused with the null character L'\0') through L'9'. The iswdigit() function returns a nonzero value (that is, true) if the wide character represents a digit; if not, it returns 0 (false).

Example

See the example for iswalpha() in this chapter.

See Also

The corresponding function for byte characters, isdigit(); iswalnum(), iswalpha(), iswblank(), iswcntrl(), iswgraph(), iswlower(), iswprint(), iswpunct(), iswspace(), iswupper(), iswxdigit(), setlocale(); the extensible wide-character classification function iswctype()

iswgraph

Ascertains whether a given wide character is graphic.

```
#include <wctype.h>
int iswgraph( wint_t wc );
```

The iswgraph() function is the wide-character version of the isgraph() character classification function. It tests whether its character argument is a graphic character; that is, whether the value represents a printable character that is not a whitespace character. In other words, iswgraph(wc) is true if and only if iswprint(wc) is true and iswspace(wc) is false.

The function call iswgraph(wc) can yield a different value than the corresponding byte-character function call isgraph(wctob(wc)) if wc is both a printing character and a whitespace character in the execution character set. In other words, isgraph(wctob(wc)) can be true while iswgraph(wc) is false, if both iswprint(wc) and iswspace(wc) are true. Or, to put it yet another way, while the space character (' ') is the only printable character for which isgraph() returns false, iswgraph() may return false for other printable, whitespace characters in addition to L' '.

Example

See the example for iswalpha() in this chapter.

See Also

The corresponding function for byte characters, isgraph(); iswalnum(), iswalpha(), iswblank(), iswcntrl(), iswdigit(), iswlower(), iswprint(), iswpunct(), iswspace(), iswupper(), iswxdigit(), setlocale(); the extensible wide-character classification function iswctype()

iswlower

Ascertains whether a given wide character is a lowercase letter.

```
#include <wctype.h>
int iswlower( wint_t wc );
```

The iswlower() function is the wide-character version of the islower() character classification function. It tests whether its character argument is a lowercase letter. If the character is a lowercase letter, iswlower() returns a nonzero value (that is, true); if not, the function returns 0 (false).

Which characters are letters and which letters are lowercase both depend on the current locale setting for the category LC_CTYPE, which you can query or change using the setlocale() function. (See the note on character classes and locales in the section on isalpha().)

For some locale-specific characters, both iswupper() and iswlower() may return true, or both may return false even though iswalpha() returns true. However, iswlower() is mutually exclusive with iswcntrl(), iswdigit(), iswpunct(), and iswspace() in all locales.

Example

See the example for iswalpha() in this chapter.

See Also

iswupper(), iswalpha(); the corresponding function for byte characters, islower(); the extensible wide-character classification function iswctype(); iswalnum(), iswblank(), iswcntrl(), iswdigit(), iswgraph(), iswprint(), iswpunct(), iswspace(), iswxdigit(), setlocale()

iswprint

Ascertains whether a given wide character is printable.

```
#include <wctype.h>
int iswprint( wint_t wc );
```

The iswprint() function is the wide-character version of the isprint() character classification function. It tests whether its argument is a printing character. If the argument is a printing wide character, iswprint() returns a nonzero value (that is, true); if not, the function returns 0 (false).

"Printing" means only that the character occupies printing space on the output medium, not that it fills the space with a glyph. In other words, iswprint() may return true for locale-specific whitespace characters, as well as for the space character, L' '.

Which character codes represent printable characters depends on the current locale setting for the category LC_CTYPE, which you can query or change using the setlocale() function.

Example

See the example for iswalpha() in this chapter.

See Also

iswspace(); the corresponding function for byte characters, isprint(); iswalnum(), iswalpha(), iswblank(), iswcntrl(), iswdigit(), iswlower(), iswpunct(), iswupper(), iswxdigit(), setlocale(); the extensible wide-character classification function iswctype()

iswpunct

Ascertains whether a given wide character is a punctuation mark.

```
#include <wctype.h>
int iswpunct( wint_t wc );
```

The iswpunct() function is the wide-character version of the ispunct() character classification function. It tests whether its wide-character argument is a punctuation mark. If the argument represents a punctuation mark, iswpunct() returns a nonzero value (that is, true); if not, the function returns 0 (false).

Which characters represent punctuation marks depends on the current locale setting for the category LC_CTYPE, which you can query or change using the setlocale() function. For all locale-specific punctuation characters, both iswspace() and iswalnum() return false.

If the wide character is not the space character L' ', but is both a printing and a whitespace character—that is, both iswprint(wc) and iswspace(wc) return true—then the function call iswpunct(wc) may yield a different value than the corresponding byte-character function call ispunct(wctob(wc)).

Example

See the example for iswalpha() in this chapter.

See Also

The corresponding function for byte characters, `ispunct()`; `iswalnum()`, `iswalpha()`, `iswblank()`, `iswcntrl()`, `iswdigit()`, `iswgraph()`, `iswlower()`, `iswprint()`, `iswspace()`, `iswupper()`, `iswxdigit()`, `setlocale()`; the extensible wide-character classification function `iswctype()`

iswspace

Ascertains whether a given wide character produces space.

```
#include <wctype.h>
int iswspace( wint_t wc );
```

The `iswspace()` function is the wide-character version of the `isspace()` character classification function. It tests whether its wide-character argument produces white-space rather than a glyph when printed—that is, a space, tabulator, newline, or the like. If the argument is a whitespace wide character, `iswspace()` returns a nonzero value (that is, `true`); if not, the function returns 0 (`false`).

Which wide characters fall into the whitespace class depends on the current locale setting for the category `LC_CTYPE`, which you can query or change using the `setlocale()` function. In all locales, however, if `iswspace()` is true for a given wide character, then `iswalnum()`, `iswgraph()`, and `iswpunct()` are false.

Example

See the example for `iswalpha()` in this chapter.

See Also

`iswblank()`, `iswprint()`; the corresponding function for byte characters, `isspace()`; `iswalnum()`, `iswalpha()`, `iswcntrl()`, `iswdigit()`, `iswgraph()`, `iswlower()`, `iswprint()`, `iswpunct()`, `iswupper()`, `iswxdigit()`, `setlocale()`; the extensible wide-character classification function `iswctype()`

iswupper

Ascertains whether a given wide character is an uppercase letter.

```
#include <wctype.h>
int iswupper( wint_t wc );
```

The `iswupper()` function is the wide-character version of the `isupper()` character classification function. It tests whether its character argument is an uppercase letter. If the character is an uppercase letter, `isupper()` returns a nonzero value (that is, `true`); if not, the function returns 0 (`false`).

Which characters are letters and which letters are uppercase both depend on the current locale setting for the category `LC_CTYPE`, which you can query or change using the `setlocale()` function. (See the note on character classes and locales in the section on `isalpha()`.)

For some locale-specific characters, both `iswupper()` and `iswlower()` may return true, or both may return false even though `iswalpha()` returns true. However, `iswupper()` is mutually exclusive with `iswcntrl()`, `iswdigit()`, `iswpunct()`, and `iswspace()` in all locales.

Example

See the example for `iswalpha()` in this chapter.

See Also

`iswlower()`, `iswalpha()`; the corresponding function for byte characters, `isupper()`; the extensible wide-character classification function `iswctype()`; `iswalnum()`, `iswblank()`, `iswcntrl()`, `iswdigit()`, `iswgraph()`, `iswprint()`, `iswpunct()`, `iswspace()`, `iswxdigit()`, `setlocale()`

iswxdigit

Ascertains whether a given wide character is a hexadecimal digit.

```
#include <wctype.h>
int iswxdigit( wint_t wc );
```

The `iswxdigit()` function is the wide-character version of the `isxdigit()` character classification function. It tests whether its character argument is a hexadecimal digit, and returns a nonzero value (that is, true) if the character is one of the digits between `L'0'` and `L'9'` inclusive, or a letter from `L'A'` through `L'F'` or from `L'a'` through `L'f'` inclusive. If not, the function returns 0 (false).

Example

See the example for `iswalpha()` in this chapter.

See Also

`iswdigit()`; the corresponding functions for byte characters, `isdigit()` and `isxdigit()`; `iswalnum()`, `iswalpha()`, `iswblank()`, `iswcntrl()`, `iswgraph()`, `iswlower()`, `iswprint()`, `iswpunct()`, `iswspace()`, `iswupper()`, `setlocale()`; the extensible wide-character classification function `iswctype()`

isxdigit

Ascertains whether a given character is a hexadecimal digit.

```
#include <ctype.h>
int isxdigit( int c );
```

The function `isxdigit()` tests whether its character argument is a hexadecimal digit. The results depend on the current locale setting for the localization category `LC_CTYPE`, which you can query or change using the `setlocale()` function. In the C locale, `isxdigit()` returns a nonzero value (that is, true) if the character is between `'0'` and `'9'` inclusive, or between `'A'` and `'F'` inclusive, or between `'a'` and `'f'` inclusive. If not, the function returns 0 (false).

Example

See the example for isprint() in this chapter.

See Also

The corresponding C99 function for wide characters, iswxdigit(); isalnum(), isalpha(), isblank(), iscntrl(), isdigit(), isgraph(), islower(), isprint(), ispunct(), isspace(), isupper(), isxdigit(); the extensible wide-character classification function iswctype()

labs

Gives the absolute value of a long integer.

```
#include <stdlib.h>
long labs( long n );
```

The parameter and the return value of labs() are long integers. Otherwise, labs() works the same as the int function abs().

Example

See the example for abs() in this chapter.

See Also

abs(), llabs(), imaxabs()

ldexp

Multiplies a floating-point number by a power of two.

```
#include <math.h>
double ldexp( double mantissa, int exponent );
float ldexpf( float mantissa, int exponent );        (C99)
long double ldexpl( long double mantissa, int exponent );        (C99)
```

The ldexp() functions calculate a floating-point number from separate mantissa and exponent values. The *exponent* parameter is an integer exponent to base 2.

The function returns the value $mantissa \times 2^{exponent}$. If the result is not representable in the function's type, a range error may occur.

Example

See the example for frexp() in this chapter.

See Also

The function frexp(), which performs the reverse operation, analyzing a floating-point number into a mantissa and an exponent to base 2.

ldiv

Performs integer division, returning quotient and remainder.

```
#include <stdlib.h>
ldiv_t ldiv( long dividend, long divisor );
```

The parameters of ldiv() are long integers, and its return value is a structure of type ldiv_t containing two long integers. Otherwise, ldiv() works the same as the int function div().

Example

See the example for div() in this chapter.

See Also

div(), lldiv(), imaxdiv()

llabs   C99

Gives the absolute value of a long long integer.

```
#include <stdlib.h>
long long llabs( long long n );
```

The parameter and the return value of llabs() are long long integers. Otherwise, llabs() works the same as the int function abs().

Example

See the example for abs() in this chapter.

See Also

abs(), labs(), imaxabs()

lldiv   C99

Performs integer division, returning quotient and remainder.

```
#include <stdlib.h>
lldiv_t lldiv( long long dividend, long long divisor );
```

The parameters of lldiv() are long long integers, and its return value is a structure of type lldiv_t containing two long long integers. Otherwise, lldiv() works the same as the int function div().

Example

See the example for div() in this chapter.

See Also

div(), ldiv(), imaxdiv()

llrint

Rounds a floating-point number to a long long integer.

```
#include <math.h>
long long llrint( double x );
long long llrintf( float x );
long long llrintl( long double x );
```

The llrint() functions round a floating-point number to the next integer value in the current rounding direction. If the result is outside the range of long long, a range error may occur (this is implementation-dependent), and the return value is unspecified.

Example

See the example for the analogous function lrint().

See Also

rint(), lrint(), round(), lround(), llround(), nearbyint(), fegetround(), fesetround()

llround

Rounds a floating-point number to a long long integer.

```
#include <math.h>
long long llround( double x );
long long llroundf( float x );
long long llroundl( long double x );
```

The llround() functions are like lround() except that they return an integer of type long long. llround() rounds a floating-point number to the nearest integer value. A value halfway between two integers is rounded away from zero. If the result is outside the range of long long, a range error may occur (this is implementation-dependent), and the return value is unspecified.

Example

See the example for lround() in this chapter.

See Also

rint(), lrint(), llrint(), round(), lround(), nearbyint()

localeconv

Obtains the conventions of the current locale.

```
#include <locale.h>
struct lconv *localeconv( void );
```

The localeconv() function returns a pointer to a structure containing complete information on the locale-specific conventions for formatting numeric and monetary information. The values returned reflect the conventions of the current locale, which you can query or set using the setlocale() function.

The structure that localeconv() fills in has the type struct lconv, which is defined in the header file *locale.h*. The members of this structure describe how to format monetary as well as non-monetary numeric values in the locale. In C99, moreover, two sets of information describing monetary formatting are present: one describing local usage and one describing international usage, which calls for standard alphabetic currency symbols and may also use a different number of decimal places.

The full set of members and their order in the structure may vary from one implementation to another, but they must include at least the members described here:

char *decimal_point;
    The decimal point character, except when referring to money. In the default locale C, this pointer refers to the value ".".

char *thousands_sep;
    The digit-grouping character: for example, the comma in "65,536". In spite of the name, not all locales group digits by thousands; for example, see the next member, grouping.

char *grouping;
    This pointer refers not to a text string but to an array of numeric char values with the following meaning: the first element in the array is the number of digits in the rightmost digit group. Each successive element is the number of digits in the next group to the left. The value CHAR_MAX means that the remaining digits are not grouped at all; the value 0 means that the last group size indicated is used for all remaining digits. For example, the char array {'\3','\0'} indicates that all digits are grouped in threes.

char *mon_decimal_point;
    Decimal point character for monetary values.

char *mon_thousands_sep;
    The digit-grouping character for monetary values.

char *mon_grouping;
    Like the grouping element, but for monetary values.

char *positive_sign;
    The sign used to indicate positive monetary values.

char *negative_sign;
    The sign used to indicate negative monetary values.

`char *currency_symbol;`

The currency symbol in *the current locale*: in the United States, this would be "$", whereas the abbreviation used in international finance, "USD", would be indicated by another structure member, `int_currency_symbol`.

`char frac_digits;`

The number of digits after the decimal point in monetary values, in local usage.

`char p_cs_precedes;`

The value 1 means the local `currency_symbol` is placed before positive numbers (as in U.S. dollars: "$10.99"); 0 means the symbol comes after the number (as in the Canadian French locale, "fr_CA": "10,99 $").

`char n_cs_precedes;`

The value 1 means the local `currency_symbol` is placed before negative numbers; 0 means the symbol comes after the number.

`char p_sep_by_space;`

The value 1 means a space is inserted between `currency_symbol` and a positive number.

`char n_sep_by_space;`

The value 1 means a space is inserted between `currency_symbol` and a negative number.

`char p_sign_posn;`

See next item.

`char n_sign_posn;`

These values indicate the positions of the positive and negative signs, as follows:

0

The number and `currency_symbol` are enclosed together in parentheses.

1

The sign string is placed before the number and `currency_symbol`.

2

The sign string is placed after the number and `currency_symbol`.

3

The sign string is placed immediately before the `currency_symbol`.

4

The sign string is placed immediately after the `currency_symbol`.

`char *int_curr_symbol;`

This pointer indicates a null-terminated string containing the three-letter international symbol for the local currency (as specified in ISO 4217), and a separator character in the fourth position.

`char int_frac_digits;`

The number of digits after the decimal point in monetary values, in international usage.

`char int_p_cs_precedes;` *(C99)*

The value 1 means that `int_curr_symbol` is placed before positive numbers; 0 means the symbol comes after the number.

`char int_n_cs_precedes;` *(C99)*

The value 1 means `int_curr_symbol` is placed before negative numbers; 0 means the symbol comes after the number.

`char int_p_sep_by_space;` *(C99)*

The value 1 means a space is inserted between `int_curr_symbol` and a positive number.

`char int_n_sep_by_space;` *(C99)*

The value 1 means a space is inserted between `int_curr_symbol` and a negative number.

`char int_p_sign_posn;` *(C99)*

See next item.

`char int_n_sign_posn;` *(C99)*

These values indicate the positions of the positive and negative signs with respect to `int_curr_symbol` in the same way that `p_sign_posn` and `n_sign_posn` indicate the sign positions with respect to `currency_symbol`.

In the default locale, C, all of the `char` members have the value `CHAR_MAX`, and all of the `char *` members point to an empty string (`""`), except `decimal_point`, which points to the string `"."`.

Example

```
long long cents;        // Amount in cents or customary fraction of
                        // currency unit.
struct lconv *locinfo;
wchar_t number[128] = { L'\0' }, prefix[32]  = { L'\0' },
        suffix[32]  = { L'\0' };

// Use system's current locale.
char *localename = setlocale( LC_MONETARY, "" );

locinfo = localeconv();

/* ... */
```

```
if ( cents >= 0 ) // For positive amounts,
                  // use 'p_...' members of lconv structure.
{
  if ( locinfo->p_cs_precedes )    // If currency symbol before number
  {                                // ... prepare prefix
    mbstowcs( prefix, locinfo->currency_symbol, 32 );
    if ( locinfo->p_sep_by_space )
      wcscat( prefix, L" " );      // ... maybe with a space.
  }
/* ... else etc. ... */
```
See Also

setlocale()

localtime

Converts a time value into a year, month, day, hour, minute, second, and so on.

```
#include <time.h>
struct tm *localtime( const time_t *timer );
```

The localtime() function converts a numeric time value (usually a number of seconds since January 1, 1970, but not necessarily) into the equivalent date-and-time structure for the local time zone. To obtain similar values for Coordinated Universal Time (UTC, formerly called Greenwich Mean Time), use the function gmtime().

The function's argument is not the number of seconds itself but a pointer to that value. Both the structure type struct tm and the arithmetic type time_t are defined in the header file *time.h*. The tm structure is described at gmtime() in this chapter.

The argument most often passed to localtime() is the current time, obtained as a number with type time_t by calling the function time(). The type time_t is usually defined in *time.h* as equivalent to long or unsigned long.

Example

See the example for gmtime() in this chapter.

See Also

asctime(), difftime(), gmtime(), localtime_s(), mktime(), strftime(), time()

localtime_s   C11

Converts a time value into a year, month, day, hour, minute, second, etc.

```
#include <time.h>
struct tm *localtime_s( const time_t * restrict timer ,
                        struct tm * restrict result);
```

The function localtime_s(), like localtime(), converts a numeric time value into the equivalent date-and-time structure for the local time zone. The results are stored in an object of the type struct tm. This structure is described in the section on gmtime() in this chapter.

Unlike localtime(), localtime_s() does not use an internal, static struct tm object, but places the results in the struct tm object addressed by its second argument. The localtime_s() function is thread-safe.

The function first tests its runtime constraints: the pointer arguments *timer* and *result* must not be null pointers. If a runtime constraint is violated or if the value of *timer* cannot be converted into a local calendar time, localtime_s() returns a null pointer. If no error occurs, the return value is the pointer *result*.

Example

```
#define __STDC_WANT_LIB_EXT1__ 1
#include <time.h>
// ...

    time_t now;    struct tm timeStruct;    char timeStr[26];

    time(&now);                  // Current time as an integer.
    // Convert to local time as a struct tm:
    if( localtime_s(&now, &timeStruct) != NULL)
    {
        timeStruct.tm_year += 1;              // One year later.
        if(asctime_s( timeStr, sizeof(timeStr), &timeStruct) == 0)
            printf("A year from today: %s", timeStr);
    }
```

See Also

localtime(), gmtime(), gmtime_s(), strftime(), time()

log

Calculates the natural logarithm of a number.

```
#include <math.h>
double log( double x );
float logf( float x );            (C99)
long double logl( long double x );        (C99)
```

The log() functions calculate the natural logarithm of their argument. The natural logarithm—called "log" for short in English as well as in C—is the logarithm to base e, where e is Euler's number, 2.718281....

The natural log of a number x is defined only for positive values of x. If x is negative, a domain error occurs; if x is zero, a range error may occur (or not, depending on the implementation).

Example

The following code prints some sample values for base 2, base e, and base 10 logarithms:

```
double x[] = { 1E-100, 0.5, 2, exp(1), 10, 1E+100 };

puts("      x              log2(x)            log(x)            log10(x)\n"
     " -----------------------------------------------------------------");
for ( int i = 0; i < sizeof(x) / sizeof(x[0]); ++i )
{
  printf("%#10.3G %+17.10G %+17.10G %+17.10G\n",
         x[i], log2(x[i]), log(x[i]), log10(x[i]) );
}
```

This code produces the following output:

```
      x            log2(x)              log(x)            log10(x)
 ---------------------------------------------------------------
1.00E-100      -332.1928095        -230.2585093                -100
    0.500                -1        -0.6931471806       -0.3010299957
     2.00                +1        +0.6931471806       +0.3010299957
     2.72      +1.442695041                  +1       +0.4342944819
     10.0      +3.321928095        +2.302585093                  +1
1.00E+100      +332.1928095        +230.2585093                +100
```

See Also

log10(), log1p(), log2(), exp(), pow()

log10

Calculates the base-10 logarithm of a number.

```
#include <math.h>
double log10( double x );
float log10f( float x );       (C99)
long double log10l( long double x );       (C99)
```

The log10() functions calculate the common logarithm of their argument. The common logarithm is the logarithm to base 10. The common logarithm of a number x is defined only for positive values of x. If x is negative, a domain error occurs; if x is zero, a range error may occur.

Example

See the example for log() in this chapter.

See Also

log(), log1p(), log2(), exp(), pow()

log1p   C99

Calculates the logarithm of one plus a number.

```
#include <math.h>
double log1p( double x );
float log1pf( float x );
long double log1pl( long double x );
```

The log1p() functions calculate the natural logarithm of the sum of 1 plus the argument x, or $\log_e(1 + x)$. The function is designed to yield a more accurate result than the expression log(x + 1), especially when the value of the argument is close to zero.

The natural logarithm is defined only for positive numbers. If x is less than -1, a domain error occurs; if x is equal to -1, a range error may occur (or not, depending on the implementation).

Example

```
// atanh(x) is defined as 0.5 * ( log(x+1) - log(-x+1).
// Rounding errors can result in different results
// for different methods.

puts("    x           atanh(x)     atanh(x) - 0.5*(log1p(x) - log1p(-x))\n"
     "-----------------------------------------------------------------");
for ( double x = -0.8; x < 1.0; x += 0.4)
{
  double y = atanh(x);
  printf("%6.2f %14f %20E\n", x, y, y - 0.5*(log1p(x) - log1p(-x)) );
}
```

This code produces the following output:

```
     x           atanh(x)     atanh(x) - 0.5*(log1p(x) - log1p(-x))
    ------------------------------------------------------------------
    -0.80        -1.098612        -1.376937E-17
    -0.40        -0.423649        -1.843144E-18
     0.00         0.000000         0.000000E+00
     0.40         0.423649         7.589415E-19
     0.80         1.098612        -4.640385E-17
```

See Also

log(), log10(), log2(), exp(), pow()

log2   C99

Calculates the logarithm to base 2 of a number.

```
#include <math.h>
double log2( double x );
float log2f( float x );
long double log2l( long double x );
```

The base-2 logarithm of a number x is defined only for positive values of x. If x is negative, a domain error occurs; if x is zero, and depending on the implementation, a range error may occur.

Example

```
double x[] = { 0, 0.7, 1.8, 1234, INFINITY };

for ( int i = 0; i < sizeof( x ) / sizeof( double ); i++ )
```

```
{
  errno = 0;
  printf( "The base 2 log of  %.1f is %.3f.\n", x[i], log2( x[i] ) );
  if ( errno == EDOM || errno == ERANGE )
    perror( __FILE__ );
}
```

This code produces the following output:

```
The base 2 log of  0.0 is -inf.
log2.c: Numerical result out of range
The base 2 log of  0.7 is -0.515.
The base 2 log of  1.8 is 0.848.
The base 2 log of  1234.0 is 10.269.
The base 2 log of  inf is inf.
```

See Also

log( ), log10( ), log1p( ), exp( ), pow( )

logb   C99

Obtains the exponent of a floating-point number.

```
#include <math.h>
double logb( double x );
float logbf( float x );
long double logbl( long double x );
```

The logb( ) functions return the exponent of their floating-point argument. If the argument is not normalized, logb( ) returns the exponent of its normalized value. If the argument is zero, logb( ) may incur a domain error, depending on the implementation. (In the example shown here, which uses the GNU C library, no domain error occurs.)

Example

```
double x[] = { 0, 0, 0.7, 1.8, 1234, INFINITY };

x[1] = nexttoward( 0.0, 1.0 );

for ( int i = 0; i < sizeof( x ) / sizeof( double ); i++ )
{
  printf( "The exponent in the binary representation of %g is %g.\n",
          x[i], logb( x[i] ) );
  if ( errno == EDOM || errno == ERANGE )
    perror( __FILE__ );
}
```

This code produces the following output:

```
The exponent in the binary representation of 0 is -inf.
The exponent in the binary representation of 4.94066e-324 is -1074.
The exponent in the binary representation of 0.7 is -1.
The exponent in the binary representation of 1.8 is 0.
```

```
The exponent in the binary representation of 1234 is 10.
The exponent in the binary representation of inf is inf.
```

See Also

ilogb( ), log( ), log10( ), log1p( ), log2( ), exp( ), pow( )

longjmp

Jump to a previously defined point in the program.

```
#include <setjmp.h>
void longjmp( jmp_buf environment, int returnval );
```

The longjmp( ) function allows the program to jump to a point that was previously defined by calling the macro setjmp( ). Unlike the goto statement, the longjmp( ) call does not need to be within the same function as its destination. The use of setjmp( ) and longjmp( ) can make a program harder to read and maintain, but they are useful as a way to escape from function calls in case of errors.

The *environment* argument contains the processor and stack environment corresponding to the destination, and must be obtained from a prior setjmp( ) call. Its type, jmp_buf, is defined in *setjmp.h*.

The longjmp( ) function does not return. Instead, the program continues as if returning from the setjmp( ) call except that the *returnval* argument passed to longjmp( ) appears as the return value of setjmp( ). This value allows the setjmp( ) caller to determine whether the initial setjmp( ) call has just returned, or whether a longjmp( ) call has occurred. setjmp( ) itself returns 0. If setjmp( ) appears to return any other value, then that point in the program was reached by calling longjmp( ). If the *returnval* argument in the longjmp( ) call is 0, it is replaced with 1 as the apparent return value after the corresponding setjmp( ) call. The longjmp( ) call must not occur after the function that called setjmp( ) returns. Furthermore, if any variables with automatic storage duration in the function that called setjmp( ) were modified after the setjmp( ) call (and were not declared as volatile), then their values after the longjmp( ) call are indeterminate.

Example

See the example for setjmp( ).

See Also

setjmp( )

lrint   C99

Rounds a floating-point number to an integer.

```
#include <math.h>
long lrint( double x );
```

```
long lrintf( float x );
long lrintl( long double x );
```

The lrint() functions round a floating-point number to the next integer value in the current rounding direction. If the result is outside the range of long, a range error may occur, depending on the implementation, and the return value is unspecified.

Example

```
double t_ambient;        // Ambient temperature in Celsius.
int t_display;           // Display permits integer values.
char tempstring[128];
int saverounding = fegetround();

/* ... Read t_ambient from some thermometer somewhere ... */

fesetround(FE_TONEAREST); // Round toward nearest integer, up or down.

t_display = (int)lrint( t_ambient );
snprintf( tempstring, 128, "Current temperature: %d° C\n", t_display );

fesetround( saverounding );   // Restore rounding direction.
```

See Also

rint(), llrint(), round(), lround(), llround(), nearbyint()

lround   C99

Rounds a floating-point number to an integer.

```
#include <math.h>
long lround( double x );
long lroundf( float x );
long lroundl( long double x );
```

The lround() functions are like round() except that they return an integer of type long. lround() rounds a floating-point number to the nearest integer value. A number halfway between two integers is rounded away from 0. If the result is outside the range of long, a range error may occur (depending on the implementation), and the return value is unspecified.

Example

```
long costnow;        // Total cost in cents.
long realcost;
double rate;         // Annual interest rate.
int period;          // Time to defray cost.

/* ... obtain the interest rate to use for calculation ... */

realcost = lround( (double)costnow * exp( rate * (double)period ));
```

```
printf( "Financed over %d years, the real cost will be $%ld.%2ld.\n",
        period, realcost/100, realcost % 100 );
```

See Also

rint(), lrint(), llrint(), round(), llround(), nearbyint()

malloc

Allocates a block of memory.

```
#include <stdlib.h>
void *malloc( size_t size );
```

The malloc() function obtains a block of memory for the program to use. The argument specifies the size of the block requested in bytes. The type size_t is defined in *stdlib.h*, usually as unsigned int.

If successful, malloc() returns a void pointer to the beginning of the memory block obtained. Void pointers are converted automatically to another pointer on assignment, so you do not need to use an explicit cast, although you may want do so for the sake of clarity. Also, in older C dialects, malloc() returned a pointer to char, which did necessitate explicit casts. If no memory block of the requested size is available, the function returns a null pointer.

Example

```
struct linelink { char *line;
                  struct linelink *next;
                };
struct linelink *head = NULL, *tail = NULL;

char buffer[2048];
FILE *fp_in;
/* ... Open input file ... */
while ( NULL != fgets(buffer, sizeof(buffer), fp_in ))
{
  if ( head == NULL ) /* Chain not yet started; add first link */
  {
    head = tail = malloc( sizeof(struct linelink));
    if ( head != NULL )
    {
      head->line = malloc( strlen( buffer  ) + 1 );
      if ( head->line != NULL )
      { strcpy( head->line, buffer); head->next = NULL; }
      else
        { fprintf( stderr, "Out of memory\n" ); return -1; }
    }
    else
      { fprintf( stderr, "Out of memory\n" ); return -1; }
  }
  else  /* Chain already started; add another link ... */
```

`free()`, `calloc()`, `realloc()`

mblen

Determines the length of a multibyte character, or whether the multibyte encoding is stateful.

```
#include <stdlib.h>
int mblen( const char *s, size_t maxsize );
```

The `mblen()` function determines the length in bytes of a multibyte character referenced by its pointer argument. If the argument points to a valid multibyte character, then `mblen()` returns a value greater than zero. If the argument points to a null character (`'\0'`), then `mblen()` returns 0. A return value of -1 indicates that the argument does not point to a valid multibyte character, or that the multibyte character is longer than the maximum size specified by the second argument. The `LC_TYPE` category in the current locale settings determines which byte sequences are valid multibyte characters.

The second argument specifies a maximum byte length for the multibyte character, and should not be greater than the value of the symbolic constant `MB_CUR_MAX`, defined in *stdlib.h*.

If you pass `mblen()` a null pointer as the first argument, then the return value indicates whether the current multibyte encoding is stateful. This behavior is the same as that of `mbtowc()`. If `mblen()` returns 0, then the encoding is stateless. If it returns any other value, the encoding is stateful; that is, the interpretation of a given byte sequence may depend on the shift state.

Example

```
size_t mbsrcat( char * restrict s1, char * restrict s2,
                mbstate_t * restrict p_s1state, size_t n )
/* mbsrcat: multibyte string restartable concatenation.
 * Appends s2 to s1, respecting final shift state of destination string,
 * indicated by *p_s1state. String s2 must start in the initial shift
 * state.
 * Returns: number of bytes written, or (size_t)-1 on encoding error.
 * Max. total length (incl. terminating null byte) is <= n;
 * stores ending state of concatenated string in *s1state.
 */
{
  int result;
  size_t i = strlen( s1 );
  size_t j = 0;

  if ( i >= n - (MB_CUR_MAX+1)) // Sanity check: room for 1 multibyte
                                // char + string terminator.
    return 0;                   // Report 0 bytes written.
```

```
    // Shift s1 down to initial state:

    if ( !mbsinit( p_s1state ))   // If not initial state, then append
    {                             // shift sequence to get initial state.
      if ( ( result = wcrtomb ( s1+i, L'\0', p_s1state )) == -1 )
        {                         // Encoding error:
          s1[i] = '\0';           // Try restoring termination.
          return (size_t)-1;      // Report error to caller.
        }
      else
        i += result;
    }
    // Copy only whole multibyte characters at a time.
    // Get length of next char w/o changing state:
    while (( result = mblen( s2+j, MB_CUR_MAX )) <= (n - ( 1 + i )) )
    {
      if ( result == 0  ) break;
      if ( result == -1 )
        {                         // Encoding error:
          s1[i] = '\0';           // Terminate now.
          return (size_t)-1;      // Report error to caller.
        }
                        // Next character fits; copy it and update state:
      strncpy( s1+i, s2+j, mbrlen( s2+j, MB_CUR_MAX, p_s1state ));
      i += result;
      j += result;
    }
    s1[i] = '\0';
    return j;
  }
```

See Also

mbrlen(), mbtowc()

mbrlen

Determines the length of a multibyte character and saves the parse state.

```
#include <stdlib.h>
size_t mbrlen( const char * restrict s, size_t maxsize,
               mbstate_t * restrict state );
```

The mbrlen() function, like mblen(), determines the length in bytes of a multibyte character referenced by its first argument. Its additional parameter, a pointer to an mbstate_t object, describes the parse state (also called the shift state) of a multibyte character sequence in the given encoding. mbrlen() updates this parse-state object after analyzing the multibyte character in the string, so that you can use it in a subsequent function call to interpret the next character correctly (hence the additional "r" in the function name, which stands for "restartable"). If the final argument is a null pointer, mbrlen() uses an internal, static mbstate_t object.

The possible return values are as follows:

Positive values
> The return value is the length of the multibyte character.

0
> The first multibyte character in the string is a null character. In this case, mbrlen() sets the parse state object to the initial state.

`(size_t)(-1)`
> The first argument does not point to a valid multibyte character. The mbrlen() function sets the errno variable to EILSEQ and leaves the mbstate_t object in an undefined state.

`(size_t)(-2)`
> The first argument does not point to a valid multibyte character within the specified maximum number of bytes. The sequence may be the beginning of a valid but longer multibyte character.

The LC_TYPE category in the current locale settings determines which byte sequences are valid multibyte characters.

Example

See the example for mblen() in this chapter.

See Also

mblen(), mbrtowc()

mbrtoc16   C11

Converts a multibyte character to a wide character of the type char16_t.

```
#include <uchar.h>
size_t mbrtoc16( char16_t * restrict pc16, const char * restrict s,
                 size_t n, mbstate_t * restrict state );
```

If *s* is not a null pointer, the function mbrtoc16() reads a maximum of *n* bytes starting at the address *s* to determine the next multibyte character. If it reads a valid multibyte character, the function converts it to the corresponding wide character of the type char16_t and stores that value in the object addressed by *pc16*, provided *pc16* is not a null pointer. The function also updates the shift state addressed by *state*. If more than one char16_t object is required to represent the character, subsequent calls to the function store the subsequent 16-bit character codes without reading more of the multibyte string.

If the wide character produced by the conversion is the null character, the function sets the shift state stored at the address *static* to the initial shift state.

If *s* is a null pointer, the values of *n* and *pc16* are ignored and the function call is equivalent to the following:

```
mbrtoc16(NULL, "", 1, ps)
```

Ordinarily, the mbrtoc16() function is thread-safe. However, if the last argument, *state*, is a null pointer, mbrtoc16() uses an internal, static mbstate_t object, and in that case, the function is not guaranteed to be thread-safe.

Implementations that define the macro __STDC_UTF_16__ use UTF-16 encoding for characters of the type char16_t. The macro is not defined if a different encoding is used.

The function mbrtoc16() returns one of the following values:

Positive value [1 ... n]
> The number of bytes read; i.e., the length of the multibyte character.

0
> The wide character produced is the null character.

(size_t)(-1)
> No valid multibyte character was found. The function mbrtoc16() sets the error variable errno to the value of EILSEQ and leaves the mbstate_t object in an undefined state.

(size_t)(-2)
> The first *n* bytes did not contain a complete multibyte character, but may be the beginning of a valid multibyte character.

(size_t)(-3)
> The function stored the next char16_t code of a character without reading additional bytes. (The representation of the character requires more than one char16_t object.)

Example

```
// The function mbsToC16s() uses mbrtoc16() to convert a string of
// multibyte characters into a string of 16-bit characters
// (typically in UTF-16 encoding).
// Return value: the number of char16_t characters produced, or
//               -1 if an error occurred.

int mbsToC16s( const char *mbStr, char16_t *c16Str, size_t len)
{
   if( mbStr == NULL || c16Str == NULL || len == 0) // Sanity checks.
      return -1;

   mbstate_t mbstate = {0};
   char16_t c16;
   int count = 0, i = 0, rv = 0,
      nBytes = (int)strlen(mbStr)+1;

   do {
      rv = (int)mbrtoc16(&c16, mbStr+i, nBytes-i, &mbstate);
```

```
            switch( rv)
            {
              case  0:  c16Str[count] = 0; i = nBytes;  // End of string.
                        break;
              case -1:                             // Encoding error.
              case -2:  count = -1;
                        break;
              default:
                if( count < (int)len-1 )
                {
                    c16Str[count++] = c16;
                    if( rv > 0)  i += rv;        // rv != -3
                }
                else count = -1;
            }
        } while( count > 0 && i < nBytes);

        return count;
    }
```

A sample function call:

```
    int main(void)
    {
       if( setlocale(LC_ALL, "en_US.utf8") == NULL)
          fputs("Unable to set the locale.\n", stderr);

       char *u8Str = u8"Grüße";
       char16_t c16Str[100];
       int nChars = 0;

       nChars = mbsToC16s( u8Str, c16Str, 100);
       if( nChars < 0)
          fputs("Error ...", stderr);
       else
       {
          printf("%d UTF-16 characters.\n", nChars);
    // ...
       }
    }
```

See Also

c16rtomb(), mbrtoc32(), c32rtomb(), mbtowc(), mbrtowc(), wcrtomb(), mbrlen()

mbrtoc32   C11

Converts a multibyte character to a wide character of the type char32_t.

```
    #include <uchar.h>
    size_t mbrtoc32( char32_t * restrict pc32, const char * restrict s>,
                     size_t n, mbstate_t * restrict state> );
```

The function mbrtoc32(), like mbrtoc16(), converts a multibyte character to the corresponding wide character, except that the wide-character output has the type char32_t.

Example

See the example for mbrtoc16() in this chapter.

See Also

c32rtomb(), mbrtoc16(), c16rtomb(), mbtowc(), mbrtowc(), wcrtomb(), mbrlen()

mbrtowc   C99

Converts a multibyte character to a wide character, and saves the parse state.

```
#include <wchar.h>
size_t mbrtowc( wchar_t * restrict widebuffer,
                const char * restrict string,
                size_t maxsize, mbstate_t * restrict state );
```

The mbrtowc() function, like mbtowc(), determines the wide character that corresponds to the multibyte character referenced by the second pointer argument, and stores the result in the location referenced by the first pointer argument. Its additional parameter, a pointer to an mbstate_t object, describes the shift state of a multibyte character sequence in the given encoding. mbrtowc() updates this shift-state object after analyzing the multibyte character in the string, so you can use it in a subsequent function call to interpret the next character correctly (hence the additional "r" in the function name, which stands for "restartable"). If the last argument is a null pointer, mbrtowc() uses an internal, static mbstate_t object.

The third argument is the maximum number of bytes to read for the multibyte character, and the return value is the number of bytes that the function actually read to obtain a valid multibyte character. If the string pointer in the second parameter points to a null character, mbrtowc() returns 0 and sets the parse state object to the initial state. If the string pointer does not point to a valid multibyte character, mbrtowc() returns (size_t)(-1), sets the errno variable to EILSEQ, and leaves the mbstate_t object in an undefined state. If the first maxsize bytes do not yield a complete multibyte character but could be the beginning of a valid multibyte character, the function returns (size_t)(-2).

Example

```
size_t mbstoupper( char *s1, char *s2, size_t n )
/* Copies the multibyte string from s2 to s1, converting all the
   characters to uppercase on the way.
   Because there are no standard functions for case-mapping in multibyte
   encodings, converts to and from the wide-character encoding (using the
   current locale setting for the LC_CTYPE category). The source string
   must begin in the initial shift state.
   Returns: the number of bytes written;
   or (size_t)-1 on an encoding error.
*/
```

```
{
  char *inptr = s2, *outptr = s1;
  wchar_t thiswc[1];
  size_t inresult, outresult;

  mbstate_t states[2], *instate = &states[0], *outstate = &states[1];

  memset( states, '\0', sizeof states );

  do
  {
    inresult = mbrtowc( thiswc, inptr, MB_CUR_MAX, instate );
    switch ( inresult )
      {
      case (size_t)-2: // The (MB_CUR_MAX) bytes at inptr do not make
                       //   a complete mb character. Maybe there is a
                       //   redundant sequence of shift codes. Treat the
                       //   same as an encoding error.
        *outptr = '\0';
        return (size_t)-1;

      case (size_t)-1:   // Found an invalid mb sequence at inptr:
        return inresult; // pass the error to the caller.

      case 0:          // Got a null character. Make a last null wc.
                       // The default action, with wcrtomb, does this
                       // nicely, so *no break statement* necessary here.

      default:         // Read <result> mb characters to get one wide
                       // character.
        /* Check for length limit before writing anything but a null.
           Note: Using inresult as an approximation for the output
           length.
           The actual output length could conceivably be different
           due to a different succession of state-shift sequences.
        */
        if (( outptr - s1 ) + inresult + MB_CUR_MAX > n )
        {   // i.e., if bytes written + bytes to write + termination > n,
            // then terminate now by simulating a null-character input.
          thiswc[0] = L'\0';
          inresult = 0;
        }
        inptr += inresult;
        if (( outresult = wcrtomb( outptr,
                                   (wchar_t)towupper(thiswc[0]),
                                   outstate )) == -1 )
        {                               // Encoding error on output:
          *outptr = '\0';              // Terminate and return error.
          return outresult;
        }
        else
          outptr += outresult;
```

```
        }
    } while ( inresult );              // Drop out after handling '\0'.
    return outptr - s1;
}
```

See Also

mbtowc( ), mbrlen( ), wcrtomb( )

mbsinit

Determines whether a multibyte parse state variable represents the initial state.

```
#include <wchar.h>
int mbsinit( const mbstate_t *state );
```

The mbsinit( ) function tests whether the multibyte parse state variable represents the initial state. The type mbstate_t is defined in *wchar.h*. An object of this type holds the parse state of a multibyte string or stream. If the parse state is the initial state, mbsinit( ) returns a nonzero value; otherwise, mbsinit( ) returns 0. mbsinit( ) also returns a nonzero value if the argument is a null pointer.

Example

See the example for mblen( ) in this chapter.

See Also

wcrtomb( ), wcsrtombs( ), mbsrtowcs( ), mbrtowc( )

mbsrtowcs

Converts a multibyte string to a wide-character string.

```
#include <wchar.h>
size_t mbsrtowcs( wchar_t * restrict dest, const char ** restrict src,
                  size_t n, mbstate_t * restrict state );
```

The function mbsrtowcs( ) is the "restartable" verion of mbstowcs( ). It begins converting the input string, not in the initial shift state, but in the shift state specified by the additional paramter *state*. Furthermore, before returning, mbsrtowcs( ) sets the pointer addressed by *src* to point to the next character to be converted, so that the conversion can be continued by a subsequent function call. If it reaches the end of the string, mbsrtowcs( ) sets the pointer addressed by *src* to NULL and lets the object addressed by *state* specify the initial shift state.

The conversion performed is equivalent to an mbrtowc( ) call for each multibyte character in the source string, beginning with the shift state specified by *state*. If mbsrtowcs( ) encounters an invalid multibyte character, it returns the value (size_t)(-1) and sets the variable errno to the value EILSEQ ("illegal sequence"). If no error occurs, the function returns the number of wide characters written, not counting the terminating null character if present.

If the return value is equal to the specified maximum *n*, the wide-character string is not terminated with a null character!

Example

```
size_t result;

char mbstring[ ] = "This is originally a multibyte string.\n";
const char *mbsptr = mbstring;

wchar_t widestring[256] = { L'\0' };

mbstate_t state;
memset( &state, '\0', sizeof state );

printf( "The current locale is %s.\n", setlocale( LC_CTYPE, "" ));

result = mbsrtowcs( widestring, &mbsptr, 256, &state );
if ( result == (size_t)-1 )
{
  fputs( "Encoding error in multibyte string", stderr );
  return -1;
}
else
{
  printf( "Converted %u multibyte characters. The result:\n", result );
  printf( "%ls", widestring );
}
```

See Also

mbstowcs(), mbrtowc(); wcsrtombs(), wcrtomb(), wcstombs(), wctomb(), and the corresponding secure functions

mbsrtowcs_s   C11

Converts a multibyte string to a wide-character string.

```
#include <wchar.h>
errno_t mbsrtowcs_s(size_t * restrict retval,
                    wchar_t * restrict dst, size_t dstmax,
                    const char ** restrict src, size_t n,
                    mbstate_t * restrict state );
```

The function mbsrtowcs_s() is the "restartable" version of mbstowcs_s(). It begins the conversion not in the initial shift state but in the shift state specified by the parameter *state*. The parameter *src* is a pointer to a char pointer. Before it returns, the function stores a pointer to the next byte to be read in **src*, and the appropriate shift state in **state*, so that subsequent function calls can continue the string conversion with that byte. If the function reaches the end of the input string, it stores a null pointer in the variable addressed by *src*.

The pointer arguments *retval*, *src*, **src*, and *state* must not be null pointers. Except for the differences described here, the function mbsrtowcs_s() is similar to mbsrtowcs(). It returns zero on success, or a nonzero value if an error occurs.

Example

```
const char *mbptr = "Any multibyte string";
wchar_t wcstr[10];      // A buffer for wide characters
size_t  len;            // and its capacity.
mbstate_t state = {0};

if( mbsrtowcs_s( &len, wcstr, 10, &mbptr, 9, &state) != 0)
    printf("The array contains an invalid multibyte character.\n");
else
{
    printf("Length: %u; text: %ls\n", len, wcstr);
    printf("The remaining characters: %s\n", mbptr);
}
```

The output from this code is:

```
Length: 9; text: Any multi
The remaining characters: byte string
```

See Also

mbsrtowcs(), mbstowcs(), mbstowcs_s(), mbtowc(), mbrtowc(), mbrtoc16(), mbrtoc32(), wcstombs(), wcsrtombs()

mbstowcs

Converts a multibyte string to a wide-character string.

```
#include <stdlib.h>
size_t mbstowcs( wchar_t * restrict dest, const char * restrict src,
                size_t n );
```

The mbstowcs() function converts a multibyte string to a wide-character string, and returns the number of wide characters in the result, not counting the wide-string terminator. The first argument is a pointer to a buffer for the result; the second argument is a pointer to the string of multibyte characters to be converted; the third argument is the maximum number of wide characters to be written to the buffer.

The conversion performed is equivalent to calling mbtowc() for each multibyte character in the original string, beginning in the initial shift state.

The mbstowcs() function terminates the resulting wide-character string with a null wide character (L'\0') only if it has not yet written the maximum number of wide characters specified by the third argument! If the return value is the same as the specified limit, then the resulting wide string has not been terminated.

If mbstowcs() encounters an invalid multibyte character, it returns (size_t)(-1).

Example

See the example for localeconv() in this chapter.

See Also

mbsrtowcs(), mbtowc(), wcstombs(), wcsrtombs(), and the corresponding secure functions

mbstowcs_s   C11

Converts a multibyte string to a wide-character string.

```
#include <stdlib.h>
errno_t mbstowcs_s(size_t * restrict retval,
                   wchar_t * restrict dst, size_t dstmax,
                   const char * restrict src, size_t n );
```

The function mbstowcs_s() is the "secure" version of the function mbstowcs(). It converts the multibyte string addressed by *src* to a string of wide characters of the type wchar_t. The conversion begins in the initial shift state, and the function's operation is equivalent to calling mbrtowc() for each multibyte character in the source string. The number of characters converted, not counting the string-terminating null character, is stored in the variable addressed by *retval*.

If *dst* is not a null pointer, then the function only converts the first *n* multibyte characters (or up to the end of the multibyte string, whichever comes first), and stores the result in the array addressed by *dst*, up to the maximum length specified by *dstmax*. In any case, the output string is terminated with L'\0'. Thus, if no terminator character was copied from the source string, and *dstmax* is at least equal to *n*+1, *dst*[*n*] contains the string terminator L'\0'. The value of any elements of the array *dst* after the terminator character is undefined.

If *dst* is a null pointer, the function ignores the argument *n* and only counts the number of multibyte characters in the string, storing the result in the variable addressed by *retval*.

The function tests the following runtime constraints: the pointer arguments *retval* and *src* must not be null pointers. If *dst* is a null pointer, the output length argument *dstmax* must also be zero. If *dst* is not a null pointer, the values of *n* and *dstmax* must not be greater than RSIZE_MAX. Furthermore, *dstmax* must be greater than the number of wide characters that actually need to be stored—that is, either greater than *n* or greater than the number of characters in the string, whichever is less.

If a runtime constraint violation occurs and *retval* is not a null pointer, mbstowcs_s() stores the value -1 in the size_t object addressed by *retval*, and also writes the string terminator character L'\0' to *dst*[0], provided *dst* is not a null pointer and *dstmax* is greater than zero.

The mbstowcs_s() also places the value -1 in the object addressed by *retval* to indicate an encoding error if the source string contains a byte sequence that does not represent a valid multibyte character.

The mbstowcs_s() function returns zero on success, or a nonzero value if an error occurs.

Example

```
char    mbstr[] = "Any multibyte string";
wchar_t wcstr[10];      // A buffer for wide characters
size_t  len;            // and the number of characters.

if( mbstowcs_s( &len, wcstr, 10, mbstr, 9) != 0)
    printf("The array contains an invalid multibyte character.\n");
else
    printf("Length: %u; text: %ls\n", len, wcstr);
```

Output:

```
Length: 9; text: Any multi
```

See Also

mbstowcs(), mbsrtowcs(), mbsrtowcs_s(), mbtowc(), mbrtowc(), mbrtoc16(), mbrtoc32(), wcstombs(), wcsrtombs()

mbtowc

Converts a multibyte character to a wide character.

```
#include <stdlib.h>
int mbtowc( wchar_t * restrict wc, const char * restrict s,
        size_t maxsize );
```

The mbtowc() function determines the wide character corresponding to the multibyte character referenced by the second pointer argument, and stores the result in the location referenced by the first pointer argument. The third argument is the maximum number of bytes to read for the multibyte character, and the return value is the number of bytes that the function actually read to obtain a valid multibyte character. If the second argument points to a null character, mbtowc() returns 0. If it does not point to a valid multibyte character, mbtowc() returns -1.

If you pass mbtowc() a null pointer as the second argument, *s*, then the return value indicates whether the current multibyte encoding is stateful. This behavior is the same as that of mblen(). If mbtowc() returns 0, then the encoding is stateless. If it returns any other value, the encoding is stateful; that is, the interpretation of a given byte sequence may depend on the shift state.

Example

The following example converts an array of multibyte characters into wide characters one at a time, and prints each one:

```
int i = 0, n = 0;
wchar_t wc;
char mbstring[256] = "This is originally a multibyte string.\n";

printf( "The current locale is %s.\n", setlocale(LC_CTYPE, "" ));

while ( (n = mbtowc( &wc, &mbstring[i], MB_CUR_MAX )) != 0 )
{
  if ( n == -1 )
  {
    fputs( "Encoding error in multibyte string", stderr );
    break;
  }
  printf( "%lc", (wint_t)wc );
  i += n;
}
```

See Also

mbrtowc(), mblen(), mbsinit()

memchr

Searches a memory block for a given byte value.

```
#include <string.h>
void *memchr( const void *buffer, int c, size_t n );
```

The memchr() function searches for a byte with the value of *c* in a buffer of *n* bytes beginning at the address in the pointer argument *buffer*. The function's return value is a pointer to the first occurrence of the specified character in the buffer, or a null pointer if the character does not occur within the specified number of bytes. The type size_t is defined in *string.h* (and other header files), usually as unsigned int.

Example

```
char *found, buffer[4096] = "";
int ch = ' ';

fgets( buffer, sizeof(buffer), stdin );

/* Replace any spaces in the string read with underscores: */
while (( found = memchr( buffer, ch, strlen(buffer) )) != NULL )
  *found = '_';
```

See Also

strchr(), wmemchr()

memcmp

Compares two memory blocks.

```
#include <string.h>
int memcmp(const void *b1, const void *b2, size_t n );
```

The memcmp() function compares the contents two memory blocks of *n* bytes, beginning at the addresses in *b1* and *b2*, until it finds a byte that doesn't match. The function returns a value greater than zero if the first mismatched byte (evaluated as unsigned char) is greater in b1, or less than zero if the first mismatched byte is greater in b2, or zero if the two buffers are identical over *n* bytes.

Example

```
long setone[5] = { 1, 3, 5, 7, 9 };
long settwo[5] = { 0, 2, 4, 6, 8 };

for ( int i = 0; i < 5; i++ )
  settwo[i] += 1;

if ( memcmp( &setone, &settwo, sizeof(settwo) ) == 0 )
  printf( "The two arrays are identical, byte for byte.\n" );
```

See Also

strcmp(), strncmp(), wmemcmp()

memcpy, memcpy_s

Copies the contents of a memory block.

```
#include <string.h>
void *memcpy( void * restrict dest,
              const void * restrict src, size_t n );
errno_t memcpy_s( void * restrict dest, size_t destmax,
              const void * restrict , rsize_t n );      (C11)
```

The memcpy() function copies *n* successive bytes beginning at the address in *src* to the location beginning at the address in *dest*. The return value is the same as the first argument, *dest*. The two pointer values must be at least *n* bytes apart, so that the source and destination blocks do not overlap; otherwise, the function's behavior is undefined. For overlapping blocks, use memmove() or memmove_s().

The function memcpy_s(), like memcpy(), copies a block of *n* successive bytes beginning at the address in *src* to the location beginning at the address in *dest*. Unlike memcpy(), memcpy_s() has the additional parameter *destmax*, which specifies the size of the destination block. The function tests the following runtime constraints: the pointer arguments *dest* and *src* must not be null pointers. The values of *destmax* and *n* must not be greater than RSIZE_MAX, and *n* must not be greater than *destmax*. The two memory blocks addressed by *src* and *dest* must not overlap.

If any of the runtime constraints is violated, memcpy_s() fills the destination block with null bytes, provided *dest* is not a null pointer and *destmax* is not greater than RSIZE_MAX.

The function memcpy_s() returns zero on success, or a nonzero value if a violation of the runtime constraints occurs.

Example

```
typedef struct record {
  char   name[32];
  double data;
  struct record *next, *prev;
} Rec_t;

Rec_t template = { "Another fine product", -0.0, NULL, NULL };
Rec_t *tmp_new;

if (( tmp_new  = malloc( sizeof(Rec_t) )) != NULL )
  memcpy( tmp_new, &template, sizeof(Rec_t) );
  // Equivalent to
  // memcpy_s( tmp_new, sizeof(Rec_t), &template, sizeof(Rec_t) );
  // or *tmp_new = template;
else
  fprintf( stderr, "Out of memory!\n" );
```

See Also

strcpy(), strncpy(), memmove(), wmemcpy(), wmemmove()

For each of these functions, there is also a corresponding "secure" function, if the implementation supports the C11 bounds-checking functions (i.e., if the macro __STDC_LIB_EXT1__ is defined)

memmove, memmove_s

Copies the contents of a memory block.

```
#include <string.h>
void *memmove( void *dest, const void *src, size_t int n );
errno_t memmove_s( void * restrict dest, size_t destmax,
                   const void * restrict src, rsize_t n );        (C11)
```

The memmove() function copies *n* successive bytes beginning at the address in *src* to the location beginning at the address in *dest*. The return value is the same as the first argument, *dest*. If the source and destination blocks overlap, copying takes place as if through a temporary buffer, so that after the function call, each original value from the *src* block appears in *dest*.

The function memmove_s(), like memmove(), copies a block of *n* bytes beginning at the location addressed by *src* to the location beginning at the address in *dest*. Unlike memmove(), memmove_s() has the additional parameter *destmax*, which specifies the size of the destination block. The function tests the following runtime constraints: the pointer arguments *dest* and *src* must not be null pointers; the values of *destmax* and *n* must not be greater than RSIZE_MAX; and *n* must not be greater than *destmax*.

If a runtime constraint is violated, memmove_s() fills the destination block with null bytes, provided *dest* is not a null pointer and *destmax* is not greater than RSIZE_MAX.

The function memmove_s() returns zero on success, or a nonzero value if a violation of the runtime constraints occurs.

Example

```
char a[30] = "That's not what I said." ;
    memmove( a+7, a+11, 13 );       // Move 13 bytes, 'w' through '\0'
// Or with memmove_s():
// memmove_s( a+7, 13, a+11, 13 );
puts( a );
```

These lines produce the following output:

```
That's what I said.
```

See Also

memcpy(), wmemmove()

memset, memset_s

Set all bytes of a memory block to a given value.

```
#include <string.h>
void *memset( void *dest, int c, size_t n );
errno_t memset_s(void *dest, rsize_t destmax, int c, rsize_t n);    (C11)
```

The function memset() stores the value of *c* (converted to the type *unsigned* char) in each byte of the memory block of *n* bytes beginning at the address in dest. The return value is the same as the pointer argument *dest*.

The function memset_s(), like memset(), sets each byte in a block of *n* bytes in memory to the value *c*. Unlike memset(), however, memset_s() has the additional parameter *destmax*, which specifies the size of the destination block. The function also tests the following runtime constraints: the pointer argument *dest* must not be a null pointer; the values of *destmax* and *n* must not be greater than RSIZE_MAX; and *n* must not be greater than *destmax*.

If any of the runtime constraints is violated, memset_s() nonetheless fills the destination block with the value of *c* (converted to the type unsigned char), provided *dest* is not a null pointer and *destmax* is not greater than RSIZE_MAX.

The function memset_s() returns zero on success, or a nonzero value if a violation of the runtime constraints occurs.

Example

```
char str[] = "Account number: 1234567890";
char digits[] = "0123456789";

size_t pos = strcspn( str, digits);  // Position of the first digit.
// puts( memset( str+pos, 'x', 7));
// or
if( memset_s( str+pos, strlen(str)-pos, 'x', 7) == 0)
    puts(str)
```

These statements produce the following output:

```
Account number: xxxxxxx890
```

See Also

wmemset(), calloc()

mktime

Determines the time represented by a struct tm value.

```
#include <time.h>
time_t mktime( struct tm *timeptr );
```

The mktime() function calculates the local calendar time represented by the member values in the object referenced by the pointer argument.

The type struct tm is defined in *time.h* as follows:

```
struct tm {
    int tm_sec;      /* Seconds (0-60; 1 leap second) */
    int tm_min;      /* Minutes (0-59) */
    int tm_hour;     /* Hours   (0-23) */
    int tm_mday;     /* Day     (1-31) */
    int tm_mon;      /* Month   (0-11) */
    int tm_year;     /* Year    (difference from 1900) */
    int tm_wday;     /* Day of week (0-6)   */
    int tm_yday;     /* Day of year (0-365) */
    int tm_isdst;    /* Daylight saving time (-1, 0, 1) */
};
```

The member tm_isdst is equal to 0 if daylight saving time is not in effect, or 1 if it is. A negative value indicates that the information is not available, in which case mktime() attempts to calculate whether daylight saving time is applicable at the time represented by the other members.

The mktime() function ignores the tm_wday and tm_yday members in determining the time, but does use tm_isdst. The other members may contain values outside their normal ranges. Once it has calculated the time represented, mktime() adjusts the struct tm members so that each one is within its normal range, and also sets tm_wday and tm_yday accordingly. The return value is the number of seconds from the epoch (usually midnight on January 1, 1970, UTC) to the time represented in the structure, or -1 to indicate an error.

Example

```
time_t seconds;
struct tm sometime;

sometime.tm_sec   = 10;
sometime.tm_min   = 80;
sometime.tm_hour  = 40;
sometime.tm_mday  = 23;
sometime.tm_mon   = 1;
sometime.tm_year  = 105;
sometime.tm_wday  = 11;
sometime.tm_yday  = 111;
sometime.tm_isdst = -1;

seconds = mktime( &sometime );

if ( seconds == -1 )
{
  printf( "mktime() couldn't make sense of its input.\n" );
  return -1;
}

printf( "The return value, %ld, represents %s",
        (long)seconds, ctime(&seconds) );

printf( "The structure has been adjusted as follows:\n"
        "tm_sec   == %d\n"
        "tm_min   == %d\n"
        "tm_hour  == %d\n"
        "tm_mday  == %d\n"
        "tm_mon   == %d\n"
        "tm_year  == %d\n"
        "tm_wday  == %d\n"
        "tm_yday  == %d\n"
        "tm_isdst == %d\n",

        sometime.tm_sec,
        sometime.tm_min,
        sometime.tm_hour,
        sometime.tm_mday,
        sometime.tm_mon,
        sometime.tm_year,
        sometime.tm_wday,
        sometime.tm_yday,
        sometime.tm_isdst );

  printf( "The structure now represents %s", asctime( &sometime ));
}
```

This program produces the following output:

```
The return value, 1109262010, represents Thu Feb 24 17:20:10 2005
The structure has been adjusted as follows:
tm_sec   == 10
tm_min   == 20
tm_hour  == 17
tm_mday  == 24
tm_mon   == 1
tm_year  == 105
tm_wday  == 4
tm_yday  == 54
tm_isdst == 0
The structure now represents Thu Feb 24 17:20:10 2005
```

See Also

asctime(), ctime(), localtime(), gmtime(), strftime()

modf

Separates a floating-point number into integer and fraction parts.

```
#include <math.h>
double modf( double x, double *intpart );
float modff( float x, float *intpart );          (C99)
long double modfl( long double x, long double *intpart );          (C99)
```

The modf() functions analyze a floating-point number into an integer and a fraction whose magnitude is less than one. The integer part is stored in the location addressed by the second argument, and the fractional part is the return value.

There is no type-generic macro for the modf() functions.

Example

```
double x, integer = 0.0, fraction = 0.0;
x = 1.23;
fraction = modf( x, &integer );
printf("%10f = %f + %f\n", x , integer, fraction );

x = -1.23;
fraction = modf( x, &integer );
printf("%10f = %f + %f\n", x , integer, fraction );
```

The example produces the following output:

```
  1.230000 = 1.000000 + 0.230000
 -1.230000 = -1.000000 + -0.230000
```

frexp()

mtx_destroy   C11

Destroys the specified mutex.

```
#include <threads.h>
void mtx_destroy(mtx_t *mtx);
```

The function mtx_destroy() frees all the resources used by the mutex object referenced by its pointer argument *mtx*. There must not be any threads blocked on the
mutex when mtx_destroy() is called.

Example

See the examples for mtx_init() and cnd_broadcast() in this chapter.

See Also

mtx_init(), mtx_lock(), mtx_unlock(), cnd_wait()

mtx_init   C11

Creates a mutex object.

```
#include <threads.h>
int mtx_init( mtx_t *mtx, int mutextype);
```

The function mtx_init() creates a mutex with the properties specified by *mutex
type*, where the value of *mutextype* is one of the following:

Table 18-6. Mutex types

mutextype	Properties of the mutex
mtx_plain	A plain, non-recursive mutex
mtx_timed	A non-recursive mutex that supports timeouts
mtx_plain|mtx_recursive	A recursive mutex
mtx_timed|mtx_recursive	A recursive mutex that supports timeouts

If it succeeds in creating a new mutex, the function mtx_init() writes the ID of the
new mutex in the object addressed by the argument *mtx*, and returns the value of
the macro thrd_success. If an error occurs, mtx_init() returns thrd_error.

Example

```
mtx_t mtx;                          // A mutex.

int main()
{
    if( mtx_init( &mtx, mtx_plain) != thrd_success)
```

```
    {
        fputs( "Error initializing the mutex.\n", stderr);
        return -1;
    }
    // Here on success.
    // ... Threads use the mutex ...
    // ... Wait for threads to end ...

    mtx_destroy(&mtx);
    return 0;
}
```

See Also

mtx_destroy(), mtx_lock(), mtx-timedlock(), mtx-trylock(), mtx_unlock(), cnd_wait(), cnd_timedwait()

mtx_lock   C11

Locks the specified mutex.

```
#include <threads.h>
int mtx_lock( mtx_t *mtx);
```

The function mtx_lock() blocks the calling thread until it obtains the mutex with the ID addressed by *mtx*. The calling thread must not already hold the mutex, unless it is a recursive one. The return value is thrd_success if no error occurs, or thrd_error if an error occurred.

Example

See the example for mtx_timedlock() in this chapter.

See Also

mtx_timedlock(), mtx_trylock(), mtx_unlock(), mtx_init()

mtx_timedlock   C11

Tries for a limited time to lock the specified mutex.

```
#include <threads.h>
int mtx_timedlock( mtx_t *restrict mtx,
                   const struct timespec *restrict ts);
```

The function mtx_timedlock() blocks the calling thread until it obtains the mutex with the ID addressed by *mtx*, or until the time specified by *ts* has elapsed. The mutex must support timeouts and the calling thread must not already hold the mutex, unless it is a recursive one. The parameter *ts* specifies a point in Coordinated Universal Time, or UTC (also called Greenwich Mean Time). The current time in UTC can be obtained using the function timespec_get().

The return value is `thrd_success` if no error occurs, `thrd_timedout` if the time limit elapsed, or `thrd_error` if an error occurred.

Example

```
mtx_t mtx;
int func(void * thrd);                          // Thread function.

int main()
{
    thrd_t th;
    if( mtx_init(&mtx, mtx_timed) != thrd_success)
    { fputs("Initialization error.\n", stderr); return 1; }

    mtx_lock(&mtx);                             // Lock the mutex.
    if( thrd_create(&th, func, "Thread A") != thrd_success)
    { fputs("Thread error.\n", stderr); return 2; }

    thrd_join(th, NULL);
    mtx_destroy( &mtx);
    return 0;
}

int func(void * thrd)
{
    struct timespec ts;
    timespec_get( &ts, TIME_UTC);              // The current time;
    ts.tv_sec += 3;                            // 3 seconds from now.

    printf("%s waiting ...\n", (char*)thrd);
    int res = mtx_timedlock(&mtx, &ts);
    switch(res)
    {
        case thrd_success:
            puts("Obtained mutex\n... releasing ...");
            mtx_unlock(&mtx);   break;
        case thrd_timedout:
            puts("Timed out.");    break;
        default:
            puts("mtx_timedlock: error.");
    };
    return res;
}
```

This code produces the following output:

```
Thread A waiting ...
Timed out.
```

See Also

`mtx_lock()`, `mtx_trylock()`, `mtx_unlock()`, `mtx_init()`

Tries to lock the specified mutex, but without blocking.

```
#include <threads.h>
int mtx_trylock( mtx_t *mtx);
```

The function mtx_trylock() tries to acquire the mutex with the ID addressed by *mtx* but does not block the calling thread if the mutex is busy. The calling thread must not already hold the mutex, unless the mutex supports recursion.

The return value is thrd_success if the function succeeds in locking the mutex, thrd_busy if the mutex could not be acquired, and thrd_error if an error occurred.

Example

```
#define NUM_THREADS 3

mtx_t mtx;
struct timespec duration = { .tv_nsec = 1 };        // One nanosecond.

int func(void * thrd_num)                            // Thread function.
{
    int num = *(int*)thrd_num;
    int res, count = 1;

    while( (res = mtx_trylock(&mtx)) == thrd_busy)
    {   ++count;  thrd_sleep( &duration, NULL); }

    if( res == thrd_success)
    {
      printf("Thread %d succeeded after %d attempts.\n", num, count);
      thrd_sleep( &duration, NULL);
      mtx_unlock(&mtx);
      return 0;
    }
    else return -1;
}

int main(void)
{
    struct { thrd_t th; int id; } th_arr[NUM_THREADS];

    if( mtx_init(&mtx, mtx_plain) != thrd_success)
       return 1;

    // Create threads:
    for( int i = 0; i < NUM_THREADS; ++i)
    {
       th_arr[i].id = i;
       if( thrd_create( &th_arr[i].th, func, &th_arr[i].id) !=
           thrd_success)
```

```
        return -2;
    }
    // Wait for threads to finish:
    for( int i = 0; i < NUM_THREADS; ++i)
        thrd_join( th_arr[i].th, NULL);

    mtx_destroy( &mtx);
    return 0;
}
```

Possible output of this program:

```
Thread 0 succeeded after 1 attempts.
Thread 2 succeeded after 2 attempts.
Thread 1 succeeded after 4 attempts.
```

See Also

mtx_lock(), mtx_timedlock(), mtx_unlock()

mtx_unlock   C11

Unlocks the specified mutex.

```
#include <threads.h>
int mtx_unlock( mtx_t *mtx);
```

The function mtx_unlock() unlocks the mutex with the ID addressed by *mtx*. The calling thread must hold the mutex. The return value is thrd_success if no error occurs; otherwise, thrd_error.

Example

See the example for mtx_trylock() in this chapter.

See Also

mtx_lock(), mtx_timedlock(), mtx_trylock(), mtx_init()

nearbyint   C99

Rounds a floating-point number to an integer value.

```
#include <math.h>
double nearbyint( double x );
float nearbyintf( float x );
long double nearbyintl( long double x );
```

The nearbyint() functions round the value of the argument to the next integer value in the current rounding direction. The current rounding direction is an attribute of the floating-point environment that you can read and modify using the fegetround() and fesetround() functions. They are similar to the rint() functions, except that the nearbyint() functions do not raise the FE_INEXACT exception when the result of the rounding is different from the argument.

Example

```
if ( fesetround( FE_TOWARDZERO) == 0)
  printf("The current rounding mode is \"round toward 0.\"\n");
else
  printf("The rounding mode is unchanged.\n");

printf("nearbyint(1.9) = %4.1f    nearbyint(-1.9) = %4.1f\n",
       nearbyint(1.9), nearbyint(-1.9) );

printf("round(1.9) = %4.1f        round(-1.9) = %4.1f\n",
       round(1.9), round(-1.9) );
```

This code produces the following output:

```
The current rounding mode is "round toward 0."
nearbyint(1.9) =  1.0    nearbyint(-1.9) = -1.0
round(1.9) =  2.0        round(-1.9) = -2.0
```

See Also

rint(), lrint(), llrint(); round(), lround(), llround(); nextafter(), ceil(), floor(), fegetround(), fesetround()

nextafter   C99

Obtains the next representable value.

```
#include <math.h>
double nextafter( double x, double y );
float nextafterf( float x, float y );
long double nextafterl( long double x, long double y );
```

The nextafter() function returns the next value to the first argument x, removed from it in the direction toward the value of y, that is representable in the function's type. If the values of the two arguments are equal, nextafter() returns the value of the second argument y.

If the argument x has the magnitude of the largest finite value that can be represented in the function's type, and the result is not a finite, representable value, then a range error may occur.

Example

```
double x = nextafter( 0.0, 1.0 );
printf("The smallest positive number "
       "with the type double: %E\n", x);
```

This code produces output like the following:

```
The smallest positive number with the type double: 4.940656E-324
```

See Also

nexttoward(), nearbyint(), rint(), lrint(), llrint(), round(), lround(), llround(), ceil(), floor()

Obtains the next representable value in the direction of a given long double value.

```c
#include <math.h>
double nexttoward( double x, long double y );
float nexttowardf( float x, long double y );
long double nexttowardl( long double x, long double y );
```

The nexttoward() functions are similar to nextafter(), except that the second parameter in all three variants has the type long double.

Example

```c
float x = nexttowardf( 0.0F, -1E-100L );
printf("The greatest negative floating-point number \n"
       "(i.e., the closest to zero) with type float: %E\n", x);
```

This code produces output like the following:

```
The greatest negative floating-point number
(i.e., the closest to zero) with type float: -1.401298E-45
```

See Also

nextafter(), nearbyint(), rint(), lrint(), llrint(), round(), lround(), llround(), ceil(), floor()

---

perror

Print an error message corresponding to the value of errno.

```c
#include <stdio.h>
void perror( const char *string );
```

The perror() function prints a message to the standard error stream. The output includes first the string referenced by the pointer argument, if any; then a colon and a space, then the error message that corresponds to the current value of the errno variable, ending with a newline character.

Example

```c
#define MSGLEN_MAX 256
FILE *fp;
char msgbuf[MSGLEN_MAX] = "";

if (( fp = fopen( "nonexistentfile", "r" )) == NULL )
{
  snprintf( msgbuf, MSGLEN_MAX, "%s, function %s, file %s, line %d",
          argv[0], __func__, __FILE__, __LINE__ );
  perror( msgbuf );
  return errno;
}
```

Assuming that there is no file available named *nonexistentfile*, this code results in output like the following on stderr:

```
./perror, function main, file perror.c, line 18: No such file
or directory
```

See Also

strerror()

pow

Raises a number to a power.

```
#include <math.h>
double pow( double x, double y );
float powf( float x, float y );          (C99)
long double powl( long double x, long double y );      (C99)
```

The pow() function calculates *x* to the power of *y*. In other words, the return value is x^y. The arguments are subject to the following rules:

- If *x* is negative, *y* must have an integer value.
- If *x* is zero, then *y* must not be negative. ($0^0 = 1.0$, but for all other positive values of *y*, $0^y = 0.0$.)

If the arguments violate these conditions, pow() may return NaN ("not a number") or infinity, and may indicate a domain error. If an overflow or underflow occurs, pow() returns positive or negative HUGE_VAL and may indicate a range error.

Example

See the example for cosh() in this chapter.

See Also

exp(), sqrt(), cpow()

printf

Writes formatted output to the standard output stream.

```
#include <stdio.h>
int printf( const char * restrict format, ... );
```

The printf() function converts various kinds of data into string representations for output, and substitutes them for placeholders in the string referenced by the mandatory pointer argument, *format*. The resulting output string is then written to the standard output stream. The return value of printf() is the number of characters printed, or EOF to indicate that an error occurred.

The placeholders in the string argument are called *conversion specifications* because they also specify how each replacement data item is to be converted, according to a protocol described shortly.

The optional arguments, represented by the ellipsis in the function prototype, are the data items to be converted for insertion in the output string. The arguments are in the same order as the conversion specifications in the format string.

Conversion specification syntax

For a general overview of data output with printf(), see "Formatted Output" on page 223. This section describes the syntax of conversion specifications in the printf() format string in detail. The conversion specifications have the following syntax:

```
%[flags][field width][.precision][length modifier]specifier
```

The *flags* consist of one or more of the characters +, ' ' (space), -, 0, or #. Their meanings are as follows:

+

Add a plus sign before positive numbers.

' '

Add a space before positive numbers (not applicable in conjunction with +).

-

Align the output with the left end of the field.

0

Pad the field with leading zeros to the left of the numeric output (not applicable in conjunction with -). Ignored for integer types if *precision* is specified.

#

Use alternative conversion rules for the following conversion specifiers:

A, a, E, e, F, f, G, g
 Format floating-point numbers with a decimal point, even if no digits follow.

G, g
 Do not truncate trailing zeros.

X, x, o
 Format nonzero hexadecimal integers with the 0X or 0x prefix; format octal integers with the 0 prefix.

The optional *field width* is a positive integer that specifies the *minimum* number of characters that the given data item occupies in the output string. If the flags include a minus sign, then the converted argument value is aligned left in the field; otherwise, it is aligned right. The remaining field width is padded with spaces (or zeros, if the flags include 0). If the converted data item is longer than the specified *field width*, it is inserted in the output string in its entirety.

If an asterisk (*) appears in place of the *field width*, then the argument to be converted for output must be preceded by an additional argument with the type int, which indicates the field width for the converted output.

For the conversion specifiers f, F, e, E, a, and A, *precision* specifies the number of decimal places to present. For the conversion specifier g, *precision* indicates the number of significant digits. The result is rounded. The default value for *precision* is 6.

For integers—that is, the conversion specifiers u, d, i, x, and o—*precision* specifies a minimum number of digits to present. The converted value is padded with leading zeros if necessary. The default value for *precision* in this case is 1. If you convert a zero integer value with zero precision, the result is no characters.

For the conversion specifier s, indicating a string argument, *precision* specifies the maximum length of the string to be inserted in the output.

If an asterisk (*) appears in place of a *precision* value, then the argument to be converted for output must be preceded by an additional argument with the type int, which indicates the precision for the converted output. If asterisks appear both for *field width* and for *precision*, then the argument to be converted must be preceded by two additional int arguments, the first for *field width* and the second for *precision*.

The *length modifier* qualifies the conversion specifier to indicate the corresponding argument's type more specifically. Each length modifier value is applicable only to certain conversion specifier values. If they are mismatched, the function's behavior is undefined. The permissible *length modifier* values and their meaning for the appropriate conversion specifiers are listed in Table 18-7.

Table 18-7. printf() conversion specifier modifiers

Modifier	With conversion specifier	Corresponding argument's type
hh	d, i, o, u, x, or X	signed char or unsigned char
hh	n	signed char *
h	d, i, o, u, x, or X	short int or unsigned short int
h	n	short int *
l (ell)	d, i, o, u, x, or X	long int or unsigned long int
l (ell)	c	wint_t
l (ell)	n	long int *
l (ell)	s	wchar_t *
l (ell)	a, A, e, E, f, F, g, or G	(The modifier is permitted, but has no effect)

Modifier	With conversion specifier	Corresponding argument's type
`ll` (two ells)	d, i, o, u, x, or X	`long long` or `unsigned long long`
`ll` (two ells)	n	`long long *`
`j`	d, i, o, u, x, or X	`intmax_t` or `uintmax_t`
`j`	n	`intmax_t *`
`z`	d, i, o, u, x, or X	`size_t` or the corresponding signed integer type
`z`	n	`size_t *` or a pointer to the corresponding signed integer type
`t`	d, i, o, u, x, or X	`ptrdiff_t` or the corresponding unsigned integer type
`t`	n	`ptrdiff_t *` or a pointer to the corresponding unsigned integer type
`L`	a, A, e, E, f, F, g, or G	`long double`

The *conversion specifier* indicates the type of the argument and how it is to be converted. The corresponding function argument must have a compatible type; otherwise, the behavior of `printf()` is undefined. The conversion specifier values are listed in Table 18-8.

Table 18-8. printf() conversion specifiers

Conversion specifier	Argument type	Output notation
d, i	`int`	Decimal
u	`unsigned int`	Decimal
o	`unsigned int`	Octal
x, X	`unsigned int`	Hexadecimal
f, F	`float` or `double`	Floating decimal point
e, E	`float` or `double`	Exponential notation
g, G	`float` or `double`	Floating decimal point or exponential notation, whichever is shorter
a, A	`float` or `double`	Hexadecimal exponential notation
c	`char` or `int`	Single character
s	`char *`	The string addressed by the pointer argument
n	`int *`	No output; instead, `printf()` stores the number of characters in the output string so far in the variable addressed by the argument
p	Any pointer type	The pointer value, in hexadecimal notation
%	None	A percent sign (%)

The exact meaning of the `a` and `A` conversion specifiers, introduced in C99, is somewhat complicated. They convert a floating-point argument into an exponential notation in which the significant digits are hexadecimal, preceded by the `0x` (or `0X`)

---

prefix, and with one digit to the left of the decimal point character. The exponential multiplier, separated from the significant digits by a p (or P), is represented as a decimal exponent to base FLT_RADIX. The symbolic constant FLT_RADIX, defined in *float.h*, indicates the base of the floating-point environment's exponent representation; this is usually 2, for binary exponent representation. Here is an example using the a conversion specifier:

```
double pi = 3.1415926;
double bignumber = 8 * 8 * 8 * pi * pi * pi;
printf("512 times pi cubed equals %.2e, or %.2a.\n",
                                bignumber, bignumber);
```

This printf() call produces the following output:

```
512 times pi cubed equals 1.59e+04, or 0x1.f0p+13.
```

The first representation shown here, produced by the e conversion specifier, reads "one point five nine times ten to the fourth power," and the second, produced by a, as "hexadecimal one point F zero times two to the (decimal) thirteenth power."

For floating-point arguments, and for the x or X conversion specifiers, the case of the conversion specifier determines the case of any letters in the resulting output: the x (or X) in the hexadecimal prefix; the hexadecimal digits greater than 9; the e (or E) in exponential notation; infinity (or INFINITY) and nan (or NAN); and p (or P) in hexadecimal exponential notation.

In Chapter 2, we described the types with specific characteristics defined in *stdint.h*, such as intmax_t for the given implementation's largest integer type, int_fast32_t for its fastest integer type of at least 32 bits, and the like (see Table 2-5). The header file *stdint.h* also defines macros for the corresponding conversion specifiers for use in the printf() functions. These conversion specifier macros are listed in Table 18-9.

Table 18-9. Conversion specifier macros for integer types defined in stdint.h

Type	Meaning	printf() conversion specifiers
intN_t uintN_t	An integer type whose width is exactly N bits	PRIdN, PRIiN PRIoN, PRIuN, PRIxN, PRIXN
int_leastN_t uint_leastN_t	An integer type whose width is at least N bits	PRIdLEASTN, PRIiLEASTN PRIoLEASTN, PRIuLEASTN, PRIxLEASTN, PRIXLEASTN
int_fastN_t uint_fastN_t	The fastest type to process whose width is at least N bits	PRIdFASTN, PRIiFASTN PRIoFASTN, PRIuFASTN, PRIxFASTN, PRIXFASTN
intmax_t uintmax_t	The widest integer type implemented	PRIdMAX, PRIiMAX PRIoMAX, PRIuMAX, PRIxMAX, PRIXMAX

Type	Meaning	printf() conversion specifiers
intptr_t	An integer type wide enough to store the	PRIdPTR, PRIiPTR
uintptr_t	value of a pointer	PRIoPTR, PRIuPTR, PRIxPTR,
		PRIXPTR

The macros in Table 18-9 expand to string literals. Therefore, when you use one in a printf() format string, you must close the quotation marks surrounding the format string on either side of the macro. Here is an example:

```
int_fast16_t counter = 1001;
while ( --counter )
  printf( "Only %" PRIiFAST16 " nights to go.\n", counter );
```

The preprocessor expands the macro and concatenates the resulting string literal with the adjacent ones on either side of it.

Example

The following example illustrates the use of the %n conversion specification to count the characters in the output string:

```
void print_line( double x)
{
  int n1, n2;
  printf("x = %5.2f   exp(x) = %n%10.5f%n\n", x, &n1, exp(x), &n2);
  assert( n2-n1 <= 10);     // Did printf() stretch the field width?
}

int main()
{
  print_line( 11.22);
  return 0;
}
```

The code produces the following output:

```
x = 11.22   exp(x) = 74607.77476
printf_ex: printf_ex.c:20: print_line: Assertion `n2-n1 <= 10' failed.
Aborted
```

See Also

The other functions in the "printf() family," fprintf(), sprintf(), and snprintf(); the printf() functions for wide characters (declared in *wchar.h*): wprintf(), fwprintf(), and swprintf(); the printf() functions that use the type va_list for the variable arguments (declared in *stdarg.h*): vprintf(), vfprintf(), vsprintf(), and vsnprintf(); the printf() functions for wide characters that use the type va_list for the variable arguments, vwprint(), vfwprint(), and vswprint(); the formatted input functions scanf(), sscanf(), and fscanf()

For each of these functions there is also a corresponding "secure" function, if the implementation supports the C11 bounds-checking functions (i.e., if the macro __STDC_LIB_EXT1__ is defined)

printf_s   C11

Writes formatted data to the standard output stream.

```
#include <stdio.h>
int printf_s( const char * restrict format>, ... );
```

The secure function printf_s(), introduced in C11, is available if the macro __STDC_LIB_EXT1__ is defined. It differs from printf() only in its runtime constraints: the format string must not contain the conversion specifier %n, and the *format* argument and all arguments corresponding to %s specifiers must not be null pointers.

Like printf(), printf_s() returns the number of characters written, or a negative value if an error occurred, such as a violation of the runtime constraints.

Example

```
#define __STDC_WANT_LIB_EXT1__  1
#include <stdio.h>
char *res = NULL;

// ...
   printf_s("Result: %s\n", res);   // The current constraint handler
                                     // will be called if res == NULL.
```

See Also

printf(), scanf(), scanf_s()

putc

Writes a character to a file.

```
#include <stdio.h>
int putc( int c, FILE *fp );
```

The macro putc() is similar to the function fputc(). It writes one character to the current file position of the specified FILE pointer. The return value is the character written, or EOF if an error occurred.

Because putc() is a macro, it may evaluate its argument more than once. Make sure the argument is not an expression with side effects—or else use fputc().

Example

This is a simple search-and-replace filter to eliminate backtick characters in text files:

```
int c;
FILE *fp;

if (( fp = fopen( "textfile", "r+" )) == NULL )
{
```

```
            fprintf( stderr, "Couldn't open input file.\n" );
            exit(-1);
         }

         while (( c = getc( fp )) != EOF ) // Read a character until EOF
         {
            if ( c == '`' )                 // If it's a backtick ...
            {
               fseek( fp, -1, SEEK_CUR ); // back up to the place it was read from,
               putc( '\'', fp );          // and replace it with a single-quote
               fflush( fp );              // character.
            }
         }
         fclose( fp );
```

See Also

fgetc(), fputc(), getc(), getchar(), putchar(); the functions to read and write
wide characters, putwc(), fputwc(), putwchar(); getwc(), fgetwc(), getwchar()

putchar

Writes a character to standard output.

```
#include <stdio.h>
int putchar( int c );
```

The macro putchar() is similar to putc(), but rather than writing a character to a
specified file, it writes to stdout, and hence has no FILE pointer argument.

Example

The following example code reads the beginning of a file repetitively, and reports its
progress on stdout.

```
long count; const long CYCLES = 5000;
FILE *fp = fopen( "infile.txt", "r" );
char readback[1024];

for (count = 0; count <= CYCLES; ++count)
{
 /* Start output with '\r' to reuse same screen line. */
  printf( "\rPerformed %li file reads. ", count );

  rewind( fp );
  fgets( readback, 1024, fp );

 /* Scroll a new screen line every hundred cycles. */
  if (count % 100 != 0) continue;
  putchar( '\n' );
}
puts( "Done." );
```

putc(), getc(), getchar(), fgetc(), fputc(); the functions to read and write wide characters, putwc(), fputwc(), putwchar(); getwc(), fgetwc(), getwchar()

puts

Writes a text line to standard output.

```
#include <stdio.h>
int puts( const char *string );
```

The puts() function writes the string referenced by its pointer argument to the standard output stream, followed by a newline character ('\n'). The return value is non-negative, or EOF if an error occurs.

Example

See the examples for qsort(), setjmp(), and signal() in this chapter.

See Also

fputs(), gets(), fputws()

putwc

Writes a wide character to a file.

```
#include <stdio.h>
#include <wchar.h>
wint_t putwc( wchar_t c, FILE *fp );
```

The function or macro putwc() is similar to the function fputwc(). It writes one character to the current file position of the specified FILE pointer. The return value is the character written, or WEOF if an error occurred.

Because putwc() may be implemented as a macro, it might evaluate its argument more than once. Make sure the argument is not an expression with side effects—or else use fputwc().

Example

See the examples for getwc() and fgetwc() in this chapter.

See Also

fputwc(), putwchar(), getwc(), fgetwc(), getwchar()

putwchar

Writes a wide character to standard output.

```
#include <wchar.h>
wint_t putwchar( wchar_t c );
```

The macro putwchar() is similar to putwc(), but writes a wide character to stdout, and has no FILE pointer argument.

Example

See the example for getwchar() in this chapter.

See Also

putwc(), fputwc(), getwc(), fgetwc(), getwchar()

qsort

Sorts an array using the quick-sort algorithm.

```
#include <stdlib.h>
void qsort( void *array, size_t n, size_t size,
            int (*compare)( const void *, const void * ) );
```

The qsort() function sorts the array referenced by its first argument according to a user-definable sorting criterion using the quick-sort algorithm. You determine the sorting criterion by defining a callback function that compares two array elements in some way and indicates which is greater. The qsort() function calls this function by the pointer passed in the last argument to qsort() each time it needs to compare two elements of the array.

The comparison function takes as its arguments two pointers to elements of the array being sorted. The corresponding parameters are declared as void pointers so that qsort() can be used with any type of array element. The comparison must return a negative value if its first argument is "less than" the second, a positive value if the first argument is "greater than" the second, or zero if they are "equal." It is up to you to define the criteria that constitute these relations for the given type of array element. The qsort() function sorts the array in ascending order. The same comparison function can be used by the bsearch() function.

Example

```
int strptrcmp( const void *sp1, const void *sp2 );

int main()
{
  char *words[] = { "Then",    "he",    "shouted", "What", "I",
                    "didn't", "hear", "what",    "you", "said" };

  int n = sizeof(words) / sizeof(char *);

  qsort( words, n, sizeof(char *), strptrcmp );

  for ( int j = 0 ; j < n ; j++ )
    puts( words[j] );
}

int strptrcmp( const void *sp1, const void *sp2 )
// Compare two strings by reference.
```

```
{
    // qsort() passes a pointer to the pointer:
    // dereference it to pass a char * to strcmp.
    const char * s1 = *(char **)sp1;
    const char * s2 = *(char **)sp2;
    return strcmp( s1, s2 );
}
```

This program sorts the words in the array in alphabetical order. As the output shows, any capital letter is less than any lowercase letter, and "he" is less than "hear":

```
I
Then
What
didn't
he
hear
said
shouted
what
you
```

See also the example for bsearch() in this chapter, as well as Example 4-1.

See Also

qsort_s(), bsearch(), bsearch_s()

qsort_s   C11

Sorts an array.

```
#include <stdlib.h>
errno_t qsort_s( const void *array, rsize_t n, rsize_t size,
        int (*compare)(const void *el1, const void *el2, void *context),
        void *context);
```

The function qsort_s(), like qsort(), sorts the array addressed by its pointer argument *array*. The array consists of *n* elements, and the size of each element is *size*. The qsort_s() function calls the function specified by the *compare()* argument to compare pairs of array elements.

Unlike qsort(), the function has an additional parameter, *context*. The qsort_s() function merely passes the *context* argument, which may be a null pointer, to the comparison function *compare* with each call. The function qsort_s() also tests the following runtime constraints: the values of *n* and *size* must not be greater than RSIZE_MAX, and if *n* is not zero, then the pointer arguments *key*, *array*, and compare must not be null pointers.

The qsort_s() function compares pairs of array elements by passing pointers to the elements to the comparison function specified by the *compare* argument. That function must return a value that is less than, equal to, or greater than zero to indicate whether the first array element is less than, equal to, or greater than the second.

If a violation of the runtime constraints occurs, qsort_s() returns a nonzero value. Otherwise, qsort_s() returns zero and leaves the array sorted in ascending order. If two array members compare equal, their order in the sorted array is undetermined.

Example

See the example for bsearch_s() in this chapter.

See Also

qsort(), bsearch(), bsearch_s()

quick_exit   C99

Ends program execution.

```
#include <stdlib.h>
_Noreturn void quick_exit( int status);
```

The function quick_exit() first calls any functions that have been registered by calls to at_quick_exit(), in the reverse order of registration. However, quick_exit() does not run any cleanup functions registered by atexit(), nor signal handlers registered by the function signal(). Then quick_exit() ends the program by calling _Exit(status).

Example

See the example for at_quick_exit().

See Also

quick_exit(), exit(), atexit(), _Exit(), abort()

raise

Raises a signal.

```
#include <signal.h>
int raise( int sig );
```

The raise() function sends the signal identified by *sig* to the program. If the program has installed a handler for the given signal by means of a call to the signal() function, then that handler routine runs when the signal is raised, and raise() does not return until the handler function has returned. If the signal handler doesn't end the program, the return value of raise() is 0 if it succeeds in raising the signal; otherwise, it is a nonzero value.

Macros for values of the argument *sig* are defined in the standard header *signal.h*, and are described under signal() in this chapter.

Example

See the example for signal() in this chapter.

See Also

abort(), signal(), feraiseexcept()

rand

Obtains a random integer value.

```
#include <stdlib.h>
int rand( void );
```

The rand() function returns a pseudo-random number between 0 and RAND_MAX. The symbolic constant RAND_MAX is defined in *stdlib.h*, and is equal to at least 32,767 (or 2^{15} -1).

To initialize the pseudo-random number generator, call the srand() function with a new seed value before the first call to rand(). This step ensures that rand() provides a different sequence of random numbers each time the program runs. If you call rand() without having called srand(), the result is the same as if you had called srand() with the argument value 1.

Example

```
printf( "Think of a number between one and twenty.\n"
        "Press Enter when you're ready." );
getchar();

srand( (unsigned)time( NULL ) );

for ( int i = 0; i < 3; i++ )         // We get three guesses.
{
  printf( "Is it %u? (y or n) ", 1 + rand() % 20 );
  if ( tolower( getchar() ) ) == 'y' )
  {
    printf( "Ha! I knew it!\n" );
    exit( 0 );
  }
  getchar();                          // Discard newline character.
}
printf( "I give up.\n" );
```

See Also

srand()

realloc

Resizes an allocated memory block.

```
#include <stdlib.h>
void *realloc( void *ptr, size_t n );
```

The realloc() function replaces a memory block dynamically allocated by malloc(), calloc(), or realloc() with a new one of size *n*, and copies the contents of the previous block to the new block, to the extent that the two blocks' sizes permit. If the new block is larger, the values of the remaining bytes are undetermined. The pointer argument passed to realloc() is the address of the block previously allocated, and the function's return value is the address of the new block. The new block may or may not begin at the same address as the old block. realloc() returns a null pointer if the new block could not be allocated as requested; in this case, it does not release the old block, and your program can continue using it.

If the first argument is a null pointer, realloc() allocates a new memory block, behaving similarly to malloc(). Otherwise, if the pointer argument does not point to a memory block allocated by malloc(), calloc(), or realloc(), or if it points to such a block that has since been released by a call to free() or realloc(), then the behavior is undefined.

Example

```
typedef struct { int len;
                 float array[];
               } DynArray_t;

DynArray_t *daPtr = malloc( sizeof(DynArray_t) + 10*sizeof(float) );
if ( daPtr == NULL ) return -1;

daPtr->len = 10;

for ( int i = 0; i < daPtr->len; ++i )
  daPtr->array[i] = 1.0F/(i+1);
/* daPtr->array[10] = 0.1F            // Invalid array index! */

DynArray_t *daResizePtr = realloc( daPtr,
                              sizeof(DynArray_t) + 11*sizeof(float));
if ( daResizePtr != NULL )
{
  daPtr = daResizePtr ;
  daPtr->len = 11;
  daPtr->array[10] = 0.1F / 12;       // OK now.
}
else
  /* We'll just have to get along with the array of 10 floats. */
```

See Also

malloc(), calloc(), free()

Calculates the remainder of a floating-point division.

```
#include <math.h>
double remainder( double x, double y );
float remainderf( float x, float y );
long double remainderl( long double x, long double y );
```

The remainder() functions return the remainder r of x / y, such that $r = x - ny$, where n is the nearest integer to the exact value of x / y (regardless of the current rounding direction). If the exact quotient is exactly halfway between two integers, then the quotient n is the nearest even integer. By this definition, the remainder can be positive or negative. If the remainder is zero, then remainder() returns zero with the same sign as the argument x.

Example

```
double apples, people, share, left;
printf( "\nHow many people? " );
scanf( "%lf", &people );
printf( "\nHow many apples? " );
scanf( "%lf", &apples );

left = remainder( apples, people );    // left may be negative!
share = ( apples - left ) / people;

printf( "If there are %.1lf of us and %.1lf apples, "
        "each of us gets %.1lf of %s, with %.1lf left over.\n",
        people, apples, share, ( share < 1 ) ? "one" : "them", left );
```

See Also

remquo( ), fmod( )

remove

Unlinks a file.

```
#include <stdio.h>
int remove( const char *filename );
```

The remove() function deletes the file (or directory) referred to by its string argument. To be exact, it "unlinks" the file, or deletes its filename from the filesystem, so that the file's contents may still exist if the file was linked to more than one name.

The remove() function may or may not be able to unlink a file while it is open, depending on the given implementation. The function returns 0 on success. If remove() fails to unlink the file, it returns a nonzero value.

Example

```
char fname_tmp[L_tmpnam] = "";
FILE *fp;
```

```
int result;

tmpnam( fname_tmp );
fp = fopen( fname_tmp, "w+" );

/* ... write something in the file, edit it ... */

fclose( fp );

result = rename( fname_tmp, "finished.txt" );
if ( result )             // Delete previous "finished.txt" and try again.
{
  remove( "finished.txt" );
  result = rename( fname_tmp, "finished.txt" );
  if ( result )                    // Give up and log the error.
    fprintf( stderr, "Error %d on trying to rename output file\n",
                                                    errno );

}
```

See Also

fopen( ), tmpfile( )

remquo   C99

Calculates the integer quotient and the remainder of a floating-point division.

```
#include <math.h>
double remquo( double x, double y, int *quo );
float remquof( float x, float y, int *quo );
long double remquol( long double x, long double y, int *quo );
```

The remquo( ) functions are similar to the remainder( ) functions, except that they also store part of the integer quotient of the division in the object referenced by the pointer argument. The entire quotient may not fit in the int object referenced by the pointer, and the ISO C standard requires only that the quotient as stored has the same sign as the actual quotient x/y, and that its absolute value matches the actual quotient in at least the lowest three bits, or modulo 8.

Example

```
double apples = 0.0, people = 0.0, left = 0.0, share = 0.0;
int quotient = 0;

printf( "\nHow many people? " );
scanf( "%lf", &people );

printf( "\nHow many apples? " );
scanf( "%lf", &apples );

share = nearbyint( apples / people );
left = remquo( apples, people, &quotient );
```

```
printf( "If there are %.2lf of us and %.2lf apples, "
        "each of us gets %.2lf apple%s, with %.2lf left over.\n",
        people, apples, share, ( share == 1 ) ? "" : "s", left );
printf( "remquo() stored %d as the quotient "
        " of the division (modulo 8).\n", quotient );

printf( "Test: share modulo 8 - quotient = %d\n",
        (int) share % 8 - quotient );
```

See Also

remainder(), modf()

rename

Renames or moves a file.

```
#include <stdio.h>
int rename( const char *oldname, const char *newname );
```

The rename() function changes the name of the file specified by *oldname* to the string referenced by *newname*. The pointer argument *oldname* must refer to the name of an existing file.

The function returns 0 on success. If rename() fails to rename the file, it returns a nonzero value.

Example

See the example for remove() in this chapter.

See Also

freopen(), remove(), tmpnam()

rewind

Resets a file's access position to the beginning of the file.

```
#include <stdio.h>
void rewind( FILE *fp );
```

The rewind() function sets the access position of the file associated with the FILE pointer *fp* to the beginning of the file, and clears the EOF and error flags.

Example

This example prints the contents of a file twice, converting each character to lowercase the first time through, and to uppercase the second time:

```
FILE *fp; int c;

if (( fp = fopen( argv[1], "r" )) == NULL )
  fprintf( stderr, "Failed to open file %s\n", argv[1] );
else
{
```

```
    puts( "Contents of the file in lowercase:" );
    while (( c = fgetc( fp )) != EOF )
      putchar( tolower( c ));

    rewind( fp );

    puts( "Same again in uppercase:" );
    while (( c = fgetc( fp )) != EOF )
      putchar( toupper( c ));

    fclose( fp );
  }
```

See Also

fseek(), ftell(), fgetpos(), fsetpos(), clearerr()

rint   C99

Rounds a floating-point number to an integer value.

```
#include <math.h>
double rint( double x );
float rintf( float x );
long double rintl( long double x );
```

The rint() functions round a floating-point number to the next integer value in the current rounding direction. The current rounding direction is an attribute of the floating-point environment that you can read and modify using the fegetround() and fesetround() functions. The rint() functions are similar to the nearbyint() functions, except that the rint() functions may raise the FE_INEXACT exception (depending on the implementation) when the result of the rounding is different from the argument.

Example

```
struct round_modes { int id; char *str; } arrModes[ ] =
{
  #ifdef FE_TONEAREST
  { FE_TONEAREST,
    "FE_TONEAREST: round to nearest representable value" },
  #endif
  #ifdef FE_DOWNWARD
  { FE_DOWNWARD, "FE_DOWNWARD: round toward -Inf" },
  #endif
  #ifdef FE_UPWARD
  { FE_UPWARD, "FE_UPWARD: round toward +Inf" },
  #endif
  #ifdef FE_TOWARDZERO
  { FE_TOWARDZERO, "FE_TOWARDZERO: round toward 0" }
  #endif
};
```

```
int nModes = sizeof( arrModes) / sizeof(*arrModes);

#pragma STDC FENV_ACCESS ON

for ( int i = 0; i < nModes; ++i)
{
  if ( fesetround( arrModes[i].id) != 0)
    break;
  printf( "Rounding mode: %s\n", arrModes[i].str );

  printf( "rint(1.4)  = %4.1f    rint(1.5)  = %4.1f\n",
          rint(1.4), rint(1.5) );
  printf( "rint(-1.4) = %4.1f    rint(-1.5) = %4.1f\n",
          rint(-1.4), rint(-1.5) );
}
```

If the implementation supports all four rounding modes, this code produces the following output:

```
Rounding mode: FE_TONEAREST: round to nearest representable value
rint(1.4)  =  1.0    rint(1.5)  =  2.0
rint(-1.4) = -1.0    rint(-1.5) = -2.0
Rounding mode: FE_DOWNWARD: round toward -Inf
rint(1.4)  =  1.0    rint(1.5)  =  1.0
rint(-1.4) = -2.0    rint(-1.5) = -2.0
Rounding mode: FE_UPWARD: round toward +Inf
rint(1.4)  =  2.0    rint(1.5)  =  2.0
rint(-1.4) = -1.0    rint(-1.5) = -1.0
Rounding mode: FE_TOWARDZERO: round toward 0
rint(1.4)  =  1.0    rint(1.5)  =  1.0
rint(-1.4) = -1.0    rint(-1.5) = -1.0
```

See Also

lrint(), llrint(); nearbyint(), nexttoward(), nextafter(); round(), lround(), llround(), ceil(), floor(), fegetround(), fesetround()

---

round   C99

Rounds a floating-point number to an integer value.

```
#include <math.h>
double round( double x );
float roundf( float x );
long double roundl( long double x );
```

The round() functions round a floating-point number to the nearest integer value, regardless of the current rounding direction setting in the floating-point environment. If the argument is exactly halfway between two integers, round() rounds it away from 0. The return value is the rounded integer value.

Example

See the example for nearbyint() in this chapter.

lround(), llround(), rint(), lrint(), llrint(), nearbyint(), nexttoward(), nextafter(); ceil(), trunc()

scalbln, scalbn   C99

Multiplies a floating-point number by a power of the floating-point radix.

```
#include <math.h>
double scalbn( double x, int n );
float scalbnf( float x, int n );
long double scalbnl( long double x, int n );

double scalbln( double x, long int n );
float scalblnf( float x, long int n );
long double scalblnl( long double x, long int n );
```

The scalbn() and scalbln() functions multiply a floating-point number x by an integer power of FLT_RADIX, providing a more efficient calculation than the arithmetic operators. The symbolic constant FLT_RADIX, defined in *float.h*, indicates the base of the floating-point environment's exponent representation; this is usually 2, for binary exponent representation. In this case, the return value of the scalbn() and scalbln() functions is $x \times 2^n$.

Example

See the example for feholdexcept() in this chapter.

See Also

frexp(), ldexp()

scanf

Reads formatted data from standard input.

```
#include <stdio.h>
int scanf( const char * restrict format, ... );
```

The scanf() function reads a sequence of characters from the standard input stream and parses it for the data items specified by the format string. The function then stores the data in the locations addressed by the subsequent pointer arguments.

The ellipsis (...) in the function prototype indicates that scanf() takes a variable number of optional arguments. All parameters after those explicitly declared can be considered to be of the type void *, which means that you can pass any type of object pointer to scanf() in that position. Each of these pointer arguments must point to a variable whose type agrees with the corresponding conversion specification in the format string. If there are more such arguments than conversion specifiers, the excess arguments are ignored. However, if there are not enough arguments to store the data converted, the function's behavior is undefined.

Conversion specification syntax

For a general overview of data conversion with scanf(), see "Formatted Input" on page 230. This section describes the syntax of conversion specifications in the scanf() format string in detail. The conversion specifications have the following syntax:

%[*][*field width*][*length modifier*]*specifier*

Before processing each conversion specification in the format string, scanf() skips over any whitespace characters in the input stream (except with the conversion specifiers c and [], which we will describe in a moment). For each conversion specification, scanf() reads one or more characters from the input stream. As soon as scanf() reads a character that cannot be interpreted under the current conversion specification, reading is interrupted, as if the first character after the data to be converted had not been read. Then scanf() converts the characters that belong to the field, and assigns the result to the variable addressed by the corresponding pointer argument.

If a conversion specification contains an asterisk after the percent sign (%*...), then the result of the conversion is not assigned to a variable but simply discarded.

The optional *field width* is a positive integer that specifies the *maximum* number of characters to read and convert for the given conversion specification.

The *length modifier* qualifies the conversion specifier to indicate the corresponding argument's type more specifically. Each length modifier value is applicable only to certain conversion specifier values. If they are mismatched, the function's behavior is undefined. The permissible *length modifier* values and their meaning for the appropriate conversion specifiers are listed in Table 18-10.

Table 18-10. scanf() conversion specifier modifiers

Modifier	With conversion specifier	Corresponding argument's type
hh	d, i, o, u, x, X, or n	signed char * or unsigned char *
h	d, i, o, u, x, X, or n	short int * or unsigned short int *
l (ell)	d, i, o, u, x, X, or n	long int * or unsigned long int *
l (ell)	c, s, or [...]	wchar_t *; conversion as by mbrtowc()
l (ell)	a, A, e, E, f, F, g, or G	double *
ll (two ells)	d, i, o, u, x, X, or n	long long * or unsigned long long *
j	d, i, o, u, x, X, or n	intmax_t * or uintmax_t *
z	d, i, o, u, x, X, or n	size_t * or a pointer to the corresponding signed integer type
t	d, i, o, u, x, X, or n	ptrdiff_t * or a pointer to the corresponding unsigned integer type
L	a, A, e, E, f, F, g, or G	long double *

The *conversion specifier* indicates the type of the argument and how the input characters are to be interpreted. The corresponding function argument must have a compatible type; otherwise, the behavior of scanf() is undefined. The conversion specifier values are listed in Table 18-11.

Table 18-11. scanf() conversion specifiers

Conversion specifier	Argument type	Input notation
d	signed int *	Decimal with optional sign
i	signed int *	Decimal, octal, or hexadecimal, with optional sign
u	unsigned int *	Decimal with optional sign
o	unsigned int *	Octal with optional sign
x	unsigned int *	Hexadecimal with optional sign and/or 0x (or 0X) prefix
a, e, f, or g	float *	Floating-point
c	char * or int *	One character, or several if a field width greater than one is specified
s	char *	Consecutive non-whitespace characters
[scanset]	char *	Consecutive characters from the specified set
n	int *	No input read; instead, scanf() stores the number of characters read from input so far in the variable addressed by the argument
p	void *	The system's notation for a pointer value; converts inversely as printf()
%	None	A single percent sign (%); no value stored

For a description of the character sequences that are interpreted as floating-point numbers, including decimal and hexadecimal exponential notation, see "Floating-Point Constants" on page 40.

If you use the conversion specifier c without a field width, it matches one character. If you specify a field width, as in the conversion specification %7c, then scanf() reads the specified number of characters, including whitespace characters, and assigns them to successive elements of an array of char addressed by the corresponding pointer argument, but does *not* append a terminating null character. It is up to you to make sure that the argument points to the first element of an array of sufficient size to accommodate the number of characters indicated by the field width.

If you use the conversion specifier c together with the length modifier l, then scanf() reads one or more bytes (according to the specified field width, if any), converting them as it goes from multibyte characters to wide characters in the same way as successive calls to the mbrtowc() function would, starting with an mbstate_t object corresponding to the initial parsing state. If you specify a field width, scanf() reads the specified number of bytes, and assigns the corresponding wide characters to successive elements of an array of wchar_t addressed by the corresponding pointer argument, but does *not* append a terminating null wide character ((L'\0')). It is up to you to make sure that the argument points to the first element of an array of sufficient size to accommodate the number of wide characters stored.

The conversion specifier s is similar to c, with these exceptions:

- scanf() with an s specifier stops reading at the first whitespace character, or when it has read the number of bytes indicated by the field length, if specified.

- scanf() with an s specifier appends a null character (or wide character, if the l modifier is present) to the sequence of characters (or wide characters) stored. The pointer argument must point to the first element of an array that is large enough to accommodate the characters read plus the null character.

The conversion specifier [...] is similar to s, with the following exceptions: rather than matching any sequence of non-whitespace characters, it matches any sequence of the characters in the set that appear between the square brackets, called the *scanset*. (The scanset may or may not include whitespace characters.) If the first character after the opening bracket is a caret (^), then it is not a member of the scanset but inverts the meaning of the set of characters that follows; the conversion specifier matches any sequence of the characters that do *not* appear in the list that follows the caret.

If the first character after the opening bracket (or after the opening bracket and an initial caret) of a [...] specifier is a right bracket (]), then that right bracket is interpreted as a member of the character list that defines the scanset, not as the closing delimiter. If the characters between the brackets (or between the initial caret and the closing bracket) include a hyphen (-) that is neither in the first nor the last position, then it is left up to the given implementation to define whether scanf() interprets the hyphen in a special way—for example, as indicating a range of characters. For example, the conversion specifier %[0-9] may match any sequence of digits, or any sequence of the characters 0, -, and 9—or the implementation may define the hyphen in some other way.

The scanf() function stops reading the input stream in whichever of the following events occurs first:

- The entire format string has been processed.

- A *matching failure*: the first non-whitespace character in an input field did not match the conversion specification, or a character in the input did not match the corresponding position in the format string.

- An *input failure*: no input could be read from the input stream, or an encoding error occurred.

Any non-whitespace character in the format string that is not part of a conversion specification is processed by reading a character from the input stream, and testing for a literal match. If the characters do not match, scanf() returns, leaving the input stream as if the mismatched character had not been read. A whitespace character in the format string matches any sequence of whitespace characters in the input stream, including an empty string.

The scanf() function returns the number of data items assigned to variables, not counting assignments due to %n conversion specifications. If an input failure occurs before any input item can be converted, scanf() returns EOF.

Example

```
double x, y;
char operation[16] = "";
scanf("%15s%lf%*[^0123456789]%lf", operation, &x, &y);
```

The format string in this scanf() call contains four conversion specifications. Let us assume that a user enters the following sequence of characters when this call occurs:

```
Divide 1.5e3 by 52.25\n
```

For the first conversion specification, %15s, scanf() reads each character up to the first space, and hence stores the string "Divide", terminated by a null character, in the array operation. After the space, the sequence 1.5e3 matches the conversion specification %lf, and scanf() assigns the value 1500.0 to the double variable x. After the next space, each of the characters 'b', 'y', and ' ' (the space) is in the very large scanset of the conversion specification %*[^01234567890]; the first character that does not match is the digit character '5'. Because the conversion specification contains the asterisk, scanf() discards the characters read, then reads to the next whitespace character, '\n', for the conversion specification %lf, and assigns the value 52.25 to the variable y.

For another example, see fscanf() in this chapter (fscanf() reads a specified file rather than stdin, but is otherwise similar to scanf()).

See Also

fscanf(), sscanf(), wscanf(), fwscanf(), swscanf(), vscanf(), vfscanf(), vsscanf(), vwscanf(), vfwscanf(), vswscanf()

For each of these functions, there is also a corresponding "secure" function, if the implementation supports the C11 bounds-checking functions (i.e., if the macro __STDC_LIB_EXT1__ is defined)

scanf_s

Reads formatted data from the standard input stream.

```
#include <stdio.h>
int scanf_s(const char * restrict format, ... );
```

The secure function scanf_s(), introduced in C11, is available if the macro __STDC_LIB_EXT1__ is defined. Like scanf(), it reads formatted data from standard input. Unlike scanf(), however, it takes two arguments for each of the conversion specifiers %c, %s, and %[ ]: in addition to an array pointer, you must provide the length of the given array in an argument with the type rsize_t. The input at runtime must fit in the array, including a string terminator character. For the conversion specifier %c, a length of 1 is sufficient, because scanf_s() reads only one character for %c and does not append a string terminator character.

The function scanf_s() tests the following runtime constraints: the pointer argument *format* and the pointer arguments for format elements must not be null pointers. Implementations may optionally test for additional conditions, such as the correctness of the format elements.

The scanf_s() function returns the number of data items converted and stored in variables. If an input error occurs before any data can be converted, or if a runtime constraint violation occurs, the function returns EOF.

Example

```
#define __STDC_WANT_LIB_EXT1__ 1
#include <stdio.h>
// ...

  char article[64] = "";
  int quantity = 0;
  printf("Enter article name and quantity: ");
  if( scanf_s("%s %d", article, sizeof(article), &quantity) < 2)
    fputs("Invalid entry.\n", stderr);
  else
  {  /* Process input.   */
```

See Also

scanf(), fscanf(), sscanf(), wscanf(), fwscanf(), swscanf(), vscanf(), vfscanf(), vsscanf(), vwscanf(), vfwscanf(), vswscanf(), and the corresponding secure functions

set_constraint_handler_s   C11

Installs a call-back function to handle violations of runtime constraints.

```
#include <stdlib.h>
constraint_handler_t set_constraint_handler_s(
                        constraint_handler_t handler);
```

The function set_constraint_handler_s() installs the function specified by its argument as an error handler for violations of the secure functions' runtime constraints. After a successful set_constraint_handler_s() call, the handler function installed is called when any of the secure standard library functions (those with names ending in _s) detects a violation of its runtime constraints.

The function pointer argument *handler* must have the type constraint_han
dler_t, which is defined in *stdlib.h* as follows:

```
typedef void (*constraint_handler_t)( const char * restrict msg,
                                       void * restrict ptr,
                                       errno_t error);
```

When the installed handler function is called, it receives the following arguments:

- A string describing the error.
- A null pointer or a pointer to an object defined by the given implementation.
- The return value of the function in which the error occurred, if the function's
  return type is error_t, or an undetermined positive value if the function's type
  is different.

There is a default error handler that is called on runtime constraint violations if no
handler has been installed by a set_constraint_handler_s() call. That default
handler may be the standard function abort_handler_s() or ignore_handler_s(),
or another implementation-specific handler function. The default handler is also
reinstalled if you call the function set_constraint_handler_s() with a null pointer
as its argument. The set_constraint_handler_s() function returns a pointer to
the previously registered handler.

Example

```
// Use a custom handler:
void myConstraintHandler(const char* msg, void * ptr, errno_t error)
{
    printf("A runtime constraint violation "
           "occurred: \n%s; ", msg);
    printf("error code: %d\n", error);  fflush(stdout);
    exit(error);
}

void func( const char *str)
{
    constraint_handler_t prevHandler =
                set_constraint_handler_s(myConstraintHandler);
    printf_s("The argument: %s\n", str);   // Error if str
                                           // is a null pointer.
    int len = strlen(str);
    char str2[len];
    strcpy_s( str2, len, str);     // Error: str2 is one byte too short.
    // . . .
    set_constraint_handler_s(prevHandler);
}
```

For example, the function call func("Hi!"); produces the following output:

```
The argument: Hi!
A runtime constraint violation occurred:
Range error; error code: 34
```

abort_handler_s(), ignore_handler_s()

setbuf

Sets up I/O buffering for an open file.

```
#include <stdio.h>
void setbuf( FILE * restrict fp, char * restrict buffer );
```

The setbuf() function is similar to setvbuf(), except that it has no return value, and no parameters to specify a buffering mode or a buffer size. The size of the buffer established by setbuf() is given by the value of the macro BUFSIZ. If the *buffer* argument is not a null pointer, the setbuf() call initiates fully buffered input and output for the specified file so that the buffer is filled completely before data appears from the source or at the destination; this behavior corresponds to the buffering mode specified by the macro _IOFBF as the *mode* argument to setvbuf(). If the *buffer* argument is a null pointer, setbuf() disables all I/O buffering for the file, so that data is written and read directly.

You may call the setbuf() function only after the file has been successfully opened, and before any file I/O operations have taken place.

Example

```
FILE *fp = tmpfile();
unsigned char *iobuffer = malloc( BUFSIZ );
if ( iobuffer != NULL )
{
  setbuf( fp, iobuffer );     // Make sure temporary file is buffered.
}
/* ... now write and read the temporary file as needed ... */
```

See Also

setvbuf(), fflush()

setjmp

Saves the calling environment as a long jump destination.

```
#include <setjmp.h>
int setjmp( jmp_buf env );
```

The setjmp() macro saves the current environment at the time of the call in a buffer specified by its argument. The environment includes the stack, and with it all variables that have automatic storage duration. Like the setjmp() macro itself, the argument's type, jmp_buf, is defined in the header file *setjmp.h*.

A later call to the longjmp() function restores the saved environment. As a result, the longjmp() function does not return but instead causes execution to continue as if control had returned from the setjmp(). However, while the original setjmp()

Library
Functions

call always returns 0, the apparent return value after longjmp() is never equal to zero.

Because the execution environment saved may not include other partial expressions, the return value of setjmp() must not be used except in simple conditional expressions, or in comparison to an integer constant value. Furthermore, if any variables with automatic storage duration in the function that called setjmp() were modified after the setjmp() call (and were not declared as volatile), then their values after the longjmp() call are indeterminate.

Example

This example shows the complete contents of two source files to illustrate how setjmp() and longjmp() allow you to escape from a function call.

```
#include <stdlib.h>
#include <stdio.h>
#include <setjmp.h>
#include <errno.h>

double calculate1( double x);      // Functions defined
double calculate2( double x);      // in calculate.c.

jmp_buf jmp_dest;                  // Destination for longjmp()

int main()
{
  double x = 0, y1, y2;
  int n = 0;

  puts("--- Demonstrating non-local jumps ---\n");

  switch( setjmp( jmp_dest))    // Jump to here for error handling
  {
  case 0:                          // The original setjmp() call
    break;
  case EDOM:                       // Arrived via longjmp() call with EDOM
    puts("Domain error. "
         "Negative numbers are not permitted.");
    break;
  case ERANGE:                     // Arrived via longjmp() call with ERANGE
    puts("Range error. "
         "The number you entered is too big.");
    break;
  default:                         // We should never arrive here.
    puts("Unknown error.");
    exit( EXIT_FAILURE );
  }

  printf("Enter a number: ");
  do
  {
```

```
    if ( (n = scanf("%lf", &x)) < 0)        // Read in a number.
        exit( EXIT_FAILURE );               // Read end of file.
    while ( getchar() != '\n')              // Clear the input buffer.
        ;
    if ( n == 0 )
        printf("Invalid entry. Try again: ");
    }while ( n == 0 );

    y1 = calculate1(x);
    y2 = calculate2(x);

    printf("\nResult of Calculation 1: %G\n", y1);
    printf(  "Result of Calculation 2: %G\n", y2);

    return 0;
}

// calculate.c: Perform some calculations.
// Functions: calculate1(), calculate2().
#include <math.h>
#include <setjmp.h>
#include <errno.h>

extern jmp_buf jmp_dest;                    // Destination for longjmp()

double calculate1( double x)
{
    if ( x < 0)
        longjmp( jmp_dest, EDOM);           // Domain error
    else
        return sqrt(x);
}

double calculate2( double x)
{
    double y = exp(x);
    if ( y == HUGE_VAL)
        longjmp( jmp_dest, ERANGE);         // Range error
    else
        return y;
}
```

See Also

longjmp()

setlocale

Gets or sets locale information.

```
#include <locale.h>
char *setlocale( int category, const char *locale_name );
```

The `setlocale()` function allows you to adapt the program to the local conditions of a given regional and cultural environment—called a *locale*—such as clocks and calendars, decimal point and currency symbol characters, and other conventions. The `setlocale()` function returns a pointer to a string that identifies the new locale, or the current locale if you pass the function a null pointer as its second argument.

The locale conventions are classed in *categories*. You can set the individual categories of the program's locale individually. The header file *locale.h* defines the following macros to identify each category in the first argument to `setlocale()`:

LC_ALL
>   Includes all the other categories.

LC_COLLATE
>   Affects the functions `strcoll()`, `strxfrm()`, `wcscoll()`, and `wcsxfrm()`.

LC_CTYPE
>   Affects the character-handling functions (such as `isalpha()`, `tolower()`, etc.), and the multibyte and wide-character functions.

LC_MONETARY
>   Affects the monetary format information provided by the `localeconv()` function.

LC_NUMERIC
>   Affects the nonmonetary numeral format information provided by the `locale conv()` function, and the decimal point used by the `printf()` and `scanf()` functions, and by string conversion functions such as `strtod()`.

LC_TIME
>   Affects the time-and-date string format produced by the `strftime()` and `wcsftime()` functions.

The second argument to `setlocale()`, *locale_name*, is a pointer to a string that indicates the desired locale. The permissible *locale_name* strings are system-dependent, except for two standard values, which are the default locale, "C", and the empty string, "". All locale categories are set to the default locale "C" on program start-up; the "C" locale corresponds to the minimum environment for compiling C programs. If you use the empty string as the locale name, `setlocale()` sets the specified category to the system's native locale. If `setlocale()` is unable to set the desired locale, it returns a null pointer.

If you pass `setlocale()` a null pointer as the *locale_name* argument, it returns the name of the current locale. You can use this string as the *locale_name* argument to restore that locale later.

Example

```
#define MAX_STRING 80

char name[MAX_STRING];
char locale[MAX_STRING];
char *newlocale;
int i;

printf( "Who are you? " );
fgets( name, sizeof(name), stdin );

printf( "What is your locale? " );
fgets( locale, sizeof(locale), stdin );

name[ strlen(name) - 1 ] = '\0';        // Chomp off the newlines.
locale[ strlen(locale) - 1 ] = '\0';

newlocale = setlocale( LC_CTYPE, locale );
if ( newlocale == NULL )
  printf( "Sorry, couldn't change the locale to %s.\n"
          "The current locale is %s. ",
          locale, setlocale( LC_CTYPE, NULL ));
else
  printf( "The new locale is %s. ", newlocale );

name[0] = toupper( name[0] );  // Force the first letter to uppercase.

i = 1;
if ( isupper( name[i] ) )       // Is the second letter also uppercase?
  {
    while ( name[i] != '\0' )  // If so, force all the rest to lowercase.
      {
        name[i] = tolower( name[i] );
        ++i;
      }
  }
printf( "Hello there, %s!\n", name );
```

This program produces output like the following, if the first setlocale() call is successful:

```
Who are you? sörEn
What is your locale? de_DE
The new locale is de_DE. Hello there, Sören!
```

In the locale "de_DE", the isupper() function recognized the second letter of sörEn as uppercase, and so the ö and E were changed to lowercase.

If the first setlocale() call fails, the output may look like this:

```
Who are you? FRÉDÉRIQUE
What is your locale? fr_CA
```

```
Sorry, couldn't change the locale to fr_CA.
The current locale is C. Hello there, FrÉdÉrique!
```

In the locale "C", the isupper() function recognized the R as uppercase, but the tolower() function was unable to convert the accented uppercase É.

See Also

The character classification functions, whose names begin with is and isw; the character conversion functions, whose names begin with to and tow; the numeral string conversion functions, whose names begin with strto and wcsto; the locale-sensitive string functions strcoll(), strxfrm(), wcscoll(), and wcsxfrm(); strftime() and wcsftime()

setvbuf

Sets up I/O buffering for an open file.

```
#include <stdio.h>
int setvbuf( FILE * restrict fp, char * restrict buffer, int mode,
          size_t size );
```

The setvbuf() function specifies the buffering conditions for input and/or output using the stream associated with the FILE pointer fp. You may call the setvbuf() function only after the file has been successfully opened, and before any file I/O operations have taken place.

The mode parameter determines the type of buffering requested. Symbolic constants for the permissible values are defined in *stdio.h* as follows:

_IOFBF

> *Fully buffered:* On read and write operations, the buffer is filled completely before data appears from the source or at the destination.

_IOLBF

> *Line buffered:* On read and write operations, characters are placed in the buffer until one of them is a newline character, or until the buffer is full. Then the contents of the buffer are written to the stream. The buffer is also written to the stream whenever the program requests, from an unbuffered stream or a line-buffered stream, input which requires characters to be read from the execution environment.

_IONBF

> *Not buffered:* Data is read from or written to the file directly. The *buffer* and *size* parameters are ignored.

You can provide a buffer for the file by passing its address and size in the arguments *buffer* and *size*. The setvbuf() function is not required to use the buffer you provide, however. If *buffer* is a null pointer, setvbuf() dynamically allocates a buffer of the specified size. Otherwise, you must make sure that the buffer remains available until you close the file. The function returns 0 on success; any other value indicates failure or an invalid *mode* argument.

Example

```
#define MAX_LINE 4096
FILE *fp_linewise = fopen( "output.txt", "a+" );
unsigned char *iobuffer = malloc( MAX_LINE );
if ( iobuffer != NULL )
{ // Buffer output up to each '\n'.
  if ( setvbuf( fp_linewise, iobuffer, _IOLBF, MAX_LINE ))
    fprintf( stderr, "setvbuf() failed; "
                     "unable to set line-buffering.\n" ),
    exit( -2 );
}
else
    fprintf( stderr,"malloc() failed; no point in calling setvbuf().\n"),
    exit( -1 );
```

See Also

setbuf(), fopen(), malloc()

signal

Installs a signal handler.

```
#include <signal.h>
void ( *signal( int sig, void (*handler)(int) ) )(int);
```

The signal() function specifies a function to be executed when the program receives a given signal. The parameter *handler* is a pointer to a function that takes one argument of type int and has no return value. This pointer may be the address of a function defined in your program, or one of two macros defined in the header file *signal.h*.

The *handler* argument works in the following ways (assuming that the call to signal() is successful):

- If the *handler* argument is a function pointer, then signal() installs this function as the routine to be called the next time the program receives the signal designated by the integer parameter *sig*.

- If the *handler* argument is equal to the macro SIG_DFL, then the next time the program receives the specified signal, the default signal handler routine is called. The default handler's action for most signals is to terminate the program.

- If the *handler* argument is equal to the macro SIG_IGN, then the specified signal will be ignored.

If the *handler* argument points to a function in the program, then that function is generally installed as a handler for only one occurrence of the signal, as if the program called signal() with the argument SIG_DFL before calling the handler. To make a handler persistent, you can have your handler function reinstall itself by calling signal() again. Alternatively, the C standard allows implementations to mask the signal *sig* while the handler is running, rather than uninstalling the handler before calling it: BSD Unix does this, for example. Refer to the documentation for your system.

The return value of signal() is also a function pointer: it has the same type as the *handler* parameter. If the signal() function succeeds in installing the new handler, it returns a pointer to the previous handler (which may be SIG_IGN or SIG_DEF, if the program has not installed any other handler for the given signal). If unsuccessful, signal() returns the value of SIG_ERR and sets the errno variable to an appropriate value.

Signals are sent through the operating system by other programs, or are raised by system interrupts, or by the program itself using the raise() function. According to the C standard, the following signals are defined in all implementations. The macros listed here represent the permissible values of the signal() function's integer argument *sig*, as well as the argument value passed to the signal handler installed when the signal occurs:

SIGFPE
: *Floating-point exception:* The program attempted an illegal arithmetic operation, such as division by zero, or caused an error such as an overflow.

SIGILL
: *Illegal instruction:* The program flow contained an invalid machine code.

SIGSEGV
: *Segmentation violation:* The program tried to perform an illegal memory access operation.

SIGABRT
: *Abort:* End the program abruptly. (See also abort() in this chapter.)

SIGINT
: *Interrupt:* The program has been interrupted interactively, by the user pressing Ctrl+C or by some similar event.

SIGTERM
: *Termination:* The program is being ordered to exit.

Specific systems may also define other signal types, as well as macros for other special values of *handler*. Furthermore, many systems do not allow programs to install signal handlers for, or to ignore, certain signals. For example, Unix systems do not allow programs to handle or ignore a SIGKILL or SIGSTOP signal. The first three signals in the previous list—SIGFPE, SIGILL, and SIGSEGV—are *non-recoverable*. In other words, if you use signal() to install a handler for one of these signals, your handler function should never return. If it does, the program's behavior is undefined. For other signal types, when a signal handler returns, the program resumes execution wherever it was when the signal occurred.

Signal handler functions are also subject to other constraints, as the state of the system and the program is undefined at the time of their execution. They must not access objects with static storage class, except objects declared with the type sig_atomic_t and the qualifier volatile. Signal handlers must also avoid calling any other functions except abort(), _Exit(), or signal(), and may call signal() only to set a handler for the signal type that caused the present function call. Otherwise the program's behavior is undefined. These restrictions do not apply to handlers invoked through calls to abort() or raise(), however. Handlers invoked through abort() or raise() must not call raise(). Certain systems specify other functions besides abort(), _Exit(), and signal() that a signal handler may call safely. In particular, the POSIX standards define such "safe functions," as well as functions for finer control of signal handling.

Example

```
# include <stdio.h>
# include <stdlib.h>
# include <stdint.h>          // Defines SIG_ATOMIC_MAX
# include <signal.h>

void sigint_handler(int sig);
volatile sig_atomic_t i;    // A counter accessed by main and the
                            // handler.

int main()
{
  if ( signal( SIGINT, sigint_handler ) == SIG_ERR )
  {
    perror("Failed to install SIGINT handler");
    exit(3);
  }

  while (1)
  {
    puts( "Press Ctrl+C to interrupt me.");
    for ( i = 0 ; i < SIG_ATOMIC_MAX ; i++ )
      if ( i % 100000 == 0)
      {
        printf( "\r%d ", i / 100000 );
        fflush( stdout );
      }
    raise( SIGINT );    // Simulate a Ctrl+C in case the user didn't
                        // type it.
  }
  return 0;
}

void sigint_handler( int sig )
{
```

```
    int c = 0;

    if ( sig != SIGINT ) exit( 1 );

    signal( SIGINT, SIG_IGN );  // Ignore a second Ctrl+C

    puts( "\nThis is the function sigint_handler()."
          "\nDo you want to exit the program now? [y/n]");
    while (( c = tolower( getchar( ) )) != 'y' && c != 'n' && c != EOF )
      ;

    if ( c != 'n' )
      exit(0);
    else
      i = 0;                              // Reset timer
    signal( SIGINT, sigint_handler );    // Reinstall this handler.

    /* No return value; just fall off the end of the function. */
}
```

See Also

raise(), abort()

signbit   C99

Ascertains whether a floating-point number is negative.

```
#include <math.h>
int signbit(x );
```

The argument of the signbit() macro can have any real floating-point type—
float, double, or long double—and can have any numeric or other value, including INFINITY, NaN, or 0. The macro ascertains whether the argument's value is negative (whether its sign bit is set, to put it more precisely), and returns a nonzero
value, or true, if it is. Otherwise, signbit() returns 0.

Example

```
double x[ ] = { -0.0,  187.234,  sqrt( -1.0 ),  1.0 / -0.0 };

for ( int i = 0 ; i < ( sizeof(x) / sizeof(double)) ; i++ )
  printf( "x[%d] equals %lF, and is%s negative.\n",
          i, x[i], signbit( x[i] ) ? "" : " not" );
```

The behavior of this example depends on whether the compiler supports negative
zero values in floating-point constants, and whether the undefined arithmetic operations in the array initialization cause fatal exceptions. Compiled with GCC 4.9.2
and the GNU C library, this code produces the following output:

```
x[0] equals -0.000000, and is negative.
x[1] equals 187.234000, and is not negative.
x[2] equals NAN, and is negative.
x[3] equals -INF, and is negative.
```

See also the example for isunordered() in this chapter.

See Also

fpclassify(), isfinite(), isinf(), isnan(), isnormal()

sin

Calculates the sine of an angle.

```
#include <math.h>
double sin( double x );
float sinf( float x );          (C99)
long double sinl( long double x );        (C99)
```

The sin() function calculates the sine of the angle represented by its argument x as a number of radians. The return value is in the range $-1 \le \sin(x) \le 1$.

Example

```
#define DEG_PER_RAD ( 180.0 / PI )

const double PI = 4.0 * atan( 1.0 );
double a[4];

printf( "\nEnter an acute angle measure, in degrees: " );

if ( scanf( "%lf", a ) < 1 || ( a[0] <= 0 || a[0] >= 90 ) )
  printf( "\nThat's not an acute angle.\n" ), exit( 1 );
else
{
  a[1] = a[0] + 90 ;
  a[2] = 180 - a[0] ;
  a[3] = 225 + a[0] ;
  for ( int i = 0 ; i < 4 ; i ++ )
    printf( "The sine of %4.2lf degrees is %6.4lf.\n",
            a[i], sin( a[i] / DEG_PER_RAD ) );
}
```

See Also

cos(), tan(), asin(), csin()

sinh

Calculates the hyperbolic sine of a number.

```
#include <math.h>
double sinh( double x> );
float sinhf( float x );         (C99)
long double sinhl( long double x );       (C99)
```

The sinh() function returns the hyperbolic sine of its argument x. If the result of sinh() is too great for the double type, a range error occurs.

Library
Functions

Example

```
// A chain hanging from two points forms a curve called a catenary.
// A catenary is a segment of the graph of the function
// cosh(k*x)/k, for some constant k.
// The length along the catenary over a certain span, bounded by the
// two vertical lines at x=a and x=b, is equal to
// sinh(k*b)/k - sinh(k*a)/k.

double x, k;
puts("Catenary f(x) = cosh(k*x)/k\n"
     "Length along the catenary from a to b: "
     "sinh(k*b)/k - sinh(k*a)/k)\n");

puts(
"           f(-1.0)   f(0.0)   f(1.0)   f(2.0)   Length(-1.0 to 2.0)\n"
"-----------------------------------------------------------------------");
for ( k = 0.5; k < 5; k *= 2)
{
  printf("k = %.1f: ", k);
  for (   x = -1.0; x < 2.1; x += 1.0)
    printf("%8.2f ", cosh(k*x)/k );

  printf("  %12.2f\n", (sinh(2*k) - sinh(-1*k))/ k);
}
```

This code produces the following output:

```
Catenary f(x) = cosh(k*x)/k
Length along the catenary from a to b:  sinh(k*b)/k - sinh(k*a)/k)

           f(-1.0)   f(0.0)   f(1.0)   f(2.0)   Length(-1.0 to 2.0)
-----------------------------------------------------------------------
k = 0.5:     2.26     2.00     2.26     3.09          3.39
k = 1.0:     1.54     1.00     1.54     3.76          4.80
k = 2.0:     1.88     0.50     1.88    13.65         15.46
k = 4.0:     6.83     0.25     6.83   372.62        379.44
```

See Also

cosh(), tanh(), asinh(), csinh(), casinh()

snprintf, snprintf_s

Stores formatted output in a string buffer.

```
#include <stdio.h>
int snprintf( char * restrict dest, size_t n,
             const char * restrict format, ... );
int snprintf_s( char * restrict dest, rsize_t n,
             const char * restrict format, ... );      (C11)
```

The snprintf() function is similar to printf() but writes its output as a string in the buffer referenced by the first pointer argument, *dest*, rather than to stdout.

Furthermore, the second argument, *n*, specifies the maximum number of characters that snprintf() may write to the buffer, including the terminating null character. If *n* is too small to accommodate the complete output string, then snprintf() writes only the first *n* − 1 characters of the output, followed by a null character, and discards the rest. The return value is the number of characters (not counting the terminating null character) that would have been written if *n* had been large enough. Consequently, the output string has been written completely if and only if the function returns a non-negative value less than *n*. To obtain the length of the output string without storing it, you can set *n* equal to zero; in this case, sprintf() writes nothing to *dest*, which may be a null pointer.

The secure function snprintf_s() is equivalent to snprintf() except for the following runtime constraints: the pointer arguments *dest*, *format*, and any arguments corresponding to %s conversion specifiers must not be null pointers; the number *n* must be greater than zero, but not greater than RSIZE_MAX; and the format string must not contain the conversion specifier %n. If a runtime constraint is violated, snprintf_s() writes the string terminator character '\0' to dest[0], provided *dest* is not a null pointer and *n* is greater than zero and less than RSIZE_MAX.

The return value of snprintf_s() is like that of snprintf(), if the runtime constraints are fulfilled. If a violation occurs, snprintf_s() returns a negative value.

 If the output overlaps with any argument that snprintf() or snprintf_s() copies data from, the behavior is undefined.

Example
```
char buffer[80];
double x = 1234.5, y = 678.9, z = -753.1, a = x * y + z;
int output_len = 0;

output_len = snprintf( buffer, 80, "For the input values %lf, %lf,"
                       " and %lf,\nthe result was %lf.\n",
                       x, y, z, a );
puts( buffer );
if ( output_len >= 80 )
  fprintf( stderr, "Output string truncated! Lost %d characters.\n",
          output_len - 79 );
```
This code produces the following output:
```
For the input values 1234.500000, 678.900000, and -753.100000,
the result was 8
Output string truncated! Lost 14 characters.
```
The first two lines are printed by puts() and the third by fprintf().

See Also

printf(), fprintf(), sprintf(), vprintf(), vfprintf(), vsprintf(), vsnprintf(); the wide-character functions wprintf(), fwprintf(), swprintf(), vwprint(), vfwprint(), vswprint(); the corresponding secure functions, if the implementation supports the C11 bounds-checking functions (i.e., if the macro __STDC_LIB_EXT1__ is defined)

Argument conversion in the printf() family of functions is described in detail under printf() in this chapter.

snwprintf_s   C11

Stores formatted output in a wide-character string buffer.

```
#include <wchar.h>
int snwprintf( wchar_t * restrict dest, size_t n,
               const wchar_t * restrict format, ... );
```

The function snwprintf_s() is equivalent to snprintf_s() except that its format string and output string are wide-character strings of the type wchar_t.

Example

See the example for swprintf() in this chapter.

See Also

snprintf_s(), swprintf()

sprintf, sprintf_s

Stores formatted output in a string buffer.

```
#include <stdio.h>
int sprintf( char * restrict dest, const char * restrict format, ... );
int sprintf_s( char * restrict dest, rsize_t n,
               const char * restrict format, ... );        (C11)
```

The sprintf() function is similar to snprintf(), except that it has no parameter to limit the number of characters written to the destination buffer. As a result, using it means risking buffer overflows, especially because the length of the output depends on the current locale as well as input variables. Use snprintf() instead.

The secure function sprintf_s() is equivalent to snprintf_s(), except that the buffer *dest* must be large enough to store the complete result string. If the number of characters required by the result string is greater than the argument *n*, a violation of the runtime constraints occurs.

A successful sprintf_s() call returns the number of characters written (not counting the terminating null character). The function returns a negative value if a conversion error occurs, and zero if another violation of the runtime constraints occurs.

Example

```
double x = 1234.5, y = 678.9, z = -753.1, a = x * y + z;
char buffer[80];
int output_len = 0;

output_len = sprintf( buffer, "For the input values %lf, %lf, and %lf,"
                              "\nthe result was %lf.\n",
                              x, y, z, a );
puts( buffer );
if ( output_len >= 80 )
  fprintf( stderr, "Output string overflowed by %d characters.\n"
                   "The variables x, y, z and a may have been corrupted:\n"
                   "x now contains %lf, y %lf, z %lf, and a %lf.\n",
                   output_len - 79, x, y, z, a );
```

This code produces the following output:

```
For the input values 1234.500000, 678.900000, and -753.100000,
the result was 837348.950000.

Output string overflowed by 14 characters.
The variables x, y, z and a may have been corrupted:
x now contains 1234.500000, y 678.900000, z -736.004971, and a 0.000000.
```

See Also

printf(), fprintf(), snprintf(), declared in *stdio.h*; vprintf(), vfprintf(), vsprintf(), vsnprintf(), declared in *stdarg.h*; the wide-character functions wprintf(), fwprintf(), swprintf(), declared in *stdio.h* and *wchar.h*; and vwprint(), vfwprint(), and vswprint(), declared in *stdarg.h*; the scanf() input functions. Argument conversion in the printf() family of functions is described in detail under printf() in this chapter.

sqrt

Calculates the square root of a floating-point number.

```
#include <math.h>
double sqrt( double x );
float sqrtf( float x );          (C99)
long double sqrtl( long double x );          (C99)
```

The sqrt() functions return the square root of the argument *x*. If the argument is less than zero, a domain error occurs.

Example

```
double x[ ] = { 0.5, 0.0, -0.0, -0.5 };

for ( int i = 0; i < ( sizeof(x) / sizeof(double) ); i++)
{
  printf("The square root of %.2F equals %.4F\n", x[i], sqrt( x[i] ) );
  if ( errno )
```

```
        perror( __FILE__ );
    }
```

This code produces the following output:

```
The square root of 0.50 equals 0.7071
The square root of 0.00 equals 0.0000
The square root of -0.00 equals -0.0000
The square root of -0.50 equals NAN
sqrt.c: Numerical argument out of domain
```

sqrt() is also used in the examples shown at erf(), feholdexcept(), frexp(), and signbit() in this chapter.

See Also

The complex arithmetic function csqrt(); the cube root function cbrt() and the hypotenuse function, hypot()

srand

Initializes the random number generator.

```
#include <stdlib.h>
void srand( unsigned n );
```

The srand() function initializes the random number generator using its argument n as the "seed." For each value of the seed passed to srand(), subsequent calls to rand() yield the same sequence of "random" numbers. For this reason, a common technique to avoid repetition is to seed srand() with the current time. If you call rand() without having called srand(), the result is the same as if you had called srand() with the argument value 1.

Example

See the example for rand() in this chapter.

See Also

rand()

sscanf, sscanf_s

Reads formatted data from a string.

```
#include <stdio.h>
int sscanf( const char * restrict src,
            const char * restrict format, ... );
int sscanf_s( const char * restrict src,
              const char * restrict format, ... );      (C11)
```

The functions sscanf() and sscanf_s() are similar to the functions scanf() and scanf_s(), except that they read from the string specified by their argument src instead of stdin.

Like scanf(), the sscanf() functions return the number of data items converted and stored in variables. If an input error occurs or the function reads to the end of the string before any data can be converted, the return value is EOF. The sscanf_s() function also returns EOF if a violation of its runtime constraints occurs.

Example

See the examples for fscanf() and strspn() in this chapter.

See Also

scanf(), fscanf(), vscanf(), vsscanf(), vfscanf(), wscanf(), fwscanf(), swscanf(), vwscanf(), vfwscanf(), vswscanf(); the corresponding secure functions, if the implementation supports the C11 bounds-checking functions (i.e., if the macro __STDC_LIB_EXT1__ is defined)

Argument conversion in the scanf() family of functions is described in detail under scanf() in this chapter.

strcat, strcat_s

Appends one string to another.

```
#include <string.h>
char *strcat( char * restrict s1, const char * restrict s2 );
errno_t strcat_s( char * restrict s1, rsize_t s1max,
                  const char * restrict s2 );        (C11)
```

The strcat() function copies the string addressed by the second pointer argument, s2, to the location following the string addressed by the first pointer, s1. The first character of s2 is copied over the terminating null character of the string addressed by s1. It is up to you, the programmer, to make sure that the char array addressed by the argument s1 is big enough to store the concatenated string. The source and destination arrays must not overlap. The function strcat() returns the value of its first argument s1, which points to the concatenated string.

Like strcat(), the secure function strcat_s() appends the second string, s2, to the end of the first string, s1, but it avoids the danger of a buffer overflow. It has the additional parameter s1max to specify the size of the destination array, and tests the following runtime constraints:

- The pointers s1 and s2 must not be null pointers, and the value of s1max must be greater than zero and less than or equal to RSIZE_MAX.
- The sum of the string lengths of s1 and s2 must be less than s1max.
- The source and destination arrays must not overlap.

If a violation of the runtime constraints occurs, strcat_s() writes the string terminator character to s1[0], provided s1 is not a null pointer and s1max is greater than zero but not greater than RSIZE_MAX.

`strcat_s()` returns zero, or a nonzero value if a violation of the runtime constraints occurs.

Example

```
typedef struct {
  char  lastname[32];
  char  firstname[32];
  _Bool ismale;
} Name;

char displayname[80];
Name *newName = calloc( 1, sizeof(Name) );

/* ... check for calloc failure; read in the name parts ... */

strcpy( displayname, ( newName->ismale ? "Mr. " : "Ms. " ) );
// strcat( displayname, newName->firstname );
// strcat( displayname, " " );
// strcat( displayname, newName->lastname );

// Better to use strcat_s() in case the fields in the Name
// structure are ever enlarged:
strcat_s( displayname, sizeof(displayname), newName->firstname );
strcat_s( displayname, sizeof(displayname), " " );
strcat_s( displayname, sizeof(displayname), newName->lastname );

puts( displayname );
```

See Also

strncat(), strncat_s(), wcscat(), wcscat_s()

strchr

Search for a given character in a string.

```
#include <string.h>
char *strchr( const char *s, int c );
```

The strchr() function returns a pointer to the first occurrence of the character value c in the string addressed by s. If there is no such character in the string, strchr() returns a null pointer. If c is a null character ('\0'), then the return value points to the terminator character of the string addressed by s.

Example

```
typedef struct { char  street[32];
                 char  city[32];
                 char  stateprovince[32];
                 char  zip[16];
               } Address;

char printaddr[128] = "720 S. Michigan Ave.\nChicago, IL 60605\n";
int sublength;
```

```
Address *newAddr = calloc( 1, sizeof(Address) );

if ( newAddr != NULL )
{
  sublength = strchr( printaddr, '\n' ) - printaddr;
  strncpy( newAddr->street, printaddr,
           ( sublength < 31 ? sublength : 31 ) );
  /* ... */
}
```

See Also

strrchr(), strpbrk(), strstr(); the wide-string functions wcschr() and wcsrchr()

strcmp

Compares two strings.

```
#include <string.h>
int strcmp( const char *s1, const char *s2 );
```

The strcmp() function compares the strings addressed by its two pointer arguments, and returns a value indicating the result as follows:

Zero
> The two strings are equal.

Greater than zero
> The string addressed by *s1* is greater than the string addressed by *s2*.

Less than zero
> The string addressed by *s1* is less than the string addressed by *s2*.

The strcmp() function compares the strings, one character at a time. As soon as it finds unmatched characters in corresponding positions in the two strings, the string containing the greater unsigned character value at that position is the greater string.

Example

```
int result = 0;
char word1[256], word2[256], *greaterlessequal;

while ( result < 2 )
{
  puts( "Type two words, please." );
  result = scanf( "%s%s", word1, word2 );
}
result = strcmp( word1, word2 );

if ( result < 0 )
  greaterlessequal = "less than";
else if ( result > 0 )
  greaterlessequal = "greater than";
```

```
else
  greaterlessequal = "the same as";

printf( "The word \"%s\" is %s the word \"%s\".\n",
        word1, greaterlessequal, word2 );
```

See also the example for qsort( ) in this chapter.

See Also

strncmp( ), memcmp( ), wcscmp( )

strcoll

Compares two strings by locale-specific sorting criteria.

```
#include <string.h>
int strcoll( const char *s1, const char *s2 );
```

Like strcmp( ), the strcoll( ) function performs a character-by-character comparison of the two strings, *s1* and *s2*. However, where strcmp( ) just compares unsigned character values, strcoll( ) can apply a locale-specific set of rules in comparing strings. The value of the locale information category LC_COLLATE determines the applicable rule set, and can be changed by the setlocale( ) function.

The return value of strcoll( ) indicates the result of the comparison as follows:

Zero
> The two strings are equal.

Greater than zero
> The string addressed by *s1* is greater than the string addressed by *s2*.

Less than zero
> The string addressed by *s1* is less than the string addressed by *s2*.

Example

```
char *samples[ ] = { "curso", "churro" };

setlocale( LC_COLLATE, "es_US.UTF-8" );

int result = strcoll( samples[0], samples[1] );

if ( result == 0 )
  printf( "The strings \"%s\" and \"%s\" are alphabetically "
          "equivalent.\n", samples[0], samples[1] );
else if ( result < 0 )
  printf( "The string \"%s\" comes before \"%s\" alphabetically.\n",
          samples[0], samples[1] );
else if ( result > 0 )
  printf( "The string \"%s\" comes after \"%s\" alphabetically.\n",
          samples[0], samples[1] );
```

Because the letter *ch* comes after the letter *c* in the Spanish alphabet, the preceding code prints this line in the es_US locale:

```
The string "curso" comes before "churro" alphabetically.
```

See Also

strcmp( ), strncmp( ), setlocale( ), wcscoll( ), strxfrm( )

strcpy, strcpy_s

Copies a string to another location.

```
#include <string.h>
char *strcpy( char * restrict dest, const char * restrict src );
errno_t strcpy_s( char * restrict dest, rsize_t destmax,
                  const char * restrict src );
```

The strcpy( ) function copies the string addressed by *src* to the char array addressed by *dest*. It is up to you, the programmer, to make sure that the char array addressed by the argument *dest* is big enough to store the string, including its terminating null character. The source and destination arrays must not overlap. The function strcpy( ) returns the pointer *dest*.

Like strcpy( ), the secure function strcpy_s( ) copies the string *src* to the character array addressed by *dest*, but it avoids the danger of a buffer overflow. It has the additional parameter *destmax* to specify the size of the destination array, and tests the following runtime constraints:

- The pointers *dest* and *src* must not be null pointers, and the value of *destmax* must be greater than zero and less than or equal to RSIZE_MAX.
- The string length of *src* must be less than *destmax*.
- The source and destination arrays must not overlap.

If a violation of the runtime constraints occurs, strcat_s( ) writes the string terminator character to *dest*[0], provided *dest* is not a null pointer and *destmax* is greater than zero but not greater than RSIZE_MAX.

strcpy_s( ) returns zero if no violation of the runtime constraints occurs—that is, if it succeeds in copying the string *src*, including the string terminator character. A nonzero return value indicates an error. The contents of the char array *dest* after the string terminator character are undetermined.

Example

```
struct guest {
        char name[64]; int age; _Bool male, smoking, discount; } this;
int result;

printf( "Last name: " );
result = scanf( "%[^\n]", this.name );
```

```
if ( result < 1 )
    strcpy( this.name, "[not available]" );
// or
// strcpy_s( this.name, sizeof(this.name), "[not available]" );
printf( "Name: %s\n", this.name );
```

See Also

strncpy(), memcpy(), memmove(), wcscpy(), wcsncpy(), wmemcpy(), and
wmemmove() and the corresponding secure functions, if the implementation supports the C11 bounds-checking functions (i.e., if the macro __STDC_LIB_EXT1__ is
defined)

strcspn

Searches for any element of one string in another.

```
#include <string.h>
int strcspn( const char *s1, const char *s2 );
```

The strcspn() function returns the number of characters at the beginning of the
string addressed by s1 that do not match any of the characters in the string
addressed by s2. In other words, strcspn() returns the index of the first character
in s1 that matches any character in s2. If the two strings have no characters in common, then the return value is the length of the string addressed by s1.

Example

```
char *path = "/usr/local/bin:/usr/bin:/bin:/usr/bin/X11:/usr/games";
int  separator;
char *basename = "aprogram";
char fullname[1024] = "";

separator = strcspn( path, ":" );    // Obtain the index of the first
                                     // colon.

strncpy( fullname, path, separator );
fullname[separator] = '\0';          // Terminate the copied string
                                     // fragment.
strncat( fullname, "/", sizeof(fullname) - strlen(fullname) -1 );
strncat( fullname, basename, sizeof(fullname) - strlen(fullname) -1 );

puts( fullname );
```

The last statement prints the following string:

```
/usr/local/bin/aprogram
```

See Also

strspn(), strpbrk(), strchr(), wcscspn()

strerror

Obtains a string that describes a given error.

```
#include <string.h>
char *strerror( int errornumber );
```

The strerror() function returns a pointer to an error message string that corresponds to the specified error number. The argument value is usually that of the errno variable but can be any integer value. The string pointed to by the return value of strerror() may change on successive strerror() calls.

The function strerror(), unlike strerror_s(), is not necessarily thread-safe.

Example

```
FILE *fp;
char msgbuf[1024] = { '\0' };

/* Open input file: */
if (( fp = fopen( "nonexistent", "r" )) == NULL)
{
  int retval = errno;
  snprintf( msgbuf, sizeof(msgbuf),
            "%s:  file %s, function %s, line %d: error %d,\n%s.\n",
            argv[0], __FILE__, __func__, __LINE__, retval,
            strerror( retval ));
  fputs( msgbuf, stderr );
  return retval;
}
```

This error-handling block prints the following message:

```
./strerror:  file strerror.c, function main, line 17: error 2,
No such file or directory.
```

See Also

strerror_s(), perror()

strerror_s, strerrorlen_s   C11

Obtains a string that describes a given error, or the length of such a string.

```
#include <string.h>
errno_t strerror_s(char *s, rsize_t maxsize, errno_t errnum);
size_t strerrorlen_s(errno_t errnum);
```

The function strerror_s() copies the locale-specific error message string that corresponds to the specified error number *errnum* to the char array addressed by *s*. If the array length specified by *maxsize* is too small to accommodate the whole string, the error message is truncated to fit. In this case, the message ends with three dots, provided *maxsize* is greater than three. The error number is usually the value of the error variable errno, but can be any int value desired.

The function strerror_s() tests the following runtime constraints: the pointer *s* must not be a null pointer, and the value of *maxsize* must be greater than zero and less than or equal to RSIZE_MAX. If the runtime constraints are not fulfilled, the function returns immediately.

Unlike strerror(), the strerror_s() function is thread-safe. It returns zero if the complete error message string was copied, and a nonzero value otherwise.

The function strerrorlen_s() returns the length of the complete error message that corresponds to the error number *errnum* (not counting the string terminator character) .

Example

```
#define __STDC_WANT_LIB_EXT1__ 1
#include <string.h>
// ...
  double x = -1.0, y = 0;
// ...
  errno = 0;
  y = sqrt(x);
  if( errno == EDOM)
  {
    char msg[30] = "";
    strerror_s( msg, sizeof(msg), errno);
    fprintf( stderr, "sqrt: %s\n", msg);
  }
```

Possible output of the preceding statements is:

```
sqrt: Mathematics argument out o...
```

See Also

strerror(), perror()

strftime

Generates a formatted time-and-date string.

```
#include <time.h>
size_t strftime( char * restrict s, size_t n,
                 const char * restrict format,
                 const struct tm * restrict timeptr );
```

The strftime() function converts date-and-time information from a struct tm object addressed by the last pointer argument into a character string, following a format specified by the string addressed by the pointer argument *format*. The strftime() function stores the resulting string in the buffer addressed by the first pointer argument, without exceeding the buffer length specified by the second argument, *n*. The locations that strftime() reads from and writes to using its restricted pointer parameters must not overlap.

Typically, the struct tm object is obtained by calling localtime() or gmtime(). For a description of this structure type, see mktime() in this chapter.

The generation of the output string is governed by the format string. In this way, strftime() is similar to the functions in the printf() family. The format string consists of ordinary characters, which are copied to the output buffer unchanged, and conversion specifications, which direct strftime() to convert a data item from the struct tm object and include it in the output string.

Conversion specification syntax

The conversion specifications have the following syntax:

```
%[modifier]specifier
```

The modifier, if present, instructs strftime() to use an alternative, locale-specific conversion for the specified data item, and is either E, for locale-specific calendars and clocks, or O, for locale-specific numeric symbols. The E modifier can be prefixed to the specifiers c, C, x, X, y, and Y. The O modifier can be prefixed to the specifiers d, e, H, I, m, M, S, u, U, V, w, W, and Y. All of the conversion specifiers are listed, with the struct tm members they refer to, in Table 18-12. The replacement value for the conversion specifiers depend on the LC_TIME category of the current locale, which can be changed by the setlocale() function.

Table 18-12. The strftime() conversion specifiers

Conversion specifier	Structure member(s)	Output notation
a	tm_wday	The name of the day of the week, abbreviated
A	tm_wday	The name of the day of the week, in full
b or h	tm_mon	The name of the month, abbreviated
B	tm_mon	The name of the month, in full
c	(all)	The date and time
C	tm_year	The year, divided by 100, as a decimal integer (00 to 99)
d	tm_mday	The day of the month, in decimal, with a leading zero on values less than 10 (01 to 31)
D	tm_mon, tm_mday, tm_year	Shorthand for %m/%d/%y
F	tm_mon, tm_mday, tm_year	Shorthand for %Y-%m-%d

Conversion specifier	Structure member(s)	Output notation
g	tm_year, tm_wday, tm_yday	The last two digits of the year in the ISO 8601 week-based calendar (00 to 99)[a]
G	tm_year, tm_wday, tm_yday	The four-digit year in the ISO 8601 week-based calendar
H	tm_hour	The hour of the 24-hour clock as a two-digit decimal number (00 to 23)
I	tm_hour	The hour of the 12-hour clock as a two-digit decimal number (01 to 12)
j	tm_yday	The day of the year as a three-digit decimal number (001 to 366)
m	tm_mon	The month as a two-digit decimal number (01 to 12)
M	tm_min	The minutes after the hour as a two-digit decimal number (00 to 59)
n	(none)	A newline character ('\n')
p	tm_hour	The AM or PM indication used with a 12-hour clock
r	tm_hour, tm_min, tm_sec	The time of day on the 12-hour clock
R	tm_hour, tm_min	Shorthand for %H:%M
S	tm_sec	The seconds after the minute as a two-digit decimal number (00 to 60)
t	(none)	A tab character ('\t')
T	tm_hour, tm_min, tm_sec	Shorthand for %H:%M:%S
u	tm_wday	The day of the week as a one-digit decimal number (1 to 7, where 1 is Monday)
U	tm_year, tm_wday, tm_yday	The week of the year as a two-digit decimal number (00 to 53), where week 1 begins on the first Sunday in January
V	tm_year, tm_wday, tm_yday	The week of the year in the ISO 8601 week-based calendar, as a two-digit decimal number (01 to 53), where week 1 begins on the last Monday that falls on or before January 4
w	tm_wday	The day of the week as a one-digit decimal number (0 to 6, where 0 is Sunday)

Conversion specifier	Structure member(s)	Output notation
W	tm_year, tm_wday, tm_yday	The week of the year as a two-digit decimal number (00 to 53), where week 1 begins on the first Monday in January
x	(all)	The date
X	(all)	The time
y	tm_year	The last two digits of the year, as a decimal number (00 to 99)
Y	tm_year	The year as a decimal number (example: 2005)
z	tm_isdst	The offset from Greenwich Mean Time if available; otherwise nothing (example: +0200 for two hours and no minutes east of GMT)
Z	tm_isdst	The name or abbreviation of the time zone if available; otherwise nothing
%	(none)	A percent sign (%)

ᵃ In this calendar, the week begins on Monday, and the first week of the year is the week that contains January 4. Up to the first three days of January may belong to week 53 of the old year, or up to the last three days of December may belong to week one of the new year.

The strftime() function returns the length of the string written to the output buffer, not counting the terminating null character. If the output is longer than the argument *n* allows, strftime() returns 0, and the contents of the output buffer are undetermined.

Example

```
time_t now;
struct tm *localnow;
char hdr_date[999] = "";

time( &now );
localnow = localtime( &now );

if ( strftime( hdr_date, 78, "Date: %a, %d %b %Y %T %z", localnow ) )
  puts( hdr_date );
else
  return -1;
```

This code prints a date field in RFC 2822 style, such as this one:

```
Date: Thu, 10 Mar 2005 13:44:18 +0100
```

See Also

asctime(), ctime(), mktime(), localtime(), gmtime(), wcsftime(), snprintf(), setlocale()

strlen

Obtains the length of a string.

```
#include <string.h>
size_t strlen( const char *s );
```

The strlen() function calculates the length of the string addressed by its argument s. The length of a string is the number of characters in it, not counting the terminating null character ('\0').

Example

```
char line[1024] =
        "This string could easily be hundreds of characters long.";
char *readptr = line;
int columns = 80;

// While the text is longer than a row:
while ( strlen( readptr ) > columns )
{ // print a row with a backslash at the end:
  printf( "%.*s\\", columns-1, readptr);
  readptr += columns -1;
}
//  Then print the rest with a newline at the end:
printf( "%s\n", readptr );
```

See Also

strnlen_s(), wcslen()

strncat, strncat_s

Appends a number of characters from one string to another.

```
#include <string.h>
char *strncat( char * restrict s1,
               const char * restrict s2, size_t n );
errno_t strncat_s(char * restrict s1, rsize_t s1max,
               const char * restrict s2, rsize_t n);
```

The strncat() function copies up to n characters of the string addressed by its second argument, s2, to the end of the string addressed by its first argument, s1. The first character copied from s2 replaces the string terminator character of s1. The function copies fewer than n characters if it first encounters a terminating null character in the string s2. In any case, strncat() appends a null character to the concatenated string. The string addressed by s1 is thus lengthened by at most n characters.

It is up to you, the programmer, to make sure that the char array addressed by the argument s1 is big enough to store the concatenated string. The source and destination arrays must not overlap. The function strcat() returns the pointer s.

Like `strncat()`, the secure function `strncat_s()` appends up to *n* characters of the second string, *s2*, to the end of the first string, *s1*, but it avoids the danger of a buffer overflow. It has the additional parameter *s1max* to specify the size of the destination array, and tests the following runtime constraints:

- The pointers *s1* and *s2* must not be null pointers. The values of *s1max* and *n* must not be greater than RSIZE_MAX, and *s1max* must be greater than zero.
- The length of the concatenated string must be less than *s1max*. In other words, either strlen(*s1*) + *n* or strlen(*s1*) + strlen(*s2*) must be less than *s1max*.
- The source and destination arrays must not overlap.

If a violation of the runtime constraints occurs, `strcat_s()` writes the string terminator character to *s1*[0], provided *s1* is not a null pointer and *s1max* is greater than zero, but not greater than RSIZE_MAX.

`strcat_s()` returns zero on success, or a nonzero value if a violation of the runtime constraints occurs.

Example

```
#define __STDC_WANT_LIB_EXT1__ 1     // For the secure functions.
#include <string.h>
#include <stdlib.h>
// ...
  char str1[]  = "hello ",    // 7 bytes
       str2[10] = "hello ",    // 7 + 3 bytes
       str3[10] = "hello ";    // 7 + 3 bytes

//  strncat( str1, "Jimi", 1);    // Severe error: buffer overflow!
//  strncat( str2, "Jimi", 3);    // OK: "hello Jim"
//  strncat( str3, "Jim", 100);   // OK.

// Or, using strncat_s(), with the variables defined above:
  int ret1, ret2, ret3;

  set_constraint_handler_s(ignore_handler_s);
  ret1 = strncat_s( str1, sizeof(str1), "Jimi", 1);  // ret1 != 0 and
                                                      // str1[0] == '\0'
  ret2 = strncat_s( str2, sizeof(str2), "Jimi", 3);  // OK: ret2 == 0
  ret3 = strncat_s( str3, sizeof(str3), "Jim", 100); // OK: ret3 == 0
```

See Also

strcat(), strcat_s(), wcsncat(), wcsncat_s()

strncmp

Compares the first *n* characters of two strings.

```
#include <string.h>
int strncmp( const char *s1, const char *s2, size_t n );
```

The strncmp() function compares at most the first *n* characters in the two strings addressed by its pointer arguments. Characters that follow a null character are ignored. strncmp() returns a value indicating the result as follows:

Zero
> The two strings, or arrays of *n* characters, are equal.

Greater than zero
> The string or array of *n* characters addressed by *s1* is greater than that addressed by *s2*.

Less than zero
> The string or array of *n* characters addressed by *s1* is less than that addressed by *s2*.

Example

```
char *weekdays[] = { "Sunday", "Monday", "Tuesday", "Wednesday",
                     "Thursday", "Friday", "Saturday" };
char date[ ] = "Thu, 10 Mar 2005 13:44:18 +0100";
int dow;
for ( dow = 0; dow < 7; dow++ )
  if ( strncmp( date, weekdays[dow], 3 ) == 0 )
    break;
```

See Also

strcmp(), wcsncmp(), wcscmp()

strncpy, strncpy_s

Copies the first *n* characters of a string to another location.

```
#include <string.h>
char *strncpy( char * restrict dest,
               const char * restrict src, size_t n );
errno_t strncpy_s(char * restrict dest, rsize_t destmax,
                  const char * restrict src, rsize_t n);
```

The strncpy() function copies at most *n* characters from the string addressed by *src* to the char array addressed by *dest*, which must be large enough to accommodate *n* characters. The strncpy() function returns the value of its first argument, *dest*. The locations that strncpy() reads from and writes to using its restricted pointer parameters must not overlap.

If strncpy() reads a null character from *src* before it has copied *n* characters, it writes null characters to *dest* until it has written a total of *n* characters.

If the first *n* characters of *src* do not contain a null character, the function does not terminate the copied string fragment with a null character!

The secure function strncpy_s() also copies up to *n* characters from the source string *src* to the *char* array addressed by dest, but it always appends a null character. If strncpy_s() reads a null character from the source string before copying *n* characters, then the number of characters it copies is less than *n*. Otherwise, it writes a terminating null character to *dest[n]*. The contents of the char array *dest* after the string terminator character are undetermined.

The function strncpy_s() has the additional parameter *destmax* to specify the size of the destination array, and tests the following runtime constraints:

- The pointers *dest* and *src* must not be null pointers. The values of *destmax* and *n* must not be greater than RSIZE_MAX, and *destmax* must be greater than zero.
- Either *n* or the string length of *src* (or both) must be less than *destmax*.
- The source and destination arrays must not overlap.

If a violation of the runtime constraints occurs, strncpy_s() writes the string terminator character to *dest[0]*, provided *dest* is not a null pointer and *destmax* is greater than zero, but not greater than RSIZE_MAX.

The strncpy_s() function returns zero, or a nonzero value if a violation of the runtime constraints occurs.

Example

For strncpy(), see the examples for strcspn() and strpbrk() in this chapter.

The example here shows three strncpy_s() calls:

```
#define __STDC_WANT_LIB_EXT1__ 1
#include <string.h>
// ...
   char dest[5], src[] = "okay";
   int r;
   r = strncpy_s( dest, 2, src, 2);    // r != 0, dest[0] == '\0'
   r = strncpy_s( dest, 3, src, 2);    // r == 0, dest == "ok"
   r = strncpy_s( dest, 5, src, 10);   // r == 0, dest == "okay"
```

See Also

strcpy(), memcpy(), memmove(), wcsncpy(), wmemcpy(), wmemmove() and the corresponding secure functions, if the implementation supports the C11 bounds-checking functions (i.e., if the macro __STDC_LIB_EXT1__ is defined)

Obtains the length of a string.

```
#include <string.h>
size_t strnlen_s(const char *s, size_t maxsize);
```

If the pointer *s* is a null pointer, the function strnlen_s() returns zero. Otherwise, strnlen_s() returns the length of the string addressed by the pointer *s*; that is, the number of characters that precede the terminating null character ('\0'). The function only examines at most the first *maxsize* characters in the string, however. If there is no null character within the first *maxsize* characters, strnlen_s() returns the value of *maxsize*.

Example

```
#define __STDC_WANT_LIB_EXT1__ 1
#include <string.h>
// ...
char str[] = "hello";
size_t len = strnlen_s( str, 1000);      // len = 5
if( strnlen_s( str, 4) == 4)
{  /* str is more than 4 characters long. */ }
```

See Also

strlen(), wcslen(), wcsnlen_s()

strpbrk

Finds the first character in a string that matches any character in another string.

```
#include <string.h>
char *strpbrk( const char *s1, const char *s2 );
```

The strpbrk() function returns a pointer to the first character in the string addressed by *s1* that matches any character contained in the string addressed by *s2*, or a null pointer if the two strings have no characters in common.

Example

```
char *story = "He shouted: \"What? I can't hear you!\"\n";
char separators[] = " \t\n.:?!\"";
char *start = story, *end = NULL;
char words[16][16];      // An array of char arrays to collect words in.
int i = 0;

while ( i < 16 && ( end = strpbrk( start, separators ) ) != NULL )
{
  if ( end != start )    // If the separator wasn't the first character,
  {                      // then save a word in an array.
    strncpy( words[i], start, end - start );
    words[i][end - start] = '\0'; // And terminate it.
    i++;
```

```
        }
        start = end + 1;              // Next strpbrk call starts with
    }                                 // the character after this separator.
    puts( story );
    for ( int j = 0 ; j < i ; j++ )
        puts( words[j] );
```

This program prints each of the words it has collected on a new line:

```
He
shouted
What
I
can't
hear
you
```

See Also

strchr(), strrchr(), strstr(), strcspn(), strtok(), wcspbrk()

strrchr

Searches for the rightmost occurrence of a given character in a string.

```
#include <string.h>
char *strrchr( const char *s, int c );
```

The strrchr() function returns a pointer to the *last* occurrence of the character value c in the string addressed by s. If there is no such character in the string, strrchr() returns a null pointer. If c is a null character ('\0'), then the return value points to the terminator character of the string addressed by s.

Example

```
char *mybasename = strrchr( argv[0], '/' );        // Find end of path.
if ( mybasename != NULL )
    mybasename++;          // Point to the first character after the slash.
else
    mybasename = argv[0];
printf( "This program was invoked as %s.\n", mybasename );
```

See Also

strchr(), strpbrk(), strstr(); the wide-string functions wcschr() and wcsrchr()

strspn

Searches a string for a character that is not in a given set.

```
#include <string.h>
int strspn( const char *s1, const char *s2 );
```

The strspn() function returns the index of the first character in the string addressed by *s1* that does not match any character in the string addressed by *s2*, or in other words, the length of the string segment addressed by *s1* that contains only characters that are present in the string addressed by *s2*. If all characters in *s1* are also contained in *s2*, then strspn() returns the index of *s1*'s string terminator character, which is the same as strlen(*s1*).

Example

```
char wordin[256];
double val;

puts( "Enter a floating-point number, please:" );
scanf( "%s", wordin );

int index = strspn( wordin, "+-0123456789eE." );
if ( index < strlen( wordin ) )
  printf( "Sorry, but the character %c is not permitted.\n",
          wordin[index] );
else
{
  sscanf( wordin, "%lg", &val );
  printf( "You entered the value %g\n", val );
}
```

See Also

strcspn(), wcsspn()

strstr

Searches a string for a replica of another string.

```
#include <string.h>
char *strstr( const char *s1, const char *s2 );
```

The strstr() function searches the string *s1* for the first occurrence of the string *s2* (not counting *s2*'s terminating null character). The return value is a pointer to the first character in the first occurrence in *s1* of the sequence contained in *s2*, or a null pointer if there is no such occurrence. If *s2* points to an empty string, then strstr() returns the value of its first argument, *s1*.

Example

```
FILE *fpTx, *fpRx, *fpLog;
char rxbuffer[1024], *found;
/* ... */
fgets( rxbuffer, 1024, fpRx );
found = strstr( rxbuffer, "assword:" );
if ( found != NULL )
{
  fputs( "Got password prompt. Sending password", fpLog );
  fputs( "topsecret", fpTx );
}
```

strchr(), strpbrk(), wcsstr()

strtod, strtof, strtold

Converts a string into a floating-point number.

```
#include <stdlib.h>
double strtod( const char * restrict s, char ** restrict endptr );
float  strtof( const char * restrict s,
               char ** restrict endptr );     (C99)
long double strtold( const char * restrict s,
                     char ** restrict endptr );     (C99)
```

The strtod() function attempts to interpret the string addressed by its first pointer argument, s, as a floating-point numeric value, and returns the result with the type double. strtof() and strold() are similar, but return float and long double, respectively. Leading whitespace characters are ignored, and the converted string ends with the last character that can be interpreted as part of a floating-point numeral. The second parameter, *endptr*, is a pointer to a pointer. If its argument value is not a null pointer, then the function stores a pointer to the first character that is not part of the numeral converted in the location addressed by the *endptr* argument. (The locations that the function reads from and writes to using its restricted pointer parameters must not overlap.) If no conversion is possible, the function returns 0.

If the resulting value exceeds the range of the function's type, then the return value is positive or negative HUGE_VAL (or HUGE_VALF or HUGE_VALL, for the float and long double variants). On an overflow, the errno variable is set to the value of ERANGE ("range error"). If the conversion produces an underflow, the magnitude of the return value is at most the smallest value greater than zero that is representable in the function's return type, and the function may set the errno variable to the value of ERANGE ("range error").

The character sequences that can be interpreted as floating-point numerals depend on the current locale. In all locales, they include those described in "Floating-Point Constants" on page 40, and the sequences "infinity" and "nan", without regard to upper- or lowercase.

Example

```
char in[1024], *this = in, *next = in;
double val;
puts( "Enter some floating-point numbers, please:" );
scanf( "%[^\n]", in );

puts( "Here are the values you entered:" );
while ( 1 )
{
  val = strtod( this, &next );
```

```
      if ( next == this )       // Means no conversion was possible.
        break ;
      printf( "\t%g\n", val );
      this = next;              // Try again with the rest of the input string.
   }
   puts( "Done." );
```

See Also

atof(); wcstof(), wcstod() and wcstold(); strtol(), strtoul(), and strtoi
max()

strtoimax   C99

Converts a string into an integer value with type intmax_t.

```
#include <inttypes.h>
intmax_t strtoimax( const char * restrict s, char ** restrict endptr,
                    int base );
```

The strtoimax() function is similar to strtol() except that it converts a string to
an integer value of type intmax_t. If the conversion fails, strtoimax() returns 0. If
the result of the conversion exceeds the range of the type intmax_t, then strtoi
max() returns the value of INTMAX_MAX or INTMAX_MIN, and sets the errno variable to
the value of ERANGE ("range error").

Example

See the example for the analogous function strtol() in this chapter.

See Also

strtoumax(), wcstoimax(), and wcstoumax(); strtol() and strtoul(); strtod(),
strtof(), and strtold(); wcstol() and wcstoul()

strtok

Divides a string into tokens.

```
#include <string.h>
char *strtok( char * restrict s1, const char * restrict s2 );
```

The strtok() function isolates tokens in the string addressed by *s1* that are delimited by any of the characters contained in the string addressed by *s2*. The tokens are
identified one at a time by successive calls to strtok(). On calls after the first, the
s1 argument is a null pointer.

On the first call, strtok() searches in *s1* for the first character that does not match
any character in *s2*, behavior that is similar to the strspn() function. The first such
character found is considered to be the beginning of a token. Then strtok()
searches further for the first character that *does* match any of the characters in *s2*—
or the null character that terminates the string, whichever comes first—similarly to
the strcspn() function. This is considered to be the delimiter that ends the token.

strtok() then replaces this ending delimiter with '\0', and returns a pointer to the beginning of the token (or a null pointer if no token was found), while saving an internal, static pointer to the next character after the ending delimiter for use in subsequent strtok() calls.

On each subsequent call with a null pointer as the *s1* argument, strtok() behaves similarly, but starts the search at the character that follows the previous delimiter. You can specify a different set of delimiters in the *s2* argument on each call. The locations that strtok() reads from using *s2* and writes to using *s1* on any given call must not overlap. Unlike strtok_s(), the function strtok() is not thread-safe.

Example

```
char *command, *arg1, *arg2, *comment;
char line[ ] = "    mul eax,[ebp+4]    ; Multiply by y\n";

command = strtok(line," \t"); // First word, between spaces or tabs.
arg1 = strtok( NULL, ",");    // From there to the comma is arg1.
                              // (Trim off any spaces later.)
arg2 = strtok( NULL, ";\n");  // From there to a semicolon or line end.
comment = strtok( NULL, "\n\r\v\f" ); // From there to end of line or
                              // page.
printf( "Command:       %s\n"
        "1st argument: %s\n"
        "2nd argument: %s\n"
        "Comment:       %s\n\n",
        command, arg1, arg2, comment );
```

This sample produces the following output:

```
Command:       mul
1st argument: eax
2nd argument: [ebp+4]
Comment:       Multiply by y
```

See Also

strtok_s(), strspn(), strcspn(), strstr(), wcstok()

strtok_s   C11

Divides a string into tokens.

```
#include <string.h>
char *strtok_s( char * restrict s1, rsize_t * restrict s1max,
                const char * restrict s2, char ** restrict ptr);
```

Like strtok(), the strtok_s() function divides the string addressed by *s1* into a sequence of tokens delimited by any of the characters contained in the string addressed by *s2*. The tokens are identified one at a time by successive calls to strtok_s(). On calls after the first, the *s1* argument is a null pointer. The string *s2* can contain different delimiter characters on each call.

Unlike strtok(), the function strtok_s() is thread-safe because it does not save its state between two calls internally. Instead, the state is saved in objects addressed by the two additional parameters, *s1max* and *ptr*. On the first call, the object addressed by *s1max* must contain the length of the char array addressed by *s1*. On each subsequent call, the strtok_s() function updates the objects addressed by *s1max* and *ptr* so that the pointer addressed by *ptr* refers to the new starting position in the string, and the variable addressed by *s1max* contains the remaining string length.

The function strtok_s() tests the following runtime constraints: the pointers *s1max*, *s2*, and *ptr* must not be null pointers. If *s1* is a null pointer, then *ptr* must not point to a null pointer. The source string must contain the end of a token within the number of characters specified by the value addressed by *s1max*, counting from the current starting position.

The strtok_s() function writes the terminator character '\0' to the first byte after the token found, and returns a pointer to the beginning of the token, or a null pointer if no token was found or a violation of the runtime constraints occurred.

Example

```
#define __STDC_WANT_LIB_EXT1__ 1
#include <string.h>
// ...
  char str[] = "Lennon, John: 10/9/1940";
  char *ptr;
  size_t size = sizeof(str);
  char *firstname, *lastname, *birthday;

  lastname = strtok_s( str, &size, ", ", &ptr);
  if( lastname != NULL)
    firstname = strtok_s(NULL, &size, ": ", &ptr);
  if( firstname != NULL)
    birthday = strtok_s(NULL, &size, "", &ptr);
  if(birthday != NULL)
    printf("%s %s was born on %s.\n",
          firstname, lastname, birthday);
```

This example would generate the following output:

```
John Lennon was born on 10/9/1940.
```

See Also

strtok(), strspn(), strcspn(), strstr(), wcstok()

strtol, strtoll

Converts a string into a `long` (or `long long`) integer value.

```
#include <stdlib.h>
long strtol( const char * restrict s, char ** restrict endptr,
             int base );
long long strtoll( const char * restrict s, char ** restrict endptr,
                   int base );        (C99)
```

The `strtol()` function attempts to interpret the string addressed by its first pointer argument, `s`, as an integer numeric value, and returns the result with the type `long`. `strtoll()` is similar but returns `long long`. The character string is interpreted as a numeral to the base specified by the third argument, `base`, which must be 0 or an integer between 2 and 36. If `base` is 36, then the letters from a to z (and likewise those from A to Z) are used as digits with values from 10 to 35. If `base` is between 10 and 35, then only those letters up to the digit value of `base` – 1 are permissible. In other locales besides the default locale, C, other character sequences may also be interpretable as numerals.

If `base` is 0, then the numeral string is interpreted as octal if it begins, after an optional plus or minus sign, with the character 0, hexadecimal if it begins with 0x or 0X, or decimal if it begins with a digit from 1 to 9. Leading whitespace characters are ignored, and the converted string ends with the last character than can be interpreted as part of the numeral.

The second parameter, `endptr`, is a pointer to a pointer. If its argument value is not a null pointer, then the function stores a pointer to the first character that is not part of the numeral converted in the location addressed by the `endptr` argument. (The locations that the function reads from and writes to using its restricted pointer parameters must not overlap.) If no conversion is possible, the function returns 0.

If the resulting value exceeds the range of the function's type, then the return value is `LONG_MAX` or `LONG_MIN`, depending on the sign (or `LLONG_MAX` or `LLONG_MIN`, for `strtoll()`), and the `errno` variable is set to the value of `ERANGE` ("range error").

Example

```
char date[ ] = "10/3/2005, 13:44:18 +0100", *more = date;
long day, mo, yr, hr, min, sec, tzone;
day = strtol( more, &more, 10 );
mo  = strtol( more+1, &more, 10 );
yr  = strtol( more+1, &more, 10 );
/* ... */
```

See Also

`strtoul()`; `strtod()`, `strtof()`, and `strtold()`; `wcstol()` and `wcstoul()`; `strtoimax()`, `strtoumax()`, `wcstoimax()`, and `wcstoumax()`

strtoul, strtoull

Converts a string into an unsigned long (or unsigned long long) integer value.

```
#include <stdlib.h>
unsigned long strtoul( const char * restrict s, char ** restrict endptr,
                       int base );
unsigned long long strtoull( const char * restrict s,
                             char ** restrict endptr,
                             int base );        (C99)
```

The strtoul() function attempts to interpret the string addressed by its first pointer argument, *s*, as an integer numeric value, and returns the result with the type unsigned long. Otherwise, the strtoul() function works in the same way as strtol(). strtoull() is similar but returns unsigned long long.

If the resulting value is outside the range of the function's type, then the return value is ULONG_MAX (or ULLONG_MAX, for strtoull()), and the errno variable is set to the value of ERANGE ("range error").

Example

This for loop uses stroul() to convert an IPv4 address from a dotted-decimal string to a 32-bit integer value:

```
char dotted[ ] = "172.16.2.10", *ptr = dotted, *nextdot = NULL;
unsigned long dest = 0;
for ( int i = 0; i < 4; i++)
{
  dest <<= 8;
  dest += strtoul( ptr, &nextdot, 10 );
  ptr = nextdot + 1;
}
```

See Also

strtol(), strtod(), strtof(), and strtold(); wcstol() and wcstoul(); strtoimax(), strtoumax(), wcstoimax(), and wcstoumax()

strtoumax   C99

Converts a string into an integer value with type uintmax_t.

```
#include <inttypes.h>
uintmax_t strtoumax( const char * restrict s, char ** restrict endptr,
                     int base );
```

The strtoumax() function is similar to strtoul() except that it converts a string to an integer value of type uintmax_t. If the conversion fails, strtoumax() returns 0. If the result of the conversion is outside the range of the type uintmax_t, then strtoumax() returns UINTMAX_MAX, and sets the errno variable to the value of ERANGE ("range error").

Example

See the example for the analogous function strtoul() in this chapter.

See Also

strtoimax(), wcstoimax(), and wcstoumax(); strtol() and strtoul(); strtod(), strtof(), and strtold(); wcstol() and wcstoul()

strxfrm

Transforms a string for easier locale-specific comparison.

```
#include <string.h>
size_t strxfrm( char * restrict dest, const char * restrict src,
                size_t n );
```

The strxfrm() function transforms the string addressed by *src*, and copies the result to the char array addressed by *dest*. The third argument, *n*, specifies a maximum number of characters (including the terminating null character) that the function may write to *dest*. The locations that strxfrm() reads from and writes to using its restricted pointer parameters must not overlap.

The transformation performed depends on the value of the locale category LC_COL LATE, which you can query or set using the setlocale() function. Furthermore, the strxfrm() transformation is related to the strcoll() function in the following way: if you use strcmp() to compare two strings produced by strxfrm() calls, the result is the same as if you use strcoll() to compare the original strings passed to strxfrm(). Using strxfrm() and strcmp() may be more efficient than strcoll() if you need to use the same string in many comparisons.

The strxfrm() function returns the length of the transformed version of the string, not counting the terminating null character. If this length is greater than or equal to *n*, then the contents of the array at *dest* are indeterminate. The value of *n* may also be 0, in which case *dest* may be a null pointer.

Example

```
typedef struct stringpair { char * original;
                            char * xformed; } Stringpair_t ;

Stringpair_t stringpairs[8] =
            { { "Chávez", NULL },      { "Carron", NULL    },
              { "Canoso", NULL },      { "Cañoso", NULL    },
              { "Carteño", NULL },     { "Cortillo", NULL },
              { "Cortiluz S.A.", NULL }, { "Corriando", NULL } };

char xformbuffer[1024];      // Space to catch each strxfrm() result.

int stringpaircmp( const void * p1, const void *p2 );
                             // Defined externally.

setlocale( LC_COLLATE, "" );   // Use the host system's locale setting.
```

```
for ( int i = 0; i < 8 ; i++ )
{
  stringpairs[i].xformed
  = malloc( strxfrm( xformbuffer, stringpairs[i].original, 1024 ) + 1);
  if ( stringpairs[i].xformed != NULL )
    strcpy(stringpairs[i].xformed, xformbuffer);
}

qsort( stringpairs, 8, sizeof(Stringpair_t), stringpaircmp );
```

The qsort() function invoked in the last line of this example would pass the transformed strings to a comparison function named stringpaircmp(). That function would compare the transformed strings using strcmp(), rather than comparing the originals using strcoll().

See Also

strcoll(), strcmp(), wcsxfrm(), setlocale()

swprintf, swprintf_s

Stores formatted output in a wide-character string buffer.

```
#include <wchar.h>
int swprintf( wchar_t * restrict dest, size_t n,
              const wchar_t * restrict format, ... );
int swprintf_s(wchar_t * restrict dest, rsize_t n,
               const wchar_t * restrict format, ...);
```

The function swprintf() is similar to the function wprintf(), except that the string generated is not written to stdout but to the array of wide characters addressed by the pointer *dest*. The function writes no more than *n* wide characters, including the string terminator character.

The return value of swprintf() is the number of wide characters written (not counting the terminating null character, so that it is always less than *n*). If a conversion error occurs or the destination array *dest* is too small to store the entire string generated, the return value is negative.

The secure function swprintf_s() is equivalent to swprintf() except for the following runtime constraints: the pointers *dest* and *format* and arguments corresponding to %s conversion specifiers must not be null pointers. Furthermore, the format string must not contain the conversion specifier %n. The number *n* must be greater than zero but not greater than RSIZE_MAX. The destination array *dest* must be large enough to store the entire string generated.

If a runtime constraint is violated, swprintf_s() writes the string terminator character L'\0' to *dest*[0], provided *dest* is not a null pointer, and *n* is greater than zero and less than RSIZE_MAX.

The return value of swprintf_s() is negative if a conversion error occurs or the destination array *dest* is too small. If a different runtime constraint violation occurs, the function returns zero.

 Unlike swprintf_s(), the snwprintf_s() function truncates the output string if it is longer than the destination array. In this case, the function writes the first *n* – 1 characters of the output string, and then the terminating null character.

Example

```
const wchar_t *dollar_as_wstr( long amount)
// Converts a number of cents into a wide string
// showing dollars and cents.
// For example, converts -123456 into the wide string L"-$1234.56"
{
  static wchar_t buffer[16];
  wchar_t sign[2] = L"";
  if ( amount < 0L)
    amount = -amount, sign[0] = '-';
  ldiv_t dollars_cents = ldiv( amount, 100);
  swprintf( buffer, sizeof(buffer),
          L"%ls$%ld.%2ld", sign, dollars_cents.quot, dollars_cents.rem);
  return buffer;
}
```

See Also

wprintf() and fwprintf(), declared in *stdio.h* and *wchar.h*; vwprint(), vfwprint(), and vswprint(), declared in *stdarg.h*; printf(), fprintf(), sprintf(), snprintf(), declared in *stdio.h*; vprintf(), vfprintf(), vsprintf(), vsnprintf(), declared in *stdarg.h*; the wscanf() input functions; the corresponding secure functions, if the implementation supports the C11 bounds-checking functions (i.e., if the macro __STDC_LIB_EXT1__ is defined)

Argument conversion in the printf() family of functions is described in detail under printf() in this chapter.

swscanf, swscanf_s

Reads in formatted data from a wide-character string.

```
#include <wchar.h>
int swscanf( const wchar_t * restrict wcs,
          const wchar_t * restrict format, ... );
int swscanf_s( const wchar_t * restrict wcs,
          const wchar_t * restrict format, ... );
```

The functions `swscanf()` and `swscanf_s()` are similar to the functions `wscanf()` and `wscanf_s()`, except that they read from the string specified by their argument *src* instead of `stdin`.

Like `wscanf()`, the `swscanf()` functions return the number of data items converted and stored in variables. If an input error occurs or the function reads to the end of the string before any data can be converted, the return value is EOF. The `swscanf_s()` function also returns EOF if a violation of its runtime constraints occurs. These constraints are described in the section on `scanf_s()` in this chapter.

Example

```
double price = 0.0;
wchar_t wstr[ ] = L"Current price: $199.90";
swscanf( wstr, L"%*[^$]$%lf", &price);     // Read price from string.
price *= 0.8;                              // Apply 20% discount.
printf( "New price: $%.2lf\n", price);
```

This code produces the following output:

```
New price: $159.92
```

See Also

`wscanf()`, `fwscanf()`; `wcstod()`, `wcstol()`, and `wcstoul()`; `scanf()`, `fscanf()`; `fwprintf()`, `wprintf()`, `vfwprint()`, and `vwprint()`; the corresponding secure functions, if the implementation supports the C11 bounds-checking functions (i.e., if the macro `__STDC_LIB_EXT1__` is defined); the example for `wcsspn()` in this chapter

system

Executes a shell command.

```
#include <stdlib.h>
int system( const char *s );
```

The `system()` function passes a command line addressed by the pointer argument *s* to an operating system shell. If *s* is a null pointer, the function returns true (a non-zero value) if a command processor is available to handle shell commands, and 0 or false if not.

How the system executes a command, and what value the `system()` function returns, is left up to the given implementation. The command may terminate the program that calls `system()` or have unspecified effects on its further behavior.

Example

```
if ( system( NULL ))
    system( "echo \"Shell: $SHELL; process ID: $$\"");
else
    printf( "No command processor available.\n" );
```

This example is not portable, but on certain systems it can produce output like this:

```
Shell: /usr/local/bin/bash; process ID: 21349
```
See Also

getenv( )

tan

Calculates the tangent of an angle.

```
#include <math.h>
double tan( double x );
float tanf( float x );          (C99)
long double tanl( long double x );          (C99)
```

The tan( ) function calculates the tangent of the angle represented by its argument *x* as a number of radians.

Example

```
const double pi = 4.0L * atan( 1.0 );          // Because tan(pi/4) = 1
double shadow_length = 85.5,
       angle = 36.2;          // Sun's elevation from the horizon, in
                              // degrees
double height = shadow_length *tan ( angle * pi/180);

printf("The tower is %.2f meters high.\n", height);
```

This code produces the following output:

```
The tower is 62.58 meters high.
```

See Also

sin( ), cos( ), atan( ); the tangent functions for complex numbers, ctan( ), ctanf( ) and ctanl( )

tanh

Calculates the hyperbolic tangent of a number.

```
#include <math.h>
double tanh( double x);
float tanhf( float x);          (C99)
long double tanhl( long double x);          (C99)
```

The tanh( ) function returns the hyperbolic tangent of its argument *x*, which is defined as $\sinh(x)/\cosh(x)$.

Example

```
double x = -0.5, y1, y2;

y1 = tanh(x);
y2 = exp(2*x);
y2 = (y2 -1) / (y2 + 1);
```

```
printf("The tanh() function returns    %.15f.\n", y1 );
printf("Using the function exp() yields %.15f.\n", y2 );
```

This code produces the following output:

```
The tanh() function returns    -0.462117157260010.
Using the function exp() yields -0.462117157260010.
```

See Also

sinh(), cosh(), atanh(); the hyperbolic tangent and inverse tangent functions for complex numbers, ctanh() and catanh()

thrd_create   C11

Starts a new thread.

```
#include <threads.h>
int thrd_create(thrd_t *thr, thrd_start_t func, void *arg);
```

The function thrd_create() starts a new thread which executes the function call *func(arg)*. If the new thread is successfully started, the function thrd_create() writes the ID of the new thread to the object addressed by the argument *thr*. The new thread starts running when the thrd_create() call ends.

thrd_create() returns the value of thrd_success if the new thread has been started, or the value of thrd_nomem if there was insufficient memory available to start a new thread, or the value of thrd_error if a different error occurred.

The type thrd_start_t is defined as int(*)(void*). Thus, the thread function *func* must take one void-pointer argument and have the return type int. Ending the thread function with a return statement is equivalent to ending it by calling thrd_exit(*return_value*). The program can obtain its return value by calling the function thrd_join() after thrd_create().

Example

```
int th_func(void * arg)              // The thread function.
{
    puts("Hello from th_func ...");
    ++*(int*)arg;
    return 0;
}

int main()
{
    thrd_t th;   int n = 1;

    if ( thrd_create(&th, th_func, &n) != thrd_success) {
        fprintf(stderr, "Error creating thread.\n"); return -1;
    }
    puts("Main thread here ...");
```

```
        thrd_join(th, NULL);
        printf("The value of n is %d\n", n);      // n == 2
        return 0;
    }
```

See Also

thrd_exit(), thrd_join(), thrd_detach(), thrd_current(), thrd_equal(),
thrd_sleep(), thrd_yield()

thrd_current   C11

Obtains the ID of the current thread.

```
    #include <threads.h>
    thrd_t thrd_current(void);
```

The function thrd_current() returns the ID of the thread in which it is called.

Example

See the example for thrd_equal() in this chapter.

See Also

thrd_equal()

thrd_detach   C11

Detaches the specified thread.

```
    #include <threads.h>
    int thrd_detach(thrd_t thr);
```

The function thrd_detach() informs the operating system that all the resources
used by the specified thread can be released as soon as the thread ends. Once a
thread has been detached, the program cannot call thrd_join() to wait for it to
end. The program can call either thrd_join() or thrd_detach() no more than
once for each thread created. After that, the object addressed by *thr* can be reused
for another thread.

The function thrd_detach() returns the value of thrd_success, or thrd_error if
an error occurs.

Example

```
    void independent_thread(void)
    {
        puts("Working independently in the background ... ");
        // . . .
        thrd_exit(0);
    }

    int create_independent_thread(void)
    {
```

```
        thrd_t th;
        if( thrd_create(&th, (thrd_start_t)independent_thread, "")
                                                != thrd_success)
            return -1;
        if( thrd_detach(th) != thrd_success)
            return -1;
        puts("Started independent thread.");
        return 0;
    }
```

See Also

thrd_join()

thrd_equal   C11

Tests whether two thread IDs are equal.

```
    #include <threads.h>
    int thrd_equal(thrd_t thr1, thrd_t thr2);
```

The function thrd_equal() tests whether the thread ID objects *thr1* and *thr2* identify the same thread. The function returns zero if *thr1* and *thr2* refer to different
threads, or a nonzero value if they refer to the same thread.

Example

```
    thrd_t mainThrd;

    int func(void)
    {
        if( thrd_equal( thrd_current(), mainThrd) )
        {   puts("Main thread here ..."); return 0;  }
        else
        {   puts("Other thread here ..."); return 1;  }
    }

    int main()
    {
        thrd_t th;
        mainThrd = thrd_current();
        if ( thrd_create(&th, (thrd_start_t)func, NULL) != thrd_success)
        {   fprintf(stderr, "Error creating thread.\n");  return -1; }
        func();
        thrd_join(th, NULL);
        return 0;
    }
```

See Also

thrd_current()

Ends the thread.

```
#include <threads.h>
_Noreturn void thrd_exit(int res);
```

The function thrd_exit() first calls the appropriate destructor for each thread-specific storage block that the thread uses, provided a destructor was specified in the tss_create() call. Then thrd_exit() ends the calling thread with the result code res. Ending a thread with the statement return res; is equivalent to the function call thrd_exit(res);.

Exiting the last remaining thread causes the program to exit normally—that is, as if ended by the function call exit(EXIT_SUCCESS). That means in particular that the program calls any functions that were registered using atexit().

Example

See the example for thrd_detach() in this chapter.

See Also

thrd_create(), thrd_join(), thrd_detach()

Wait for a thread to finish.

```
#include <threads.h>
int thrd_join(thrd_t thr, int *res);
```

The function thrd_join() blocks the calling thread until the thread specified by the thr argument ends. Then thrd_join() writes the result code of the finished thread to the int variable addressed by the pointer argument res, provided res is not a null pointer. The program must not have already called either of the functions thrd_join() and thrd_detach() with the given thread ID thr.

The function thrd_join() returns the value of thrd_success, or thrd_error if an error occurs.

Example

See the example for thrd_create() in this chapter.

See Also

thrd_detach(), thrd_create(), thrd_exit()

Suspends the calling thread for a certain time.

```
#include <threads.h>
int thrd_sleep(const struct timespec *duration,
               struct timespec *remaining);
```

The function thrd_sleep() blocks the calling thread for the specified *duration*. The function can return earlier if it receives a signal that is not being ignored. In that case, the function saves the remaining countdown time in the object addressed by *remaining*, provided *remaining* is not a null pointer. The pointers *duration* and *remaining* may point to the same object.

The function thrd_sleep() returns zero if the full duration has elapsed, or –1 if it was interrupted by a signal. Other negative return values indicate errors.

The timespec structure has at least the following two members:

```
time_t tv_sec;     // seconds >= 0
long   tv_nsec;    // 0 <= nanoseconds <= 999,999,999
```

The order of the members in the structure is not specified.

Example

Block the calling thread for a half second (500 million nanoseconds):

```
struct timespec d = { .tv_nsec = 500*1E6 };
while( thrd_sleep( &d, &d) == -1)      // Sleep 500 ms.
    ;
```

See Also

thrd_yield()

Suspends the calling thread for a certain time.

```
#include <threads.h>
void thrd_yield(void);
```

The function thrd_yield() advises the operating system's scheduler to interrupt the calling thread and give CPU time to another thread.

Example

See the example on atomic_fence_op() in this chapter.

See Also

thrd_sleep()

time

Obtains the current calendar time.

```
#include <time.h>
time_t time( time_t *timeptr );
```

The time() function returns the current calendar time as a single arithmetic value. The return type, time_t, is defined in *time.h*, generally as long or unsigned long. If the argument is not a null pointer, the return value is also assigned to the location it references.

Many operating systems specify that the type time_t represents an integer number of seconds, and that the time() function returns the number of seconds passed since a specified epoch, such as midnight on January 1, 1970, Greenwich Mean Time. However, according to the C standard, neither of these conditions is required. The type time_t is an arithmetic type whose range and precision are defined by the implementation, as is the encoding of the time() function's return value.

Example

```
time_t sec;
time(&sec);
printf("This line executed at %.24s.\n", ctime(&sec));
```

This code produces output like the following:

```
This line executed at Thu Jan 29 08:30:17 2015.
```

See also the examples for asctime(), ctime(), fprintf(), freopen(), gmtime(), rand(), and strftime() in this chapter.

See Also

timespec_get(), asctime(), ctime(), gmtime(), localtime(), strftime()

timespec_get   C11

Obtains the current calendar time.

```
#include <time.h>
int timespec_get(struct timespec *ts, int base);
```

The function timespec_get() sets the timespec object addressed by the argument *ts* to reflect the current calendar time in accordance with the time base specified by the argument *base*. The timespec structure has at least two members for storing seconds and nanoseconds:

```
time_t tv_sec;     // seconds >= 0
long   tv_nsec;    // 0 <= nanoseconds <= 999,999,999
```

The order of the members in the structure is not defined. The positive constant TIME_UTC is always a permissible value of the argument *base*, and indicates universal time (also called Greenwich Mean Time). (Implementations may define other time-base constants.) For UTC, `timespec_get()` stores the calendar time as follows:

`ts->tv_sec`
> The number of seconds elapsed since an implementation-dependent epoch (usually January 1, 1970, at 00:00:00 UTC).

`ts->tv_nsec`
> The number of nanoseconds elapsed in addition to the whole seconds, rounded to reflect the resolution of the system clock.

On success, the function `timespec_get()` returns the positive value *base*. The return value zero indicates an error.

Example

```
struct timespec ts;
if( timespec_get( &ts, TIME_UTC) != 0)
    printf("The exact local time:\n"
    "%.24s and %09lu nanoseconds\n", ctime(&ts.tv_sec), ts.tv_nsec);
```

Typical output:

```
The exact local time:
Sun Apr 12 11:40:43 2015 and 030395137 nanoseconds
```

See Also

`time()`, `ctime()`, `gmtime()`, `localtime()`, `mktime()`, `strftime()`

tmpfile, tmpfile_s

Opens a temporary file with a unique name.

```
#include <stdio.h>
FILE *tmpfile( void );
errno_t tmpfile_s(FILE * restrict * restrict streamPtr);    (C11)
```

The `tmpfile()` function opens a temporary file for reading and writing, and returns the corresponding FILE pointer. The file is guaranteed to have a distinct name and FILE pointer from all other files, and is automatically deleted when closed, whether by `fclose()` or by normal program termination. The file is opened with the mode string "wb+" (see `fopen()` in this chapter for a description of mode strings).

If `tmpfile()` is unable to open a temporary file, it returns a null pointer. Whether temporary files are deleted after an abnormal program termination depends on the given implementation. The number of temporary files a program may create is at least equal to the value of the macro TMP_MAX. This macro is defined in *stdio.h* and is greater than or equal to 25 (see `tmpnam()` in this chapter).

Like `tmpfile()`, the secure function `tmpfile_s()` opens a temporary file for reading and writing with the access mode "wb+". The caller receives the corresponding FILE pointer not as the function's return value but in the object addressed by the parameter *streamPtr*. In other words, the argument is a pointer to a pointer. A run-time constraint of tmpfile_s() is that *streamPtr* must not be a null pointer.

The access mode corresponds to the mode string "wb+" as interpreted by the function fopen_s(): the file is opened for exclusive access, if the operating system supports that feature. The number of temporary files a program may create is at least equal to the value of the macro TMP_MAX_S, which is at least 25 (see tmpnam_s() in this chapter).

If the file has been opened successfully, tmpfile_s() returns zero and places the new FILE pointer in the variable referenced by *streamPtr*. If unsuccessful, the function returns a nonzero value and places a null pointer in the variable referenced by *streamPtr*, provided *streamPtr* is not a null pointer itself.

Example

```
FILE *fpTmp, *fpRx;
int c;

/* ... open Rx stream ... */

// if (( fpTmp = tmpfile() ) == NULL )
// or
if( tmpfile_s( &fpTmp) != 0 )
  fputs( "Unable to open a temporary file.", stderr );
else
{
  while (( c = fgetc( fpRx )) != EOF )
    if ( fputc( c, fpTmp ) == EOF )
      break;
}
fclose( fpRx );

/* ... process the data captured in fpTmp ... */
```

See Also

fopen(), fopen_s(), tmpnam(), tmpnam_s()

tmpnam, tmpnam_s

Generates a unique filename.

```
#include <stdio.h>
char *tmpnam( char *s );
errno_t tmpnam_s(char *s, rsize_t maxsize);        (C11)
```

The tmpnam() function generates a unique filename suitable for using for temporary files, and returns a pointer to the name string. If the pointer argument s is not a null pointer, then tmpnam() places the name string in a buffer addressed by s. The size of the buffer is assumed to be at least equal to the macro L_tmpnam. If s is a null pointer, then the return value points to the filename in tmpnam()'s internal, static buffer, where it may be modified by subsequent tmpnam() calls.

The `tmpnam()` function generates a different name each time it is called, and can generate at least `TMP_MAX` distinct names (some of which may be used by `tmpfile()`). The macros `L_tmpnam` and `TMP_MAX` are defined in *stdio.h*. `TMP_MAX` is greater than or equal to 25. The `tmpnam()` function returns a null pointer on failure.

Like `tmpnam()`, the secure function `tmpnam_s()` generates a unique name suitable for use as the name of a temporary file. The function is governed by the values of the macros `L_tmpnam_s` and `TMP_MAX_S`. `TMP_MAX_S`, like `TMP_MAX`, is at least equal to 25. The function `tmpnam_s()` also has the additional parameter *maxsize* to specify the size of the `char` array addressed by *s*. The function has the following runtime constraints: the parameter *s* must not be a null pointer, and *maxsize* must be greater than the length of the name generated but not greater than `RSIZE_MAX`.

The `tmpnam_s()` function returns zero if it was able to generate and store a suitable string. If not, the function writes the string terminator character to *s*[0], provided *s* is not a null pointer and *maxsize* is greater than zero but not greater than `RSIZE_MAX`, and returns a nonzero value.

 If you use a name supplied by `tmpnam()` to create a file, that does not mean the file is a temporary file in the sense of `tmpfile()`; it will not be automatically deleted on closing.

Example

```
// char fname[L_tmpnam];
// or
char fname[L_tmpnam_s];
FILE *fpOut;

// if( tmpnam( fname) == NULL)
// or
if( tmpnam_s( fname, sizeof(fname)) != 0)
{
  fputs( "Error generating a temporary file name.", stderr );
  return -1;
}

fpOut = fopen( fname, "w+" );
/* ... write and edit something in the file ... */
fclose( fpOut );
printf( "The results have been saved in %s.\n", fname );
```

See Also

`tmpfile()`, `tmpfile_s()`, `rename()`, `remove()`

tolower

Converts an uppercase alphabetic character to lowercase.

```
#include <ctype.h>
int tolower( int c );
```

The tolower() function returns the lowercase letter corresponding to the character value of its argument c. If c is not an uppercase letter, or if there is no lowercase letter that corresponds to it, its value is returned unchanged.

Which characters are considered uppercase, and which of those have a corresponding lowercase character, depends on the current locale setting for the localization category LC_CTYPE, which you can query or change using the setlocale() function. The uppercase characters are those for which isupper() returns true; the lowercase characters are those for which islower() returns true.

Accented characters, umlauts, and the like are considered alphabetic only in certain locales. Moreover, other locales may have characters that are alphabetic but are neither uppercase nor lowercase, or both uppercase and lowercase.

Example

See the examples for getchar() and setlocale() in this chapter.

See Also

islower(), toupper(), isupper(), towupper(), towlower(), towctrans()

toupper

Converts a lowercase alphabetic character to uppercase.

```
#include <ctype.h>
int toupper( int c );
```

The toupper() function returns the uppercase letter corresponding to the character value of its argument c. If c is not an lowercase letter, or if there is no uppercase letter that corresponds to it, its value is returned unchanged.

The note concerning locales under tolower() in this chapter applies to toupper() as well.

Example

See the example for setlocale() in this chapter.

See Also

isupper(), tolower(), islower(), towupper(), towlower(), towctrans()

towctrans

Performs a locale-specific conversion on a wide character.

```
#include <wctype.h>
wint_t towctrans( wint_t wc, wctrans_t desc );
```

The towctrans() function returns a wide character that corresponds to the wide-character value of its first argument, wc, according to a locale-specific mapping described by the second argument, desc. Values of desc are obtained by calling the wctrans() function. The behavior of both wctrans() and towctrans() depends on the locale setting of the category LC_CTYPE, which must not change between the two function calls.

Example

```
wint_t before = L'\0', after = L'\0';
wctrans_t mapping;
mapping = wctrans("toupper");

while (( before = getwchar() ) != WEOF )
{
  after = towctrans( before, mapping );
  putwchar( after );
  if ( after == L'Q' )
    break;
}
```

See Also

wctrans(), towlower(), towupper()

towlower

Converts an uppercase wide character to lowercase.

```
#include <wctype.h>
wint_t towlower( wint_t wc );
```

The towlower() function is like tolower() in all respects except that it operates on wide characters. An uppercase wide character is one for which iswupper() returns true in the current locale; a lowercase wide character is one for which iswlower() returns true.

Example

See the example using the analogous function towupper() under mbrtowc() in this chapter.

See Also

iswlower(), iswupper(), tolower(), toupper(), towupper(), towctrans()

towupper

Converts a lowercase wide character to uppercase.

```
#include <wctype.h>
wint_t towupper( wint_t wc );
```

The towupper() function is like toupper() in all respects except that it operates on wide characters. An uppercase wide character is one for which iswupper() returns true in the current locale; a lowercase wide character is one for which iswlower() returns true.

Example

See the example for mbrtowc() in this chapter.

See Also

iswlower(), iswupper(), tolower(), toupper(), towlower(), towctrans()

trunc   C99

Rounds a floating-point number toward 0 to an integer value.

```
#include <math.h>
double trunc( double x );
float truncf( float x );
long double truncl( long double x );
```

The trunc() functions round the value of their argument, x, to the nearest integer value whose magnitude is not greater than that of x—in other words, toward 0.

Example

```
printf("trunc(-1.7) = %.2f   trunc(1.4) = %.2f   trunc(1.5) = %.2f\n",
        trunc(-1.7),  trunc(1.4), trunc(1.5) );

printf("round(-1.7) = %.2f   round(1.4) = %.2f   round(1.5) = %.2f\n",
        round(-1.7), round(1.4), round(1.5) );
```

This code produces the following output:

```
trunc(-1.7) = -1.00   trunc(1.4) = 1.00   trunc(1.5) = 1.00
round(-1.7) = -2.00   round(1.4) = 1.00   round(1.5) = 2.00
```

See Also

rint(), lrint(), llrint(), round(), lround(), llround(), nearbyint()

tss_create   C11

Creates a key for thread-specific storage.

```
#include <threads.h>
int tss_create(tss_t *key, tss_dtor_t dtor);
```

The function tss_create() creates a new key for a pointer to access thread-specific storage (TSS) and sets the object addressed by the argument *key* to a value that uniquely identifies a TSS pointer. Each thread has its own instance of the pointer associated with that key. The pointer is initially null; each thread that needs thread-specific storage must call the function tss_set() to make the pointer address its thread-specific storage block.

The second parameter, *dtor*, is a pointer to a destructor function. It may be a null pointer. The type tss_dtor_t is defined as void(*)(void*). If *dtor* is not a null pointer, the destructor is called automatically with the TSS pointer as its argument when the thread terminates.

The tss_create() function returns the value of thrd_success if it succeeds in creating a TSS pointer. Otherwise, it returns thrd_error and leaves the object addressed by *key* with an undefined value.

Example

The following example illustrates the use of tss_create() and tss_delete(). See also the example for tss_set() and the more complete code example in "Using Thread-Specific Storage" on page 257.

```
tss_t key;              // Global key for a TSS pointer
void destructor(void *data);          // Destructor function

int main()
{
    // Create the TSS key:
    if( tss_create(&key, destructor) != thrd_success)
      return -1;

    // Create threads and wait for them to finish.
    // . . .

    tss_delete(key);  // Free all resources of the TSS pointer.
    return 0;
}
```

See Also

tss_delete(), tss_set(), tss_get()

tss_delete   C11

Deletes a key for thread-specific storage.

```
#include <threads.h>
void tss_delete(tss_t *key);
```

The function tss_delete() is the counterpart to tss_create() and frees all the resources used by the TSS key that its parameter *key* addresses.

Example

See the example for tss_create() in this chapter.

See Also

tss_create(), tss_set(), tss_get()

tss_get C11

Obtains a pointer to the thread-specific storage associated with a given key.

```
#include <threads.h>
void *tss_get(tss_t *key);
```

The function tss_get() returns a pointer to the calling thread's instance of the thread-specific storage block identified by the parameter *key*. The function returns NULL if the pointer could not be set or an error occurred.

Example

See the example for tss_set() in this chapter.

See Also

tss_set(), tss_create(), tss_delete()

tss_set C11

Sets a pointer to the thread-specific storage associated with a given key.

```
#include <threads.h>
int tss_set(tss_t *key, void * ptr);
```

The tss_set() function sets the TSS pointer designated by *key* to the memory block addressed by *val*.

The function tss_set() returns the value thrd_success if it succeeds in setting the TSS pointer, or thrd_error if an error occurs.

Example

The following example illustrates the use of tss_set() and tss_get(). See also the example for tss_create() and the more complete code example in "Using Thread-Specific Storage" on page 257.

```
tss_t key;                  // Global key for a TSS pointer
                            // tss_create(&key, ...) has been called.
// Process some data of some type Data_t:
int process_data(void)      // Use thread-specific storage.
{
   Data_t *ptr = (Data_t*)tss_get(key);    // Pointer to TSS
   // Process data ...
   return 0;
}
```

```
int thread_func( void* arg)
{
    size_t size = size_data( arg);   // A helper function to find the
                                     // required storage size.
    // Set thread-specific storage:
    if( tss_set(key, malloc(size)) != thrd_success)
        return -1;

    // Store and process data ...
    return process_data();           // return calls the destructor, if
}                                    // the tss_create() call set one.
```

See Also

tss_get(), tss_create(), tss_delete()

ungetc

Pushes a character back onto a file buffer to be read next.

```
#include <stdio.h>
int ungetc( int c, FILE *fp );
```

The ungetc() function reverses the effect of a getc() call; it pushes the character c back onto the file buffer associated with the FILE pointer fp, so that c becomes the first character to be read in a subsequent read operation. (However, if the program successfully calls fseek(), fsetpos(), or rewind() before reading from the file again, then the pushed-back character is lost.) The ungetc() function does not change the file on disk.

You can push at least one character onto the file buffer with unget(). Multiple calls in succession are possible, but are not guaranteed to succeed without intervening read operations. If successive unget() calls succeed, the characters pushed will be read in last-in, first-out order.

If successful, the ungetc() function returns the character pushed back onto the file buffer, and clears the file's EOF flag. On failure, ungetc() returns EOF. You cannot push an EOF value onto a file buffer.

The file associated with fp must be open for reading in either text or binary mode. If the file is in text mode, then ungetc() leaves the file access position indicator in an unspecified state until all pushed-back characters have been read again. If the file is in binary mode, ungetc() reduces the file position indicator by one. In either case, once all pushed-back characters have been read again, the file position indicator is the same as before the first ungetc() call.

Example

```
char file[ ]  = "input.dat";
FILE *fp;
int c;
char numstr[64];
```

```
if (( fp = fopen( file, "r" )) == NULL )
  fprintf( stderr, "Can't read the file %s\n", file), exit(1);

while ( (c = getc(fp)) != EOF )
{
  if ( isdigit(c) )       // Collect a sequence of digits.
  {
    int i = 0;
    do
    {
      numstr[i++] = (char)c;
      c = getc(fp);
    }while ( isdigit(c) && i+1 < sizeof(numstr) );

    numstr[i] = '\0';              // Terminate the numeral string.

    /* ... process the numeral string ... */

    if ( ungetc( c, fp) == EOF) // Put back the first non-digit.
      break;
    continue;
  }
  /* ... process any non-digit characters ... */
}
if ( !feof( fp))
  fprintf( stderr, "Error processing the file %s\n", file);

return 0;
```

See Also

getc(), ungetwc(), getwc()

ungetwc

Pushes a wide character back onto a file buffer to be read next.

```
#include <stdio.h>
#include <wchar.h>
wint_t ungetwc( wint_t wc, FILE *fp );
```

The ungetwc() function is the wide-character version of ungetc(), and works analogously, returning WEOF on failure or the wide character pushed back onto the file buffer if successful.

Example

See the example for the corresponding byte-character function, ungetc().

See Also

getwc(), getc()

va_arg, va_copy, va_end, va_start

Manage variable-argument lists.

```
#include <stdarg.h>
void va_start( va_list argptr, last_fixed_arg );
type va_arg( va_list argptr, type );
void va_copy( va_list dest, va_list src );        (C99)
void va_end( va_list argptr );
```

The macros va_arg(), va_start(), and va_end() allow you to define C functions with variable numbers of arguments. Such functions use these macros to access the optional arguments, which are managed as anonymous objects in a list referenced by a pointer object of type va_list.

The prototype syntax for a function that takes a variable number of arguments is as follows:

```
fn_type fn_name(
    [arg_type_1 fixed_arg_1, [arg_type_2 fixed_arg_2, [etc.]]]
    last_arg_type last_fixed_arg, ... );
```

The ellipsis (...) after last_fixed_arg in this syntax is a literal ellipsis, which must appear in the function prototype to represent the optional arguments. A function with optional arguments must also take at least one mandatory argument. The ellipsis representing the optional arguments must be the last item in the parameter list, after the last mandatory parameter. The following example shows the prototype of the function vop(), which takes two mandatory arguments—one with the type pointer to const char and one with the type int—and a variable number of optional arguments:

```
double vop( const char * op, int argcount, ... );
```

In a function definition, the macros va_start(), va_arg(), va_copy(), and va_end() allow you to access the optional arguments.

va_start

The macro va_start() initializes a va_list object so that it can be used in a va_arg() call to access the first optional argument in the variable-arguments list. The va_start() macro takes as its arguments the va_list object argptr, and the identifier of the last mandatory parameter, represented in this description by last_fixed_arg. Because va_start() makes certain assumptions about the alignment of the parameters in memory, last_fixed_arg must not be declared with the register storage class specifier, and must not have a function or array type, nor an integer type that is narrower than int.

Once you have called va_start(), you can access the optional arguments in the list one by one through successive va_arg() calls. You must not call va_start() again for the same va_list object until you have passed it to the va_end() macro.

va_arg

To obtain each optional argument, call the va_arg() macro. The va_arg() macro takes as its arguments the va_list object *argptr*, and the type of the argument being read. Each such call to va_arg() returns one argument from the optional arguments list, and adjusts *argptr* so that the next call returns the next argument.

If there is no argument left to be read when you call va_arg(), the behavior is undefined. The behavior is likewise undefined if the type indicated in the va_arg() call does not match the actual argument's type, with two exceptions: a signed integer type may match an unsigned integer type, if the value of the argument is representable in both types; and a pointer to void can match a pointer to char, signed char, or unsigned char.

 The *type* argument to va_arg() must be in such a notation that appending an asterisk to it yields the type of a pointer to *type*. For example, the *type* argument may be char *, but not char [8], because char ** means "pointer to a pointer to char"; but char [8]* does not mean "pointer to an array of 8 char elements." (That type's name would be written char (*) [8].)

va_copy

The macro va_copy() copies the state of the argument list referenced by the va_list object *src* to the object *dest*. If you have already called va_arg() for the same va_list object, then the copy produced by va_copy() is set to access the same argument as the original at the time it was copied. Otherwise, the copy is initialized to access the first argument in the list. You must call va_end() both for the copy and for the original after use.

va_end

To facilitate a clean return, a function that takes a variable number of arguments must call the macro va_end() after it has finished reading its optional arguments. The va_end() macro may render *argptr* unusable until it is reinitialized by calling va_start().

Example

```
#include <stdarg.h>
#include <stdio.h>
#include <string.h>
#include <math.h>

double vproduct( int n, va_list argptr );
double vsum( int n, va_list argptr );

double vop( const char * op, int argcount, ... );
// main() calls vop() to perform calculations. vop()'s arguments are:
// (1) the name of the operation ("sum", "product",
//     "sum minus the product");
```

```
// (2) the number of operands;
// (3 through n) the operands themselves.
// Iterates through operations twice: once with three operands, once
// with six.

int main()
{
  double d1, d2, d3, d4, d5, d6;

  puts( "Enter six floating-point numbers, please:" );
  scanf( "%lf%lf%lf%lf%lf%lf", &d1, &d2, &d3, &d4, &d5, &d6 );

  char *operation[] = {"sum", "product", "product minus the sum",NULL};

  printf("\nUsing the three numbers %lf, %lf, and %lf.\n", d1, d2, d3);
  for ( int i = 0; operation[i] != NULL; i++ )
    {
      printf( "The %s of these %d numbers is %lf\n",
              operation[i], 3,
              vop( operation[i], 3, d1, d2, d3 ) );
    }

  printf( "\nUsing six numbers:"
          "\n\t%lf \t%lf \t%lf \n\t%lf \t%lf \t%lf\n",
          d1, d2, d3, d4, d5, d6 );
  for ( int i = 0; operation[i] != NULL; i++ )
    {
      printf( "The %s of these %d numbers is %lf\n",
              operation[i], 6,
              vop( operation[i], 6, d1, d2, d3, d4, d5, d6 ) );
    }
}

double vop( const char * op, int argcount, ... )
{
  va_list argptr;
  double  result;

  va_start( argptr, argcount );

  if ( strcmp( op, "sum" ) == 0 )
    result = vsum( argcount, argptr );

  else if ( strcmp( op, "product" ) == 0 )
    result = vproduct( argcount, argptr );

  else if ( strcmp( op, "product minus the sum" ) == 0 )
    {
      va_list duplicate_argptr;     // Clone the va_list in its present
                                    // state.

      va_copy( duplicate_argptr, argptr );
```

```
      result = vproduct( argcount, argptr )
                - vsum( argcount, duplicate_argptr );
    va_end( duplicate_argptr );                // Clean up the clone.
  }

  else result = NAN;

  va_end( argptr );                            // Clean up the original.
  return result;
}

double vproduct( int n, va_list argptr )
{
  double product = 1.0;

  for ( int i = 0; i < n; i ++ )
    product *= va_arg( argptr, double );

  return product;
}

double vsum( int n, va_list argptr )
{
  double sum = 0.0;

  for ( int i = 0; i < n; i ++ )
    sum += va_arg( argptr, double );

  return sum;
}
```

In this example, the helper functions vproduct() and vsum() take as their second argument a va_list object that has already been initialized, and also leave the cleaning up to the caller. In this respect, they are similar to the vprintf() and vscanf() function families.

See also the example for vfscanf() in this chapter.

See Also

vfprintf(), vprintf(), vsnprintf(), and vsprintf(); vfscanf(), vscanf(), and vsscanf(); vfwprint(), vswprint(), and vwprint(); vfwscanf(), vswscanf(), and vwscanf()

vfprintf, vprintf, vsnprintf, vsprintf

Writes formatted output using a variable argument list object.

```
#include <stdio.h>
#include <stdarg.h>
int vfprintf( FILE * restrict fp, const char * restrict format,
              va_list argptr );
```

```
int vprintf( const char * restrict format, va_list argptr );
int vsprintf( char * restrict buffer, const char * restrict format,
             va_list argptr );
int vsnprintf( char * restrict buffer, size_t n,
             const char * restrict format, va_list argptr );  (C99)
```

The functions vfprintf(), vprintf(), vsprintf(), and vsnprintf() work in the same way as fprintf(), printf(), sprintf(), and snprintf(), respectively, except that their last argument, *argptr*, is a variable-argument list object with type va_list. The program must initialize this object by calling the va_start() macro before calling the vfprintf(), vprintf(), vsprintf(), or vsnprintf() function, and must call the va_end() macro after the function returns. Because these functions use the va_arg() macro internally to advance *argptr* through the argument list, its value is indeterminate after the vfprintf(), vprintf(), vsprintf(), or vsnprintf() function call has returned.

 The va_start(), va_arg(), and va_end() macros and the type va_list are declared in the header file *stdarg.h*.

Like the fprintf() and printf() functions, vfprintf() and vprintf() return the number of characters written to the output stream. The function vsprintf() returns the number of characters written to the string buffer, not counting the terminator character; and vsnprintf() returns the number of characters that would have been written to the string buffer if the parameter *n* had been sufficiently large, again not counting the terminator character.

Example

```
// write_log appends a line to the log file associated with the
// FILE pointer fp_log.
// The format string and optional arguments are the same as for printf().

void write_log(const char *function_name, unsigned int line_num,
               const char *format_str, ...)
{
  if ( fp_log == NULL)
    return;
  time_t timestamp = time(NULL);
  va_list argptr;
  // Set argptr to the first optional argument:
  va_start( argptr, format_str);

  // First print the timestamp, function name, and line number:
  fprintf( fp_log, "%.8s %s (line %u): ",
                   ctime(&timestamp)+11, function_name, line_num);
  // Then print the rest of the message:
  vfprintf( fp_log, format_str, argptr);
```

```
    va_end(argptr);
}

void myFunc( int param)
{
    write_log( __func__, __LINE__, "param = %d\n", param);
    /* ... */
}
```

Calling myFunc() in this example with the argument value 777 results in the following log file entry:

```
13:32:44 myFunc (line 62): param = 777
```

See Also

va_start(), va_arg(), va_copy() and va_end(); fprintf(), printf(), sprintf(), and snprintf(); vfwprint(), vwprint(), and vswprint(); the corresponding secure functions, if the implementation supports the C11 bounds-checking functions (i.e., if the macro __STDC_LIB_EXT1__ is defined)

vfprintf_s, vprintf_s, vsnprintf_s, vsprintf_s   C11

Writes formatted output using a variable argument list object.

```
#include <stdio.h>
#include <stdarg.h>
int vfprintf_s( FILE * restrict fp, const char * restrict format,
                va_list argptr );
int vprintf_s( const char * restrict format, va_list argptr );
int vsprintf_s( char * restrict buffer, const char * restrict format,
                va_list argptr );
int vsnprintf_s(char * restrict buffer, rsize_t n,
                const char * restrict format, va_list argptr);
```

The secure functions, introduced in C11, are available if the macro __STDC_LIB_EXT1__ is defined. They differ from the corresponding functions vfprintf(), vprintf(), vsprintf(), and vsnprintf() only in their runtime constraints: the format string must not contain the conversion specifier %n, and any pointer arguments, including all arguments corresponding to %s specifiers, must not be null pointers. In the vsnprintf_s() function, the value of n must be greater than zero but not greater than RSIZE_MAX.

The functions' return values and error handling, in particular with regard to violations of the runtime constraints, are the same as those of the functions fprintf_s(), printf_s(), sprintf_s(), and snprintf_s().

Example

See the example for vfprintf() in this chapter.

va_start(), va_arg(), va_copy() and va_end(); vfprintf(), vprintf(), vsprintf() and vsnprintf(); fprintf_s(), printf_s(), sprintf_s() and snprintf_s(); the corresponding wide-character functions vfwprintf_s(), vwprintf_s(), and vswprintf_s()

vfscanf, vscanf, vsscanf

Reads formatted data using a variable argument list.

```
#include <stdio.h>
#include <stdarg.h>
int vfscanf( FILE * restrict fp, const char * restrict format,
          va_list argptr );
int vscanf( const char * restrict format, va_list argptr );
int vsscanf( const char * restrict src, const char * restrict format,
          va_list argptr );
```

The functions vfscanf(), vscanf(), and vsscanf() work in the same way as fscanf(), scanf(), and sscanf(), respectively, except that their final argument, *argptr*, is a variable-argument list object with type va_list. The program must initialize this object by calling the va_start macro before calling the vfscanf(), vscanf(), or vsscanf() function, and must call the va_end() macro after the function returns. Because these functions use the va_arg() macro internally to advance the pointer through the argument list, its value is indeterminate after the vfscanf(), vscanf(), or vsscanf() function call has returned.

The va_start(), va_arg(), and va_end() macros and the type va_list are declared in the header file *stdarg.h*.

Like the fscanf(), scanf(), and sscanf() functions, vfscanf(), vscanf(), and vsscanf() return the number of input items that have been assigned to variables referenced by elements of the argument list.

Example

```
typedef struct {
  char lastname[20];
  char firstname[20];
  int dob_month;
  int dob_day;
  int dob_year;
} person;

person employee;

int read_person( char *lname, char *fname, ... )
```

```
// As variable arguments (...) use NULL
// or three int pointers (month, day, year).
{
  va_list args;
  int count;

  puts( "Enter the last name and first name (Example: Smith, Sally)");
  count = scanf( "%[^,], %[^\n]", lname, fname );   // Read the name.

  va_start(args, fname); // Initialize args to start with the argument
                         // that follows fname in the function call.
  if ( count == 2 && va_arg(args, int*) != NULL )
  {
    va_end( args);
    va_start( args, fname);  // Initialize args again.

    printf( "Enter the date of birth. (Example: 9/21/1962)\n");
    count += vscanf( "%d/%d/%d", args );        // Read date of birth.
  }
#ifdef DEBUG
  fprintf( stderr, "Read %d fields.\n", count);
#endif // def DEBUG

  va_end( args );
  return count;
}

int main()
{
  person *pEmployee = &employee;
  int result;

  result = read_person( pEmployee->lastname,
                        pEmployee->firstname,
                        &pEmployee->dob_month,
                        &pEmployee->dob_day,
                        &pEmployee->dob_year );

#ifdef DEBUG
  fprintf( stderr, "Fields read: %s, %s; born %d-%d-%d\n",
           pEmployee->lastname,
           pEmployee->firstname,
           pEmployee->dob_month,
           pEmployee->dob_day,
           pEmployee->dob_year );
#endif // def DEBUG
}
```

va_start(), va_arg(), va_copy() and va_end(); fscanf(), scanf(), and sscanf(); vfwscanf(), vwscanf(), and vswscanf(); the corresponding secure functions, if the implementation supports the C11 bounds-checking functions (i.e., if the macro __STDC_LIB_EXT1__ is defined)

vfscanf_s, vscanf_s, vsscanf_s   C11

Reads formatted input using a variable argument list object.

```
#include <stdio.h>
#include <stdarg.h>
int vfscanf_s( FILE * restrict fp, const char * restrict format,
               va_list argptr );
int vscanf_s( const char * restrict format, va_list argptr );
int vsscanf_s( const char * restrict src, const char * restrict format,
               va_list argptr );
```

These secure functions work in the same way as fscanf_s(), scanf_s(), and sscanf_s(), except that their last argument, *argptr*, is a variable-argument list object with the type va_list. The program must initialize this object by calling the va_start() macro before calling the vfscanf_s(), vscanf_s(), or vsscanf_s() function, and must call the va_end() macro after the function returns.

The functions test the following runtime constraints: all pointers, including the indirectly provided pointers for format elements, must not be null pointers. The functions return the number of data items converted and stored in variables. If an input error occurs before any data can be converted, or if a runtime constraint violation occurs, the functions return EOF.

Example

See the example for vfscanf() in this chapter.

See Also

va_start() and va_end(); vfscanf(), vscanf(), and vsscanf(); fscanf_s(), scanf_s(), and sscanf_s(); vfwscanf_s(), vwscanf_s(), and vswscanf_s()

vfwprintf, vswprintf, vwprintf

Prints formatted wide-character output using a variable argument list object.

```
#include <stdarg.h>
#include <wchar.h>
int vswprintf( wchar_t * restrict s, size_t n,
               const wchar_t * restrict format, va_list argptr );
int vwprintf( const wchar_t * restrict format, va_list argptr );

#include <stdio.h>        // In addition to <stdarg.h> and <wchar.h>
int vfwprintf( FILE *fp, const wchar_t * restrict format,
               va_list argptr );
```

The functions vfwprintf(), vswprintf(), and vwprintf() are like fwprintf(), swprintf(), and wprintf(), respectively, except that their last argument, *argptr*, is a variable-argument list object with type va_list. The program must initialize this object by calling the va_start() macro before calling the vfwprintf(), vswprintf(), or vwprintf() function, and must call the va_end() macro after the function returns. Because these functions use the va_arg() macro internally to advance the pointer through the argument list, its value is indeterminate after the vfwprintf(), vswprintf(), or vwprintf() function call has returned.

The vfwprintf() and vwprintf() functions return the number of wide characters written to the output stream, or a negative value if an error occurred. The vswprintf() function returns the number of wide characters written to the output buffer, not counting the terminating null wide character, or a negative value if an encoding error occurred or if the complete output string would have contained more than *n* wide characters.

Example

See the example for the corresponding byte-character function vfprintf() in this chapter.

See Also

va_start() and va_end(); wprintf(), fwprintf(), and swprintf(); vfwscanf(), vswscanf(), and vwscanf(); the corresponding secure functions, if the implementation supports the C11 bounds-checking functions (i.e., if the macro __STDC_LIB_EXT1__ is defined)

vfwprintf_s, vswprintf_s, vsnwprintf_s, vwprintf_s   C11

Writes formatted wide-string output using a variable-arguments list object.

```
#include <stdarg.h>
#include <wchar.h>
int vswprintf_s( wchar_t * restrict s, rsize_t n,
                const wchar_t * restrict format, va_list argptr );
int vsnwprintf_s( wchar_t * restrict s, rsize_t n,
                const wchar_t * restrict format, va_list argptr );
int vwprintf_s( const wchar_t * restrict format, va_list argptr );

#include <stdio.h>          // In addition to <stdarg.h> and <wchar.h>
int vfwprintf_s( FILE * restrict fp, const wchar_t * restrict format,
                va_list argptr );
```

These secure functions work in the same way as fwprintf_s(), swprintf_s(), snwprintf_s(), and wprintf_s, except that their last argument, *argptr*, is a variable-argument list object with the type va_list. The program must initialize this object by calling the va_start() macro before calling one of the variadic output functions, and must call the va_end() macro after the function returns.

The function `vsnwprintf_s()` truncates its output string if the destination array `s` is too small. If the destination array is too small for the output of `vswprintf_s()`, however, a runtime constraint violation occurs.

Example

See the example for `vfprintf()` in this chapter.

See Also

`va_start()` and `va_end()`; `fwprintf_s()`, `wprintf_s()`, `swprintf_s()`, and `snwprintf_s()`; the corresponding byte-character functions `vfprintf_s()`, `vprintf_s()`, `vsprintf_s()`, and `vsnprintf_s()`

vfwscanf, vswscanf, vwscanf

Reads formatted wide-character input using a variable argument list object.

```
#include <stdarg.h>
#include <wchar.h>
int vswscanf( const wchar_t * restrict s,
              const wchar_t * restrict format, va_list argptr );
int vwscanf( const wchar_t * restrict format, va_list argptr );

#include <stdio.h>    // In addition to <stdarg.h> and <wchar.h>
int vfwscanf( FILE * restrict fp, const wchar_t * restrict format,
              va_list argptr );
```

The functions `vfwscanf()`, `vswscanf()`, and `vwscanf()` are like `fwscanf()`, `swscanf()`, and `wscanf()`, respectively, except that their final argument, *argptr*, is a variable-argument list object with type `va_list`. The program must initialize this object by calling the `va_start()` macro before calling the `vfwscanf()`, `vswscanf()`, or `vwscanf()` function, and must call the `va_end()` macro after the function returns. Because these functions use the `va_arg()` macro internally to advance the pointer through the argument list, its value is indeterminate after the `vfwprintf()`, `vswprintf()`, or `vwprintf()` function call has returned.

The `vfwscanf()`, `vswscanf()`, and `vwscanf()` functions return the number of input items assigned to variables, which may be 0; or `EOF` if an input failure occurs before any conversion takes place.

Example

See the example for the corresponding byte-character function `vfscanf()` in this chapter.

See Also

`va_start()`, `va_arg()`, `va_copy()`, and `va_end()`; `fwscanf()`, `swscanf()`, and `wscanf()`; `vfwprint()`, `vswprint()`, and `vwprint()`; the corresponding secure functions

---

Reads formatted wide-character input using a variable-argument list object.

```
#include <stdarg.h>
#include <wchar.h>
int vswscanf_s( const wchar_t * restrict s,
                const wchar_t * restrict format, va_list argptr );
int vwscanf_s( const wchar_t * restrict format, va_list argptr );

#include <stdio.h>          // In addition to <stdarg.h> and <wchar.h>
int vfwscanf_s( FILE * restrict fp, const wchar_t * restrict format,
                va_list argptr );
```

These secure functions work in the same way as fwscanf_s(), wscanf_s(), and swscanf_s(), except that their last argument, *argptr*, is a variable-argument list object with the type va_list. The program must initialize this object by calling the va_start() macro before calling the vfscanf_s(), vscanf_s(), or vsscanf_s() function, and must call the va_end() macro after the function returns.

The functions test the following runtime constraints: all pointers, including the indirectly provided pointers for format elements, must not be null pointers. The functions return the number of data items converted and stored in variables. If an input error occurs before any data can be converted, or if a runtime constraint violation occurs, the function returns EOF.

Example

See the example for vfscanf() in this chapter.

See Also

va_start() and va_end(); fwscanf_s(), swscanf_s(), and wscanf_s(); vfwprint(), vwprint(), vswprint(), vsnwprintf()_s; the corresponding byte-character functions vfscanf_s(), vscanf_s(), and vsscanf_s()

wcrtomb

Converts a wide character to a multibyte character.

```
#include <wchar.h>
size_t wcrtomb( char restrict *dest, wchar_t wc,
                mbstate_t * restrict state );
```

The wcrtomb() function is the restartable version of wctomb(). The third argument is a pointer to a variable with type mbstate_t, which holds the current parse state of a multibyte string being formed in the buffer that the first argument by successive function calls. Each call to wcrtomb() converts a wide character into a multibyte character, and stores the result in the buffer pointed to by its first argument. The return value indicates the number of bytes written to the output buffer. The maximum number of bytes that wcrtomb() writes to the buffer is the value of

`MB_CUR_MAX`. `wcrtomb()` also updates the state variable referenced by the third argument to represent the new parse state of the string written. The locations that `wcrtomb()` reads from and writes to using its restricted pointer parameters must not overlap.

If the wide character is the null character (`L'\0'`), then `wcrtomb()` writes to the buffer a shift sequence, if necessary, to restore the multibyte string to the initial parse state, and then writes a null character. The state variable is updated to represent the initial state. If the second argument is not a valid wide character, `wcrtomb()` returns -1, sets the `errno` variable to `EILSEQ`, and leaves the parse state variable in an undefined state. If the first argument is a null pointer, then `wcrtomb()` only sets the state variable to represent the initial state. The return value is then the number of bytes that would have been written to the output buffer.

Example

See the example for `mbrtowc()` in this chapter.

See Also

`wctomb()`, `mbrtowc()`, `wctob()`, and `btowc()`; `wcsrtombs()`, `wcstombs()`, and `mbstowcs()`; the corresponding secure functions.

wcrtomb_s   C11

Converts a wide character into a multibyte character.

```
#include <wchar.h>
errno_t wcrtomb_s(size_t * restrict retval,
                  char * restrict dest, rsize_t destmax,
                  wchar_t wc, mbstate_t * restrict ps);
```

The function `wcrtomb_s()` is the restartable version of `wctomb_s()`. Instead of storing the parse state of its multibyte output string internally, it stores it between successive calls in a variable with the type `mbstate_t` addressed by its last argument, *ps*.

If *dest* is not a null pointer, `wcrtomb_s()` stores the multibyte character corresponding to the wide character *wc* in the `char` array addressed by *dest*, and puts the length of the multibyte output in the variable addressed by *retval*. The length is always less than or equal to the value of `MB_CUR_MAX`. The function also updates the parse state variable addressed by *ps*.

If *dest* is a null pointer, `wcrtomb_s()`, unlike `wctomb_s()`, does not determine whether the multibyte character encoding is state-dependent, but only sets the state variable addressed by *ps* to the initial shift state.

The function has the following runtime constraints: the pointers *retval* and *ps* must not be null pointers. If *dest* is not a null pointer, the size of the `char` array specified by *destmax* must not be less than the length of the multibyte character to be written, and must not be greater than `RSIZE_MAX`. If *dest* is a null pointer, the length argument *destmax* must be zero.

If a violation of the runtime constraints occurs, wcrtomb_s() writes the string terminator character to *dest*[0], provided *dest* is not a null pointer and *destmax* is greater than zero, but not greater than RSIZE_MAX.

The wcrtomb_s() function returns zero if no error occurs. If a violation of the runtime constraints occurs, or if the value of *wc* does not correspond to any valid multibyte character, the function returns a nonzero value and sets the variable addressed by *retval* to the value of (size_t)(-1), provided *retval* is not a null pointer.

Example

```
wchar_t wc = L'\u00b1';        //'±'
char mbStr[MB_CUR_MAX];
size_t nBytes = 0;
mbstate_t state = {0};

if( wcrtomb_s( &nBytes, mbStr, sizeof(mbStr), wc, &state ) != 0)
{ /* Handle the error ... */ }
printf("Character: '%lc';  multibyte code:", wc);          // '±'
for( unsigned i = 0; i < nBytes; ++i)
    printf(" %#04x", (unsigned char)mbStr[i]);       // 0xc2 0xb1
```

See Also

wctomb_s(),   wcrtomb(),   wctomb()   wctob();   wcstombs(),   wcstombs_s(),
wcsrtombs(), wcsrtombs_s();

wcscat, wcscat_s

Appends one wide string to another.

```
#include <wchar.h>
wchar_t *wcscat( wchar_t * restrict s1, const wchar_t * restrict s2 );
errno_t wcscat_s( wchar_t * restrict s1, rsize_t s1max,
                  const wchar_t * restrict s2);
```

The wcscat() function copies the wide-character string addressed by the second pointer argument, *s2*, to the location following the string addressed by the first pointer, *s1*. The first wide character of *s2* is copied over the terminating null wide character of the string addressed by *s1*. The function returns the value of its first argument, which points to the concatenated string. It is up to you, the programmer, to make sure that the array of wchar_t addressed by the argument *s1* is big enough to store the concatenated string. The source and destination arrays must not overlap. The function wcscat() returns the pointer *s1*.

Like wcscat(), the secure function wcscat_s() appends the second wide string, *s2*, to the end of the first wide string, *s1*, but it avoids the danger of a buffer overflow. It has the additional parameter *s1max* to specify the size of the destination array—as a number of wide characters—and tests the following runtime constraints:

- The pointers *s1* and *s2* must not be null pointers, and the value *s1max* must be greater than zero and less than or equal to RSIZE_MAX.

- The sum of the string lengths of *s1* and *s2* must be less than *s1max*.

- The source and destination arrays must not overlap.

If a violation of the runtime constraints occurs, wcscat_s() writes the string terminator character to *s1*[0], provided *s1* is not a null pointer and *s1max* is greater than zero but not greater than RSIZE_MAX.

The wcscat_s() function returns zero on success, or a nonzero value if a violation of the runtime constraints occurs.

Example

```
typedef struct {
  wchar_t  lastname[32];
  wchar_t  firstname[32];
  _Bool ismale;
} Name;

Name *newName = calloc( 1, sizeof(Name) );

/* ... check for calloc failure; read in the name parts ... */

// Then display the new name
wchar_t displayname[80];
wcscpy( displayname, ( newName->ismale ? L"Mr. " : L"Ms. " ) );
wcscat( displayname, newName->firstname );
wcscat( displayname, L" " );
wcscat( displayname, newName->lastname );
wcscat( displayname, L"\n" );

// Better to use wcscat_s() in case the fields in the Name
// structure are ever enlarged:
// wcscat_s( displayname, sizeof(displayname), newName->firstname );
// wcscat_s( displayname, sizeof(displayname), L" " );
// wcscat_s( displayname, sizeof(displayname), newName->lastname );
// wcscat_s( displayname, sizeof(displayname), L"\n" );
fputws( displayname, stdout );
```

See Also

wcsncat(), wcsncat_s(), strcat(), strcat_s(), strncat(), strncat_s()

wcschr

Searches for a given character in a string.

```
#include <wchar.h>
wchar_t *wcschr( const wchar_t *s, wchar_t c );
```

The wcschr() function returns a pointer to the first occurrence of the wide-character value *c* in the wide string addressed by *s*. If there is no such character in the string, wcschr() returns a null pointer. If *c* is a null wide character (L'\0'), then

the return value points to the terminator character of the wide string addressed by
s.

Example

```
typedef struct {
  wchar_t  street[32];
  wchar_t  city[32];
  wchar_t  stateprovince[32];
  wchar_t  zip[16];
} Address;

wchar_t printaddr[128] = L"720 S. Michigan Ave.\nChicago, IL 60605\n";
int sublength;
Address *newAddr = calloc( 1, sizeof(Address) );

if ( newAddr != NULL )
 {
   sublength = wcschr( printaddr, L'\n' ) - printaddr;
   wcsncpy( newAddr->street, printaddr,
            (sublength < 31 ? sublength : 31) );
   /* ... */
 }
```

See Also

strchr(), wcsrchr()

wcscmp

Compares two wide strings.

```
#include <wchar.h>
int wcscmp( const wchar_t *s1, const wchar_t *s2 );
```

The wcscmp() function compares the wide strings addressed by its two pointer
arguments, and returns a value indicating the result as follows:

Zero
> The two strings are equal.

Greater than zero
> The string addressed by *s1* is greater than the string addressed by *s2*.

Less than zero
> The string addressed by *s1* is less than the string addressed by *s2*.

The wcscmp() function compares the strings one wide character at a time. As soon
as it finds unmatched characters in corresponding positions in the two strings, the
string containing the greater wide-character value at that position is the greater
string.

Example

```
int result = 0;
wchar_t word1[255], word2[256], *greaterlessequal;

while ( result < 2 )
{
  fputws( L"Type two words, please:  ", stdout );
  result = wscanf( L"%255ls%255ls", word1, word2 );
  if ( result == EOF )
    return EOF;
}
result = wcscmp( word1, word2 );

if ( result < 0 )
  greaterlessequal = L"less than";
else if ( result > 0 )
  greaterlessequal = L"greater than";
else
  greaterlessequal = L"the same as";

wprintf( L"The word \"%ls\" is %ls the word \"%ls\".\n", word1,
         greaterlessequal, word2 );
```

See Also

wcsncmp(), strcmp()

wcscoll

Collates two wide strings.

```
#include <wchar.h>
int wcscoll( const wchar_t *s1, const wchar_t *s2 );
```

Like wcscmp(), the wcscoll() function performs a wide-character-by-wide-character comparison of the two strings, *s1* and *s2*. However, where wcscmp() just compares unsigned character values, wcscoll() can apply a locale-specific set of rules in comparing strings. The value of the locale information category LC_COLLATE determines the applicable rule set, and can be changed by the setlocale() function. The return value of wcscoll() indicates the relation between the two wide strings as follows. If the return value is:

Zero
> The two strings are equal.

Greater than zero
> The string addressed by *s1* is greater than that addressed by *s2*.

Less than zero
> The string addressed by *s1* is less than that addressed by *s2*.

Example

```
wchar_t *samples[ ] = { L"anejo", L"añeja",};

setlocale( LC_COLLATE, "es_US.UTF-8" );

int result = wcscoll( samples[0], samples[1] );

wprintf( L"In the locale %s, ", setlocale( LC_COLLATE, NULL ));

if ( result == 0 )
  wprintf( L"the wide strings \"%ls\" and \"%ls\" are alphabetically "
          "equivalent.\n", samples[0], samples[1] );
else if ( result < 0 )
  wprintf( L"the wide string \"%ls\" precedes \"%ls\" "
          "alphabetically.\n", samples[0], samples[1] );
else if ( result > 0 )
  wprintf( L"the wide string \"%ls\" comes after \"%ls\" "
          "alphabetically.\n", samples[0], samples[1] );
```

See Also

wcscmp(), wcsncmp(), and wcsxfrm(); strcoll(), strcmp(), strncmp(), and strxfrm()

wcscpy, wcscpy_s

Copies a wide string to another location.

```
#include <wchar.h>
wchar_t *wcscpy(wchar_t * restrict dest, const wchar_t * restrict src);
errno_t wcscpy_s(wchar_t * restrict dest, rsize_t destmax,
                const wchar_t * restrict src);
```

The functions wcscpy() and wcscpy_s() copy the wide-character string addressed by *src* to the array of *wchar_t* addressed by dest. These functions are equivalent to strcpy() and strcpy_s() except that they copy wide characters instead of byte characters.

Example

```
struct record {
  wchar_t name[64];
  int age;
  _Bool male, smoking, discount;
} this;
int results;

wprintf( L"Last name: " );
results = wscanf( L"%63l[^\n]", this.name );
if ( results < 1 )
    wcscpy( this.name,  L"[Name not available]" );
// or:
// wcscpy_s( this.name, sizeof(this.name)/sizeof(wchar_t),
```

```
//            L"[Name not available]" );
wprintf( L"%ls\n", this.name );
```
See Also

wcsncpy(), wcsncpy_s(), strcpy(), strcpy_s(), strncpy(), strncpy_s()

wcscspn

Searches for any element of one wide string in another.

```
#include <wchar.h>
size_t wcscspn( const wchar_t *s1, const wchar_t *s2 );
```

The wcscspn() function returns the number of wide characters at the beginning of
the string addressed by *s1* that do not match any of the wide characters in the string
addressed by *s2*. In other words, wcscspn() returns the index of the first wide character in *s1* that matches any wide character in *s2*. If the two strings have no wide
characters in common, then the return value is the length of the string addressed by
s1.

Example

```
wchar_t *path
        = L"/usr/local/bin:/usr/bin:/bin:/usr/bin/X11:/usr/games";
int  separator;

wchar_t *basename = L"aprogram";
wchar_t fullname[1024] = L"";

separator = wcscspn( path, L":" );

wcsncpy( fullname, path, separator );
fullname[separator] = '\0';
wcsncat( fullname, L"/", sizeof(fullname) - wcslen(fullname) -1 );
wcsncat( fullname, basename, sizeof(fullname) - wcslen(fullname) -1 );

fputws( fullname, stdout );
```
See Also

wcsspn(), wcspbrk(), and wcschr(); strcspn(), strspn(), strpbrk(), and
strchr()

wcsftime

Generates a formatted wide string of date-and-time information.

```
#include <time.h>
#include <wchar.h>
size_t wcsftime( wchar_t * restrict s, size_t n,
                 const wchar_t * restrict format,
                 const struct tm * restrict timeptr );
```

The wcsftime() function is similar to strftime() except that its format string argument and the output string it generates are wide-character strings. Accordingly, the length *n* and the function's return value indicate numbers of wide characters, not byte characters. The locations that wcsftime() reads from and writes to using its restricted pointer parameters must not overlap.

Example

```
#define MAX_HDR 1024

time_t now;
struct tm *localnow;
wchar_t hdr_date[MAX_HDR] = L"";

time( &now );
localnow = localtime( &now );

if( wcsftime( hdr_date, MAX_HDR, L"Date: %a, %d %b %Y %T %z", localnow))
  fputws( hdr_date, stdout );
else
  return -1;
```

See Also

strftime(), setlocale()

wcslen

Obtains the length of a wide-character string.

```
#include <wchar.h>
size_t wcslen( const wchar_t *s );
```

The wcslen() function calculates the length of the string addressed by its argument *s*. The length of a wide string is the number of wide characters in it, not counting the terminating null character (L'\0').

Example

```
wchar_t line[1024] =
        L"This string could easily be 400 or 500 characters long. "
        L"This string could easily be 400 or 500 characters long. "
        L"\n";
wchar_t *readptr = line;
int columns = 80;
while( wcslen( readptr ) > columns) // While remaining text is too long,
{                                    // print a chunk with a final
  wprintf(L"%.*ls\\n", columns-1, readptr);  // backslash and newline.
  readptr += columns -1;
}
wprintf( L"%ls\n", readptr);   // Print the rest, ending with a newline.
```

See Also

wcsnlen_s(), strlen(), strnlen_s(); the example for mbtowc()

wcsncat, wcsncat_s

Appends a number of wide characters from one string to another.

```
#include <wchar.h>
wchar_t *wcsncat( wchar_t * restrict s1,
                  const wchar_t * restrict s2, size_t n );
errno_t wcsncat_s(wchar_t * restrict s1, rsize_t s1max,
                  const wchar_t * restrict s2, rsize_t n );
```

The functions wcsncat() and wcsncat_s() copy up to n characters of the string addressed by their second argument, s2, to the end of the string addressed by their first argument s1. The first wide character copied from s2 replaces the string terminator character of s1. The functions copy less than n characters if they encounter a terminating null character before the nth character in the source string s2. In all cases, both functions append a null character to the concatenated string.

The functions wcsncat() and wcsncat_s() are similar to the functions strncat() and strncat_s() except that they copy wide characters instead of byte characters.

Example

See the examples for strncat() and wcscspn() in this chapter.

See Also

wcscat(), strncat(), strcat(), and the corresponding secure functions

wcsncmp

Compares the first n wide characters of two strings.

```
#include <wchar.h>
int wcsncmp( const wchar_t *s1, const wchar_t *s2, size_t n );
```

The wcsncmp() function compares at most the first n wide characters in the two strings addressed by its pointer arguments. Characters that follow a null wide character are ignored. wcsncmp() returns a value indicating the result as follows:

Zero
> The two wide strings, or arrays of n wide characters, are equal.

Greater than zero
> The string or array of n wide characters addressed by s1 is greater than that addressed by s2.

Less than zero
> The string or array of n wide characters addressed by s1 is less than that addressed by s2.

Example

```
wchar_t *months[] = { L"January", L"February", L"March", L"April",
                      L"May", L"June", L"July", L"August",
                      L"September", L"October", L"November", L"December"};

wchar_t date[ ] = L"Thu, 10 Mar 2005 13:44:18 +0100";
int mo = 0;
while (( mo < 12 ) && ( wcsncmp( date + 8, months[mo], 3 ) != 0 ))
    mo++;
```

See Also

wcscmp(), wcscoll(), strncmp(), strcmp()

wcsncpy, wcsncpy_s

Copies the first *n* wide characters of a string to another location.

```
#include <wchar.h>
wchar_t *wcsncpy( const wchar_t * restrict dest,
                 const wchar_t * restrict src, size_t n );
errno_t wcsncpy_s(wchar_t * restrict dest, rsize_t destmax,
                 const wchar_t * restrict src, rsize_t n);
```

The functions wcsncpy() and wcsncpy_s() copy up to *n* wide characters from the string addressed by *src* to the array of *wchar_t* addressed by dest. These functions are equivalent to strncpy() and strncpy_s() except that they copy wide characters instead of byte characters.

 If there is no null wide character in the first *n* wide characters of *src*, then the wcsncpy() function does not append a terminating null character to the copied string!

If wcsncpy() reads a null wide character from *src* before it has copied *n* wide characters, then the function writes null wide characters to *dest* until it has written a total of *n* wide characters.

Example

See the examples for wcscspn() and wcspbrk() in this chapter.

See Also

strcpy(), strncpy(), memcpy(), memmove(), wcscpy(), wmemcpy(), wmemmove(); the corresponding secure functions, if the implementation supports the C11 bounds-checking functions (i.e., if the macro __STDC_LIB_EXT1__ is defined)

Obtains the length of a wide string.

```
#include <wchar.h>
size_t wcsnlen_s(const wchar_t *s, size_t maxsize);
```

If the pointer *s* is a null pointer, the function wcsnlen_s() returns zero. Otherwise, wcsnlen_s() returns the length of the wide string addressed by the pointer *s*; that is, the number of wide characters that precede the terminating null character (L'\0'). The function only examines at most the first *maxsize* wide characters in the string, however. If there is no null wide character within the first *maxsize* wide characters, wcsnlen_s() returns the value of *maxsize*.

Example

```
#define __STDC_WANT_LIB_EXT1__ 1
#include <wchar.h>
// ...
wchar_t ws[] = L"hello";
size_t len = wcsnlen_s( ws, 100);         // len = 5
if( wcsnlen_s( ws, 4) == 4)
{ /* The string contains more than 4 wide characters. */ }
```

See Also

wcslen(), strlen(), strnlen_s()

wcspbrk

Finds the first wide character in a string that matches any wide character in another string.

```
#include <wchar.h>
wchar_t *wcspbrk( const wchar_t *s1, const wchar_t *s2 );
```

The wcspbrk() function returns a pointer to the first wide character in the string addressed by *s1* that matches any wide character contained in the string addressed by *s2*. If the two strings have no wide characters in common, then wcspbrk() returns a null pointer.

Example

```
wchar_t *story = L"He shouted: \"What? I can't hear you!\"\n";
wchar_t separators[ ] = L" \t\n.:?!\"";
wchar_t *start = story, *end = NULL;
wchar_t words[16][16];
int i = 0;

while ( i < 16 && ( end = wcspbrk( start, separators ) ) != NULL )
{
  if ( end != start )              // If the separator wasn't the first
  {                                // character in the substring,
```

```
    wcsncpy( words[i], start, end - start );  // then save a word.
    words[i][end - start] = L'\0';            // And terminate it.
    i++;
  }
  start = end + 1;                            // Next wcspbrk call starts with the
}                                             // character after this separator.

fputws( story, stdout );
for ( int j = 0 ; j < i ; j++ )
{
  fputws( words[j], stdout );
  fputwc( L'\n', stdout );
}
```

See Also

wcschr(), wcsrchr(), wcsstr(), wcscspn(), strpbrk()

wcsrchr

Searches for the rightmost occurrence of a given wide character in a string.

```
#include <wchar.h>
wchar_t *wcsrchr( const wchar_t *s, wchar_t wc );
```

The wcsrchr() function returns a pointer to the *last* occurrence of the wide-character value *wc* in the string addressed by *s*. If there is no such wide character in the string, wcsrchr() returns a null pointer. If *wc* is a null wide character (L'\0'), then the return value points to the terminator of the string addressed by *s*.

Example

```
int main( int argc, char ** argv )
{
  wchar_t wmyname[256];
  size_t result = mbstowcs( wmyname, argv[0], 256 );
  if ( result == -1 )
    return -1;
  wchar_t *mybasename = wcsrchr( wmyname, L'/' );   // End of path
  if ( mybasename != NULL )
    mybasename++;
  else
    mybasename = wmyname;
  wprintf( L"This program was invoked as %ls.\n", mybasename );
}
```

See Also

wcschr(), wcsstr(), wcsspn(), wcscspn(), wcspbrk(); the byte character string functions strchr(), strrchr(), strpbrk(), strstr(), strspn(), strcspn()

wcsrtombs

Converts a wide-character string into a multibyte string and saves the parse state.

```
#include <wchar.h>
size_t wcsrtombs( char * restrict dest, const wchar_t ** restrict src,
                  size_t n, mbstate_t * restrict state );
```

The wcsrtombs() function converts one or more wide characters from the array indirectly addressed by *src* into a string of multibyte characters, beginning in the parse state indicated by the *state* argument, and stores the results in the array of char addressed by *dest*. (*dest* may also be a null pointer, in which case wcsrtombs() does not actually store any output characters, and does not modify the pointer in the location addressed by *src*. The function therefore merely returns the number of bytes that a multibyte representation of the wide-character string would occupy.)

The third argument, *n*, specifies the maximum number of characters that can be written to the output buffer. The conversion performed on each wide character is the same as that which would be performed by the wcrtomb() function, updating the mbstate_t object addressed by *state*.

Conversion ends on the first of three possible events:

When a terminating null character has been written to the output buffer
> In this case, wcsrtombs() stores a null pointer in the location addressed by *src*, and returns the number of bytes in the multibyte sequence resulting from the conversion. The object addressed by *state* represents the initial parse state, and the terminating null character stored in the output buffer is preceded by any shift sequence required to reach the initial parse state.

When writing another multibyte character would exceed the maximum length of n bytes
> In the location addressed by *src*, wcsrtombs() stores a pointer to the location that follows the last wide character read, and the object addressed by *state* represents the current parse state of the incomplete output string so that subsequent function calls can continue the string conversion. The function returns the number of bytes in the multibyte sequence resulting from the conversion.

When a wide character read cannot be converted into a valid multibyte character
> In this case, wcsrtombs() sets the errno variable to the value of EILSEQ ("illegal sequence") and returns (size_t)(-1). The state of the object addressed by *state* is unspecified.

Example

```
int i = 0, n = 0;
size_t result;
wchar_t wc;
char mbstring[256] = { '\0' };
```

```
wchar_t widestring[]
        = L"This is originally a string of wide characters.";
const wchar_t *wcsptr = widestring;
mbstate_t state;

printf( "The current locale is %s.\n", setlocale(LC_CTYPE, "") );

memset( &state, '\0', sizeof state );
result = wcsrtombs( mbstring, &wcsptr, 256, &state );

printf("The return value: %d\n", (int)result );
if( result > 0 && wcsptr == NULL )
    printf("The multibyte string: \"%s\"\n", mbstring);
```

See Also

wcstombs(), wcrtomb(), wctomb(), mbsrtowcs(), mbstowcs(), mbrtowc(),
mbtowc(); the corresponding secure functions, and the example for wcsrtombs_s()

wcsrtombs_s   C11

Converts a wide string to a multibyte string.

```
#include <wchar.h>
errno_t wcsrtombs_s(size_t * restrict retval,
                char * restrict dest, rsize_t destmax,
                const wchar_t ** restrict src, rsize_t n,
                mbstate_t * restrict state);
```

The function wcsrtombs_s() is the "restartable" version of wcstombs_s(). It begins
the conversion, not in the initial shift state, but in the shift state specified by the
parameter *state*. The parameter *src* is a pointer to a wchar_t pointer that
addresses the next wide character to be converted. Before it returns, the function
stores a pointer to the next wide character to be read in the object addressed by *src*,
and stores the parse state of the multibyte output string in the object addressed by
state, so that subsequent function calls can continue the string conversion. If the
function finds that the end of the input string has been reached, it puts a null
pointer in the object addressed by *src* and sets the object addressed by *state* to the
initial shift state.

The pointers *retval*, *src*, *src*, and *state* must not be null pointers. Except for the
differences described here, the function wcsrtombs_s() is similar to wcstombs_s().
It returns zero on success, or a nonzero value if an error occurs.

Example

```
#define __STDC_WANT_LIB_EXT1__ 1
#include <wchar.h>
// ...
    wchar_t widestr[] = L"A wide-character string ...";
    const wchar_t *wcptr = widestr;     // A pointer to a wide character.
    char mbstr[100] = "";               // For the multibyte string.
```

```
      size_t mblen = 0;
      mbstate_t mbstate = {0};                    // Conversion state.

      if( wcsrtombs_s( &mblen, mbstr, sizeof(mbstr),
                       &wcptr, 3, &mbstate) == 0)
      {
         printf("Multibyte length: %zu;  character codes: [", mblen);
         for( size_t i = 0; i < mblen; ++i)
            printf(" %X", (unsigned char)mbstr[i]);
         puts(" ]");
         if( wcptr != NULL)
            printf("Wide characters remaining: \"%ls\"\n", wcptr);
      }
```

This example produces the following output:

```
      Multibyte length: 3;  character codes: [ 41 20 77 ]
      Wide characters remaining: "ide character string ..."
```

See Also

wcstombs_s(), wcstombs(), wcsrtombs(), mbstowcs(), mbstowcs_s(), mbsrtowcs(), mbsrtowcs_s()

wcsspn

Searches a wide string for a wide character that is not in a given set.

```
      #include <wchar.h>
      size_t wcsspn( const wchar_t *s1, const wchar_t *s2 );
```

The wcsspn() function returns the index of the first wide character in the string addressed by *s1* that does not match any wide character in the string addressed by *s2*. In other words, the return value is the length of the wide-string segment addressed by *s1* that contains only wide characters which are present in the wide string addressed by *s2*. If all of the wide characters in *s1* are also contained in *s2*, then wcsspn() returns the index of *s1*'s string terminator character, which is the same as wcslen(*s1*).

Example

```
      wchar_t wordin[256];
      double val;
      fputws( L"Enter a floating-point number, please: ", stdout );
      wscanf( L"%ls", wordin );
      int index = wcsspn( wordin, L"+-0123456789eE." );
      if ( index < wcslen( wordin ) )
        wprintf ( L"Sorry, but the character %lc is not permitted.\n",
                wordin[index] );
      else
      {
        swscanf( wordin, L"%lg", &val );
        wprintf( L"You entered the value %g\n", val );
      }
```

See Also

wcscspn(), wcschr(), wcsrchr(), wcsstr(), wcspbrk(), strspn(), strcspn(), strchr(), strrchr(), strstr(), strpbrk()

wcsstr

Searches a wide string for a replica of another wide string.

```
#include <wchar.h>
wchar_t *wcsstr( const wchar_t *s1, const wchar_t *s2 );
```

The wcsstr() function searches the wide string addressed by *s1* for the sequence of wide characters contained in *s2*, not counting the terminating null wide character. The return value is a pointer to the first wide character in the first occurrence in *s1* of the sequence contained in *s2*, or a null pointer if there is no such occurrence. If *s2* points to an empty wide string, then wcsstr() returns the value of its first argument, *s1*.

Example

This simple program prints each line in a file that contains a given keyword:

```
#define MAX_LINE 1024

int main( int argc, char **argv )
{
  FILE *fpIn = NULL;
  wchar_t keyword[MAX_LINE] = { L'\0' };
  wchar_t line[MAX_LINE] = { L'\0' };

  if ( argc != 3 )
  {
    wprintf( L"Syntax: %s <keyword> <filename>\n", argv[0] );
    return -1;
  }

  if (( fpIn = fopen( argv[2], "r" )) == NULL )
    return -2;
  else
    fwide( fpIn, 1 );

  if ( mbstowcs( keyword, argv[1], MAX_LINE ) == -1 )
    return -3;

  int count = 0;
  while ( fgetws( line, MAX_LINE, fpIn ) != NULL )
    if ( wcsstr( line, keyword ) != NULL )
      {
        ++count;
        fputws( line, stdout );
      }
```

```
        if ( !feof( fpIn ))
          return -4;
        else
          return count;
    }
```

See Also

wcspbrk(), wcsspn(), wcscspn(), wcschr(), wcsrchr(), strstr(), strpbrk(), strspn(), strcspn(), strchr(), strrchr()

wcstod, wcstof, wcstold

Converts a wide string into a floating-point number.

```
#include <wchar.h>
double wcstod( const wchar_t * restrict wcs,
               wchar_t ** restrict endptr );
float wcstof( const wchar_t * restrict wcs,
              wchar_t ** restrict endptr );          (C99)
long double wcstold( const wchar_t * restrict wcs,
                     wchar_t ** restrict endptr );   (C99)
```

The wcstod() function attempts to interpret the wide string addressed by its first pointer argument, *wcs*, as a floating-point numeric value, and returns the result with the type double. wcstof() and wcsold() are similar but return float and long double, respectively. Leading whitespace wide characters are ignored, and the converted string ends with the last wide character that can be interpreted as part of a floating-point numeral. The second parameter, *endptr*, is a pointer to a pointer. If its argument value is not a null pointer, then the function stores a pointer to the first wide character that is not part of the numeral converted in the location addressed by the *endptr* argument. (The locations that the function reads from and writes to using its restricted pointer parameters must not overlap.) If no conversion is possible, the function returns 0.

If the resulting value exceeds the range of the function's type, then the return value is positive or negative HUGE_VAL (or HUGE_VALF or HUGE_VALL, for the float and long double variants). On an overflow, the errno variable is set to the value of ERANGE ("range error"). If the conversion produces an underflow, the magnitude of the return value is at most the smallest value greater than 0 that is representable in the function's return type, and the function may set the errno variable to the value of ERANGE ("range error").

The wide-character sequences that can be interpreted as floating-point numerals depend on the current locale. In all locales, they include those described in "Floating-Point Constants" on page 40, and the sequence L"infinity", without regard to uppercase or lowercase, or any sequence of letters, digits, and underscores that begins with L"nan" without regard to case.

Example

```
wchar_t in[1024], *this = in, *next = in;
double val;
fputws( L"Enter some floating-point numbers, please:\n", stdout );
wscanf( L"%l[^\n]", in );

fputws( L"Here are the values you entered:\n", stdout );
while ( 1 )
{
  val = wcstod( this, &next );
  if ( next == this )        // Means no conversion possible.
    break ;
  this = next;
  wprintf( L"\t%g\n", val );
}
fputws( L"Done.\n", stdout );
```

See Also

wcstol(), wcstoul(), and wcstoimax(); strtof(), strtod(), and strtold()

wcstoimax   C99

Converts a wide string into an integer value with type intmax_t.

```
#include <stddef.h>
#include <inttypes.h>
intmax_t wcstoimax( const wchar_t * restrict wcs,
                    wchar_t ** restrict endptr, int base );
```

The wcstoimax() function is similar to wcstol() except that it converts a wide string to an integer value of type intmax_t. If the conversion fails, wcstoimax() returns 0. If the result of the conversion exceeds the range of the type intmax_t, then the wcstoimax() returns INTMAX_MAX or INTMAX_MIN, and sets the errno variable to the value of ERANGE ("range error").

Example

See the example for the analogous function wcstoumax() in this chapter.

See Also

wcstoumax(), wcstol(), and wcstoul(); wcstod(), wcstof(), and wcstold(); strtoimax() and strtoumax()

wcstok

Divides a wide string into tokens.

```
#include <wchar.h>
wchar_t *wcstok( wchar_t * restrict s1, const wchar_t * restrict s2,
                 wchar_t ** restrict ptr );
```

Library
Functions

The wcstok() function isolates tokens in the wide string addressed by *s1* that are delimited by any of the wide characters contained in the string addressed by *s2*. The tokens are identified one at a time by successive calls to wcstok(). On calls after the first, the *s1* argument is a null pointer. The third argument is a pointer to a wchar_t pointer; wcstok() stores caller-specific information at the location addressed by this pointer for use on successive calls in the same sequence.

On the first call, wcstok() searches in *s1* for the first character that does not match any character in *s2*, similarly to the wcsspn() function. The first such wide character found is considered to be the beginning of a token. Then wcstok() searches further for the first wide character that *does* match any of the wide characters in *s2* or the null wide character that terminates the string—whichever comes first, similarly to the wcscspn() function. The first such wide character found is considered to be the delimiter that ends the token. wcstok() then replaces this ending delimiter with L'\0', which modifies the string *s1*. The function returns a pointer to the beginning of the token (or a null pointer if no token was found), after storing a value in the location addressed by the *ptr* argument for use in subsequent wcstok() calls.

On each subsequent call with a null pointer as the *s1* argument and the same value as before for the *ptr* argument, wcstok() behaves similarly but starts the search at the wide character that follows the previous delimiter. You can specify a different set of delimiters in the *s2* argument on each call. The locations that wcstok() reads from and writes to using its restricted pointer arguments must not overlap on any given call.

Example

```
wchar_t *mnemonic, *arg1, *arg2, *comment, *ptr;
wchar_t line[ ] = L"    mul eax,[ebp+4]    ; Multiply by y\n";
// First word between spaces or tabs
mnemonic = wcstok( line, L" \t", &ptr );
arg1 = wcstok( NULL, L",", &ptr );   // From there to the comma is arg1.
                                     // Trim off any spaces later.
arg2 = wcstok( NULL, L";\n", &ptr ); // From there to the semicolon is
                                     // arg2.
// To line or page end is comment:
comment = wcstok( NULL, L"\n\r\v\f", &ptr );

wprintf( L"Mnemonic:     %ls\n"
         L"1st argument: %ls\n"
         L"2nd argument: %ls\n"
         L"Comment:      %ls\n\n",
         mnemonic, arg1, arg2, comment );
```

This code produces the following output:

```
Mnemonic:     mul
1st argument: eax
2nd argument: [ebp+4]
Comment:      Multiply by y
```

wcstok_s   C11

Divides a wide string into tokens.

```
#include <string.h>
wchar_t *wcstok_s( wchar_t * restrict s1, rsize_t * restrict s1max,
                   const wchar_t * restrict s2,
                   wchar_t ** restrict ptr);
```

Like wcstok(), the secure function wcstok_s() divides the string addressed by *s1* into a sequence of tokens delimited by any of the characters contained in the string addressed by *s2*. The tokens are identified one at a time by successive calls to wcstok_s(). On calls after the first, the *s1* argument is a null pointer. The function returns a null pointer if no further token is present in the remaining string. The function modifies the string *s1* by substituting a null wide character (L'\0') for the first delimiter character that follows the token found.

Unlike wcstok(), the secure function wcstok_s() has an additional parameter, *s1max*. On the first function call, the *s1max* argument must point to a variable that contains the length of the wchar_t array *s1*. On each subsequent call, the wcstok_s() function updates the objects addressed by *s1max* and *ptr* so that *ptr* refers to the new starting position in the string, and the variable addressed by *s1max* contains the remaining string length.

The function wcstok_s() also tests the following runtime constraints: the pointers *s1max*, *s2*, and *ptr* must not be null pointers. If *s1* is a null pointer, then *ptr* must not point to a null pointer. The string segment of **s1max* characters from the current starting position must contain the end of a token. If a violation of the runtime constraints occurs, the pointer addressed by *ptr* is not modified and the function returns a null pointer.

Example

See the examples for the functions wcstok() and strtok_s() in this chapter.

See Also

wcstok(), strtok(), strtok_s(), wcsspn(), wcscpn(), and wcsstr()

wcstol, wcstoll

Converts a wide string into a long (or long long) integer value.

```
#include <wchar.h>
long int wcstol( const wchar_t * restrict wcs,
                 wchar_t ** restrict endptr, int base );
```

```
long long int wcstoll( const wchar_t * restrict wcs,
                       wchar_t ** restrict endptr, int base );      (C99)
```

The wcstol() function attempts to interpret the wide string addressed by its first pointer argument, wcs, as an integer numeric value, and returns the result with the type long. wcstoll() is similar, but returns long long. These functions are the wide-string equivalents of strtol() and strtoll(), and they work in the same way, except that they operate on strings of wchar_t rather than char. See the description under strtol() in this chapter.

Example

```
wchar_t date[ ] = L"10/3/2005, 13:44:18 +0100", *more = date;
long day, mo, yr, hr, min, sec, tzone;
day = wcstol( more, &more, 10 );       // &more is the address of a
mo  = wcstol( more+1, &more, 10 );     // pointer
yr  = wcstol( more+1, &more, 10 );
hr  = wcstol( more+1, &more, 10 );
min = wcstol( more+1, &more, 10 );
sec = wcstol( more+1, &more, 10 );
tzone = wcstol( more+1, &more, 10 );

wprintf( L"It's now %02ld:%02ld o'clock on %02ld-%02ld-%02ld.\n",
         hr, min, mo, day, yr % 100 );
```

This code produces the following output:

```
It's now 13:44 o'clock on 03-10-05.
```

See Also

wcstoul(), wcstoull(), wcstod(), wcstof(), and wcstold(); strtol(), strtoll(), strtoul(), and strtoull()

wcstold

See the description under wcstod().

wcstoll

See the description under wcstol().

wcstombs

Converts a wide-character string into a multibyte string.

```
#include <stdlib.h>
size_t wcstombs( char * restrict dest, const wchar_t * restrict src,
                 size_t n );
```

The wcstombs() function converts one or more wide characters from the array addressed by src into a string of multibyte characters, beginning in the initial parse state, and stores the results in the array of char addressed by dest. The third argument, *n*, specifies the maximum number of characters that can be written to the output buffer; conversion ends either when a terminating null character has been written to the output buffer, or when writing another multibyte character would exceed the buffer size of *n* bytes. The wcstombs() function returns the number of bytes written, not including the terminating null character if any, or (size_t)(-1) if an encoding error occurs. The conversion performed on each wide character is the same as that which would be performed by the wctomb() function.

The wcstombs() function terminates the resulting multibyte string with a null character ('\0') only if it has not yet written the maximum number of characters specified by the third argument! If the return value is the same as the specified limit, then the resulting string has not been terminated.

Example

```
wchar_t fmt_amount[128] = { L'\0' };
wchar_t prefix[32]  = L"-";
wchar_t suffix[32]  = L"€";
wchar_t number[128] = L"123.456,78";
char output_amount[256];

wcscpy( fmt_amount, prefix );
wcscat( fmt_amount, number );
wcscat( fmt_amount, suffix );

if ( -1 != wcstombs( output_amount, fmt_amount, 256 ))
    printf( "Full amount: %s\n", output_amount );
```

See Also

wcsrtombs(), mbstowcs(), and wcrtomb(); wctomb(), mbtowc(), and mbrtowc(); the corresponding secure functions

wcstombs_s   C11

Converts a wide string to a multibyte string.

```
#include <stdlib.h>
errno_t wcstombs_s(size_t * restrict retval,
                   char * restrict dest, rsize_t destmax,
                   const wchar_t * restrict src, rsize_t n);
```

The function wcstombs_s() is the "secure" version of the function wcstombs(). It converts the wide string addressed by *src* to a multibyte string. The conversion begins in the initial shift state, and the function's operation is equivalent to calling wcrtomb() for each wide character in the source string.

If *dest* is a null pointer, wcstombs_s() only writes the number of bytes in the multibyte string that would otherwise result, not counting the terminating null character, to the variable addressed by *retval*.

If *dest* is not a null pointer, the multibyte characters are copied to the char array with the length *destmax* addressed by *dest*. The argument *n* specifies the maximum number of bytes that the function may write to the destination. If the length of the complete multibyte string is less than *destmax* and less than or equal to *n*, then the function writes the whole string. Otherwise, *destmax* must be greater than *n*, and the conversion ends when writing the next multibyte character would make the number of output bytes exceed *n*. In any case, the null character '\0' is appended after the last multibyte character, and the number of bytes written (not counting the null character) is stored in the variable addressed by *retval*.

The function wcstombs_s() tests the following runtime constraints: The pointers *retval* and *src* must not be null pointers. If *dest* is a null pointer, the output length argument *destmax* must be zero. If *dest* is not a null pointer, the values of *n* and *destmax* must not be greater than RSIZE_MAX. Furthermore, *destmax* must be greater than the number of bytes that actually need to be stored—that is, either greater than *n* or greater than the number of bytes in the multibyte string, as the case may be.

If a runtime constraint violation occurs and *retval* is not a null pointer, wcstombs_s() stores the value (size_t)(-1) in the object addressed by *retval*. Furthermore, the function writes the string terminator character '\0' to *dest*[0], provided *dest* is not a null pointer and *destmax* is greater than zero and less than RSIZE_MAX.

The wcstombs_s() function also writes the value of (size_t)(-1) to the object addressed by *retval* if an encoding error occurs. The wcstombs_s() function returns zero on success, or a nonzero value if an error occurs.

Example

```
#define __STDC_WANT_LIB_EXT1__ 1
#include <stdlib.h>
// ...
  wchar_t widestr[] = L "A wide-character string ...";
  char mbstr[100] = "";              // For the multibyte string.
  size_t mblen = 0;

  printf("The current locale is %s.\n",
       setlocale(LC_CTYPE, "" ));

  if( wcstombs_s( &mblen, mbstr, sizeof(mbstr), widestr, 5) == 0)
  {
    printf("Multibyte length: %u;  text: \"%s\"\n", mblen, mbstr);
  // ...
  }
```

This example produces the following output:

```
Multibyte length: 5; text: "A wid"
```

wcstombs(), wcsrtombs(), wctomb(), wcrtomb(), mbstowcs(), mbsrtowcs(), mbtowc(), mbrtowc(); the corresponding secure functions

wcstoul, wcstoull

Converts a wide string into an unsigned long (or unsigned long long) integer value.

```
#include <wchar.h>
unsigned long int wcstoul( const wchar_t * restrict wcs,
                      wchar_t ** restrict endptr, int base );
unsigned long long int wcstoull( const wchar_t * restrict wcs,
                            wchar_t ** restrict endptr,
                            int base );      (C99)
```

The wcstoul() function attempts to interpret the wide string addressed by its first pointer argument, wcs, as an integer numeric value, and returns the result with the type unsigned long. wcstoull() is similar, but returns unsigned long long. These functions are the wide-string equivalents of strtoul() and strtoull(), and they work in the same way except that they operate on strings of wchar_t rather than char. See the description for strtol() in this chapter.

If the resulting value is outside the range of the function's type, then the return value is ULONG_MAX, depending on the sign (or ULLONG_MAX, for wcstoull()), and the errno variable is set to the value of ERANGE ("range error").

Example

See the example for the analogous function wcstol() in this chapter.

See Also

wcstol(), wcstod(), wcstof(), and wcstold(); strtol() and strtoul()

wcstoumax   C99

Converts a wide string into an integer value with type uintmax_t.

```
#include <stddef.h>
#include <inttypes.h>
uintmax_t wcstoumax( const wchar_t * restrict wcs,
               wchar_t ** restrict endptr, int base );
```

The wcstoumax() function is similar to wcstoul() except that it converts a wide string to an integer value of type uintmax_t. If the conversion fails, wcstoumax() returns 0. If the result of the conversion exceeds the range of the type uintmax_t, then the wcstoumax() returns UINTMAX_MAX and sets the errno variable to the value of ERANGE ("range error").

Example

```
typedef struct {
  uintmax_t packets, bytes;
  wchar_t   policy[16];
  wchar_t   protocol[6];
  /* ... */
} stats_t ;
stats_t iface_in;

wchar_t wcsstat[] =
        L"25183 1633438 ACCEPT tcp -- eth2 * 0.0.0.0/0 tcp dpts:80";
wchar_t *wcsptr = wcsstat;

iface_in.packets = wcstoumax( wcsptr, &wcsptr, 10 );
iface_in.bytes = wcstoumax( ++wcsptr, &wcsptr, 10 );
/* ... */
wprintf( L"Packets: %" PRIuMAX "; bytes: %" PRIuMAX "; policy: ...\n",
         iface_in.packets, iface_in.bytes );
```

This code produces the following output:

```
Packets: 25183; bytes: 1633438; policy: ...
```

See Also

wcstoimax(), wcstol(), and wcstoul(); wcstod(), wcstof(), and wcstold(); strtoimax() and strtoumax()

wcsxfrm

Transforms a wide string for easier locale-specific comparison.

```
#include <wchar.h>
size_t wcsxfrm( wchar_t * restrict dest, const wchar_t * restrict src,
                size_t n );
```

The wcsxfrm() function transforms the wide string addressed by *src*, and copies the result to the wchar_t array addressed by *dest*. The third argument, *n*, specifies a maximum number of wide characters (including the terminating null wide character) that the function may write to *dest*. The locations that wcsxfrm() reads from and writes to using its restricted pointer parameters must not overlap.

The transformation performed depends on the value of the locale category LC_COLLATE, which you can query or set using the setlocale() function. Furthermore, the wcsxfrm() transformation is related to the wcscoll() function in the following way: if you use wcscmp() to compare two strings produced by wcsxfrm() calls, the result is the same as if you use wcscoll() to compare the original strings passed to wcsxfrm(). Using wcsxfrm() and wcscmp() may be more efficient than wcscoll() if you need to use the same string in many comparisons.

The wcsxfrm() function returns the length of the transformed version of the string, not counting the terminating null character. If this length is greater than or equal to *n*, then the contents of the array at *dest* are indeterminate. The value of *n* may also be 0, in which case *dest* may be a null pointer.

Example

```
typedef struct stringpair { wchar_t * original;
                            wchar_t * xformed;
                          } Stringpair_t ;

int stringpaircmp( const void *p1, const void *p2 );

int main()
{
  wchar_t *originals[] = { L"Chávez", L"Carron",  L"Canoso",
                           L"Cañoso", L"Carteño", L"Corriando",
                           L"Carilo", L"Carillón", };
  wchar_t xformbuffer[1024];

  /* Make an array of structures out of the strings and their
     xformations */

  const int elementcount = sizeof(originals) / sizeof(wchar_t *);
  Stringpair_t stringpairs[elementcount];

  setlocale( LC_ALL, "es_US.UTF-8" );   // Set the locale to US Spanish
  wprintf( L"Sorting order in the locale %s:\n",
           setlocale( LC_COLLATE, NULL ));

  for ( int i = 0; i < elementcount ; i++ )
  {
    stringpairs[i].original = originals[i];
    stringpairs[i].xformed
                = malloc( wcsxfrm( xformbuffer, originals[i], 1024 ));
    if ( stringpairs[i].xformed != NULL )
      wcscpy( stringpairs[i].xformed, xformbuffer );
  }

  qsort( stringpairs, elementcount,
         sizeof(Stringpair_t), stringpaircmp );

  for ( int i = 0; i < elementcount ; i++ )
  {
    fputws( stringpairs[i].original, stdout );
    fputwc( L'\n', stdout );
  }
} // end of main()

/* A comparison function for use by qsort. Uses wcscmp() rather
 * that wcscoll(), assuming strings are paired with their wcsxfrm()
 * results in a Stringpair_t structure.
 */
int stringpaircmp( const void *p1, const void *p2 )
{
```

Library
Functions

```
    const Stringpair_t * sp1 = (Stringpair_t *)p1;
    const Stringpair_t * sp2 = (Stringpair_t *)p2;

    return wcscmp( sp1->xformed, sp2->xformed );
}
```

This code produces the following output:

```
Sorting order in the locale es_US.UTF-8:
Canoso
Cañoso
Carilo
Carillón
Carron
Carteño
Corriando
Chávez
```

See Also

wcscoll(), wcscmp(), strxfrm(), setlocale()

wctob

Obtains the single-byte equivalent of a wide character, if any.

```
#include <stdio.h>
#include <wchar.h>
int wctob( wint_t wc );
```

The wctob() function returns the single-byte member of the extended character set, if there is one, that corresponds to its wide-character argument, wc.

To be more exact, wctob() determines whether there is a character in the extended character set that corresponds to the wide-character value wc, and whose multibyte character representation is expressed in a single byte in the initial shift state of the locale's multibyte encoding. If this is the case, then wctob() returns that character, converted from unsigned char to int. If not, wctob() returns EOF.

Example

```
FILE *fp_inwide;
wchar_t wc;
int bc;

/* ... open the files ... */

fwide( fp_inwide, 1 );
while (( wc = fgetwc( fp_inwide )) != WEOF )
  if (( bc = wctob( wc )) != EOF )
    fputc( c, stdout );
  else                        // If no byte-character equivalent,
    fputc( '?', stdout );     // print a question mark instead.
```

wctomb(), wcrtomb(), wcstombs(), and wcsrtombs(); btowc(), mbtowc(), mbrtowc(), mbstowcs(), and mbsrtowcs()

wctomb

Converts a wide character to a multibyte character, or determines whether the multibyte encoding is stateful.

```
#include <stdlib.h>
int wctomb( char *s, wchar_t wc );
```

The wctomb() function determines the multibyte representation that corresponds to the wide-character value wc, and stores it, including any necessary shift sequences, in the char array addressed by the pointer argument s. The size of this array is assumed to be at least MB_CUR_MAX to accommodate the multibyte character representation. If wc is a null wide character (L'\0'), wctomb() stores a null character, preceded by any necessary shift sequences to restore the initial shift state, in the char array addressed by s. The function returns the number of bytes in the multibyte sequence written, or -1 if the value of wc does not correspond to any valid multibyte character.

If you pass wctomb() a null pointer as the first argument, then the return value indicates whether the current multibyte encoding is stateful. This behavior is the same as that of mblen(). If wctomb() returns 0, then the encoding is stateless. If it returns any other value, the encoding is stateful; that is, the interpretation of a given byte sequence may depend on the shift state.

Example

```
char mbbuffer[MB_LEN_MAX] = { '\0' };
wchar_t wcs[] = L"Wir stehen auf den Füßen von Riesen";
int n = 0, i = 0;

printf( "The current locale is %s.\n", setlocale( LC_CTYPE, "" ));
printf( "The locale's multibyte encoding is %s.\n",
        (wctomb( NULL, L'\0' ) ? "stateful" : "stateless" ));
do {
  n += wctomb( mbbuffer, wcs[i] );
} while ( wcs[i++] != L'\0' );

printf( "The wide string \"%ls\" \nis %u wide characters long.\n"
        "Its multibyte representation requires a buffer of %u bytes.\n",
        wcs, wcslen( wcs ), n );
```

This code produces output like this:

```
The current locale is en_US.UTF-8.
The locale's multibyte encoding is stateless.
The wide string "Wir stehen auf den Füßen von Riesen"
is 35 wide characters long.
Its multibyte representation requires a buffer of 38 bytes.
```

wctob(), wcrtomb(), wcstombs(), and wcsrtombs(); btowc(), mbtowc(), mbrtowc(), mbstowcs(), and mbsrtowcs(); the corresponding secure functions

wctomb_s   C11

Converts a wide character to a multibyte character, or determines whether the multibyte encoding is stateful.

```
#include <stdlib.h>
errno_t wctomb_s( int * restrict status, char * restrict s,
                  rsize_t smax, wchar_t wc);
```

Like wctomb(), the secure function wctomb_s() determines the multibyte representation that corresponds to the wide-character value *wc*, and stores it—including any necessary shift sequences—in the char array addressed by the pointer argument *s*. The length of the multibyte character—that is, the number of bytes written to represent it—is always less than or equal to the value of MB_CUR_MAX. The two functions differ in the following respects:

- The function wctomb_s() provides information about the statefulness of the multibyte encoding, not as the return value but in the int variable addressed by the pointer argument *status*:

  If *s* is not a null pointer, wctomb_s() stores in the object addressed by *status* the length of the multibyte character, or -1 if the value of *wc* does not correspond to a valid multibyte character.

  If *s* is a null pointer, wctomb_s() stores in the object addressed by *status* the value zero if the multibyte character encoding is not stateful, and a nonzero value if it is stateful.

- The function wctomb_s() tests the following runtime constraints: if *s* is not a null pointer, then the value of *smax*, specifying the size of the char array addressed by *s*, must not be less than the length of the multibyte character to be written, and must not be greater than RSIZE_MAX. If *s* is a null pointer, then the length argument *smax* must be zero.

  The variable addressed by *status* is not modified if a violation of the runtime constraints occurs.

The wctomb_s() function returns zero if no error occurs. If a violation of the runtime constraints occurs, or if the value of *wc* does not correspond to any valid multibyte character, the function returns a nonzero value.

Example

```
#define __STDC_WANT_LIB_EXT1__ 1  // For wctomb_s()
#include <stdlib.h>
// ...
int main()
```

```
    {
        setlocale(LC_ALL, "en_US.utf8");

        wchar_t wc = L'\u03B1';        // Greek lowercase alpha α
        char mbStr[MB_CUR_MAX];
        int nBytes = 0;

    // if( (nBytes = wctomb( mbStr, wc )) < 0)
    // is equivalent to
        if( wctomb_s( &nBytes, mbStr, sizeof(mbStr), wc ) != 0)
            { /* error: */ return -1; }
        printf("Wide-character code: %#06x; character: '%lc'; "
                "multibyte code:", wc, wc);
        for( int i = 0; i < nBytes; ++i)
            printf(" %#04x", (unsigned char)mbStr[i]);
        putchar('\n');
        return 0;
    }
```

This example generates the following output:

```
Wide-character code: 0x03b1; character: 'α'; multibyte code: 0xce 0xb1
```

See Also

wctob(), wctomb(), wcrtomb(), wcrtomb_s()

wctrans

Provides a transformation argument for towctrans().

```
#include <wctype.h>
wctrans_t wctrans( const char *property );
```

The wctrans() function obtains a value of type wctrans_t that you can use as an argument to the towctrans() function, and that represents a wide-character mapping in the current locale. The permissible values of the string argument *property* depend on the current locale setting for the LC_CTYPE category, but "tolower" and "toupper" are permissible values in all locales. If the string addressed by *property* does not identify a valid mapping, wctrans() returns 0.

Example

See the example for towctrans() in this chapter.

See Also

towctrans(), towupper(), towlower()

wctype

Provides a property argument for iswctype().

```
#include <wctype.h>
wctype_t wctype( const char *property );
```

The wctype() function constructs a value with type wctype_t that describes a class of wide characters identified by the string argument *property*.

If *property* identifies a valid class of wide characters according to the LC_CTYPE category of the current locale, the wctype() function returns a nonzero value that is valid as the second argument to the iswctype() function; otherwise, it returns 0.

The strings listed in the description of the iswctype() function are valid in all locales as *property* arguments to the wctype() function.

Example

```
wctype_t wct_kanji, wct_kata, wct_hira /* , ... */ ;

setlocale( LC_CTYPE, "ja_JP.UTF-8" );

if (( wct_kata = wctype( "jkata" ) ) == 0 )
   { wprintf( L"The locale doesn't support the wide-character type "
              "string \"jkata\".\n" ); return -1; }
/* ... */
wc = fgetwc( stdin );
if ( iswctype( wc, wct_kata ) )              // Mainly 0xFF66 - 0xFF9F.
   wprintf( L"%lc is a katakana character.\n", wc );
```

See Also

iswctype()

wmemchr

Searches a memory block for a given wide-character value.

```
#include <wchar.h>
wchar_t *wmemchr( const wchar_t *buffer, wchar_t wc, size_t n );
```

The wmemchr() function searches for a wide character with the value of *wc* in a buffer of *n* wide characters beginning at the address in the pointer argument *buffer*. The function returns a pointer to the first occurrence of the specified wide character in the buffer, or a null pointer if the wide character does not occur within the specified number of wide characters.

Example

See the example for wmemcpy() in this chapter.

See Also

wcschr(), wcsrchr(), wcsstr(), wcsspn(), and wcscspn(); memchr(), strchr(), strrchr(), strstr(), strspn(), and strcspn()

wmemcmp

Compares two blocks of wide characters.

```
#include <wchar.h>
int wmemcmp( const wchar_t * restrict b1, const wchar_t * restrict b2,
            size_t n );
```

The wmemcmp() function compares the contents of two memory blocks of *n* wide characters, beginning at the addresses in *b1* and *b2*, until it finds a pair of wide characters that don't match. The function returns a value greater than 0 if the mismatched wide character is greater in b1, or less than 0 if the first mismatched wide character is greater in b2, or 0 if the two buffers are identical over *n* wide characters.

Example

```
#define BUFFERSIZE 4096

wchar_t  first[BUFFERSIZE] = { L'\0' };
wchar_t second[BUFFERSIZE] = { L'\0' };

/* ... read some data into the two buffers ... */

if ( wmemcmp( first, second, BUFFERSIZE ) == 0 )
  printf( "The two buffers contain the same wide-character text.\n" );
```

See Also

wcscmp(), memcmp(), strcmp()

wmemcpy, wmemcpy_s

Copies the contents of a block of wide characters.

```
#include <wchar.h>
wchar_t *wmemcpy( wchar_t * restrict dest, const wchar_t * restrict src,
                 size_t n );
errno_t wmemcpy_s(wchar_t * restrict dest, rsize_t destmax,
                 const wchar_t * restrict src, rsize_t n);
```

The wmemcpy() function copies *n* successive wide characters beginning at the address in *src* to the location beginning at the address in *dest*. The return value is the same as the first argument, *dest*. The two pointer values must be at least *n* wide characters apart so that the source and destination blocks do not overlap; otherwise, the function's behavior is undefined. For overlapping blocks, use wmemmove().

Like wmemcpy(), the function wmemcpy_s() copies a block of *n* wide characters. Unlike wmemcpy(), however, wmemcpy_s() has the additional parameter *destmax*, which specifies the size of the destination block as a number of wide characters. The secure version also tests the following runtime constraints: the pointers *dest* and *src* must not be null pointers. The values of *destmax* and *n* must not be greater than

RSIZE_MAX, and *n* must not be greater than *destmax*. The two memory blocks addressed by *src* and *dest* must not overlap.

If any of the runtime constraints is violated, wmemcpy_s() fills the destination block with null wide characters, provided *dest* is not a null pointer and *destmax* is not greater than RSIZE_MAX.

The function wmemcpy_s() returns zero on success, or a nonzero value if a violation of the runtime constraints occurs.

Example

```
#define BUFFERSIZE 2048          // Size as a number of wchar_t elements.

wchar_t inputbuffer[BUFFERSIZE] = { L'\0' },
        *writeptr = inputbuffer;

struct block { wchar_t *text;
  struct block *next;
  struct block *prev;
} firstblock = { NULL },   // The first block is the list head.
  *tmp = NULL;

struct block *newblock( struct block *lastblock );
                                  // Creates a linked-list member.
wchar_t *storetext( struct block *listhead,
                    wchar_t *buffer,
                    size_t bufsize );
                    // Copies input buffer to a new linked-list member.

int main()
{

  while( fgetws( writeptr, BUFFERSIZE - (writeptr-inputbuffer), stdin)
         != NULL )
    {
      // Set writeptr to end of the input string:
      writeptr = wmemchr( inputbuffer, L'\0',
                          sizeof(inputbuffer) / sizeof(wchar_t) );

      if ( BUFFERSIZE - (writeptr - inputbuffer) < 80 )
                                  // If block full, or nearly so:
          {                       // copy buffer to a data block.
            writeptr = storetext( &firstblock, inputbuffer, BUFFERSIZE );
            if ( writeptr == NULL )      // Out of memory!
              abort();
          }
    }           // Here if fgetws() returns NULL.
  writeptr = storetext( &firstblock, inputbuffer, BUFFERSIZE );
  if ( writeptr == NULL )        // Out of memory!
    abort();
}
// ----------------------------
```

```
wchar_t *storetext(struct block *listhead,
                   wchar_t *buffer, size_t bufsize)
    // Copies input buffer to a new chained-list member;
    // returns pointer to input buffer, or NULL on failure.
{
  struct block *tmp = listhead;  // create new block on end of list ...
  while ( tmp->next != NULL )
    tmp = tmp->next;
  if (( tmp = newblock( tmp )) != NULL )
    wmemcpy( tmp->text, buffer, bufsize ); // ... and copy the text.
  // Or:
  // wmemcpy_s( tmp->text, BUFFERSIZE, buffer, bufsize );
  else  // Out of memory!
    return NULL;

#ifdef DEBUG
  fwprintf( stderr, L"\nStored a block with this text:\n%ls\n",
            tmp->text );
#endif

  return buffer;     // Return pointer to buffer, now ready for reuse.
}
// ---------------------------
struct block *newblock( struct block *lastblock )
    // Allocates a new block and appends it to the chained list;
    // returns pointer to new block, or NULL on failure.
{
  if (( lastblock->next = malloc( sizeof(struct block) )) != NULL
      && ( lastblock->next->text
             = malloc( BUFFERSIZE * sizeof(wchar_t) )) != NULL)
    {
      lastblock->next->prev = lastblock;
      lastblock->next->next = NULL;
      return lastblock->next;
    }
  else                         // Out of memory!
    return NULL;
}
```

See Also

wmemmove(), wcscpy(), wcsncpy(), memcpy(), strcpy(), strncpy(), memmove(); the corresponding secure functions, if the implementation supports the C11 bounds-checking functions (i.e., if the macro __STDC_LIB_EXT1__ is defined)

wmemmove, wmemmove_s

Copies the contents of a block of wide characters.

```
#include <wchar.h>
wchar_t *wmemmove( wchar_t *dest, const wchar_t *src, size_t n );
```

```
errno_t wmemmove_s(wchar_t *dest, rsize_t destmax,
                   const wchar_t *src, rsize_t n);
```

The wmemmove() function copies *n* successive wide characters beginning at the address in *src* to the location beginning at the address in *dest*. The return value is the same as the first argument, *dest*. If the source and destination blocks overlap, copying takes place as if through a temporary buffer; after the function call, each original value from the *src* block appears in *dest*.

Like wmemmove(), the function wmemmove_s() copies a block of *n* wide characters. Unlike wmemmove(), however, wmemmove_s() has the additional parameter *destmax*, which specifies the size of the destination block as a number of wide characters. The function tests the following runtime constraints: the pointers *dest* and *src* must not be null pointers. The values of *destmax* and *n* must not be greater than RSIZE_MAX, and *n* must not be greater than *destmax*.

If any of the runtime constraints is violated, wmemmove_s() fills the destination block with null wide characters, provided *dest* is not a null pointer and *destmax* is not greater than RSIZE_MAX.

The function wmemmove_s() returns zero on success, or a nonzero value if a violation of the runtime constraints occurs.

Example

```
#define LINESIZE   2048      // Sizes as numbers of wchar_t elements.
FILE *fp_input, *fp_tmp;
w_char inputblock[LINESIZE*128], *writeptr;

/* ... Input some lines to the input block ... */

/* Dump most of the block to a temporary file: */
fp_tmp = tmpfile();
fwrite( inputblock, sizeof(wchar_t), LINESIZE*127, fp_tmp );

/* ... push the rest of the block to the front ... */
wmemmove( inputblock, inputblock + LINESIZE*127, LINESIZE );
// or
// wmemmove_s( inputblock, sizeof(inputblock)/sizeof(wchar_t),
//             inputblock + LINESIZE*127, LINESIZE );

/* ... and continue input: */
writeptr -= LINESIZE*127;
/* ... */
```

See Also

wmemcpy() and wcsncpy(); memmove(), memcpy(), and strncpy(); the corresponding secure functions, if the implementation supports the C11 bounds-checking functions (i.e., if the macro __STDC_LIB_EXT1__ is defined)

wmemset

Sets all wide characters in a memory block to a given value.

```
#include <wchar.h>
wchar_t *wmemset( wchar_t *buffer, wchar_t c, size_t n );
```

The wmemset() function sets each wide character in a block of *n* wide characters to the value *c*, beginning at the address in *dest*. The return value is the same as the pointer argument *dest*.

Example

```
#define BLOCKSIZE 2048        // Size as a number of wchar_t elements.
wchar_t *inputblock;

if (( inputblock = malloc( BLOCKSIZE * sizeof(wchar_t))) != NULL )
    wmemset( inputblock, L'~', BLOCKSIZE );
/* ... */
```

See Also

memset(), calloc()

wprintf, wprintf_s

Prints formatted wide-character string output.

```
#include <wchar.h>
int wprintf( const wchar_t * restrict format, ... );
int wprintf_s( const wchar_t * restrict format, ... );      (C11)
```

The functions wprintf() and wprintf_s() are equivalent to the printf() and printf_s() functions except that the format string is a wide-character string and the functions write wide characters to stdout.

Example

See the examples for iswalnum() and wscanf() in this chapter.

See Also

swprintf() and fwprintf(), declared in *stdio.h* and *wchar.h*; vwprint(), vfwprint(), and vswprint(), declared in *stdarg.h*; printf(), fprintf(), sprintf(), and snprintf(), declared in *stdio.h*; vprintf(), vfprintf(), vsprintf(), and vsnprintf(), declared in *stdarg.h*; the wscanf() input functions. Argument conversion in the printf() family of functions is described in detail under printf() in this chapter.

For each of these functions, there is also a corresponding "secure" function, if the implementation supports the C11 bounds-checking functions (i.e., if the macro __STDC_LIB_EXT1__ is defined)

wscanf, wscanf_s

Reads in formatted wide-character data from standard input.

```
#include <stdio.h>
#include <wchar.h>
int wscanf( const wchar_t * restrict format, ... );
int wscanf_s( const wchar_t * restrict format, ... );    (C11)
```

The functions wscanf() and wscanf_s() are similar to scanf() and scanf_s(), except that the format string and the input stream consist of wide characters. The conversion specifications are the same as for the function scanf(), except those described in Table 18-13.

Table 18-13. wscanf() conversion specifications that differ from scanf()

Conversion specification	Argument type	Remarks
%c	char *	Conversion as by wcrtomb()
%lc	wchar_t *	No conversion, no string terminator
%s	char *	Conversion as by wcrtomb()
%ls	wchar_t *	No conversion

Example

```
wchar_t perms[12];
wchar_t name[256];
unsigned int ownerid, groupid, links;
unsigned long size;
int count;

count = wscanf( L"%11l[rwxsStTld+]%u%u%u%lu%*10s%*5s%256ls",
                perms, &links, &ownerid, &groupid, &size, name );

wprintf( L"The file %ls has a length of %lu bytes.\n", name, size );
```

Assume that this code is executed with the following input (produced by the Unix command ls -ln --time-style=long-iso):

```
-rw-r--r--  1 1001 1001 15 2005-03-01 17:23 überlänge.txt
```

The wscanf() function call in the example copies the string "-rw-r--r--" to the array perms, and assigns the integer values 1 to the links variable, 1,001 to ownerid and groupid, and 15 to size. Then it reads and discards the date-and-time information, and copies the rest of the input string, up to a maximum length of 256 wide characters, to the name array. The resulting output is:

```
The file überlänge.txt has a length of 15 bytes.
```

fwscanf(), swscanf(); wcstod(), wcstol(), wcstoul(); scanf(), fscanf(), sscanf(); the wide-character output functions fwprintf(), wprintf(), vfwprint(), and vwprint()

For each of these functions there is also a corresponding "secure" function, if the implementation supports the C11 bounds-checking functions (i.e., if the macro __STDC_LIB_EXT1__ is defined)

Basic Tools

19

Compiling with GCC

This chapter explains how to use GCC to compile executable programs from C source code. First, we present the basic program control options in the order of the corresponding steps in the compiling process. Then we look at how you can use GCC's warning options to troubleshoot your programs. Finally, we summarize the options for optimized compiling.

This chapter should provide you with a basic working knowledge of GCC. If you later need information on special details, such as architecture-specific or system-specific options, this basic orientation will enable you to find what you need in the GCC manual. The manual is included in Texinfo format in the GCC distribution, and is also available in PostScript and HTML formats (*http://gcc.gnu.org/online docs/*).

The GNU Compiler Collection

GCC originally stood for the "GNU C Compiler." Since its beginnings, the program has grown to support a number of other programming languages besides C, including C++, Ada, Objective-C, Fortran, and Java. The acronym GCC has therefore been redefined to mean "GNU Compiler Collection." The compiler incorporates a number of frontends to translate different languages. In this book, of course, we are concerned only with the C frontend.

GCC is also a *multitarget* compiler; in other words, it has interchangeable backends to produce executable output for a number of different computer architectures. As the modular concept would suggest, GCC can also be used as a cross-compiler; that is, you can produce executable programs for machines and operating systems other than the one GCC is running on. However, doing so requires special configuration and installation, and most GCC installations are adapted to compile programs only for the system on which they are hosted.

GCC not only supports many "dialects" of C, but also distinguishes between them; that is, you can use command-line options to control which C standard the compiler adheres to in translating your source code. For example, when you start GCC with the command-line argument -std=c99, the compiler supports the C99 standard. Support for the C11 standard in GCC is incomplete, especially in regard to the multithreading functions declared in the header *thread.h*. This is because GCC's C library has long supported very similar multithreading capabilities under the POSIX standard. For more details, see the page on C11 support (*https://gcc.gnu.org/wiki/C11Status*) in the GCC developers' wiki.

Obtaining and Installing GCC

If you have a Unix-like system, there's a fair chance that GCC is already installed. To find out, type cc --version at the command prompt. If GCC is installed and linked to the default C compiler name cc, you will see the compiler's version number and copyright information:

```
$ cc --version
cc (GCC) 4.9.2
Copyright (C) 2014 Free Software Foundation, Inc.
This is free software; see the source for copying conditions.
There is NO warranty; not even for MERCHANTABILITY or FITNESS
FOR A PARTICULAR PURPOSE.
```

 In the examples in this chapter, the dollar sign ($) at the beginning of a line represents the command prompt. The text that follows it is a command line that you would enter at a console to invoke GCC (or whatever program is named in the command).

It's possible that GCC is installed but not linked to the program name cc. Just in case, try calling the compiler by its proper name:

```
$ gcc --version
```

If GCC is not installed, consult your system vendor to see whether GCC is available in a binary package for your system's software installation mechanism. GCC binary packages are also included in free software systems such as MacPorts (*https://www.macports.org/*) and Homebrew (*http://brew.sh/*) for OS X, and Cygwin (*http://cygwin.org/*) and MinGW (*http://www.mingw.org/*) for Windows.

Cygwin is an extensive collection of GNU and other open source tools that provide a Unix-like environment, oriented after the POSIX standard, on Windows. The foundation of Cygwin is the dynamically shared library *cygwin1.dll*, which provides Unix-like system functions to the Cygwin programs while interacting with the underlying Windows system. Programs compiled with GCC for Cygwin also require the runtime library *cygwin1.dll*. The Cygwin setup program (*https://cygwin.com*) initially installs the base packages, and launches a package manager in which you can select other Cygwin software to install, including *gcc*, *make*, and *gdb*. You can run the setup program at any time to add, remove, and update programs.

MinGW also provides the GCC compiler for Windows, but unlike Cygwin, the MinGW version of GCC generates native 32-bit Windows programs that require no special runtime library. The variant MinGW-w64, also called MinGW64, can also produce 64-bit programs. You can install the latest version of MinGW using the setup program available at *http://sourceforge.net/projects/mingw* or *http://source forge.net/projects/mingw-w64*.

Note that the Cygwin package manager also allows you to install MinGW-GCC packages. GCC then functions as a cross-compiler, running on Cygwin but producing Windows programs that do not use *cygwin1.dll*.

The GCC website maintains a list of GCC binary packages compiled by third parties for a variety of systems at *http://gcc.gnu.org/install/binaries.html*. Otherwise, if your system has another C compiler, you can obtain the source code of GCC from the Free Software Foundation and compile it on your system according to the step-by-step instructions at *http://gcc.gnu.org/install/*.

Compiling C Programs with GCC

When you run GCC, its default behavior is to produce an executable program file from one or more specified source code files. To start with a simple example, we'll run GCC to make a finished executable program from the C source code in Example 1-1:

```
$ gcc -Wall circle.c
```

This command line contains only the compiler's name, the source filename, and one option: -Wall instructs GCC to print warnings if it finds certain problems in the program (see "Compiler Warnings" on page 683 for more information). If there are no errors in the source code, GCC runs and exits without writing to the screen. Its output is a program file in the current working directory with the default name *a.out* (in Windows, the default name is *a.exe*). We can run this new program file:

```
$ ./a.out
```

The program then produces the screen output shown in Example 1-1.

If you do not want the executable program file to be named *a.out*, you can specify an output filename on the command line using the -o option:

```
$ gcc -Wall -o circle circle.c
```

This command produces the same executable, but it is now named *circle*.

Step by Step

The following sections present GCC options to let you control each stage of the compiling process: *preprocessing, compiling, assembling,* and *linking.* You can also perform the individual steps by invoking separate tools, such as the C preprocessor *cpp*, the assembler *as*, and the linker *ld*. GCC can also be configured to use such external programs on a given host system. For the sake of a uniform overview, however, this chapter shows you how to perform all four steps by invoking GCC and letting it control the process.

Preprocessing

Before submitting the source code to the compiler, the preprocessor executes directives and expands macros in the source files (see steps 1 through 4 in "The C Compiler's Translation Phases" on page 19). GCC ordinarily leaves no intermediate output file containing the results of this preprocessing stage. However, you can save the preprocessor output for diagnostic purposes by using the -E option, which directs GCC to stop after preprocessing. The preprocessor output is directed to the standard output stream, unless you indicate an output filename using the -o option:

```
$ gcc -E -o circle.i circle.c
```

Because header files can be large, the preprocessor output from source files that include several headers is often unwieldy.

You may find it helpful to use the -C option as well, which prevents the preprocessor from removing comments from source and header files:

```
$ gcc -E -C -o circle.i circle.c
```

The following commonly used options affect GCC's behavior in the preprocessor phase:

-D*name*[=*definition*]
:   Defines the symbol *name* before preprocessing the source files. The macro *name* must not be defined in the source and header files themselves. Use this option together with #ifdef *name* directives in the source code for conditional compiling. If you do not specify a replacement value, the macro is defined with the value 1.

-U*name*
:   "Undefines" the symbol *name*, if defined on the command line or in GCC's default settings. The -D and -U options are processed in the order in which they occur on the command line.

-I*directory*[:*directory*[...]]
:   When header files are required by #include directives in the source code, search for them in the specified directory (or directories), in addition to the system's standard *include* directories.

-iquote *directory*[:*directory*[...]]
:   This option is new in recent versions of GCC, and specifies a directory to be searched for header files named in quotation marks, not angle brackets, in an #include directive.

-isystem *directory*[:*directory*[...]]

This option specifies a directory to be searched for system header files in addition to, and before, the standard system include directories. An equals sign at the beginning of the directory specification is treated as a placeholder for the system root directory, which you can modify for this purpose using the --sysroot or -isysroot option.

-isysroot *directory*

This option specifies the system root directory for the purpose of searching for header files. For example, if the compiler would ordinarily search for system header files in */usr/include* and its subdirectories, this option causes it to search for them in *directory*/usr/include and its subdirectories instead. (The --sysroot option, with a second hyphen instead of the *i*, does the same thing for library searches—or for both library and header file searches if no isysroot option is present.)

-I-

This deprecated option has been made unnecessary in newer GCC versions by the -iquote option. It was formerly used to divide all the -I*directory* options on the command line into two groups. All directories appended to an -I option to the *left* of -I- are treated as if named in -iquote options; that is, they are searched only for header files named in quotation marks in the #include directive.

All directories appended to an -I option to the *right* of -I- are searched for header files named in any #include directive, whether the filename is enclosed in quotation marks or in angle brackets.

Furthermore, if -I- appears on the command line, then the directory containing the source file itself is no longer automatically searched first for header files.

The usual search order for *include* directories is:

1. The directory containing the given source file (for filenames given in quotation marks in an #include directive).

2. Directories specified by -iquote options, in command-line order. These directories are searched only for header files named in quotation marks in the #include directive.

3. Directories specified by -I options, in command-line order.

4. Directories specified in the environment variable CPATH.

5. Directories specified by -isystem options, in command-line order.

6. Directories specified in the environment variable C_INCLUDE_PATH.

7. The system's default *include* directories.

See also the section on #include directives, "Inserting the Contents of Header Files" on page 262.

Compiling

At the heart of the compiler's job is the translation of C programs into the machine's assembly language.[1] Assembly language is a human-readable programming language that correlates closely to the actual machine code. Consequently, there is a different assembly language for each CPU architecture.

 Assembly language is often referred to more simply as "assembler." Strictly speaking, however, the term "assembler" refers to the program that translates assembly language into machine code. In this chapter, we use "assembly language" to refer to the human-readable code and "assembler" to refer to the program that translates assembly language into a binary object file.

Ordinarily, GCC stores its assembly-language output in temporary files, and deletes them immediately after the assembler has run. But you can use the -S option to stop the compiling process after the assembly-language output has been generated. If you do not specify an output filename, GCC with the -S option creates an assembly-language file with a name ending in *.s* for each input file compiled. Here is an example:

```
$ gcc -S circle.c
```

The compiler preprocesses *circle.c* and translates it into assembly language, and saves the results in the file *circle.s*. To include the names of C variables as comments on the assembly language statements that access those variables, use the additional option -fverbose-asm:

```
$ gcc -S -fverbose-asm circle.c
```

Assembling

Because each machine architecture has its own assembly language, GCC invokes an assembler on the host system to translate the assembly-language program into executable binary code. The result is an *object file*, which contains the machine code to

---

1 Actually, as a *retargetable* compiler, GCC doesn't translate C statements directly into the target machine's assembly language, but uses an intermediate language called *Register Transfer Language* or *RTL*, between the input language and the assembly-language output. This abstraction layer allows the compiler to choose the most economical way of coding a given operation in any context. Furthermore, an abstract description of the target machine in an interchangeable file provides a structured way to retarget the compiler to new architectures. From the point of view of GCC users, though, we can ignore this intermediate step.

---

perform the functions defined in the corresponding source file, and also contains a *symbol table* describing all objects in the file that have external linkage.

If you invoke GCC to compile and link a program in one command, then its object files are only temporary, and are deleted after the linker has run. Most often, however, compiling and linking are done separately. The -c option instructs GCC not to link the program but to produce an object file with the filename ending *.o* for each input file:

```
$ gcc -c circle.c
```

This command produces the object file *circle.o*.

You can use GCC's option -Wa to pass command-line options to the assembler itself. For example, suppose we want the assembler to run with the following options:

-as=circle.sym

Print the module's symbol table in a separate listing, and save the specified listing output in a filenamed *circle.sym*.

-L

Include local symbols—that is, symbols representing C identifiers with internal linkage—in the symbol table. (Don't confuse this assembler option with the GCC option -L!)

We can have GCC add these options to its invocation of the assembler by appending them as a comma-separated list to GCC's own -Wa option:

```
$ gcc -v -o circle -Wa,-as=circle.sym,-L circle.c
```

The list must begin with a comma after -Wa and contain no spaces. You can also use additional -Wa options in the same command. The -v option, which makes GCC print the options applied at each step of compiling, allows you to see the resulting assembler command line (along with a great deal of other information).

You can append several switches to the assembler's -a option to control the listing output. For a full reference, see the assembler's manual. The default listing output, produced when you simply specify -a with no additional switches, contains the assembly language code followed by the symbol table.

GCC's -g option makes the compiler include debugging information in its output. If you specify the -g option in addition to the assembler's -a option, then the resulting assembly language listing is interspersed with the corresponding lines of C source code:

```
$ gcc -g -o circle -Wa,-a=circle.list,-L circle.c
```

The resulting listing file, *circle.list*, allows you to examine, line by line, how the compiler has translated the C statements in the program *circle*.

Linking

The linker joins a number of binary object files into a single executable file. In the process, it has to complete the external references among your program's various modules by substituting the final locations of the objects for the symbolic references. The linker does this using the same information that the assembler provides in the symbol table.

Furthermore, the linker must also add the code for any C standard library functions you have used in your program. In the context of linking, a *library* is simply a set of object files collected in a single archive file for easier handling.

 When you link your program to a library, only its member object files containing the functions you use are actually linked into your program. To make libraries of your own out of object files that you have compiled, use the utility *ar*. See its manual page for information.

The bulk of the standard library functions are ordinarily in the file *libc.a* (the ending *.a* stands for "archive") or in a shareable version for dynamic linking in *libc.so* (the ending *.so* stands for "shared object"). These libraries are generally in */lib/* or */usr/lib/*, or in another library directory that GCC searches by default.

Non-standard libraries. Certain functions are contained in separate library files, and for many applications you will want to use library functions that are not part of the C standard library. To see how to link such libraries, let's write another version of *circle.c* from Example 1-1 that uses the ncurses console output library available on many systems.

Example 19-1. A version of circle.c with ncurses console output

```
// circle.c: Calculate the areas of circles and
// print them in ncurses mode

#include <curses.h>            // Console control functions
double circularArea( double r );  // Function for the math
void circle();                 // Function for output

int main()       // Starts and stops curses display mode
{

/* Set up the console behavior: */
    (void) initscr();     // Initialize the curses system
    keypad(stdscr, TRUE); // Enable keyboard mapping
    (void) nonl();        // Disable line-end translation
    (void) cbreak();      // Take single input characters

/* Run the circle routine: */
```

```
    circle();
    printw( "Press any key to exit." );
    refresh();              // Put the output on the screen

/* Finish: */
    getch();                // Wait for user to press a key
    endwin();               // Shut down the ncurses console
    return 0;
}

// The circle.c program from Example 1.1 but replacing the
// standard library function printf() with printw() from the
// ncurses library.
void circle()
{
  double radius = 1.0, area = 0.0;
  printw("    Areas of Circles\n\n" );
  printw("    Radius          Area\n"
         "-----------------------\n" );
  area = circularArea( radius );
  printw( "%10.1f    %10.2f\n", radius, area );
  radius = 5.0;
  area = circularArea( radius );
  printw( "%10.1f    %10.2f\n", radius, area );
}

// Return the area of a circle with radius r
double circularArea( double r )
{
  const double pi = 3.1415926536; // Pi is a constant
  return  pi * r * r;
}
```

Example 19-1 adds the directive #include <curses.h> at the beginning of the source file to declare the new external functions, because the ncurses functions initscr(), printw(), refresh(), etc. are not defined in the source code, nor in the C standard library. To compile this *circle.c*, we have to use the -l option to link the ncurses library as well:

```
$ gcc -o circle circle.c -lncurses
```

The filename of the ncurses library is *libncurses.a*. (On systems that support dynamic linking, GCC automatically uses the shared library *libncurses.so*, or *libncurses.dylib* on Darwin if it is available. See "Dynamic Linking and Shared Object Files" on page 680 for more details.) The prefix *lib* and the suffix *.a* are standard, and GCC adds them automatically to whatever base name follows the -l on the command line—in this case, *ncurses*.

Normally, GCC automatically searches for a file with the library's name in standard library directories, such as */usr/lib*. There are three ways to link a library that is not in a path where GCC searches for it. One is to present GCC with the full path and filename of the library as if it were an object file. For example, if the library were named *libncurses.a* and located in */usr/local/lib*, the following command would make GCC compile *circle.c*, and then link the resulting *circle.o* with *libncurses.a*:

```
$ gcc -o circle circle.c /usr/local/lib/libncurses.a
```

In this case the library filename must be placed after the name of the source or object files that use it. This is because the linker works through the files on its command line sequentially, and does not go back to an earlier library file to resolve a reference in a later object.

The second way to link a library that is not in GCC's search path is to use the -L option to add another directory for GCC to search for libraries:

```
$ gcc -o circle -L/usr/local/lib -lncurses circle.c
```

You can add more than one library directory either by using multiple -L options, or by using one -L followed by a colon-separated path list. The third way to make sure GCC finds the necessary libraries is to make sure that the directories containing your libraries are listed in the environment variable LIBRARYPATH.

Passing options to the linker. You can pass options directly to the linker stage using -Wl followed by a comma-separated list, as in this command:

```
$ gcc -lncurses -Wl,-Map,circle.map circle.c circulararea.c
```

The option -Wl,-Map,circle.map on the GCC command line passes the option -Map,circle.map to the linker command line, instructing the linker to print a link script and a memory map of the linked executable to the specified file, circle.map.

The list must begin with a comma after -Wl, and must contain no spaces. In case of doubt, you can use several -Wl options in the same GCC command line. Use the -v option to see the resulting linker command.

All of the above

There is another GCC option that offers a convenient way to obtain all the intermediate output files at once, and that is -save-temps. When you use that option, GCC will compile and link normally, but will save all preprocessor output, assembly language, and object files in the current directory. The intermediate files produced with the -save-temps option have the same base filename as the corresponding source files, with the endings *.i*, *.s*, and *.o* for preprocessor output, assembly language, and object files, respectively.

None of the above

If you invoke GCC with the option -fsyntax-only, it does not preprocess, compile, assemble, or link. It merely tests the input files for correct syntax. See also "Compiler Warnings" on page 683.

Multiple Input Files

In Chapter 1, we went on to divide *circle.c* into two separate source files (see Examples 1-2 and 1-3). Compiling multiple source files results in multiple *object files*, each containing the machine code and symbols corresponding to the objects in one source file. GCC uses temporary files for the object output, unless you use the option -c to instruct it to compile only, and not link:

```
$ gcc -c circle.c
$ gcc -c circulararea.c
```

These commands produce two object files in the current working directory named *circle.o* and *circulararea.o*. You can achieve the same result by putting both source filenames on one GCC command line:

```
$ gcc -c circle.c circulararea.c
```

In practice, however, the compiler is usually invoked for one small task at a time. Large programs consist of many source files, which have to be compiled, tested, edited, and compiled again many times during development, and very few of the changes made between builds affect all source files. To save time, a tool such as *make* (see Chapter 20) controls the build process, invoking the compiler to recompile only those object files that are older than the latest version of the corresponding source file.

Once all the object files have been compiled from current source files, you can use GCC to link them:

```
$ gcc -o circle circle.o circulararea.o -lncurses
```

GCC assumes that files with the filename extension *.o* are object files to be linked.

File types

The compiler recognizes a number of file extensions that pertain to C programs, interpreting them as follows:

.c

    C source code, to be preprocessed before compiling.

.i

    C preprocessor output, ready for compiling.

.h

    C header file. (To save time compiling many source files that include the same headers, GCC allows you to create "precompiled header" files, which it then uses automatically as appropriate.)

.s

    Assembly language.

.S

Assembly language with C preprocessor directives, to be preprocessed before assembling.

GCC also recognizes the file extensions *.ii*, *.cc*, *.cp*, *.cxx*, *.cpp*, *.CPP*, *.c++*, *.C*, *.hh*, *.H*, *.m*, *.mi*, *.f*, *.for*, *.FOR*, *.F*, *.fpp*, *.FPP*, *.r*, *.ads*, and *.adb*; these file types are involved in compiling C++, Objective-C, Fortran, or Ada programs. A file with any other filename extension is interpreted as an object file ready for linking.

If you use other naming conventions for your input files, you can use the option `-x`*file_type* to specify how GCC should treat them. *file_type* must be one of the following: `c`, `c-header`, `cpp-output`, `assembler` (meaning that the file contains assembly language), `assembler-with-cpp`, or `none`. All files that you list on the command line following an `-x` option will be treated as the type that you specify. To change types, use `-x` again. For example:

```
$ gcc -o bigprg mainpart.c -x assembler trickypart.asm -x c otherpart.c
```

You can use the `-x` option several times on the same command line to indicate files of different types. The option `-x none` turns off the file type indication, so that subsequent filenames are interpreted according to their endings again.

Mixed input types

You can mix any combination of input file types on the GCC command line. The compiler ignores any files that cannot be processed as you request. Here is an example:

```
$ gcc -c circle.c circulararea.s /usr/lib/libm.a
```

With this command line, assuming all the specified files are present, GCC compiles and assembles *circle.c*, assembles *circulararea.s*, and ignores the library file, because the `-c` option says not to do any linking. The results are two object files: *circle.o* and *circulararea.o*.

Dynamic Linking and Shared Object Files

Shared libraries are special object files that can be linked to a program at runtime. The use of shared libraries has a number of advantages: a program's executable file is smaller, and shared modules permit modular updating, as well as more efficient use of the available memory.

To create a shared object file, use GCC's `-shared` option. The input file must be an existing object file. Here is a simple example using our *circle* program:

```
$ gcc -c circulararea.c
$ gcc -shared -o libcirculararea.so circulararea.o
```

The second of these two commands creates the shared object file *libcirculararea.so*. To link an executable to a shared object file, name the object file on the command line like any other object or library file:

```
$ gcc -c circle.c
$ gcc -o circle circle.o libcirculararea.so -lncurses
```

This command creates an executable that dynamically links to *libcirculararea.so* at runtime. Of course, you will also have to make sure that your program can find the shared library at runtime—either by installing your libraries in a standard directory, such as */usr/lib*, or by setting an appropriate environment variable such as LIBRARY_PATH. The mechanisms for configuring dynamic loading vary from one system to another.

If shared libraries are available on your system but you want to avoid using them— to exclude a potential opening for rogue code, for example—there are two ways to build statically linked executables with GCC. One is to use the -static option, as in the following command:

```
$ gcc -static -o circle circle.o circulararea.o -lncurses
```

The other is to specify a statically linking version of the external library instead of using the -l option on the command line:

```
$ gcc -o circle circle.o circulararea.o /usr/lib/libncurses.a
```

The resulting program file may be much larger than the dynamically linked one, however.

Freestanding Programs

In addition to the object and library files you specify on the GCC command line, the linker must also link in the system-specific startup code that the program needs in order to load and interact smoothly with the operating system. This code is already on hand in a standard object file named *crt0.o*, which contains the actual entry point of the executable program. (The *crt* stands for "C runtime.") On most systems, GCC also links programs by default with initialization and clean-up routines in object files named *crtbegin.o* and *crtend.o*.

However, if you are writing a freestanding program, such as an operating system or an application for an embedded microcontroller, you can instruct GCC not to link this code by using the -ffreestanding and -nostartfiles options. The option -nostdlib allows you to disable automatic linking to the C standard library. If you use this option, you must provide your own versions of any standard functions used in your program. Finally, in a freestanding environment, a C program need not begin with main(). You can use the linking option -e*name* on the GCC command line to specify an alternative entry point for your program.

C Dialects

When writing a C program, one of your first tasks is to decide which of the various definitions of the C language applies to your program. GCC's default dialect is "GNU C11," which is largely the ISO/IEC 9899:2011 standard, with a certain number of extensions, and without the C11 standard's optional multithreading features.

These extensions include many features that have since been standardized in C99—such as complex floating-point types and long long integers—as well as other features that have not been adopted, such as complex integer types and zero-length arrays. The full list of extensions is provided in the GCC documentation (*https://gcc.gnu.org/onlinedocs/*). To turn off all the GNU C extensions, use the command-line option -ansi.

GCC's language standardization options are:

-std=iso9899:1990, -std=c90, -std=c89, -ansi
> These options all mean the same thing: conform to ISO/IEC 9899:1990, including Technical Corrigenda of 1994 and 1996. They do *not* mean that no extensions are accepted: only those GNU extensions that conflict with the ISO standard are disabled, such as the typeof operator.

-std=iso9899:199409
> Conform to "AMD1," the 1995 internationalization amendment to ISO/IEC 9899:1990.

-std=iso9899:1999, -std=c99
> Conform to ISO/IEC 9899:1999, with the Technical Corrigendum of 2001. GCC supports nearly all provisions of C99. See *http://gcc.gnu.org/c99status.html* for details.

-std=iso9899:2011, -std=c11
> Conform to ISO/IEC 9899:2011. Support for the mandatory features of the C11 is largely complete (although the GNU standard C library, GLIBC, does not support the multithreading features defined in *threads.h*). See *https://gcc.gnu.org/wiki/C11Status* for details.

-std=gnu89, -std=gnu90
> These options are equivalent and mean: Support ISO/IEC 9899:1990 and the GNU extensions. This dialect was GCC's default before version 5.

-std=gnu99
> Conform to ISO/IEC 9899:1999 with the GNU extensions.

-std=gnu11
> Conform to ISO/IEC 9899:2011 with the GNU extensions. The GNU dialect of C11 is the default beginning in GCC version 5.

With any of these options, you must also add the option -pedantic if you want GCC to issue all the warnings that are required by the given standard version, and to reject all extensions that are prohibited by the standard. The option -pedantic-errors causes compiling to fail when such warnings occur.

Earlier versions of GCC also offered a -traditional option, which was intended to provide support for pre-ANSI or "K&R-style" C. Currently, GCC supports this option only in the preprocessing stage, and accepts it only in conjunction with the -E option, which directs GCC to perform preprocessing and then exit.

Furthermore, a number of GCC options allow you to enable or disable individual aspects of different standards and extensions. For example, the -trigraphs option enables trigraphs (see "Digraphs and Trigraphs" on page 12) even if you have not used the -ansi option. For the full list of available dialect options, see the GCC manual (*https://gcc.gnu.org/onlinedocs/*).

Compiler Warnings

You'll get two types of complaints from GCC when compiling a C program. *Error messages* refer to problems that make your program impossible to compile. *Warnings* refer to conditions in your program that you might want to know about and change—for stricter conformance to a given standard, for example—but that do not prevent the compiler from finishing its job. You may be able to compile and run a program in spite of some compiler warnings—although that doesn't mean it's a good idea to do so.

GCC gives you very fine control over the warning messages that it provides. For example, if you don't like the distinction between errors and warnings, you can use the -Werror option to make GCC stop compiling on any warning as if it were an error. Other options let you request warnings about archaic or nonstandard usage, and about many kinds of C constructs in your programs that are considered hazardous, ambiguous, or sloppy.

You can enable most of GCC's warnings individually by using options that begin with -W. For example, the option -Wswitch-default causes GCC to produce a warning message whenever you use a switch statement without a default label, and -Wsequence-point provides a warning when the value of an expression between two sequence points depends on a subexpression that is modified in the same interval (see "Side Effects and Sequence Points" on page 70).

The easiest way to request these and many other warnings from GCC is to use the command-line option -Wall. However, the name of this option is somewhat misleading: -Wall does not enable *all* of the individual -W options. Quite a few more must be asked for specifically by name, such as -Wshadow; this option gives you a warning whenever you define a variable with block scope that has the same name as, and thus "shadows," another variable with a larger scope. Such warnings are not among those produced by -Wall.

If you use the -Wall option but want to disable a subset of the warnings it causes, you can insert no- after the -W in the names of individual warning options. For example, -Wno-switch-default turns off warnings about switch statements without default. Furthermore, the -w option (that's a lowercase w) anywhere on the command line turns off all warnings.

The option -Wextra (formerly named simply -W, with no suffix) adds warnings about a number of legal but questionable expressions, such as testing whether an unsigned value is negative or non-negative:

```
unsigned int u;
/* ... */
if ( u < 0 )
    { /* ... this block is never executed ... */ }
```

The -Wextra option also warns about expressions that have no side effects and whose value is discarded. The full set of conditions it checks for is described in the GCC reference manual (*https://gcc.gnu.org/onlinedocs/*).

Furthermore, if you are updating older programs, you may want to use -Wtraditional to request warnings about constructs that have different meanings in old-style C and ISO standard C, such as a string literal in a macro body that contains the macro's argument:

```
#define printerror(x)    fputs("x\n", stderr)
```

In older, "traditional" C, this macro would work as intended, but in ISO standard C, it would print the letter "x" and a newline character each time you use it. Hence for this line -Wtraditional would generate a warning such as the following:

```
file:line:column: warning: macro argument "x" would be stringified in
traditional C
```

Optimization

GCC can apply many techniques to make the executable program that it generates faster and/or smaller. These techniques all tend to reduce still further the "word-for-word" correspondence between the C program you write and the machine code that the computer reads. As a result, they can make debugging more difficult, and are usually applied only after a program has been tested and debugged without optimization.

There are two kinds of optimization options. You can apply individual optimization techniques by means of options beginning with -f (for *flag*), such as -fmerge-constants, which causes the compiler to place identical constants in a common location, even across different source files. You can also use the -O options (-O0, -O1, -O2, and -O3) to set an optimization level that cumulatively enables a number of techniques at once.

The -O Levels

Each of the -O options represents a number of individual optimization techniques. The -O optimization levels are cumulative: -O2 includes all the optimizations in -O1, and -O3 includes -O2. For complete and detailed descriptions of the different levels, and the many -f optimization options that they represent, see the GCC reference manual. The following list offers a brief description of each level:

-O0

Turn off all optimization options.

-O, -O1

Try to make the executable program smaller and faster, but without increasing compiling time excessively. The techniques applied include merging identical constants, basic loop optimization, and grouping stack operations after successive function calls. A -O with no number is interpreted as -O1.

-O2

Apply almost all of the supported optimization techniques that do not involve a tradeoff between program size and execution speed. This option generally increases the time needed to compile. In addition to the optimizations enabled by -O1, the compiler performs *common subexpression elimination*, or *CSE*, which involves detecting mathematically equivalent expressions in the program and rewriting the code to evaluate them only once, saving the value in an unnamed variable for reuse. Furthermore, instructions are reordered to reduce the time spent waiting for data moving between memory and CPU registers. Incidentally, the data flow analysis performed at this level of optimization also allows the compiler to provide additional warnings about the use of uninitialized variables.

-O3

Generate inline functions and enable more flexible allocation of variables to processor registers. Includes the -O2 optimizations.

-Os

Optimize for size. This option is like -O2, but without those performance optimizations that are likely to increase the code size. Furthermore, block reordering and the alignment of functions and other jump destinations on power-of-two byte boundaries are disabled. If you want small executables, you should be compiling with the GCC option -s, which instructs the linker to strip all the symbol tables out of the executable output file after all the necessary functions and objects have been linked. This makes the finished program file significantly smaller, and is often used in building a production version.

The following example illustrates how -O options are used:

```
$ gcc -Wall -O3 -o circle circle.c circulararea.c -lncurses
```

This command uses -O3 to enable the majority of the supported optimization techniques.

The -f Flags

GCC's many -f options give you even finer control over optimization. For example, you can set a general optimization level using an -O option, and then turn off a certain technique. Here is an example:

```
$ gcc -Wall -O3 -fno-inline-functions -o circle circle.c \
circulararea.c -lncurses
```

The options -O3 -fno-inline-functions in this command enable all the optimizations grouped in -O3 except inline compiling of functions.

There are also flags to enable many optimizations that are not included in any -O level, such as -funroll-loops; this option replaces loop statements that have a known, small number of iterations with repetitive, linear code sequences, thus saving jumps and loop-counter operations. A full list of the hundred or so -f options that control GCC's individual optimization flags would be too long for this chapter, but the examples in this section offer a hint of the capabilities available. If you need a certain compiler feature, there's a good chance you'll find it in the GCC manual (*https://gcc.gnu.org/onlinedocs/*).

Floating-Point Optimization

Some of the optimization options that are not included in the -O groups pertain to floating-point operations. The C99 floating-point environment supports scientific and mathematical applications with a high degree of numeric accuracy, but for a given application, you might be more interested in speed than in the best floating-point math available. For such cases, the -ffast-math option defines the preprocessor macro __FAST_MATH__, indicating that the compiler makes no claim to conform to IEEE and ISO floating-point math standards. The -ffast-math flag is a group option, which enables the following six individual options:

-fno-math-errno
> Disables the use of the global variable errno for math functions that represent a single floating-point instruction.

-funsafe-math-optimizations
> The "unsafe math optimizations" are those that might violate floating-point math standards, or that do away with verification of arguments and results. Using such optimizations may involve linking code that modifies the floating-point processor's control flags.

-fno-trapping-math
> Generates "nonstop" code on the assumption that no math exceptions will be raised that can be handled by the user program.

-ffinite-math-only
> Generates executable code that disregards infinities and NaN ("not a number") values in arguments and results.

-fno-rounding-math
> This option indicates that your program does not depend on a certain rounding behavior, and does not attempt to change the floating-point environment's default rounding mode. This setting is currently the default, and its opposite, -frounding-math, is still experimental.

`-fno-signaling-nans`

This option permits optimizations that limit the number of floating-point exceptions that may be raised by signaling NaNs. This setting is currently the default, and its opposite, `-fsignaling-nans`, is still experimental.

Architecture-Specific Optimization

For certain system architectures, GCC provides options to produce optimized code for specific members of the processor family, taking into account features such as memory alignment, model-specific CPU instructions, stack structures, increased floating-point precision, prefetching and pipelining, and others. These machine-specific options begin with the prefix `-m`. If you want to compile your code to make the most of a specific target system, read about the available options in the GCC reference manual.

For several processor types, such as the Sparc, ARM, and RS/6000-PowerPC series, the option `-mcpu=`*cpu* generates machine code for the specific CPU type's register set, instruction set, and scheduling behavior. Programs compiled with this option may not run at all on a different model in the same CPU family. The GCC reference manual lists the available *cpu* abbreviations for each series.

The option `-mtune=`*cpu* is more tolerant. Code generated with `-mtune=`*cpu* uses optimized scheduling parameters for the given CPU model but adheres to the family's common instructions and registers, so that it should still run on a related model.

For the Intel x86 series, the `-mcpu=`*cpu* option is the same as `-mtune=`*cpu*. The option to enable a model-specific instruction set is `-march=`*cpu*. Here's an example:

```
$ gcc -Wall -O -march=athlon-4 -o circle circle.c circulararea.c \
-lncurses
```

This command line compiles a program for the AMD Athlon XP CPU.

Why Not Optimize?

Sometimes there are good reasons not to optimize. In general, compiling with optimization takes longer and requires more memory than without optimization. How much more depends on the techniques that are applied. Furthermore, the performance gains obtained by a given optimization technique depend on both the given program and the target architecture. If you really need optimum performance, you need to choose the techniques that will work in your specific circumstances.

You can combine both `-O` and `-f` optimization options with GCC's `-g` option to include debugging information in the compiled program, but if you do, the results may be hard to follow in a debugging program; optimization can change the order of operations, and variables defined in the program may not remain associated with one register, or may even be optimized out of existence. For these reasons, many developers find it easier to optimize only after a program has been debugged.

Some optimization options may also conflict with strict conformance to the ISO C standard, such as merging variables declared with const as if they were constants. If standards-conformance is critical, and sometimes it is, there are certain optimizations you may not wish to pursue.

Another issue you may encounter is that some optimization techniques result in nondeterministic code generation. For example, the compiler's guess as to which branch of a conditional jump will be taken most often may involve randomness. If you are programming real-time applications, you'll probably want to be careful to ensure deterministic behavior.

Finally, when developing multithreaded programs, you need to be aware of how shared memory access works and the features that the threads library offers to control it (see Chapter 14), because optimization can involve rearranging the order of memory access operations, and even eliminate operations that appear superfluous to the compiler in the scope of a single thread.

In any case, if you want to be sure of getting the greatest possible runtime performance, or if you need to know in detail how GCC is arriving at the exact machine code for your C program, there is no substitute for testing and comparing your specific program's performance with the various optimization options.

Debugging

Use the -g option to have GCC include symbol and source-line information in its object and executable output files. This information is used by debugging programs to display the contents of variables in registers and memory while stepping through the program. (For more on debugging, see Chapter 21.) There are a number of formats for this symbol information, and GCC uses your system's native format by default.

You can also use a suffix to the -g option to store the symbol information in a different format from your system's native format. You might want to do this in order to conform to the specific debugging program that you are using. For example, the option -ggdb chooses the best format available on your system for debugging with the GNU debugger, GDB.

Because the symbol information can increase and even multiply the size of your executable file, you will probably want to recompile without the -g option and link using the -s option when you have completed debugging and testing. However, some software packages are distributed with debugging information in the binaries for use in diagnosing subsequent users' problems.

Profiling

The -p option adds special functions to your program to output profiling information when you run it. Profiling is useful in resolving performance problems, because it lets you see which functions your program is spending its execution time on. The profiling output is saved in a file called *mon.out*. You can then use the *prof* utility to analyze the profiling information in a number of ways; see the *prof* manual for details.

For the GNU profiler, *gprof*, compile your program with the `-pg` option. The default output filename for the profiling information is then *gmon.out*. *gprof* in conjunction with the GCC option `-pg` can generate a call graph showing which functions in your program call which others. If you combine the `-pg` option with `-g`, the GCC option that provides source-line information for a debugger, then *gprof* can also provide line-by-line profiling.

Option and Environment Variable Summary

This section summarizes frequently used GCC options for quick reference, and lists the environment variables used by GCC.

Command-Line Options

`-c`
> Preprocess, compile, and assemble only (i.e., don't link).

`-C`
> Leave comments in when preprocessing.

`-D`*name*`[=`*definition*`]`
> Defines the symbol *name*.

`-e`*name*
> Start program execution at *name*.

`-E`
> Preprocess only; output to `stdout`, unless used with `-o`.

`-ffast-math`
> Permit faster floating-point arithmetic methods at the cost of accuracy or precision.

`-ffinite-math-only`
> Disregard infinities and NaN ("not a number") values.

`-ffreestanding`
> Compile as a freestanding (not hosted) program.

`-finline-functions, -fno-inline-functions`
> Enable/disable inline functions.

`-fno-math-errno`
> Disable the `errno` variable for simple math functions.

`-fmerge-constants`
Put identical constants in a single location.

`-fno-trapping-math`
Generate "nonstop" floating-point code.

`-frounding-math`
Don't disregard the rounding-mode features of the floating-point environment (experimental).

`-fsignaling-nans`
Allow all exceptions raised by signaling NaNs (experimental).

`-fsyntax-only`
Don't compile or link; just test input for syntax.

`-funroll-loops, -fno-unroll-loops`
Enable/disable loop optimization.

`-funsafe-math-optimizations`
Permit optimizations that don't conform to standards and/or don't verify values.

`-fverbose-asm`
Include C variable names as comments in assembly language.

`-g[`*`format`*`]`
Compile for debugging.

`-I`*`directory`*`[:`*`directory`*`[…]]`
Search for header files in the specified path.

`-I-`
Distinguish between `-I`*`path`* for #include *`<filename>`* and `-I`*`path`* for #include *`"filename"`* (deprecated).

`-iquote`*`directory`*`[:`*`directory`*`[…]]`
Search the specified path for header files specified in quotation marks (#include *`"filename"`*).

`-isysroot`*`directory`*
Prepend the specified directory to the system root directory to find header files.

`-l`*`basename`*
Link with library `lib`*`basename`*`.so` or `lib`*`basename`*`.a`.

`-L`*`directory`*`[:`*`directory`*`[…]]`
Search for library files in the specified path.

`-march=`*cpu*

> *Intel x86*: Generate model-specific code.

`-mcpu=`*cpu*

> *Sparc, ARM, and RS/6000-PowerPC:* Generate model-specific code.

> *Intel x86:* Optimize scheduling for the specified CPU model.

`-mtune=`*cpu*

> Optimize scheduling for the specified CPU model.

`-nostartfiles`

> Don't link startup code.

`-nostdlib`

> Don't link with the standard library.

`-o` *filename*

> Direct output to the specified file.

`-O0`

> Turn off all optimization options.

`-O, -O1`

> Perform some optimization without taking much time.

`-O2`

> Perform more optimization, including data flow analysis.

`-O3`

> Perform still more optimization, including inline function compilation.

`-Os`

> Optimize for size.

`-p`

> Link in code to output profiling information.

`-pedantic-errors`

> Fail on nonstandard usage.

`-pg`

> Link in code to output profiling information for *gprof.*

`-s`

> Strip symbol tables from executable file.

`-S`

> Preprocess and translate into assembly language only.

-save-temps

Save intermediate output files.

-shared

Create a shared object file for dynamic linking.

-static

Don't link to shared object files.

-std=iso9899:1990, -std=c89, -ansi

Support ISO/IEC 9899:1990.

-std=iso9899:199409

Support ISO/IEC 9899:1989 and AMD1.

-std=c99

Support ISO/IEC 9899:1999.

-std=c11

Support ISO/IEC 9899:2011.

-std=gnu89

Like -ansi, plus GNU extensions (GCC's default before version 5).

-std=gnu99

Like -std=c99, plus GNU extensions.

-std=gnu11

Like -std=c11, plus GNU extensions (GCC's default beginning with version 5).

--sysroot*directory*

Prepend the specified directory to the system root directory to find header and library files. If the -isysroot option is not used, the --sysroot option affects both library and header file searches.

-traditional

Support old-style C. Deprecated; supported only with -E.

-trigraphs

Support ISO C trigraphs.

-U*name*

"Undefine" the symbol *name*.

-v

Be verbose: print the options applied at each step of compiling.

--version

Output GCC version and license information.

-W
> Disable all warnings.

-Wa,*option*[,*option*[…]]
> Pass options to assembler command line.

-Wall
> Output warnings about a broad range of problems in source code.

-Wl,*option*[,*option*[…]]
> Pass options to linker command line.

-Werror
> Fail on all warnings.

-Wextra
> Output warnings about legal but questionable usage.

-Wtraditional
> Warn about differences to old-style C.

-x *filetype*
> Treat subsequent files as being of the specified type.

Environment Variables

CPATH, C_INCLUDE_PATH
> Colon-separated list of directories to search for header files, after those indicated by -I*directory* on the command line.

COMPILER_PATH
> Colon-separated list of directories to search for GCC's own subprogram files.

GCC_EXEC_PREFIX
> A prefix for GCC to add to the names of its subprograms when invoking them. May end with a slash.

LIBRARY_PATH
> Colon-separated list of directories to search for linker and library files, after directories specified by -L*directory* on the command line.

LD_LIBRARY_PATH
> Colon-separated list of directories to search for shared library files. Read not by GCC but by executables dynamically linked against shared libraries.

TMPDIR
> Directory to use for temporary files.

20

Using make to Build C Programs

As you saw in Chapter 18, the commands involved in compiling and linking C programs can be numerous and complex. The *make* utility automates and manages the process of compiling programs of any size and complexity, so that a single *make* command replaces hundreds of compiler and linker commands. Moreover, *make* compares the timestamps of related files to avoid having to repeat any previous work. And most importantly, *make* manages the individual rules that define how to build various targets, and automatically analyzes the dependency relationships between all the files involved.

There are a number of different versions of *make*, and their features and usage differ to varying degrees. They feature different sets of built-in variables and targets with special meanings. In this brief chapter, rather than trying to cover different varieties, we concentrate on GNU *make*, which is widely available. (On systems that use a different default *make*, GNU *make* is often available under the executable name *gmake*.) Furthermore, even as far as GNU *make* is concerned, this chapter sticks more or less to the basics: in this book, we want to use *make* only as a tool for building programs from C source code. If you want to go on to exploit the full capabilities of *make*, an inevitable step is to read the program's documentation itself. For a well-structured course in using *make*'s advanced capabilities, see also *Managing Projects with GNU make* by Robert Mecklenburg (O'Reilly).

Targets, Prerequisites, and Commands

Before we describe the *make* solution, we will briefly review the problem. To make an executable program, we need to link compiled object files. To generate object files, we need to compile C source files. The source files in turn need to be preprocessed to include their header files. And whenever we have edited a source or header file, then any file that was directly or indirectly generated from it needs to be rebuilt.

The *make* utility organizes the work just described in the form of *rules*. For C programs, these rules generally take the following form: the executable file is a *target* that must be rebuilt whenever certain object files have changed—the object files are its *prerequisites*. At the same time, the object files are *intermediate targets*, which must be recompiled if the source and header files have changed. (Thus, the executable depends indirectly on the source files. *make* manages such dependency chains elegantly, even when they become complex.) The rule for each target generally contains one or more commands, called the *command script*, that *make* executes to build it. For example, the rule for building the executable file says to run the linker, while the rule for building object files says to run the preprocessor and compiler. In other words, a rule's prerequisites say *when* to build the target, and the command script says *how* to build it.

The Makefile

The *make* program has a special syntax for its rules. Furthermore, the rules for all the operations that you want *make* to manage in your project generally need to be collected in a file for *make* to read. The command-line option `-f filename` tells *make* which file contains the rules you want it to apply. Usually, though, this option is omitted and *make* looks for a file with the default name *makefile*, or failing that, *Makefile*.[1]

When you read makefiles, remember that they are not simply scripts to be executed in sequential order. Rather, *make* first analyzes an entire makefile to build a dependency tree of possible targets and their prerequisites, then iterates through that dependency tree to build the desired targets.

In addition to rules, makefiles also contain comments, variable assignments, macro definitions, include directives, and conditional directives. These will be discussed in later sections of this chapter, after we have taken a closer look at the meat of the makefile: the rules.

Rules

Example 20-1 shows a makefile that might be used to build the program in Example 1-2.

Example 20-1. A basic makefile

```
# A basic makefile for "circle".

CC = gcc
CFLAGS = -Wall -g -std=c99
```

---

1 Before *makefile* or *Makefile*, GNU *make* without the `-f` option first looks for a file named *GNUmakefile*.

```
LDFLAGS = -lm

circle : circle.o circulararea.o
        $(CC) $(LDFLAGS) -o $@ $^

circle.o : circle.c
        $(CC) $(CFLAGS) -o $@ -c $<

circulararea.o: circulararea.c
        $(CC) $(CFLAGS) -o $@ -c $<
```

The line that begins with the character # is a comment, which *make* ignores. This makefile begins by defining some variables, which are used in the statements that follow. The rest of the file consists of rules, with the following general form:

```
target [target [...]] : [prerequisite[prerequisite[...]]]
        [command
        [command
        [...]]]
```

The first *target* must be placed at the beginning of the line, with no whitespace to the left of it. Moreover, each *command* line must start with a tab character. (It would be simpler if all whitespace characters were permissible here, but that's not the case.)

Each rule in the makefile says, in effect: if any *target* is older than any *prerequisite*, execute the *command* script. More importantly, *make* also checks whether the prerequisites have other prerequisites in turn before it starts executing commands.

Both the prerequisites and the command script are optional. A rule with no command script tells only *make* about a dependency relationship; and a rule with no prerequisites tells only *how* to build the target, not *when* to build it. You can also put the prerequisites for a given target in one rule, and the command script in another. For any target requested, whether on the *make* command line or as a prerequisite for another target, *make* collects all the pertinent information from *all* rules for that target before it acts on them.

Example 20-1 shows two different notations for variable references in the command script. Variable names that consist of more than one character—in this case, CC, CFLAGS, and LDFLAGS—must be prefixed with a dollar sign and enclosed in parentheses when referenced. Variables that consist of just one character—in our example, these happen to be the automatic variables ^, <, and @—need just the dollar sign, not the parentheses. We discuss variables in detail in a separate section later in this chapter. The following program output shows how *make* expands both kinds of variables to generate compiler commands:

```
$ make -n -f Makefile19-1 circle
gcc -Wall -g -std=c99 -o circle.o -c circle.c
gcc -Wall -g -std=c99 -o circulararea.o -c circulararea.c
gcc -lm -o circle circle.o circulararea.o
```

The command-line option -n instructs *make* to print the commands it would otherwise execute to build the specified targets. This option is indispensable when testing makefiles. (A complete reference list of *make* options is included at the end of this chapter.) The final line of output corresponds to the first rule contained in Example 20-1. It shows that *make* expands the variable reference $(CC) to the text gcc and $(LDFLAGS) to -lm. The automatic variables $@ and $^ expand to the target circle and the prerequisite list circle.o circulararea.o. In the first two output lines, the automatic variable $< is expanded to just one prerequisite, which is the name of the C source file to be compiled.

The Command Script

The command script for a rule can consist of several lines, each of which must begin with a tab. Comments and blank lines are ignored, so that the command script ends with the next target line or variable definition.

Furthermore, the first line of the command script may be placed after a semicolon at the end of the dependency line, as in the following syntax:

```
target_list : [prerequisite_list] ; [command
    [command
    [...]]]
```

This variant is rarely used today, however.

The important thing to remember about the command part of a *make* rule is that it is not a shell script. When *make* invokes a rule to build its target, each line in the rule's command section is executed individually in a separate shell instance. For that reason, you must make sure that no command depends on the side effects of a preceding line. For example, the following commands will not run *etags* in the *src/* subdirectory:

```
TAGS:
        cd src/
        etags *.c
```

In trying to build TAGS, *make* runs the shell command cd src/ in the current directory. When that command exits, *make* runs etags *.c in a new shell, again in the current directory.

There are two ways to cause several commands to run in the same shell: putting them on one line, separated by a semicolon, or adding a semicolon and a backslash to place them virtually on one line:

```
TAGS:
            cd src/ ; etags *.c ;\
            cd .. ; ls src/TAGS
```

Another reason for running multiple commands in the same shell could be to speed up processing, especially in large projects.

Pattern Rules

The last two rules in Example 20-1 show a repetitive pattern. Each of the two object files, *circle.o* and *circulararea.o*, depends on a source file with the same name and the suffix *.c*, and the commands to build them are the same. *make* lets you describe such cases economically using *pattern rules*. Here is a single rule that replaces the last two rules in Example 20-1:

```
circulararea.o circle.o: %.o: %.c
        $(CC) $(CFLAGS) -o $@ -c $<
```

The first line of this rule has three colon-separated parts rather than two. The first part is a list of the targets that the rule applies to. The rest of the line, `%.o: %.c`, is a pattern explaining how to derive a prerequisite name from each of the targets, using the percent sign (`%`) as a wildcard. When *make* matches each target in the list against the pattern `%.o`, the part of the target that corresponds to the wildcard `%` is called the *stem*. The stem is then substituted for the percent sign in `%.c` to yield the prerequisite.

The general syntax of such pattern rules is:

```
[target_list :] target_pattern : prerequisite_pattern
        [command-script]
```

You must make sure that each target in the list matches the target pattern. Otherwise, *make* issues an error message.

If you include an explicit target list, the rule is a *static pattern rule*. If you omit the target list, the rule is called an *implicit rule*, and applies to any target whose name matches the target pattern. For example, if you expect to add more modules as the *circle* program grows and evolves, you can make a rule for all present and future object files in the project like this:

```
%.o: %.c
        $(CC) $(CFLAGS) -o $@ -c $<
```

And if a certain object needs to be handled differently for some reason, you can put a static pattern rule for that object file in the makefile as well. *make* then applies the static rule for targets explicitly named in it, and the implicit rule for all other *.o* files. Also, *make* refrains from announcing an error if any object file's implicit prerequisite does not exist.

The percent sign is usually used only once in each pattern. To represent a literal percent sign in a pattern, you must escape it with a backslash. For example, the filename *app%3amodule.o* matches the pattern `app\%3a%.o`, and the resulting stem is `module`. To use a literal backslash in a pattern without escaping a percent sign that happens to follow it, you need to escape the backslash itself. Thus, the filename *app \module.o* would match the pattern `app\\%.o`, yielding the stem `module`.

Suffix Rules

The kind of pattern rule in which the percent sign represents all but the filename's suffix is the modern way of expressing a *suffix rule*. In older makefiles, you might see such a rule expressed in the following notation:

```
.c.o:
        $(CC) $(CFLAGS) ...
```

The "target" in this rule consists simply of the target and source filename suffixes—and in the opposite order; that is, with the source suffix first, followed by the target suffix. This example with the target `.c.o:` is equivalent to a pattern rule beginning with `%o: %c`. If a suffix rule target contains only one suffix, then that is the suffix for source filenames, and target filenames under that rule are assumed to have no suffix.

GNU *make* also supports suffix rules, but that notation is considered obsolete. Pattern rules using the `%` wildcard character are more readable, and more versatile.

Every suffix used in the target of a suffix rule must be a "known suffix." *make* stores its list of known suffixes in the built-in variable SUFFIXES. You can add your own suffixes by declaring them as prerequisites of the built-in target .SUFFIXES (see "Special Targets Used as Runtime Options" on page 728 for more about this technique).

Built-In Rules

You don't have to tell *make* how to do standard operations like compiling an object file from C source; the program has a built-in default rule for that operation, and for many others. Example 20-2 shows a more elegant version of our sample makefile that takes advantage of built-in rules.

Example 20-2. A makefile using built-in rules

```
# A slightly more elegant makefile for "circle".

CC = gcc
CFLAGS = -Werror -std=c99
OBJS =  circle.o circulararea.o

circle: $(OBJS) -lm
```

This makefile does away with the rule for compiling source code into objects, depending instead on *make*'s built-in pattern rule. Furthermore, the rule that says the executable *circle* depends on the two object files has no command script. This is because *make* also has a built-in rule to link objects to build an executable. We will look at those built-in rules in a moment. First, suppose we enter this command:

```
$ touch *.c ; make circle
```

This produces roughly the same output as before:

```
gcc -Werror -std=c99    -c -o circle.o circle.c
gcc -Werror -std=c99    -c -o circulararea.o circulararea.c
gcc circle.o circulararea.o  /usr/lib/libm.so  -o circle
```

None of these commands is visible in the new makefile in Example 20-2, even if individual arguments are recognizable in the variable assignments. To display *make*'s built-in rules (as well as the variables at work), you can run the program with the command-line switch -p. The output is rather long. Here are the parts of it that are relevant to our example (including the comments that *make* generates to identify where each variable or rule definition originates):

```
# default
OUTPUT_OPTION = -o $@

# default
LINK.o = $(CC) $(LDFLAGS) $(TARGET_ARCH)

# default
COMPILE.c = $(CC) $(CFLAGS) $(CPPFLAGS) $(TARGET_ARCH) -c

%: %.o
#   commands to execute (built-in):
        $(LINK.o) $^ $(LOADLIBES) $(LDLIBS) -o $@

%.o: %.c
#   commands to execute (built-in):
        $(COMPILE.c) $(OUTPUT_OPTION) $<
```

Note that the linking step was handled by a combination of two rules: *make* automatically applied the command defined by the built-in rule using the information about the prerequisites provided by the dependency rule in the makefile.

Finally, the makefile in Example 20-2, unlike Example 20-1, does not define a variable for linker options. Instead, it correctly lists the C math library as a prerequisite of the executable *circle*, using the same -lm notation as the compiler's command line. The output shown illustrates how *make* expands this notation to the full library filename.

Implicit Rule Chains

make tries to use implicit rules, whether built-in ones or pattern rules from the makefile, for any target that doesn't have an explicit rule with a command script. There may be many implicit rules that match a given target. For example, *make* has built-in rules to generate an object file (matching the pattern %.o) from source code in C (%.c), C++ (%.cpp), or even assembler (%.s). Which rule does *make* use, then? It selects the first one in the list for which the prerequisites are available or can be made by applying appropriate rules. In this way, *make* can automatically apply a *chain* of implicit rules to generate a target. If *make* generates any *intermediate* files that are not mentioned in the makefile, it deletes them after they have served their purpose. For example, suppose that the current directory contains only the file *square.c*, and the makefile contains the following:

```
%: %.o
        cc -o $@ $^

%.o : %.c
        cc -c -o $@ $<
```

To disable all the built-in rules and use only the two implicit rules we can see in the makefile, we'll run *make* with the -r option:

```
$ ls
Makefile  square.c
$ make -r square
cc -c -o square.o square.c
cc -o square square.o
rm square.o
$ ls
Makefile square   square.c
```

From the target, the two implicit rules in the makefile, and the available source file, *make* found the indirect way to build the target, and then automatically cleaned up the intermediate object file because it isn't mentioned in the makefile or on the command line.

Double-Colon Rules

Before we move away from rules, another kind of rule that you should know about is the *double-colon rule*, so named because it has not one but two colons between the targets and the prerequisites:

```
target :: prerequisites
      commands
```

Double-colon rules are the same as single-colon rules unless your makefile contains multiple double-colon rules for the same target. In that case, *make* treats the rules as alternative rather than cumulative: instead of collating all the rules' prerequisites into a single set of dependencies for the target, *make* tests the target against each rule's prerequisites separately to decide whether to execute that rule's script. Example 20-3 shows a makefile that uses double-colon rules.

Example 20-3. Double-colon rules

```
# A makefile for "circle" to demonstrate double-colon rules.

CC = gcc
RM = rm -f
CFLAGS = -Wall -std=c99
DBGFLAGS = -ggdb -pg
DEBUGFILE = ./debug
SRC = circle.c circulararea.c
```

```
circle :: $(SRC)
        $(CC) $(CFLAGS) -o $@ -lm $^

circle :: $(DEBUGFILE)
        $(CC) $(CFLAGS) $(DBGFLAGS) -o $@ -lm $(SRC)

.PHONY : clean
clean  :
        $(RM) circle
```

The makefile in Example 20-3 builds the target *circle* in either of two ways, with or without debugging options in the compiler command line. In the first rule for *circle*, the target depends on the source files. *make* runs the command for this rule if the source files are newer than the executable. In the second rule, *circle* depends on a file named *debug* in the current directory. The command for that rule doesn't use the prerequisite *debug* at all. That file is empty; it just sits in the directory for the sake of its timestamp, which tells *make* whether to build a debugging version of the *circle* executable. The following sample session illustrates how *make* can alternate between the two rules:

```
$ make clean
rm -f circle
$ make circle
gcc -Wall -std=c99 -o circle -lm circle.c circulararea.c
$ make circle
make: `circle' is up to date.
$ touch debug
$ make circle
gcc -Wall -std=c99 -ggdb -pg -o circle -lm circle.c circulararea.c
$ make circle
make: `circle' is up to date.
$ make clean
rm -f circle
$ make circle
gcc -Wall -std=c99 -o circle -lm circle.c circulararea.c
```

As the output shows, *make* applies only one rule or the other, depending on which rule's prerequisites are newer than the target. (If both rules' prerequisites are newer than the target, *make* applies the rule that appears first in the makefile.)

Comments

In a makefile, a hash mark (#) anywhere in a line begins a comment, unless the line is a command. *make* ignores comments, as if the text from the hash mark to the end of its line did not exist. Comments (like blank lines) between the lines of a rule do not interrupt its continuity. Leading whitespace before a hash mark is ignored.

If a line containing a hash mark is a command—that is, if it begins with a tab character—then it cannot contain a *make* comment. If the corresponding target needs to be built, *make* passes the entire command line, minus the leading tab character, to the shell for execution. (Some shells, such as the Bourne shell, also interpret the hash mark as introducing a comment, but that is beyond *make*'s control.)

Variables

All variables in *make* are of the same type: they contain sequences of characters, never numeric values. Whenever *make* applies a rule, it evaluates all the variables contained in the targets, prerequisites, and commands. Variables in GNU *make* come in two "flavors," called *recursively expanded* and *simply expanded* variables. Which flavor a given variable has is determined by the specific assignment operator used in its definition. In a recursively expanded variable, nested variable references are stored verbatim until the variable is evaluated. In a simply expanded variable, on the other hand, variable references in the value are expanded immediately on assignment, and their expanded values are stored, not their names.

Variable names can include any character except :, =, and #. However, for robust makefiles and compatibility with shell constraints, you should use only letters, digits, and the underscore character.

Assignment Operators

Which assignment operator you use in defining a variable determines whether it is a simply or a recursively expanded variable. The assignment operator = in the following example creates a recursively expanded variable:

```
DEBUGFLAGS = $(CFLAGS) -ggdb -DDEBUG -O0
```

make stores the character sequence to the right of the equals sign verbatim; the nested variable $(CFLAGS) is not expanded until $(DEBUGFLAGS) is used.

To create a simply expanded variable, use the assignment operator := as shown in the following example:

```
OBJ = circle.o circulararea.o
TESTOBJ := $(OBJ) profile.o
```

In this case, *make* stores the character sequence circle.o circulararea.o profile.o as the value of $(TESTOBJ). If a subsequent assignment modifies the value of $(OBJ), $(TESTOBJ) is not affected.

You can define both recursively expanded and simply expanded variables not only in the makefile, but also on the *make* command line, as in the following example:

```
$ make CFLAGS=-ffinite-math-only circulararea.o
```

Each such assignment must be contained in a single command-line argument. If the assignment contains spaces, you must escape them or enclose the entire assignment in quotation marks. Any variable defined on the command line, or in the shell environment, can be cancelled out by an assignment in the makefile that starts with the optional override keyword, as this one does:

```
override CPPLFAGS = -DDEBUG
```

Use `override` assignments with caution, unless you want to confuse and frustrate future users of your makefile.

make also provides two more assignment operators. Here is the complete list:

=

Defines a recursively expanded variable.

:=

Defines a simply expanded variable.

+=

Also called the *append operator*. Appends more characters to the existing value of a variable. If the left operand is not yet defined, the assignment defines a recursively expanded variable. Or, to put it another way, the result of the append operator is a recursively expanded variable, unless its left operand already exists as a simply expanded variable.

This operator provides the only way to append characters to the value of a recursively expanded variable. The following assignment is wrong, as recursive expansion would cause an infinite loop:

```
OBJ = $(OBJ) profile.o
```

Here is the right way to do it:

```
OBJ += profile.o
```

The += operator automatically inserts a space before appending the new text to the variable's previous value.

?=

The *conditional assignment* operator. Assigns a value to a variable, but only if the variable has no value.

The conditional assignment operator can only define recursively expanded variables. If its left operand already exists, it remains unaffected, regardless of whether it is a simply expanded or a recursively expanded variable.

In addition to these operations, there are two more ways to define *make* variables. One is the `define` directive, used to create variables of multiple lines; we will discuss this later in "Macros" on page 714. Another is by setting environment variables in the system shell before you invoke *make*. We will discuss *make*'s use of environment variables later in the chapter as well.

Variables and Whitespace

In a variable assignment, *make* ignores any whitespace between the assignment operator and the first non-whitespace character of the value. However, trailing whitespace up to the end of the line containing the variable assignment, or up to a comment that follows on the same line, becomes part of the variable's value. Usually this behavior is unimportant because most references to *make* variables are options in shell command lines, where additional whitespace has no effect. However, if you use variable references to construct file or directory names, unintended whitespace at the end of an assignment line can be fatal.

On the other hand, if you develop complex makefiles, you might sometimes need a literal space that *make* does not ignore or interpret as a list separator. The easiest way is to use a variable whose value is a single space character, but defining such a variable is tricky. Simply enclosing a space in quotation marks does not have the same effect as in C. Consider the following assignment:

```
ONESPACE := ' '
TEST = Does$(ONESPACE)this$(ONESPACE)work?
```

In this case, a reference to $(TEST) would expand to the following text:

```
Does' 'this' 'work?
```

Double quotation marks are no different: they also become part of the variable's value. To define a variable containing just the space and nothing else, you can use the following lines:

```
NOTHING :=
ONESPACE := $(NOTHING) # This comment terminates the variable's value.
```

The variable reference $(NOTHING) expands to zero characters, but it ends the leading whitespace that *make* trims off after the assignment operator. If you do not insert a comment after the space character that follows $(NOTHING), you may find it hard to tell when editing the makefile whether the single trailing space is present as desired.

Target-Specific Variable Assignments

You can make any of the assignment operations apply to only a specific target (or target pattern) by including a line in your makefile with the form:

```
target_list: [override]assignment
```

While *make* is building the given target—or its prerequisites—the target-specific or pattern-specific variable supersedes any other definition of the same variable name elsewhere in the makefile.

Example 20-4 shows a sample makefile illustrating different kinds of assignments.

Example 20-4. Variable assignments

```
# Tools and options:
CC = gcc
CFLAGS = -c -Wall -std=c99 $(ASMFLAGS)
DEBUGCFLAGS = -ggdb -O0
RM = rm -f
```

```
MKDIR = mkdir -p

# Filenames:
OBJ = circle.o circulararea.o
SYMTABS = $(OBJ:.o=.sym)
EXEC = circle

# The primary targets:
production: clean circle

testing: clean debug

symbols: $(SYMTABS)

clean:
        $(RM) $(OBJ) *.sym circle circle-dbg

# Rules to build prerequisites:
circle debug: $(OBJ) -lm
        $(CC) $(LDFLAGS) -o $(EXEC) $^

$(OBJ): %.o: %.c
        $(CC) $(CFLAGS) $(CPPFLAGS) -o $@ $<

$(SYMTABS): %.sym: %.c
        $(CC) $(CFLAGS) $(CPPFLAGS) -o $*.o $<

# Target-specific options:
debug: CPPFLAGS += -DDEBUG
debug: EXEC = circle-dbg
debug symbols: CFLAGS += $(DEBUGCFLAGS)
symbols: ASMFLAGS = -Wa,-as=$*.sym,-L
```

For the targets debug and symbols, this makefile uses the append operator to add the value of DEBUGCFLAGS to the value of CFLAGS, while conserving any compiler flags already defined.

The assignment to SYMTABS illustrates another feature of *make* variables: you can perform substitutions when referencing them. As Example 20-4 illustrates, a substitution reference has this form:

> $(*name*:*ending=new_ending*)

When you reference a variable in this way, *make* expands it, and then checks the end of each word in the value (where a word is a sequence of non-whitespace characters followed by a whitespace character, or by the end of the value) for the string *ending*. If the word ends with *ending*, *make* replaces that part with *new_ending*. In Example 20-4, the resulting value of $(SYMTABS) is circle.sym circulararea.sym.

The variable CFLAGS is defined near the top of the makefile, with an unconditional assignment. The expansion of the nested variable it contains, $(ASMFLAGS), is deferred until *make* expands $(CFLAGS) in order to execute the compiler command. The value of $(ASMFLAGS), for example, may be -Wa,-as=circle.sym,-L, or it may be nothing. When *make* builds the target symbols, the compiler command expands recursively to:

```
gcc -c -Wall -std=c99 -Wa,-as=circle.sym,-L -ggdb -O0
-o circle.o circle.c
gcc -c -Wall -std=c99 -Wa,-as=circulararea.sym,-L -ggdb -O0
-o circulararea.o circulararea.c
```

(Each of these two gcc commands is generated in a single line, which is split in two here to fit the page.) As you can see, if there is no variable defined with the name CPPFLAGS at the time of variable expansion, *make* simply replaces $(CPPFLAGS) with nothing.

 Unlike C, *make* doesn't balk at undefined variables. The only difference between an undefined variable and a variable whose value contains no characters is that a defined variable has a determined flavor: it is either simply expanded or recursively expanded, and cannot change its behavior, even if you assign it a new value.

Like many real-life makefiles, the one in Example 20-4 uses variables to store the names of common utilities like *mkdir* and *rm* together with the standard options that we want to use with them. This approach not only saves repetition in the makefile's command scripts but also makes maintenance and porting easier.

The Automatic Variables

The command scripts in Example 20-4 also contain a number of single-character variables: $@, $<, $,, and $*. These are *automatic variables*, which *make* defines and expands itself in carrying out each rule. Here is a complete list of the automatic variables and their meanings in a given rule:

$@

The target filename.

$*

The stem of the target filename—that is, the part represented by % in a pattern rule.

$<

The first prerequisite.

$,

The list of prerequisites, excluding duplicate elements.

$?

The list of prerequisites that are newer than the target.

$+

The full list of prerequisites, including duplicates.

$%

If the target is an archive member, the variable $% yields the member name without the archive filename, and $@ supplies the filename of the archive.

The last of these automatic variables brings up a special target case. Because most programs depend not only on source code but also on library modules, *make* also provides a special notation for targets that are members of an archive:

```
archive_name(member_name): [prerequisites]
        [command_script]
```

The name of the archive member is enclosed in parentheses immediately after the filename of the archive itself. Here is an example:

```
AR = ar -rv
```

```
libcircularmath.a(circulararea.o): circulararea.o
        $(AR) $@ $%
```

This rule executes the following command to add or replace the object file in the archive:

```
ar -rv libcircularmath.a circulararea.o
```

In other *make* versions, these special variables also have long names that start with a dot, such as $(.TARGET) as a synonym for $@. Also, some *make* programs use the symbol $> for all prerequisites rather than GNU *make*'s $^.

When an automatic variable expands to a list, such as a list of filenames, the elements are separated by spaces.

To separate filenames from directories, there are two more versions of each automatic variable in this list whose names are formed with the suffixes D and F. Because the resulting variable name is two characters, not one, parentheses are required. For example, $(@D) in any rule expands to the directory part of the target, without the actual filename, while $(@F) yields just the filename with no directory. (GNU *make* supports these forms for compatibility's sake, but provides more flexible handling of filenames by means of functions; see "Built-In Functions" on page 715.)

Other Built-In Variables

The variables that *make* uses internally are described in the following list. You can also use them in makefiles. Remember that you can find out the sources of all variables in the output of make -p:

CURDIR

This variable holds the name of the current working directory after *make* has processed its -C or --directory command-line options. You can modify this variable, but doing so doesn't change the working directory.

.LIBPATTERNS

A list of filename patterns that determines how *make* searches for libraries when a prerequisite starts with -l. The default value is lib%.so lib%.a. A prerequisite called -lncurses causes *make* to search for *libncurses.so* and *libncurses.a*, in that order.

MAKE

This variable holds the name of the *make* executable. When you use $(MAKE) in a command, *make* automatically expands it to the full path name of the program file so that all recursive instances of *make* are from the same executable.

MAKECMDGOALS

make stores any targets specified on the command line in this variable. You can modify this variable, but doing so doesn't change the targets *make* builds.

MAKEFILES

A list of standard makefiles that *make* reads every time it starts.

MAKEFILE_LIST

A list of all the makefiles that the present invocation of *make* is using.

MAKEFLAGS

This variable contains the command-line options with which *make* was invoked, with some exceptions. Each instance of *make* reads this variable from the environment on starting, and exports it to the environment before spawning a recursive instance. You can modify this variable in the environment or in a makefile.

MAKELEVEL

When *make* invokes itself recursively, this variable holds the degree of recursion of the present instance. In exporting this variable to the environment, *make* increments its value. Child instances of *make* print this number in square brackets after the program name in their console output.

MAKESHELL

On Windows, this variable holds the name of the command interpreter for *make* to use in running command scripts. MAKESHELL overrides SHELL.

SHELL

The name of the shell that *make* invokes when it runs command scripts, usually /bin/sh. Unlike most variables, *make* doesn't read the value of SHELL from the environment (except on Windows), as users' shell preferences would make *make*'s results less consistent. If you want *make* to run commands using a specific shell, you must set this variable in your makefile.

SUFFIXES

make's default list of known suffixes (see "Suffix Rules" on page 700). This variable contains the *default* list, which is not necessarily the list currently in effect;

---

the value of this variable does not change when you clear the list or add your own known suffixes using the built-in target .SUFFIXES.

VPATH
> The directory path that *make* uses to search for any files not found in the current working directory.

Environment Variables

If you want, you can set environment variables in the shell before starting *make*, and then reference them in the makefile using the same syntax as for other *make* variables. Furthermore, you can use the export directive in the makefile to copy any or all of *make*'s variables to the shell environment before invoking shell commands, as in the following example:

```
INCLUDE=/usr/include:/usr/local/include:~/include
export INCLUDE
export LIB := $(LIBS):/usr/lib:/usr/local/lib

%.o: %.c
        $(CC) $(CFLAGS) -o $@ -c $<
```

When the C compiler is invoked by the pattern rule in this example, it can obtain information defined in the makefile by reading the environment variables INCLUDE and LIB. Similarly, *make* automatically passes its command-line options to child instances by copying them to and then exporting the variable MAKEFLAGS. See "Recursive make Commands" on page 724 for other examples.

The shell environment is more restrictive than *make* with regard to the characters that are permitted in variable names and values. It might be possible to trick your shell into propagating environment variables containing illegal characters, but the easiest thing by far is just to avoid special characters in any variables you want to export.

Phony Targets

The makefile in Example 20-4 also illustrates several different ways of using targets. The targets debug, testing, production, clean, and symbols are not names of files to be generated. Nonetheless, the rules clearly define the behavior of a command like **make production** or **make clean symbols debug**. Targets that are not the names of files to be generated are called *phony targets*.

In Example 20-4, the phony target clean has a command script but no prerequisites. Furthermore, its command script doesn't actually build anything: on the contrary, it deletes files generated by other rules. We can use this target to clear the board before rebuilding the program from scratch. In this way, the phony targets testing and production ensure that the executable is linked from object files made with the desired compiler options by including clean as one of their prerequisites.

You can also think of a phony target as one that is never supposed to be up to date: its command script should be executed whenever the target is called for. This is the case with clean—as long as no file with the name *clean* happens to appear in the project directory.

Often, however, a phony target's name might really appear as a filename in the project directory. For example, if your project's products are built in subdirectories, such as *bin* and *doc*, you might want to use subdirectory names as targets. But you must make sure that *make* rebuilds the contents of a subdirectory when out of date, even if the subdirectory itself already exists.

For such cases, *make* lets you declare a target as phony regardless of whether a matching filename exists. The way to do so is to add a line like the following one to your makefile, making the target a prerequisite of the special built-in target .PHONY:

```
.PHONY: clean
```

Or, to use an example with a subdirectory name, suppose we added these lines to the makefile in Example 20-4:

```
.PHONY: bin
bin: circle
        $(MKDIR) $@
        $(CP) $< $@/
        $(CHMOD) 600 $@/$<
```

This rule for the target bin actually does create bin in the project directory. However, because bin is explicitly phony, it is never up to date. *make* puts an up-to-date copy of *circle* in the bin subdirectory even if *bin* is newer than its prerequisite, *circle*.

You should generally declare all phony targets explicitly, as doing so can also save time. For targets that are declared as phony, *make* does not bother looking for appropriately named source files that it could use with implicit rules to build a file with the target's name. An old-fashioned, slightly less intuitive way of producing the same effect is to add another rule for the target with no prerequisites and no commands:

```
bin: circle
        $(MKDIR) $@
        $(CP) $< $@/
        $(CHMOD) 600 $@/$<
bin:
```

The .PHONY target is preferable if only because it is so explicit, but you may see the other technique in automatically generated dependency rules, for example.

Other Target Attributes

There are also other attributes that you can assign to certain targets in a makefile by making those targets prerequisites of other built-in targets like .PHONY. The most important of these built-in targets are listed here (other special built-in targets that can be used in makefiles to alter *make*'s runtime behavior in general are listed at the end of this chapter):

`.IGNORE`

For any target that is a prerequisite of `.IGNORE`, *make* ignores any errors that occur in executing the commands to build that target. `.IGNORE` itself does not take a command script.

You can also put `.IGNORE` in a makefile with no prerequisites at all, although it is probably not a good idea. If you do, *make* ignores all errors in running any command script.

`.INTERMEDIATE`

Ordinarily, when *make* needs to build a target whose prerequisites do not exist, it searches for an appropriate rule to build them first. If the absent prerequisites are not named anywhere in the makefile and *make* has to resort to implicit rules to build them, they are called *intermediate* files. *make* deletes any intermediate files after building its intended target (see "Implicit Rule Chains" on page 701). If you want certain files to be treated in this way even though they are mentioned in your makefile, declare them as prerequisites of `.INTERMEDIATE`.

`.LOW_RESOLUTION_TIME`

On some systems, the timestamps on files have resolution of less than a second, yet certain programs create timestamps that reflect only full seconds. If this behavior causes *make* to misjudge the relative ages of files on your system, you can declare any file with high-resolution timestamps as a prerequisite of `.LOW_RESOLUTION_TIME`. Then *make* considers the file up to date if its timestamp indicates the same whole second in which its prerequisite was stamped. Members of library archives are automatically treated as having low-resolution timestamps.

`.PHONY`

Any targets that are prerequisites of `.PHONY` are always treated as out of date.

`.PRECIOUS`

Normally, if you interrupt *make* while running a command script—if *make* receives any fatal signal, to be more precise—*make* deletes the target it was building before it exits. Any target you declare as a prerequisite of `.PRECIOUS` is not deleted in such cases, however.

Furthermore, when *make* builds a target by concatenating implicit rules, it normally deletes any intermediate files that it creates by one such rule as prerequisites for the next. However, if any such file is a prerequisite of `.PRECIOUS` (or matches a pattern that is a prerequisite of `.PRECIOUS`), *make* does not delete it.

`.SECONDARY`

> Like `.INTERMEDIATE`, except that *make* does not automatically delete files that are prerequisites of `.SECONDARY`.

> You can also put `.SECONDARY` in a makefile with no prerequisites at all. In this case, *make* treats all targets as prerequisites of `.SECONDARY`.

A few other built-in targets act like general runtime options, affecting *make*'s overall behavior just by appearing in a makefile. These are listed in "Running make" on page 722.

Macros

When we talk about macros in *make*, you should remember that there is really no difference between them and variables. Nonetheless, *make* provides a directive that allows you to define variables with both newline characters and references to other variables embedded in them. Programmers often use this capability to encapsulate multiline command sequences in a variable, so that the term *macro* is fairly appropriate. (The GNU *make* manual calls them "canned command sequences.")

To define a variable containing multiple lines, you must use the `define` directive. Its syntax is:

```
define macro_name
macro_value
endef
```

The line breaks shown in the syntax are significant: `define` and `endef` both need to be placed at the beginning of a line, and nothing may follow `define` on its line except the name of the macro. Within the `macro_value`, though, any number of newline characters may also occur. These are included literally, along with all other characters between the `define` and `endef` lines, in the value of the variable you are defining. Here is a simple example:

```
define installtarget
@echo Installing $@ in $(USRBINDIR) ... ;\
$(MKDIR) -m 7700 $(USRBINDIR)            ;\
$(CP) $@ $(USRBINDIR)/                   ;\
@echo ... done.
endef
```

The variable references contained in the macro `installtarget` are stored literally as shown here, and expanded only when *make* expands `$(installtarget)` itself, in a rule like this, for example:

```
circle: $(OBJ) $(LIB)
        $(CC) $(LDFLAGS) -o $@ $^
ifdef INSTALLTOO
        $(installtarget)
endif
```

Functions

GNU *make* goes beyond simple macro expansion to provide functions—both built-in and user-defined functions. By using parameters, conditions, and built-in functions, you can define quite powerful functions and use them anywhere in your makefiles.

The syntax of function invocations in makefiles, like that of macro references, uses the dollar sign and parentheses:

```
$(function_name argument[,argument[,...]])
```

Whitespace in the argument list is significant. *make* ignores any whitespace before the first argument, but if you include any whitespace characters before or after a comma, *make* treats them as part of the adjacent argument value.

The arguments themselves can contain any characters, except for embedded commas. Parentheses must occur in matched pairs; otherwise, they will keep *make* from parsing the function call correctly. If necessary, you can avoid these restrictions by defining a variable to hold a comma or parenthesis character, and using a variable reference as the function argument.

Built-In Functions

GNU *make* provides more than 20 useful text-processing and flow-control functions, which are listed briefly in the following sections.

Text-processing functions

The text-processing functions listed here are useful in operating on the values of *make* variables, which are always sequences of characters:

$(subst *find_text,replacement_text,original_text*)
> Expands to the value of *original_text*, except that each occurrence of *find_text* in it is changed to *replacement_text*.

$(patsubst *find_pattern,replacement_pattern,original_text*)
> Expands to the value of *original_text*, except that each occurrence of *find_pattern* in it is changed to *replacement_pattern*. The *find_pattern* argument may contain a percent sign as a wildcard for any number of non-whitespace characters. If *replacement_pattern* also contains a percent sign, it is replaced with the characters represented by the wildcard in *find_pattern*. The patsubst function also collapses each unquoted whitespace sequence into a single space character.

$(strip *original_text*)
> Removes leading and trailing whitespace, and collapses each unquoted internal whitespace sequence into a single space character.

$(findstring *find_text,original_text*)
> Expands to the value of *find_text*, if it occurs in *original_text*; or to nothing if it does not.

$(filter *find_patterns,original_text*)
> *find_patterns* is a whitespace-separated list of patterns like that in patsubst. The function call expands to a space-separated list of the words in *origi nal_text* that match any of the words in *find_patterns*.

$(filter-out *find_patterns,original_text*)
> Expands to a space-separated list of the words in *original_text* that do *not* match any of the words in *find_patterns*.

$(sort *original_text*)
> Expands to a list of the words in *original_text*, in alphabetical order, without duplicates.

$(word *n,original_text*)
> Expands to the *n*th word in *original_text*.

$(firstword *original_text*)
> The same as $(word 1,*original_text*).

$(wordlist *n,m,original_text*)
> Expands to a space-separated list of the *n*th through *m*th words in *origi nal_text*.

$(words *original_text*)
> Expands to the number of words in *original_text*.

Filename-manipulation functions

These functions operate on a whitespace-separated list of file or directory names, and expand to a space-separated list containing a processed element for each name in the argument:

$(dir *filename_list*)
> Expands to a list of the directory parts of each filename in the argument.

$(notdir *filename_list*)
> Expands to a list of the filenames in the argument with their directory parts removed.

`$(suffix filename_list)`
> Expands to a list of the filename suffixes in the argument. Each suffix is the filename ending, beginning with the last period (.) in it; or nothing, if the filename contains no period.

`$(basename filename_list)`
> Expands to a list of the filenames in the argument with their suffixes removed. Directory parts are unchanged.

`$(addsuffix suffix,filename_list)`
> Expands to a list of the filenames in the argument with *suffix* appended to each one. (*suffix* is not treated as a list, even if it contains whitespace.)

`$(addprefix prefix,filename_list)`
> Expands to a list of the filenames in the argument with *prefix* prefixed to each one. (*prefix* is not treated as a list, even if it contains whitespace.)

`$(join prefix_list,suffix_list)`
> Expands to a list of filenames composed by concatenating each word in *prefix_list* with the corresponding word in *suffix_list*. If the lists have different numbers of elements, the excess elements are included unchanged in the result.

`$(wildcard glob)`
> Expands to a list of existing filenames that match the pattern *glob*, which typically contains shell wildcards.

Conditions and flow control functions

The functions listed here allow you to perform operations conditionally, process lists iteratively, or execute the contents of a variable:

`$(foreach name,list,replacement)`
> The argument *name* is a name for a temporary variable (without dollar sign and parentheses). The *replacement* text typically contains a reference to $(*name*). The result of the function is a list of expansions of *replacement*, using successive elements of *list* as the value of $(*name*).

`$(if condition,then_text[,else_text])`
> Expands to the value of *then_text* if *condition*, stripped of leading and trailing spaces, expands to a nonempty text. Otherwise, the function expands to the value of *else_text*, if present.

`$(eval text)`
> Treats the expansion of *text* as included makefile text.

Operations on variables

The argument *variable_name* in the descriptions that follow is just the name of a variable (without dollar sign and parentheses), not a reference to it. (Of course, you may use a variable reference to obtain the name of another variable.)

$(value *variable_name*)
>   Expands to the "raw" value of the variable named, without further expansion of any variable references it may contain.

$(origin *variable_name*)
>   Expands to one of the following values to indicate how the variable named was defined:

>>   undefined
>>   default
>>   environment
>>   environment override
>>   file
>>   command line
>>   override
>>   automatic

$(call *variable_name,argument*[,*argument*[,…]])
>   Expands the variable named, replacing numbered parameters in its expansion ($1, $2, etc.) with the remaining arguments. In effect, this built-in function allows you to create user-defined function-like macros. See "User-Defined Functions" on page 718.

System functions

The functions in the following list interact with *make*'s environment:

$(shell *text*)
>   Passes the expansion of *text* to the shell. The function expands to the standard output of the resulting shell command.

$(error *text*)
>   *make* prints the expansion of *text* as an error message and exits.

$(warning *text*)
>   Like the error command except that *make* doesn't exit. The function expands to nothing.

User-Defined Functions

You can define functions in the same way as simply expanded variables or macros, using the define directive or the := assignment operator. Functions in *make* are simply variables that contain numbered parameter references ($1, $2, $3, etc.) to

---

represent arguments that you provide when you use the built-in function `call` to expand the variable.

In order for these parameters to be replaced with the arguments when *make* expands your user-defined function, you have to pass the function name and arguments to the built-in *make* function `call`.

Example 20-5 defines the macro `getmodulename` to return a filename for a program module depending on whether the flag `STATIC` has been set, to indicate a statically linked executable, or left undefined, to indicate dynamic object linking.

Example 20-5. The user-defined function getmodulename

```
# A conditional assignment, just as a reminder that
# the user may define STATIC=1 or STATIC=yes on the command line.
STATIC ?=

# A function to generate the "library" module name:
# Syntax: $(call getmodulename, objectname, isstatic)
define getmodulename
  $(if $2,$1,$(addsuffix .so,$(basename $1)))
endef


all: circle


circle: circle.o $(call getmodulename,circulararea.o,$(STATIC))
        $(CC) -o $@ $^

ifndef STATIC
%.so: %.o
        $(CC) -shared -o $@ $<
endif
```

The `$(call …)` function expands the macro `getmodulename` either to the text `circulararea.o`, or, if the variable `STATIC` is not defined, to `circulararea.so`.

The rule to build the object file *circulararea.o* in Example 20-5 brings us to our next topic, as it illustrates another way to query the `STATIC` flag: by means of the *conditional directive* `ifndef`.

Directives

We have already introduced the `define` directive, which produces a simply expanded variable or a function. Other *make* directives allow you to influence the effective contents of your makefiles dynamically by making certain lines in a makefile dependent on variable conditions, or by inserting additional makefiles on the fly.

Conditionals

You can also make part of your makefile conditional upon the existence of a variable by using the ifdef or ifndef directive. They work the same as the C preprocessor directives of the same names, except that in *make*, an undefined variable is the same as one whose value is empty. Here is an example:

```
OBJ = circle.o
LIB = -lm

ifdef SHAREDLIBS
  LIB += circulararea.so
else
  OBJ += circulararea.o
endif

circle: $(OBJ) $(LIB)
        $(CC) -o $@ $^

%.so : %.o
        $(CC) -shared -o $@ $<
```

As the example shows, the variable name follows ifdef or ifndef without a dollar sign or parentheses. The makefile excerpt shown here defines a rule to link object files into a shared library if the variable SHAREDLIBS has been defined. You might define such a general build option in an environment variable, or on the command line, for example.

You can also make certain lines of the makefile conditional upon whether two expressions—usually the value of a variable and a literal string—are equal. The ifeq and ifneq directives test this condition. The two operands whose equality is the condition to test are either enclosed together in parentheses and separated by a comma, or enclosed individually in quotation marks and separated by whitespace. Here is an example:

```
ifeq ($(MATHLIB), /usr/lib/libm.so)
  # ... Special provisions for this particular math library ...
endif
```

That conditional directive, with parentheses, is equivalent to this one with quotation marks:

```
ifeq "$(MATHLIB)" "/usr/lib/libm.so"
  # ... Special provisions for this particular math library ...
endif
```

The second version has one strong advantage: the quotation marks make it quite clear where each of the operands begins and ends. In the first version, you must remember that whitespace within the parentheses *is* significant, except immediately before and after the comma (see also "Variables and Whitespace" on page 705).

---

make's handling of whitespace in the `ifeq` and `ifneq` directives is not the same as in function calls!

Includes

The `include` directive serves the same purpose as its C preprocessor counterpart but works slightly differently. To start with an example, you might write a makefile named *defaults.mk* with a set of standard variables for your environment, containing something like this:

```
BINDIR = /usr/bin
HOMEBINDIR = ~/bin
SRCDIR = project/src
BUILDDIR = project/obj

RM = rm -f
MKDIR = mkdir -p
# ... etc. ...
```

Then you could add these variables to any makefile by inserting this line:

```
include defaults.mk
```

The `include` keyword may be followed by more than one filename. You can also use shell wildcards like * and ?, and reference *make* variables to form filenames:

```
include $(HOMEBINDIR)/myutils.mk $(SRCDIR)/*.mk
```

For included files without an absolute path, *make* searches in the current working directory first, then in any directories specified with the -I option on the command line, and then in standard directories determined when *make* was compiled.

If *make* fails to find a file named in an `include` directive, it continues reading the makefile, and then checks to see whether there is a rule that will build the missing file. If so, *make* rereads the whole makefile after building the included file. If not, *make* exits with an error. The `-include` directive (or its synonym `sinclude`) is more tolerant: it works the same as `include` except that *make* ignores the error and goes on working if it can't find or build an included file.

Other Directives

Of the other four *make* directives, three are used to control the interplay between *make*'s internal variables and the shell environment, while the fourth instructs *make* where to look for specific kinds of files. These directives are:

`override` *variable_assignment*
>   Ordinarily, variables defined on the command line take precedence over definitions or assignments with the same name in a makefile. Prefixing the `override` keyword makes an assignment in a makefile take precedence over the com-

mand line. The *variable_assignment* may use the =, :=, or += operator, or the define directive.

export [*variable_name*|*variable_assignment*]

You can prefix export to a variable assignment or to the name of a variable that has been defined to export that variable to the environment, so that programs invoked by command scripts (including recursive invocations of *make*) can read it.

The export directive by itself on a line exports all *make* variables to the environment.

 make does not export variables whose *names* contain any characters other than letters, digits, and underscores. The *values* of variables you export from makefiles may contain characters that are not allowed in shell environment variables. Such values will probably not be accessible by ordinary shell commands. Nonetheless, child instances of *make* itself can inherit and use them.

The *make* variables SHELL and MAKEFLAGS, and also MAKEFILES if you have assigned it a value, are exported by default. Any variables that the current instance of *make* acquired from the environment are also passed on to child processes.

unexport *variable_name*

Use the unexport directive to prevent a variable from being exported to the environment. The unexport directive always overrides export.

vpath *pattern directory*[:*directory*[:…]]

The *pattern* in this directive is formed in the same way as in *make* pattern rules, using one percent sign (%) as a wildcard character. Whenever *make* needs a file that matches the pattern, it looks for it in the directories indicated, in the order of their appearance. Here is an example:

```
vpath %.c  $(MYPROJECTDIR)/src
vpath %.h  $(MYPROJECTDIR)/include:/usr/include
```

On Windows, the separator character in the directory list is a semicolon, not a colon.

Running make

This section explains how to add dependency information to the makefile automatically, and how to use *make* recursively. These two ways of using *make* are common and basic, but they do involve multiple features of the program. Finally, the remainder of this section is devoted to a reference list of GNU *make*'s command-line options and the special pseudotargets that also function as runtime options.

The command-line syntax of *make* is as follows:

```
make [options] [variable_assignments] [target [target [...]]]
```

If you don't specify any target on the command line, *make* behaves as though you had specified the default target; that is, whichever target is named first in the make-file. *make* builds other targets named in the makefile only if you request them on the command line or if they need to be built as prerequisites of any target requested.

Generating Header Dependencies

Our program executable *circle* depends on more files than those we have named in the sample makefile up to now. To begin with, just think of the standard headers included in our source code—not to mention the implementation-specific header files they include in turn.

Most C source files include both standard and user-defined header files, and the compiled program should be considered out of date whenever any header file has been changed. Because you cannot reasonably be expected to know the full list of header files involved, the standard *make* technique to account for these dependencies is to let the C preprocessor analyze the #include directives in your C source and write the appropriate *make* rules. The makefile lines in Example 20-6 fulfill this purpose.

Example 20-6. Generating header dependencies

```
CC = gcc
OBJ = circle.o circulararea.o
LIB = -lm

circle: $(OBJ) $(LIB)
        $(CC) $(LDFLAGS) -o $@ $^

%.o: %.c
        $(CC) $(CFLAGS) $(CPPFLAGS) -o $@ $<

dependencies: $(OBJ:.o=.c)
        $(CC) -M $^ > $@

include dependencies
```

The third rule uses a special kind of *make* variable reference, called a *substitution reference*, to declare that the target dependencies depend on files like those named in the value of $(OBJ) but with the ending *.c* instead of *.o*. The command to build dependencies runs the compiler with the preprocessor option -M, which instructs it to collate dependency information from source files. (The GCC compiler permits fine control of the dependency output by means of more preprocessor options that start with -M, which are listed in "GCC Options for Generating Makefile Rules" on page 729.)

The first time you use this makefile, *make* prints an error message about the `include` directive because no file named *dependencies* exists. When this happens, however, *make* automatically treats the missing file named in the `include` directive as a target, and looks for a rule to build it. The `include` directive itself is placed below the target rules to prevent the included file's contents from defining a new default target.

Recursive make Commands

Your makefile rules can include any command that is executable on your system. This includes the *make* command itself, and recursive invocation of *make* is in fact a frequently used technique, especially to process source code in subdirectories. *make* is designed to be aware of such recursive invocation, and incorporates certain features that help it work smoothly when you use it in this way. This section summarizes the special features of "recursive *make*."

The most typical recursive use of *make* is in building projects that are organized in subdirectories with a makefile in each one. The following snippet illustrates how a top-level makefile can invoke recursive instances of *make* in three subdirectories named *utils*, *drivers*, and *doc*:

```
.PHONY: utils drivers doc

utils drivers doc:
    $(MAKE) -C $@
```

The variable `MAKE` is not defined in the makefile; it is defined internally to yield the full pathname of the currently running program file. Your makefiles should always invoke *make* in this way to ensure consistent program behavior.

The command-line option `-C`, or its long form, `--directory`, causes *make* to change to the specified working directory on startup, before it even looks for a makefile. This is how *make* "passes control" to the makefile in a subdirectory when used recursively. In this example, the command does not name a target, so the child *make* will build the first target named in the default makefile in the given subdirectory.

The subdirectories themselves are declared as prerequisites of the special target `.PHONY` so that *make* never considers them up to date (see "Phony Targets" on page 711 for more details). However, if files in one subdirectory depend on files in a parallel subdirectory, you must account for these dependencies in the makefile of a higher-level directory that contains both subdirectories.

There are a few things to remember about command-line options and special variables when you use *make* recursively. A more complete list of *make* options and environment variables appears in the following section. The following list merely summarizes those with a special relevance to the recursive use of *make*:

- Some of *make*'s command-line options instruct it not to execute commands but to only print them (-n), touch the files (-t), or indicate whether the targets are up to date (-q). In these cases, if the subordinate *make* command were not executed, then these options would be incompatible with the recursive use of *make*. To ensure recursion, when you run *make* with one of the -t, -n, or -q options, commands containing the variable reference $(MAKE) *are* executed even though other commands are not. You can also extend this special treatment to other commands individually by prefixing a plus sign (+) to the command line as a command modifier.

- The variable MAKELEVEL automatically contains a numeral indicating the recursion depth of the current *make* instance, starting with 0 for a *make* invoked from the console.

- The parent instance of *make* passes its command-line options to child instances by copying them to the environment variable MAKEFLAGS. However, the options -C, -f, -o, and -W are exceptions: these options, which take a file or directory name as their argument, do not appear in MAKEFLAGS.

- The -j option, whose argument tells *make* how many commands it can spawn for parallel processing, is passed on to child instances of *make* but with the parallel job limit decreased by one.

- By default, a child instance of *make* inherits those of its parent's variables that were defined on the command line or in the environment. You can use the export directive to pass on variables defined in a makefile.

Like any other shell command in a makefile rule, a recursive instance of *make* can exit with an error status. If this happens, the parent *make* also exits with an error (unless it was started with the -k or --keep-going option), so that the error cascades up the chain of recursive *make* instances.

When using *make* recursively with multiple makefiles in subdirectories, you should use the include directive to avoid duplicating common definitions, implicit rules, and so on. See "Includes" on page 721 for more information.

Command-Line Options

The following is a brief summary of the command-line options supported by GNU *make*. Some of these options can also be enabled by including special targets in the makefile. These targets are described in "Special Targets Used as Runtime Options" on page 728.

-B, --always-make
> Build unconditionally. In other words, *make* considers all targets out of date.

-C *dir*, --directory=*dir*
> > *make* changes the current working directory to *dir* before it does anything else. If the command line includes multiple -C options (which is often the case when

make invokes itself recursively), each directory specified builds on the previous one. Here is an example:

```
$ make -C src -C common -C libs
```

These options would have the same effect as -C src/common/libs.

-d
Print debugging information.

-e, --environment-overrides
In the case of multiple definitions of a given variable name, variables defined on the *make* command line or in makefiles normally have precedence over environment variables. This command-line option makes environment variables take precedence over variable assignments in makefiles (except for variables specified in override directives).

-f *filename*, --file=*filename*, --makefile=*filename*
Use the makefile *filename*.

-h, --help
Print *make*'s command-line options.

-i, --ignore-errors
Ignore any errors that occur when executing command scripts.

-I *dir*, --include-dir=*dir*
If a makefile contains include directives that specify files without absolute paths, search for such files in the directory *dir* (in addition to the current directory). If the command line includes several -I options, the directories are searched in the order of their occurrence.

-j [*number*], --jobs[=*number*]
Run multiple commands in parallel. The optional integer argument *number* specifies the maximum number of simultaneous jobs. The -j argument by itself causes *make* to run as many simultaneous commands as possible. (Naturally, *make* is smart enough not to start building any target before its prerequisites have been completed.) If the command line includes several -j options, the last one overrides all others.

Parallel jobs spawned by *make* do not share the standard streams elegantly. Console output from different jobs can appear in random order, and only one job can inherit the stdin stream from *make*. If you use the -j option, make sure none of the commands in your makefiles read from stdin.

`-k, --keep-going`

This option tells *make* not to exit after a command has returned a nonzero exit status. Instead, *make* abandons the failed target and any other targets that depend on it but continues working on any other goals in progress.

`-l [number], --load-average[=number], --max-load[=number]`

In conjunction with the `-j` option, `-l` (that's a lowercase L) prevents *make* from executing more simultaneous commands whenever the system load is greater than or equal to the floating-point value *number*. The `-l` option with no argument cancels any load limit imposed by previous `-l` options.

`-n, --just-print, --dry-run, --recon`

make prints the commands it would otherwise run, but doesn't actually execute them.

`-o filename, --old-file=filename, --assume-old=filename__`

make treats the specified file as if it were up to date, and yet older than any file that depends on it.

`-p, --print-data-base`

Before executing any commands, *make* prints its version information and all its rules and variables, including built-ins and those acquired from makefiles.

`-q, --question`

make builds nothing and prints nothing, but returns an exit status as follows:

Exit status	Meaning
0	All specified targets are up to date.
1	At least one target is out of date.
2	An error occurred.

`-r, --no-builtin-rules`

This option disables *make*'s built-in implicit rules, as well as the default list of suffixes for old-style suffix rules. Pattern rules, user-defined suffixes, and suffix rules that you have defined in makefiles still apply, as do built-in variables.

`-R, --no-builtin-variables`

Like `-r`, but also disables *make*'s built-in rule-specific variables. Variables you define in makefiles are unaffected.

`-s, --silent, --quiet`

Ordinarily, *make* echoes each command on standard output before executing it. This option suppresses such output.

`-S, --no-keep-going, --stop`

This option causes a recursive instance of *make* to ignore a `-k` or `--keep-going` option inherited from its parent *make*.

`-t, --touch`

make simply touches target files—that is, it updates their timestamps—instead of rebuilding them.

`-v, --version`

make prints its version and copyright information.

`-w, --print-directory`

make prints a line indicating the working directory before and after processing the makefile. This output can be useful in debugging recursive make applications. This option is enabled by default for recursive instances of make, and whenever you use the -C option.

`--no-print-directory`

Disable the working directory output in cases where -w is automatically activated.

`-W filename, --what-if=filename, --new-file=<filename,`
`--assume-new=filename`

make treats the file filename as if it were brand new.

`--warn-undefined-variables`

Normally, make takes references to undefined variables in its stride, treating them like references to variables with empty values. This option provides warnings about undefined variables to help you debug makefiles.

Special Targets Used as Runtime Options

The built-in targets listed in this section are ordinarily used in makefiles to alter make's runtime behavior in general. Other built-in targets are used primarily to assign attributes to certain targets in a makefile, and are listed in "Other Target Attributes" on page 712.

`.DEFAULT`

You can use the built-in target .DEFAULT to introduce a command script that you want make to execute for any target that is not covered by any other explicit or implicit rule. make also executes the .DEFAULT command script for every prerequisite that is not a target in some rule.

`.DELETE_ON_ERROR`

You can include the built-in target .DELETE_ON_ERROR anywhere in a makefile to instruct make to delete any target that has been changed by its command script if the script returns a nonzero value on exiting.

`.SILENT`

Normally, make prints each command to standard output before executing it. However, if a given target is a prerequisite of .SILENT, then make does not print the rules when building that target.

If you include .SILENT with no prerequisites in a makefile, it applies to all targets, like the command-line options -s or --silent.

.EXPORT_ALL_VARIABLES

This target acts as an option telling *make* to export all the currently defined variables before spawning child processes (see "Recursive make Commands" on page 724).

.NOTPARALLEL

This built-in target is a general option; any prerequisites are ignored. The target .NOTPARALLEL in a makefile overrides the command-line option -j for the current instance of *make*, so that targets are built in sequence. If *make* invokes itself, however, the new instance of make still executes commands in parallel, unless its makefile also contains .NOTPARALLEL.

.SUFFIXES

This built-in target defines the list of suffixes that *make* recognizes for use in old-style suffix rules (see "Suffix Rules" on page 700). You can add suffixes to the built-in list by naming them as prerequisites of .SUFFIXES, or clear the list by declaring the target .SUFFIXES with no prerequisites.

GCC Options for Generating Makefile Rules

-M

Generate a rule showing the prerequisites for the object file that would result from compiling a given source file. The -M option implies the -E option (preprocess only; don't compile), but the -MD and -MMD variants do not. By default, the dependency rules are written to standard output.

-MD

Like -M, but allows GCC to compile source files (unless -E is also present) in addition to running the preprocessor. The dependency output is written to a file whose name is taken from the -o argument, if any, but with the filename ending .d.

-MM

Like -M, but omit header files located in system header directories (and any files they depend on in turn) from the dependency list.

-MMD

Combines the effects of -MM and -MD.

The following options are modifiers used in addition to -M, -MD, -MM, or -MMD:

-MF *filename*

Writes the dependency information to *filename* rather than to standard output or to a preprocessor output file.

`-MG`
> Include nonexistent header files in the dependency list.

`-MP`
> Include a phony target for each header file in the dependency output. The effect is that *make* doesn't complain about header files that have been removed from the project but not from the dependency list.

`-MT` *target*
> Substitute *target* for the actual target in generating dependency rules.

`-MQ` *target*
> Like -MT, but quote any special characters.

21

Debugging C Programs with GDB

An important part of software development is testing and troubleshooting. In a large program, programming errors—or *bugs*—are practically inevitable. Programs can deliver wrong results, get hung up in infinite loops, or crash due to illegal memory operations. The task of finding and eliminating such errors is called *debugging* a program.

Many bugs are not apparent by simply studying the source code. Extra output provided by a testing version of the program is one helpful diagnostic technique. You can add statements to display the contents of variables and other information during runtime. However, you can generally perform runtime diagnostics much more efficiently by using a debugger.

A *debugger* is a program that runs another program in a finely controlled environment. For example, a debugger allows you to run the program step by step, observing the contents of variables, memory locations, and CPU registers after each statement. You can also analyze the sequence of function calls that lead to a given point in the program.

This chapter is an introduction to one powerful and widely used debugger, the GNU debugger (GDB). The sections that follow describe GDB's basic options and commands. Most of the features and working principles described here are similar to those of other debugging tools. For a complete description of GDB's capabilities, see the program manual "Debugging with GDB" (*http://www.gnu.org/software/gdb/documentation/*) by the Free Software Foundation, which is available in PDF and HTML. If your system also has the GNU Texinfo system installed, you can browse the full manual by entering the shell command info gdb.

Installing GDB

If the GNU C compiler, GCC, is available on your system, then GDB is probably already installed as well. You can tell by running the following command, which displays the debugger's version and copyright information:

```
$ gdb -version
```

As in the preceding chapters, the dollar sign character ($) followed by a space represents the shell command prompt.

If GDB is installed, a message like the following appears:

```
GNU gdb (GDB) 7.8
Copyright (C) 2014 Free Software Foundation, Inc.
License GPLv3+: GNU GPL version 3 or later
<http://gnu.org/licenses/gpl.html>
This is free software: you are free to change and redistribute it.
There is NO WARRANTY, to the extent permitted by law.
Type "show copying" and "show warranty" for details.
This GDB was configured as "x86_64-pc-cygwin".
...
```

If GDB is not installed, you can download the source code and compile it (*http://www.gnu.org/software/gdb/download*). This is seldom necessary, though. Most Unix-like systems provide a convenient method to install a binary GDB package, including the documentation. On Windows systems, we recommend that you install the Cygwin software. Cygwin provides a standard Unix environment on Windows platforms, including the GCC compiler, GDB debugger, and other GNU tools (see *http://www.cygwin.com* or *http://www.redhat.com/software/cygwin/*).

A Sample Debugging Session

This section describes a sample GDB session to illustrate the basic operation of the debugger. Many problems in C programs can be pinpointed using just a handful of debugger commands. The program in Example 21-1, *gdb_example.c*, contains a logical error. We'll use this program in the following subsections to show how GDB can be used to track down such errors.

Example 21-1. A program to be debugged in a GDB session

```
// gdb_example.c:
// Test the swap() function, which exchanges the contents
// of two int variables.
// -------------------------------------------------------------
#include <stdio.h>

void swap( int *p1, int *p2 );          // Exchange *p1 and *p2

int main()
{
```

```
  int a = 10, b = 20;
/* ... */
  printf( "The old values: a = %d; b = %d.\n", a, b );

  swap( &a, &b );

  printf( "The new values: a = %d; b = %d.\n", a, b );
/* ... */
  return 0;
}

void swap( int *p1, int *p2 )        // Exchange *p1 and *p2
{
  int *p = p1;
  p1 = p2;
  p2 = p;
}
```

Symbol Information

GDB is a symbolic command-line debugger. "Symbolic" here means that you can refer to variables and functions in the running program by the names you gave them in your C source code. In order to display and interpret these names, the debugger requires information about the types of the variables and functions in the program, and about which instructions in the executable file correspond to which lines in the source files. Such information takes the form of a *symbol table*, which the compiler and linker include in the executable file when you run GCC with the -g option:

```
$ gcc -g gdb_example.c
```

In a large program consisting of several source files, you must compile each module with the -g option.

Finding a Bug

The following command runs the program from Example 21-1:

```
$ ./a.out
```

The program produces the following output:

```
The old values: a = 10; b = 20.
The new values: a = 10; b = 20.
```

Although the swap() function call is plain to see in the source code, the contents of the variables a and b have not been swapped. We can look for the reason using GDB. To begin the debugging session, start GDB from the shell, specifying the name of the executable file as a command-line argument to the debugger:

```
$ gdb ./a.out
```

```
GNU gdb (GDB) 7.8
Copyright (C) 2014 Free Software Foundation, Inc.
...
(gdb)
```

The debugger loads the program executable but waits for your instructions before running it. GDB prints (gdb) at the beginning of a new line to prompt you for a debugging command. You can start by entering the command list, or just its initial l for short, to list a few lines of source code of the program you are debugging. By default, the listing shows 10 lines, centered on the source line that is ready to be executed next. In our example, the program has just been started, and the next line is line 8, where the function main() begins:

```
(gdb) l
5
6         void swap( int *p1, int *p2 );          // Exchange *p1 and *p2
7
8         int main()
9         {
10            int a = 10, b = 20;
11            /* ... */
12
13            printf( "The old values: a = %d; b = %d.\n", a, b );
14
(gdb)
```

If you follow one list command with another, GDB prints the next few lines of source code.

Before you instruct GDB to run the program, you should tell it where you want it to stop. You can do this by setting a *breakpoint*. When the debugger reaches the breakpoint, it interrupts the execution of your program, giving you an opportunity to examine the program's state at that point. Furthermore, once the program has been interrupted at a breakpoint, you can continue execution line by line, observing the state of program objects as you go.

To set a breakpoint, enter the command break, or b for short. Breakpoints are usually set at a specific line of source code or at the beginning of a function. The following command sets a breakpoint at line 15 of the current source file, which is the line containing the swap() function call:

```
(gdb) b 15
Breakpoint 1 at 0x80483aa: file gdb_example.c, line 15.
```

The command run, or r, starts the program:

```
(gdb) r
Starting program: /home/peter/src/c/gdb/a.out
Breakpoint 1, main () at gdb_example.c:15
15              swap( &a, &b );
```

Upon reaching the breakpoint, the debugger interrupts the execution of the program and displays the line containing the next statement to be executed. Because we suspect the bug in our example is in the swap() function, we want to execute that function step by step. For this purpose, GDB provides the commands next, or n, and step, or s. The next and step commands behave differently if the next line to be executed contains a function call. The next command executes the next line, including all function calls, and interrupts the program again at the following line. The step command, on the other hand, executes a jump to the function called in the line, provided that the debugging symbols are available for that function, and interrupts the program again at the first statement in the function body. In our example session, the command step takes us to the first statement in the swap() function:

```
(gdb) s
swap (p1=0xbffff234, p2=0xbffff230) at gdb_example.c:24
24          int *p = p1;
```

The debugger displays the values of the function arguments (here, these are the addresses of the variables a and b), and once again the next line to be executed. At this point, we can check to see whether the values of the variables referenced by the function's pointer arguments are correct. We can do this using the print command (p for short), which displays the value of a given expression:

```
(gdb) p *p1
$1 = 10
(gdb) p *p2
$2 = 20
```

The expression *p1 has the value 10, and *p2 has the value 20. The output of GDB's print command has the form $number = value, where $number is a GDB variable that the debugger creates so that you can refer to this result later. (See "Displaying Data" on page 756 for more information about GDB's variables.)

If we now type n (for next) three times, the debugger executes lines 24, 25, and 26:

```
(gdb) n
25          p1 = p2;
(gdb) n
26          p2 = p;
(gdb) n
27      }
(gdb)
```

As long as the program flow has not yet returned from the swap() function to main(), we can use the print command to display the contents of the local variables:

```
(gdb) p *p1
$3 = 20
(gdb) p *p2
$4 = 10
```

Now *p1 has the value 20, and *p2 has the value 10, which seems correct. We can continue the examination of the program state with two more print commands:

```
(gdb) p p1
$5 = (int *) 0xbffff230
(gdb) p p2
$6 = (int *) 0xbffff234
(gdb)
```

As these print commands show, the values of the pointers p1 and p2 have been swapped—not the contents of the memory locations referenced as *p1 and *p2. That was the bug in swap(). The function needs to be amended so that it exchanges the int values addressed as *p1 and *p2, rather than the pointer values stored in p1 and p2. A correct version would be the following:

```
void swap( int *p1, int *p2 )           // Exchange *p1 and *p2
{
    int tmp = *p1;
    *p1 = *p2;
    *p2 = tmp;
}
```

The command continue, abbreviated c, lets program execution continue until it reaches the next breakpoint or the end of the program:

```
(gdb) c
Continuing.
The new values: a = 10; b = 20
Program exited normally.
(gdb)
```

As the (gdb) prompt indicates, the debugger is still running. To stop it, enter the command quit or q. The quit command terminates the debugger even if the program you are debugging is still running. However, GDB does prompt you for confirmation in this case:

```
(gdb) q
The program is running.  Exit anyway? (y or n) y
$
```

Starting GDB

You can start GDB by entering gdb at the shell command prompt. GDB supports numerous command-line options and arguments:

```
gdb [options] [executable_file [core_file | process_id]]
```

For example, the following command starts the debugger without displaying its sign-on message:

```
$ gdb -silent
(gdb)
```

In this example, the command line does not name the executable file to be debugged. You can specify the program you want to test in GDB using the debugger's `file` command, described in "Using GDB Commands" on page 741.

Command-Line Arguments

Ordinarily, the program to be debugged is named on the GDB command line. In the following example, the GDB command loads the executable *myprog* for debugging:

```
$ gdb myprog
(gdb)
```

As an additional argument after the name of the program to be tested, you may specify a process ID number or the name of a core dump file. In the following example, the number after the program name is a process ID (or "PID"):

```
$ gdb myprog 1001
(gdb)
```

This command instructs GDB to connect to a process that is already running on the system, and has the program name *myprog* and the process ID 1001. If GDB finds such a process, you can interrupt its execution to begin debugging by pressing Ctrl+C. If there is no running process with this ID, however, and the debugger finds a file in the current working directory named *1001*, it will interpret that argument as the name of a core file rather than a process ID. A core file is a file containing the memory dump representing the state of a process. For details about debugging with core files, see "Analyzing Core Files in GDB" on page 763.

Command-Line Options

Most of the command-line options for the GDB debugger have both short and long forms. The descriptions in the following list and subsections show both forms for the most frequently used options. You can also truncate the long form if you type enough of it to be unambiguous. For options that take an argument, such as `-tty` *device*, the option and its argument can be separated by a space or by an equals sign (=), as in `-tty=/dev/tty6`. Options may be introduced by one or two hyphens: `-quiet`, for example, is synonymous with `--quiet`.

 This section lists the most commonly used GDB options. For a complete list, see the program manual (*http://www.gnu.org/software/gdb/documentation*).

`--version, -v`
GDB prints its version and copyright information to the console, and then exits without starting a debugging session.

`--quiet, --silent`
> GDB starts an interactive session without displaying its version and copyright information.

`--help, -h`
> GDB displays its command-line syntax with a brief description of all the options, and then exits without starting a debugging session.

Passing arguments to the program being debugged

GDB has one special command-line option that serves to separate the debugger's own command line from that of the program you want it to load for debugging:

`--args`
> Use the `--args` option on starting a debugging session to pass command-line arguments to the program that GDB loads for debugging. In the following example, myprog is the program to be debugged:
>
> ```
> $ gdb --args myprog -d "$HOME"
> (gdb)
> ```
>
> The `--args` option must be immediately followed by the command invoking the program you wish to debug. That command should consist of the program name and then its arguments, just as they would appear if you were starting that program without GDB. In the previous example, `-d` and `"$HOME"` are command-line arguments for *myprog*, not for *gdb*. If you want to specify options for GDB at the same time, you must place them before `--args` on the command line. In other words, `--args` must be the last GDB option.

You can also specify arguments for the program you are debugging after GDB has started by using one of the interactive commands `run` or `set args`, described in "Running a Program in the Debugger" on page 744.

Selecting files

The following command-line options tell GDB which input files to use:

`-symbols` *filename*, `-s` *filename*
> If the table of debugging symbols is not contained in the executable file, use the `-symbols` option to load a separate symbol table file. GDB reads the symbol table from the specified file.

`-exec` *filename*, `-e` *filename*
> The `-exec` option specifies the executable file to be debugged.

`-se` *filename*
> The specified file is the executable you want to test in GDB and contains the symbol table. This option is not usually necessary; if the GDB command line contains a filename that is not an argument to any option, GDB treats the first such file as if it were an argument to the `-se` option.

-core *filename,* **-c** *filename,* **-c** *number,* **-pid** *number,* **-p** *number*

>The -core and -pid options are actually synonymous. If the argument to either one is a decimal number, GDB connects to a running process with that process ID, if there is one. If there is no process with that ID, GDB attempts to open a core file with the name *number.* If you want to force GDB to open a core file whose name is a decimal number, you can prefix the directory to the filename. For example, gdb -p ./32436 instructs GDB to open a core file named *32436* in the current directory, regardless of whether there is a running process with that PID.

>Like the -se option, the -core option is often unnecessary. If the GDB command line contains a second filename that is not an argument to any option, GDB treats that file as if it were an argument to the -core option.

Selecting the user interface

In GDB's customary command-line mode, the console I/O of the program being debugged appears interspersed with the debugger's own commands and diagnostic output. If this behavior is inconvenient, you can prevent it by specifying a separate terminal for the input and output of the program you are debugging:

-tty *device,* **-t** *device*

>The debugger uses *device* as the standard input and output streams of the program you are debugging. In the following example, the standard I/O streams of the program *myprog* are attached to the terminal */dev/tty5:*

> $ **gdb myprog -t /dev/tty5**

-windows, -w

>GDB may also be built with an integrated GUI. This user interface provides separate display windows for the source code, assembler code, and CPU registers of the program you are debugging. The -w option instructs GDB to run with its GUI, if possible. If the GUI is not available, this option has no effect.

-nowindows, -nw

>The -nw option instructs GDB to run in console mode, even if a GUI is available. If the GUI is not available, this option has no effect.

There are a number of separate "frontend" programs that provide GUIs for GDB. The best known of these is DDD, the Data Display Debugger (*http://www.gnu.org/software/ddd/*). DDD's capabilities include displaying dynamic data structures such as linked lists and trees. But even without a GUI, you may be able to use separate display windows with GDB:

-tui

>If the help text displayed by the command gdb -h includes the option --tui, then your GDB installation provides a text-based user interface, or TUI, to manage a number of console windows. The TUI is a program module that uses the *curses* library.

The -tui option starts GDB with the text-based full-screen user interface, or TUI. The initial display consists of two windows: the upper window displays the C source code, with the current line highlighted and breakpoints indicated in the left margin. Below it is the command window, which displays the same (gdb) command prompt and diagnostic output as a line-based GDB session. You can also open a third window to display the program in assembly language or the contents of CPU registers. For details about working with the TUI, see the section "GDB Text User Interface" in the GDB manual (*http://www.gnu.org/software/gdb/documentation/*).

 If you use the Emacs editor, you can run GDB using the Emacs buffer windows for its display. Start GDB within Emacs using the command M-x gdb. The debugger's command window appears as a new Emacs buffer. When you begin running a program in GDB, a second buffer is created displaying the source code. The Emacs "debugger" mode also provides commands to control GDB, which are described in the section "Using GDB under GNU Emacs" in the GDB manual, and also documented in Emacs itself through the C-h m command.

Executing command scripts

-command *command_file*, -x *command_file*

The -command or -x option instructs GDB to carry out the commands in the specified file on starting. A command file is a text file whose lines are GDB commands. Blank lines and comments, which are lines beginning with the hash character (#), are ignored. If you want the debugger to execute one or more command files and then exit, use the -batch option in addition to the -x or -command option.

-batch

The -batch option instructs GDB to exit after executing all command files specified in -x commands. If no errors occur, GDB exits with the status 0. Any other exit status indicates an error.

Initialization Files

On starting, GDB ordinarily processes an initialization file, if present, with the name *.gdbinit*. On certain systems with a special debugger configuration, the initialization file may have a different name. Initialization files have the same internal syntax as command files, consisting of GDB commands, comments, and blank lines. GDB processes the initialization files it finds in the current directory and your home directory. The initialization files, command line, and command files are processed in the following order:

1. Upon starting, GDB first reads the initialization file in your home directory, if present, and carries out the commands it contains. On Windows, GDB deter-

mines the home directory from the value of the environment variable HOME. The initialization file typically contains general commands to configure the debugger, such as set listsize 5 to limit the default output of the list command to five lines.

2. Next, GDB processes the command-line options. Any command files specified in -x or -command options are not executed at this point, though.

3. If the current directory is not your home directory, and if the current directory contains an initialization file, GDB executes the commands in that file. Usually, the current directory contains the files of a program in development, and the local initialization file *.gdbinit* contains commands to configure the debugger for the program's special requirements.

4. Finally, GDB executes the commands in files specified by the -x or -command options on the command line.

GDB also lets you skip any *.gdbinit* files by specifying the following command-line option:

-nx, -n
Instructs GDB to ignore all initialization files. The option takes no argument.

Using GDB Commands

Upon starting, the debugger prompts you to enter commands—for example, to set a breakpoint and run the program that you specified on the command line to load for debugging.

Each command you issue to GDB is a line of text beginning with a command keyword. The remainder of the line consists of the command's arguments. You can truncate any keyword, as long as you type enough of it to identify a command unambiguously. For example, you can enter q (or qu or qui) to exit the debugger with the quit command.

If you enter an empty command line—that is, if you press the Enter key immediately at the GDB command prompt—then GDB repeats your last command, if that action is plausible. For example, GDB automatically repeats step and next commands in this way, but not a run command.

If you enter an ambiguous or unknown abbreviation, or fail to specify required command arguments, GDB responds with an appropriate error message, as in this example:

```
(gdb) sh
Ambiguous command "sh": sharedlibrary, shell, show.
```

Command Completion

The GDB debugger can reduce your typing by completing the names of commands, variables, files, and functions. Type the first few characters of the desired word, and then press the Tab key. For example, the program *circle.c* in Example 1-1 contains the function `circularArea()`. To display this function in a GDB session, all you have to type is the following:

(gdb) **list ci**

Then press the Tab key. Automatic completion yields this command line:

(gdb) **list circularArea**

Press Enter to execute the command. If there are several possible completions for a word, GDB inserts the next letters that are common to all possible completions, and then prompts you for more input. You can type another letter or two to make your entry more specific, and then press the Tab key again. If you press the Tab key twice in a row, GDB displays all possible completions of the word. Here is an example of command completion in several steps:

(gdb) **break ci<tab>**

GDB appends two letters, and then pauses for more input to resolve an ambiguity:

(gdb) break circ

If you press the Tab key twice, GDB displays the possible completions, and then repeats the prompt:

```
(gdb) break circ<tab><tab>
circle.c       circularArea
(gdb) break circ
```

Displaying Help for Commands

GDB has a help function, which divides its many commands into classes to help you find the one you need. When you enter the `help` (or `h`) command with no argument, GDB prints the list of command classes:

```
(gdb) h
List of classes of commands:
aliases -- Aliases of other commands
breakpoints -- Making program stop at certain points
data -- Examining data
files -- Specifying and examining files
internals -- Maintenance commands
obscure -- Obscure features
running -- Running the program
stack -- Examining the stack
status -- Status inquiries
support -- Support facilities
tracepoints -- Tracing of program execution without stopping the
program
user-defined -- User-defined commands
Type "help" followed by a class name for a list of commands in that
class.
Type "help" followed by command name for full documentation.
```

```
Command name abbreviations are allowed if unambiguous.
(gdb)
```

To read about the commands in a given class, type help followed by the class name. To read about how a given command works, type help followed by the name of the command.

Status Information

To display information about the status of the debugger and the program being debugged, GDB provides the commands info and show, as the help text shows:

```
(gdb) help status
Status inquiries.
List of commands:
info -- Generic command for showing things about the program being
debugged
show -- Generic command for showing things about the debugger
```

Status information on the program being debugged

The info command with no argument lists all the items that you can query about the program you are testing:

```
(gdb) info
List of info subcommands:

info address -- Describe where symbol SYM is stored
info all-registers -- List of all registers and their contents
info args -- Argument variables of current stack frame
info breakpoints -- Status of user-settable breakpoints
 ...
```

When you specify one of the info arguments listed, GDB displays the corresponding information. Like commands, these arguments can be abbreviated, as in the following command:

```
(gdb) info all-reg
```

This command displays the contents of all processor registers, including floating-point and vector registers. The command info register, on the other hand, displays only the CPU registers, without the floating-point or vector registers.

The following command displays information about the *current source file*; that is, the source file containing the function that is currently being executed. If you have not yet started the program that you want to test, then the current source file is the one that contains the function main():

```
(gdb) info source
Current source file is circle.c
Compilation directory is /home/peter/C_in_a_Nutshell/tests/Ch21/
 ...
(gdb)
```

Some of the subcommands take another argument. For example, the info subcommand address in the following example takes the name of an object or function as its argument:

```
(gdb) info address radius
Symbol "radius" is a local variable at frame offset -8.
(gdb)
```

Status information on the debugger

Like info, the show command also has numerous subcommands to display various kinds of information about the debugger itself. The help text on show describes its subcommands:

```
(gdb) help show
Generic command for showing things about the debugger.
List of show subcommands:

show annotate -- Show annotation_level
show archdebug -- Show architecture debugging
show architecture -- Show the current target architecture
show args -- Show argument list to give program being debugged when it
is started
...
```

The following command displays information about GDB's current logging behavior:

```
(gdb) show logging
Future logs will be written to gdb.txt.
Logs will be appended to the log file.
Output will be logged and displayed.
(gdb)
```

Most of the settings displayed by show can be modified by the set command. For example, the following command turns on logging:

```
(gdb) set logging on
Copying output to gdb.txt.
(gdb) show logging
Currently logging to "gdb.txt".
...
```

The online help also describes the subcommands. For example, the following help command displays a description of possible logging settings:

```
(gdb) help set logging
```

Running a Program in the Debugger

The following GDB commands allow you to control programs running in the debugger:

file *filename*

If you have not specified the program you want to debug in the GDB command line, you can indicate it at GDB's prompt using the file command. GDB reads the symbol table from the executable file *filename*, and starts the program if you enter a subsequent run command. If *filename* is not in the debugger's working directory, the debugger searches for it in the directories named in the environment variable PATH.

set args [*arguments*]

If you have not specified the command-line arguments for the program you want to debug in the GDB command line, you can define them at GDB's prompt using the set args command. For example, the following command specifies two arguments for the program being tested:

```
(gdb) set args -d $HOME
```

To clear the argument list without setting new arguments, enter the set args command with no further arguments.

show args

Displays the currently set command-line arguments for the program being debugged:

```
(gdb) show args
Argument list to give program being debugged when it is started
is "-d $HOME".
```

run [*arguments*]

When you start a program using the run command (r for short), you can also specify command-line arguments for it. On Unix-like systems, the *arguments* may contain shell metacharacters such as * and $. You can also redirect the program's input and output using <, >, and >>. The debugger uses a shell to interpret the program's command line so that all special characters have the same effect as they would in an ordinary shell environment. GDB uses whichever shell is indicated by the SHELL environment variable, or the default shell */bin/sh* if SHELL is not defined.

The run command with no arguments starts the program with the arguments currently set for it in GDB. If you have not yet set any arguments for the program, whether in a previous run command, on the GDB command line, or in a set args command, then run starts the program with no arguments.

Once you start the program using the run command, it runs until it exits or until it reaches a breakpoint that you have set in the debugger. The program can also be interrupted by a signal, such as the SIGINT signal, which is usually raised by the key combination Ctrl+C.

kill

If you have found one or more errors to correct and want to edit and recompile a program outside the debugger, you should first terminate it. You can do this using the `kill` command, as in the following example:

```
(gdb) kill
Kill the program being debugged? (y or n) y
```

The settings, including the command-line arguments for the program, remain unchanged as long as you do not exit the debugger. The next time you start the program using the `run` command, GDB detects the fact that the executable file has been modified, and reloads it.

Displaying Source Code

You can display a program's source code in the debugger using the `list` (or `l`) command. By default, GDB displays ten lines at a time, starting five lines before the next statement to be executed. The `list` command supports arguments that allow you to specify which part of the program you want to display:

list *filename*:*line_number*
Displays source code centered around the line with the specified line number.

list *line_number*
If you do not specify a source filename, then the lines displayed are those in the current source file.

list *from*,[*to*]
Displays the specified range of the source code. The *from* and *to* arguments can be either line numbers or function names. If you do not specify a *to* argument, `list` displays the default number of lines beginning at *from*. For example, the following command displays the first 10 lines of the `main()` function:

```
(gdb) list main,
```

list *function_name*
Displays source code centered around the line in which the specified function begins.

list, l
The `list` command with no arguments displays more lines of source code following those presented by the last `list` command. If another command executed since the last `list` command also displayed a line of source code, then the new `list` command displays lines centered around the line displayed by that command. For example, if the debugger has just interrupted execution of the program at a breakpoint, the next `list` command displays lines centered around that breakpoint.

If you have not yet started the program, the first `list` command with no arguments displays source code centered around the beginning of the `main()` function, as the following example illustrates:

```
$ gdb -silent circle
(gdb) l
1    // Circle.c: Calculate and print the areas of circles
2    #include <stdio.h>                // Preprocessor directive
3
4    double circularArea( double r );  // Function declaration
5                                      // (prototype form)
6    int main()                        // Definition of main() begins
7    {
8      double radius = 1.0, area = 0.0;
9
10     printf( "    Areas of Circles\n\n" );
(gdb)
```

Two other commands are useful in controlling the output of your `list` commands:

`set listsize` *number*
Sets the default number of lines displayed by `list` commands to *number*.

`show listsize`
Shows the default number of lines displayed by `list` commands.

Working with Breakpoints

On reaching a breakpoint, the debugger interrupts the running program and displays the line at which you have set the breakpoint. To be exact, the line displayed is the line containing the next statement that will be executed when the program resumes. Once the program flow has been interrupted by a breakpoint, you can use GDB commands to execute the program line by line, and to display the contents of variables and registers.

Breakpoints can also be made conditional, so that on reaching such a breakpoint, the debugger interrupts the program only if a specified condition is fulfilled.

Setting and displaying breakpoints

Set breakpoints using the `break` command, which you can also abbreviate b. You can specify the location of a breakpoint in several ways. Here are the most common forms of the `break` command:

`break [`*filename:*`]`*line_number*
Sets a breakpoint at the specified line in the current source file, or in the source file *filename*, if specified.

`break` *function*
Sets a breakpoint at the first line of the specified function.

break

Sets a breakpoint at the next statement to be executed. In other words, the program flow will be automatically interrupted the next time it reaches the point where it is now. (To be more exact, the break command with no arguments sets a breakpoint at the next statement in the currently selected stack frame; see "Analyzing the Stack" on page 753. For now, we assume that you have not explicitly selected any stack frame, so that the current frame corresponds to the function in which the program flow is currently interrupted, and the break command with no arguments sets a breakpoint at the current statement.)

Referring now to the program *gdb_example.c* from Example 21-1, the following command sets a breakpoint at the beginning of the function swap():

```
(gdb) b swap
Breakpoint 1 at 0x4010e7: file gdb_example.c, line 27.
```

The output from the b command tells you that the breakpoint was set on line 27. You can issue the list command to confirm that line 27 is, in fact, the first line of the swap function:

```
(gdb) list 27
22          return 0;
23      }
24
25      void swap( int *p1, int *p2 )            // Exchange *p1 and *p2
26      {
27          int *p = p1;
28          p1 = p2;
29          p2 = p;
30      }
31
```

The following command sets a second breakpoint before the end of the function:

```
(gdb) b 30
Breakpoint 2 at 0x4010f9: file gdb_example.c, line 30.
```

You can use the info command to display all the breakpoints that are currently defined:

```
(gdb) info breakpoints
Num Type           Disp Enb Address    What
1   breakpoint     keep y   0x004010e7 in swap at gdb_example.c:27
2   breakpoint     keep y   0x004010f9 in swap at gdb_example.c:30
```

The breakpoint numbers shown at left in the info output are used to identify the individual breakpoints in other commands, such as those used to delete or disable a breakpoint. In the info output just shown, the letter y for "yes" in the column labeled Enb indicates that both breakpoints are enabled. The third column, labeled Disp for "disposition," indicates whether each breakpoint will be retained or deleted the next time the program flow reaches it. If a breakpoint is temporary, GDB automatically deletes it as soon as it is reached. To set a temporary breakpoint, use the tbreak command instead of break, as in the following example:

```
(gdb) tbreak 16
Breakpoint 3 at 0x4010c0: file gdb_example.c, line 16.
```

Deleting, disabling, and ignoring breakpoints

The following commands take as their argument either a single breakpoint number or a *range* of breakpoints (a range consists of two breakpoint numbers separated by a hyphen, such as 3-5):

delete [*bp_number* | *range*], d [*bp_number* | *range*]
> Deletes the specified breakpoint or range of breakpoints. A delete command with no argument deletes all the breakpoints that have been defined. GDB prompts you for confirmation before carrying out such a sweeping command:
>
> ```
> (gdb) d
> Delete all breakpoints? (y or n)
> ```

disable [*bp_number* | *range*]
> Temporarily deactivates a breakpoint or a range of breakpoints. If you don't specify any argument, this command affects all breakpoints. It is often more practical to disable breakpoints temporarily than to delete them. GDB retains the information about the positions and conditions of disabled breakpoints so that you can easily reactivate them.

enable [*bp_number* | *range*]
> Restores disabled breakpoints. If you don't specify any argument, this command affects all disabled breakpoints.

ignore *bp_number iterations*
> Instructs GDB to pass over a breakpoint without stopping a certain number of times. The ignore command takes two arguments: the number of a breakpoint, and the number of times you want it to be passed over.

Here is an example using all of the commands listed:

```
(gdb) del 2
(gdb) dis 1-3
No breakpoint number 2.
(gdb) ena 1
(gdb) ign 1 5
Will ignore next 5 crossings of breakpoint 1.
(gdb) info b
Num Type           Disp Enb Address    What
1   breakpoint     keep y   0x004010e7 in swap at gdb_example.c:27
        ignore next 5 hits
3   breakpoint     del  n   0x004010c0 in main at gdb_example.c:16
```

As the info output indicates, breakpoint 2 no longer exists, the temporary breakpoint 3 is disabled, and breakpoint 1 will not stop the program until the sixth time the program reaches it.

Conditional breakpoints

Normally, the debugger interrupts a program as soon as it reaches a breakpoint. If the breakpoint is conditional, however, then GDB stops the program only if the specified condition is true. You can specify a break condition when you set a breakpoint by appending the keyword if to a normal break command:

```
break [position] if expression
```

In this syntax, *position* can be a function name or a line number, with or without a filename, just as for an unconditional breakpoint (see "Setting and displaying breakpoints" on page 747). The condition can be any C expression with a scalar type, and may include function calls. Here is an example of a conditional breakpoint:

```
(gdb) s
27        for ( i = 1; i <= limit ; ++i )
(gdb) break 28 if i == limit - 1
Breakpoint 1 at 0x4010e7: file gdb_test.c, line 28.
```

This command instructs the debugger to interrupt the program at line 28 if the variable i at that point has a value one less than the variable limit.

 Any variables you use in a break condition must be visible at the breakpoint's position. In other words, the breakpoint must be located within the variables' scope.

If you have already set a breakpoint at the desired position, you can use the condition command to add or change its break condition:

```
condition bp_number [expression]
```

The argument *expression* becomes the new condition of the breakpoint with the number *bp_number*. The output of the info breakpoints (or info b) command includes any break conditions, as the following example illustrates:

```
(gdb) condition 2 *p1 != *p2
(gdb) info b
Num Type           Disp Enb Address    What
1   breakpoint     keep y   0x004010ae in main at gdb_example.c:12
2   breakpoint     keep y   0x004010e7 in swap at gdb_example.c:21
        stop only if *p1 != *p2
3   breakpoint     del  y   0x004010f9 in swap at gdb_example.c:24
(gdb)
```

To delete a break condition, use the condition command without an *expression* argument:

```
(gdb) condition 2
Breakpoint 2 now unconditional.
```

Resuming Execution After a Break

When you have finished analyzing the state of a stopped program, there are several ways of resuming execution. You can step through the program line by line, let the program run to the next breakpoint, or let it run to a specified position such as the end of the current function. The commands you can use to proceed after a break in execution are listed here (examples of all four commands are given after the list):

continue [*passes*], c [*passes*]

Allows the program to run until it reaches another breakpoint, or until it exits if it doesn't encounter any further breakpoints. The *passes* argument is a number that indicates how many times you want to allow the program to run past the present breakpoint before GDB stops it again. This is especially useful if the program is currently stopped at a breakpoint within a loop. See also the ignore command, described in "Working with Breakpoints" on page 747.

step [*lines*], s [*lines*]

Executes the current line of the program, and stops the program again before executing the line that follows. The step command accepts an optional argument, which is a positive number of source code lines to be executed before GDB interrupts the program again. However, GDB stops the program earlier if it encounters a breakpoint before executing the specified number of lines. If any line executed contains a function call, step proceeds to the first line of the function body, provided that the function has been compiled with the necessary symbol and line number information for debugging.

next [*lines*], n [*lines*]

Works the same way as step except that next executes function calls without stopping before the function returns, even if the necessary debugging information is present to step through the function.

finish

To resume execution until the current function returns, use the finish command. The finish command allows program execution to continue through the body of the current function, and stops it again immediately after the program flow returns to the function's caller. At that point, GDB displays the function's return value in addition to the line containing the next statement.

Remember that the lines of a program are not always executed in the order in which they appear in the source code. For example, consider the following function to compute a factorial:

```
(gdb) list factorial
21
22     // factorial() calculates n!, the factorial of a non-negative n.
23     // For n > 0, n! is the product of all integers from 1 to n.
24     // 0! equals 1.
25
26     long double factorial( register unsigned int n )
27     {
28       long double f = 1;
29       while ( n > 1 )
30         f *= n--;
31       return f;
32     }
```

The following excerpt of a GDB session demonstrates that lines of code can execute outside of their linear order. The `frame` command shows that the program execution has been stopped at line 30. The `step` command executes line 30, whereupon line 29 is displayed as the next one to be executed:

```
(gdb) frame
#0  factorial (n=10) at factorial.c:30
30            f *= n--;
(gdb) s
29          while ( n > 1 )
(gdb)
```

In this particular example, the execution of line 31 does not follow that of line 30. Instead, line 29 follows line 30. The reason, of course, is that the loop condition has to be evaluated after every iteration of the loop body.

If any line executed by a `step` command contains a function call, and GDB has the necessary symbol table and line number information for the function, then execution stops again at the first line within the function called. In the following example, the `step` command enters the `factorial()` function but not the `printf()` function:

```
(gdb) frame
#0  main () at factorial.c:14
14          printf( "%u factorial is %.0Lf.\n", n, factorial(n) );
(gdb) s
factorial (n=10) at factorial.c:28
28          long double f = 1;
(gdb)
```

In this example, the function `printf()`, unlike `factorial()`, was linked into the program from a standard library that was compiled without debugging information. As a result, GDB is able to display the contents of `factorial()` but not of `printf()`.

You can use the `next` command to skip over function calls; that is, to avoid stepping into functions. The following example is the same as the preceding one except that it substitutes `next` for `step` to illustrate the difference in behavior between the two commands:

```
(gdb) frame
#0  main () at factorial.c:14
14          printf( "%u factorial is %.0Lf.\n", n, factorial(n) );
(gdb) n
10 factorial is 3628800.
16          return 0;
(gdb)
```

As you can see, the use of next prevented the debugger from stepping into either factorial() or printf().

Finally, here is an example illustrating the finish command, again using the factorial() function:

```
(gdb) s
14          printf( "%u factorial is %.0Lf.\n", n, factorial(n) );
(gdb) s
factorial (n=10) at factorial.c:28
28          long double f = 1;
(gdb) finish
Run till exit from #0  factorial (n=10) at factorial.c:28
0x0040112b in main () at factorial.c:14
14          printf( "%u factorial is %.0Lf.\n", n, factorial(n) );
Value returned is $2 = 3628800
(gdb)
```

In this case, finish caused execution to continue until the return from the factorial() function call. (If there had been breakpoints within the factorial() function block, GDB would have stopped the program there.) The call to printf() has not yet been executed at this point, however.

Analyzing the Stack

The *call stack*, usually called the *stack* for short, is an area of memory organized on the LIFO principle: "last in, first out." Each time a program performs a function call, it creates a data structure on the stack called a *stack frame*. The stack frame contains not only the caller's address and register values, which enable the program to return control to the caller after completing the function, but also the function's parameters and local variables. When a function returns, the memory that its stack frame occupied is free again.

Displaying a call trace

When the debugger stops a program, it is often helpful to know what sequence of function calls has brought the flow of execution to the current position. GDB provides this information in the form of a *call trace*, which shows each function call that is currently in progress, with its arguments. To display the call trace, use the backtrace command (abbreviated bt). The backtrace command has two more synonyms: where and info stack (or info s).

The following example shows the call trace when the program *circle.c* is stopped within the function circularArea():

```
(gdb) bt
#0  circularArea (r=5) at circle.c:30
#1  0x0040114c in main () at circle.c:18
```

The trace shows that the circularArea() function is called from main() at line 18, with the argument value 5. The debugger numbers the stack frames from last to first so that the current function's frame always has the number 0. The highest numbered stack frame is that of the main() function.

The address that follows the frame number in the backtrace output is the return address; that is, the address of the next instruction to be executed after the return from the function call for which the stack frame was generated. However, this address is omitted from the stack frame display if it corresponds to the same source code line at which the program is stopped.

We'll illustrate backtraces using the following recursive function named factorial():

```
34    long double factorial( register unsigned int n)
35    {
36        if ( n <= 1 )
37            return 1.0L;
38        else
39            return n * factorial( n-1 );
40    }
```

The following GDB output shows the call stack during the final, recursive call to factorial(). By definition, that final call occurs when n is 1. To stop the program in the last recursive iteration of the factorial() function, we can set a breakpoint with the condition n == 1:

```
(gdb) b factorial if n == 1
Breakpoint 1 at 0x40114f: file factorial.c, line 36.
(gdb) r
...
Breakpoint 1, factorial (n=1) at factorial.c:36
36            if ( n <= 1 )
(gdb) bt
#0  factorial (n=1) at factorial.c:36
#1  0x0040117c in factorial (n=2) at factorial.c:39
#2  0x0040117c in factorial (n=3) at factorial.c:39
#3  0x0040117c in factorial (n=4) at factorial.c:39
#4  0x0040117c in factorial (n=5) at factorial.c:39
#5  0x0040112b in main () at factorial.c:14
(gdb)
```

The backtrace in this example shows that the main() function started things off by requesting the value of 5! (the factorial of 5). The factorial() function then recursively invoked itself to compute 4!, and then 3!, followed by 2!, and finally by 1!.

Displaying and changing the current stack frame

Most of the commands for examining the stack operate on the *current stack frame*. For example, you can address the local variables in the current stack frame by their names. When multiple frames are available, GDB lets you choose among them.

When the debugger stops the program at a breakpoint, the current stack frame is the frame corresponding to the function currently being executed—that is, the frame numbered 0 in the backtrace list. The frame command allows you to display the current stack frame, or to select a different frame:

```
frame [number]
```

The command frame, abbreviated as f, selects and displays the frame with the specified number. That frame is then the current stack frame. The frame command with no argument simply displays information about the current frame.

The output of the frame command always consists of two lines of text: the first contains the name of the function called and the values of its arguments, and the second is the current source code line in the corresponding function.

In the following example, the program *circle* has been stopped in the function circularArea():

```
(gdb) bt
#0  circularArea (r=5) at circle.c:27
#1  0x0040114c in main () at circle.c:18
(gdb) f 1
#1  0x0040114c in main () at circle.c:18
18          area = circularArea( radius );
(gdb) p radius
$1 = 5
(gdb)
```

The command f 1 selects the stack frame that contains the call to the current function. In this example, that is the frame corresponding to the main() function. Once that stack frame has been selected, local variables in main() can be accessed by their names, as the command p radius demonstrates.

Displaying arguments and local variables

The info command has three subcommands that are useful in displaying the contents of the current stack frame:

info frame
Displays information about the current stack frame, including its return address and saved register values.

info locals
Lists the local variables of the function corresponding to the stack frame, with their current values.

```
info args
```
List the argument values of the corresponding function call.

In the following example, the program has been stopped at the beginning of the swap() function. This swap() is the corrected version of the function in Example 21-1:

```
25    void swap( int *p1, int *p2 )              // Exchange *p1 and *p2
26    {
27        int tmp = *p1;
28        *p1 = *p2;
29        *p2 = tmp;
30    }
```

On an Intel-based system with Windows XP, the info frame command displays the following information:

```
(gdb) info frame
Stack level 0, frame at 0x22f010:
 eip = 0x4010e7 in swap (gdb_example.c:27); saved eip 0x4010c0
 called by frame at 0x22f030
 source language c.
 Arglist at 0x22f008, args: p1=0x22f024, p2=0x22f020
 Locals at 0x22f008, Previous frame's sp is 0x22f010
 Saved registers:
  ebp at 0x22f008, eip at 0x22f00c
```

The register eip (the "extended instruction pointer") contains the address of the next machine instruction to be executed, corresponding to line 27. The ebp register ("extended base pointer") points to the current stack frame. The info args command produces the following display:

```
(gdb) info args
p1 = (int *) 0x22f024
p2 = (int *) 0x22f020
```

GDB indicates the pointers' type, int *, as well as their values. The info locals command displays the following information:

```
(gdb) info locals
tmp = 0
```

Displaying Data

Usually, you can use the print command to display the values of variables and other expressions. In addition, you can use the command x to examine unnamed blocks of memory.

Displaying values of expressions

The print or p command takes any C expression as its argument:

```
p [/format] [expression]
```

This command evaluates *expression* and displays the resulting value. A `print` command with no *expression* argument displays the previous value again, without reevaluating the previous expression. If you want, you can specify a different output format.

The optional argument /*format* allows you to specify an appropriate output format for the expression (see "Output formats" on page 758). Without a format argument, `print` formats the output as appropriate for the data type.

Expressions in `print` commands can also have side effects, as the following example illustrates. The current stack frame is that of the `circularArea()` function in the *circle* program:

```
(gdb) p r
$1 = 1
(gdb) p r=7
$2 = 7
(gdb) p r*r
$3 = 49
```

In this example, the expression r=7 in the second `print` command assigns the value 7 to the variable r. You can also change the value of a variable using the `set` command:

```
(gdb) set variable r=1.5
```

The `print` command's output displays an expression's value as the value of a variable $*i*, where *i* is a positive integer. You can refer to these variables in subsequent commands, as in the following example:

```
(gdb) p  2*circularArea($2)
$4 = 307.87608005280003
```

This command calls the function `circularArea()` with the value of $2 (which was 7 in our preceding example), and then multiplies the return value by 2 and saves the result in the new variable $4.

You can also use the `p` and `set` commands to define new variables in GDB, with names that start with a dollar sign. For example, the command set $var = *ptr creates a new variable named $var and assigns it the value currently referenced by the pointer `ptr`. The debugger's variables are separate from those of the program being debugged. GDB also stores the values of CPU registers in variables whose names are the standard register names, with the dollar sign prefix.

To access variables in other stack frames without first changing the current stack frame, prefix the function name and the double-colon operator (::) to the variable's name, as the following example illustrates:

```
(gdb) p main::radius
$8 = 1
```

Output formats

The optional */format* argument to the `print` command consists of a slash followed by a single letter that specifies an output format. The letters permitted are mostly similar to the conversion specifiers in the format string argument of the C function `printf()`. For example, the command `print /x` displays the previous value as an integer in hexadecimal notation.

The print command converts the value to the appropriate type, if necessary. The following list describes all of the format options for integer values:

d

    Decimal notation. This is the default format for integer expressions.

u

    Decimal notation. The value is interpreted as an unsigned integer type.

x

    Hexadecimal notation.

o

    Octal notation.

t

    Binary notation. Do not confuse this with the x command's option b for "byte," described in the next subsection.

c

    Character, displayed together with the character code in decimal notation.

As the following example illustrates, the format option can follow the p command immediately, without an intervening space:

```
(gdb) p/x 65
$10 = 0x41
(gdb) p/t
$11 = 1000001
(gdb) p/c
$12 = 65 'A'
(gdb) p/u -1
$13 = 4294967295
```

Each `print` command without an *expression* argument in this example displays the same value as the previous command, but formatted as specified by the */format* argument.

The `print` command accepts two more format options for non-integer expressions:

a

    Displays an address, such as a pointer value, in hexadecimal notation, along with its offset from the nearest named address below it in memory, if any.

---

f

Interprets the bit pattern of the expression's value as a floating-point number, and displays it.

Here are some examples using these format options:

```
(gdb) p/a 0x401100
$14 = 0x401100 <swap+31>
(gdb) p/f 123.0
$15 = 123
(gdb) p/f 123
$16 = 1.72359711e-43
```

Displaying memory blocks

The x command allows you to examine unnamed memory blocks. The command's arguments include the block's beginning address and size, and an optional output format:

```
x [/nfu] [address]
```

This command displays the contents of the memory block starting at the specified address, with the block size and output format determined by the /nfu option. The address argument can be any expression whose value is a valid address. If you omit the address argument, the x command displays the next memory block following the last memory location displayed by an x or print command.

The /nfu argument can consist of up to three parts, all of which are optional:

n

A decimal number specifying how many units of memory to display. The size of each such unit is determined by the third part of the /nfu option, u. The default value of n is one.

f

A format specifier, which may be one of those supported by the print command (described in "Output formats" on page 758), or one of the following two additional format specifiers:

s   Display the data at the specified address as a null-terminated string.

i   Display machine instructions in assembly language.

The default format is initially x, and later the format that you last specified in an x or print command.

u

The third part of the /nfu argument, the u option, defines the size of each memory unit displayed, and can have one of the following values:

b   One byte

h   Two bytes (a "half word")

w   Four bytes (a "word")

g   Eight bytes (a "giant word")

The default value of *u* is initially w, and later whichever unit you last specified in an x command. It makes no sense to specify a unit size with the format option s or i. If you do so, GDB ignores the unit size option.

The following examples illustrate the use of the x command. In these examples, assume that the following variables are defined in the current scope:

```
char msg[100] = "Hello world!\n";
char *cPtr = msg + 6;
```

Each line of the x command's output begins with the starting address of the memory location displayed, and the corresponding name from the symbol table, if any. The first x command displays the string msg:

```
(gdb) x/s msg
0x402000 <msg>:  "Hello world!\n"
```

The next command displays the first 15 bytes of the msg string in hexadecimal:

```
(gdb) x/15xb msg
0x402000 <msg>:   0x48   0x65   0x6c   0x6c   0x6f   0x20   0x77   0x6f
0x402008 <msg+8>:        0x72   0x6c   0x64   0x21   0x0a   0x00   0x00
```

Two 32-bit words, in hexadecimal notation, at the address msg:

```
(gdb) x/2xw msg
0x402000 <msg>: 0x6c6c6548       0x6f77206f
```

The string that begins at the pointer value of cPtr:

```
(gdb) x/s cPtr
0x402006 <msg+6>:    "world!\n"
```

Beginning at the same address, eight decimal character codes, with the corresponding character values:

```
(gdb) x/8cb cPtr
0x402006 <msg+6>: 119 'w' 111 'o' 114 'r' 108 'l' 100 'd' 33 '!'
10 '\n' 0 '\0'
```

The value of the pointer cPtr itself, in hexadecimal and in binary:

```
(gdb) x/a &cPtr
0x22f00c:        0x402006 <msg+6>
(gdb) x/tw &cPtr
0x22f00c:        00000000010000000010000000000110
```

Watchpoints: Observing Operations on Variables

GDB lets you take notice of read and write access to variables by setting *watchpoints*. A watchpoint is like a breakpoint except that it is not bound to a specific line of source code. If you set a watchpoint for a variable, then GDB stops the program whenever the value of the variable changes. In fact, GDB can watch not only individual variables but also expressions. You can set different kinds of watchpoints using the commands watch, rwatch, and awatch. All three commands have the same syntax:

watch *expression*
> The debugger stops the program when the value of *expression* changes.

rwatch *expression*
> The debugger stops the program whenever the program reads the value of any object involved in the evaluation of *expression*.

awatch *expression*
> The debugger stops the program whenever the program reads or modifies the value of any object involved in the evaluation of *expression*.

The most common use of watchpoints is to observe when the program modifies a variable. When a watched variable changes, GDB displays the variable's old and new values, and the line containing the next statement to be executed. To illustrate the use of watchpoints, we will provide some examples based on the following simple program:

```
1       #include <stdio.h>
2
3       int main()
4       {
5           int a = 10;
6           int b = 20;
7           int *iPtr = &a;
8
9           ++*iPtr;
10          puts( "This is the statement following ++*iPtr." );
11
12          printf( "a = %d;  b = %d.\n", a, b );
13          return 0;
14      }
```

Before you can set a watchpoint for a local variable, you must begin executing the program until the program flow enters the scope of the desired variable. For this reason, we will start by running the program to an ordinary breakpoint at line 9:

```
(gdb) b 9
Breakpoint 1 at 0x4010ba: file myprog2.c, line 9.
(gdb) r
Starting program: ...
```

```
Breakpoint 1, main () at myprog2.c:9
9               ++*iPtr;
```

Now we can set a watchpoint for the variable a, and continue execution:

```
(gdb) watch a
Hardware watchpoint 2: a
(gdb) c
Continuing.
Hardware watchpoint 2: a

Old value = 10
New value = 11
main () at myprog2.c:10
10              puts( "This is the statement following ++*iPtr." );
```

Because iPtr points to a, the expression ++*iPtr modifies the value of a. As a result, the debugger stops the program after that operation, and displays the next statement about to be executed.

To continue this example, we can set a "read watchpoint" on the variable b. Watchpoints are included in the list of breakpoints displayed by the command info break points (or info b for short):

```
(gdb) rwatch b
Hardware read watchpoint 3: b
(gdb) info b
Num Type           Disp Enb Address    What
1   breakpoint     keep y   0x004010ba in main at myprog2.c:9
        breakpoint already hit 1 time
2   hw watchpoint  keep y               a
        breakpoint already hit 1 time
3   read watchpoint keep y              b
(gdb) c
Continuing.
This is the statement following ++*iPtr.
Hardware read watchpoint 3: b

Value = 20
0x004010ce in main () at myprog2.c:12
12              printf( "a = %d;  b = %d.\n", a, b );
(gdb) c
Continuing.
a = 11;  b = 20.
...
```

When the program leaves a block—that is, when the flow of program execution passes a closing brace (})—the debugger automatically deletes all watchpoints for expressions involving local variables that are no longer in scope.

To conclude this section, let us look at how the debugger behaves when you set a watchpoint for an expression with several variables. GDB stops the program each time it accesses (or modifies, depending on the type of watchpoint) any variable in

---

the expression. For the following session, we restart the program examined in the previous examples. When it stops at the breakpoint in line 9, we set a read watchpoint for the expression a + b:

```
(gdb) b 9
Breakpoint 1 at 0x4010ba: file myprog2.c, line 9.
(gdb) r
Starting program: ...

Breakpoint 1, main () at myprog2.c:9
9           ++*iPtr;
(gdb) rwatch a+b
Hardware read watchpoint 2: a + b
```

If we now let the program continue, the debugger stops it at the next statement that reads either of the variables a or b. The next such statement is the printf call in line 12. Because that statement reads both a and b, the debugger stops the program twice, displaying the value of the watch expression a + b each time:

```
(gdb) c
Continuing.
This is the statement following ++*iPtr.
Hardware read watchpoint 2: a + b

Value = 31
0x004010ce in main () at myprog2.c:12
12          printf( "a = %d;  b = %d.\n", a, b );
(gdb) c
Continuing.
Hardware read watchpoint 2: a + b

Value = 31
0x004010d5 in main () at myprog2.c:12
12          printf( "a = %d;  b = %d.\n", a, b );
(gdb) c
Continuing.
a = 11;  b = 20.
...
```

Analyzing Core Files in GDB

A core file, or core dump, is a file containing an image of the memory used by a process. Unix systems generally write a core dump in the working directory when a process terminates abnormally. (On Unix systems, you can read which signals trigger a core dump under man signal.) By passing the name of a core file to GDB on the command line, you can examine the state of the process at the moment it was terminated.

A GDB session to analyze a core file is similar to an ordinary debugging session except that the program you are debugging has already been stopped at a certain position, and you can't use the run, step, next, or continue commands to make it go again. We'll walk through a sample "postmortem" session to illustrate how to debug the program using the other GDB commands. To begin, suppose the program *myprog*, located in the current directory, has been compiled with the -g option. The following command runs the program:

```
$ ./myprog
Segmentation fault (core dumped)
```

The error message indicates that *myprog* aborted due to an illegal memory access. The system has generated a core file in the current directory with the name *core*. To analyze the program's error, we will start GDB, passing it the name of the core file as well as the executable file on the command line. On starting, the debugger immediately displays the address and the function in which the program was terminated:

```
$ gdb myprog core
GNU gdb (GDB) 7.8
Copyright (C) 2014 Free Software Foundation, Inc.
...
Core was generated by `./myprog'.
Program terminated with signal 11, Segmentation fault.

Reading symbols from /lib/tls/libc.so.6...done.
Loaded symbols for /lib/tls/libc.so.6
Reading symbols from /lib/ld-linux.so.2...done.
Loaded symbols for /lib/ld-linux.so.2
#0  0x4008ff06 in strcpy () from /lib/tls/libc.so.6
(gdb)
```

The last output line indicates that the error took place in the standard library function `strcpy()`. If we assume that `strcpy()` itself is bug-free, then *myprog* must have made an error in calling it. The command `backtrace`, abbreviated `bt`, displays the function calls that have led to the current point in the program flow (for more details on backtraces, see "Analyzing the Stack" on page 753):

```
(gdb) bt
#0  0x4008ff06 in strcpy () from /lib/tls/libc.so.6
#1  0x080483f3 in main () at myprog.c:13
(gdb)
```

The output indicates that the `strcpy()` call occurs at line 13 of the source file *myprog.c*, in the function `main()`. Each of the numbered lines in the output of the `backtrace` command corresponds to a *stack frame*, which is a data structure created on the stack to hold the data required for a function call. The command `frame` n (or `f` n for short), where n is the number of a stack frame displayed in the backtrace, selects the stack frame corresponding to the current function's caller, and displays the source code line containing the function call:

```
(gdb) f 1
#1  0x080483f3 in main () at myprog.c:13
13          strcpy( name, "Jim" );
```

Because the function call shows that the second argument to strcpy() is a string literal, we can assume that the other argument, name, is an invalid pointer. To verify its value, use the print command:

```
(gdb) p name
$1 = 0x0
(gdb)
```

The value of name is zero: *myprog* crashed by trying to write using a null pointer. To correct this bug, you would have to make sure that name points to a char array of sufficient size to hold the string copied to it.

Debugging
C Programs

22

Using an IDE with C

An *integrated development environment*, or *IDE*, is a program that provides convenient interaction with the tools used to create programs in C under a unified graphical interface. The integration of the various software tools used in program development can increase your productivity dramatically compared to separate command-line tools. The minimum equipment of an IDE includes an editor, a compiler, a linker, and a debugger. Other tools are often included as well, or can be added, such as a design tool for GUI elements or a version-control system to support collaboration with other developers.

IDEs are available for all common programming languages and platforms. Many IDEs support multiple languages and platforms. For a thorough overview of the characteristics of different IDEs, sorted by programming language, see the Wikipedia page on "Comparison of integrated development environments" (*https://en.wiki pedia.org/wiki/Comparison_of_integrated_development_environments*).

IDEs for C

One of the first IDEs for C was *Turbo C*, published by the Borland company in 1987. Although it was a text-based program for a single-tasking operating system, it was a complete IDE capable of producing and debugging PC applications. On Windows systems, the dominant IDE today is Microsoft's Visual Studio. Other important IDEs for the Windows platform include Open Watcom and Pelles C, both of which include a resource editor for creating graphical user interfaces. The Watcom C/C++ compiler generates native DOS and Windows applications. Pelles C is remarkable in that it contains a C compiler for Windows applications that supports all features of the C11 standard (since late 2012).

Software for OS X is often developed using Apple's IDE *Xcode*. For Unix-like systems, including Linux, FreeBSD, Solaris, and OS X, a number of free IDEs are available, such as *Kdevelop*, for example. Unlike the other IDEs mentioned up to now, Kdevelop does not contain its own compiler but uses an external C compiler such as GCC or Clang. Other free IDEs that function as frontends for external compilers include *Eclipse* and *Code::Blocks*, both of which are also available for Windows and support the GNU Compiler Collection (GCC).

Modern IDEs for C and C++ include a source code editor that not only highlights the various elements of C syntax but also provides intelligent text completion and other convenient features, such as the ability to display a function's call hierarchy; that is, a structured list of the functions that call it and the functions it calls.

For each software product you want to develop, you create a *project* in the IDE. A project incorporates all the information necessary to build the program, such as the names of the source files and the compiler options. The IDE uses an external or internal *make* tool, and is able to export an appropriate makefile to build the C program from the command line (see Chapter 20)—or, conversely, to import a makefile to create a corresponding IDE project.

The sections that follow introduce the workflow of C software development with an IDE using *Eclipse CDT* as a typical example.

The Eclipse IDE for C/C++

Eclipse is descended from the IBM product *Visual Age for Java*. In 2004, the *Eclipse Foundation* was created to take over the development of that IDE as free software under the name Eclipse. Since 2006, the foundation has released a new version in the middle of each year with an individual version nickname. Version 4.4 of 2014 is called *Luna*; version 4.5 of 2015 is named *Mars*. Eclipse is free, open source software published under the terms of the *Eclipse Public License* (EPL).

Eclipse uses plug-ins to provide the various capabilities of the IDE. Because a majority of Eclipse users are still Java developers, the most commonly used Eclipse plug-in is JDT, which provides the *Java development tools*. There are also plug-ins for many other languages, including Fortran, Perl, PHP, and Python, to name just a few. In particular, C development is supported by the Eclipse plug-in CDT (*C/C++ Development Tooling*), first released in 2006 and continuously developed since then (see *http://www.eclipse.org/cdt*).

Installing Eclipse CDT

Eclipse itself is a Java program, and requires the Java Runtime Environment (JRE) to run. If the JRE is not yet installed on your system, you can download it from *http://java.com*. (You may also choose to use another IDE that does not require Java, such as Code::Blocks.) If you intend to use Eclipse to produce Java programs (or if you want to use Eclipse on OS X), you need to install the Java Development Kit (JDK). Both the JRE and the JDK are available at *http://www.oracle.com/technetwork/java/javase/downloads*.

To develop C programs, you will also need a C compiler. Eclipse CDT is most often used with the GNU Compiler Collection (GCC). If GCC is not yet installed on your system, see "Obtaining and Installing GCC" on page 670.

On Windows, Eclipse can use either the Cygwin or the MinGW version of GCC. To ensure that Eclipse on Windows finds the directory with your MinGW (or MinGW64) installation, set the environment variable `MINGW_HOME` to the directory path. You can set environment variables in the System applet in the Control Panel under "Advanced System Settings". You may also have to add the directory `%MINGW_HOME%\bin` to the `PATH` variable.

Once you have installed Java and the "GCC toolchain," download and install the "Eclipse IDE for C/C++ Developers" from *http://www.eclipse.org/downloads/*. This package contains the CDT plug-in. If you also want to use Eclipse for Java development, install the "Eclipse IDE for Java Developers" first, and then start Eclipse and add the CDT plug-in by clicking "Install New Software" in the Help menu. Select "C/C++ Development Tools" in the list of available plug-ins.

Running Eclipse

The first time you start Eclipse, you will be prompted to choose a *workspace*, which is a directory in which you want Eclipse to save your work. Click OK to use the default directory. If you want to change to a different directory later, you can go to File -> Switch workspace. (This does not move any files from your previous workspace.) After you have chosen a workspace, Eclipse displays a "welcome" window with links to helpful documents about the program. You can go to Help -> Welcome at any time to display this window again. When you close the welcome window, the main Eclipse window shows your *workbench*.

Perspectives and Views

The workbench window shows your work in one of several possible *perspectives*. A perspective is a window layout that groups certain commands and *views* that are appropriate for a given type of project or workflow phase. A *view* is a pane in the workbench window that displays a given kind of information in an appropriate format. When several views share the same section of the window layout, they are managed by tabs.

The concept of perspectives allows the various plug-ins to provide the appropriate commands and views depending on your current task. You can have several workbench windows open at the same time. (On OS X, you need to add an Eclipse plug-in called the OS X Eclipse Launcher for this capability.)

A small toolbar at the top right in the workbench window allows you to open or close a perspective, or to switch between the currently open perspectives. When you click the Open Perspective icon (see Figure 22-1), Eclipse displays a list of the available perspectives for you to choose from. If the "C/C++" perspective is not already active, open or switch to it.

Figure 22-1. The Open Perspective icon

Developing a C Program with Eclipse

For each C program, you must start by creating a *project* in which Eclipse will save all the information necessary to build the program.

Creating a New C Project

To create a new C project, open the C/C++ perspective and select File -> New -> C Project. In the dialog that appears, enter a name for the project (such as *First* for your first trial project). Under Project Types, choose the type Executable -> Empty project (or Hello World ANSI C project) and a compiler toolchain, such as Cygwin GCC. Eclipse automatically detects the C/C++ toolchains installed on your system. If you have installed both Cygwin and MinGW on Windows, for example, both are shown for you to choose from. Click on the Next button to open the Select Configuration dialog. Keep the default options to build Release and Debug versions of your program. Click Finish, and your new project will appear in the Project Explorer pane on the left.

To add a new C source file to your project, right-click on the project in the project explorer and select New -> Source File in the context menu. If you prefer to create a new subdirectory first, select New -> Source Folder in the context menu. There are also icons for these options in the default toolbar.

Editing

When you create a new source file, it is automatically opened in the editor pane. To edit a source file that is not yet open, double-click on the filename in the Project Explorer. A useful feature of the IDE's editor is *code completion*, which you can activate by pressing Ctrl+Space. Eclipse then displays a list of suggested completions of the word or line you are typing. For example, when you type #include, it lists the most likely header filenames to insert in the line, as shown in Figure 22-2.

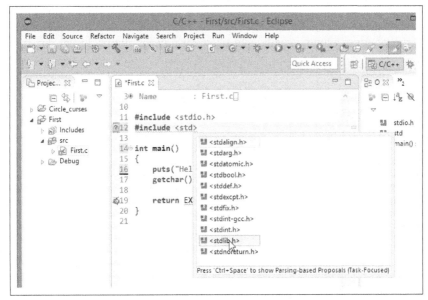

Figure 22-2. Code completion

When the code completion list shows a function name as a suggested completion, it also displays the prototypes and brief descriptions of the possible functions.

Compiling and Running a Program

Right-click on the project and select Build Project in the context menu to compile and link the program. Or you can select Build Project in the Project menu to compile and link the program currently selected in the Project Explorer. (Note that the source file currently displayed in the editor may belong to a different project from that selected in the Project Explorer view!) The command Build All, which you can also invoke by pressing Ctrl+B, performs the Build command for every project open in the Project Explorer, except those that are up to date (i.e., those that have not been edited since they were last built).

If the attempt to build the program produces compiler warnings or error messages, they are summarized in the Problems tab, and the full compiler output is displayed in the Console tab at the bottom of the window. Compiler warnings are highlighted in yellow, errors in red. Furthermore, the Console and Problems tabs are helpfully integrated with the source code view in the editor: the line referred to in each warning or error is flagged in the left margin of the editor with the appropriate color. And you can simply double-click on a highlighted warning in the Console view to jump to the faulty source code line in the editor, where you can correct it. When you can build the program without producing any errors, you can run it.

To run a program, simply select the Run command in the Run menu, or click the Run icon in the toolbar (see Figure 22-3). If you have edited any of the source files or settings since the last build, Eclipse builds the program anew before running it. The program's output appears in the console view at the bottom of the window. If the program is waiting for keyboard input, click in the console to put the focus there before typing your input.

Figure 22-3. The Run icon

Some programs require other information to run, such as command-line arguments or certain environment variable values. You can set such information in the Run Configuration dialog. To open it, select the Run Configurations command in the Run menu, or in the drop-down list attached to the Run icon in the toolbar. Figure 22-4 illustrates a run configuration with the command-line arguments for the sample program in Example 7-6 from Chapter 7.

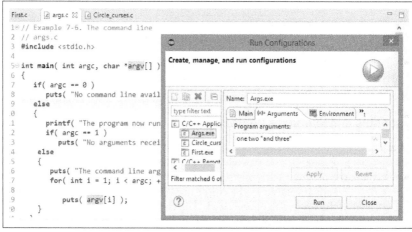

Figure 22-4. Run configuration

The Environment tab in the Run Configurations dialog allows you to define and modify environment variables for the environment in which Eclipse runs your program. This may be necessary for programs that read an environment variable to find certain files, for example. If you are using Cygwin GCC on Windows, and have not added the Cygwin *bin* directory to the Windows PATH variable, you can simply add it to the Path variable in the Run Configuration. Then your programs will be able to load the runtime library *cygwin1.dll*. Changes you make to these settings only affect the current project.

Project Properties

All the information necessary to build a C program is stored in a project. In particular, this includes the toolchain to build the program and all the compiler and linker options. You can verify and adjust these settings in the Properties dialog. To open the dialog, right-click on the project and select the command Properties in the context menu. (Or select Properties in the Project menu, or press Alt+Enter.)

To change the command-line options of the compiler or linker, click on C/C++ Build -> Settings in the left pane of the Properties dialog.

- Then click on the Tool Settings tab and select "… Compiler" in the list of tools. The text fields at the right show the command gcc and all the command-line options with which gcc is invoked to build your program. The items in the list under "… Compiler" are specific categories of compiler options. To set the option for C11, for example, select Dialect in the list, and in the drop-down list "Language standard," choose the option "ISO C11 (-std=c11)."

- If you expand the node "… Linker" in the list of tools on the Tool Settings page, and then click on Libraries, you can specify the names of libraries to link with your program (such as ncurses for the program in Example 19-1), and additional paths to search for libraries.

Debugging a C Program in Eclipse

Having the debugger integrated in the graphical user interface is perhaps the greatest feature of an IDE for efficient software development. Eclipse CDT's Debug perspective is a graphical frontend for the GDB debugger. Different views offer synchronized views of the program's source code, values of variables and CPU registers, memory blocks, and console I/O.

The GDB debugger is described in detail in Chapter 21. The program in Example 21-1, containing a logic error in the swap() function, is used in this section as well to illustrate the basic commands used in a debugging session in Eclipse. In this section, we assume that you have created a new project named *GDB-Example* that contains the source file *gdb_example.c*, with the content shown in Example 21-1. When you run the program, its console output shows that the contents of the variables are not exchanged. Now you want to find the problem by stepping through the program in a debugging session.

Starting the Debugger

To start debugging the program, select the command Debug in the Run menu, or click on the Debug icon (see Figure 22-5) in the toolbar. Or simply press the function key F11. If you have not built the program since the last modification, Eclipse first builds it again. Then confirm the prompt to change to the Debug perspective by clicking on Yes (unless you already switched to the Debug perspective beforehand). The debugger immediately starts the program and interrupts it at the first line in the main() function.

Figure 22-5. The Debug icon

If you want to debug a program started with certain command-line arguments or environment variables, you can enter the desired information in the Debug Configuration. Select the command Debug Configuration; in the Run menu, or in the drop-down list attached to the Debug icon in the toolbar. The contents of the dialog are similar to those of the Run Configurations dialog (see Figure 22-4) with the addition of tabs for GDB options and source code paths.

Setting Breakpoints

Because the error in the sample program has to be in the swap() function, we will set a breakpoint at the line that contains the swap() function call. To set the breakpoint, simply double-click in the left margin next to that line in the editor.

The breakpoint is indicated by a blue disc in the left margin of the source code editor (see Figure 22-6). Double-click again in the margin beside the line to clear the breakpoint.

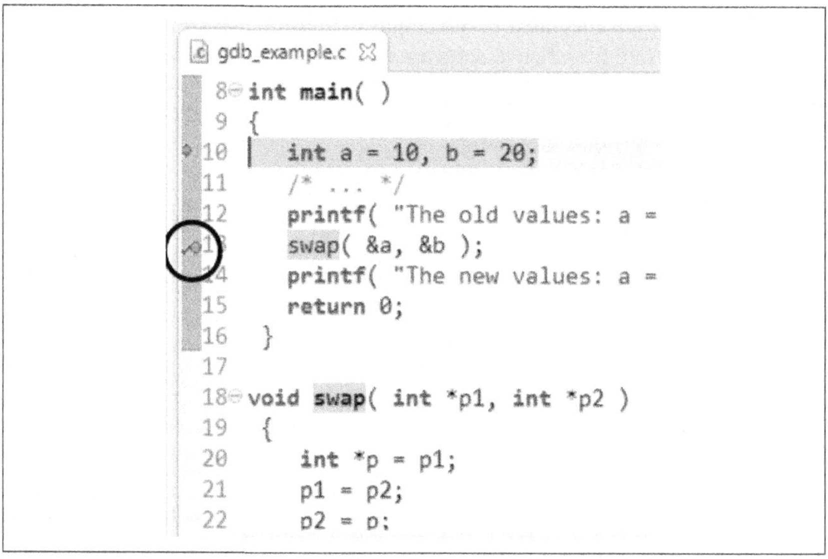

```
 gdb_example.c

 8  int main( )
 9  {
10      int a = 10, b = 20;
11      /* ... */
12      printf( "The old values: a =
13      swap( &a, &b );
14      printf( "The new values: a =
15      return 0;
16  }
17
18  void swap( int *p1, int *p2 )
19  {
20      int *p = p1;
21      p1 = p2;
22      p2 = p;
```

Figure 22-6. A breakpoint in the source code editor

All the breakpoints are shown in the Breakpoints view. Click on the Breakpoints tab in the upper-right pane, or select Show View -> Breakpoints in the Window menu if the tab has been closed. Other views in this pane display the values of variables and registers. Right-click on a breakpoint in the list (or on the blue disc in the left margin of the editor) to open a context menu in which you can deactivate the breakpoint, or select Breakpoint Properties to specify a condition for the breakpoint. See "Conditional breakpoints" on page 750.

Controlling Program Execution in the Debugger

To run the program to the next breakpoint (in our example, the breakpoint is before the call to swap()), click on the Resume icon in the toolbar shown in Figure 22-7 (or press F8). The highlighted line always indicates the statement that will be executed next.

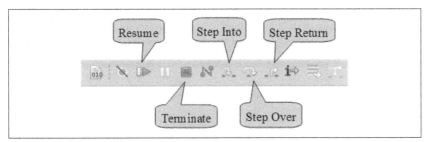

Figure 22-7. The Debug toolbar

Click on Step Into to begin the function call, jumping to the first line in the swap() function. The Variables view, shown in Figure 22-8, now shows the values of the local pointers p1 andp2, and the values of the variables to which they point.

Name	Type	Value
▲ ◆ p1	int *	0x23caac
(x)= *p1	int	10
▲ ◆ p2	int *	0x23caa8
(x)= *p2	int	20

Figure 22-8. The Variables view

In the Debug perspective, the value of a variable is also shown when you hold the mouse pointer over a variable in the source code editor. In the Variables view, you can also change the value of a variable between steps in the program, and without changing the source code. This is practical when you want to test the program's behavior with a different value only in the current debugging session.

If you click on Step Return, the program runs to the end of the current function, or more exactly, up to the first statement after the function call. But because we want to watch the values of the function's local variables, we'll step through the three lines of the swap() function. (Another option would be to set a breakpoint at the end of the function, and examine the values of the variables again there.) In the Variables view, you can see that only the values of the pointers are swapped—not the values of the variables they point to, *p1 and *p2. That was the bug in swap(). For the corrected version, see the end of the section "A Sample Debugging Session" on page 732.

Further Information on Eclipse

The most important resources on Eclipse are accessible from the program itself: go to Welcome -> Overview in the Help menu. To make the most efficient use of Eclipse CDT, you should certainly have a look at the C/C++ Development User Guide. The Overview page also contains the link "Workbench basics," which opens the Workbench User Guide. This document explains the basic concepts of the Eclipse user interface, such as views and perspectives, and explains how to customize the Workbench layout. The Workbench User Guide contains a section on collaborative version control in Eclipse titled "Team Programming with CVS". An interface to the distributed version control system Git is also integrated in Eclipse, and is described in a separate document: the link Git in the Overview page opens the EGit User Guide.

The complete Eclipse documentation is also available on the Web (*http://help.eclipse.org/luna/index.jsp*).

There is also an Eclipse forum (*http://www.eclipse.org/forums/*) where you can discuss questions with the community of Eclipse users and developers.

Index

Symbols

& (ampersand)
  address operator, 87, 122, 141
  bitwise AND operator, 84
&& (ampersand, double), logical AND
  operator, 82
&= (ampersand, equal sign), bitwise AND
  assignment operator, 76, 77
< > (angle brackets), enclosing filenames
  in include directives, 262
* (asterisk)
  automatic variable in makefiles, 708
  in pointer declarations, 142, 182-186
  indirection operator, 69, 87, 145
  multiplication operator, 73
  specifying array length, 121
*= (asterisk, equal sign), multiplication
  assignment operator, 76, 77
@ (at sign), automatic variable in makefiles, 708
\ (backslash)
  beginning character codes, 45
  beginning escape sequences, 9, 10,
    44-45
  escape sequence for, 44
  in makefile rules, 699
  in preprocessor directives, 261
  trigraph representing, 13
{ } (braces)
  digraphs representing, 12
  enclosing array initialization lists, 132,
    137
  enclosing block statements, 100

enclosing enumeration values, 33, 90
enclosing initialization lists, 191
enclosing structure members, 160
trigraphs representing, 13
^ (caret)
  automatic variable in makefiles, 708
  bitwise exclusive OR operator, 84
  trigraph representing, 13
^= (caret, equal sign), bitwise exclusive
  OR assignment operator, 76, 77
: (colon)
  in makefiles, 699
  preceding bit-field width, 172
:: (colon, double), double-colon rule for
  makefiles, 702
:= (colon, equal sign)
  assignment operator in makefiles, 704
  function definition in makefiles, 718
, (comma), sequential evaluation operator, 90, 103
$ (dollar sign)
  preceding function calls in makefiles,
    715
  preceding variable references in make-
    files, 697, 708
" " (double quotes)
  enclosing filenames in include direc-
    tives, 262
  enclosing string literals, 45
  escape sequence for, 44
… (ellipsis), indicating optional parameters, 7, 121, 267
= (equal sign)
  assignment operator, 76

enclosing character constants, 42

escape sequence for, 44

[ ] (square brackets)

digraphs representing, 12

enclosing array element designators, 133, 138

in array declarations, 182-186

in array definitions, 129, 136

indicating array parameters, 116

subscript operator, 69, 87, 131

trigraphs representing, 13

~ (tilde)

bitwise NOT operator, 84

trigraph representing, 13

| (vertical bar)

bitwise OR operator, 84

trigraph representing, 13

|| (vertical bar, double), logical OR operator, 82

|= (vertical bar, equal sign), bitwise OR assignment operator, 76, 77

0 (zero)

preceding octal constants, 39

return value, 119

\0 null character, 9

0x (zero, x), preceding hexadecimal constants, 39, 41

A

a (append), in access mode string, 214, 215

\a alert character, 9, 44

.a files, 676

-a option, gcc command, 675

A or a conversion specifier, 228, 234

abort function, 350

abort_handler_s function, 351

abs function, 352

access modes for files, 214-215

acos function, 352

acosh function, 353

addition assignment operator (+=), 76, 77

addition operator (+), 73

addprefix function, make, 717

address constants, 98

address operator (&), 87, 122, 141

addresses

determining (see address operator)

pointers containing (see pointers)

printing, 142

addsuffix function, make, 717

aggregate types, 24

alert character, 9

alignas specifier, 37, 303

_Alignas specifier, 36-37, 176

__alignas_is_defined macro, 303

alignment of objects in memory, 36-37

alignof operator, 37, 303

_Alignof operator, 36-37, 90

__alignof_is_defined macro, 303

ampersand (&)

address operator, 87, 122, 141

bitwise AND operator, 84

ampersand, double (&&), logical AND operator, 82

ampersand, equal sign (&=), bitwise AND assignment operator, 76, 77

and operator, 298

and_eq operator, 298

angle brackets (< >), enclosing filenames in include directives, 262

anonymous structures, 171-172

anonymous unions, 171-172

-ansi option, gcc command, 682

ar command, 676

--args option, GDB, 738

arguments (see parameters)

arithmetic constant expressions, 98

arithmetic operators, 73-76

(see also mathematical functions)

arithmetic types, 24

conversion rank of, 50-51

conversions involving, 50-58, 74-74, 335-336

array designators, type conversions with, 58-59

array pointers, 152-154

arrays, 129-131

of characters (see strings)

declaring, 137, 177

default values of, 132

defining, 129-131, 136

elements of, accessing, 88, 131-132

fixed-length, 130

flexible array members of structures, 166-167

initializing, 132-134, 136, 137-138

G

-g option, gcc command, 675, 687, 688, 733

G or g conversion specifier, 228, 234

GCC (GNU Compiler Collection), 669-670
(see also make utility)
assembling stage, 674
C dialect used by, 681
compiler warnings from, 683
compiling stage, 674
debugging options with, 688
environment variables used by, 693
file types recognized by, 679
freestanding programs with, 681
include directories, order searched, 673
installing, 670-671
linking stage, 676-678
multiple source files with, 679-680
operation of, 671-681
optimization options, 684-688
options, list of, 689-693
(see also specific options)
preprocessing, 672-674
profiling options with, 688
shared object files with, 680
version of, 670

gcc command, 670, 671

GCC_EXEC_PREFIX environment variable, 693

GDB (GNU debugger), 731, 736-741
breakpoints, 734, 747-753
call stack, analyzing, 753-756
command completion in, 741
command help, 742
command scripts, executing, 740
command-line options, 737-740
core files, analyzing, 763-765
displaying source code, 746-747
example debugging session, 732-736
initialization files for, 740
input files for, 738
installing, 732
passing arguments to program, 738, 745
process ID number for, 737
program data, displaying, 756-760

program to debug, 737, 745
running program to debug, 744-746
starting, 736-740
status information, displaying, 743-744
symbol table used by, 733
user interface for, 739
version of, 732
watchpoints, 761-763

gdb command, 732

.gdbinit file, 740

_Generic keyword, 68, 272-272

generic selection, 68-69, 272-272

getc function, 218, 453

getchar function, 218, 454

getenv function, 454

gets function, 220-220, 456

gets_s function, 220-220, 457

getwc function, 218, 458

getwchar function, 218, 459

gmake utility (see make utility)

gmtime function, 460

gmtime_s function, 461

GNU Compiler Collection (see GCC)

goto statement, 110-112

greater-than operator (>), 80

greater-than or equal-to operator (>=), 80

H

.h files, 7, 679

-h option, GDB, 738

hash mark (#)
beginning preprocessor directives, 7, 261
digraph representing, 12
preceding comments in makefiles, 697, 703
stringify operator, 268
trigraph representing, 13

hash mark, double (##), token-pasting operator, 269

header files, 7
including, 262-264
location of, 263
for standard libraries (see standard headers)

help (h) command, GDB, 742

--help option, GDB, 738

value ranges of, 28-28, 298-299, 308

integrated development environment (see IDE)

.INTERMEDIATE target attribute, make, 713

internal linkage (see static specifier)

international characters, 9-11

internationalization, 299, 340-340

INTMAX_C macro, 310

INTnn_C macros, 310

inttypes.h header, 30, 296-297, 323, 335

_IOFBF macro, 311

_IOLBF macro, 311

_IONBF macro, 311

-iquote option, gcc command, 672

isalnum function, 465

isalpha function, 466

isblank function, 467

iscntrl function, 468

isdigit function, 468

isfinite function, 469

isfinite macro, 301

isgraph function, 469

isgreater function, 470

isgreaterequal function, 470

isinf function, 471

isinf macro, 301

isless function, 471

islessequal function, 471

islessgreater function, 471

islower function, 472

isnan function, 473

isnan macro, 301

isnormal function, 473

isnormal macro, 301

iso646.h header, 298

isprint function, 474

ispunct function, 475

isspace function, 476

isunordered function, 477

isupper function, 478

iswalnum function, 478

iswalpha function, 480

iswblank function, 481

iswcntrl function, 482

iswctype function, 482

iswdigit function, 484

iswgraph function, 484

iswlower function, 485

iswprint function, 485

iswpunct function, 486

iswspace function, 487

iswupper function, 487

iswxdigit function, 488

isxdigit function, 488

-isysroot option, gcc command, 673

-isystem option, gcc command, 673

iteration statements, 101-105

controlling expression of, 101

do … while statement, 104

for statement, 102-104

nested, 105

not using in inline functions, 124

while statement, 101-102

J

jmp_buf type, 302

join function, make, 717

jump statements, 108-112

break statement, 109

continue statement, 109-110

goto statement, 110-112

nonlocal jumps, 112, 341

return statement, 112

K

K&R (Kernighan-Ritchie) style function definitions, 115

Kdevelop, 767

keywords, reserved, 15

kill command, GDB, 746

kill_dependency macro, 307

L

-L option, gcc command, 675

L or l, suffix for constants, 40, 41, 42

L, prefix for wide string literals, 46, 135

L, prefix for wide-character constants, 42, 43

labels, goto statement, 110, 175

labs function, 489

ld command, 671

ldexp function, 489

ldiv function, 490

ldiv_t type, 312

LD_LIBRARY_PATH environment variable, 693
left angle bracket (<)
    automatic variable in makefiles, 708
    less-than operator, 80
left angle bracket, double (<<), shift left operator, 85
left angle bracket, double, equal sign (<<=), shift left assignment operator, 76, 77
left angle bracket, equal sign (<=), less-than or equal-to operator, 80
less-than operator (<), 80
less-than or equal-to operator (<=), 80
.LIBPATTERNS variable, make, 710
libraries, 349
    (see also shared object files)
    headers for (see header files; standard headers)
    non-standard, linking, 676-678
    standard (see standard library functions)
LIBRARY_PATH environment variable, 678, 693
limits.h header, 28, 298-299
#line directive, 274
line-buffered streams, 212
__LINE__ macro, 274, 277
linkage for identifiers, 179, 187-189, 284
linker, 19
list (l) command, GDB, 734, 746
literals, 39-48
    character constants, 42-45
    floating-point constants, 40-42
    integer constants, 39-40
    string literals, 45-48
LL or ll, suffix for constants, 40
llabs function, 490
lldiv function, 490
lldiv_t type, 312
llrint function, 491
llround function, 491
locale.h header, 299, 340
localeconv function, 299, 491
locales, 299, 340-340
    (see also international characters)
localtime function, 495
localtime_s function, 495
locking

mutexes using, 246
streams using, 210
log function, 496
log10 function, 497
log1p function, 497
log2 function, 498
logb function, 499
logical AND operator (&&), 82
logical NOT operator (!), 82
logical operators, 82-83, 298
logical OR operator (||), 82
long double imaginary type, 33
long double type, 30-32
long double _Complex type, 33
long long type, 24, 26
long type, 24, 26
longjmp function, 112, 500
loops (see iteration statements)
.LOW_RESOLUTION_TIME target attribute, make, 713
lrint function, 500
lround function, 501
lvalues, 69-70
L_tmpnam macro, 311
L_tmpnam_s macro, 312

M

-m options, gcc command, 687
macros, 264-272
    comparison, 326
    conditionally defined, list of, 278-279
    defining, 264-266
    for floating-point math, 325-326
    in makefiles, 714
    other macros within, 270
    parameters of, 266-270
    predefined, list of, 277-279
    redefining, 271
    scope of, 271
    standard library functions implemented as, 286-286
    type-generic, 68, 272-272, 325
    undefining, 271
main function, 4, 113, 118-120, 284
make utility, 695-696
    automatic variables, 708
    built-in rules, 700
    command script, 696, 698

R

r (read), in access mode string, 214
\r carriage return character, 9, 44, 210
race condition (see data race)
raise function, 540
rand function, 541
random file access, 235
RAND_MAX macro, 313
range errors, 329
read-only pointers, 64, 123
reading data (see I/O (input and output))
real floating-point types, 30-32, 57-58
realloc function, 196-197, 542
records, 159
  (see also structures)
recursive functions, 126-127
register specifier, 116, 179
register storage class, 69
relational operators (see comparative
  operators)
remainder function, 543
remove function, 211, 543
remquo function, 544
rename function, 211, 545
reserved identifiers, 287
reserved keywords, 15
restrict qualifier, 63, 117, 149, 150-152,
  180-181
restricted pointers, 150-152
return statement, 54, 112, 122
rewind function, 545
right angle bracket (>), greater-than operator, 80
right angle bracket, double (>>), shift
  right operator, 85
right angle bracket, double, equal sign
  (>>=), shift right assignment operator,
  76, 77
right angle bracket, equal sign (>=),
  greater-than or equal-to operator, 80
rint function, 546
Ritchie, Dennis, 3
round function, 547
rounding modes, 328
rounding, of floating-point types, 32
RSIZE_MAX macro, 288
rsize_t type, 288, 308
run (r) command, GDB, 734

run command, GDB, 745
runtime constraints, for secure functions,
  288-289
rvalues, 69
rwatch command, GDB, 761

S

s conversion specifier, 226, 233
.s files, 674, 679
.S files, 679
-S option, gcc command, 674
-s option, GDB, 738
-save-temps option, gcc command, 678
scalar types, 24
scalbln function, 548
scalbn function, 548
scanf functions, 230-235, 297, 548
scanf_s function, 552
scientific notation, for constants, 40, 41
SCN prefix for conversion specifier macros, 297
scope of identifiers, 17-18, 100
-se option, GDB, 738
searching functions, 336
.SECONDARY target attribute, make, 714
secure (bounds-checking) functions,
  287-289
  error handling, 351
  for I/O functions, 209, 214
  printf_s functions, 224
  scanf_s functions, 230
  support for, determining, 209
SEEK_CUR macro, 311
SEEK_END macro, 311
SEEK_SET macro, 311
selection statements, 105-108
  if statement, 106-107
  switch statement, 107-108
self-referential structures, 160
semicolon (;)
  ending statements, 99
  in command scripts for make, 698
sequence points, 70-71
sequential evaluation operator (,), 90, 103
set args command, GDB, 745
set listsize command, GDB, 747
setbuf function, 212, 555
setjmp function, 555

U

u conversion specifier, 227, 234
\u escape sequence, 12, 44
\U escape sequence, 12, 44
-U option, gcc command, 672
U or u, prefix for wide string literals, 46, 135
U or u, prefix for wide-character constants, 42, 43
U or u, suffix for constants, 40
u8, prefix for UTF-8 string literal, 46
uchar.h header, 10, 29, 317
UINTMAX_C macro, 310
UINTnn_C macros, 310
unbuffered streams, 212
unconditional jumps (see jump statements)
#undef directive, 271
underflows, 330
unexport directive, make, 722
unformatted data, reading and writing, 218-222
ungetc function, 219, 614
ungetwc function, 219, 615
Unicode characters, 10, 12, 317
union keyword, 170
unions, 159, 169-172
    anonymous, 171-172
    bit-fields as members of, 172-174
    defining, 170-171
    initializing, 171
    members of, accessing, 89-90
universal character names, 12, 44
unsigned char type, 25, 25-26
unsigned int type, 25
unsigned integer types, conversions involving, 55-56
unsigned long long type, 25
unsigned long type, 25
unsigned short type, 25
unsigned types, 23, 25

V

-v option, gcc command, 675
\v vertical tab character, 44
value function, make, 718
variables, 23

(see also objects)
condition variables, 251-255
in makefiles, 704-711
variadic functions, 127-128
va_arg function, 616
va_arg macro, 128, 304
__VA_ARGS__ identifier, 267
va_copy function, 616
va_copy macro, 128, 304
va_end function, 616
va_end macro, 128, 304
va_list type, 127, 304
va_start function, 616
va_start macro, 128, 304
--version option, GDB, 737
-v option, GDB, 737
vertical bar (|)
    bitwise OR operator, 84
    trigraph representing, 13
vertical bar, double (||), logical OR operator, 82
vertical bar, equal sign (|=), bitwise OR assignment operator, 76, 77
vfprintf function, 224, 619
    (see also printf functions)
vfprintf_s function, 621
vfscanf function, 230, 622
    (see also scanf functions)
vfscanf_s function, 624
vfwprintf function, 224, 624
    (see also printf functions)
vfwprintf_s function, 625
vfwscanf function, 230, 626
    (see also scanf functions)
vfwscanf_s function, 627
Visual Age for Java, 768
Visual Studio, 767
void pointers, 143-144
void type, 34-35, 62-63, 194
volatile qualifier, 63, 117, 148-149, 180-181
vpath directive, make, 722
VPATH variable, make, 711
vprintf function, 224, 619
    (see also printf functions)
vprintf_s function, 621
vscanf function, 230, 622
    (see also scanf functions)
vscanf_s function, 624

About the Authors

Peter Prinz is a seminar leader and key course developer, teaching courses to thousands of software developers for Unix and Windows systems. As the chief developer and cofounder of the IT company Authensis AG in Germany, he has gained extensive experience in software development for computer telephony. Peter is also the author of several other books on software development in C/C++, most of them as coauthor with Ulla Kirch-Prinz, including O'Reilly's *C Pocket Reference*.

Tony Crawford is a freelance writer, editor, and translator in Berlin, Germany.

Colophon

The animal on the cover of *C in a Nutshell* is a cow, in the broad sense that it is a member of the domesticated species generally known as Western or European cattle (*Bos taurus*). In cattle terminology, the word "cow" refers to an adult female (or more specifically, a female who has given birth), as opposed to a heifer (young female), steer (castrated male), or bull (intact male).

All domesticated cattle evolved from aurochs, ancient long-horned oxen that stood six feet at the shoulder and had roughly half the mass of a rhinoceros. The head of an aurochs (the term is both singular and plural) is currently featured on the Romanian coat of arms and the Moldovan flag, tracing back to the royal standard adopted in 1359 by Bogdan I, founder of the Romanian principality of Bogdania (later renamed Moldova). Full-body profiles of the animal survive in Paleolithic European cave paintings, and animated renderings can be found in video games; aurochs have been objects of fear and worship in a number of societies through the ages.

Aurochs are believed to have originated in India some two million years ago; over time, they spread to neighboring continents and split into at least three genetically distinct groups, which were domesticated independently. Domestication of aurochs began 8,000 to 10,000 years ago in the southern Caucasus and northern Mesopotamia; European cattle descended from this group. Wild aurochs survived in dwindling numbers in the forests of eastern Europe through the Middle Ages (the last one was killed by a poacher in 1627). Attempts were made in Germany in the early twentieth century to breed aurochs back into existence (guided by a pre-Darwinian concept of atavism), using primitive varieties of cattle such as Highland cattle; the result is a breed known as Heck cattle.

European cattle, brought to the Americas by Columbus on his second voyage, now number in the hundreds of breeds. It is a popular misconception that only the males have horns; in fact, both sexes are born with horns (except in a few breeds that are polled, or naturally hornless). Seeing horns other than on isolated bulls is unusual because of the common practice in modern cattle management of debudding calves at or shortly after birth (that is, removing the immature base, or horn bud, before an actual horn develops).

Cow horns, which consist of a bony core sheathed in keratinous material, figure in the history of book manufacturing and the promulgation of the alphabet. In sixteenth- to eighteenth-century Europe and in colonial America, a common type of primer was composed of the alphabet (plus other text that varied) printed or written on one side of a piece of paper or parchment, which was then attached to a wooden board and covered with a thin, transparent sheet culled from the outer layer of a cow horn. The board was shaped like a small paddle (with a hole in the handle for attachment to a girdle) to make it easy to transport and share among students. The protective layer of horn extended the life of the paper (a scarce and expensive resource) and inspired the name of the device: a hornbook.

Many of the animals on O'Reilly covers are endangered; all of them are important to the world. To learn more about how you can help, go to *animals.oreilly.com*.

The cover image is an original illustration created by Susan Hart. The cover fonts are URW Typewriter and Guardian Sans. The text font is Adobe Minion Pro; the heading font is Adobe Myriad Condensed; and the code font is Dalton Maag's Ubuntu Mono.

Have it your way.

Get even more for your money.

Join the O'Reilly Community, and register the O'Reilly books you own. It's free, and you'll get:

- $4.99 ebook upgrade offer
- 40% upgrade offer on O'Reilly print books
- Membership discounts on books and events
- Free lifetime updates to ebooks and videos
- Multiple ebook formats, DRM FREE
- Participation in the O'Reilly community
- Newsletters
- Account management
- 100% Satisfaction Guarantee

Signing up is easy:

1. Go to: oreilly.com/go/register
2. Create an O'Reilly login.
3. Provide your address.
4. Register your books.

Note: English-language books only

To order books online:
oreilly.com/store

For questions about products or an order:
orders@oreilly.com

To sign up to get topic-specific email announcements and/or news about upcoming books, conferences, special offers, and new technologies:
elists@oreilly.com

For technical questions about book content:
booktech@oreilly.com

To submit new book proposals to our editors:
proposals@oreilly.com

O'Reilly books are available in multiple DRM-free ebook formats. For more information:
oreilly.com/ebooks